TIMKEN

TIMKEN

From Missouri to Mars—

A Century of Leadership

in Manufacturing

Bettye H. Pruitt

with the assistance of Jeffrey R. Yost

HARVARD BUSINESS SCHOOL PRESS

Boston, Massachusetts

Copyright © 1998 The Timken Company
All rights reserved
Printed in the United States of America

02   01   00   99   98   5   4   3   2   1

Library of Congress Cataloging-in-Publication Data

Pruitt, Bettye Hobbs.
    Timken : from Missouri to Mars—a century of leadership / Bettye
Hobbs Pruitt.
        p.   cm.
    Includes bibliographical references (p.).
    ISBN 0-87584-887-7 (alk. paper)
    1. Timken Company—History. 2. International business
enterprises—United States—History. 3. Bearings industry—United
States—History. 4. Machine parts industry—United States—History.
5. Steel alloy industry—United States—History. 6. Roller
bearings—United States—History. I. Title.
HD9705.5.B434T567 1998
338.7'669142'0973—dc21   98-42263
                                                                CIP

Front jacket photographs: Henry Timken (front left) in a horseless carriage entered by
H. Mueller & Co. of Decatur, Illinois, in a race sponsored by the *Chicago Times Herald*
and held Thanksgiving Day, 1895. A communications satellite making use of Timken
bearings. Photo courtesy of TRW Inc.

The paper used in this publication meets the requirements of the American National
Standard for Permanence for Printed Library Materials Z39.49-1984.

Contents

Acknowledgments   *vii*

Introduction   *xi*

1 Henry Timken: Immigrant, Carriage Maker, Visionary   *1*

2 "Famous Automotive Brothers": The Formative Years, 1900–1915   *33*

3 H. H. Timken, Organization Builder: Securing Independence in a Consolidating Industry   *67*

4 Crisis and Transition: Timken in the 1930s   *103*

5 Timken at War   *133*

6 Timken at Midcentury: The Umstattd Era   *163*

FOCUS CHAPTER Bucyrus   *197*

7 Timken Bearings on a Roll: Expansion of Markets at Home and Abroad   *211*

8 Competition on an International Scale   *245*

9 Chasing Demand   *277*

FOCUS CHAPTER Faircrest   *313*

10 Crisis and Transition: The Challenge of Global Competition   *331*

11 The New Century Approaches   *363*

CONCLUSION Timken at Ninety-Nine: Continuity and Change   *399*

Appendix A: The Timken Company Officers and Directors, 1899–1998   *411*

Appendix B: History of Sales, Income, and Stock Prices for
The Timken Company   *419*

Appendix C: The Timken Company—Timeline of Key Events   *421*

Appendix D: Offices and Plants of The Timken Company   *435*

A Note on Sources and List of Interviewees   *437*

Notes   *445*

Index   *493*

Acknowledgments

By definition, a commissioned corporate history involves collaboration be-tween author and company. This book, however, has received exceptional atten-tion and care from many individuals within The Timken Company. The chairman, W. R. (Tim) Timken, Jr., has been actively engaged from the beginning through many meetings and interviews as well as several readings of the evolving manu-script. Most important, he set the tone and the goals for the project as an objective historical study. In the many letters he sent to prospective interviewees, both within and outside the company, he urged open and frank discussion and stated clearly, "We are not interested only in the good things about The Timken Com-pany." Joseph F. Toot, Jr., retired president and CEO, now chairman of the exec-utive committee of the board of directors, participated at the same high level of engagement and in the same spirit of openness and inquiry. His insightful read-ings of the manuscript have been particularly helpful.

Two individuals within Timken's corporate communications department have also been integral and essential to the history project that produced this book. Marjorie Peterson, communications manager, played a critical role of both coordination and collaboration in every phase from the first interview through the final edit. In particular, she is responsible for the selection of the visual images that enhance this text, and she provided essential support in pulling together the information for the appendices. The book has benefited greatly from her tireless drive for accuracy and completeness. Michael L. Johnson, vice president of communications, championed the idea of a full-scale company history well before it took shape as a formal project. He provided support at every stage, particularly with editorial work on the manuscript that helped to make it more concise and readable.

In addition to the individual contributions noted, each of those four people participated in a history advisory committee that oversaw the development of an outline and successive manuscript drafts. Other Timken Company members of that committee included Ward J. Timken, vice president, and George L. Deal, retired vice president—finance. Two outsiders also participated: Bela Gold, Fletcher Jones Professor of Technology & Management, The Claremont Graduate School; and Carroll W. Pursell, Jr., Adeline Barry Davee Distinguished Professor of History, Case Western Reserve University. Each of the committee members brought valuable perspective, both in wide-ranging group discussions and in their responses to the outline and manuscript.

The technical history of The Timken Company deserves a volume by itself. A number of people within the company have made special contributions to presenting it accurately and placing it appropriately within the broad stream of the company's evolution. Robert L. Leibensperger is executive vice president, chief operating officer, and president—bearings. He provided invaluable assistance with the technical history of the Timken bearing. Jack D. Stover, retired senior research specialist, developed the illustrations of bearing technology and its advancement and helped with the timeline in Appendix C. George T. Matthews, general manager (now retired), quality assurance—steel, provided insight on both the technical and business history of Timken Steel for the text and the timeline. Both Jack and George gave helpful readings of the manuscript and provided much-needed assistance in fact finding. Gregory W. Duggan, global project manager—human resources/finance, contributed to the solidity of the financial history by reviewing text, tables, and graphs. Dennis Vernier, general manager—accounting, compiled the data in Appendix B.

Many people both inside and outside Timken have contributed time and attention to the history as interviewees. It simply could not have been done without their assistance. They are listed with the Note on Sources. The success of the interviewing, particularly in Great Britain and France, also depended on the assistance of Timken personnel who helped develop interview lists, handled the logistics, and in many cases participated in the discussions. They were invariably gracious hosts and enthusiastic supporters of the project. Special thanks in that regard go to George Foale, Anthony Edmonds, Keith Tunnicliff, John Hunt, Wendy Lewis, and Robert Senior at British Timken; to Klaus Schulze, Maurice Amiel, Klaus Behnke, Jon Elsasser, Isabelle Yau, and Pascale Kieny in Colmar; and to Yves Peyronnaud in Paris.

Thanks also to Nancy Blake at Latrobe Steel Company for assistance in gathering Latrobe historical materials and to Samuel Williams at the Columbus railroad bearing plant for organizing a group discussion and interview on Timken's railroad business. Russell Fowler, James Oberlander, and Glen Wilson all provided helpful commentary on a draft of the Bucyrus chapter. Ann Stauffer transcribed with admirable accuracy and speed the many interviews conducted in the course of the history project.

A number of people outside The Timken Company were also important project participants. Among those, Jeffrey R. Yost deserves special recognition. He was the chief documentary researcher for this history. He mined the corporate archives and other local sources, summarized documents, and prepared background essays with impressive thoroughness and thoughtfulness. His Ph.D. dissertation for Case Western Reserve University, which examined Timken along with several other companies in the early automotive supply industry, provided additional information and insight.

Timken commissioned The Winthrop Group, Inc.—where I served as a partner through June 1997—to write its history in 1993. Davis Dyer played a leading role in its original conceptualization. Subsequently, he and another Winthrop Group colleague, Margaret Graham, provided valuable support by reading draft chapters.

Barbara Griffith conducted numerous interviews and collaborated in the development of an outline. Judith Gurney contributed essential library research, pulled together the story of British Timken in the 1950s, helped to organize research materials, and provided intellectual and moral support throughout the drafting of chapters. In the latter stages of writing the first-draft manuscript, Jeffrey Moran provided invaluable assistance by writing early versions of the chapter on Timken in the 1990s and the sections on Latrobe Steel Company and MPB Corporation. At the very beginning of the project Paul Barnhill compiled a timeline and database of historical financial information that helped to get us off to a good start. The staff of the Phillips Exeter Academy Library provided helpful assistance on this project, as they have done on many others over the years.

Special thanks are also due to individuals at the Harvard Business School Press who have helped to shepherd this book through publication—Carol Franco and her staff, in particular Nikki Sabin and Barbara Roth. Holly Webber gave the manuscript a thoughtful copyedit. Three anonymous readers provided helpful criticism and advice. A fourth reader, Hugo Uyterhoeven, the Timken professor at the Harvard Business School, pushed me, as he has done in the past, to humanize the story. The author gratefully acknowledges the help of all.

Finally, as anyone who reads acknowledgments sections must know, books can be hard on authors' families and friends. To mine, once again, thank you.

Introduction

A farm boy boards a ship in Germany bound for America. He is seven and the year is 1838. With his family, he makes the hazardous Atlantic crossing to New Orleans. There they pause, then take a steamer that bucks the current up the Mississippi to St. Louis.

The hundred-year journey of The Timken Company has its roots in that 1830s odyssey, which calls to mind some of history's great adventures. The hero of the tale develops a bold strategy. He gathers resources, sets out, innovates and improvises, encounters early hurdles, stays the course and overcomes them, progresses, stumbles, rights himself, and continues on to ultimate success.

The Timken story includes all of that and more. It includes lessons that the company has drawn from its own history, which can also be applied more broadly. It is a story of being born in Missouri, growing in Ohio, and gradually branching out to the world's farthest corners. It is a story of manufacturing, of working to meet the needs of manufacturing customers, and eventually diversifying into distribution and service. It is a story of inventiveness, boldness, perseverance, loyalty, leadership, and achievement. Legend—not altogether verifiable—also is part of it. Those are threads that tie the story together and give it meaning for the generation embarking on the company's second century.

The Timken Company's corporate life spans one hundred years of manufacturing anti-friction bearings and more than eighty years of producing specialty alloy steel. Its antecedents reach back into the nineteenth-century carriage industry. It has ranked among the largest 250 U.S. manufacturing corporations since the 1920s. Its story is an important chapter in the history of industrialization and of the automotive industry in particular.[1]

The bearing industry has received scant attention from historians of business and technology. Yet it would be difficult to overstate the importance of anti-friction bearings in the advancement of twentieth-century work and living standards. They are some of the most highly engineered equipment components, and they have been essential to the progress made in power, speed, fuel efficiency, reliability, and effective life of virtually all types of machinery. Timken's claim to manufacturing leadership rests in large part on contributions it has made both to the diffusion of that critical technology and to its steady improvement, which has kept pace with and in some cases driven technical advances made by the company's customers. Its history provides a valuable case study of the mechanisms—for example, sales engineering linked to in-house research and development—by which a business organization has pushed technological development on a broad front in pursuit of its own profitability and growth.[2]

Timken's history also offers a striking example of the interdependence of innovations in products and processes. It presents a rare and fascinating case in which a single firm has committed itself to process development in both steel making and precision manufacturing, as well as the steps in between. It calls attention to and illuminates the critical role that advances in materials have played in technological progress. At the same time, Timken's experience, like that of other technology-driven companies, adds to our understanding of how technical capabilities and personnel influence and enable corporate strategy.[3]

Timken's hundred-year evolution also offers rich material for reflection on the nature of organizational life. The celebration of a centennial is in itself a noteworthy achievement—the life expectancy for existing large multinational firms is less than fifty years. Timken has not only survived as an independent firm but has remained a leader in two industries, bearings and steel, where international competition and restructuring have been particularly intense. In the closing decades of the century, the question of how successful, long-lived companies survive dramatic changes in the business environment seems especially pressing because so many venerable firms have either lost positions of leadership or succumbed to industry consolidation brought about by global competition. Several important studies based on collective histories of multiple firms have produced useful theories about the factors that contribute to corporate success and longevity. Timken's history shows those factors at work in the life of an old but still dynamic organization.[4]

The work of Alfred D. Chandler, Jr., based on analysis of hundreds of large industrial firms in the United States, Britain, and Germany, provides a compelling argument for the overriding importance of early and sustained investment in manufacturing processes and organizational capabilities. Those investments and organization building created the large manufacturing companies that became the leaders in basic industries in the early decades of the twentieth century. They also created the productive capacities and capabilities in marketing and distribution that were the basis for competition and expansion in international markets. Because they were so successful, large-scale corporations, directed by ranks of salaried managers, became the central institution of industrial activity. That was particularly true in the United States, where the managerial enterprise became the dominant force in world industry in the decades following World War II. Within the framework of that historical evolution, Chandler has attributed the subsequent loss of competitiveness in U.S. industry to a failure of management, both in abandoning strategies firmly grounded in core capabilities and in neglecting critical investments. The lessons he draws from the devastation wreaked on U.S. companies by the long merger wave launched in the 1960s presents some clear guidelines for corporate survival: maintain strategic focus on core businesses and keep up investments in organizational capabilities.[5]

In contrast, two other recent studies based on collective corporate histories examine quite a different set of factors, which may broadly be termed cultural, including corporate purpose and values as well as corporate culture. They offer some alternative explanations for organizational success and longevity, and their findings provide a necessary complement to Chandler's analysis. Both books—*Built to Last* (1994) by James C. Collins and Jerry I. Porras, and *The Living Company* (1997) by Arie de Geus—set out to address the question of what characteristics enable companies to survive and prosper over the long term by looking at some that have done so. They differ in emphasis, but they agree on basic principles.[6]

The most critical factor in making a company enduring, they suggest, is a clear corporate purpose around which shared values and identity can form. Collins and Porras argue that "a fundamental element" of success and long life is "a core ideology—core values and sense of purpose beyond just making money—that guides and inspires people throughout the organization and remains relatively fixed for long periods of time." The very definition of a "living company" derives from sense of purpose. "The living company," writes de Geus, "exists primarily for its own survival and improvement: to fulfill its potential and to become as great as it can be." In enduring companies, corporate purpose transcends financial objectives such as revenue and earnings growth, but does not exclude them by any means. Over the long term, such companies perform better than others, these studies report. But financial performance and even core businesses, though important, are means to an end, not ends in themselves. Says de Geus, a long-time executive of Royal Dutch/Shell Group, "Shell does not 'exist to pump oil.' We pump oil to exist." At the same time, even in very large, diversified, decentralized firms such as Shell, everyone has an understanding of "'what this company stands for,' or 'what this company is about.'"[7]

The key to that kind of understanding is a cohesive corporate culture through which company values become shared values and are sustained from one generation to the next. Such cultures are not for everyone. Only those who embrace the values will thrive. Yet for those who do fit, according to Collins and Porras, the reward is a feeling of "elitism—a sense of belonging to something special and superior."[8]

Yet the stable core is only part of the formula. It must be matched by the capacity for change if the organization is to endure over the very long term. Along with conformity around shared mission and values there must also be openness to new ideas, both from the outside and from within. Living companies, de Geus writes, are "sensitive to their environment in order to learn and adapt [and are] tolerant of unconventional thinking and experimentation." Similarly, Collins and Porras suggest that "ideological control" must be balanced by "operational autonomy" that encourages individual initiative and accepts both trial and error.[9]

Strategic focus, investment, corporate purpose and identity, corporate culture, and the capacity for change—all of those factors figure prominently in Timken's story. At the same time, Timken's story shows how they can come together and play out over time within a single, long-lived corporation.

Timken presents a clear case in which timely and sustained investments in its core businesses have been critical factors in success and longevity. Largely on that basis, it became one of the three major U.S. bearing producers in the early years of the industry. More dramatically, having set itself apart with a bold investment in vertical integration into steel production, Timken remained independent as the other two industry leaders, Hyatt Roller Bearing Company and New Departure Company, were absorbed in the consolidation of the U.S. automotive industry in the second decade of the twentieth century. Just after World War II, Timken set itself apart again by leading the bearing industry into automated high-volume production. Subsequently, a long stream of investments in new plants and organizational capabilities kept the company competitive through the 1970s as Japanese bearing manufacturers began to make inroads in other segments of the industry. And, in the early 1980s, when seriously challenged on steel quality and bearing price and performance, Timken doubled its investment in research and development and committed to building a leading-edge steel mill in its hometown of Canton, Ohio. During the worst years of the 1980s, it invested heavily in computerization throughout its offices and plants. In 1989, the company launched a $1-billion capital spending program through which it continued to upgrade its steel-making technologies and existing bearing factories and built two new flexible manufacturing plants for bearings. It has continued that pattern in the 1990s.

People within the company and outsiders who know it well would certainly point to that history of strategic focus and investment—especially the new steel mill, which came on line in the depths of the crisis of U.S. manufacturing in the 1980s—as a defining aspect of the firm. Yet they would hardly recognize its story if it were told only in those terms. Over the years, Timken's distinctive corporate culture, strong values, and clear sense of mission have been even more defining. Moreover, its history of the past twenty years has been about nothing so much as deep cultural change around a solid core of corporate identity and purpose.

Both the distinctiveness and the strength of Timken's character have derived largely from the sustained role of its founding family, which has maintained a financial stake in the firm (currently 19 percent) and has provided leadership over four generations. Indeed, the central thread in its hundred-year history is the translation of the family's values and its sense of mission for the Timken bearing into the strategic choices and corporate policies that shaped the company's organizational capabilities and determined its course. The process by which those values and mission came to be broadly shared within the management culture and the positive effect they had on performance are essential pieces of the story of Timken's growth, international expansion, and sustained competitive strength from the earliest days through the 1970s.

At the same time, in Timken's recent history one sees clearly that the crisis of competitiveness it faced in the 1980s had a significant cultural component. The company came into that era with a highly cohesive management culture based on a shared sense of purpose built around pride of product. It had a strong identity embodied in the Timken name, which had come to stand for many worthy things—ethical business practices, responsibility to community, technical leadership, quality products, strong customer support. But Timken did not have a corporate culture that was open, either to the outside or within. Rather, it was quite insular, its management culture was strongly hierarchical and top-down, and that style was magnified in the way it ran its manufacturing operations. Its purpose and values were not widely shared by production personnel. Those characteristics were barriers to adoption of the flexible manufacturing technology and the practices supporting continuous improvement in product quality and productivity that were the foundation of the competitive threat coming from Japanese bearing and steel manufacturers. Cultural change was thus, by necessity, as much a part of

Timken's emergence from the competitive crisis as its substantial investments in new technology and research and development. In the process, it has begun to take on the characteristics of openness to ideas from the outside and empowerment of people on the inside that Collins, Porras, and de Geus have judged to be attributes of enduring organizations.

In its broad outlines, that pattern of cultural change—both the rigidities in the old culture and the openness and inclusiveness of the culture that is emerging—is hardly unique to Timken. On the contrary, though less studied, it is as much a part of the history of big business in America as is the development of organizational capabilities. Hierarchy is fundamental to the nature of the managerial enterprise. Yet the cultures of firms have also been shaped by the times through which they have lived. Timken's cultural history reflects the impact of the two great crises in the industrial history of the twentieth century—the Great Depression of the 1930s and the globalization of competition, completed with the shift to worldwide over-supply in most industries in the 1980s. The deep ideological divisions that formed in the company after the institutionalization of organized labor profoundly influenced corporate culture in the years when the managerial hierarchy was growing most rapidly and the policies that shaped its character were established. The hierarchical structure and top-down culture served well enough in an era when the opportunities for growth were expansive—the need then was for high-volume production of standardized products. But with the onset of global competition, the barriers to productivity gains created by Timken's structure and culture were no longer tolerable. Two key Timken plants symbolize the technological and cultural differences between the two eras. One is Bucyrus, built in the late 1940s, a pioneering facility for automated production of bearings, and the first to be situated in a non-union environment. The other is Faircrest, the new steel plant of the 1980s, made possible by the union's no-strike agreement and concessions on work rules, but also embodying both empowering technology and management practices that became the inspiration and model for spreading cultural change.[10]

That most recent, dramatic chapter in Timken's history illuminates both the competitive crisis faced by all U.S. manufacturing companies in the 1980s and the nature of the industrial revival that has taken place in the 1990s. The company's experience suggests that an open, inclusive culture was not always essential for survival but has now become so. On the other hand, it suggests the timeless importance of corporate purpose and identity. Timken has become a lasting institution through a multigenerational process of making family mission and values into a shared sense of purpose—first within management and now companywide. That purpose, still residing in the Timken name and all it represents, provided the solid core that made change possible. At the same time, change has refreshed the corporate purpose and deepened its meaning.

The many Timken readers of this book will find much to take pride in and learn from in the hundred-year adventure it describes. Yet, considering the full sweep of the company's history and the challenges it faces going forward, the accomplishments of the present generation seem at least as significant as those of the heroes of the past. A financial measure of Timken's vitality is the fact that, from 1987 to 1997, its ten-year rate of earnings growth outperformed 96 percent of all U.S. corporations of its size or larger—an outstanding achievement for a manufacturer in two basic industries such as bearings and steel. It expresses concretely the dynamic nature of the organizational renewal that is carrying Timken boldly into the twenty-first century.

CHAPTER ONE

Henry Timken: Immigrant, Carriage Maker, Visionary

*T*o understand how a large, complex organization has evolved, one must begin with the idea that inspired its creation. This is particularly true for The Timken Company, which has pursued its original mission with remarkable consistency for one hundred years. Henry Timken's creative inspiration lay in envisioning a business built on solving a critical technical problem. The problem was friction, the force that impedes the motion of objects in contact with each other. "The man who could devise something that would reduce friction fundamentally," Timken observed, "would achieve something of real value to the world."[1] Embodied in a patented anti-friction device—the Timken bearing—that basic concept of value provided the motivating force for a century of organizational vitality and achievement.

The Founder's Legacy: From Missouri to Mars

When Timken patented a tapered roller bearing and formed a company to produce it, in St. Louis in 1898 and 1899, he was at the end of a long and highly successful career as a carriage manufacturer. He did not involve himself actively in the new business after its founding, but retired to San Diego, where he pursued investments in real estate and other business ventures. His sons, Henry Heinzelman Timken and William Robert Timken—known to the outside world as "H. H." and "W. R."—moved the company to Canton, Ohio, in 1901 and carried the burden of producing and selling the Timken bearing in the early years. Henry Timken died in 1909, shortly before the company completed its first decade.

Four generations of Timken family members have led the company through its first one hundred years. From left, back row, are Henry (1831–1909); William R. (1866–1949); William R. (1910–95); Henry H. (1868–1940). Front row, from left, are Henry H., Jr. (1906–68); and William R., Jr. (1938–   ). A fifth-generation Timken, Ward J., Jr., joined the company in 1993.

Yet he contributed a number of essential ingredients. One was the patented bearing design that gave the company a competitive product in the formative era of a rapidly developing industry. Another was capital, including both his initial investment and continuing financial support through a difficult start-up period. Beyond those tangible contributions, he provided intangibles of inestimable value. Indeed, Timken's influence has been pervasive and long-lasting primarily because he gave the business a sense of purpose sufficiently robust to motivate three succeeding generations of Timken family members to remain financially and personally committed to the enterprise, to enlist and maintain the support of talented non-family personnel, and to anchor the company firmly enough to withstand and adapt to the dramatic changes in the business environment that have occurred over the course of the twentieth century. (See Figure 1.1.)

This is not to say that either he or his sons ever drafted a definitive mission statement. Our knowledge of Henry Timken's ideas comes indirectly. He was not a public speaker or writer, and though he probably had a substantial personal and business correspondence, his heirs did not save it. Timken's sons took after him in the respect that, while they had strong opinions, they shied away from voicing them in public forums. In 1924, however, the business journalist O. D. Foster conducted an interview with H. H. Timken, the only one he ever gave, in which he talked at length about the origins and early years of the company. Foster's article in *Forbes* magazine provides evidence of the lessons Henry Timken drew from the experiences of his life and work, and of the way in which they influenced the company through his son. Since H. H. Timken

FIGURE 1.1

Four Generations of Timken Family Leadership as Officers and/or Directors

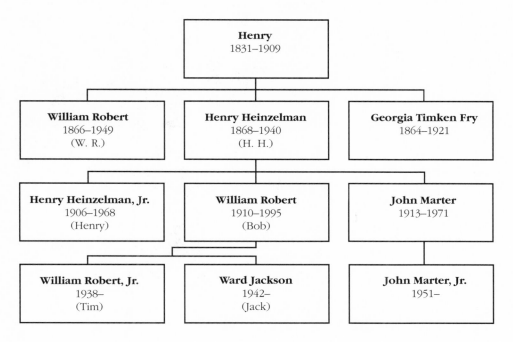

Note: See Appendix A for titles.

was most responsible for building the organization and shaping its character—
W. R. ended his active involvement in 1915; H. H. remained engaged well into
the 1930s—this source is especially significant.

Among the elements of the corporate purpose that emerge from the interview, the concept of value in an effective friction-reducing device is central. Said
H. H., this was "one of the first things my father impressed on me in those early
days," when the work of bearing development was just beginning. The impression
was lasting because, throughout his life, Henry Timken had communicated both
his excitement at the advance of technology and his eagerness to be part of it. He

Below: *Passing
along the vision,
ca. 1907: Henry
(left), H. H., and
H. H., Jr.*

Above: *H. H. Timken, as shown here in 1911, was the
organization builder who shaped the company's
character.*

had urged his sons at an early age "to look into the future and try to foresee events." H. H. recalled, "As a growing boy I learned some very important lessons from his clear-sighted vision, for he had a remarkable sense of foresight along mechanical lines." An example of that foresight was Timken's expansive view of the automotive industry's prospects. "From the first introduction of the automobile he predicted its success," said H. H. "Not only did he see it as a popular form of transportation, but he also sensed its unlimited possibilities for haulage. And he bent all his efforts toward devising a bearing which would be his contribution to that phase of progress." Working intensively on bearing development between 1895 and 1898, Henry Timken thus set his sights not just on the large potential market in the carriage industry, but also on the infant auto industry. That would, in fact, be the first major market for Timken bearings and the largest single market, with applications in wheels, transmissions, and steering and braking systems.[2]

Yet the problem of friction—and therefore the potential applications of effective bearings—extended throughout industry. Timken's framing of that general problem, along with his admonition to be always forward-looking, fueled his son's ambition for success in that broad field. By the 1920s, expanding beyond the automotive market was a central corporate concern. "Wherever there is resistance to motion we not only have serious mechanical strain but waste[d] effort," H. H. explained. The costs of friction were thus exacted not only in high maintenance expense, shortened equipment life, and wasted energy, but particularly in "lowered efficiency of man [and] machine." As H. H. understood, increased mechanical efficiency was a critical element of the revolution in productivity that was transforming industry in the early decades of the twentieth century. To aid in that increase, he said, was to contribute "materially to industrial progress." That was his ambition for the Timken bearing. Summed up by Foster, his strategy was to grow "by making things run smoothly for others."[3]

If the company's sense of purpose was built around an expansive concept of value, however, its product focus was narrow. Quite simply, the Timkens believed that their bearing—a tapered roller bearing—went further than any other toward a fundamental solution to the problem of friction. The type of bearing dominant in industry when Henry Timken began his development work was the plain, or "friction" bearing, which had been in use with little change since ancient times. It was essentially a metal liner in the hole around a rotating shaft, with the main work of friction reduction depending on lubrication. The first anti-friction bearing—the type that uses balls or rollers to create rolling motion—was developed by Leonardo da Vinci around 1500 A.D., and subsequent inventors had come up with a variety of alternative designs. But industrial production of anti-friction bearings did not begin until development of the Bessemer process in 1856 made steel an economically viable industrial material, new machine tools made it possible to work hardened steel into more precise forms, and the rise of the bicycle industry in France and England in the late 1860s created a demand for an effective and widely available anti-friction device. The use of ball bearings spread to the United States with the "bicycle craze," which began in the late 1880s and peaked in 1896–97 with production of more than 1 million bicycles per year. By 1895 at least two companies had ball-bearing-equipped axles for carriages on the market.[4]

When Timken began experimenting with ball bearings on his carriages, however, he found that they failed rapidly from wear. Working on that problem with a nephew, Reginald Heinzelman, he determined that roller bearings held greater promise for vehicle applications, because the weight of the load—so much heavier than on a bicycle—could be carried along the full length of the rollers, as opposed to weighing on a single point of contact on each ball in ball bearings. They tried straight roller bearings but ultimately settled on tapered roller bearings. The advantage of the tapered roller bearing was in its geometry, which permitted it to sustain forces from all directions. (See Bearing Basics, p. 7.) This was critical in certain applications, notably in the hubs of carriage wheels, where heavy loads were exerted from above by the weight of the vehicle (radial load), and also from the side, as the vehicle turned (thrust load). "Neither the ball bearings nor the straight roller bearings seemed to solve the problem [of friction] completely," H. H. explained to Foster, because neither could sustain both radial and thrust loads.[5]

From the beginning, the company faced competition from other manufacturers of tapered roller bearings (a fact *not* discussed in the article). Making the Timken bearing the best of its kind was therefore, of necessity, an important objective. However, both in H. H.'s day and for much of the company's history, an equally important goal was to expand the range of applications of Timken tapered roller bearings, in competition with other types. H. H. was fiercely competitive, a fact he explained by reference to another of his father's admonitions— "above all, don't set your name to anything you will ever have cause to be ashamed of." H. H. said, "If there was any one thing that fixed it in my mind that we must continue to make our product better and better, it was the thought that it carried the family name."[6] Rooted in the Timken family culture, that pride of product, with its imperative for continuous improvement, was another key element of the corporate purpose.

That mission—to make the Timken bearing the best in its field and continually expand the range of its applications—provides a framework for understanding many of the company's distinctive characteristics and unusual steps it has taken that have set it apart within its industry and among manufacturing firms in general. Timken's most striking departure from the norm was its backward integration into steel making in 1916. With the exception of Henry Ford's bold effort

Bearing Basics

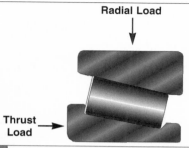

Radial Load

Thrust Load

Above: *The tapered rollers and angled raceways allow the bearing to perform best where heavy loads are exerted from above by a vehicle's weight (radial load) and from the side as a vehicle turns (thrust load). In a given volume of space, the tapered roller bearing will carry more radial and thrust loads than any other anti-friction bearing.*

Above: *Anti-friction bearings have four basic components: inner and outer races, rolling elements, and cage. Different types of bearings use different rolling elements. Some use balls, while others use rollers of the tapered, straight (cylindrical), needle, or spherical type. On tapered roller bearings, the inner race is called the cone; the outer race is the cup.*

Right: *A modern, assembled tapered roller bearing, which reduces friction as either the cup or cone rotates while the other remains stationary. The cup, cone, and rollers bear the load, while the cage spaces the rollers and retains them on the cone. Shaded area on cup cross-section shows the hard outer surface with a softer, more shock-resistant inner core.*

Cup

Cage

Cone

Rollers

Case-Hardened Steel

to control all the raw inputs to his giant River Rouge plant, this action was unique in U.S. manufacturing. The business historian Alfred Chandler has suggested that "metal makers and metal users did not integrate their operations . . . [because] there were few economic advantages in coordinating two processes that were so different technologically and required different types of working forces and managerial skills." For Timken, however, it was a question of gaining for its bearing business a *competitive* advantage—a combination of economics and material quality—by controlling its steel supply. The critical role of materials in the rapid technological progress of the twentieth century is a story historians have yet to develop fully, and it is a central thread in Timken's history. While advances in design and manufacturing have been essential, over the years the competitive success of the Timken bearing has been inextricably linked to the quality of Timken steel and to the understanding of steel properties as they affect bearing performance. The company's strength in both respects stemmed directly from its vertical integration. On the other hand, when Timken steel began to emerge as a separate business after a large-scale expansion in the late 1920s, the exacting requirements of its most demanding customer, Timken's bearing division, were a major factor in making it a leader in its segment of the steel industry. The company's Faircrest steel mill, built in the 1980s in an act of boldness comparable to undertaking steel making in 1916, ensures that both Timken steel and bearings will remain highly competitive for some time to come.[7]

Along with its 1999 centennial, The Timken Company is celebrating the 1998 induction of Henry Timken into the National Inventors Hall of Fame. H. H. Timken, the organization builder, was a 1977 inductee into the Automotive Hall of Fame. More than in most companies, those two colorful personalities and the pioneering roles they played remain a vital part of Timken's sense of identity. Indeed, the continuity of family leadership is, if anything, more central to that identity than the company's sustained focus on its signature product, the Timken bearing. From H. H. through his sons, H. H. Timken, Jr., and W. R. Timken, to his grandsons, W. R. Timken, Jr., who has served as chairman since 1975, and Ward J. Timken, vice president and long-time director, the founding family has been one of the few to remain engaged as owner-managers as their company evolved into a large public corporation. The hallmark of their leadership, particularly in the present generation, has been to provide not only consistency of purpose and values but also the resolve to change when necessary in response to the changing business environment. Both are fundamental to the character of the company today.

After nearly a century of corporate endeavor, Timken's identity and sense of purpose are no longer as closely tied to the Timken tapered roller bearing as they once were. Its steel business in 1997 sold 81 percent of its output to outside customers and contributed about one-third of the company's $2.6 billion in revenues.

In recent years it has been growing faster than the bearing business, in part through extensions into the manufacture of steel parts and steel distribution, the latter through its subsidiary, Latrobe Steel Company, a 1975 acquisition. Timken is the largest manufacturer of tapered roller bearings, holding roughly one-third of the $4.5 billion world market, and remains committed to leadership in the tapered segment of anti-friction bearings. But it is now also a leading manufacturer of super-precision and miniature ball bearings through another subsidiary, MPB Corporation, acquired in 1990. It has developed specialized straight roller bearings for production at a flexible manufacturing facility opened in Asheboro, North Carolina, in 1994. And, through the 1997 acquisition of a controlling interest in Romanian bearing manufacturer Rulmenti Grei, S.A., Timken now produces a full line of anti-friction bearings for Central European markets.[8]

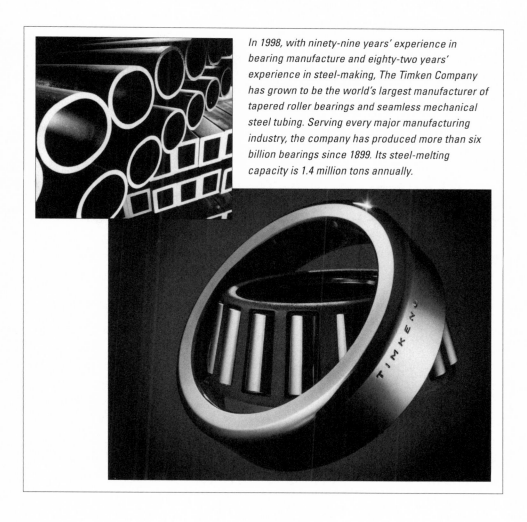

In 1998, with ninety-nine years' experience in bearing manufacture and eighty-two years' experience in steel-making, The Timken Company has grown to be the world's largest manufacturer of tapered roller bearings and seamless mechanical steel tubing. Serving every major manufacturing industry, the company has produced more than six billion bearings since 1899. Its steel-melting capacity is 1.4 million tons annually.

Yet the inner logic of its original corporate purpose—to focus narrowly and be the best in the field—still holds force. For the company, that purpose is both a link to the past and the door to the future. It explains why the Timken tapered roller bearing, a one-hundred-year-old product, is an enabling technology for high-speed trains, a critical part of the landing gear of most of the world's commercial aircraft, as well as the space shuttle, and an integral component of the designs for the next generation of military aircraft and quieter commercial jet engines. It also frames the significance of Timken steel and MPB bearings on the Mars Pathfinder spaceship. The Mars mission, arguably the most electrifying event in the U.S. space program since the first walk on the moon in 1969, is symbolic not only of what technology has achieved but of the next phase of space exploration and the new technological challenges on the horizon. For Timken, it is symbolic of the fact that the company today retains the lofty ambitions and the drive to achieve them that were so much a part of the spirit in which it was founded.[9]

Henry Timken's life up to the development of the Timken bearing was a classic American success story of the nineteenth century. An emigrant from Germany at the age of seven, he would become a successful inventor/entrepreneur and a respected businessman. He made a fortune on a patented carriage spring. A headline for his obituary—"Rose from Humble Blacksmith to Millions by his Own Energy"—captured the Horatio Alger quality of his life, which has been and remains an important part of the company's sense of identity. Like a Horatio Alger hero, Timken won success in the carriage business far more through his wits and nerve, and his recognition of an opportunity when he saw one, than by sheer hard work or the originality of his inventions. The story of his life has been recounted often in company literature and elsewhere, but only in its barest outlines. Examined in greater detail, it provides the basis for understanding how he came to set the company on its future path and for appreciating the many less dramatic but still significant ways he influenced its character.

Catching the American Fever

Up to the 1830s, Timkens had lived for centuries as farmers in the small rural village of Tarmstedt, Germany, near the city of Bremen. They had deep roots in an agrarian society that was only beginning in the nineteenth century to emerge from a feudal system of land ownership. By no means, though, should they be thought of as peasants. The Germanic states during that era were still rigid, class-ridden societies, but the entire population was literate. There had been church schools in every town since the sixteenth century and compulsory education in the region since 1681. Nearly every village had a reading club organized by the local pastor. The early decades of the nineteenth century, moreover, were a time of political and religious ferment and cultural flowering, the era of emerging liberalism and the first stirrings of nationalism, of Goethe and Beethoven. Those social currents originated mainly in urban centers but swept broadly through German society and contributed to widespread discontent and desire for change. This restlessness channeled into a fascination with the more open land and democratic society of the United States. Numerous German travelers, the most famous of whom was Gottfried Duden, visited America and returned to extol its virtues in articles and books that became popular fare in reading clubs. America, said one historian, became "a fever in the German blood." That was the backdrop against which the Timken family emigrated to Missouri.[10]

Henry's father, Jacob Timken, was an independent farmer in an area of commercialized agriculture. He owned some 60 to 100 acres, plus rights to common moor and woodland, and was one of a relatively small group that had been able to take advantage of land reforms in the early 1800s to buy the farm the family had worked for generations as tenants. The impulse to leave Germany was therefore surely not the desperation of poverty. Yet it may well have been that Jacob Timken, captivated by the effusive descriptions of Duden and others, envisioned far greater opportunity for his family in the American Midwest. He was fifty-seven in 1838. His wife, Trine Mahnken Timken, had died the year before at age forty-six. The family included a fifteen-year-old daughter, Adelheid, and six sons ranging from mid-twenties to four years old. Henry, the second youngest, had been born August 16, 1831. The oldest son, Johann, was planning to marry in the fall of 1838. Perhaps to Jacob, emigration seemed the best, if not the only, way to provide a promising future for this rising generation of young men and women.[11]

The journey to America must have been quite an adventure for seven-year-old Henry Timken. The family left Tarmstedt just days after Johann's wedding and followed a well-traveled route: through the port of Bremerhaven to New Orleans, then by steamer up the Mississippi River to St. Louis. Like New York, the other great gateway to the United States, the teeming port city of New Orleans provided a dramatic introduction to America. Wrote one German immigrant of that era, "The enormous number of ships which lie in port here, the great number of steamboats that roar back and forth with a great din, the colossal warehouses and countless streets of this city, but even more the dense crowds of black and white people which one sees here, the very great variety of fruits which are offered for sale in large quantities, all of these things provide much for the eye to see." One can imagine how fantastic and exhilarating, if not terrifying, it must have seemed to a young boy from a settled farming region.[12]

The journey also brought trauma to the Timken family. Shortly after their arrival in St. Louis in March 1839, Jacob applied on behalf of himself, Adelheid, and his three youngest sons for admission to a group of evangelical Lutherans from the German state of Saxony. The group was led by Martin Stephan, whose purpose was to establish a colony of the faithful in Missouri. It is likely that the Timkens made their ocean voyage on one of the four ships carrying the Stephanites, and that Jacob Timken first heard the teachings of this charismatic preacher and began to consider joining his community while on board. His application accepted, he pledged to adhere to the so-called Emigration Code, which granted near absolute authority to Stephan and other senior spiritual leaders. He also contributed $560 to the Credit Fund for the financial support of the mission. Within just three months, however, the Stephanite community unraveled under a cloud of scandal. The religious leaders of the group, Stephan in particular, were revealed to have squandered much of the Credit Fund on a lavish and promiscuous lifestyle and on the purchase of an unpromising tract of land for their proposed American Zion. Most of the laymen who could afford to leave the group, including Jacob Timken, did so. But they left much of their money behind. As passed down in family lore, recorded with some exaggeration by a great-grandson, he had been "swindled out of $10,000 in gold coin" through his brief attachment to the Stephanites.[13]

Earlier in the spring of 1839, Johann Timken had bought 80 acres of good Missouri farmland to the west of St. Louis, near Sedalia, an area chosen by a number of families from the region around Tarmstedt. In July, Jacob followed his eldest son there and purchased 680 acres adjacent to Johann's farm, for $1,150. After much adventure, Henry Timken had arrived at the place where he would spend the remainder of his boyhood.[14]

Henry Timken's two-page autobiography covers the next phase of his life by stating simply that he was "educated in a country school" in his Missouri farm community. He does not mention the hard labor that he, along with his sister and brothers, must have contributed to help their father make a farm out of 680 acres of unbroken land. Nor does he mention what was most certainly a devoutly religious upbringing. Jacob's brief involvement with the Stephanites indicates his affinity for the Protestant fundamentalism of his day. Once settled in Missouri, he and some of his neighbors moved as quickly as possible to build a church and summon a minister to conduct services. Jacob's second son, Gerhard, twenty years old in 1839, would later become a minister. Henry's boyhood home thus provided an environment that fostered conservative values and steady habits.

But for a youth with the mechanical gifts and enterprising nature that were clearly part of Henry's makeup, it could have provided precious little excitement. The religious life was not for him, nor did he see great opportunity in farming. At sixteen, his formal schooling completed, he left for an apprenticeship in St. Louis.

In fact, all of the Timken brothers eventually left. In 1846, in his mid-sixties, Jacob did, too. He sold most of his land, including a large parcel to his son-in-law, Gerhard Ringen, whom Adelheid had married in 1841. Shortly thereafter, Jacob went to live with the Ringens, where he stayed until his death in 1866.[15]

Henry Timken, Carriage Maker

Henry Timken arrived in St. Louis at an opportune time. French fur traders had established the city in the 1760s, and it had prospered by sending furs and buffalo skins down the Mississippi. It was an important way station for migrants and goods being carried to the West. When Henry moved to St. Louis in 1847, it was a boom town. The population increased from about 15,000 in 1840 to 450,000 by 1890. Moreover, the city had a substantial German community that was also growing rapidly. By 1850, Germans would be the largest single ethnic group in St. Louis and one of its most successful. St. Louis papers of the era characterized them as enterprising and hard-working, highly sociable and devoted to family life, though rather clannish and resistant to abandoning their native language and German identity. In short, they did well and took care of their own. All in all, St. Louis in the mid-nineteenth century would prove to be an excellent environment for young Henry Timken to make his way in life.[16]

The carriage business in 1847 was a traditional craft industry, and Henry entered it in the traditional way, as an apprentice to a master wagon maker, Caspar Schurmeier. He emerged after three years as a journeyman carriage maker. His apprenticeship likely involved all the elements of the craft, including wheelwrighting, body making, machining, trimming (cutting leather for carriage seats and dashboards), stitching, striping, painting, and varnishing. Blacksmithing proved to be Henry's strongest skill. He next went to work in the "factory" of D. T. Card, "at that time one of the leading carriage builders of St. Louis," and an establishment large enough to allow Henry to specialize. Yet, in opening his own shop in 1855, he set himself up as a master carriage builder, to build vehicles from start to finish.[17]

Just the year before, on September 28, 1854, Henry married Fredericka Heinzelman. Her father, John Heinzelman, was also a carriage maker and helped his son-in-law get started in his own shop. Gaining a foothold was far from easy. The industry was dominated by long-established firms in New York and New England. Carriages and wagons were expensive items with a limited market in the West, even in a thriving city such as St. Louis. The internal reports of the credit-rating firm R. G. Dunn & Co. characterized Henry Timken as an "honest clever owner" and a good mechanic. Yet, by the end of 1857, his business was mainly in carriage repair and his "means limited," according to the Dunn investigator. In

1858, Henry sold his shop to George D. English & Co. and moved to Belleville, Illinois, where he and his father-in-law opened a new business, Timken & Heinzelman. Belleville at that time was a flourishing town in its own right, situated directly across the Mississippi from St. Louis on the major route from St. Louis to Louisville, Kentucky. It was also a "little Germany" where German was spoken and printed in several newspapers, most of the local officials were German, and the city presented "a Teutonic sense of order, neatness, and precision," with "small brick houses, built close to the sidewalks without porches or lawns in the old German fashion."[18]

Yet Belleville, whatever its charms and advantages, held little appeal once Henry Timken caught gold-rush fever. In 1860, he headed to Colorado with John Ringen, the husband of Fredericka's sister, Louisa, and a distant cousin to Adelheid and Gerhard Ringen. Ultimately, like Henry, John Ringen would make his mark in industry—in the stove business—but in 1860 they both were bent on making their fortunes as quickly as possible. To raise money for their trip they sold what they could, including Henry's share of the carriage business, and set out for the West, leaving Fredericka and Louisa in their parental home in Belleville. After only six months, Henry and John were back in St. Louis. In his brief autobiography, written in his sixties, Henry summed up this adventure succinctly: "I got the gold fever, sold out my business and went to Pike's Peak, Colorado, but found gold scarce and returned to St. Louis and started in the carriage business again."[19]

Within the year, however, both young men were swept up in the Civil War. The German-American community of St. Louis was staunchly pro-Union: "an antislavery colony surrounded by slave owners and their adherents." The St. Louis Home Guard, in which Henry served for three months in 1861, was almost entirely German. In the first few weeks of the war, the Home Guard occupied the large U.S. arsenal at St. Louis and defended it against attack from the pro-South state militia, an action that effectively kept Missouri out of the Confederacy. After his time in the Home Guard, Timken enlisted again and served three years as a captain in the 13th regiment of the Missouri militia. John Ringen also fought for the Union, and the two men would remain the closest of friends throughout their lives.[20]

After his mustering out, Henry returned to the carriage trade. But the business was by that time in the midst of dramatic changes. Change had begun in the early 1850s with the development of specialized machine tools for woodworking operations central to carriage making, in particular for wheel making. Soon there were factories in New York and New England that specialized in producing wagon parts in great quantities by machine. Individual carriage makers could purchase components and assemble vehicles in a fraction of the time it had formerly taken to build them from the ground up. Other, vertically integrated, carriage factories adopted metalworking and woodworking machinery for every phase of production and organized their labor around specialized tasks. The Civil War hastened the development of such production methods through the tremendous demand it created for wagons and ambulances. In the postwar years, mechanization and factory organization around the assembly of interchangeable parts—the American system—spread rapidly within the industry with some notable effects. Production in greater quantities at lower cost brought about the "democratization of the carriage." The price of wheeled vehicles dropped to the point where, said one trade journal in 1875, "every man among us who can afford to keep a horse can afford to have a good buggy."[21]

The tradeoff between quantity and quality in carriage production was a subject of much debate in the trade journals of the 1870s: not all vehicle builders embraced the new mode of production. But Henry Timken certainly did. In 1864 fire destroyed his shop, on Sixth Street in St. Louis. Fire was a chronic problem in carriage shops, where blacksmith forges, lumber, and quantities of paint and varnish made a volatile combination. But in an era of rapidly changing technology it could be an opportunity as well as a disaster. Henry rebuilt his shop immediately, undoubtedly adding some new machinery and improving the efficiency of his production setup. The business flourished, and in 1877, he built a large new factory on St. Charles Street, following the most up-to-date ideas about how such an operation should be housed and organized.

As described in the carriage trade journal *The Hub*, this was a four-story building 64-by-106 feet in dimensions, with tall ceilings and lots of natural light. The first floor contained a showroom in front and blacksmith shop in back, "running 4 fires." The building, said *The Hub*, was "complete and convenient in all its parts, making one of the best carriage factories in the South or West." In such a factory, the well-equipped blacksmith shop had a power blast to drive the fires, a drop forge, power drills, hammers, lathes, grinders, and a drill press. The second floor typically contained a wagon assembly area with a wood shop and lumber room. There, power saws, planers, and dressing machines were all available to reduce both labor requirements and production time. "The ordinary dressing-machines and horizontal planers," *The Hub* noted, "will dress and reduce more work in one hour than we can possibly do by hand in ten." On the third floor were trimming rooms, a space for painting and varnishing gears (the spring assembly on which the body rested), and a paint shop, which had a "washing floor, water pipes, and all conveniences." In the trimming rooms, sewing machines, perhaps power driven, helped to assure even stitching of upholstery. In the paint shop there was machinery to grind colors into powder that could do the work in one-fourth the time required for hand grinding. The top floor contained the body-varnishing room, "plastered and painted, and with sliding partitions, making a dark room where bodies can be set to dry without disturbance from flies." A steam-powered hoist conveyed materials and vehicles between floors.[22]

The new Timken factory was by no means the nation's largest. It was only about the size of the blacksmith shop in the Studebaker factory, in South Bend, Indiana, which *was* the largest in the country and could produce a completed vehicle every seven minutes. Yet on its own scale, Timken's factory embodied all of the fundamental principles guiding construction of the "modern American carriage factory." The first of these principles, *The Hub* stated, was "arrangement of the different mechanical departments in such a manner that there shall be economy of time and labor in passing carriages through the works." As in all the industries transformed by the American system of manufacturing in the nineteenth century, efficiency was the gospel of the vehicle industry of the 1870s, and Henry Timken was a firm believer. His aggressiveness in adopting new production technologies and methods prefigured H. H. Timken's approach to building a manufacturing organization for bearings thirty years later.[23]

Just twenty-five years after launching his career in St. Louis, at age forty-six, Henry was an established manufacturer in one of the fastest growing industries of that era. He and Fredericka had five children: two sons and three daughters, Amelia, Cora, and Georgia. His younger son, H. H., nine years old when the new factory was built, was his father's "constant companion." He spent his time after school and during vacations at the carriage factory. There, he "observed first-hand the processes of manufacturing," imbibed his father's business values, and began to take to heart his father's motto: "Only in efficiency is there progress." Ultimately, though, Henry Timken's fortune would be made not as a carriage maker but as an inventor and patent holder.

Henry Timken, Patentee and Promoter

The patenting and licensing of new technology was a thriving business in the nineteenth century, one that Timken understood and from which he profited greatly. In all, he would patent fourteen inventions. United States patent law, as established in the Constitution, allowed individuals to realize returns on successful inventions by granting a temporary monopoly on an original idea. By the 1860s, thousands of individuals had obtained patents, and many of those had realized substantial gains from the sale or licensing of their patent rights. Information on patented technology was widely available to interested parties. *Scientific American* and other journals published weekly lists of new patents and articles on those of greatest significance, and industry trade journals regularly featured new

Henry and Fredericka, and their five children (ca. 1900), were the owners of The Timken Roller Bearing Axle Company. Majority ownership remained in the family until 1922, when H. H. and W. R. took the company public.

developments of particular interest. Those were channels through which inventors could advertise their patents or technology, and there were plenty of advice manuals on how to profit from new inventions.[24]

Henry Timken made several tries over nearly ten years before he hit on a patentable idea with significant market potential—the Timken Cross-Spring. Springs were a competitive field of improvement in the 1870s. Steel springs had been imported from England since the mid-eighteenth century, and English steel remained the preferred material. But English designs were aimed at providing maneuverability for heavy coaches and carriages in narrow city streets and country lanes. They had proven to be inappropriate for America, where vehicles had to be lightweight and durable enough to cover long distances at good speeds over bad roads. In the typical English end-spring design, the carriage body was suspended on two springs—one at the front and one in back—with no other support. The rival American design of the 1870s was one in which so-called side bars ran the length of the carriage on either side to provide support so that the carriage body could be lighter in construction. The springs could then be placed longitudinally on the side bars, or they could span the width: the cross-spring design. This entire structure—the side bars, the springs, and their attachments to the body and the axles—was called a gear. In 1873 James B. Brewster patented a cross-spring gear that became extremely popular and was widely copied until he successfully asserted his patent rights in court, forcing other manufacturers to license his design. Timken's cross-spring, patented in 1877, benefited from the popularity of Brewster's gear but ultimately surpassed it, less because of superior design than because of Henry Timken's aggressive campaign of advertising and promotion.[25]

Timken was an early and devoted user of advertising. From the beginning, he placed ads in the leading carriage trade magazines of the day, *The Hub* and *The Carriage Monthly*. He arranged for the Timken spring to be produced under license by established spring manufacturers in Connecticut, New Jersey, and Chicago. This step ensured marketing and distribution in key markets without a large investment. In November 1881, *The Hub* pronounced that the Timken spring was "becoming as well known as anything in the trade." A month later, Henry Timken announced to *The Hub* that he was expanding his factory in St. Louis. "Have just put in a 40 horse power engine and boiler," he noted, "as those formerly used proved entirely too small to meet the increasing demand for my gears and bodies." Reportedly, by that time, hundreds of thousands of Timken cross-springs were in use. In 1883, Timken began running weekly ads in a popular general-interest magazine with national circulation, *Harper's Weekly*.[26]

As aggressive as he was about advertising, Timken was equally so in defending his patent rights. He was also savvy enough about publicity to make the most of a high-profile legal contest. In 1883, Timken launched a patent infringement suit, seeking $50,000 in damages from one of the most prominent carriage manufacturers in the country, Columbus Buggy Company. Columbus Buggy was then a rival of Studebaker, with a factory employing nearly 1,000 men and producing 25,000 carriages a year. It was owned and managed by George M. Peters, Oscar G. Peters, and C. D. Firestone, an older first cousin of Harvey Firestone, who got his start in business and first experimented with rubber tires as a young manager in the Detroit office of Columbus Buggy. C. D. Firestone was a prominent figure in the carriage industry—he would become president of the Carriage Builders National Association in 1888—and he was not to be intimidated by a legal challenge. Columbus Buggy immediately filed a countersuit on behalf of its "Automatic" spring, and for two months verbal war was waged in the trade press. The court decided in Timken's favor in December 1884. The January newspapers greeted the industry with the image of a crowing rooster over the headline "Timken Victorious in his Suit against Columbus Buggy Company!" The rest of the large ad printed the decision of the District Court in its entirety, including notice of the $3,000 damages Columbus Buggy was obliged to pay. The conflict had an amicable ending. Columbus Buggy started using Timken springs on several of its models in 1886, and the Timken and Firestone families maintained friendly relations throughout. Yet while the litigation lasted, Henry played it for all it was worth and in the process greatly enhanced both the reputation of his product and his own stature in the industry.[27]

Ironically, Timken's cross-spring patent would ultimately be judged by the U.S. Supreme Court to be lacking in invention and thereby void. This decision resulted from a patent infringement suit brought by Timken against Thomas D. and

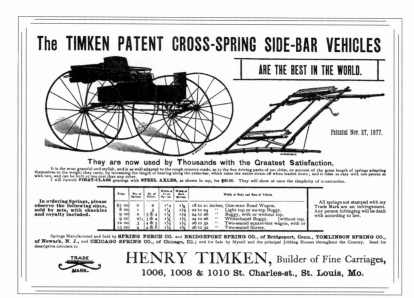

Henry capitalized on his carriage cross-spring patent through aggressive advertising in leading carriage trade magazines such as The Hub. Henry had a total of fourteen patents, including two for tapered roller bearings.

Edwin D. Olin, of Terre Haute, Indiana, who produced springs and spring assemblies for sale to carriage manufacturers. The case was originally decided in Timken's favor, in 1890, and the rooster crowed again over the announcement that the court had ordered the Olins to pay nearly $28,000 in damages. On appeal, however, the U.S. Supreme Court found that Timken's spring embodied only minor mechanical changes from a previously patented cross-spring. "While the patented article may have been popular and met with large sales," the justices stated, "those facts are not important when the alleged invention is without patentable novelty." This decision, handed down in November 1894, was one of the few significant reversals of Henry Timken's business career. [28]

Yet by the time the ruling came, it had little practical effect. Timken had long since made his fortune in sales and royalties on the cross-spring and, to a lesser extent, on his numerous other patents. In the process he had become a well-known and respected figure in one of the nation's leading industries.

The Pinnacle of Success

Tenacious in pursuit of business goals, Henry Timken was also a sociable man who enjoyed the rewards of his labor. By the last quarter of the nineteenth century, many of the Germans who immigrated to St. Louis in the 1830s and 1840s had achieved success in commerce, industry, science, literature, and public life. Timken was part of that group. He and his family moved in a lively social circle, in which music, theater, and art played a large part. Henry played the piano and pipe organ. Georgia and Cora Timken both pursued careers as artists—they lived for a time in Paris in the 1890s. In later life, Amelia would endow the San Diego Museum of Art, and W. R. Timken, in New York, would assemble one of the country's most outstanding private art collections. In the mid-1880s, when the annual convention of the Carriage Builders National Association gathered in St. Louis, Timken personally entertained the entire group with a tour of the city and "an *al fresco* lunch at the Fairgrounds." As reported admiringly in *The Hub*, "So princely an entertainment [had] never before been offered by an individual member of the Association."[29]

In 1887, at fifty-six years old, Henry Timken retired from the carriage business and moved to San Diego. "There I built a fine residence," he recalled in his autobiography, "and concluded to take life easy for the balance of my days." Timken turned his attention to real-estate investments and traveled both in America and in Europe, where he and Fredericka particularly enjoyed visiting German family and friends. Despite these diversions, however, Henry grew restless. In his own words, he "found that an active mind cannot be contented without being occupied." So, "after five years of idleness," he returned to St. Louis and the carriage business.[30]

Yet, if inactivity drove him out of "retirement," there was also much to attract him back into the carriage business. Indeed, he had never fully abandoned it. Though he had turned over the management of his business to his daughter Amelia's husband, Appleton S. Bridges, Timken maintained connections to the industry and kept his eye on the marketplace. Carriage springs remained one of the most competitive areas of the industry, and, retired or not, Timken was unwilling to abandon his position in the field. This meant he had to keep updating his product. He did this first by joining forces with the other market leader, James Brewster, to offer the Timken-Brewster Combination Spring. He also set to work to devise further improvements of his own and was granted three new patents on carriage springs in 1891 and 1892. Declared *The Hub* in November 1892, "The name of Timken is so clearly identified with carriage springs that every carriage builder and user knows of it."[31]

Beyond looking out for his own interests, however, Timken may also have been motivated to end his temporary retirement by the fact that his two sons were launching their careers. Twenty-six years old in 1892, W. R. had for some time been an investor in The Mutual Wheel Company. In January 1891, he and a partner, Charles Heflinger, each contributed their shares in that company and some additional cash to launch a new business, The St. Louis Carriage Manufacturing Company. W. R. served as secretary and treasurer of the company; Heflinger was president and oversaw manufacturing operations.[32]

H. H. was twenty-four in 1892. He had been in college, at Washington University in St. Louis, when his father moved to San Diego, but he had moved with the family and had completed his education at the University of California, receiving a law degree in 1890. The following year he was admitted to the Missouri bar and took up the practice of law in St. Louis. In later years, H. H. would place great value on his legal training. The law was a discipline, he said, that could help a man greatly in business because it taught him "to think straight, to plan wisely, to see the adverse side and realize the obstacles he is going to meet." However, early on it became evident that a legal career, at least as he wished to practice it, would be difficult for him because of partial deafness that made it hard to argue effectively in court. (This was likely a genetic illness, since W. R. Timken was also partially deaf and H. H.'s three sons were all quite hard of hearing.) As a child, H. H. had been fascinated by the carriage factory and the principles of efficiency by which Henry Timken had sought to run it. As an adult he was increasingly attracted by his father's zest for competition and his inventiveness, particularly when it focused on the problem of friction.[33]

By the time his original cross-spring patent was disallowed in 1894, Timken was successfully marketing the New Timken Side Spring, which had won a First Premium Award at the 1893 Columbian Exposition in Chicago. He had also started construction of a large new factory for wholesale production of carriages, and in January 1895, he incorporated his business as The Timken Carriage Company with $50,000 of paid-in capital. Of the 500 shares of this new corporation, Timken held 250, H. H. held 249, and a nephew, Cord Ringen, held 1. An immediate consolidation of Timken Carriage with the St. Louis Carriage Manufacturing Company, of which W. R. Timken was half owner, brought both of Henry's sons into business with him. W. R. ran the office and served as secretary. H. H. set out to learn manufacturing from the bottom up, starting as a laborer on the carriage factory floor. Near the end of 1895, the Timkens bought out W. R.'s partner, Charles Heflinger.[34]

Also in this period, Henry Timken assumed a leading role in the Carriage Builders National Association, serving on the executive committee in 1894 and as president in 1895 and 1896. That position gave him an excellent vantage point from which to assess the prospects of the emerging U.S. automotive industry. In November 1895, he served as one of two judges of a race for horseless carriages sponsored by the Chicago *Times Herald*. That contest was modeled on a dramatic Paris-to-Bordeaux race six months earlier, which had demonstrated the advanced state of automotive technology in Europe and created an instant market for motor vehicles. The French race had been run over a 745-mile course, which the contestants had to complete, nonstop, in 100 hours or less. Twenty-three autos started and nine finished. The winner, Emile Levassor, averaged 15 miles per hour—a testimony both to the power of his engine (built by the German firm, Daimler) and the good quality of French roads. The resulting boom in European auto sales would last for more than a decade.[35]

By contrast, the Chicago race demonstrated mainly the rudimentary state of American automotive technology. Of sixty would-be entrants that responded to the notice of the race and its $5,000 in prizes, only six started the race, and only two finished: H. Mueller of Decatur, Illinois, driving a German car built by Karl Benz; and J. Frank Duryea, driving a gasoline-powered car produced by Duryea Motor Wagon Company of Springfield, Massachusetts. Duryea had a clear victory, but took 10 hours and 23 minutes to complete the 53-mile course. Given the rough roads and snowy conditions (the judges and umpires followed the race in sleighs), just finishing was a triumph. Far from sparking widespread admiration and demand for the new mode of transportation, as in Europe, the *Times Herald* race left the public skeptical and largely negative.[36]

Yet the race was an important event for the American automotive industry. Until then the industry had consisted of a dispersed group of individual inventors laboring largely in ignorance of work going on elsewhere in the United States, not to mention in Europe. Since both vehicles completing the race used gasoline engines—the two competing autos with electric motors broke down within the first mile—the outcome gave confidence and renewed incentive to the inventors working on that technology. That group included Hiram Percy Maxim, who was to develop a successful gasoline-powered car for the country's leading bicycle maker, the Pope Manufacturing Company, and the young Henry Ford. Said Ford some twenty years later, "I never wanted anything so badly in my life as to go to that race, but I could not get anyone to loan me the car fare to Chicago."[37]

In contrast to the youthful group of inventors and entrepreneurs that Ford represented—working in relative isolation, full of ideas and ambition, but with limited financial resources to pursue them—Henry Timken had traveled extensively in Europe, making a six-month tour in 1892 and another visit in 1895. Carriage manufacturers were naturally intensely interested in the progress of the horseless carriage, although it would be the bicycle makers who led the way in creating the U.S. automotive industry. As the head of his industry, Timken had undoubtedly taken note of the progress in engine technology made by Daimler and Benz. He had also observed the advanced state of automobile manufacturing in France, and the way in which the spectacle of powerful vehicles racing at high speed over good roads had captured the public imagination in Europe. At a time when enthusiasts generally tended to think of the automobile as a toy for wealthy sportsmen, he had experienced firsthand over the course of his career in the carriage business how the introduction of machine-made interchangeable parts and factory methods of production had transformed a large, luxury item into a product that was widely available and affordable to individual businessmen and middle-class families. He thus had good reason to be excited by the signs of an emerging domestic auto industry in the Chicago race. In 1896, the Duryea brothers, Frank and Charles, formally launched it with a production run of 13 cars. By that time, Timken was deeply engaged in bearing development.

Invention of the Timken Bearing

The U.S. carriage industry had been awakened en masse to the potential significance of anti-friction bearings by the electrifying appearance on the horse racing scene of the so-called bicycle sulky, which had ball-bearing-equipped axles and bicycle-sized pneumatic tires (tubular rubber filled with compressed air). In 1892 a mare, Nancy Hanks, shaved seven seconds off the existing trotting record for a mile pulling the bicycle sulky. In the same year, Henry and H. H. Timken traveled together in Europe for six months. On this trip, as H. H. later recalled, they "studied in considerable detail the progress being made by foreign inventors toward anti-friction bearings." Europe was then well ahead of the United States in bearing development. Yet it must have been clear to the Timkens that there was considerable room for improvement in bearing performance, since they returned to St. Louis determined to develop a bearing "superior to anything on the market."[38]

There was much to observe abroad. In Britain, where bearing manufacture had first taken off, five English companies were producing ball bearings, four of them bicycle makers located in Coventry and Birmingham, cities that would later become the center of the English automotive industry. However, in the 1880s the leading edge of the bearing industry had begun to shift to Germany. There, in Schweinfurt in 1883, Phillipp Fischer, an instrument maker and inventor of the first pedal bicycle, and his son Friederich, who ran a repair shop for bicycles and sewing machines, pioneered the mass production of balls for bearings with a grinding machine that was not only faster but also achieved far greater uniformity in roundness and size than the existing method of turning the balls on a lathe. The Fischers built a factory to produce their bearings, and in 1885 a locksmith, Georg Schaefer, opened a second bearing factory in Schweinfurt. (Those two companies would merge in 1909 to form Kugelfischer Georg Schaefer.) Friederich Fischer patented the ball mill in 1890. In the same year, another German company, Deutsche Waffen-und-Munitionsfabriken in Berlin took delivery on ball-grinding machinery designed and built in the United States by the Cleveland Machine Screw Company. It soon advanced the use of this American-made equipment to the point that its product was recognized as superior to anything made in the United States. The German companies established a dominant position in the industry, to the extent that up until World War I most of the ball bearings used in the United States would be imported from Germany.[39]

Thus, by the time the Timkens began their investigation, the importance of manufacturing technology was already apparent, and that was doubtless part of the intelligence they brought home with them from their European tour. Before they could focus on that issue, however, they would have to address questions of bearing design. About the time they returned from Europe, Henry was approached by two nephews for support of their work toward developing an improved ball bearing. Reginald and Edmund Heinzelman were the grandsons of John Heinzelman and the third generation in the family carriage business in Belleville, Illinois. They arrived in St. Louis with a prototype of a bearing that aimed at solving a critical weakness in existing designs. In the type of ball bearings used in the bicycle industry, loose balls posed a major problem because they could easily slip out, either in assembly or when the bearings were removed for cleaning and adjustment. The solution was to form the races with deep grooves inside, to hold the balls more securely. But this new type—the annular ball bearing—posed another problem: how to get the balls into the enclosed raceway created by the grooves. The only answer available in the 1890s was to make one of the races in two halves, leaving significant weak points in the bearing where the halves were joined. The Heinzelmans came up with an alternative solution. The bearing they showed to Henry Timken had a hole in the side of the outer raceway, through which the balls could be inserted. Henry was sufficiently impressed by the idea that he hired Reginald to stay on in St. Louis to develop it further.[40]

When several sets of the Heinzelman ball bearing were made up and tested, however, they failed quickly with wear, and it was at that point that Henry determined to move on to experiment with roller bearings. Annular ball bearings with filling slots would be patented by others and widely manufactured. But, as reported later by Reginald Heinzelman, "it was the consensus of opinion that roller bearings would be more suitable for vehicles [i.e., carriages] as a line contact would have more bearing surface and therefore a greater carrying load."[41]

From his travels, Henry Timken doubtless knew that, while scores of roller bearing designs had been patented, practically none had been proven by commercial production or use. If anything, the manufacturing challenges were greater for roller bearings than for ball bearings. Even imperfect spheres would roll inside a ball bearing, and engineering studies of bicycle bearings published in the 1880s showed that, as they were worn down with use, the balls tended to become more round and even in size so that the amount of wear became less with extended use. In contrast, when an English bicycle maker, J. H. Hughes, adopted roller bearings in 1882, he was forced to abandon them immediately because uneven hardness and shape of the rollers made it impossible to obtain smooth rolling motion.[42]

That situation was beginning to change in the early 1890s. The first breakthrough came in the United States in 1891 when John Wesley Hyatt developed a process for making rollers by winding a strip of steel in a spiral around a form. The hollow, flexible rollers that resulted did away with the problems of unevenness that plagued designs with solid rollers, and Hyatt's bearing exceeded the ability of ball bearings to withstand shocks and run at high speeds. Though designed specifically for application in sugar-cane crushing mills, it was soon adopted more broadly for various types of heavy industrial machinery. The company that Hyatt formed in 1892 expanded rapidly. At the same time, development of grinding machines presented the means by which hardened steel parts could be shaped with enough precision to make it feasible to produce solid roller bearings on an industrial scale. In 1895, Arthur W. Grant of Springfield, Ohio, applied for a patent on a tapered roller bearing for vehicle axles. His patent was allowed in April 1897, by which time he had launched the Grant Axle and Wheel Company to provide roller-bearing-equipped axles to the carriage trade.[43]

About the time that Grant was applying for his patent, Timken and Heinzelman, dissatisfied with straight roller bearings, began their own experiments with tapered. In an episode now deeply ingrained in Timken Company lore, they equipped a wagon with a set of handmade bearings and sent it out on the streets of St. Louis with a load so large that the driver was arrested for cruelty to the small mule pulling it. W. R. Timken, the owner of the wagon, showed off the bearings in court—and he avoided a fine. The event, if it actually took place, was a definitive and colorful demonstration of the ability of tapered roller bearings both to carry a heavy load relative to their size and to reduce friction on the axle to the point that much less force was required to move the load.[44] Yet considerable work remained to develop an effective bearing design on which a patent position could be established. In addition to Grant's, there were more than thirty European and American patents on tapered roller bearings, dating back to 1802. At the same time, there remained some critical design issues to be addressed. Carr & Carr, a St.

Louis firm of patent attorneys, assisted Timken and Heinzelman in reviewing this extensive patent literature. H. H. and W. R. lent a hand in the blacksmith shop of the carriage factory, where further prototypes were made for testing.[45]

One problem with tapered roller bearings was that the rollers had a tendency to creep up the cone, causing the roller ends to rub against a constraining surface. The friction thus created not only reduced the effectiveness of the bearing but also greatly increased the rate of wear. The need to secure the rollers in a way that allowed them to roll freely but still maintain their proper position presented a difficult design challenge, but also an opportunity for innovation. In the course of the development work, roller alignment emerged as the critical problem to be solved. Its solution became the centerpiece of the Timken-Heinzelman patents.

Many prior designs employed a rib-and-groove construction, in which raised ribs on the cup and cone fitted into a corresponding groove near the narrow end of each roller and restrained the tendency of the roller to creep. Timken and Heinzelman adopted this approach at the outset but were forced to reevaluate after numerous prototypes failed in wear tests. In fact, they found, the single rib and groove caused the roller to become skewed. Skewing not only created friction, it also reduced the area of contact between the rollers and races and thus limited bearing capacity. To correct this problem, they began to experiment with a design that added an additional rib-and-groove construction near the large end of the roller. Another change they made was to eliminate the ribs from the cup, so that only the ribs on the cone engaged the roller grooves. This change was designed to permit adjustment of the rollers and cone within the cup, in order to compensate for wear. With those key features—a second rib and groove, and adjustability for wear—they applied for a patent in August 1897.[46]

A second, critical phase of development began with that patent application. Over a period of months it was rejected twice because the language used to state the patent's claims was deemed too broad and too vague. Finally accepted, it was then held up by technicalities—the drawing submitted with the application was mutilated in the patent office; the replacement was submitted without a signature. It was still pending when Timken and Heinzelman submitted an application on a new bearing design, in February 1898. This second application was also denied once, but an amended version passed expeditiously and both patents were issued on June 28, 1898. The successive iterations of the patent application and supporting documentation show that, during the time between the first and final applications, Timken and Heinzelman conducted an intensive review of existing knowledge as captured in the patent literature. Simultaneously, they experimented with their own and competing designs. Out of that work came an improved design, as represented in the second patent. This included the addition of thin cylindrical rollers to separate the tapered rollers, which were reduced in number from 19 to 11. This change reduced the internal friction that had existed in the previous design having a full complement of working rollers, in which the rollers revolved against each other in opposite directions. The separating rollers prevented that and helped to maintain alignment. (See patent drawings below.) By 1899, when the Timken bearing went into commercial production, the intermediate rollers would evolve into a cage, a distinct unit that held the rollers on the cone and helped to maintain alignment. (See Evolution of the Timken Tapered Roller Bearing on pages 90–92.)

Just as important as the design, however, the work of this period produced a clearer understanding of the critical issue of roller alignment. According to Herbert W. Alden, Timken's chief engineer in 1908, this was "the feature of greatest importance . . . [and] the rock on which many a roller bearing has gone down." It would drive development of tapered roller bearing design into the 1920s.[47]

The Timken-Heinzelman design proved to have solved the problem admirably. Sets of bearing-equipped carriage axles, provided to a few friends on an

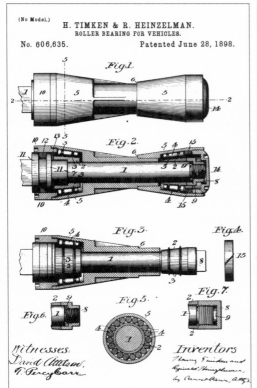
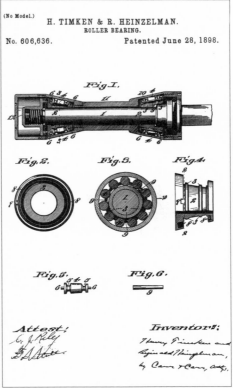

Compare Fig. 5 of Patent 606,635 with Fig. 3 of Patent 606,636 to see the two critical changes: tapered rollers are fewer in number and are separated by intermediate rollers. Additional improvements were made by 1899, when Timken began commercial production.

experimental basis while the patents were still pending, worked effectively and showed minimal wear even with heavy use. The Timkens and Heinzelman determined to organize for commercial production. On December 15, 1899, a momentous day for everyone involved, they incorporated The Timken Roller Bearing Axle Company with $100,000 of paid-in capital. This marked the official beginning of what would become The Timken Company. The corporate edifice would gain solidity only through years of heavy capital investment and the building of an organization with the capabilities to develop the business. Yet it rested upon the solid foundation of an effective solution to the problem of friction provided by the patented Timken bearing.[48]

The Founder's Legacy Revisited

With the new business launched, Henry Timken at the end of 1899 again retired to California. He retained the title of president of The Timken Roller Bearing Axle Company but left the management of it to his sons—H. H. as vice president and general manager, and W. R. as secretary and treasurer. This time, Timken found much to keep him busy in San Diego. He formed the Timken Investment Company to pursue his interest in real estate and became one of the leading developers of the city, then in a period of dynamic growth. He returned to his roots in agriculture, taking an active interest in a large citrus grove. And, in this second retirement, he indulged a fascination of his youth, investing in a Nevada gold mine, the Bonnie Claire, and serving as the mining company's president. With all those new interests to engage him, Timken would remain in the background of his sons' effort to build a business on the tapered roller bearing. Yet his continuing support would be absolutely essential in the difficult early years. Well beyond that, his life experiences and his personality would exert influence through the family culture, which, in effect, became the management culture of the fledgling company.

H. H. Timken remembered his father as a man who wanted his sons to pursue their own visions, as he had. He had studiously avoided urging them to join him in the carriage business and had sent them to college to enable them to "map out their own careers." At the same time, H. H. said, he gave them this advice:

> To be successful you must be independent. If you want to lead in any line you must bring to it independence of thought, unfailing industry, aggression, and indomitable purpose. If you have an idea which you think is right, push it to a finish. Don't let any one else influence you against it. If we all thought the same way there would be no progress. But above all don't set your name to anything you will ever have cause to be ashamed of.[49]

That statement, in particular its emphasis on independence, would take on a life of its own under later generations of company leaders. H. H. drew from it three important lessons. One was that business is hard work and success does not come to the timid. With that mindset, the Timken brothers would persevere through a difficult start-up period. In H. H., it was expressed in an almost grim tenacity and an unrelenting work ethic, which characterized the company throughout his long career and has remained an element of the corporate culture.

Another lesson was the value of independent thinking in young people trying to make their way in the world. Henry Timken had wanted to encourage that in his sons, and H. H., the organization builder, looked for it in the men he hired. He was eager to have "young blood" in the business and willing to let them try out their ideas and make good if they could. "But," said H. H. (perhaps reflecting his own upbringing), "I believe in giving them a little opposition so that they will have a chance to show their initiative. What we need in the business world is the quick wit to think our way out of a difficult situation, the independence of mind to see a new track, the courage to make a quick decision even if it does not coincide with the general opinion, and the backbone to put it over when we know we are right."[50]

By following through on those convictions in hiring and developing new leaders, H. H. put a permanent stamp on the company's character. He surrounded himself with individuals who were willing to challenge him, gave them plenty of opposition, and created an environment in which men with strong wills and strong personalities could flourish. And many did, enjoying long careers as Timken plant managers and department heads. Such men were often autocratic within their own realms. Persisting well into the 1970s, this aspect of the corporate culture would rigidify in a kind of organizational insularity and short sightedness that constrained the company's ability to respond to a changing competitive environment. Yet, overall, Timken benefited from the fact that these men of considerable energy and talent could find room within the company to pursue their personal ambitions and exercise leadership.

Henry Timken's final admonition—*"But above all, don't set your name to anything you will ever have cause to be ashamed of"*—was, of course, the most powerful one. That pride of ownership, continued over one hundred years of active family involvement, would prove to be one of the company's greatest assets, not least because of the ability of H. H., his sons, and his grandsons to inspire others to value the Timken name as they themselves did. In keeping with the founder's own style, H. H. and other family members provided inspiration mainly by their actions. The most significant is the family's sustained commitment both to the company and the communities in which it is located.

In no more than a handful of large, old public companies does the founding family maintain a significant financial stake, much less a leadership role. The Timken brothers took their company public in 1922, offering one-third of its shares for sale on the New York Stock Exchange. By the 1990s, the extended family's stake remained substantial, at 19 percent. During the intervening years, the patient capital provided by the family bloc profoundly influenced the strategic choices the company made, particularly in the 1980s and early 1990s when Timken invested heavily to improve its long-term competitive position in a business climate that strongly discouraged such investments. Henry Timken set a precedent for that: within the first five years, he doubled his initial capitalization. His support both kept the company alive and made possible sustained investment in manufacturing technology at a time when Timken's long-term competitiveness depended on keeping up with rapid advances in machine-tool technology.

Investing for the long term became a Timken Company hallmark. It has also been the hallmark of the family's approach to philanthropy, which was developed by H. H. but influenced by his father's example. Henry Timken, according to his son, was a man who acknowledged the responsibilities of wealth and "manfully and properly . . . carried them out." In San Diego, his adopted home, he made a great deal of money for his heirs with investments in real estate. But he and they also gave a great deal back. In his obituary, the *San Diego Union* commented that he had been "one of the first men" of the city in his support for "charitable enterprises, never refusing to donate to institutions or purposes which were shown to be deserving." He particularly liked to give large gifts for building projects. At the time of his death, the paper noted, his church was building an addition that he financed, and construction was under way to remodel a building for the Fredericka Home for Aged Women, named after Henry's wife because it was a charity in which they were both interested and active.[51]

Similarly, when H. H. and his brother and sisters created the Timken Foundation in 1934, they set as its mission to give large grants for capital investments in the communities where the company operated. H. H. said that the family's philanthropic efforts should focus first and foremost on the city of Canton, Ohio, "where the real foundation of the Timken fortune was made."[52] This policy, carried on and expanded to plant communities around the world by his descendants, has helped to foster the sense of pride people have felt in being associated with The Timken Company.

In short, while the Timken brothers, and particularly H. H., were the organization builders to whom must go the credit for making the company a success, any explanation of why the firm evolved as it did must encompass the contributions of Henry Timken beyond the patents and early infusions of capital. Henry's values remain alive in The Timken Company today because they were articulated and enacted by H. H. and passed on by him to successive generations of managers, both family and non-family. In the twentieth century, the rise of mass markets, a technological revolution, and two world wars would completely transform the business environment in which Henry Timken had thrived. Yet his legacy of a compelling sense of purpose and a cohesive corporate culture would play a central role in the survival and success of the company he founded.

"Famous Automotive Brothers": The Formative Years, 1900–1915

"**F**amous Automotive Brothers," a two-part article published in *Automotive Industries* in 1927, featured thirty-four brother combinations active in the early years of the auto industry. These included the four Firestone brothers, the five Studebakers, the three Davidson brothers of Harley Davidson, the Macks of Mack trucks, the Fishers, the Dodges, the Appersons, the Duryeas, and the Timkens. "Although other industries have also had their famous brother combinations," said the author, "it is doubtful if any can produce such an array as has contributed to automotive history in the last 30 years."[1] He offered this fact only as an interesting demographic anomaly, but it is a useful reminder of how many businesses originate in family entrepreneurship. Most family firms do not survive the first generation. Of those that have survived and grown large, few remain in family hands. The outcome in all cases has been largely determined by the culture and values of the founding family and by the capabilities, personalities, and personal decisions of individual members. This was clearly true for the Timkens.

H. H. and W. R. Timken worked together in the family business for fifteen years before W. R. began to withdraw from active involvement. During that time, they saw it through its start-up struggles and built the organizational capabilities in production, sales, and product and process development that were essential for long-term success. Together they engineered a dramatic expansion—including separating bearings and axles into two companies, Timken Roller Bearing and Timken-Detroit Axle—as their products took off in step with the automotive industry. And they navigated an uncertain period when competition and industry consolidation, combined with personal issues, made either selling out or merging with another bearing manufacturer an appealing option.

Fortunately, a large body of their correspondence still exists. Those letters reveal a brotherly relationship based on mutual respect and deference. H. H. and W. R. had much in common outside of business. They were both hard of hearing, and both struggled with serious illness at different times. California became a refuge for both men. H. H. spent the months of January through March in San Diego virtually every winter, and W. R. moved to Pasadena in 1915. They shared a love of travel and of sailing and other sports, though H. H. was by far the more active. Indeed, what differentiated the two men most as they matured was W. R.'s increasing desire for leisure, in contrast to the intensity with which H. H. continued to engage both in the bearing business and in a broad range of outside activities.

H. H. belonged to a ballooning club in the early years in Canton and ballooned with Wilbur Wright when he visited there. Later, he got into powerboat racing and was the first person to go over 100 miles per hour in a boat. After 1910 he ran a 3,000-acre farm in California, on which he experimented with growing flax, and in 1920 he added a cattle ranch in Arizona. Active in the Canton Chamber of Commerce, H. H. took part in politics as a Progressive and later as a Republican. From 1913 to 1929, he owned the *Canton Daily News*, which he had bought with the idea of transforming a rather "run-down" operation into "a first-class paper for this size town." H. H. contributed a great deal of time as an organizer of support activities in Ohio during World War I, and he chided W. R. for expressing strong patriotic views in his letters but declining to take an active role in the war effort. "Take it from me," he wrote to his brother in 1917, in one of his many efforts to get his brother to re-engage, "you will get more out of life by being in the game than being on the sidelines."[2]

From 1915 onward, the Timken brothers collaborated most actively on decisions relating to their joint investments. Chief among those, after the two Timken companies, was a large stake in Chalmers Motor Company. This was a connection they both viewed as problematic, as it obliged them to give Chalmers advantageous prices on bearings and axles. They vowed thereafter not to take a financial stake in any auto company. In the 1920s, this investment involved them in the reorganization by Walter Chrysler of the troubled Maxwell-Chalmers concern. Out of this emerged the Chrysler Corporation, with the Timkens as substantial stockholders. By that time, though, the Timken brothers' investment interests had further diverged. W. R. became intrigued by the opportunities on Wall Street, while H. H. preferred to continue investing in business concerns in Canton and in association with men he knew well.[3] He played a prominent role as both investor and director in the First National Bank, First Trust and Savings Bank, and Hercules Motor Corporation, all in Canton, and, with Canton associates, in the Louisiana Land & Exploration Company.

Overall, their differences were far outweighed by their likenesses and shared beliefs. This was particularly true of their collaboration in the business in the crucial formative years. They were two strong-willed, opinionated individuals, both capable of being quite overbearing and of delivering withering criticism when moved to do so. Yet there is no trace of that in their correspondence on company affairs. Their letters show that they consulted fully on important issues and tended to trust each other's judgment. That tendency was undoubtedly strengthened by the fact that they divided the responsibilities of management along clear lines. While they both handled sales, particularly in the early years, W. R. took the lead in developing sales as a function. He was president of Timken-Detroit Axle, and he handled financial and administrative matters and directed sales and advertising for both companies. H. H. from the beginning took charge of manufacturing and engineering and had primary responsibility for The Timken Roller Bearing Company. Even in the issues they handled together, however, there is no evidence in their correspondence of serious disagreement, much less conflict. Thus, they may be jointly credited for the way the business developed between 1899 and 1915.

Difficult Early Years

The Timken tapered roller bearing was a technical success from the beginning, but commercial success was longer in coming. Between the maturity of the carriage industry and the infancy of the auto industry, the company had a serious timing problem in the early years. Large-scale manufacturing had vastly expanded the market for wagons and carriages but had also made most buyers sensitive to price. The $20 price of a set of Timken bearing-equipped axles in 1900 was high for a market in which $50 buggies were widely available. Automobiles, on the other hand, were still being produced in scattered, small shops, and the market was almost entirely the province of wealthy sportsmen. Price was not an obstacle, but the potential for sales was limited. At the same time, there were large investments to be made in manufacturing processes, to ensure the competitiveness of the Timken product in both quality and price. A recession in 1903–4, a setback for the young auto industry, would further delay Timken's takeoff. After 1904, business would boom, and the company would have a difficult time expanding production fast enough to meet demand. Until then, building sales was an arduous task and profitability an elusive goal.

Reginald Heinzelman left the company in 1900, shortly after his uncle's retirement. Up to that time, he was an equal partner with Timken and his sons. He and Henry Timken had assigned half of their rights in the roller bearing patents to H. H. and W. R., and the four held equal shares in The Timken Roller Bearing Axle Company. What is known is that Heinzelman sold his stock back to the company in June 1900, and returned to Belleville, Illinois. Within a year he filed an application for a patent on a new tapered roller bearing design. That fact suggests there may have been a conflict over technical issues, but it may also have been the case that the three cousins simply found it impossible to work together once Henry Timken was no longer actively involved.[4]

The Timken brothers were both strong personalities. William Hosfeld, who joined the company in 1901, said of them, "In those days the Timken boys had the appearance of prize fighters, and they did not deceive their looks." H. H., in particular, was known for defending his opinions tenaciously, occasionally with his fists. Whatever the specific cause of Heinzelman's departure—personal or professional—it must be said that he left at a time when the future of the enterprise was far from certain. The Heinzelman family carriage business may well have seemed to offer a more promising future than the fledgling bearing company under the direction of the Timken brothers.[5]

The business lost money steadily in its first two years of operation, though not because its product was lacking. The Timken bearing-equipped axle was designed to be retrofitted into existing carriages or wagons as readily as it was incorporated into new models. To work properly, tapered roller bearings had to be mounted in pairs, facing each other on either side of the wheel hub. Each axle thus carried four Timken bearings. For ease of assembly, they came premounted in housings, or "boxes," so that the axle could be fitted directly into the wheel. (See illustration on page 37.) In 1901, at the Pan-American Exposition in Buffalo, the company staged an exhibition using two flatbed wagons, each loaded with 4,000 pounds of lead bars. One was equipped with Timken axles. A pulley-and-weight apparatus demonstrated that the wagon with ordinary axles required a force of 48 pounds to start, the Timken-equipped wagon only 8—a sixfold reduction in draft "under ideal conditions." The Timken bearing took a gold medal from this exhibition.[6]

When the Timkens solicited comments from their early customers, they received many enthusiastic testimonials, a sampling of which helps to show the practical value of an effective bearing. F. O. Bailey, a carriage maker in Portland, Maine,

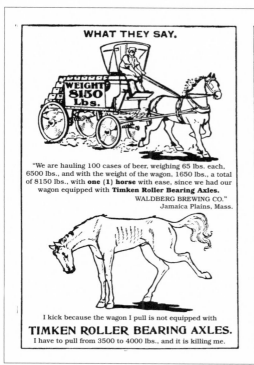

WHAT THEY SAY.

WEIGHT 8150 Lbs.

"We are hauling 100 cases of beer, weighing 65 lbs. each, 6500 lbs., and with the weight of the wagon, 1650 lbs., a total of 8150 lbs., with **one (1) horse** with ease, since we had our wagon equipped with **Timken Roller Bearing Axles.**
WALDBERG BREWING CO."
Jamaica Plains, Mass.

I kick because the wagon I pull is not equipped with
TIMKEN ROLLER BEARING AXLES.
I have to pull from 3500 to 4000 lbs., and it is killing me.

IT MAKES A HORSE LAUGH

To Equip His Vehicle with
TIMKEN ROLLER BEARING AXLES

BECAUSE
His work is made easy.
He can do double the work he could formerly.
His life-time is doubled.

HIS OWNER LAUGHS EVEN MORE

BECAUSE
The draft on his vehicle is reduced over 50 per cent.
The earning capacity of his vehicle is doubled.
He has the fastest vehicle if not the fastest horse.
He has to oil his axles only twice a year.

Early ads emphasized the Timken tapered roller bearing's ability to reduce the load and stress to horses while increasing a vehicle's speed.

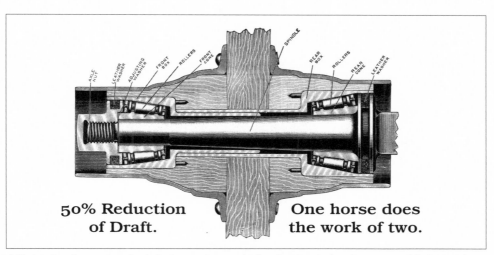

50% Reduction of Draft.

One horse does the work of two.

A Timken bearing-equipped axle for horse-drawn vehicles showing the bearings mounted facing each other on either side of the hub. Inner bearings were larger to carry the greater thrust loads when a vehicle turned. For automotive applications, where bearings were placed individually and adjusted, rather than contained in premounted boxes as shown here, Timken developed outer races (cups).

described the difference in two identical wagons, one of which was equipped with a set of Timken axles. "[O]ur lightest horse . . . weighing 300 lbs. less than the large horse, will haul the same load with ease while the big horse has to exert himself pretty hard." St. Louis veterinarian S. E. Phillips declared, "I call them the horse's friend." Many letters praised the way in which Timken bearings held up under severe and extended use with minimal maintenance—indirect testimony that the company had found solutions to the manufacturing as well as the design challenges of making an effective anti-friction bearing. One correspondent made the connection explicitly. "We think you have the right principle," wrote the manager of the Buckeye Buggy Company of Columbus, Ohio, "and that that principle is made a success by the painstaking care which you exercise in fitting up the boxes and rollers."[7]

Yet, if the quality of the product was satisfactory, the economics of production were not. The company had no in-house manufacturing capability but assembled parts obtained from outside suppliers, all of them far removed from the Timken factory in St. Louis. Axles came from Sheldon Axle Company in Wilkes Barre, Pennsylvania, and Cleveland Axle Company in Canton, Ohio. Otto Konigslow of Cleveland supplied cages and pins. Timken purchased cups and cones from Miami Cycle & Manufacturing Company and Middletown Cycle Company, in Miamisburg and Middletown, Ohio; rollers from Western Automatic Machine Screw Company, of Elyria, Ohio; and boxes from the Crosby Company of Buffalo, New York. In addition, the company was dependent on an outside firm for technical expertise. In March 1901, H. H. Timken engaged the firm of Wolf & Colthar to provide technical assistance on its own premises in Cincinnati, Ohio. He agreed to pay 75¢ per hour for design and drawing work and 50¢ per hour for experimental and machine work. He apparently foresaw a substantial need for development work—the contract anticipated $2,500 in the first year and $1,500 in subsequent years. In contracting for this level of business he extracted an agreement that Wolf & Colthar would keep its work for Timken secret and would not work on any other anti-friction bearings or devices for vehicles of any kind during the life of the contract.[8]

All of this made the cost of the company's products very high. In 1900, Timken charged its customers $20 for a set of bearing-equipped axles. During 1901 it raised the price to $26, $30, and finally to $40. Yet even at $40 per set, the cost of parts purchased, plus freight charges, amounted to 78 percent of revenues. From November 1900 through October 1901 monthly sales grew steadily and dramatically, from $20,000 to $316,000, but the business lost money consistently.[9]

The price increases made all but the high end of the carriage market largely inaccessible at a time when sales to automotive companies were relatively rare. In the summer of 1900, Timken sold three sets of bearing-equipped axles to the St. Louis Motor Carriage Company. George P. Dorris, vice president

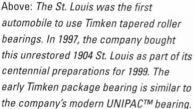

Above: *The St. Louis was the first automobile to use Timken tapered roller bearings. In 1997, the company bought this unrestored 1904 St. Louis as part of its centennial preparations for 1999. The early Timken package bearing is similar to the company's modern UNIPAC™ bearing.*

Right: *Chairman, president, and CEO Tim Timken (left) and his brother Jack, vice president, admire the condition of the original bearings removed from the rear axle of the 1904 St. Louis.*

and chief engineer of that company, was a neighbor and friend of Henry Timken. He and the Timken brothers briefly considered getting into automaking together, and in later years Dorris would take great pride in having built the first automobile with Timken roller bearing axles. He was a skilled engineer and inventor. The model he introduced in 1899, the St. Louis, had an innovative one-cylinder engine with integral transmission and was designed and built entirely in his shop. Not every St. Louis used the Timken bearing-equipped axle in those early years, but it became a standard feature in 1903. Henry Timken drove a St. Louis automobile in San Diego and provided an enthusiastic testimonial for the St. Louis Carriage Company catalog of that year. The Buckeye Manufacturing Company of Anderson, Illinois, was another early Timken customer. A producer of carriage parts that switched to making motorcars, Buckeye bought its first set of Timken axles in August 1900, possibly for an automotive application. In 1901 another St. Louis firm, H. F. Borbein & Company, adopted Timken bearings for the automobile running gears it produced.[10]

Those were important early sales, but hardly enough to set the company on its feet. H. H. and W. R. threw themselves into building the automotive market. In later years, H. H. recalled how they combed the streets of Cleveland and Detroit, "hot on the trail of every new inventor of a car. . . . When we got hold of him we did not let up until we had persuaded him that the future success of his car lay in his adoption of our particular equipment."[11] What the company needed as much as anything, however, was to internalize its manufacturing processes. This, the Timkens recognized, would have to be done *before* a substantial automotive business could be created. In 1901, they began to consider relocating the business to a place better suited to establishing a complete manufacturing facility.

The Move to Canton, Ohio

The Timkens considered and were courted by a number of communities seeking to attract industrial firms. However, one city in particular—Canton, Ohio—came to their attention through an important supplier, the Cleveland Axle Company, which had itself moved to Canton from Cleveland in 1892. Gordon Mather, the Cleveland Axle salesman who called on the Timkens in St. Louis, had struck up a friendship with H. H. that would later blossom into a broad-ranging business partnership and would endure through the rest of their lives. When H. H. married Edith Kitzmiller of Pittsburgh in February 1904, Mather would be a groomsman. In 1901, he invited the Timken brothers to visit Canton. They declared themselves favorably impressed, and he alerted the city's Board of Trade to their interest in moving their operations.[12]

In 1901, Canton was well known to virtually every U.S. citizen as the hometown of President William McKinley. In the election of 1896, McKinley had conducted his campaign from the front porch of his home. There, he addressed some 750,000 people from thirty states, who came in delegations to Canton over the course of the four-month campaign. He followed the same successful strategy in 1900. McKinley's assassination early in his second term, in September 1901, brought the era of Canton's political prominence to an end. Yet by that time, the Board of Trade, and especially its president Charles A. Dougherty, was actively engaged in building up the city's industrial base.[13]

There were good reasons for the Timken brothers to favor Canton, quite apart from the connection to Gordon Mather. Stark County, in which the city is situated, had extensive coal deposits, and for that reason it had long enjoyed a good position in the nation's railway system. Canton was on three major trunk lines: the Pennsylvania, from New York to Chicago; the Baltimore and Ohio, connecting Cleveland to Philadelphia, Washington, and Baltimore; and the Wabash, which provided a link to the South. Access to coal also made Canton a desirable location for steel producers. The Canton Steel Company had been in operation since 1872, and two other large steel companies, Stark Rolling Mill and Carnahan Tin Plate and Steel, were moving into town in 1901. Along with nearby Massillon, Ohio, the city was on its way to becoming a major center of steel production, which greatly added to its attraction for companies like Timken that manufactured steel products.[14]

Just as important, by 1901, Ohio had taken over from Massachusetts and other eastern states as the center of the machine-tool industry. The Timkens were doubtless conscious of that fact. In organizing for commercial production, they had found all of their most essential suppliers in Ohio within industries then on the leading edge of machine-tool development—bicycle makers Otto Konigslow, Miami Cycle & Manufacturing, and Middletown Cycle; and screw manufacturer, Western Automatic Machine Screw Company. The emergence of the region's automotive industry, Timken's target market, depended on such machine-tool makers. In 1901, Alexander Winton in Cleveland was arguably the nation's leading auto manufacturer. In Detroit that year Ransom Olds pioneered factory production of automobiles to produce a $650 Oldsmobile that would account for nearly one-fourth of all auto sales in 1902, and Henry Ford built a single car—a racer, in which he competed with Winton for the speed record on a new racetrack at Grosse Pointe.[15]

In fact, Canton lay near the center of what would become the heartland of manufacturing in America and remain so for most of the twentieth century. The future of the auto industry, the great engine of industrial development, was uncertain in 1901, but the combination of railroads, steel, and machine tools offered suggestions of what was to come. Canton's Board of Trade was not shy about making predictions. Its secretary, John E. Monnot, promised, "The great manufacturing and industrial belt of the future will be between Pittsburgh and Chicago from east to west and [between] Detroit, Michigan, and Louisville, Kentucky from north to south."[16] Timken's decision to move to Canton placed it on the forward edge of a wave of expansion that would increase the value of the city's industrial output fivefold and nearly triple its population by 1920.

In July 1901, Dougherty struck a deal with the Timken brothers to provide them with a factory site comprising five lots on Dueber Avenue, on the city's southwest side. The Board of Trade agreed to raise the $2,500 needed to buy the lots and to be ready to transfer the deeds by August 15. In return, The Timken Roller Bearing Axle Company agreed to place buildings and machinery worth at least $50,000 on the site, to open its factory by December 1, and to employ at least 50 people for a period of five years. Both parties made good on their side of the contract. In July Timken ordered machinery costing $15,000 from Connecticut machine-tool manufacturer Brown & Sharpe (by the end of the year the

The company's first plant in Canton, Ohio, opened with 40 employees on December 2, 1901, less than four months after the land deed was signed.

total investment in machinery would be $70,000). It broke ground in August, virtually the day the deed was handed over. The construction crew worked furiously, laying some 375,000 bricks in ten weeks; and the new factory—an L-shaped building the equivalent of 60 by 200 feet, with two stories facing Dueber Avenue—opened with 40 employees on Monday, December 2, 1901.[17]

In retrospect, it seems an auspicious beginning. Within five years, the automotive industry would be growing rapidly, Cleveland and Detroit would be predominant in automobile production, and The Timken Roller Bearing Axle Company would be on its way to having a majority of automakers as customers. Yet all of that success lay in the future when the Timkens moved to Canton. At the turn of the century the public was still skeptical of the automobile as a practical replacement for horse-drawn vehicles, mainly because the models available tended to be unreliable. With no established practices for the supply of replacement parts, it was difficult and costly to maintain them. Scores of manufacturers were entering the field each year, and nearly as many dropping out, so that there was a confusing array of automotive designs, and no industry standard. Those factors, too, discouraged potential buyers and slowed the movement toward large-scale production. Just 7,000 American-made cars were sold in the United States in 1901, 9,000 in 1902, and 11,000 in 1903, as compared with roughly 1.5 million horse-drawn vehicles produced annually in those years.[18]

A large part of the carriage market was out of reach due to price, so in deciding to bring manufacturing in-house and move to Canton, the Timkens were betting on the potential for growth in the automotive market. It was a bold move that set the company's future course. But when the automotive market was slow to develop, they faced financial ruin. In 1902 the new factory produced and shipped 120,000 bearings (about 30,000 bearing-equipped axles) and lost money. By the end of the year, the Timken brothers were broke and forced to turn to their father for support.

"We're pretty blue around here and fearfully hard up," H. H. wrote to Henry Timken in December that year. "The vehicle axle [i.e., carriage] end of the business does not improve. . . . it looks like the people won't pay the price." Sales to

Some of the company's first employees gathered under the company sign for a photo, ca. 1905.

automakers were promising but still small. "I believe we can work up a very large trade in that line," he continued, "for ball bearings do not stand up. But it takes a lot of stock to do a considerable business in the automobile line, and that means money." If they could just hold on for six more months, he reasoned, they had a chance to turn a small profit between both the carriage and the automobile business. "It's up to you," wrote H. H., "to decide whether you want to put the money in, and if you say yes we have got to have some of it soon." He assured his father that he and W. R. were "straining every nerve to make this business go" and expressed confidence that ultimately they would succeed:

From my experience on the road seeing the automobile trade, I am sure that we can get enough of that business alone to make the business a success. . . . I still have every faith that ultimately we'll make big money out of the axle. We'll hang on like grim death and never say die. We've got grit, if we haven't got sense or cents.[19]

Henry Timken willingly invested the requested money, though he stipulated that some of it be used for newspaper advertising, following his own successful strategy for publicizing the Timken spring. In 1902, he doubled the company's capitalization, to $200,000. The year 1903 was another tough one. The financial panic and recession of that year took a heavy toll on the auto market. However, having secured their father's continued backing, H. H. and W. R. were able not only to hang on until the market revived, but also to make investments in key personnel, in product and process development, and in promotion. Those were the investments that every industrial firm had to make in order to prosper and grow. By forging ahead in the midst of an economic downturn, the Timken brothers, with their father's support, established a pattern that would hold down to the present day, evidenced dramatically in the building of the Faircrest Steel plant.

Essential Investments

Timken's first salesman, Eugene W. Lewis, produced a memoir of the early days of the auto industry. He recalled that, shortly after the company moved to Canton, Alexander Winton, one of its earliest automotive customers, visited the new factory. Winton looked out the windows and advised the Timken brothers to secure options to buy the land behind them and across the street. "If you handle your business properly," said Winton, "and make a good product, you will need it all. The motor car business is going to be a very large industry."[20]

Winton was prophetic on all counts, and bringing Eugene Lewis on board was an important early step toward making his prophecy come true for the company. Carrying in his pocket a sample bearing wrapped in flannel and chain-smoking cigars, Lewis visited all the major automakers, as well as all the "so-called 'motor car manufacturers,'" whom he found "in all sorts of nooks and crannies in odd places, small shops, alleys, tumble-down and partially leased buildings." He also took the company's display to the all-important exhibits and auto shows. He explained the advantages of Timken bearings to the likes of Thomas Edison and Charles Steinmetz, as well as to the many manufacturers and potential car buyers who made the auto shows, in particular, important industry events.[21]

Lewis was especially valuable as a salesman because he understood automotive design and construction and could give advice on how Timken bearings and axles should be applied. While the extent of his own formal technical training is not clear, he knew enough to be scornful of the state of knowledge within the industry. "Any man who claimed to be an engineer of whatever sort, had a fair chance to enter the business of making motor cars," he recalled. For example, some of those "engineers" asserted that the tapered shape of its rollers would cause a Timken bearing to "wedge going around the corners." Lewis set up a demonstration at one of the early motor shows at Madison Square Garden to disprove that theory. Just as important, in his day-to-day work, Lewis was able to advise auto manufacturers how to design for and properly install Timken bearings and bearing-equipped axles. Often they would specify axles that Lewis could tell were too small for the weight of the car. Part of the sale was to persuade them to order correctly, so that the performance of Timken's product would not be compromised. Quite a few auto parts suppliers were technical leaders in this early era, when there were many automakers but few with much in-house expertise. In most areas of component design that balance shifted dramatically as the industry matured and consolidated and large-scale manufacturers created strong internal design capabilities. In contrast, sales engineering remained a permanent fixture, and a differentiating capability, at Timken.[22]

Another advantage to hiring Lewis early was to provide some relief for H. H., whose attention was necessarily focused primarily on developing manufacturing processes. Another of Lewis's stories highlights the problems he faced. The legendary inventor Thomas Edison visited the company's booth at one of the auto shows in Madison Square Garden. "He said he had heard of the Timken Tapered Roller Bearing but had never seen it," recalled Lewis. "After looking at it a few moments, he asked dozens of pertinent, pointed questions, and we were all impressed with the final nod of his head when he said, 'That bearing is all right in principle and if made with good steel will give a satisfactory account of itself.'"[23] Edison was on the mark. Ultimately, the critical connection between steel quality and bearing performance would push Timken into making its own steel. And, in the short run, materials problems posed some of the greatest challenges in bringing production in-house.

By mid-1901, Timken had begun using (and was advertising the use of) case-hardened steel. This was a departure from the common practice in bearing manufacture of using high-carbon, high-chrome tool steel that was through hardened, a process in which alloy steel is heated and then allowed to cool at room temperature, to produce an even degree of hardness throughout. In case hardening, the steel is heated and then quenched, so that only the exterior surfaces harden fully, while the inner core remains softer, hence less brittle and more resistant to shock.

In the early years in Canton, working with its steel suppliers, Timken adopted a nickel steel with a small amount of chrome. This steel was well suited to case hardening, and, unlike tool steels, in its "green" state (before hardening) it could readily be formed by screw machines into cups, cones, and rollers. Since carbon was still an essential element for maximum hardness, the bearing parts had to be carburized after green machining. That step involved heating them in a furnace with carbon to a temperature at which the carbon fused with the surface of the steel. After cooling they were case-hardened—placed in another furnace, heated, then removed and quenched in oil. The final steps were grinding, to achieve a smooth surface and more accurate dimensions, and bearing assembly. H. H. recalled in the 1924 *Forbes* interview the struggle to get those basic production processes in place with the business on the brink of going broke: "We just about sweated our souls out down at the plant."[24]

Yet it was by expanding sales capability and solving critical manufacturing problems that the company ensured its fortunes would rise when the economy recovered. Beyond that, while sales were especially slow in 1903, H. H. launched a program to produce a new axle design specifically for trucks. In March 1904, the company mounted a large exhibit at the World's Fair in St. Louis—and brought home another first prize for the Timken bearing. By the end of the year, when the local paper ran an article on the bright business prospects following the election of Republican Theodore Roosevelt as president, W. R. was able to report nearly a year's worth of booked business. Now The Timken Roller Bearing Axle Company would face a different problem, but a good one: producing to keep up with demand. "To work night and day during the entire year," said W. R., "is the sort of indication of prosperity that we appreciate."[25]

In 1906, the company hired Herbert Alden, and in doing so took another big step toward building the organizational capabilities it would need for long-term success. Alden was a true automotive engineer. An 1893 mechanical engineering graduate of MIT, he had worked for Pope Manufacturing Company, which became the Electric Vehicle Company, and was part of a team that designed early gasoline engines, transmissions, and axles. In 1905, he helped to found the Society of Automotive Engineers (originally named the Society of Automobile Engineers). Alden brought to Timken both his considerable stature within the industry and the technical expertise the company needed to make continuing advances in product design.[26]

By early 1907, Alden developed a new cage for the Timken bearing. This was a single unit with pockets for the rollers that served to hold them on the cone and maintain alignment. One advantage of the new cage design was that it could be stamped from sheet metal, a crucial savings in cost over parts that had to be machined individually. More important, this improvement opened the way to a redesign of the cone and roller that eliminated the rib-and-groove feature on the large end. The result was shorter rollers and smaller bearings overall, capable of carrying the same loads as larger bearings of the older design. The changes also reduced friction between the parts of the bearing, allowing it to run at higher speeds and extending its life. In 1908, the company introduced the new design as the Short Series. (See Evolution of the Timken Tapered Roller Bearing on pages 90–92.) As H. H. told one customer, "The use of the short series bearings is an advantage, as it means you can use smaller hubs, smaller gear box, etc. [They are] superior in every way to the old type." Significantly, the more compact short series also helped to widen the field of application to automotive transmissions. Timken bearings of the original production design had been used on the gears of differentials and steering mechanisms since 1904. The short series bearings came into use for transmissions on some 1908 models.[27]

Improvements in bearing performance in this era came from advances in manufacturing as well as design. Under H. H.'s leadership, the company was struggling to make quality a Timken hallmark. Precision manufacturing, as measured by the interchangeability of parts, was still unknown in all but a few industries. Pioneered by the U.S. national armories in the nineteenth century, the manufacture of interchangeable parts depended on two developments: machine tools that could position and hold the part to be shaped in a way that ensured accuracy on a repeatable basis; and gauges that could measure with enough precision to verify the accuracy and the uniformity of the parts produced. Cadillac was the only auto manufacturer that approached precision manufacturing in the first decade of the twentieth century. Henry M. Leland, developer of the Cadillac and head of Cadillac Automobile Company from 1902 until 1917, had come to automaking from arms manufacturing and from tool builders Brown & Sharpe, where he had contributed significantly to developing both the machines and the system required for precision manufacturing. He gained widespread recognition in 1908, when Britain's Royal Automobile Club disassembled three Cadillac cars, scrambled the parts, then reassembled them into working machines that successfully completed a 500-mile test run. Alfred Sloan, the great organization builder of General Motors, recalled how, as a young salesman for Hyatt roller bearings, he had received a memorable lesson in manufacturing when Leland produced a micrometer to demonstrate that Hyatt's bearings were not close enough to the size specified. "You must grind your bearings," said Leland. "Even though you make thousands, the first and the last should be precisely alike."[28]

Coming out of the carriage industry, the Timkens were familiar with machine production of standardized parts and factory assembly methods, though hardly with the standards of accuracy required for bearing production. Henry Timken's motto had been "Only in efficiency is there progress." H. H. would amend that to

In the early years, grinders were driven by belts attached to massive pulleys, which were suspended from the ceiling and connected to a single power source.

Precision manufacturing involved manual gauging of every piece.

"Only in efficiency *and precision* is there progress." Chasing the goal of precision meant upgrading equipment frequently to keep abreast of the rapid evolution of machine-tool technology, and working closely with equipment suppliers to adapt improvements to bearing production. Timken started production in Canton with a single universal grinder for bearings but by 1909 had scores of specialized machines with automatic feeding devices and controls, an improvement introduced after 1905. Significantly, by 1907, some machine builders had adopted Timken bearings, a byproduct of the company's efforts to procure and adapt the latest equipment for its own needs.[29]

Equipment alone did not ensure quality, however. By 1907 at least, and probably earlier, standard procedure at the Canton factory included gauging every roller produced—after green machining, heat treatment, and grinding to final size and finish—then sorting by size, so that the rollers in each bearing would be as close to the same size as possible. By 1909, the company claimed that the variation in rollers was less than .002 of an inch. This was not the highest standard of the day, nor the most advanced process. Henry Leland had been seeking uniformity to within .001 of an inch in 1905, and by 1908 it was possible to obtain a grinder for cylindrical and tapered parts with an automatic sizing device that could make adjustments as fine as .000125 of an inch. Still, Timken's manufacturing process was good enough to support a two-year guarantee of the product at a time when ninety-day warranties were rare in the automobile and parts industry. Cadillac placed its first order with Timken—bearings for the rear axle of a four-cylinder car—in July 1907.[30]

Takeoff

Those early investments in human resources and process and product development laid the foundation for future, dramatic growth in an era when the U.S. auto industry was also moving into its takeoff phase. By 1905, standardization of auto body design became a reality as automakers abandoned the horseless carriage, popular in America, for the standard French design, which had the motor in front of the vehicle rather than under the driver's seat, and which employed a steering wheel instead of a tiller. That done, the industry was collectively able to focus on developing manufacturing processes to make more reliable automobiles on a scale that would permit lowering the price into a widely affordable range, much as the carriage industry had done in the 1860s and 1870s. The year 1908 was a turning point—it saw the introduction of the Ford Model T and the formation of General Motors by William Durant, who brought together Buick, Cadillac, Olds, and numerous lesser companies. GM was the future industry leader, but

Ford's innovations drove industry growth in this era. Having developed a suitable design and a manufacturing organization that set new standards for productivity—ten finished cars per hour in 1908—Ford was able to sell the Model T at an affordable price, $850. The immediate market success of this car and the profits it generated financed a continuous stream of manufacturing improvements, in particular the adoption of more advanced and specialized machine tools and labor-saving factory equipment. Ford was thus able to improve quality, increase output, and, after 1910, further reduce the price of the Model T. Those trends accelerated after the introduction of the moving assembly line in 1913, which enabled Ford to increase production to the point that, almost single-handedly, it created a mass market for the automobile.[31]

The auto industry's era of most rapid growth came in the decade from 1907 to 1917, during which time annual sales grew by a factor of forty. Consolidation in the industry began early. The four largest automakers—Ford, Buick, Maxwell, and Willys-Overland—held 43 percent of the market in 1908, 52 percent by 1911. Timken was in a strong position, with an enviable mix of customers that included, by 1909, all of the major automakers except Ford and Maxwell. Ford would remain elusive until 1918; Maxwell started using Timken bearings in 1911. Significantly, though, Timken also sold to a large portion of the smaller auto and truck manufacturers and, by 1909, to ten companies producing transmissions only. As a result, it was not overly dependent on any single account.[32]

The company's biggest challenge in this era was increasing production fast enough to meet the requirements of its customers, many of which were themselves expanding rapidly. Buick, for example, increased its order from 100 to 500 sets of bearings per month between early 1906 and the end of 1907. The Panic of 1907, which caused some customers to cut their orders substantially, afforded a welcome opportunity to catch up. Two important policies helped make Timken successful in this period of rapid growth. One was product standardization. From the beginning, the company resisted requests for special-order bearings. Said W. R. Timken in 1909, "Had we in the past ten years made everything that we had calls or orders for, we would probably be in bankruptcy today." By that time, although it had nearly one hundred automotive customers, Timken offered just three bearing designs—the original production bearing, the short series, and a third designed as a replacement for annular ball bearings—and a fixed list of standard sizes.[33]

Timken's credit policy was also significant. This was W. R.'s area of responsibility, and he prided himself on being tough and savvy in his handling of it. Through the first decade of the twentieth century, the more established auto parts suppliers typically helped to finance auto manufacturers by allowing thirty to ninety days for payment on deliveries, even though the automakers could get payment in cash almost as soon as a car was assembled. W. R. would have none of that. "We are the shortest term house in the United States, the strictest collectors, and the most particular regarding the cash discount," he wrote to Timken's British licensee in 1910. As an incentive for quick payment, Timken offered a 5 percent discount on orders paid for in cash within ten days. Said W. R., "We get 85% of our money within 15 days after goods are shipped. We never take a note, don't know what it looks like, and turn down each and every order offered us on longer than 30 days time." Though evidence indicates the company made a few exceptions to those rules, the general approach was well designed to keep cash flow strong at a time when continuing investments in expansion required it. Like product standardization, Timken's credit policy was both a sign of and a contributing factor to its strong position in the industry.[34]

Timken also benefited from the fact that competition in the U.S. market was rather limited during this formative period. American Ball Bearing Company in Cleveland was a large-scale producer of bearing-equipped axles, still expanding in 1904. However, its bicycle-type ball bearings, though a significant improvement over friction bearings, in the long run could not compete successfully against either annular ball bearings or roller bearings. German and British patents covered critical improvements for inserting the balls in the deeply grooved races of annular ball bearings. In 1906, the Hess-Bright Manufacturing Company of Hartford, Connecticut, obtained a license under the British patent of Robert Conrad, but it became tied up in litigation and was unable to exercise its license until 1913. Partly for that reason, American ball bearing makers, with one major exception—The New Departure Company—simply were not competitive prior to World War I. European imports, primarily from Germany, dominated the ball bearing field. H. H. Timken was at first concerned that imported ball bearings would provide tough competition. Yet annular ball bearings proved relatively ill suited to the heavy-duty automotive applications in which Timken bearings performed best, for example on front wheels, where the load and the thrust created on turns were the greatest. In about 1909, Timken introduced its bearing designed to replace annular ball bearings on existing cars, according to W. R., "simply because we had such a large demand for bearings to replace the annulars owing to the fact that all of them gave dissatisfaction more or less."[35]

With Timken's patents still in force, the flexible roller bearing produced by Hyatt was the only competing roller bearing of significance. Hyatt's business was closely tied to the Weston-Mott Axle Company, a leader in its own field. Hyatt and Weston-Mott had many of the same customers as Timken, but they also had Ford, which Timken did not. In 1909, New Departure entered the field with a double-row ball bearing that was capable of taking thrust from all directions. Formed in the 1890s in Bristol, Connecticut, by another brother combination, Albert F. and Edward

D. Rockwell, New Departure had started out making bells, then moved into brakes for bicycles and from there into ball bearings. It began making autos in 1907 and produced the Houpt-Rockwell and the Rockwell Cab, which became the basis for the first Yellow Taxicab Company in New York City. With the development of the double-row bearing, the company began to focus on that field and quickly became a serious competitor to Timken and Hyatt. Yet, between the rising production of autos and trucks and the opportunity to expand market share against plain bearings and single-row ball bearings, there was plenty of room for all three to grow.[36]

By late 1908 it became clear that the Canton plant could not feasibly accommodate the continuing growth of the business. The Timkens decided to separate the manufacture of axles and bearings and to relocate the axle business close to its largest customer base. In January 1909, they purchased a "large and modern" facility on Clark Avenue in Detroit, and in May they created a new corporation, The Timken-Detroit Axle Company, with $1 million of paid-in capital. W. R. and H. H. Timken were the president, secretary, and principal stockholders, but they sold a one-third stake in the new company to the three key employees who went to Detroit to manage it—Eugene Lewis, Herbert Alden, and A. R. Demory, who had been superintendent of the Canton plant. The original corporation, now the smaller of the two businesses, changed its name to The Timken Roller Bearing Company. In September the Detroit business community welcomed the opening of Timken-Detroit's new "million-dollar plant," which was offering employment to 1,200 men.[37]

The Timkens announced the separation of the axle business as a sign of their confidence in the "continuing and permanent growth of the automobile business." Equally, though, it was a sign that the tapered roller bearing was the core product on which they wished to focus their attention. Not only was it clear by 1909 that application of the Timken bearing would extend beyond vehicle axles, but it was also apparent that the bearing's market could extend geographically beyond the limits of the United States.

On a working vacation in 1908, W. R. had succeeded in selling Timken bearings to a leading British automaker, Wolseley Motors. Wolseley had been founded by Herbert Austin, but since 1901 had been a subsidiary of Vickers, Ltd., a diversified industrial giant that produced battleships, guns, electric motors, and steel. At that time, European automakers were using ball bearings exclusively. Vickers became interested in producing Timken bearings for that large, untapped market. As a result, Timken was able to negotiate licensing agreements with another Vickers subsidiary, The Electric & Ordnance Accessories Company, Ltd. (E&OA). For a royalty of 15 percent of net sales, Timken granted the exclusive right to produce and sell bearings in the United Kingdom, continental Europe, and all of the British Empire except Canada. The agreement stipulated that E&OA could not produce or sell any other type of anti-friction bearing, that the name "Timken" must always be used to identify the product, and that Timken's manufacturing practices must be followed scrupulously, "particularly those pertaining to the quality of steel used and its analysis, the method of case hardening, the system of grinding, gauging, etc." The licensing agreement laid the foundation for Timken's future expansion abroad. In the short run, it created a source of revenue that would help to fund continuing investments in the business at home.[38]

Henry Timken died unexpectedly on March 16, 1909, from an intestinal ailment suffered on a business trip from San Diego to Los Angeles.[39] He did not see the completion of the plans for Timken-Detroit Axle Company or of the negotiations with Vickers. Yet he surely knew and approved of them—indeed, the licensing strategy bears his stamp. The state-of-the-art equipment and dedication to efficiency and quality in the Canton plant likewise reflect the same approach to manufacturing that he took in his St. Louis carriage factory in 1873. From the beginning, Henry's vision for the Timken bearing was an expansive one, always international in scope and, possibly for that reason, unperturbed by the comparatively slow takeoff of the automotive industry in the United States. The patient capital he provided at a critical time betokened that long-term view, a hallmark of the Timken family's role in the business. Of course, he could not have envisioned the extent to which Timken bearings would be applied across the full spectrum of mechanical equipment, from steel mills to spaceships. Yet in his lifetime he saw the first steps in that direction, and he watched the Timken bearing become a leader in automotive applications and the company one of the strongest in the industry.

Organization Building

In the absence of corporate financial data for this era, the extent of Timken's growth and profitability cannot be determined precisely, but it can be inferred from the company's expansion of output. In 1902, its first year of operation in Canton, Timken had produced just over 100,000 bearings. By the beginning of 1910, the Canton plant was manufacturing 4,000 bearings per day, about 1.2 million per year, and the company was still struggling to keep up with orders. "The only trouble here now is to make the bearings in sufficient quantities," H. H. wrote. "We are adding machinery constantly."[40] Six years later, daily production would reach 19,000. The Timken brothers would not have been able to expand operations so rapidly if their profits had not been substantial. At the same time, their continuing investment in organizational capabilities laid the foundation for future profitable growth.

Some key personnel joined the bearing company following the departure of Alden, Lewis, and Demory to Timken-Detroit. As W. R. began to withdraw from active management, it was these men who collaborated most closely with H. H. on decisions both large and small. By all indications, H. H. was not an easy man to work for. Yet he formed strong relationships, based on mutual respect, with a few key associates who worked with him daily in the Canton plant. Heman Ely joined Timken in 1909 to provide support across the range of W. R.'s activities—sales, administration, and finance. H. H. came to rely on him greatly. In 1911, Timken hired a metallurgical engineer, Marcus T. Lothrop, from Halcomb Steel Company in Syracuse, New York. As Timken's chief metallurgist, Lothrop won the trust of H. H. and played a central role in developing Timken's steel-making capability. In 1929, he would become the company's first non-family president.

George Obermier, in particular, became a close personal friend, and he would play an invaluable role in building Timken's manufacturing capability. When Timken moved to Canton in 1901, Obermier was the superintendent at the Cleveland Axle Company plant across the street. He and H. H. became friendly business associates and soon H. H. launched an effort to recruit him. Obermier resisted for some time, on the grounds that they were too much alike and would not be able to get along. In 1912, he finally agreed to become Timken's factory manager, but with a warning: "The first time you try to shout me down, you'll meet your match." By all accounts, H. H. and Obermier waged "many bitterly fought battles" but worked together effectively on a broad range of issues related to engineering, production, and labor. The Timken brothers took pains to help all of these senior managers purchase stock in the company, both to reward them and to ensure their continued loyalty.[41]

By the terms laid down by Alfred Chandler, the great historian of managerial capitalism, Timken would not become a managerial firm—the dominant form in twentieth-century U.S. industry—because the founding family would remain engaged in running the company rather than relinquish control to salaried professionals. Yet, H. H. and W. R. Timken followed the best practices of the day, creating the management structure and procedures required to run an increasingly large and complex industrial organization. Bringing in non-family managers at the top was an essential first step. Working together with these men, the Timkens put in place the middle managers who, by purchasing materials, coordinating production, and advertising, selling, and distributing Timken's products, would be largely responsible for its competitive success.[42]

The organizational structure and administrative systems that emerged at the Canton plant mirrored developments in all major industrial companies. Each operating department—cage making, roller grinding, etc.—had its foreman and assistant foreman, with the plant superintendent coordinating them all. The engineering and metallurgical departments had their chiefs as well. They, along with the superintendent, reported to factory manager George Obermier. Pervasive throughout the organization was a system of documentation and reporting designed to communicate instructions from the top down and to collect and transmit basic operating information upward, all for the purpose of maintaining

Left: *Marcus Lothrop served as the company's first non-Timken-family president from 1929 to 1932.*

Right: *From 1912 to 1934, J. George Obermier was one of H. H. Timken's most trusted lieutenants and head of the company's bearing manufacturing operations.*

control and maximizing productivity. This kind of "control through communication" was an innovation of the late nineteenth and early twentieth centuries, made practicable by the commercialization of the typewriter in the 1880s and advanced by the development of carbon paper, mimeograph machines, and filing systems.[43]

In the spirit of Henry Timken, H. H. embraced such forms of systematic management with enthusiasm and was closely involved in developing information systems for the Canton plant. While there were numerous consultants available, he scorned such outside assistance. "I would have no efficiency experts in the Canton factory," he said. "[B]ecause I know so much more about the conduct of this business than any efficiency man in existence . . . I can evolve a better system than any expert can." Most important, in his view, was the system for monitoring the daily output of the factory. "It seems clear to me," wrote H. H., "that the one essential in a manufacturing business . . . is to get the maximum output from each machine. That is the bull's-eye to be aimed at." Timken's system was based on a calculation of the normal capacity of each machine on the plant floor. This made it possible to check up on productivity during the course of the day and to analyze trends over time. Once the reporting system was properly set up, H. H. noted, it became possible "to know on practically one or two sheets of paper" exactly what the plant was doing.[44]

In its continual drive to increase productivity and improve product quality, Timken worked closely with equipment suppliers to develop improvements specific to bearing manufacture. However, many innovations were made completely in-house, and the capacity to generate improvements internally was one of the most critical organizational capabilities. The bearing industry was a leader in the development of precision manufacturing, although similar advances were being made by all the major automobile and parts manufacturers. At Canton, "Master Mechanic" Jack Flaherty ran an engineering department focused entirely on manufacturing processes. He designed specialized machinery that was built in Timken's own tool room. The introduction of automatic machines in many areas—for example, roller making—greatly increased productivity in this era. Said George Betts, foreman of the roller screw-machine department in 1913: "It's a fact that when we started, fourteen years ago, a machinist would have to hustle to make 200 rollers in ten hours; now he can attend to six automatics, his production is seldom less than 10,000 and the rollers are more accurate in every dimension and in the angle of their taper." In cone assembly—the step that clamped the cage and rollers onto the cone—automatic machines reduced the task to a single operation on an electrically powered press. This replaced a process in which an operator had worked around the cage pocket by pocket, clamping each one down with his own force, exerted through a foot pedal. A company write-up of this improvement noted that it allowed one man to do the work of three, that it increased accuracy by "completely eliminat[ing] the human equation in adjusting the relationships of cone, cage, and rollers," and that it was an innovation that came to Canton from the Birmingham factory of Timken's British licensee, E&OA.[45]

Timken similarly improved cage making, green machining of cups and cones, and roller grinding. In contrast, in the grinding of cups and cones the skill of the operator remained essential. Grinding machines, abrasive materials, and even gauges were sensitive to variation in temperature and humidity, so the man operating the equipment had to adjust the machine continually and the way he ran it in order to maintain a high level of precision. In the grinding room, therefore, the ratio necessarily remained one man to one machine. Productivity gains came through the expansion of the department and improvement of working conditions, including better lighting and ventilation. Yet, if grinding remained an art, there were still ways to advance the art through technology, for example with magnetic chucks that held the pieces in place and specially designed gauging attachments that made it easier to check accuracy frequently.[46]

While H. H. Timken drove the development of manufacturing processes in Canton, W. R. took the lead in building a sales and advertising function. In 1911, sales for both Timken Roller Bearing and Timken-Detroit were handled by a small group that included W. R., Lewis, Ely, and one dedicated salesman, E. B. Lausier, who divided his time equally between bearings and axles. Important sales, though, might draw in Alden, Herbert Vanderbeek (Alden's replacement as chief engineer in Canton), Demory, and H. H., a reflection of the degree to which technical understanding was essential to effective sales, particularly in the case of bearings. Timken bearings were larger than plain bearings but smaller than ball bearings of the same capacity, and they had to be mounted in pairs. The manufacturers that adopted them generally needed to make some design changes to accommodate them. It was also important to adjust Timken bearings properly at installation, because overtightening made them wear rapidly. Since the expansion of the business largely involved supplanting other types of bearings in existing designs, it made great sense for the company to provide technical expertise, both to facilitate the changeover and to ensure that the bearings performed properly in its customers' applications.

In expanding the sales department, W. R. took pains to find individuals with the right mix of skills. He insisted on looking outside the company and on paying top salaries to get people with both the technical understanding and the sales experience he considered necessary. By 1914 the two Timken companies had in place a joint sales force of five men. It was organized by region, although some of the men clearly excelled at selling bearings, others at selling axles. Within a few years, Timken Roller Bearing and Timken-Detroit would have separate sales organizations.

Complementing the sales effort was a strong program of advertising, which also started out as a joint effort of the two Timken companies. In 1911, they hired an in-house advertising specialist, Edwin Walton, and the following year Walton launched *Timken Magazine,* a sociable, informative newsletter aimed at car dealers and car service men. It had a circulation of 20,000 by 1914. By far the largest segment of Timken's advertising expenditure, however—following Henry Timken's example—was devoted to popular national magazines. Not everyone was convinced of the efficacy of Timken's national advertising program. A. R. Demory, for one, was skeptical and at one point came close to quitting in frustration over the fact that more than 10 percent of his overhead at Timken-Detroit was made up of advertising expense. But, as 70 percent owners of the Detroit company, W. R. and H. H. were not averse to asserting their authority in important matters, and they strongly believed in the value of educating the public about the virtues of Timken products. Timken's leading competitors apparently believed it was effective. Though Timken had pioneered advertising in this venue, by 1916 Hyatt Roller Bearing and New Departure were each spending about as much on national magazine advertising as the two Timken companies combined. In 1917, The Timken Roller Bearing Company hired its own advertising manager, and its budget for national weeklies and monthlies increased by nearly 60 percent.[47]

The Timken Detroit-Axle Company launched Timken Magazine *in 1912 for car dealers and servicemen. Using a similar format, The Timken Roller Bearing Company published* The Timken Triangle *from 1918 to 1920 for internal readership. This was followed by* The Trading Post *in 1942,* Timken *in 1960, and* Timken World *in 1993. Many local and regional publications have supplemented these, such as* Exchange *in the United States and* Contact *in Europe.*

The impact of Timken's advertising cannot be measured precisely, but in at least two cases the growth of its business was definitely attributable to public awareness. One example was the dissatisfaction of car owners with the performance of annular ball bearings, which led to the development of the annular replacement series in 1909. Again, nearly ten years later, the company would finally succeed in winning Ford as a customer, at least in part because Model T owners were demanding a replacement Timken bearing for their cars. To be sure, Timken was not the only automotive parts supplier to advertise in venues such as *The Saturday Evening Post*. However, at a time when the great majority of metal parts manufacturers relied on agents to sell their products, Timken's highly evolved sales organization and aggressive use of advertising placed it in the ranks of the most progressive industrial firms.[48]

Moreover, the combination of sales engineering and strong in-house product engineering gave the company an edge in an increasingly competitive industry. Sales engineers helped to open the door to collaboration with customers in the

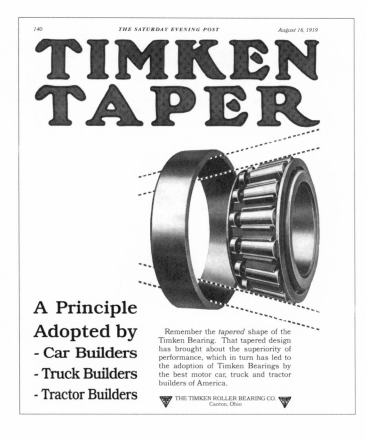

As part of the company's early promotional program, ads like this one in 1919 appeared regularly in magazines such as The Saturday Evening Post and Harper's Weekly.

critical design phase. As the volume of autos and trucks produced by the larger manufacturers grew, Timken became more willing to modify its standard sizes and designs for specific vehicle applications and thereby became more able to win and secure important accounts and to continue expanding the range of applications. By 1915, it was also looking beyond the automotive industry and planning a campaign to develop markets in agricultural and general industrial machinery. Those plans were necessarily suspended during World War I but taken up vigorously thereafter. Thus, even after the automakers developed in-house technical capabilities and took over from their suppliers most aspects of automotive design, Timken would continue to provide engineering support and to consider that an essential aspect of its sales function.[49]

All of the company's investments in state-of-the-art machine tools and essential organizational capabilities enabled it to operate profitably and expand its market steadily, while growing sales and profits in turn made possible continuing investments. One sign of its financial health was the increase in wages Timken paid to its shop-floor personnel. By 1914 it had abandoned the straight piecework calculation of pay for machine operators and replaced it with a system of base pay plus premiums for productivity, reduced scrap, and lower rates of machine repair. This system and the rates of pay it produced were apparently quite competitive, since during two years (1914–16) of intensive union activity and numerous extended strikes in Canton, Timken's workforce did not strike and resisted the overtures of union organizers.[50]

In 1917, the company undertook a major revision of its wage system, which was urged on H. H. by Heman Ely as a complement to the large capital investments Timken was then making. While they had raised wages and created bonuses from time to time, noted Ely, "none of this was done on a broad, comprehensive plan, but simply as an expedient to meet conditions that arose at the time." H. H. took up the problem and, as a great admirer of Henry Ford, decided to implement a version of the $5-per-day minimum wage and bonus plan inaugurated at Ford in 1914. He established a $4 minimum wage and an eight-hour day and even went so far as to emulate Ford in creating an Advisory Department, which visited every eligible employee at home for an interview and collection of financial information, to determine if he—Timken employed women in its inspection departments but did not include them in the plan—met the requirements for bonuses "as to age, home conditions, and thrift."[51]

Timken abandoned the bonus plan just six months after it was up and running. For all his admiration of Ford, H. H. was apparently less than zealous about Ford's social agenda. The administration of the system was complex, and it seemed unfair to many employees in the way it established the skill levels on which base compensation was founded. And the wage-plus-bonus formula did not, in management's view, provide much incentive for improving productivity. The company returned to calculating wages on an hourly-wage-plus-premium basis, maintaining the eight-hour day and a basic level of compensation close to its original minimum wage. The hard data on wages are scarce, but in 1920 the standard hourly rate for screw-machine operators was 55¢. At any rate, the company largely avoided the labor strife of the immediate post–World War I years, when its biggest problem was having sufficient human resources to keep up with business growth.[52]

H. H. Timken's experimentation with the Ford system was short-lived. Yet in general during this period he took the position that the only way to attract and secure the loyalty of capable employees was to "pay more wages than other factories in similar lines." As much as his openness to Ford's ideas, that view set him at odds philosophically with most industrialists of the era. In contrast, according to Alfred Sloan, the prevailing approach was "to set wages low, the lower the better. Reduce when you could, increase when you must." Yet Timken's wage scale was as much a reflection of its profitability as of the fair-mindedness of its management. That profitability rested on the successful organization building that took place in the company's formative years.[53]

By 1915, the increasing dominance of Ford, GM, and other large-scale auto manufacturers and their drive for vertical integration were creating pressures in the automotive supply industry that seemed to threaten Timken's strong position. Those pressures combined with personal issues to create a period of great uncertainty, and ultimately of transition, for the Timken brothers. During that time, they seriously considered selling one or both of the family businesses.

Unsettled Times

W. R.'s disengagement from the company began after he suffered a serious bout with tonsillitis and diphtheria in early 1912. That spring, William Durant, between his two terms as head of General Motors, approached the Timkens with the idea of creating an auto supply company, building on the core of Timken Roller Bearing and Timken-Detroit Axle. He and W. R. put together a deal by which the Timkens would sell out for a combination of cash and five-year notes. "My physical condition . . . has considerable to do with my personal desire to sell out the business," W. R. wrote to his brother from Florida, where he was attempting to recuperate.[54] In the end, the deal fell through because it would have required the Timken brothers to stay on and oversee the management of the bearing company for five years. Neither was interested in doing that.

By the winter of 1914–15, W. R. had largely regained his health but continued on a path of disengagement. About that time his marriage ended in divorce, an event that would surely have been viewed as scandalous in Canton, as in most cities in that era. W. R. moved to Cleveland in 1914, where he conducted business from a personal office in the Leader News Building. He continued to participate in sales to a few important customers and to oversee the financial and legal affairs of both Timken companies, but he was determined to withdraw from day-to-day management. To that end, in the fall of 1915, he moved to California. W. R. was frank about wanting more leisure time. He was earning a substantial income in dividends from the two Timken companies. The Timken Roller Bearing Company, of which he owned one-third, paid out $3 million in 1914. Increasingly, he would become less interested in selling bearings and axles to auto companies and more interested in buying their stock, and in the stock market in general.[55]

As W. R. withdrew from management, relations between H. H. in Canton and the managers of Timken-Detroit became increasingly strained, adding to the general uncertainty about the future. Since 1909 there had been a formal agreement between the two companies that Timken-Detroit would use only Timken bearings on its axles and Timken Roller Bearing would not sell to competing axle manufacturers. Both companies had grown and prospered under that arrangement, which had made Timken-Detroit Canton's largest customer by a good margin. The axle company had expanded rapidly and by 1915 had three axle plants at two separate Detroit locations. It had also formed a joint venture with a British firm, David Brown and Sons, to make worm gears—a spiral gear drive system for steering mechanisms first popularized in Europe—in another large Detroit factory. As the majority owners, H. H. and W. R. Timken had profited greatly from that growth. Yet they also had endured great frustration when Demory, Alden, and Lewis lagged behind H. H. and his lieutenants in Canton in getting their operations under control and in implementing systems. In particular, they continued to have difficulties producing and delivering products to customers on schedule long after Timken Roller Bearing had solved that problem. The Detroit managers naturally felt their share of frustration and annoyance as well, and they sometimes resisted the Timkens' criticism. But they had little leverage on the situation.

Moreover, as H. H. strove to grow the bearing business in the face of increasing competition, he came to view the agreement that prohibited the sale of bearings to competing axle manufacturers as an unacceptable restraint. Timken Roller Bearing was pushing hard to expand its position with General Motors, but that meant supplying bearings to Weston-Mott, one of Timken-Detroit's major competitors. H. H. first argued that the agreement with Timken-Detroit should be relaxed in this instance, but he soon progressed to the assertion that it was time to do away with the agreement altogether. When the Detroit managers resisted, he threatened to market a bearing under a different trade name in order to circumvent the agreement's provisions. Finally, they submitted. Once the change was made, Timken Roller Bearing made only slow progress with axle makers, finding them less than eager to adopt the bearing that was Timken-Detroit's trademark. H. H. had won his point, but from late 1915 onward he remained disposed to sell Timken-Detroit Axle if possible.

In the meantime, the Timkens had become engaged once again in serious talks with a potential suitor for the bearing company, this time Alfred Sloan, now the principal owner of Hyatt Roller Bearing. Increasing competitiveness in the bearing industry made the idea of combination appealing to both parties. While they were on friendly terms personally and had been able to expand their businesses without directly competing against each other, they both felt the pressure to win and keep contracts with the largest automakers. Hyatt was

An advertisement from a 1922 Society of Automotive Engineers' journal shows the different configuration of a competitor's product. Timken acquired The Bock Bearing Company in 1926.

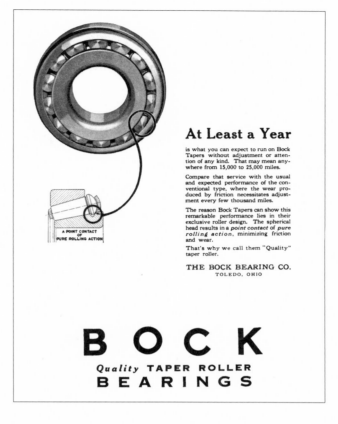

At Least a Year

is what you can expect to run on Bock Tapers without adjustment or attention of any kind. That may mean anywhere from 15,000 to 25,000 miles.

Compare that service with the usual and expected performance of the conventional type, where the wear produced by friction necessitates adjustment every few thousand miles.

The reason Bock Tapers can show this remarkable performance lies in their exclusive roller design. The spherical head results in a *point contact* of *pure rolling action*, minimizing friction and wear.

That's why we call them "Quality" taper roller.

THE BOCK BEARING CO.
TOLEDO, OHIO

A POINT CONTACT
OF
PURE ROLLING ACTION

BOCK
Quality TAPER ROLLER
BEARINGS

a larger company than Timken Roller Bearing, producing more than 30,000 bearings per day to Timken's 19,000. Yet Sloan had a problem: most of Hyatt's output went to two huge accounts, Ford and GM. "If either Ford or General Motors should start making their own bearings or use some other type of bearings," he noted, "our company would be in a desperate situation." In fact, at the time GM was moving toward a new axle design for which flexible roller bearings were unsuitable. "Sloan is very much scared," W. R. reported to his brother in February 1915.[56]

Timken, on the other hand, had all the major car makers except Ford as customers and was expanding its business all the time. Yet H. H. and W. R. were nervous, too, not only because of the ongoing competition with Hyatt and New Departure, but also because of the rise of new competitors in the tapered roller bearing field. For example, The Bock Bearing Company of Toledo, Ohio, was just entering the field with a new tapered roller bearing design and was talking to General Motors in January 1915. H. H. was respectful of Bock's product, which effectively solved the problem of roller alignment with a knob on the large end of the roller that maintained contact with the bearing cone. (See ad above.) He proposed a substantial reduction in price to General Motors in order to capture its business quickly before Bock could get established. Then, he suggested, Timken should attempt to acquire Bock. "I feel that in a way a critical period has arrived for our bearing business," said H. H. "You must not overlook this fact," he continued, "namely, that . . . heretofore we have had no substantial competition in the tapered bearing business [because] we knew a great deal more about the manufacture of such bearings than anybody else in the world, but that condition exists no longer in the same degree." H. H. did not mention the fact that the Timken patents were expiring in 1915, but it surely contributed to his anxiety.[57]

The Timkens lost interest in acquiring Bock when it developed that its bearing might become embroiled in patent litigation. But H. H. saw the threat posed by Bock as only part of a larger problem. He was most concerned about the possibility that an established bearing or automobile maker would acquire a manufacturer of tapered roller bearings that might pose an insignificant threat on its own but could become a real competitor in the hands of a larger firm. In 1912, for example, GM had briefly considered purchasing The Standard Roller Bearing of Philadelphia, producer of Grant roller bearing axles. Again, in early 1915, Timken learned that Willys-Overland was about to purchase The Bower Company. H. H. judged Bower's bearing to be poorly designed, yet this was just the kind of move by an important customer that he most feared. John Willys ultimately decided not to buy Bower, but he impressed upon H. H. his determination to make Willys-Overland independent for all its parts, including bearings. H. H. continued to worry about the threat posed by vertical integration in the auto industry. He also feared companies like Bower and Bock would continue to enter the tapered roller bearing field and would drive prices down regardless of the quality of their product.[58]

Just as worrisome was the possibility that a more competitive bearing maker such as Hyatt or New Departure would add tapered roller bearings to its product line. H. H. reasoned that, since Timken's continued growth would increasingly have to come at the expense of its major competitors, they, in response, would move to compete directly by making tapered roller bearings. If that happened, he believed, they would be in a stronger position than Timken, "in that they would each be making quite a general line of bearings."[59] W. R. suggested that Timken should start making straight roller bearings in the Canton plant, an option that H. H. had also considered but rejected. H. H. argued that orders for Timken bearings were too heavy and conditions in the plant too crowded to undertake such a development. As a result, the Timkens were more interested in diversifying through merger or acquisition.

Hence, they were open to Sloan's overture, and over a two-month period in the spring of 1915, they gave serious consideration to a three-way combination joining Timken, Hyatt, and The Standard Roller Bearing Company. Though Standard produced roller bearing axles, it was primarily a manufacturer of ball bearings and so would have rounded out the line. The three companies looked each other over carefully. H. H. decided rather quickly to abandon the idea of merging with Standard. He had visited its plant in Philadelphia and was scornful of its "junk machinery." In contrast, he found Hyatt's Harrison, New Jersey, plant to be well equipped and well organized, and he was most interested in Hyatt's large contract with Ford. W. R. in this case turned down the deal for financial reasons. However well run the plant might be, in his view the business was not making sufficient return on assets. "The one glaring difference between [Sloan's] business and ours is this," he wrote to H. H., "that he has $4,000,000 tangible assets which produce yearly less than our $2,000,000 tangible assets, so if we issue preferred stock dollar for dollar, we will be giving him $2 for our $1 for a plant that produces less than ours."[60]

By mid-April 1915, the Timkens had firmly decided not to merge with Hyatt. Rather than suffering from increased competition, Timken Roller Bearing seemed on the verge of significant expansion. "We have a very good look in with the General Motors," noted W. R., "and if we get a large share of that business and don't lose the Willys business, we will have a very handsome increase, due also to the general and large demand." The demand he referred to reflected the rapid growth of the industry then under way. Automobile production and sales increased by more than 60 percent between 1914 and 1915 and would increase again by 70 percent in 1916. World War I, which started in Europe in August 1914, had begun to create a strong demand for larger-sized bearings for trucks. All in all, W. R. was optimistic about the prospects for both Timken companies and increasingly reluctant to consider selling out. In November 1915, H. H. and the managers of Timken-Detroit developed an opportunity to sell that company, and all were in favor of doing so. W. R. opposed the deal on the grounds that they had just invested to expand operations there and were in a good position to take advantage of a strong market.[61]

Early in 1916 Sloan and Heman Ely began discussing a plan to form a joint venture to provide service and sell replacement bearings. By the time the new Bearing Service Company—jointly owned by Timken, Hyatt, and New Departure—was launched, in September 1916, both Hyatt and New Departure had been sold to William Durant and merged with three other automotive parts suppliers to form United Motors Company, with Sloan as president. Two years later, General Motors absorbed United Motors. Sloan became a vice president of GM, a shift in career path that was, as far as H. H. was concerned, rather fortunate for Timken.[62] The Bearing Service Company operated as a joint venture until 1923. By then, Timken was eager to internalize this function, while United Motors had built up a strong sales and service organization including all of its businesses except bearings, so that participation in Bearing Service Company had begun to seem an unnecessary duplication of effort. The partnership was dissolved by mutual agreement, and Timken took over most of its facilities for its Sales and Service Division. Also in 1923, Alfred Sloan became president of General Motors.

Sloan recorded in his memoirs that the chief reason he sold Hyatt Roller Bearing Company in 1916 was neither competitive pressure nor the money offered, though both were important. Rather, he said, the decisive factor was his recognition that the flexible roller bearing "was destined through the evolution of automobile design to be supplemented and perhaps superseded by other types."[63] His concerns provide a contrast to the growing confidence and optimism of the Timkens in 1916. Having gotten a close look at the companies they took to be their major competitors, they had decided they were much better off on their own. The scope of applications for the tapered roller bearing seemed to be growing, not shrinking, as automakers pushed toward heavier, faster vehicles. The market for truck bearings was expanding, and a new market, for tractor bearings, was just opening up. While W. R. was continuing to withdraw from management responsibility—he would submit his resignation as president and director of Timken-Detroit in 1919—he had turned away completely from the idea that the businesses should be sold. For his part, H. H. had become highly focused on putting into effect his decision to undertake production of steel and tubing, and beyond that on winning the business of the great Ford Motor Company. Threats from competition and the consolidation of the automotive industry did not, of course, disappear. But increasingly H. H. would draw confidence from the competitive advantages conferred by vertical integration and continuing improvements in manufacturing.

H. H. Timken, Organization Builder: Securing Independence in a Consolidating Industry

*I*n 1926, H. H. Timken had occasion to write to Frederick J. Fisher, formerly head of Fisher Body Company but by then a vice president of General Motors, which had acquired his company some five years before. There had been, it seems, an attempt by unidentified agents ("some stock broker's representatives trying to work out a commission") to elicit an offer from GM to purchase Timken Roller Bearing. "The purpose of this letter," said H. H., "is to state very frankly that we are not seeking to sell this company. We expect to continue right along in our regular business." Indeed, he pointed out, the entire focus of the company's efforts for many years had been to secure its position as an independent producer of bearings. This had been accomplished largely by the development of manufacturing capabilities that made Timken the low-cost producer in its field. By 1926 The Timken Roller Bearing Company had itself integrated vertically and was producing its own steel and converting that steel to seamless tubing in its own mill. In addition, the company had developed specialized machinery for bearing production and had originated and patented new production processes. Through those investments, H. H. declared, "we feel that we have gotten ourselves into the position . . . to manufacture tapered roller bearings of the highest quality at an absolute minimum cost."[1]

All of this had come about, said H. H., as a result of the company's concentration on its core product: "The entire efforts of our whole organization for many years have been along this one line." Timken had been asked on numerous occasions to undertake production of ball bearings and straight roller bearings, and the company had even investigated what it would take to do so. But, he said, "we have not considered it advisable to engage in that business, nor do we at this time consider it advisable that we should do so." This decision and the resulting intense focus on the tapered roller bearing were, he suggested, the principal reasons that the company was in such a strong position.

In fact, H. H.'s letter indicated that Timken was becoming less dependent on its large automotive customers as it opened up new applications for the tapered roller bearing. That had become, for him, the most interesting part of the business. He congratulated Fisher on being—along with Alfred Sloan of Hyatt Roller Bearing and Charles Mott of Weston-Mott Axle Company—among the "prominent original parts makers who were wise enough to get into the automobile business direct." As leaders of General Motors they had become some of the "very strongest men" in the industry. At the same time H. H. made it clear he was quite content with his own situation. "I myself expect to continue in this bearing business and am getting considerable satisfaction out of developing new uses for Timken bearings. Doubtless all three of you are like me," he added, "in that the money end of the business is no longer very interesting but the constructive end of the business is more interesting than ever."

By 1926, H. H. Timken had stood alone at the head of the company for a decade. (His brother, W. R., had given up an active management role in 1915.) Those were eventful, defining years, during which the distinctive character of The Timken Company took shape. They encompassed the disruptions of World War I, a postwar cycle of economic boom and bust, some key acquisitions, and the public sale of one-third of the company's stock. Yet, as Timken's letter to Fisher implies, two developments were of overriding significance: vertical integration into steel production; and the mobilizing of the company's resources for expansion of bearing applications outside the automotive field. It was in this era that the sales engineering function became a truly differentiating capability. At the same time, integration of steel production with precision manufacturing opened the door to a stream of bearings-driven improvements in steel making and materials-related improvements in bearing performance. In the long term, those developments would have a profound impact, not only on the company's fortunes, but also on the ability of its expanding group of industrial customers to make continuing advances in their own technologies.

Firing Up the Furnaces

As the Timken brothers flirted with the possibilities of selling or merging Timken Roller Bearing, H. H. developed two strong impressions—first, that his physical plant and manufacturing processes were at least equal to those of any competing bearing company and, second, that major changes were needed in order to survive in the consolidating automotive industry. The industry as a whole was growing dramatically. Between 1909 and 1929, the number of cars sold annually in the United States rose from 124,000 to 4.5 million, and the proportion of families owning a car increased from less than one percent to more than 75 percent. At the same time, the largest auto manufacturers wielded increasing power. Ford, GM, and a number of lesser but still large-scale producers were integrating vertically and were gaining a bigger share of the market. The two largest automakers accounted for nearly half of auto and truck sales in 1915, and more than 60 percent by 1925. Timken's actions in this era were strongly influenced by the pressures that those trends created.[2]

The company's broad base of automotive customers gave it a degree of independence that Hyatt, for example, did not have. Yet H. H. clearly saw that Timken would have to win and keep a substantial share of the business of the largest companies in order to survive and grow. He recognized that to do so would mean being competitive on price, relative not just to other independent bearing manufacturers but also to the vertically integrated auto companies that were taking shape. For the short run, H. H. took the approach of lowering prices immediately to win the large contracts that would enable his bearing plant to operate at efficient levels of production. "We must get away from the fancy prices we have been charging in the past and not in a year or two, but right away," he wrote to the managers of Timken-Detroit in January 1915. In the future, he argued, it would be necessary to accept lower margins and prosper by selling a larger volume of goods.[3] Following that line of thinking, he began to focus on reducing his production cost. Over the course of the ensuing year, he would come to see vertical integration as a necessary step toward achieving that goal.

The reasons for that highly unusual strategy, however, cannot be understood simply in terms of production costs. Securing a reliable supply of steel was also a critical issue. Both problems—cost and supply—were closely linked to the special considerations of steel quality that bearing manufacturers faced. From their first experiments with anti-friction bearings, Henry Timken and Reginald Heinzelman had become aware of the fundamental relationship between material quality and bearing performance. Yet it would fall primarily to H. H. Timken to put that understanding into practice, and it was far easier to specify good steel than to obtain it in commercial quantities.

To ensure the quality of the material coming from its steel suppliers, Timken put in place a program of inspection and metallurgical testing, and in the process launched its first formal research program. As chief metallurgist, Marcus Lothrop's charge was, broadly, to improve the quality of Timken's steel, through research as well as through inspection and control. In 1913, under his direction, Timken built a new metallurgical and chemical laboratory in a separate facility situated in the center quadrangle formed by the Canton factory's main buildings. This location afforded good natural light, plus the advantages of being "removed from the din and vibration of machinery." According to James Howland, who came to Timken about this time as head chemist, the laboratory was equipped with "every up-to-date appliance for accurate and rapid [chemical] determinations" and was "one of the finest chemical and physical laboratories in the country." Howland indicated that his methods were also the most advanced and rigorous, noting that he followed strictly the procedures dictated by the U.S. Bureau of Standards. The metallurgical laboratory was equipped with wear-testing machines, both for steel and for assembled bearings, high-magnification microscopes, and equipment for microphotography. Pyrometers linked to the carburizing and case-hardening furnaces allowed the metallurgical staff to monitor and control Timken's own metallurgical processes.[4]

The new laboratory and organization made possible experimental work aimed at improving Timken's basic material. It also set up a powerful screen for steel coming into the plant. But the company's rigorous standards exacted a heavy price. To begin with, Timken bought steel "on a fifty-fifty basis," meaning that it would only consider the bottom portion of each ingot, because the impurities in the molten metal tended to rise to the top as it solidified. Said the *Timken Magazine* author who described that practice, "Timken pays the highest price and gets the pick of the mills." That still did not ensure that all the steel that came through would be up to specifications, however. In 1914, the company began placing inspectors on site in its suppliers' plants. After checking for visible defects, the inspector drilled out samples and sent them to the laboratory in Canton for analysis and approval, a process that saved Timken and its suppliers the cost of shipping material that did not measure up. By 1915, the Canton plant was producing 3.5 million bearings per year, about three times the production of early 1910. At the same time, it was rejecting on average one million pounds of steel per year. As noted in *Timken Magazine,* "This represented an economic waste for which some one had to pay." Since there was no shortage of willing steel suppliers, the writer reasoned, it was likely The Timken Roller Bearing Company that "paid in the end for its rigid specifications."[5]

In 1915, however, supply was at least as pressing a problem as cost. The waging of World War I in Europe was beginning to affect U.S. industry. In 1910, Timken had begun buying steel for its cups and cones in the form of seamless tubing, which could be cut and machined to precise dimensions far more economically than bar stock. As the war progressed, the company found it difficult and then impossible to buy seamless tubing in the full range of sizes it required. Large tubes could be machined down to size, but that was an expensive option. On the other hand, it was still possible to obtain piercing rounds—solid cylinders that could be fabricated into tubes in a piercing mill. H. H. took the first step into steel production when, in mid-1915, he decided to erect such a mill at the Canton plant. He hired R. E. Brock, a master mechanic from the Shelby Steel Company, to design the mill—a large T-shaped building fronting on Harrison Avenue—supervise its construction, and become its first superintendent. Brock brought in an associate from Shelby Steel, Harry Y. McCool, to help install the equipment and start up the mill. On December 17, 1915, the new facility launched its operations: steel billets were heated, then pierced to form rough tubes, rolled to approximate size, cold-drawn to exact dimensions, straightened, annealed (heated again to obtain final properties), and sent to the bearing factory. "It's a fortunate thing, indeed, that we have this Tube Mill," wrote H. H. to W. R. at this time. Without it, he indicated, the bearing plant would have been shut down to half its capacity. Heman Ely wrote to W. R., seconding the sentiment. "This Tube Mill, as a matter of fact, is about the most important investment we have made for some time," Ely said. "The thing that I am most anxious about now is to see our yard full of billets, which are as good as wheat, whether we use them this week or six months from now."[6]

A wartime need for more seamless tubing to make bearings prompted the company to build its first piercing mill in 1915.

Yet the tube mill only partially addressed the supply problem. Timken's sources of supply were limited both by wartime constraints and because the company was attempting to switch from open-hearth to electric-furnace steel, a change directly related to material quality. Electric-arc steel making was a new technology. It was based on an 1899 invention by Frenchman Paul L. T. Heroult, which was, in turn, made possible by the development of large-scale hydroelectric generators and electric-transmission systems in the 1880s. The Heroult furnace was an enclosed unit in which a mixture of scrap steel and iron was melted by a powerful charge passed between two electrodes. Though smaller in scale than the existing processes—open hearth, Bessemer, and crucible—the electric furnace made it possible to control temperatures and alloying elements with more precision. Electric-furnace steel was finer grained and had less porosity and more consistent properties and quality.[7]

The switch to electric-furnace steel originated in one of Marcus Lothrop's very first research assignments: to investigate improved steels for Timken bearings. By early 1914, Timken had begun working with key customers to test and evaluate bearings with rollers made of a new high-chrome alloy and cups and cones made with electric-furnace steel. Such collaborative testing was essential, since so little was conclusively known about the properties of different materials. As Lothrop described the problem to H. H. Timken, "Mr. Beall [of Packard] stated that if we used high carbon, high chrome steel in our cups and cones, that he would not use Timken bearings. Mr. Sweet states that if we don't put high carbon, high chrome steel in pivot bearings that we can't make pivot bearings for the Cadillac Co. . . . Apparently there is a difference of opinion regarding bearings in the city of Detroit." But tests of the new materials produced exciting results. Timken's former bearings had performed no better in tests for wear than bearings made by Standard Roller Bearing Company—both failed at about 29,000 miles. Its new bearings, Lothrop reported to H. H., had been operating under test conditions for 50,000 miles and were "still in perfect condition." In-house tests showed similar improvement. "Our old bearings never gave us 5,000,000 revolutions without failure of rolls, or cones, or both," noted Lothrop. "The electric cones under the present methods of case hardening . . . give us 20,000,000 [revolutions] without failure." In all, Timken had conducted seventy-eight different tests of the new bearings, and they had shown "a vast improvement as regards wear over what we have had in the past."[8]

Yet moving to electric-furnace steel exacerbated the company's supply problems. In 1913 there were only ten Heroult furnaces in the United States. The United Steel Company of Canton installed a 4-ton electric furnace in 1914 and in early 1916 was struggling to bring a second furnace on line to meet Timken's need. By then, however, H. H. was desperate to get steel, and felt forced to abandon the plan to switch entirely to electric-furnace steel. "Our gravest trouble now is to get steel," he wrote to W. R. in January 1916. He had agreed to make a large personal investment in the start-up of Central Steel Company in nearby Massillon, Ohio, on the condition that Central Steel supply Timken 5,000 tons of its open-hearth steel at an advantageous price. "But the principal thing is," said H. H., *"we have to have the steel."*[9]

By that time, H. H. was investigating what it would take to produce steel in-house. When apprised of H. H.'s plans, W. R. expressed some not unreasonable concerns. "That looks to me to be a big project, and one that must be looked into very carefully," he counseled. "Not being steel manufacturers, how can we as novices look into it properly? Is there not some way that you could get expert knowledge on it, aside from the information and data that you and Lothrop can secure?" Implicit in those questions was a healthy respect for the fundamental differences between steel making and bearing manufacture—in technology, labor requirements, and, not least, in capital requirements. Economical operation was much more dependent on scale in steel production, and capacity increases necessarily came in much larger increments. W. R. was respectfully skeptical that the anticipated savings could be realized over the long run. "Can we operate a small unit for our requirements, or something over it, and make it as cheap as we can buy it over a period of years?" he asked. "To be sure we could make it cheaper today because of the demand and increased price of steel, but what about the lean years?"[10]

But H. H. was determined to move ahead and to act quickly. He had decided that entering steel making would place the company on a whole new footing relative to its bearing competitors and, simultaneously, address the threat of auto companies integrating vertically into bearing production. "We must not overlook the fact of the huge combinations being made in the automobile business," he told W. R. "The result is going to be that they will . . . make their own goods unless they can buy them at very little above the cost to them of making the goods themselves." Buick and Willys-Overland were already in a position to manufacture their own ball bearings, he pointed out. They would move into roller bearings "sure as fate" if Timken did not act quickly. If just a few of "the big fellows" started making their own bearings, he reasoned, it would no longer be possible to have the "quantity business" that permitted low prices. H. H. stated firmly, "I want to build up here a stable business of large volume based on a small profit."[11]

The numbers, as he and Lothrop worked them out, appeared quite attractive. One of the biggest cost savings would come from recycling the scrap from bearing production. In this era, Timken's manufacturing processes had an extremely high scrap rate. "By the addition of a little pig iron," H. H. said, "we would have material to make our steel." Taking all things together, he and Lothrop calculated that two 5-ton electric furnaces could produce all of Timken's steel requirements of 20,000 tons per year at $40 per ton or less. The cheapest the company had ever bought electric-furnace steel was $45 per ton, and in January 1916, it was paying $80 per ton. If those numbers proved accurate, H. H. reasoned, they could make $400,000 from six months' savings in the cost of steel, on a facility that they estimated would cost $100,000 to build and equip. "From all of this," he said to W. R., "you will see that I have personally made up my mind that the thing for us to do is to proceed with this steel mill forthwith."[12]

It was a bold decision that, as events proved, was based on some overly optimistic financial calculations. Most of W. R.'s concerns, in fact, were on the mark. During the first half of 1916, Timken's chief engineer, Herbert Vanderbeek, and George Obermier planned the layout of the new steel plant, working closely with H. H. As early as February, they decided to increase the number of 5-ton electric furnaces in the plant from two to four, making it the largest electric-furnace facility in the country, with a theoretical capacity of 100 tons per day, when it came on line in early 1917. Difficulties plagued the operation in its first year. Some of those were beyond the company's control: shortages of labor and power were especially intense after the United States entered the war in Europe. But, as H. H. later admitted to his brother, many of the problems were self-inflicted. "We made a great many mistakes in the layout of the steel mill and got some awful poorly made equipment," he said. Those problems had prevented the plant from reaching the level of production planned for it and hence its goals for cost per ton of steel produced. Instead of $40 per ton, its steel cost over $100 per ton. Over and above the issue of cost, Timken Roller Bearing, in a rare but extreme "fall-down," was unable to supply the bearings and steel for which it had contracted. The customer worst hit was Timken-Detroit Axle, and H. H. was sufficiently embarrassed to propose compensating the Detroit company, still Timken's largest bearing customer, for the losses incurred.[13]

By 1918, Timken had spent, not $100,000, but nearly $1 million getting into steel making. And, to gain greater economies of scale, Lothrop was proposing a capacity expansion costing $1.8 million. The steel-making proposition was clearly far more formidable than H. H. had foreseen, yet he remained solidly committed to his strategy of vertical integration.[14]

Timken was not the only company to pursue such a strategy, but it was still exceptional. As the modern industrial corporation took shape in the early twentieth century, it was common for primary steel production to be integrated with the manufacture of secondary steel products such as wire, nails, rails, and structural materials. It was quite *uncommon* for steel making to be linked to the production of more complex products, for example, machinery or precision-manufactured machinery parts, such as bearings. Alfred Chandler points to a handful of cases in Germany and Great Britain, including some in which steel makers acquired machinery producers and others in which machinery companies backward integrated

H. H. Timken (foreground) observes the steel-pouring process at the company's first melt shop, the largest electric-furnace facility in the country in 1917.

into steel. The French automaker, Renault, was another exceptional case. In the United States Bethlehem Steel and, during World War I, United States Steel engaged in shipbuilding. But, in general, steel producers did not manufacture final products, particularly precision products. And, once the giant integrated steel companies came into being in the first years of the twentieth century, metal fabricators, in Chandler's words, "did not feel the need to have their own large steelworks." Henry Ford's huge River Rouge plant, which came on-line in 1918, had the internal capacity to make steel, but this was part of a much larger effort by Ford to control all the raw inputs to auto production, and it did not become a model for industrial organization.[15]

Chandler explained the limited amount of integration between steel production and fabrication of final products by the lack of significant economic advantages to be gained. Even in the production of secondary steel products, the processes of the day did not permit linkage into a continuous stream to drive economies of scale. Savings in transaction costs could come from locating plants next to each other, but where integration occurred, Chandler suggested, it was motivated primarily by the drive to secure a reliable source of supply (or, in the case of steel makers integrating forward, a reliable outlet). That analysis, however, does not speak to the question of material quality, which in bearings was critical to product performance. From the very beginning, George Obermier made it clear that the bearing plant would be every bit as rigorous in screening Timken steel as it was with that of outside suppliers. "I will not have any tubes delivered to the screw room that can't stand our inspection," he warned H. H. in early 1916. Over the years, the exacting demands of the bearing business would push its captive steel maker to stay on the leading edge of electric-steel technology. That dynamic made both businesses highly competitive in their respective fields and was surely one of the major advantages of vertical integration.[16]

Unfortunately, the internal financial data that would permit analysis of the economic impact on Timken have not been preserved. Certainly, H. H. believed at the outset that significant economies would ensue from taking up steel making. The fact that Lothrop immediately proposed a major capacity expansion indicates an early recognition that their projections had been far too optimistic, and that it would be much more difficult than first estimated to produce steel at competitive rates. Nevertheless, Timken remained in the business and waited another eight years to make the proposed expansion, suggesting that integration one way or another served its strategic objectives. Significantly, the Swedish bearing manufacturer, Svenska Kullagerfabriken (SKF), already an international force in ball bearings, also backward integrated into steel production in 1916, through the acquisition of a centuries-old mining, smelting, and steel-making company, Hofors Bruk. Its motivation was to gain greater control over the quality of its steel supply. That simultaneous but quite independent move by another industry leader lends further support to the notion that some unique conditions applied in bearing manufacture making vertical integration a logical strategy.[17]

The superiority of bearings made with electric-furnace steel had been proven decisively, and Timken was the only American bearing maker with its own supply. In addition, with a metallurgical research program in place, the company was better able than ever to continue making materials-related improvements in its product. In December 1917, H. H. wrote to C. Harold Wills, Henry Ford's right-hand man, to obtain a sample of molybdenum steel, a new alloy with which Ford Motor Company was experimenting at the time. The Timken brothers owned molybdenum mines in Arizona, H. H. told Wills, and he was very interested in determining if this rare metal held potential for improving bearings.[18] Thus began an investigation that would result, by the early 1920s, in Timken's adoption of a nickel-molybdenum alloy as its basic bearing material, a change of long-term significance to the technical success of the Timken bearing. In fact, by late 1917, H. H. was devoting much of his attention to winning a contract with Ford, the one major auto manufacturer that had not yet

adopted Timken bearings for any application. In that effort, the in-house production of steel was an important part of a broad-ranging program to develop a
better-performing, lower-priced bearing and to gain the approval and the business of Henry Ford.

Aiming for Ford

The Ford Motor Company was a commanding presence in the automotive
industry. In the words of Henry Ford's biographer, Allan Nevins, it "towered above
its associates like a massive skyscraper soaring upward from a village, to contain
almost as many people and as much activity as the rest of the community combined." The years between the outbreak of war in Europe and the entry of the
United States into World War I brought prosperity, rising incomes, and greatly increased demand for automobiles. Ford benefited disproportionately by driving
mass production and decreasing the price of the Model T. By late 1917, its share
of the market was greater than 50 percent. Gaining Ford as a customer, H. H. understood, would put The Timken Roller Bearing Company on an entirely new
level, both in scale of production and in prominence within the industry. With a
little serendipity, all of the organizational capabilities that had been built up within
the company came together to enable it to reach that goal.[19]

Ford had long resisted even considering Timken tapered roller bearings.
Henry Ford was happy with the bearings he was using—annular ball bearings
produced by Gurney. He was also highly skeptical of the adjustable feature of
Timken bearings, by which wear in the rollers could be taken up by tightening the
nut holding the bearing in place. Early in 1917, the automaker accepted some
truck bearings for testing but, as Heman Ely reported, it proved to be a difficult
customer, unwilling to cooperate with Timken in working out the proper installation and evaluating test results, "i.e., they are very secretive about whether the
bearings are in test, or when they will be in test, and it is certainly a tough job to
pry any information out of them that they don't wish to give." Some chinks in the
armor began to appear, however. H. H. succeeded in persuading Harold Wills to
consider Timken-David Brown worm gears for its trucks. He also interested Wills
in the Timken brothers' molybdenum mines. In addition, Timken had begun receiving unsolicited letters from Ford owners and dealers around the country who
wanted to buy Timken replacement bearings for their Ford cars. "We are keeping
a record of all such letters as we receive them," reported Ely, "and can at any time
pull out of our files a pretty stiff array of this stuff." When he succeeded in getting
an audience with Wills about the truck bearings, Ely made sure to show him a
sample of the requests.[20]

H. H. took advantage of these openings to establish communication with the Ford organization. In the spring of 1917, he spent a an eye-opening day with Harold Wills in Detroit. Wills told H. H. frankly that he considered Timken's manufacturing processes outdated. He pointed out that machining cups and cones from seamless tubing, then grinding them to precise dimensions after heat treatment was an inefficient method compared to hot pressing, which could form a metal blank on a die to a precise shape in a single operation. Without some change in process, Wills suggested, Timken would not be able to produce bearings inexpensively enough to sell to Ford. "I learned a lot from you that day," H. H. later told Wills, "and, when I came home, immediately started to look the situation squarely in the face." Even before this encounter, Marcus Lothrop had been experimenting with hot and cold forming processes. That work now became a high-priority program. In July, H. H. reported to Wills that Timken was testing a Ford replacement bearing and was also making progress on new processes. He concluded, "I sincerely believe that if you will give us a real opportunity some day before long we will be able to show you a real bearing on a Ford car that you could afford to use."[21]

By the end of 1917, the team in Canton was well along in developing processes for making cups and rollers without grinding. Timken continued to use seamless tubing to ensure surface quality, but otherwise had largely followed Harold Wills's suggestions. Cups and cones were formed to shape by hot pressing (cups) or rolling (rollers), then polished to a smooth finish, a process called "burnishing." Along with this process change came a new cup design— the so-called tapered cup—on which the outer surface was tapered slightly, whereas in the standard design only the inner cup surface was tapered. This would later prove to be an undesirable change, but in the short run it appeared to offer an advantage, since it made the bearing tend to fit more snugly in the socket of the hub. More important, perhaps, it made the cup easier to manufacture with the new forming process, hence less costly. Timken was also by this time ready to begin marketing its replacement bearings for Ford Model T and truck front axles, on which ball bearings were standard. H. H. announced those developments in a December letter to Joseph Galamb, head of Ford's engineering department. Just then, illness prevented him from traveling to Detroit to make a presentation to Galamb and Henry Ford. He was leaving for an extended, recuperative trip to California, H. H. explained, and would pick up the matter immediately on his return.[22]

However, by the time H. H. came back to Canton in early April, the sale was largely made. As it happened, another line of communication between the two companies had opened up, presenting another avenue for Timken to make its case informally to decision makers at Ford. This opening came through Hercules Motor Company, which was located near Timken in Canton. H. H. had helped to launch Hercules in 1915 as one-fourth owner with Gordon Mather and some other investors from Canton and Toledo. In early 1918, the company was on the verge of landing a large contract to produce motors for Fordson tractors and so was in contact with Henry Ford. George Obermier served (in effect, moon-lighted) as president of Hercules, but it was managed by Charles Balough, who as a young apprentice had worked with Ford on the Model T. On a visit to De-troit on Hercules' behalf, Balough showed Ford a set of Timken bearings and de-scribed their advantages. Ford asked to keep the bearings for testing, and Balough promptly arranged to have a dozen more sets sent. Then Timken got some additional help from an unexpected quarter, as Balough described to H. H.: "A little later on, I had a request from Mr. Ford's chauffeur to send a set for him, stating that he has constant trouble with the ball bearings in the front wheels." Balough was hopeful about this development, "because this man is probably in closer contact with Mr. Ford daily than anybody else, and, if this set of bearings would do away with his front axle bearing trouble, I think he would keep up Mr. Ford's interest constantly."[23]

On hearing that news, H. H. pressed Ely and Lothrop to prepare a quote to Ford and to plan on lowering prices to a point that would be competitive with the Gurney ball bearings Ford used. H. H. also instructed them to reassure Ford on the question of capacity: "I want you to impress on him that if we get their business we will immediately equip far beyond what their requirements would actually demand so as to assure them of an adequate source of supply under any and all conditions."[24]

As it turned out, however, the entering wedge for Timken was truck bear-ings. Reassurances from H. H. notwithstanding, production managers at Ford were skeptical that Timken had the capacity to handle the volume requirement of its "pleasure cars." In April 1918, Ford contracted to purchase 2,000 bearings per day for the front axles of Ford trucks. Later in the year the order expanded to include 1,200 more bearings per day for Ford's "closed" pleasure car; and in January 1919, it jumped dramatically with an agreement to supply replacement bearings to Ford dealers around the country, an additional 10,000 per day, be-ginning April 1. The total commitment to Ford at that point—13,200 bearings per day—was more than half the average daily output of the Canton plant in De-cember 1918. Timken therefore contracted to buy $100,000 of new equipment, to be dedicated solely to the Ford order. By May 1919, H. H. was negotiating to supply Timken bearings for Ford's entire output of cars and trucks, a deal that would more than double the daily requirement.[25]

The Challenges of Success

Those sales to Ford put great pressure on manufacturing operations that were already struggling to keep up with the demand for Timken bearings. When the United States entered World War I in the summer of 1917, Timken had quickly geared up to produce large bearings for military trucks under government contracts. During the war it supplied a substantial proportion of the nation's total requirement. In the same period, the company had for the first time opened up a sizable market outside the automotive field—in tractor bearings. Timken in 1918 created a new sales organization, the Tractor Department, to develop this new line. During the war, severe shortages of fuel, steel, and labor created disruptions and made it difficult to sustain output, but space and equipment were constraints on production as well.[26]

Moreover, in contrast to Ford's mass-production automotive plants, in which the steps of production were arranged sequentially and sped along with moving assembly lines, bearing manufacture in this era remained a large-scale batch process. Timken had to expand rapidly—adding more screw machines to the green machining department, grinders to the grinding department, and so forth—to have the capacity to keep pace with Ford's tremendous output. In the spring of 1918, Timken added a large new building to the Canton bearing plant, and it continued to add new machinery throughout the year. This kind of expansion put a great deal of pressure on the tooling department in particular, because so many of Timken's machine tools required specialized jigs and fixtures, the mechanisms that made precision manufacturing possible. In October, H. H. reported that the Canton plant was buying more large-sized machinery to make truck bearings and taking the additional step of installing a conveyor system to mechanize the movement of materials within the factory. The conclusion of the war in November 1918 brought an end to government contracts but no respite from the pressure to expand capacity. The auto industry was poised to return swiftly to peacetime production and Timken's commitments to Ford were growing rapidly.[27]

A new factory seemed inevitable, so in anticipation of winning the large new order from Ford, H. H. initiated plans in the spring of 1919 to build a new bearing factory outside of Canton. The war's end had brought conflict between labor and management in many industries. The anxiety that automakers felt about the potential for disruption of parts supply strongly influenced that decision. Ford, for example, was beginning to talk about developing a second source of supply for tapered roller bearings, as its commitment to Timken grew. A strike at Bock Bearing Company had shut down its plant for many weeks. "Every Bock customer has tried to buy bearings from us and we have not been able to take on a single one," H. H. wrote to W. R. in May. "This large strike has called to the attention of our large customers very forcibly their precarious position [in] depending solely on one source for their bearings." Just a few days later, Timken-Detroit's personnel struck its Clark Street plants. The wisdom of having a second location was affirmed in this instance, as its third plant, on Waterloo Avenue, was able to continue at full capacity and take up some of the slack. W. R. at first expressed concern over an expansion of capacity in advance of firm orders, but H. H. was determined it was the proper course. Thus was born Timken's Columbus, Ohio, bearing plant.[28]

Winning Ford as a customer substantially increased demand for Timken bearings. As a result, Timken built the Columbus bearing plant in 1920. It would expand in 1958 to include automated, high-volume railroad bearing production.

The Columbus plant took shape quickly. H. H. and Obermier rushed through the design phase and set up tooling shops in rented space in Columbus and Cincinnati, so that equipment could be built and ready to install as soon as the factory was completed. When first envisioned, the Columbus plant was expected to add 15,000 bearings per day to Timken's output, which was then running at about 40,000 per day. Within a few months, however, Canton was building a small addition and planning to increase its daily output to 55,000, and plans for the Columbus plant had been enlarged to allow it to add another 20,000 to 25,000. The new factory came on-line early in 1920. For the first time in its history—but only for a brief time—the company was capable of making more bearings than it had contracts to sell. The new manufacturing processes developed for Ford contributed to Timken's rapid expansion of output. Likewise, the new product Timken developed for Ford, the tapered-cup axle bearing, could be sold at an aggressively low price. This created an opportunity to expand Timken's share of the automotive market. Truck and tractor bearings presented further opportunities for growth. "Everywhere you go in the country you find new paved highways being built," observed H. H., "and the higher the [railroad] freight rates go, the more the trucking business will grow."[29] Near the end of 1919 the company moved its general sales department, with engineering support, to Detroit.

Another challenge of rapid growth was to secure a large enough workforce to man Timken's expanding plants. H. H. resolved to keep wages up in the Canton plant, despite the loosening of the labor market. A wave of strikes in the steel industry in the fall of 1919 left the company largely unaffected, perhaps because he and Marcus Lothrop, who ran Timken's steel operations, promised their men that when United States Steel Corporation raised its wages, Timken would follow suit. They kept that promise in February 1920. In the same period, a severe shortage of living space in town was limiting Canton's labor supply. Some local companies resorted to building bunkhouses for men coming from out of town to work. Timken instead undertook to build what became the Maryland Road housing development, and to guarantee mortgages for company employees who bought the new homes there. At the plant, in a new office building erected on Dueber Avenue in 1920, H. H. insisted on including a store and restaurant to serve all employees. "These two things will help us very much, in my opinion, in getting and maintaining help," he wrote to W. R.[30]

By a rough estimate in January 1920, H. H. calculated that all the investments—the new plant in Columbus, the housing project, the new office building and restaurant, the new store, plus an addition to the tube mill and increased material to run the factory on a larger scale—were going to cost about $4.5 million. In addition, Timken Roller Bearing, like all U.S. corporations, had for the first time been assessed a federal income tax of 37 percent on its 1919 profits. With a reduced cash flow, the only way to finance continued investments was through borrowing. "We have been spending vast sums of money in new plant, equipment, etc., and our program for the balance of the year calls for a large expenditure," H. H. wrote to W. R. in May 1920, informing him that Timken had borrowed a little over $2 million from New York banks. By early the next year, the company's indebtedness, all in the form of bank loans, reached $3.5 million. It was an unfamiliar position for a firm that had, since its first few years in business, financed growth internally. It became uncomfortable when the post–World War I recession hit Timken in 1921, roughly halving net sales, from $20.4 million to $10.6 million. (See Table 3.1.) "Thank goodness we are out of debt once again," Ely wrote W. R. in September 1921. "I'd like to stay that way for some time to come."[31]

Ely's concerns aside, the recession came later and was far less disruptive to Timken than to its automotive customers and many other large corporations. Consumer demand dropped sharply in the summer of 1920, not to revive until early 1922. Many companies were caught by surprise or did not respond quickly enough, and quite a few failed. In other cases, owner-entrepreneurs lost control

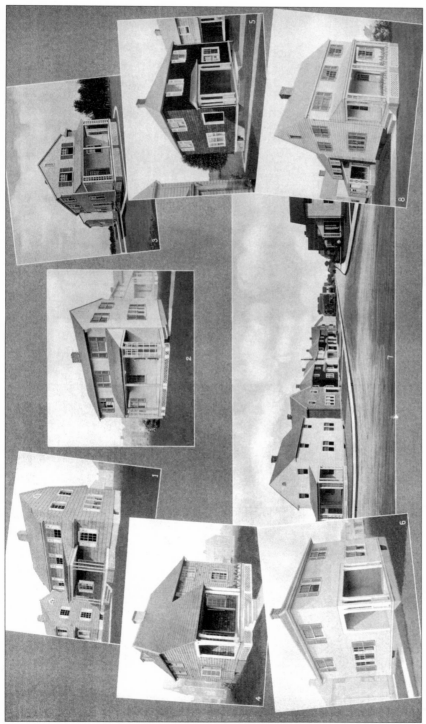

In 1920, to attract workers, Timken built homes in a variety of styles on Canton's Maryland Road for employees and guaranteed their mortgages. The October 1920 issue of The Timken Triangle featured these typical styles and groupings: (1) Dutch Colonial or Gambrel; (2) Italian, with front porch; (3) Italian, with side porch; (4) English, with shingled sides; (5) Low Colonial, square, shingled; (6) Low Colonial, square, stucco finish; (7) Roslyn Ave., looking north from intersection of Arbor Road; (8) High Colonial, with lap-siding.

TABLE 3.1

The Timken Company Comparative Financial Data, 1919–1929 (in Thousands of Dollars, except per Share Data)

	1919	1920	1921	1922	1923	1924	1925	1926	1927	1928	1929
Net sales	$18,200	$20,400	$10,600	$19,700	$25,500	$22,200	$26,400	$26,400	$27,700	$38,200	$42,700
Operating income				9,604	10,057	7,114	8,793	10,725	10,866	15,814	16,194
Operating income as a percentage of sales				48.8%	39.4%	32.0%	33.3%	40.6%	39.2%	41.4%	37.9%
Net income	$4,900	$2,400	$2,200	$7,724	$8,097	$5,806	$8,088	$8,474	$9,554	$13,730	$14,155
Total assets				$20,179	$24,175	$24,379	$28,561	$32,002	$35,524	$45,523	$52,073
Total capital and earnings invested in the business				16,829	20,725	21,780	25,065	28,110	31,679	39,515	46,458
Return on sales				39.2%	31.8%	26.2%	30.6%	32.1%	34.5%	35.9%	33.1%
Return on assets				38.3	33.5	23.8	28.3	26.5	26.9	30.2	27.2
Return on capital and earnings				45.9	39.1	26.7	32.3	30.1	30.2	34.7	30.5
Earnings per share				$3.22	$3.37	$2.42	$3.37	$3.53	$3.98	$5.72	$5.88
Dividends per share				1.14	1.75	2.00	2.00	2.25	2.50	2.62	3.00

Sources: The Timken Roller Bearing Company Annual Reports, 1922–29; C. L. Van Horn to G. L. Deal (February 3, 1966) in The Timken Company Archives.

Note: All net sales and net income for 1919–21 are rounded to the nearest $100,000; all per share data adjusted for 2-for-1 stock split (January 10, 1929).

of their businesses to investors and professional managers, William Durant of General Motors being a notable example. By contrast, Timken's sales, under contracts made months earlier, continued strong until early 1921, hitting a high of $2.4 million in February. By the summer, monthly sales fell below $1 million. They would reach a low point of just $300,000 in December. During the winter of 1921–22, the company's largest customers, Ford and Dodge, both closed their plants completely. Yet Timken had anticipated the continued slump. After building up a large inventory of bearings over the summer, it had closed the steel and tube mills and the Columbus plant in October. The Canton plant remained open but cut back to a single shift and finally laid off a portion of the workforce. By the turn of the year, business began to revive slowly.[32]

The nation and the automotive industry emerged from the postwar depression over the course of 1922. The Columbus plant reopened in April, and by the end of the year, a new addition there had further expanded its capacity. Timken was once again running at full capacity and was, if anything, stronger than it had been going into the crisis. Its operations had contracted but had remained profitable. Timken's metallurgical and engineering organizations had made good use of the time gained by the slowdown in business, continuing to develop the burnishing process for making cups, cones, and rollers without grinding and patenting it. That patent was among twelve obtained by H. H. in his years of work on the company's products and processes. Priced 5 to 10 percent lower than before, the Timken bearing was more competitive than ever.[33]

While the postwar recession did not have the dramatic impact on Timken that it did on many large industrial companies, it did form the backdrop to a significant change—the public sale of one-third of the company's stock. Since 1915 the possibility of selling one or both Timken companies had surfaced a number of times, including another overture from Durant in 1919, during his second term as president of General Motors. At that time, H. H. was eager to sell Timken-Detroit but not the bearing company. W. R. resisted selling either concern to General Motors, at least in part out of loyalty to Timken's many other customers ("these firms who have made us rich").[34]

In September 1921, H. H. asked his brother to get the bearing company's stock listed for public sale as quickly as possible, so that family members could divest some of their large holdings. One of his objectives was to become less dependent on dividend income, which had recently become taxable. He also sought to make the family's wealth more liquid by creating a market for the stock, which would enable them to raise cash if necessary. In addition, taking the company public lessened the family's burden of financing its continued growth and, conversely, opened the way to further growth beyond what the family could finance on its own. The correspondence of the Timken brothers does not touch on those considerations. Yet the timing of H. H.'s request—he had seen Timken's business fall off by nearly 90 percent just as it had completed a major program of capital investment that had required borrowing for the first time in twenty years—strongly suggests a connection. From 1899 through 1921, the Timkens had invested more than $11 million in the company. In H. H.'s view, it was time to convert some of that investment to cash, in order to get the family's finances in order. The unexpected death of his sister, Georgia Fry, on a trip to China in 1921, only increased the impetus to do so.[35]

In the end, despite the fact that he usually relied upon W. R. to handle financial negotiations, H. H. was the one to put together a deal that worked. By March 1922, W. R. had gotten offers to underwrite a stock sale from Goldman Sachs, J. S. Bache, and Harriman, but he had deemed all of them too low. He wrote that he would be ready to make a new attempt in early fall, at which point H. H. took matters into his own hands. By July, after visiting the Canton plant and reviewing the company's books, the New York banking and brokerage firm of Hornblower & Weeks agreed to underwrite a public sale of one-third of the company's shares for $10.4 million. When W. R. proposed that they wait for a higher price, H. H. responded sharply, and with a rare expression of resentment over his brother's retirement. "You do not know anything about this business, nor do you pretend to know, for you have given up every effort to be of any assistance in the business for the last six years," he wrote. "Now . . . you want to speculate and let this thing go over in the future on the theory perhaps that you might get a little higher price. Don't block the rest of us in consummating a good sale and providing a good future market in order that you may make a little extra gambling profit." W. R. fell in line, and Timken shares went on the New York Stock Exchange in the fall of 1922. A year or so later, Hornblower & Weeks underwrote a public sale of Timken-Detroit Axle stock as well.[36]

Going public finally ended the long flirtation with the possibility of merging with an automotive company. It also put the business on a firm footing for continued growth, just as it entered the expansive 1920s. It did not, however, lead to the professionalization of management that occurred in most public companies in the United States from the 1920s onward. A rare case, the Timken family would remain owner-managers down to the present day. Moreover, the company would retain a narrow product focus and centralized organization long after the strategy of diversification, along with the decentralized multidivisional structure pioneered by GM and DuPont in the aftermath of the recession of 1920–21, had become the dominant pattern for large industrial firms. In the 1920s, H. H. remained deeply engaged in the competition for market share in the automotive industry and also, as he wrote to Fred Fisher, got "considerable satisfaction out of developing new uses for Timken bearings." That tightly focused strategy carried the company into the ranks of the two hundred largest U.S. industrials by 1930.[37]

Keeping the Timken Bearing Competitive

With the continuing advance of manufacturing processes made during the post–World War I recession, H. H. was convinced that the Timken bearing was overwhelmingly superior to any of its competitors. When, in 1922, a hapless Timken salesman expressed the opinion that a number of bearings on the market were just as good, H. H. wrote him a long, forceful letter pointing out that the Timken bearing had supplanted all types of bearings in various applications but had never once itself been replaced in an application for failure to perform satisfactorily. Only Timken, he pointed out, had its own steel- and tube-making facilities to ensure the quality of materials. No other company could manufacture with the same accuracy and economy. "Timken bearings," H. H. asserted, "are in a class by themselves as far as superiority and durability are concerned."[38]

Strong words. But contrary evidence began to come in from customers in the 1920s, indicating that Timken, in its all-out push to expand in step with its Ford contracts, had fallen behind the competition in some important areas. The automakers, like Timken itself, were becoming more sophisticated in their analytical capabilities. For example, Heman Ely reported that Reo had "made microphotographs of cross sections, surfaces, etc., and found much in our product to be condemned." Those results indicated the need to improve both steel-making and bearing-manufacturing processes. In addition, it emerged in the early 1920s that the design of the Timken bearing was less effective at maintaining roller alignment—the critical factor in reducing wear—than some competing designs that had entered the market. In the new designs, the shape of the roller was changed to create continuous contact between the large roller end and the inside rib of the cone. That rib-roller contact solved the alignment problem much more completely than Timken's design, which relied upon the combined effects of the cage and the rib-and-groove construction at the small end of the roller. The result was a more elegant roller shape that made possible a bearing at once more compact and higher performing. (See Evolution of the Timken Tapered Roller Bearing, pages 90–92.)

Two patents covered this improvement. One had been granted in 1918 to Elmer Neal of Standard Bearing Company, which had since been acquired by Marlin-Rockwell Corporation. Another patent, granted to George Lee Miller in 1921, was owned by a Canton concern, the Gilliam Manufacturing Company. H. H. had been dismissive when Gilliam started up in 1919, writing to W. R., "They will no doubt develop a small mediocre concern manufacturing tapered bearings." Within a few years, however, Gilliam was making inroads with some of Timken's established customers.[39]

Timken engineers assessed the situation. They found that rib-roller contact reduced friction inside the bearing by 65 to 75 percent, and they recognized they could not develop a competitive bearing without infringing either the Neal or the Miller patent. The situation was embarrassing on a number of levels. George Lee Miller had been working on Timken's factory floor when he came up with his improved bearing design. He had attempted unsuccessfully to win support from Timken managers, all the way up to H. H. himself. In frustration, Miller had left the company and sought backing outside, which he found at Gilliam. In 1921, Timken acknowledged the superiority of Miller's design by launching a suit against Gilliam for theft of its corporate intellectual property. Since the bearing drawings had been transferred to Gilliam on Timken company blueprints, albeit with Miller's signature attached, H. H. felt justified in this litigation, but it was far from the high point of his career. The granting of Miller's patent in 1922 strengthened Gilliam's position substantially.[40]

As it turned out, however, Timken got a break. Henry K. Smith, president of Marlin-Rockwell, was focused in the mid-1920s on a series of mergers that would strengthen his company's position as a ball bearing manufacturer. In 1924, he sold the Neal patent to Timken. A large-scale effort ensued to change all of its bearings to the new design as quickly as possible. At the same time, Timken adopted nickel-molybdenum steel. A number of auto companies, notably Studebaker, had already adopted "nickel-moly" steel for critical parts such as gears and steering knuckle pins. It tended to be a cleaner, hence stronger, steel, and with case hardening, it proved to be far tougher and more wear-resistant than the nickel-chrome material Timken had been using. With those two changes, in design and materials, the Timken bearing once again became the superior product H. H. had always believed it to be. Moreover, it assumed the basic form it would maintain into the twenty-first century. To be sure, there would be continuing improvements in bearing performance, accumulating over decades into dramatic changes. But those would come as the result of improvements in material quality (rather than changes in material), advances in manufacturing leading to tighter tolerances and better finishes, and changes in internal geometry that had a big impact on performance but did not change the outward appearance of the bearing. (See Evolution of the Timken Tapered Roller Bearing, pages 90–92.)[41]

In 1925 the company gained full control of the improved bearing design by acquiring Gilliam. The litigation over the Miller patent had become acrimonious, but the parties were able to settle the case, allowing Timken to make the acquisition. In 1926, Timken further solidified its position by acquiring Bock Bearing Company. On taking possession of Gilliam, H. H. gained some eye-opening information: its manufacturing cost had been higher than Timken's own, but so had been the prices Gilliam could command for its product. "They were getting from 2.5 to 12% more for their goods," he wrote to W. R. "About two years ago we did not keep up with the procession in the design of the bearing, the quality of the steel, and somewhat in the workmanship. They undoubtedly endeavored then to get higher prices than we were getting. When we woke up to this fact you know we purchased the Neal patent, went to the molybdenum steel and jerked up our factory on quality of workmanship. . . . In this one respect, the Gilliam Company did us a good turn, namely, we were too prosperous and getting dead on our feet."[42]

Newly invigorated, Timken became a beehive of activity. With George Obermier, H. H. continued to push on manufacturing technology. He informed W. R. in 1925, "We have definitely made up our minds to spend a very large sum of money in new machinery and simply throw out a lot of our present machinery, which is in good shape but has become obsolete in pattern." To finance this, H. H. proposed discontinuing an "extra" dividend of 25¢ per share that the company usually paid, which would provide more than $1 million for such investments.[43]

In addition, having picked up the ball on bearing design, Timken engineers began to run with it. One big advantage of the new design, they soon learned, was that the rollers maintained constant full-line contact with the cup and cone. This feature greatly increased the bearing's load capacity, and by mid-1925 Timken was experimenting successfully with automotive bearings half the size of what it was then selling. The new Timken bearing could also run much faster than the old. It had long been a rule of thumb that ball bearings should be used for speed, tapered roller bearings for load. Improved alignment, and the consequent reduction of friction inside the bearing, created the possibility of high-speed applications previously out of reach for Timken bearings.[44]

From 1924—the pivotal year in which Timken acquired the Neal patent and switched to nickel-molybdenum steel—through 1929, the company's sales and net income roughly doubled. (See Table 3.1.) Timken bearings were used on 80 percent of all motor vehicles produced in the United States in 1924. Going forward, its leadership in the tapered roller bearing field would open the way to further growth in that market. At the same time, however, H. H.'s drive to win a measure of independence from the automotive industry, in large part to balance out the cyclical pattern of ups and downs that developed in the 1920s as it matured, created important new avenues of growth—new bearing applications for nonautomotive markets, and expansion of Timken's steel-making capacity into a full-fledged line of business.

Evolution of the Timken® Tapered Roller Bearing

1899: The first production bearing had a built-up cage with the end rings tied together by riveted pins. Both pintles and nibs on the ends of the rollers held them in position. Outside cups or raceways were first introduced on this bearing when it was adapted for automobiles.

1907: A one-piece patented cage formed from sheet steel allowed removal of the pintles from the ends of the rollers. Tabs on each side of the pockets in the cage guided the rollers and held them in place on the cone. Patent No. 912,656 was issued on May 9, 1909, to Herbert W. Alden, assignor to The Timken Roller Bearing Axle Company.

1908: The nibs were eliminated on the large ends of the rollers, making the bearing more compact without sacrifice of load capacity.

1912: A further refined cage permitted the tabs or wings on each side of the pockets to be bent inward to provide roller guidance and alignment. After the rollers were assembled in the cage, the large-end flange was scalloped inwardly, locking the cage and rollers on the cone. Patent No. 1,144,451 was issued on June 29, 1915, to Herbert Vanderbeek, assignor to The Timken Roller Bearing Company.

1917: The flanges on the sides of the cage pockets were eliminated, and the perforated pockets were formed by a series of press operations. The cages were stretched or spread at the small end just enough to permit roller assembly and then were pushed into a closing-in die to bring the cage back to size.

1924: The nibs were removed from the small end of the rollers, reducing the width of the bearing and making it more compact without sacrificing load-carrying capacity. A flange was added to the cage small-end I.D. The present Timken standard single-row bearing design differs little in appearance from this.

These two bearings illustrate the dramatic changes in the Timken bearing's load-carrying capabilities within the basic bearing design: today, the smaller bearing can carry the same load as the larger bearing carried fifty years ago. This represents a reduction of 50 percent in size and 76 percent in weight. In automotive applications, for example, this means customers can redesign

a transaxle, without increasing its size, to perform with three times more horsepower. Since 1926, when the company first established a formula for bearing load ratings, the Timken bearing has undergone eight rating increases. Those performance improvements are due to increased precision in bearing manufacture and a myriad of changes in internal geometry and material. The cone rib and roller end geometry have been modified many times, not only to obtain better roller alignment, but also to improve the torque and heat-generation characteristics of the bearing. The roller and raceway contacting surfaces have undergone numerous contour and surface finish changes. The chemistry of the steel, its cleanness, and the methods of carburizing and heat-treating all have been optimized. Since 1927, an extensive performance-testing program has verified the integrity of these improvements.

Engines of Growth

Timken had long sold bearings to some manufacturers of nonautomotive machinery, and it had planned to make a concerted effort to develop that market as early as 1915. But, in the struggle to develop steel making, keep up with wartime demand for bearings, and win Ford contracts, it had put that plan on hold. Nevertheless, by 1918 Timken sales engineers had successfully opened a new market with a variety of applications on tractors, and the company created a Tractor Department within its sales organization to focus on expanding in that field. Inspired by those developments, Timken organized the Industrial Department in 1919. Renamed the Industrial Division, it took off after 1923, when Louis Klinedinst took over its direction.

Klinedinst had joined the company in 1905 as an inspector on the factory floor. By winning recognition from Ely and Obermier, he had gained the opportunity to try his hand at sales, and he had been head of the Tractor Department for a number of years. Now, as head of the Industrial Division, he made his mark immediately by determining to hire a sales force of men with formal engineering training and professional degrees and then train them further for the post in a two-to-three year program in Canton's engineering department—changes that took Timken's long-time requirement of technical competence to a new level entirely. Prior practice had been for a salesman and an engineer to make sales calls together. In the 1920s, Timken's new force of industrial sales engineers was posted by regions. Each made a thorough study of all the industries in his area, then approached potential customers to pitch Timken bearings and, if necessary, help work out the design issues involved in adopting them. In 1926, the company published the *Timken Engineering Journal,* providing detailed technical information for potential customers considering adoption of Timken bearings.[45]

The opening of industrial markets gained momentum in the 1920s, as Klinedinst's organization took shape. The annual reports from the era track this progress, although they do not, unfortunately, provide specific revenue information. Between 1924 and 1925, for example, Timken increased by 83 percent the number of its customers in eleven major categories of equipment: machine tools (the largest category), industrial trucks and trailers, cranes and hoists, pumps, electrical machinery, road-building equipment, conveyors, speed reducers, woodworking machinery, clay machinery, and paper-mill machinery. It had also by that time penetrated twenty other industrial markets ranging from elevators to lawn mowers and household appliances.[46]

Making those sales in most cases depended on convincing manufacturers to abandon relatively inexpensive plain bearings in order to gain the greater friction reduction, hence power savings and lower maintenance, of tapered roller bearings. That often required providing support in redesigning the manufacturer's equipment to accommodate them and, beyond that, to take full advantage of their significantly greater performance in friction reduction, load-carrying capacity, and maintenance-free life. In quite a few instances, Timken also convinced its industrial customers to advertise their products as "Timken equipped," to reflect the improved characteristics of their own products. It was not the only company to inaugurate sales engineering in the 1920s, but it developed the function into an extremely effective formula for expanding the market for Timken bearings.[47]

Sales engineering made new product development another key element of industrial sales, as Timken salesmen in the field identified the specialized needs of a variety of industrial customers. In 1926, Timken offered three new types of bearings tailored for specific applications: large bearings (up to 35 inches in outside diameter) for heavy duty in steel mills, cement mills, sugar mills, and the like; "all thrust bearings" for equipment such as valves, pivots, crane hooks, and oil-well swivels; and a line of double-row bearings for electric motors, turbines, and pumps. From that point forward, the company's product engineers would produce a steady stream of new designs for industrial applications. Though such bearings were manufactured in relatively small numbers, the business was profitable because customers accepted prices that permitted healthy margins. They could afford to do so because of the dramatic improvement Timken bearings offered over plain bearings. In the case of roll-neck bearings for heavy mills, Timken's 1928 annual report pointed out, there were numerous instances in which the bearings paid for themselves in less than a year through cost savings in power generation and maintenance. Such facts help explain the success of the Industrial Division. In the 1940s, Louis Klinedinst recalled that he had had to struggle initially against the high-volume, low-margin mentality that governed the production of automotive bearings, in order to get specialized grinders installed at the Canton plant to produce high-precision bearings for new machine-tool applications. Yet, when the automotive industry began experiencing periodic downturns in its market, in the mid-1920s, Timken found the impact was moderated by its sales in the industrial field. Non-automotive applications—industrial and railroad together—would grow to be the largest segment of bearing sales after World War II.[48]

In the short run, however, the expansion of steel-making operations drove the company's growth as much as anything. By the mid-1920s, Marcus Lothrop and his staff convinced H. H. that a good market existed for electric-furnace steel. Timken's metallurgical research group had made some valuable advances in the control of grain size that gave the company a unique product. A major capacity expansion could establish a solid line of business while reducing the cost of the company's basic raw material.

The decision was in the works for a few years in the mid-1920s, but once it was taken a whole series of expansion moves were made in rapid succession between 1926 and 1929. These included the addition of four new Heroult furnaces of different sizes, including one of 100 tons capacity, for many years the largest in the world. Timken also added three 100-ton open-hearth furnaces, plus new rolling mills and supporting facilities including new chemical and metallurgical laboratories. The company built a new tube mill at its Canton site in 1928, and the next year it purchased another tube mill in nearby Wooster, Ohio. In Gambrinus, Ohio, bordering Canton on the southwest, Timken built a new bearing factory, steel-finishing plant, and piercing mill in 1928–29. By the time this $6 million building program was complete, Timken's productive capacity was 200,000 bearings per day and 30,000 tons of steel per month.[49]

Timken's new steel-making facilities made a splash in the technical press. *Electrical World* noted it was "one of the most completely electrified plants in existence," including its electric-arc furnaces and most of the equipment for moving material around the mill. The plant had an innovative layout: a straight line from melting to finishing, to allow a higher volume of production. Last but not least, the steel mill was equipped with Timken bearings throughout—a practical demonstration of many new industrial applications.[50]

The products the new steel facility could make were wide ranging: 150 grades of steel in rounds, squares, flats, and wire as well as tubes. Timken sold its steel through manufacturers' agents, who worked on commission and maintained their own offices in Boston, New York, and Los Angeles. Its first steady steel customers were Mack Truck Company, Nash Motors, and Timken-Detroit Axle. Soon, though, Timken had a good-sized business selling steel to U.S. ball bearing manufacturers, who otherwise were dependent on Swedish or German suppliers for the grades required for bearing production. In 1928, Timken created a steel sales subsidiary, the Timken Steel and Tube Company. H. H. was chairman of the board and Marcus Lothrop president.[51]

The growth of the steel side of the business, like the expansion of industrial markets for Timken bearings, helped to lessen Timken's dependence on its automotive customers and to secure its future as an independent firm in the midst of a consolidating auto supply industry. By contrast, the situation of Timken-Detroit Axle Company deteriorated markedly in the 1920s. "When you look the thing square in the face a blind man can see that there is no future in the axle business," commented H. H. in 1925. "As a matter of fact when any automobile maker of any kind gets a reasonably large output he can make his axles cheaper than any axle maker can manufacture them for him." H. H. was reasonably happy with the management at Timken-Detroit by that time. Lewis and Demory had both left the company, and the new president, Frederick Glover, was an experienced factory manager who had become acquainted with Timken as the officer in charge of procurement of trucks and tractors for the U.S. military during World War I.[52]

With H. H.'s blessing, Glover narrowed Timken-Detroit's product line to heavy-duty axles and other parts for trucks. He also investigated a variety of possible new products to balance the declining axle business. His preference was for something that would be sold direct to consumers, not to manufacturers, a field "with more opportunities to control our business and with a very much greater potential market." Late in 1927 Glover decided on oil-burning stoves.[53] The Timken Automatic stove became a popular product. In addition, in 1929 Timken-Detroit acquired the Wisconsin Parts Company, an axle maker owned by Willard F. Rockwell. Rockwell joined the Timken-Detroit board. In 1933 he would succeed Glover as president of the company, while his younger brother, Walter F. Rockwell, became general manager.

When H. H. passed the presidency of The Timken Roller Bearing Company to Mark Lothrop in 1929, the company was in an enviable position. It was those large increases in capacity for both bearings and steel that raised the value of Timken's physical plant from $15 million to $31 million and made the company one of the two hundred largest industrial firms in the United States. Its bearing business was more secure than ever before, as its control of the Neal and Miller patents effectively cut the ground out from under other makers of tapered roller bearings. Its broadened focus on new applications and markets outside the automotive industry, along with the expansion of its steel-making capacity, bolstered its hard-won independence in the auto supply industry. To be sure, all U.S. business was riding high in 1929, coming off an extended period of spectacular growth and earnings. Yet Timken was as well positioned as any to face the crises that lay ahead. Just at that time, moreover, the company launched a high-profile effort to open up a large new market in the railroad industry by building its own demonstration locomotive, dubbed the Four Aces. The initiative brought Timken to a level of recognition that few manufacturers of producer durable goods such as bearings and steel ever enjoyed.[54]

The Four Aces

The railroad market was potentially a large one. To crack it, Timken went beyond working with customers to develop and demonstrate railroad bearings in anticipation of customer demand. Timken's locomotive, the Four Aces, represented that approach to new applications on a grand scale. It and the breakthrough in the railroad market also provided a rare bit of publicity for the company's main product.

The nation's railway system in the 1920s was still the preeminent means by which people and goods moved. Dramatic improvements in the comfort and safety of passenger trains had made travel a regular part of business life, and ordinary Americans were able to travel widely and in a style unknown elsewhere in the world, with electric lighting, steam heat, flush toilets, and access to a dining car on day coaches as well as overnight trains. A sharp increase in fares for travel on Pullman sleeping cars after World War I made that a first-class-only mode of travel, but it became more and more fashionable as the accommodations became more luxurious. At the same time, the volume of business on the nation's rail freight system continued to expand, despite the challenge from trucking over short-haul routes.[55]

Henry Ford had suggested to H. H. in 1920 that he should aim at putting tapered roller bearings on railroad cars, but it was not until Tracy V. Buckwalter became vice president for engineering in 1925 that the company began to pursue that market in earnest. Buckwalter had joined Timken to succeed Herbert Vander-beek as chief engineer in 1916. Though he lacked a formal engineering education, he had proven his capabilities over a fifteen-year career with the Pennsylvania Rail-road, and he came to Timken with some sixty patents. After eight years of work on automotive and then industrial bearings—he developed the large-sized roll-neck bearing for steel-rolling mills—Buckwalter, as vice president, was finally able to concentrate on railroad applications, where there was a crying need for an im-proved anti-friction device.[56]

The plain bearings then in use were a flimsy defense against the extreme forces exerted by the movement of heavy cars and locomotives, especially on turns. They frequently became overheated. When smoke began to pour from the housing around the axle, it was a "hot box." The train had to stop so it could be fixed. Hot boxes were a major cause of delays and high maintenance costs, and in the mid-1920s the railroads were eager to find a remedy. There were competi-tors: Hyatt Roller Bearing, as a division of General Motors, offered a flexible roller bearing for railroad applications; and SKF Industries, Inc., a U.S. subsidiary of the Swedish bearing maker, was in the field with a straight roller bearing. Buckwal-ter's goal was to crack the huge market for rail freight cars. He aimed to get a jump on the competition by developing an inboard truck—that is, an axle unit with the bearings mounted on the inside of the wheels—which he designed and had built by the American Car and Foundry Company.[57]

Because of the hot-box problem, the standard design placed the bearing and its housing (the "journal") on the outside for easy access. The inboard truck was smaller and lighter, due to the reduction in the length of the axles and other transverse parts supporting the weight of the car. The benefits from the weight savings were potentially quite large. "On coal cars," H. H. explained to his brother, "if we save three tons in the trucks themselves and they increase the size of the body to carry three tons more coal they would, of course, convert that three ton saving into three tons of freight paid on every loaded coal car. This sav-ing, of course, is outside of any saving due to anti-friction bearings." Timken bearings were priced higher than plain bearings to begin with, and the company had developed a more expensive double-cone bearing with two sets of rollers to handle the heavy loads on rail-car axles without a proportionate increase in over-all size. Its selling point—a rationale that worked well in industrial markets—was that the savings in operating cost, plus the greater payload, would more than off-set that high initial price.[58]

Yet some serious obstacles blocked the application, in particular the organi-zation of the nation's rail freight system. In order to move goods effectively, the railroad companies—fiercely competitive in most areas—had to cooperate by moving each other's freight cars. A particular car was thus destined to travel many lines and carry many different loads across the United States and Canada before it returned to its owner. Under this system the company that made the initial investment in bearings would have to share the operating economies with its competitors, a prospect few railroad executives relished.[59]

The first opportunity to demonstrate Timken's railroad bearings and the inboard truck came not on freight cars but on luxury passenger trains, where the business clearly justified investment in improving the smoothness of ride. In 1926 the Chicago, Milwaukee & St. Paul Railroad decided to equip one of its most luxurious trains—the Pioneer Limited, which connected Chicago and Minneapolis-St. Paul—with anti-friction bearings. The Milwaukee (as the railroad company was called) invited Timken, Hyatt, and SKF to compete for this business, and Timken won out, gaining a high-profile showcase for the company's bearings. Before its maiden run, in May 1927, the Pioneer sat on exhibit for two days in Chicago's Union Station, where it was viewed by some 32,000 people. Those who toured the train could examine a Timken bearing-equipped axle, on display in the baggage car, with part of the housing removed so that the construction of the bearing could be seen clearly. Syndicated articles carried in papers across the country detailed the advantages conferred by Timken bearings—including the comfort of the ride ("the old days of sudden jerking starts and equally unpleasant stops will be over") and the elimination of hot boxes ("there will be no more of the familiar torchlight processions, to an accompaniment of nerve-wracking poundings on journal boxes, that have for so long been a feature of travel"). In addition, the papers noted, bearing-equipped trains could be started from a standstill with one-seventh of the force required for standard trains, and a standard locomotive could pull a train of 21 cars as easily as 12 cars equipped with plain bearings. While the Pioneer Limited was still on its maiden run, the Milwaukee announced that it had ordered 130 new Pullman cars equipped with Timken bearings. The first big test of Timken's railroad bearings was a resounding success.[60]

Yet, Timken's ultimate goal remained rail freight cars—far more numerous than passenger cars—where considerations of comfort had no bearing on economic calculations. Buckwalter continued to pursue that market, but not directly. He turned his attention instead to the locomotive, the part of the train no railroad executives could ignore. With considerable farsightedness, Buckwalter realized he would have to sell them first on that application, for which they could readily calculate the economic benefit of using Timken bearings. On locomotives, the hurdle was to place tapered roller bearings on the driving axle, which required a larger-than-normal bearing to handle the extremely high loads encountered in normal operation. Timken could not demonstrate the bearing until a railroad company undertook, at considerable expense, to refit an existing engine to accommodate it. After a couple of years, during which more than 30 steam locomotives

Timken built the Four Aces locomotive to convince railroad customers of its advances in steel technology as well as tapered roller bearings. Northern Pacific bought the 1111 in 1933. It made its last run on August 4, 1957.

Tracy Buckwalter, vice president of engineering, and the man behind the Four Aces idea.

were equipped with Timken bearings on all *but* the driving axles, Tracy Buckwalter proposed that the company build its own locomotive to prove this application. In the summer of 1929, Timken set out to do just that.[61]

At that time, locomotives for passenger trains had larger wheels and were lighter than those for freight trains, because they had to pull less weight but travel at higher speeds. Buckwalter's idea was to design the Timken engine to pull either freight or passenger trains. Railroad engineers were already projecting that such a design would become most common in the future. The Timken locomotive would show the way, and it would be versatile enough to permit demonstration of Timken bearings under the widest possible range of conditions. The engine was built by the American Locomotive Company, but altogether fifty-two specialty locomotive manufacturers agreed to supply parts "on open account," that is, without payment until the engine was purchased at the end of its two-year demonstration period. In addition to its distinctive design, the Timken locomotive was a showcase for advanced materials: nickel-alloy steel, not just in the bearings but in critical parts of the power-generating system; and carbon-vanadium steel in the axles. Such high-strength steel alloys had not yet been applied to the axles of locomotives because they could not tolerate the extreme temperature changes that were unavoidable with the use of plain bearings.[62]

All of those features created excitement in the ranks of the railroad industry. The new locomotive emerged from construction—painted dark green with gold stripes—in Schenectady, New York, in April 1930. Officially named TRBX 1111, it was known as the Four Aces. The numbers on its headlight were mounted over the shapes of a heart, a diamond, a spade, and a club. A bronze plaque on its tender listed the companies that had furnished parts. Every conceivable measuring device was aboard, so that its performance could be tracked in minute detail. The first trial was a prosaic one, a "125-car freight drag" on the New York Central Railroad. The nation's largest railroad company, the Pennsylvania Railroad,

A popular promotion by railroads was to have three women in high heels pull the Timken Four Aces locomotive, weighing more than 355 tons, down the track. The Pennsylvania Railroad staged this demonstration in Chicago on August 7, 1930.

got its turn with the Four Aces in June and mounted an unusual test. Three men tried to pull the 355-ton locomotive with a rope, on a level track, and they succeeded. Two months later, in Chicago, the Pennsylvania bested that feat by staging a demonstration in which the engine was moved by three young women, all wearing high heels. After that, the Four Aces was operated by the Chesapeake & Ohio Railroad, the Erie, the New Haven, the Boston & Maine, and many others. Train crews tested the equipment by deliberately falling behind schedule, then pushing the speed to make up lost time. The Four Aces demonstrated its capabilities on long hauls and steep grades under all conditions, and at the same time Timken bearings proved their worth by running trouble-free with only minimal maintenance.[63]

The spectacle of three people—women or men—moving a huge locomotive made for great publicity. But railroad executives were most interested in the mundane operating statistics of the Four Aces. After 100,000 miles of operation in service to fourteen different railroad companies, there was a lot of such information available. One of the most significant findings was that all the working parts of the engine, indeed all the cars of the train, could run for long periods with comparatively few problems and limited wear. This improvement came from the elimination of some of the worst running conditions related to friction on the axles: lurching starts, vibration, swaying on turns, and passenger-train "surging" (the latter occurred when the cars of the train picked up speed on the locomotive as the driver eased up on the throttle, then snapped back into position when he opened the throttle and began pulling the train again). The Four Aces consumed less fuel and water yet was far more powerful than comparable engines not equipped with anti-friction bearings. The cost savings on maintenance and lubricants in a single year was nearly enough to pay for the initial cost of the bearings, which had a life expectancy of three years on driving axles and six years elsewhere. Photographs showing crusted snow and ice on the bearing housing of a train that had just completed a long passenger run on the Northern Pacific proved convincingly that the hot-box problem had been solved once and for all.[64]

Buckwalter's ultimate objective for the Four Aces—opening up rail freight applications for the Timken bearing—would not be realized until the company developed a much less expensive bearing in the 1950s. Yet it laid the essential foundation for that breakthrough. Moreover, the whole railroad initiative of which the Four Aces was part was immeasurably important to Timken in its efforts to increase its stature and expand its market reach beyond the automotive industry. Outside of a small coterie of railroad buffs, public awareness of the exploits of the Four Aces would quickly fade. But within the technical and business communities Timken's accomplishment made a lasting impression. In the 1940s, Tracy Buckwalter's career would be crowned by winning a major prize, the Henderson Medal—for his work "in applying anti-friction bearings to railroad locomotives and cars"—from an old and prestigious scientific and engineering organization, the Franklin Institute. In the depths of the Depression, Timken's boldness and ultimate success with the Four Aces won the admiration of industrialists in every field. As one commentator noted in *Machinery* magazine in 1932: "The building of a large passenger locomotive for demonstration purposes is a remarkable example of the progressive attitude of the company that undertook the work."[65]

Crisis and Transition: Timken in the 1930s

By 1929, the basic elements of the modern Timken Company were in place. Steel making—undertaken to secure the supply of high-quality raw materials for Timken bearings—had expanded in capacity to the point of becoming a business in its own right. On the bearing side, Timken had firmly established its position in an industry that, like other core industries within the U.S. economy, had settled into an oligopoly. GM's New Departure-Hyatt division was the only other bearing producer of comparable scale. The company's independence within the automotive supply industry was secure, its path into new industrial markets clearly marked out. The essential organizational capabilities—in production, sales, product and process engineering, and operational and financial control—were in place to enable the company to continue to expand its business on a profitable basis. More important, those organizational capabilities were well fitted to the corporate purpose that had been built upon the founding principle of value in the reduction of friction. Sales engineering put Timken in a position to work directly with customers in solving their specific friction problems and at the same time guided Timken's development of bearings for new applications. In-house steel-making capabilities were a critical complement to bearing product and process engineering, opening the door to materials-related improvements in bearing performance. Those elements, developed over the course of H. H. Timken's thirty-year term of leadership, would continue to define the firm through the 1930s and beyond. But at the same time, both the company and the environment in which it operated would change in a number of important ways.

The severe, prolonged depression that followed the U.S. stock market crash of 1929 definitively separated weak companies from strong—and Timken would prove to be among the strong ones. At the same time, its harsh effects brought on a change in public attitudes toward "Big Business" that led to the rise of "Big Government" and "Big Labor" as counterbalancing forces—a momentous, fundamental shift in the business environment. At Timken, as in many companies, the rise of Franklin D. Roosevelt and the policies of the New Deal not only opened the door to unionization—the United Steelworkers (USW) would win a companywide vote in 1942—but also created a division between management and labor along political lines that would persist to the present day. Hostility to the union and to the growing role of the federal government in business affairs would become as ingrained in the management culture as commitment to the tapered roller bearing.

Other changes, less dramatic but still of long-term significance, also worked to reshape the company in this era. One of those was a changing competitive environment. In the United States, Timken's position would not be seriously threatened, but the company would have to learn to live with some established competitors in the tapered roller bearing field, as dictated by the automakers' insistence on having multiple suppliers. In addition, SKF—smaller than Timken in this era, but growing aggressively on an international basis—became more competitive in U.S. markets in the 1930s. As Timken focused more attention on expanding internationally, it would meet some strong opposition from SKF, as well as the leading German bearing manufacturers.

Last but not least, the 1930s brought a transition in leadership, as H. H. relied increasingly on a group of managers that had grown up around him over some twenty years. While he remained in close touch with the business and continued to play a central role in important decisions up to the mid-1930s, those men took over responsibility for the business on a day-to-day basis and, increasingly, for its long-term direction as well. The decade would provide an eventful coming of age for this rising generation of corporate leaders.

Leadership Transition

From about 1928—the year he turned sixty—until his death in 1940, H. H. was often in ill health. He suffered from asthma, had several bouts of pneumonia, and in the mid-1930s developed emphysema. Increasingly his deafness cut him off from the world. "I am so deaf," H. H. wrote in 1927, "that it is very difficult for me to meet people I do not know and understand much of what they say."[1] He extended his annual visits to California and Arizona in those years and also began spending time in Naples, Florida, where his wife, Edith Timken, had established a winter residence. In the summer he vacationed with his family in Little Current, Ontario, in a home he built on the North Channel of Lake Huron. When in Canton, he spent much of his time at home in the mansion he had built in 1916 near the McKinley monument in the northwest part of the city. He maintained a small circle of close friends, with whom he loved to play cards, especially cribbage and bridge.

Not surprisingly perhaps, the more H. H. withdrew into his private sphere, the more his public image became a caricature of the real person. In the early 1930s, he attracted considerable attention by putting up more than $1 million to build a clinic for Dr. Orval H. Cunningham, a practitioner of hyperbaric (high-pressure) medicine, who claimed to be able to cure diabetes, cancer, and other severe diseases by exposing patients to a highly pressurized atmosphere for extended periods of time. The new clinic, on the shore of Lake Erie, in Cleveland, included a round steel hyperbaric "tank" more than three stories high. In many people's minds, H. H. would forever be associated with that giant tank.[2]

His wealth was a source of public fascination. The *New York Times* had placed him on a list of the nation's wealthiest individuals in the mid-1920s, and *Time* magazine liked to call him "The Millionaire Nobody Knows." With a large measure of myth and some downright inaccuracies (not the least of which was getting his name wrong, as Henry Holiday—not Heinzelman—Timken), a *Time* article reporting on The Timken Roller Bearing Company's dividends for 1935 captured the view from the outside world. "Canton's No. 1 citizen lives in baronial splendor," said *Time*.

> Around his estate is a high iron fence guarded by watchmen who question all who attempt to enter. Deaf, Mr. Timken expresses himself in curious ways. On his office floor is a fine thick carpet. It is said that when something displeases him, he stalks the floor scattering live cigarette butts. No one is allowed to pick them up, for later Mr. Timken likes to look across a carpet pock-marked with burned spots, evidence of successful rages. In gentler moods Chairman Timken is generous with

his money. He pays high wages, has provided food and coal for old employees now idle. To Canton he once donated a $250,000 swimming pool.[3]

"I do not know how they get up such stuff," wrote Cora Burnett to her brother about the description of his incendiary rages. In fact, H. H.'s legendary temper had mellowed considerably. "I think any intelligent and honest man, as he grows older, softens towards other people," he wrote, commenting on this change in himself. In particular, he noted that he had gained "a keener consideration for the other fellow's view point." His correspondence of the late 1920s and 1930s bears this out. Though he always spoke his mind frankly and forcefully, H. H. was both respectful and supportive of the men who took over running the company.[4]

H. H.'s bouts with serious illness undoubtedly hastened the transition to new leadership, but he had already prepared the way for change by building up the executive ranks and the board of directors. In 1929, when Marcus Lothrop became president of both The Timken Roller Bearing Company and The Timken Steel and Tube Company, there was a solid organization in place in the parent company, with long-time Timken employees at the head of the functional divisions. H. H.'s old friend George Obermier was vice president in charge of production, and Tracy Buckwalter was vice president of engineering. H. J. (Harry) Porter, vice president of sales, had been hired by W. R. Timken some fifteen years earlier. Timken's secretary-treasurer, J. F. (Fred) Strough, had worked many years with Heman Ely and succeeded him in 1925. Strough's assistant, R. C. (Charley) Brower, would take over that position in 1930. W. R. Timken remained a vice president, without portfolio, and a member of the board.

In 1929, the company's board of directors expanded from five members to seven, to include all of the vice presidents plus an outside director, Alwin C. Ernst. A founder of one of the nation's leading accounting firms, Ernst & Ernst, "A. C." was a long-time friend and advisor to H. H., as well as the company's accountant. He immediately made his presence felt on the board, as Strough reported: "Mr. Ernst suggested that we ought to have actual regular Directors' meetings from now on, with discussions of the Company's affairs and corresponding recording in the corporate minutes; otherwise, we will be open to criticism in his opinion for doing business as a family affair and not as a stock company with many stockholders."[5] Thus, after thirty years of shouldering the lion's share of responsibility for the company, H. H. had secured its future by ensuring it could carry on without him.

His plans were temporarily, but painfully, derailed in April 1932. H. H. returned from his winter stay in California that year to a directors' meeting that ratified the resignation of Mark Lothrop, whose behavior off the job had become erratic and an embarrassment to the company. In the aftermath, H. H. resumed the title of president, but problems with the management of the steel business persisted.

In 1931, Timken had hired Fred J. Griffiths to be president of The Timken Steel and Tube Company. Griffiths was an established leader in Canton's alloy steel industry, a knowledgeable metallurgist, and an effective salesman with a strong reputation in the industry. Yet he caused a great deal of disruption at Timken by insisting on bringing with him a cadre of managers from the outside, many of whom were relatively young and seemed inexperienced and inept to the old hands in the business. By 1936, the organization was in turmoil, and Timken's new president, William Umstattd, asked Griffiths to resign. The Timken Steel and Tube Company was dissolved, and the steel business became a division of The Timken Roller Bearing Company.[6]

Given those difficulties, it was fortunate for Timken that Umstattd had been identified early as a possible successor to Lothrop. A protégé of George Obermier, he had come up through the ranks in the Canton bearing factory and he knew that side of the business intimately. William Earle Umstattd was born in Tennessee in 1894, the son of a department-store manager. He had helped to organize and recruit college students for the U.S. Army's ambulance corps, which went to France during World War I. He was an officer of the corps and served in many campaigns, including some of the most brutal, on the Marne and in the Argonne. Like many others engaged in that war, he had been impressed by the superior performance of trucks equipped with Timken bearings. After the Armistice in November 1918, Umstattd served for a time in the Army of the Occupation in the German Rhineland. A number of men in his command were from Canton, and they told him that Timken was a good place to work. An ambitious young man, Umstattd headed for Ohio after mustering out. He interviewed at Timken and also at Goodyear Tire and Rubber Company in Akron, and received offers from both. The director of Canton's YMCA, where Umstattd was living at the time, advised him to choose Timken. He started work in November 1919 as an inspector of finished bearings in the Canton plant. In his first year he moved through a variety of jobs—helper in the hardening and automatic screw-machine departments and stock chaser—but before the end of 1920 he was promoted to foreman in the Canton assembly department. In 1922 he became assistant factory manager, in 1929 factory manager, and early in 1932 executive vice president. After Lothrop's untimely departure, he served a brief, but doubtless intensive, apprenticeship under H. H. In 1933 Umstattd joined the board of directors. He became president in June 1934, at the age of thirty-nine.[7]

For most of the 1930s, depression, recovery, and the structural changes precipitated by the crisis would command the attention of Timken's management group. Yet other changes—less dramatic, but still of long-term significance—were on the horizon in the late 1920s and would play out in the following decade. Chief among those was that Timken, for the first time, was to face the prospect of significant competition in tapered roller bearings, both at home and abroad.

A Changing Competitive Environment

The purchase of the Neal patent and the acquisition of the Miller patent through purchase of Gilliam, followed by the purchase of Bock Bearing Company in 1926, gave Timken a commanding lead in tapered roller bearings. As Fred Strough reported to W. R. in 1928: "We find ourselves in the position of having no additional business available to us with the automobile producers, outside of General Motors." As for GM, its bearing subsidiary, New Departure-Hyatt, continued to compete in the automotive field with improved ball bearing designs and made gradual inroads into established Timken applications in GM cars, such as Cadillac and Chevrolet. But it did not threaten to venture into production of tapered roller bearings. In 1926, when H. H. had expressed concern over reports that an outside agent was attempting to interest GM in purchasing Timken, GM vice president Frederick J. Fisher had provided reassurance. "I told him," said Fisher, "[that] you controlled the roller bearing business and we the ball bearing, and both concerns were happy, so why change it? I am sure we have no other intentions." That position would hold until after World War II.[8]

Yet Timken's enviable "virtual monopoly" on the production of tapered roller bearings was destined to give way in the 1930s. One force for change was the growing insistence of Timken's major customers—Ford Motor Company in particular—on having multiple sources of supply. Ford in the early 1920s had developed a second supplier for tapered roller bearings, the Imperial Bearing Company of Detroit. A maker of ball bearings and wound roller bearings, Imperial had begun to produce tapered roller bearings under the Bock patent of 1915, almost exclusively for Ford. In 1924, The Hoover Steel Ball Company purchased the assets of Imperial and hired its general manager, Silas A. Strickland, to oversee roller bearing production. Hoover continued to supply Ford with tapered roller bearings for the Model T and was shipping 150,000 bearings per month—10 to 15 percent of Ford's total requirement—in early 1927. (Timken was producing more than 200,000 bearings per day at that time.) In May of that year, however, the last Model T rolled off the assembly line, and Ford shut down production for the changeover to the Model A. The new Ford car specified bearings of a design covered by the Neal and Miller patents—that is, Timken bearings. Hoover was stuck with thousands of unsalable bearings. After this debacle, Hoover Steel Ball Company regrouped and reoriented itself to produce radial ball bearings. Silas Strickland, most likely with Ford's encouragement, moved to Bower Roller Bearing Company, where he became a vice president and general manager.[9]

H. H. and others at Timken at first discounted Bower as serious competition. The company had fared poorly over the years. But they did not fully appreciate Ford's determination to avoid dependence on one supplier. By 1931, Bower was producing a bearing that, in Timken's view, clearly infringed the Neal patent. It had expanded its business with Ford and was beginning to work on sales to Chrysler and Hudson. Lothrop, Ernst, and H. H. considered the options of buying Bower and, alternatively, of launching a patent infringement suit. In the end, however, they did neither. Ford's business constituted half of Timken's bearing revenues in the early 1930s. Henry Ford was not averse to making his preferences known and had the clout to get his way. "I was hoping that we could win out on an infringement suit," W. R. commented, "and in that way control a larger share of the Ford business and keep the Bower people from undermining us elsewhere." But Ford would not have it: "Evidently he has brought about a different situation so as to permit him to have two sources of supply for our bearings." W. R. accurately predicted that Timken would soon lose more business, "now that Bower is privileged to make our bearing." In 1935—the year the Neal patent expired—Chrysler, also citing the desire to have two sources of supply, specified Bower bearings for its Dodge passenger car.[10]

Ultimately, Timken would retain the lion's share of the market for tapered roller bearings. In the mid-1930s, seven other U.S. manufacturers were in the field, but only Bower, whose business was about one-fourth of Timken's, competed on a significant scale. The *Magazine of Wall Street* in 1936 described Timken's position as "at least semi-monopolistic." Ironically, though, within this success lurked another, potentially more threatening, competitive challenge. The danger: through its leadership in the market for tapered roller bearings, the Timken name would become so completely identified with the product as to become generic. In the mid-1930s, this was a real possibility and one the company was anxious to forestall.[11]

To that end, Timken sued two bearing distributors for trademark infringement. It charged Leterstone Sales Company with passing off the bearings of other manufacturers as Timken bearings. It accused the second company, L. C. Smith Bearings and Parts Company, of refinishing used Timken bearings and selling them as new. In addition, Timken asserted that both companies had reground Timken bearings of one size in order to make them fit an application calling for a bearing of larger internal diameter. The two cases were tried together in December 1936. In court, the defendants called numerous auto repairmen to testify that they did not care what brand they got when ordering "Timkens"—all they wanted was a set of tapered roller bearings. On its side, Timken provided extensive detail on the company's evolution, on how its bearings were manufactured, on its broad program of advertising, and on the competition it had faced over the years from other types of bearings. Timken prevailed, arguing that its name stood for much more than tapered roller bearings. It also stood for steel and a variety of steel products, and in all the products Timken manufactured its name stood for "reliability, great engineering, skill and accuracy . . . and excellence of workmanship."[12]

The Smith-Leterstone case was important in two respects. It confirmed the strength of the Timken trademark, but equally, it demonstrated the company's willingness to defend it. Compared to total bearing sales, the market for replacement bearings was small, but the business was significant because of its relatively high margins. Timken sold into this market through the Timken Roller Bearing Service and Sales Company, which maintained sales offices ("factory branches") at thirty-three locations around the country. This organization supplied replacement bearings directly to Timken's customers and to distributors. Of the roughly 10,000 auto parts distributors in business in the mid-1930s, the Service and Sales Company sold direct to only about 1,700. But through those 1,700, Timken bearings made their way into the broader distribution network. It was a diffuse market in which aggressive defense of the trademark in the courts was one of the only levers of control.[13]

Thus, while Timken remained strong in its home market, the situation was becoming more complex. On one hand there was the growing power of a few large automotive customers to dictate the terms of competition; on the other was the more nebulous, but still insidious, threat to the Timken trademark from the nibbling infractions of small-scale distributors. Moreover, as became evident in the early 1930s, a powerful force for change in the industry was developing abroad in the form of a strong, aggressive competitor, the Swedish firm, Svenska Kullagerfabriken. SKF had been organized in 1907 to capitalize on Sven Wingquist's important invention, a double-row, self-aligning ball bearing. Wingquist was a talented engineer but above all a bold entrepreneur with an expansive vision. By 1914, SKF had associate companies or sales representatives in twenty-seven countries around the world—including a U.S. sales company, SKF Industries, Inc.—and was manufacturing bearings in France, Britain, and Germany. During World War I, SKF Industries began producing bearings in the United States. Besides integrating backward into steel production in 1916, the same year as Timken, SKF had built capabilities in product testing and new product development. Its first research laboratory opened in 1912. In 1920, SKF's chief engineer, Dr. Arvid Palmgren, patented a tapered roller bearing, which went into production in Europe in 1924.[14]

SKF by the late 1920s was producing a variety of ball and roller bearings. Its strategy, in contrast to Timken's focus on the tapered roller bearing, was to be able to provide "the right bearing in the right place." A number of its products—the double-row ball bearing and a spherical roller bearing developed by Palmgren in 1927—offered alternatives for the heavy-duty applications where Timken bearings typically excelled. In Europe, SKF was driving hard to consolidate its position through acquisitions. In 1928 and 1929 it acquired a second French ball bearing company and seven German companies. It was then the largest bearing manufacturer in Germany, with production consolidated in two factories in Schweinfurt and one in Cannstatt. SKF was still considerably smaller than Timken: its annual bearing output was 13.3 million in 1927 and would grow to 25 million by the late 1930s, as opposed to Timken's high of 40 million bearings in 1929. Yet it was a dynamic company firmly established in international markets.[15]

At just that time, Timken's British licensee was also becoming more aggressive in its plans to expand both at home and in Europe. It was not long before the managing director of SKF in Sweden, Björn G. Prytz, proposed an agreement to divide the bearing business internationally. SKF would give up tapered roller bearings in return for Timken's agreement not to undertake making ball bearings. "I assume you know," wrote Strough to W. R. in conveying this news, "that in England and other foreign countries they do not have anything similar to our Sherman and Clayton [antitrust] Acts; in fact, the sentiment is almost the opposite and in favor of amalgamation, trusts and price agreements." Discussions arising from this proposal continued for two years, 1929–31, as Prytz persisted in trying to find some formula for cooperation in which Timken would be willing and able, within the constraints of U.S. antitrust law, to participate. One option discussed was that SKF would purchase Timken's European companies and Timken would buy SKF Industries and acquire the Palmgren tapered roller bearing patent.[16] Another involved an international merger into a single entity producing all types of bearings. In August 1930, Mark Lothrop visited SKF's bearing and steel plants in Sweden and pronounced them nearly up to Timken's standards. "To All the Boys" back home in Canton, he wrote: "They are doing a very good job of it—not as good as you are, but almost." Lothrop favored the merger and professed himself ready to take on the challenge of running a much larger company producing a full line of bearings.[17]

In the end, of course, those discussions led nowhere. SKF would eventually become the largest bearing manufacturer worldwide, and Timken would remain the leading producer in its own field. Though willing to consider proposals, the Timken brothers—H. H. in particular—were simply not disposed to make such a combination when all was said and done.

With the questions of buying Bower and merging with SKF on the table in January 1931, H. H. expressed his views clearly to Lothrop. In the first place, he noted, such consolidations would "sit very poorly" with key customers like Ford. But, more broadly, he suggested it was simply time to face the changing realities in the industry. "With reference to . . . the Bower Company, or the S. K. F. or anybody else," H. H. wrote, "I think we have got to make up our minds that the day has passed when we can buy all competition and thereby keep up fancy profits. . . . I realize that you, myself and all the rest of our organization have never been thoroughly trained in combating competent competitors. I have no doubt that it is going to be a difficult lesson for us all to learn, but I think the time has arrived when we might as well all make up our minds that that is the future condition we must face." Under these circumstances, said H. H., "the only stability we can ever hope to have is [in] meeting all competition by superior management. . . . When you look our whole proposition over, don't you agree with me that we have arrived at the point in our business of making profits through more efficiency, more capital, stronger reputation and good will, and better management than our competitors?"[18]

Thus, while it remained largely unchallenged in its effort to expand applications in diverse industrial markets, Timken settled down to coexistence with the competition in other fields. In the United States, Bower and others would share the automotive market, while SKF Industries and Hyatt went after the railroad axle business with their competing (spherical and wound) types of roller bearing. Timken's effort to extend its market reach in Europe, meanwhile, would hit some roadblocks just as it was getting into high gear.

Timken Expands Abroad

Timken's position in Europe had begun to change at the time of World War I. From 1909 until the start of war in 1914, its British licensee, Electric & Ordnance Accessories Company, made steady headway competing against annular ball bearings in British-made cars. Many of the bearings it sold in the early years were shipped from Canton, but gradually, with a great deal of technical support, E&OA began manufacturing bearings in a small plant on Cheston Road in the Aston section of Birmingham. One of its first automotive customers was Wolseley Motors, then one of Britain's five largest automakers and, like E&OA, a subsidiary of Vickers. In 1914, E&OA's entire productive capacity was redirected to Britain's wartime needs, its bearing output earmarked for military trucks, cars, and later tanks. In 1917, under great pressure to expand its other operations, Vickers commandeered the Cheston Road plant and dispersed the departments of E&OA among its other subsidiaries. Bearing production moved to Wolseley Motors at another Birmingham location, and with the consent of Timken in Canton, Wolseley took over the Timken license from E&OA.[19]

At the end of the war, in 1918, the bearing-making operation under Wolseley Motors was still small—the plant employed fewer than 100 men and produced well under 4,000 bearings per week. But the market opportunities were great, mainly because the war had introduced Europe to Timken bearings on the cars, trucks, and tanks shipped to the battlefield from the United States and Britain. In both France and Germany, where ball bearings had wholly dominated automotive applications, the performance of Timken bearings under wartime conditions made a big impression in engineering circles. "There is a great vogue for Timken

Bearings in Europe," H. H. wrote to W. R. in 1919, "and there are going to be a lot of them produced there." After the war, Wolseley Motors invested in new machinery to increase production in Britain. In France, a ball bearing company, La Société de Mécanique de Gennevilliers, of Paris—which had been pressed into service to assemble Timken bearings during the war in order to supply replacements for American trucks—agreed to continue as a sublicensee. In addition, Wolseley negotiated a license agreement with a German entrepreneur, Max Prausnitzer. Prausnitzer incorporated Deutsche Timken GmbH in Berlin in 1918, apparently with the intention of manufacturing bearings there. In 1920, Wolseley itself incorporated a new company, British Timken Limited, to which it transferred its license to make Timken bearings. Those developments were particularly gratifying to H. H., who was mindful that European manufacturers had led the field by a wide margin when he and his father had first become acquainted with antifriction bearings nearly thirty years before.[20]

British Timken remained under the control of Wolseley Motors until 1927. During that time, the plans to establish manufacturing on the Continent stalled, as the sublicensee in France remained primarily a producer of ball bearings and the company in Berlin developed into a sales agency only. In Britain, the business grew and was consistently profitable. Wolseley doubled its capital investment in British Timken in 1926. However, the following year, when Vickers undertook a major reorganization, it determined to sell both Wolseley Motors and British Timken. At that point, an enterprising British industrialist, Michael Bruce Urquhart Dewar, entered the scene and changed it dramatically.[21]

British Timken under Michael Dewar

A mechanical engineer educated at Cambridge University, Dewar had started his career as an apprentice with Vickers. During World War I he had served initially with the Royal Engineers but had moved in 1915 to the Ministry of Munitions. By the end of the war, Dewar had risen to a position of responsibility for all of Britain's shell and gun manufacturing plants. He received the Order of the British Empire in 1918 in recognition of those services. After the war, Dewar had returned to private business, but he also served on a number of postwar committees created by Britain and its allies to make comparative studies of manufacturing and industrial conditions. It was on one of those committees that he visited the United States in 1926 and had the opportunity to tour Timken's Canton plant. When he learned of Vickers' desire to sell British Timken, Dewar approached The Timken Roller Bearing Company with a proposal to buy it jointly. Timken responded favorably and, in May 1927 joined Dewar in purchasing British Timken for just under $486,000. Of that amount, the company put up a little more than half (52.5 percent). Dewar arranged with Vickers to lease the Aston factory where E&OA had first produced Timken bearings, and British Timken was launched on an entirely new footing.[22]

Michael Dewar became British Timken's managing director, with a contract stipulating that he would retain control of its operations as long as it remained profitable and paid dividends. Dewar proved to be an eager student of Canton's manufacturing methods and an energetic promoter of Timken bearings in Europe. For its part, the company helped ensure his success with solid financial support through some difficult early years. In 1928, the whole proposition expanded significantly, as Dewar and U.S. Timken became convinced of the need to get into manufacturing on a larger scale on the European continent. British Timken's first large sale, to Citroën, prompted this decision. The company's sublicensee in Paris was neither willing nor able to produce the large number of bearings required, while French protective tariffs made it impossible to supply them from Britain or the United States at competitive prices. The only practical solution was to establish a French manufacturing subsidiary. At the same time, the growth of the market in Germany seemed to warrant reorganizing the business in Berlin to produce

Michael Dewar contributed leadership and capital to the company's successful 1928 start-up of the first Timken plant in France—in Asnières, a suburb of Paris.

bearings, as had been planned in 1918. Accordingly, Timken and Dewar jointly established La Société Anonyme Française Timken in Paris and recapitalized Deutsche Timken GmbH in Berlin. They invested $40,000 in each company, Timken putting up 59 percent of the capital, Dewar 39 percent, and British Timken 2 percent. Dewar leased a plant on the Seine in Asnières, a suburb of Paris, and hired a plant manager and chief engineer from La Société de Mécanique de Gennevilliers. (The engineer, Charles Nouhaud, would remain with Timken in France for nearly forty years, until 1967.) Max Prausnitzer, still the general manager of Deutsche Timken, purchased a plant on Germaniastrasse in Berlin, and both new Timken factories were in production by the end of 1928.[23]

Soon, however, the two European companies required large infusions of working capital. Early in 1929, Citroën placed orders for delivery of 1,200 bearings per day from the plant in Asnières. As originally set up, the plant had grinding machinery only. It was finishing and assembling parts that had been formed and heat-treated by British Timken. To equip the plant to meet Citroën's needs, Dewar estimated, would take an investment of $280,000. He was not in a position to increase his investment, so Timken furnished the funds by setting up a bank loan to Timken France through the Paris branch of National City Bank, with the loan guaranteed by British Timken.[24]

Deutsche Timken apparently struggled from the beginning. In 1929, Dewar hired Max Wrba to be its general manager. Wrba had an engineering degree and had worked for a bearing manufacturer, Riebe Werke AG, and for the automaker BMW in Augsburg. With Wrba in place, noted Strough to W. R. Timken in August 1929, "we should begin to get some results." Unfortunately, though, all of this transpired virtually on the eve of the U.S. stock market crash and ensuing worldwide economic depression. Both Timken France and Deutsche Timken lost money steadily from 1929 through 1932. British Timken remained profitable and initially was able to advance working capital to keep the French and German operations going. But by 1931, it fell to U.S. Timken to take over the indebtedness of Timken France and put additional money into Deutsche Timken. By the end of 1932 Timken had invested nearly $1 million in the two companies, raising its ownership to about 70 percent. Of that investment, Timken's treasurer, Fred Strough, calculated only about one-fourth was salvageable.[25]

It soon developed, however, that the situation was not nearly that bleak. The British and French auto industries were affected far less severely by the Depression than those of Germany and the United States. Timken France became profitable in 1933 and improved steadily thereafter. Meanwhile, British Timken under Michael Dewar, general manager William Dallow, and financial officer John Pascoe, made steady progress. Relatively unscathed by the Depression, the British automotive industry grew rapidly between 1932 and 1935 to become the largest producer in Europe and the second largest in the world after the United States. British Timken won a good share of that market—Ford, the third largest British automaker, was a major customer for both car and tractor bearings. More broadly in Europe, Dewar was successful in establishing a solid network of distributors and so had a good share of the profitable replacement market. He pushed the business into South Africa with the creation of British Timken S.A. Proprietary, Ltd., in Johannesburg, in 1932. In addition, he did a large business with the Soviet Union, which was rapidly expanding its auto production under an ambitious Five-Year Plan. By the early 1930s the Aston plant was able to produce some larger bearings for railroad applications and steel-rolling mills, and British Timken made inroads in those markets. The plant expanded (to 1,000 employees by 1937) and also made solid improvements in both quality and productivity. It called on Canton for technical expertise when needed and imported a fair amount of U.S.-made manufacturing equipment.[26]

In 1935, at Michael Dewar's insistence, British Timken recapitalized, doubling the number of its shares and selling half to the public. This step allowed Dewar and The Timken Roller Bearing Company to cash out a portion of what had become a very good investment. The value of the public sale was about $1.3 million, of which Timken's share was $673,000 (52.5 percent). A major concern at Timken was to ensure against the possibility that the management control of British Timken could pass to someone other than Dewar or itself. To that end, the company and Dewar negotiated an agreement that prohibited either one from selling more shares without the other's consent. The agreement granted Dewar management control, as before, contingent on British Timken's performance; and it provided an option for Timken to buy Dewar's shares in the event of his death. Timken and Dewar still controlled 50 percent of British Timken's stock between them (the U.S. company held 26.25 percent). In addition, Timken purchased enough stock on the open market to bring its stake up to 30 percent. From the cash that Dewar received in the public offering he repaid Timken the money it had advanced to sustain Timken France and Deutsche Timken and became a 50 percent owner of the two companies. Between that and the royalties earned on its licenses, Timken's investment to support the expansion into France and Germany was solidly profitable.[27]

Subsequently, Dewar and Timken decided to discontinue the business in Germany. By the spring of 1936, all of Deutsche Timken's machinery had been shipped to Asnières, and the Berlin factory was up for sale. Though the records indicate that this company lost money every year, there is no evidence to say exactly why the venture failed. The strength of competition in Germany must have been a critical factor, however. A decision was made in Canton to start scaling back on operations in Germany as early as 1931. SKF was the largest competitor, but Germany, of course, had its own strong companies in the ball bearing field, particularly Kugelfischer Georg Schaefer AG (FAG). The Depression hit Germany and its automotive industry hard. Yet the Nazi government that came to power in 1933 invested heavily to develop a highway system and increase auto production as part of a broad program of industrialization and rearmament. German bearing manufacturers became stronger than ever as a result. FAG modernized and expanded its facilities in the mid-1930s, and in 1937—the year Deutsche Timken sold its factory and disappeared forever—it launched a manufacturing subsidiary in Britain.[28]

The devastation of World War II would drastically alter the competitive landscape in Europe, and the postwar rebuilding would open up significant new opportunities to expand the market for Timken bearings. At the same time, an antitrust decision in the U.S. courts would force U.S. Timken to compete with British Timken and Timken France throughout the 1950s. However, none of that could be foreseen in the mid-1930s as Timken resolved the issues around its European investments and adjusted to the fact of strong competition at home. Moreover, the company's leaders in Canton were naturally focused primarily on the economic and social questions raised by the Great Depression, which maintained its grip on business in the United States much longer than it did in Europe.

The Fallout from "Black Friday"

Timken went into the Depression in a strong financial position. It had used a short-term bank loan to purchase Gilliam Manufacturing Company in 1925 and since then had accumulated cash reserves, out of which it had funded the dramatic expansion of the late 1920s. (While sales and earnings roughly doubled from 1925 through 1929, dividends paid out increased by only 50 percent.) Nevertheless, "Black Friday," October 28, 1929, hit Timken hard. Its business declined sharply following the stock market crash. (See Table 4.1.) In 1930 the company's revenues fell off by more than a third from the year before, and by 1932, the worst year of the Depression, they were little more than one-fifth of the 1929 high. Timken's stock lost more than 80 percent of its value. Through the long bull market of the late 1920s, the stock price had risen steadily, from $41 per share in 1924 to $154 in 1928. Timken had split the stock, two-for-one, in January 1929, but the price per share resumed its rise immediately, hitting $139 by October. During 1932, it traded as low as $7 and no higher than $23 per share.[29]

Much of the decline in Timken's business came in the automotive segment of bearing sales. But the steps the company had taken in the 1920s to expand into nonautomotive markets helped to soften the impact. In 1929, roughly half of Timken's total revenues came from automotive bearings. Its largest customer, by far, was Ford. The auto industry as a whole was hard hit by the slowdown, and among the Big Three producers Ford fared worst, GM best. While nationwide factory auto sales declined by 75 percent from 1929 to 1932, Timken's automotive

TABLE 4.1

The Timken Company Comparative Financial Data, 1930–1939 (in Thousands of Dollars, except per Share Data)

	1930	1931	1932	1933	1934	1935	1936	1937	1938	1939
Net sales	$27,400	$16,600	$9,200	$15,800	$22,200	$31,300	$39,600	$46,700	$24,500	$40,100
Net income (loss)	7,524	2,571	(483)	2,173	3,486	7,484	9,257	10,837	1,428	7,288
Total assets	$50,977	$45,831	$41,074	$42,707	$43,951	$45,855	$46,745	$45,954	$43,423	$46,913
Total capital and earnings invested in the business	46,782	43,305	39,506	40,080	40,793	41,042	41,256	40,559	39,726	41,054
Return on sales	27.5%	15.5%	(5.3%)	13.8%	15.7%	23.9%	23.4%	23.2%	5.8%	18.2%
Return on assets	14.8	5.6	(1.2)	5.1	7.9	16.3	19.8	23.6	3.3	15.5
Return on capital and earnings	16.1	5.9	(1.2)	5.4	8.5	18.2	22.4	26.7	3.6	17.8
Earnings per share	$3.12	$1.07	($0.20)	$0.90	$1.45	$3.10	$3.84	$4.49	$0.59	$3.02
Dividends per share	3.00	2.50	1.38	0.70	1.15	3.00	3.75	5.00	1.00	2.50

Sources: The Timken Roller Bearing Company Annual Reports, 1930–39; C. L. Van Horn to G. L. Deal (February 3, 1966), in Timken Company Archives.

Note: All net sales are rounded to the nearest $100,000.

bearing sales dropped by 83 percent. Yet the expansion of industrial and railroad applications was far enough along in the early 1930s to provide a steady stream of offsetting sales. In addition, Timken had built up the sales and service organization taken over from Hyatt and New Departure in 1922 and had extended it into Canada in 1929. Its sales of replacement bearings also helped to mitigate the revenue decline. Automotive bearings constituted 80 percent of total bearing sales in 1925 and just 49 percent in 1936. As a whole, the bearing business managed to produce an operating profit every year, even in 1932. Still, the entire decade of the 1930s would pass without regaining the levels of sales and profitability attained in 1929.[30]

Timken's steel division also struggled throughout the Depression. Hard times hit just as the newly formed Timken Steel and Tube Company set out to establish itself as an independent business. The large fixed investment in steel-making capacity was a terrible drag on profitability when the market for steel crashed, and the business lost money in the toughest years: 1931, 1932, and the recession year of 1938. Overall, though, the division grew in the 1930s, opening up new markets for Timken's basic steel products, especially seamless tubing. In addition, the company's engineering organization developed some new products to create outlets for its alloy steels. One of those, fuel-injection equipment, proved to be a product before its time and never really got off the ground. Yet another, a removable steel bit for drilling equipment, was highly successful. The Timken Rock Bit was the foundation for a small but profitable line of business that would remain a division of the company until 1986. In the 1930s, all those endeavors contributed something toward balancing out the slow recovery of the bearing business.[31]

All in all, however, the financial performance of The Timken Roller Bearing Company during the Great Depression placed it in the ranks of the most solid, well-managed industrial firms. (See Table 4.2.) The company's reputation grew accordingly. Throughout the crisis, industry watchers praised Timken for its expansion into new markets for bearings, its bold move to become a major producer of alloy steel and the leader in seamless tubing, and its strong financial position, having financed those moves out of earnings rather than by debt. Along with a solid record of earnings and dividends, the publicity attached to the development of railroad bearings, as well as Timken's continuing campaign of national advertising—"now familiar to every reader"—burnished the company's reputation. The financial community touted Timken stock as a good investment throughout the Depression years. Even when the company reported a net loss in 1932, analysts focused instead on its longer-term prospects. "Whatever the course of earnings in the early future," wrote the *Magazine of Wall Street* in 1933, "Timken will ride out the storm and will return to satisfactory profits whenever normal industrial revival sets in." That prediction proved accurate.[32]

Still, as the people of Timken—and anyone who lived through those times—knew, the steps required for companies to "ride out the storm" of the Depression had painful consequences. Business fell off rapidly in the first few months of 1930. The recently acquired tube mill in Wooster was shut down in May. In June, H. H. called a meeting of all company executives and department heads to urge upon them the need to reduce all possible costs. Already by that time there were reports that automakers—Chrysler, Dodge, and Willys-Overland—were operating only three days a week. Timken began laying off some people in all departments and instituted a four-day week in the Canton and Columbus factories.[33]

All of Timken's plants were shut down completely for two weeks in July. In this early stage of the crisis, the company tried to protect its most experienced personnel, particularly in engineering and production divisions, by requesting that they take off a few days each month, unpaid, in order to avoid being laid off altogether. All plants were shut down again for two weeks in late September, after which Timken instituted a three-day week throughout, with the standard day reduced from ten to eight hours. By November 1930, layoffs had reduced the ranks of Timken's salaried employees by one-fourth. The board of directors voted to adopt a sliding scale of salary reductions ranging from 5 percent for those earning less than $1,200 per year to 10 percent for those earning more than $1,800 per year. Timken's top executives took larger cuts—Timken president, Mark Lothrop, 12 percent and H. H. Timken 26 percent. As the crisis deepened, H. H. would draw a smaller and smaller salary—$12,000 in 1934, down from $100,000 in 1929.[34]

TABLE 4.2

Net Income, Comparative, 1929–1934 (in Millions of Dollars)

	1929	1930	1931	1932	1933	1934
Timken Roller Bearing Company	$14.2	$7.5	$2.6	($0.5)	$2.2	$3.5
General Motors Corporation	236.5	144.3	87.5	(9.0)	74.0	85.6
Chrysler Corporation	21.9	11.1	2.1	(11.3)	12.1	9.5
Other auto industry firms*	74.4	(28.6)	(47.7)	(55.3)	(38.1)	(28.7)
Average, several thousand industries	4.5	1.4	(0.5)	(1.6)	0.2	1.2

Sources: The Timken Roller Bearing Company Annual Reports, 1929–34; Laurence H. Sloan, "Two Cycles of Corporation Profits" (New York: Standard Statistics Company, Inc., 1935); data on "several thousand industries" taken from *Chicago Journal of Commerce* (June 15, 1938) by Timken for its own purposes of comparison, in the files of R. C. Brower, Timken Company Archives.

*Aggregate data for six independent automakers and eight auto parts suppliers.

Writing from California in the winter of 1930–31, H. H. urged Lothrop to make deeper cuts, "not further in salaries, but in actual expenditures. . . . We must close even small leaks," he wrote. "Now is our time to force real economy in the organization. Our backs are not yet against the wall but they are getting mighty close. What of it; let's make the whole organization realize this and we will get the results we are after." As the economy continued to deteriorate, however, such brave words proved futile. Indeed, to businessmen accustomed to driving hard and getting results, the feeling of helplessness was extreme. In December, Lothrop reported that the steel business was "at a standstill." By February 1931, the entire company was stalled, as he wrote to H. H.: "It seems strange to say this to you, but things are so quiet here it is difficult for any of us to feel that we are constructively occupied. We go over the same things over and over and over again, study them the best we can, take the action we think necessary, and then of course wait until something happens to see whether the action was wise or not. So little happens it is hard to tell where we are going. We are like a sailing vessel in a calm—just drifting."[35]

During 1931 the company continued to make layoffs and began to institute cuts in hourly wages. In October, Timken shut down its Columbus bearing factory entirely, employing a skeleton crew of eight—five men to act as watchmen, one engineer, and two men to handle the work of filling customer orders from finished inventory. In February 1932, virtually all of Timken's productive capacity was idle.[36]

H. H. and other Timken managers were sensitive to the suffering and dislocations caused by the actions they took to protect the businesses. H. H. personally supplied food and coal to many laid-off Timken employees. The company increased its annual donations to Canton's community fund by 60 percent. H. H., already a large donor, encouraged his siblings to increase their contributions. When in Canton, he was active in helping to organize the relief effort. "I have spent a lot of time on this," he reported to his sister Cora in May 1932, "but not as much as some of the other men in town." In the spring of 1931 H. H. donated a building for the city to establish a community store. During the winter of 1931–32 this facility provided food to 3,100 Canton families, about one-eighth of the city's total population of 100,000. By buying provisions in car lots, the city was able to provide a balanced diet for just 10.5¢ per day, per person. Like other communities across the country, Canton set up programs to provide work for the unemployed. One of the more unusual ones made use of the specialized facilities of the area's brick-making industry—long tunnels in which bricks were heated and dried gradually as they were pulled through slowly on carts. In the emergency, the tunnels were used to dry much of the produce of the large gardening projects mounted as part of the work-relief program.[37]

"These things of course are all merely palliative and not fundamental," said H. H. Like thoughtful people across the political spectrum, by mid-1932 he had come to believe that the federal government had to address the problem of unemployment on a national basis. "My guess is that before long we will have in this country, or should have, unemployment insurance, or dole or call it what you please." The enormity of the problem simply overwhelmed the capabilities of local governments and concerned individuals such as he. "With all these efforts everywhere," H. H. commented, "still we are hardly able to take care of necessities that the terrible condition requires."[38]

H. H. Timken's concern for and contributions to the people of Canton long predated the Depression. However, his most notable and long-lasting act of philanthropy came about largely because of that crisis. When the stock market crashed in 1929, W. R. Timken was heavily invested and lost a great deal of money. Worse, he had borrowed to finance his investments and had secured his loans with a large block of Timken Roller Bearing Company stock. H. H. was reluctant to allow this stock to be sold off to pay the debt. The family's stake in the firm would be diminished, and the sale of a large number of shares at depressed prices would injure the remaining shareholders and the company. To avert this possibility, H. H. mobilized his sisters, Cora Burnett and Amelia Bridges, to join him in loaning W. R. $3 million to settle his obligations. Subsequently, having no wish to profit from his brother's troubles, H. H. asked A. C. Ernst to help him devise a plan whereby the stock reclaimed from W. R.'s creditors could be used to establish a philanthropic foundation in the family's name. Thus was born, in 1934, the Timken Foundation. The foundation's mission, in the words of a long-time secretary-treasurer, Edward Forrest, was "to benefit the workers of the Timken factories by sending back into the areas around the factories the money that came from dividends on the Timken stock." To the great satisfaction of H. H., it created the "happy situation" in which the family as a whole took up the work of fulfilling an obligation he had long carried largely on his own, to return a share of their wealth to the community in which "the real foundation of the Timken fortune was made."[39]

Timken's business, and the economy as a whole, began to revive in mid-1933. On July 1 the company raised wages and salaries 11 percent, restoring the most recent across-the-board cut that had been made just four months before. Timken also began rehiring some of the men it had been forced to lay off. By mid-August the total number of Timken employees was a little over 5,000—about two-thirds of the 1929 peak. That month's payroll, reported Brower to H. H., represented "a sizable increase over any period for the past several months." Brower added, "We are not running into any difficulties. The morale of the organization is good." The restoration of normal operations proceeded at a moderate pace. By the end of 1934, the Columbus plant was running again but with only 40 percent of its 1929 workforce. Employment in the Canton bearing factory had been restored to 50 percent of the 1929 high, the steel and tube mills to a little more than 80 percent. The company as a whole returned to 1929 levels during the following year. Timken's recovery suffered a setback in the recession of 1938, but otherwise the second half of the 1930s saw the solid fundamentals of the business once again controlling its fortunes.[40]

Yet the story of the Great Depression is not one of disruption followed by return to the *status quo ante*. Far from it. The prolonged crisis brought about a profound shift in public attitudes toward corporations. That shift reflected in the election of Franklin D. Roosevelt and embodied in the legislation and executive policies known collectively as the New Deal, brought a number of significant, and permanent, changes in the way Timken and all U.S. corporations did business.

The New Deal: Strong Medicine

Out of the pain of the Great Depression came the political will to limit the power of corporate executives by setting up countervailing powers in the form of strong government agencies and labor unions. The notion that such limitations were necessary and legitimate was not new. Anti-big-business sentiment in America was as old as big business itself. The federal government's role in the economy—exerted through tariffs, antitrust legislation, and regulatory agencies such as the Interstate Commerce Commission, the Federal Trade Commission, and the Federal Reserve Board—was an established fact of life by the time of World War I. During that war, the decades-long struggle for recognition by the nation's labor unions was temporarily rewarded, as the right of workers to bargain collectively with their employers was guaranteed by the National War Labor Board.

In the 1920s, labor unions lost public support and much of their membership amid popular fears of communism and a rising tide of prosperity that lifted wages and supported both a broad range of worker-friendly policies and a concerted corporate anti-union campaign. At the same time, the federal government, under Republican presidents Warren G. Harding, Calvin Coolidge, and Herbert Hoover, built a new relationship with business that emphasized partnership rather than control. For their part, the nation's manufacturing corporations increased productivity (measured in terms of output per unit of labor) nearly twofold, an achievement that contributed to an unprecedented level of public confidence in, and support for, business. Yet the height of corporate America's success in 1929 prefigured the extreme depth of disillusionment four years later. Corporate executives were powerless to stem the tide of economic collapse once it started and equally powerless to forestall the effects of public reaction to it.[41]

Since the stock market boom and crash had played such a pronounced role in precipitating the crisis, and since the crash exposed many egregious abuses of power by the financial community, regulation of the securities industry was a priority item for New Deal legislators. Congress passed numerous regulations in this area, and in 1934 it created the Securities and Exchange Commission (SEC) to oversee the new regulatory system. Many of those initiatives had a direct effect on companies such as Timken, whose stock was traded on the New York Stock Exchange. Under rules and accounting standards developed under the aegis of the SEC, U.S. corporations had to begin providing investors with a range of financial information unknown anywhere else in the world. Although the changes helped to strengthen U.S. financial markets over the long term, they were unpleasant medicine for the business community. Disclosure of items such as executive salaries went against deeply held views about what was legitimately private information. The requirement to report annual revenues made public data that companies had rigorously guarded from their competitors.

As Charley Brower wrote to H. H. in December 1935, it was a shock when the SEC began releasing such information on some 250 companies that had filed it "in confidence." It appeared that the agency was planning to implement the disclosure policy in stages and that Timken might be in an industry group not required to divulge its information for some time. Brower and the others in the Canton office considered the course taken by some companies, of appealing the SEC's decision in court rather than submitting to the new rules. But they decided against it, thinking that a trial would only draw attention to the information "to a greater extent than the mere announcement in the usual press notices." Thus quietly, though unhappily and no sooner than it had to, Timken adapted to the new situation. The company would begin including sales figures in its annual reports in 1949.[42]

Timken's managers accommodated themselves in similar fashion to the dramatically changed environment for labor relations brought about by the New Deal and to the unionization of Timken's plants. The National Industrial Recovery Act of 1933 guaranteed the right of labor to organize and bargain collectively, but its provisions were ambiguous and the government's will to enforce them was limited. As a result, companies had little difficulty fending off union-organizing efforts until the act was judged unconstitutional in 1935. During that two-year period, however, the union movement had grown stronger, and strikes loomed in many industries. Two critical developments in 1935 turned the tide in favor of organized labor. The first was the passage of the National Labor Relations Act, commonly known as the Wagner Act, which not only guaranteed the rights to organize and bargain collectively but also outlawed "unfair labor practices," including setting up company unions and firing and blacklisting employees for union activities. Just as important, the Wagner Act established the National Labor Relations Board and gave it the power to enforce the law's provisions.[43]

The second development of critical importance in 1935 was the formation of the Congress of Industrial Organizations (CIO). Since the nineteenth century, the labor movement had been dominated by the American Federation of Labor (AFL), which had its roots in unions of skilled craftsmen and was ill suited to represent the masses of semiskilled factory workers employed in the nation's leading industries. In contrast, the unions of the CIO—for example, the United Mine Workers and the United Auto Workers (UAW)—embraced all of an industry's workers in a single organization, without regard to skill. The new approach reinvigorated the labor movement. The developments of 1935 inaugurated a period of intense conflict between management and labor. The CIO set out to organize the nation's leading industries starting with automotive, steel, and oil. Wagner Act opponents challenged its constitutionality without success. In 1937, the Supreme Court upheld the Wagner Act, ensuring that unions would have a role to play in the relations between labor and management for the foreseeable future.

Timken was swept up in those developments. In late 1933, as the company's business was beginning to revive and it was rehiring some of the people it had laid off, Timken management proposed a plan of employee representation—a company union—a step that many corporations were taking in this period. It was voted down by some 60 percent of the nearly 5,000 employees in Canton. In contrast, the plan was accepted by a large majority in Columbus, although that plant had only 230 employees. Management was reluctant to read much into those results but took little comfort from them either. "The conclusions to be drawn from this vote are not that the employees favor an outside union instead of a company employee representation," wrote Brower to W. R. Timken. "Although we feel that outside unions are not heavily represented by members in our plants, they may become stronger as union organization increases."[44]

In the following months, Timken went about the business of rebuilding, while around it the labor-management conflict escalated on many fronts. The UAW was actively organizing throughout 1934, establishing chapters in bearing companies such as Bower and SKF Industries as well as in automotive companies. Closer to home, in Akron, the AFL organized a massive strike early in 1935 against the big three rubber companies, Goodyear, Goodrich, and Firestone. The rubber companies, Brower reported to H. H., had "prepared for a long drawn out fight. They have actually erected new wire fencing, have secured cots and supplies to house men within the plants, and at present are taking a census of the employees to see how many will stay on the job when and as the strike is called."

In Canton, the local bus company accepted the Bus Drivers' Union without a fight. Anticipating disruption of its business one way or another, Timken built up its cash reserves.[45]

Though the situation remained quiet at Timken, national events had a polarizing effect. The company's top managers, like the vast majority of corporate executives, were strongly anti-union. They became highly politicized in the mid-1930s and vocally opposed many New Deal policies, including increased regulation, progressive taxation, and deficit spending. Brower and others became active in the National Association of Manufacturers, which coordinated much of industry's opposition to the New Deal, and to labor unionism in particular. As the Wagner Act was under consideration, Timken executives mounted a letter-writing campaign to state the case against it to members of Congress. The bill, wrote Timken's new president William Umstattd, was "un-American class legislation" that would benefit no one other than "the paid organizers of the labor unions." During the 1936 presidential campaign, Timken foremen brought into the plants large baskets of buttons for Roosevelt's opponent, Alf Landon, and campaigned actively on the factory floor, a tactic that helped to drive their subordinates into the Democratic fold. The rhetoric of the era was extreme. U.S. Steel's vice president of industrial relations, Arthur Young, stated publicly that he would "go to jail or be arrested as a felon" before he would obey the Wagner Act. Roosevelt, angry at the business community's resistance to New Deal initiatives, railed in campaign speeches against "economic royalists" who took "other people's money" and sought to impose a "new industrial dictatorship." The CIO was the largest single contributor to Roosevelt's campaign.[46]

The emotion-laden political divisions of that era would remain in place for decades to come. Yet, once the president won reelection by a wide majority and the Wagner Act passed judicial review, resistance to the union movement quickly became an untenable position. Some companies, notably Republic Steel and Ford, would resist to the point of violence and hold out against unionization, only to capitulate in the early 1940s. Most, however, bowed to the new reality. In the winter of 1936–37, GM was brought to a standstill by a massive sit-down strike staged by the UAW. The decision to accept the union, in February 1937, was one of Alfred Sloan's last acts as GM president. In March, U.S. Steel, one of organized labor's most bitter opponents, accepted the United Steelworkers (USW) without a strike. By that time, the USW was active in Timken's Canton plants. The company signed an agreement making the union the bargaining agent for the workers in its Canton plants on April 17, just five days after the Supreme Court's decision upholding the Wagner Act. Despite the high feelings, the moment was calm and the change orderly. "It's the law of the land," counseled H. H. "You've got to obey the law."[47] Going forward, Timken would battle the union unrelentingly but would do so within the legally established framework.

Timken managers, like so many others in corporate America, adopted and would persist in the view that the union was an external force intervening in the natural relationship between employer and employee. Yet the union came into the company on a wave of determination among industrial wage earners to win greater job security, gain protection from arbitrary management practices, and push for higher pay and employment benefits through collective bargaining. That wave swept through a broad range of industries in the spring and summer of 1937. With it, Timken's Canton hourly workforce embraced the USW, despite the fact that the company paid relatively high wages and had virtually no history of management-labor conflict. To be sure, Timken's homegrown union leadership was some of the strongest in the movement. I. W. Abel was born in 1908, in Magnolia, Ohio, about 15 miles south of Canton. His father was a blacksmith and clay worker, and his older brothers went into the steel and mining industries. After graduating from high school, Abel attended Canton Actual Business College, but at the age of 17, he went to work at the Canton rolling mill of American Sheet and Tin Mill Works. He later moved on to the Canton Malleable Iron Company and then to Timken. Abel became a CIO member in 1936 and was an active union organizer in the company. In later years, he would proudly claim the reputation he earned in the 1930s as "the biggest union hell raiser in Canton." He helped to form local union 1123 (the Golden Lodge) and was, by turns, its financial secretary, vice president, and president. From 1942 to 1952 he was the district director of the USW in the Canton area, and he went on to become president of the national union in 1965. Abel was both an effective mobilizer of grassroots sentiment and a tough negotiator on the union's behalf.[48]

At the same time, in Timken's plants, as in most manufacturing organizations, there was a good deal of sentiment for men like Abel to build on. The hierarchical and highly departmentalized management structure that had made it possible to run large-scale manufacturing operations efficiently in the first place had created a situation in which the foreman in each department had nearly absolute control over hiring, firing, promotions, and practically every aspect of life on the job. Infused with the widely held management view of hourly personnel as basically lazy and untrustworthy, the system invited high-handedness, if not abuse, particularly in the polarized atmosphere of the mid-1930s. Harry Mayfield was a union activist in Timken's Columbus plant during the Depression who went on to become a leader of the regional USW, highly respected on both sides of the fence. He recalled the atmosphere at Timken in the 1930s: "Anytime we had a complaint and went to the foremen and tried to talk to them, they all said, 'Don't let the door hit you on your way out.' We got a little bit fed up with that." One of the most important benefits that unionization offered was a multistep grievance process in which the union acted as an advocate for the individual worker's interests.[49]

It should also be noted, however, that the pro-union sentiment in Timken's plants was not monolithic. On the factory floor and in the community there were diverse interests and opinions where unions were concerned. Even in mass production facilities such as Timken's bearing factories there were skilled workers in the plant—tool makers, electricians, pipe fitters—who had different working conditions and pay scales from machine operators and had no interest in joining forces with them under the banner of an industrial union. Others willingly signed up with the union but were turned off by the undemocratic leadership style of some CIO organizers. Up to the 1970s, when Timken's unionized plants became a closed shop (with mandatory union membership), some hourly workers declined to join. In the public at large, many people feared that unionism, especially the CIO, was a communist movement in disguise, and indeed some union activists were openly communist. The movement was especially divisive in the less heavily industrialized and more conservative communities of Columbus and Wooster. "People disowned you, wouldn't speak to you," recalled Mayfield. "It was pretty bitter back then. You lost a lot of good friends. There were a lot of fights." Though Mayfield and a handful of others worked to bring the CIO into the Columbus plant in the late 1930s, it would not happen until a companywide vote was taken in 1942. That lack of cohesion within the hourly workforce would bolster Timken's management in its determination to resist the union at every turn.[50]

The rise of new competitors and the growing importance of international markets, along with more vigorous government regulation and the new role of organized labor within the company, were all significant changes that differentiated the late 1930s business environment from what it had been in the days when H. H. was running the company. Another New Deal initiative, the strengthening of the Antitrust Division of the U.S. Department of Justice under Assistant Attorney General Thurman Arnold, would alter the landscape further. In 1946, the government would launch an antitrust suit against the company for its licensing agreements with British Timken and Timken France. All of those changes, plus the onset of World War II, made an eventful coming of age for the generation of corporate leaders that emerged in the 1930s. In meeting the challenges that lay ahead, they would stand firmly on the foundation H. H. Timken had built, but they would have to chart a course without him.

The Passing of an Era

Since he served as Timken's president for twenty-five years, William Umstattd can hardly be called a transitional figure. Yet he played a critical role in facilitating the generational transition in Timken family leadership from H. H. to his sons, H. H. (Henry) Timken, Jr., and William R. (Bob) Timken. As Bob Timken later recalled, his father often talked about business and "about the way the family had produced the company by invention and hard work and how he would like to see it continue in the family tradition." H. H. made it clear, as his own father had done, that his sons could pursue any career they wished, with his blessing. They were also wealthy enough to choose not to work at all. But, H. H. insisted, "If you want to work for the company, you'd better intend to work, and devote yourself to it entirely." Said Bob, "You didn't come here to be a loafer." Both he and Henry decided to take up this challenge. Yet neither of them was ready to take charge in the 1930s as H. H.'s health began to fail.[51]

The Timkens were a close family, but there was a large age gap between father and sons. H. H. was thirty-eight when Henry was born in 1906; Bob followed in 1910; and a third son, John Marter Timken, was born in 1913. All three children attended grade school in Canton, but Henry was tutored at home to prepare for college, while Bob and John attended the Adirondack-Florida School. One of the nice aspects about that school, Bob recalled, was that its winter term convened in Florida, where the boys could see more of their parents. The Timkens all attended Harvard University: Henry stayed for about three years; Bob graduated and went on to Harvard Business School; John also graduated and took a postgraduate year in English literature. He became an editor with G. P. Putnam & Company, publishers, but after serving in the U.S. Coast Guard during World War II, he took up a career in naval architecture. John would serve on Timken's board of directors from 1956 to 1971 but otherwise was not active in the company. In contrast, both of his brothers launched Timken careers immediately upon graduation—Henry in 1930 and Bob in 1935.[52]

Naturally, H. H. took an interest in the training his sons received in their early years with the company. Both Henry and Bob were elected to the board of directors within a year of starting work, a step that enabled them to get a high-level view of the business from the beginning and was appropriate considering that the family and the Timken Foundation jointly controlled about 38 percent of Timken's stock. Henry Timken had a strong mechanical bent and a love of manufacturing equipment and processes, though he lacked formal technical education. He started out working in The Timken Steel and Tube Company as a sales assistant, but as the Depression crisis deepened, much of his training necessarily focused on controlling costs. One of his first assignments was to implement a system monitoring the company's experimental programs to ensure their cost effectiveness. In 1933, Henry became assistant to the president, where he had the chance to work more closely with his father and with executive vice president Umstattd. The following year, Umstattd rose to president and Henry to vice president. In the late 1930s, he took on the additional job of steel division general manager. Bob's strength was in financial management. Under the wing of Charley Brower, he worked his way through all the areas of Timken's accounting department,

Henry H. Timken, Jr., the eldest of H. H.'s sons, played a key role in advancing the company's process technologies. He would assume the role of chairman of the board when H. H. died in 1940.

learning the ropes in each. He also took on special assignments—for example, studying Timken's power requirements and costs and traveling to Britain to participate in discussions with Michael Dewar about the public sale of British Timken stock.

One of Bob's duties in this period was to visit his uncle, W. R. Timken, who lived in New York in his later years, to consult with him and keep him abreast of events. Through the late 1920s and the Depression, W. R. retained the position of vice president and remained on the board of directors, and he kept up a steady correspondence with Charley Brower, as he had with his predecessors, Heman Ely and Fred Strough. Indeed, he became quite piqued at times when he felt he was not being kept fully informed about developments at Timken. Although he deferred to H. H. in all matters, W. R. freely offered advice to the company's treasurers.[53] A particular concern was to publish as little financial information as possible, and to that end he always gave drafts of the company's annual reports a close reading. W. R. resigned from both of his positions in the company in 1938. His only child, Valerie Timken Whitney, like other women in the Timken family, owned a small amount of stock but did not play an active role in the company. In the years after 1915, W. R.'s most important contribution was to provide solid financial support for his brother's efforts to develop the business, as a one-third owner up to 1922 and a substantial stockholder thereafter. He would continue to do that for his brother's successors until his death in June 1949.

In the final decade of his life, H. H. Timken was frustrated at being kept away from the business so much. Once asked why he received daily reports from his office, even on hunting trips and vacations, he said it was because he felt responsible for the business and its employees. This was particularly true in the crisis years of the early 1930s. "I feel like a slacker, because I am not on the job continuously," he confided to Gordon Mather in the winter of 1930–31. At that time he was feeling better than he had for several years but was afraid a return to Canton would risk another bout of pneumonia. Despite his illness, H. H. continued to delight in exciting activity and remained open to new experiences. At the urging of his oldest son, Henry, he bought a Ford tri-motor plane in 1929. Having flown balloons and raced speedboats, H. H. took to plane travel immediately and began using the available airline transportation whenever possible on his trips to and from California. Of a planned fourteen-hour flight from Los Angeles to Dallas, he wrote to Mather, "I am anxious to fly over that country, as I have never flown there before. Take it from me, it is the only way to get about and see the country in all its magnificence. I am sorry for you land-locked people."[54]

In 1936 George Obermier's death dealt him a terrible blow. It was just at that time that he became seriously disabled by emphysema. After that, he spent all of his time in Canton at home, confined to a wheelchair. His major interest was the first big project undertaken by the Timken Foundation, the creation of a vocational high school in Canton. Some years before, H. H. had been approached to contribute a substantial sum to Ohio State University but had declined to do so. "I feel much more interested in the education of the masses than I do in the education of the few," H. H. wrote. "I would infinitely rather contribute to manual training

The Timken Foundation built and fully equipped Timken Vocational High School, presenting it to Canton City Schools in September 1939. An imposing edifice in downtown Canton at the time, it quickly became the center for learning skilled trades such as accounting, cosmetology, printing, secretarial, welding, and various machine operations.

schools than I would to colleges, for I believe that in so doing I would help accomplish real beneficial purpose of greater value." The cornerstone for Timken Vocational High School was laid in December 1938, and the school opened for the 1939–40 school year. Bob worked closely with his father to investigate such schools and plan the one for Canton, including the most modern equipment on which the students could learn their trades. H. H. was too ill to attend the dedication ceremony, but he toured the school the day before in his wheelchair.[55]

As always, in these years H. H. kept up with company affairs. Charley Brower and Bob visited him regularly to report and consult. He had been a voracious reader throughout his life, and even when laid low by illness and its many discomforts, he remained engaged and mentally sharp, and he kept abreast of political developments and world events. In the late 1930s, he followed the coming of war in Europe with the help of a "listening device," used in combination with his hearing aid for listening to the radio. Thus, after Germany invaded Poland on September 1, 1939, it was H. H. who called a meeting of company executives to initiate the planning to raise Timken's bearing production to the highest possible level.[56]

When H. H. died, on October 14, 1940, the top-management team that would lead The Timken Roller Bearing Company through the crisis of World War II was in place and accustomed to working together. Bill Umstattd was president; Henry Timken was vice president and took the additional title of chairman of the board of directors at his father's death. Bob Timken became a vice president in 1941. The two other key members of this group were Charley Brower, the corporate secretary-treasurer, and Louis Klinedinst, who had led the development of Timken's industrial bearings division and was now a vice president for sales.

The company was fortunate to have such a smooth transition—developing a strong successor was H. H.'s last critical act of organization building. No less important, however, he had passed along to his sons the sense of purpose that had made a long career interesting to him, and it would do so for them. They would grow up in the business, working closely with Bill Umstattd, and would provide a continuity of family engagement that helped to preserve the fundamental character of the company H. H. had created. Umstattd, though a strong personality with his own style of leadership, was also firmly grounded in the same sense of purpose and committed to preserving the management culture of which he was an exemplary product. World War II and its aftermath would bring dramatic changes in the scale and reach of operations, but the company would retain its focus on core products and the pattern of sustained investment in manufacturing processes and organizational capabilities that had served it so well through H. H. Timken's long career.

Timken at War

*I*n the 1940s, world war challenged U.S. manufacturing organizations to rise to new heights of ingenuity and efficiency. Their collective response to that challenge was a deciding factor in the Allied victory. Timken's contributions to the war effort would be many and varied. As the company historian of the 1940s noted, they took "two definite forms: the work done in the plant itself, and the tremendous work done by Timken products in the outer world—on thousands upon thousands of machines." The energy and resourcefulness of Timken managers and the dedication of all its personnel in the crisis naturally had much to do with the company's wartime achievements. Yet its increased productivity, new products, and product quality and performance also rested upon significant new technologies and organizational capabilities developed in the 1930s. Many of the nation's leading industrial companies, including Timken, had built up in-house technical departments in the early decades of the twentieth century. They used the slack time created by the Depression to strengthen their resources in preparation for the revival of market demand. Hence, the demands of war found them ready.[1]

Timken's associated companies, British Timken and Timken France, each had their own wartime challenges to meet, but under vastly different circumstances than those that prevailed in Canton, Ohio. All three would be permanently changed by war's end. British and U.S. Timken were greatly strengthened and enlarged, and Timken France emerged with deep divisions caused by its experience under German occupation. At the same time, the relationship among them would be drastically altered by the antitrust proceedings against U.S. Timken that began in 1946 and concluded in 1950 with a court order requiring the three Timken companies to compete against one another. That outcome would have a lasting impact on the way the business developed in the postwar era.

Technical Progress in the 1930s

In the Depression decade, the management group that H. H. Timken had assembled maintained his long-term pattern of investment in the company's products and processes. In the early 1930s, when business conditions were at their worst, the company cut back on its experimental and developmental programs, but did not eliminate them. So, for example, it reduced advertising personnel and expenditures substantially, but largely sustained its sales and application engineering programs. In the absence of market demand, Timken sales engineers continued to work with industrial customers to design and test new bearing applications. When railroad companies drastically cut back their purchases of new equipment, Timken set about redesigning the company's railroad bearings so that they could be retrofitted to existing equipment. On the steel side, where the business slowdown was initially even more damaging than in bearings, Timken turned to its engineering organization to develop products that would create new outlets for its alloy steels—fuel-injection equipment and Timken rock bits.[2]

Timken's research was not confined to new product development. It also encompassed process improvement, development of new materials, and an effort to build the company's base of knowledge in key areas. William Umstattd, looking back on Depression-era R&D from an era when the company's technical programs had become centralized and more highly programmed, noted that the work was done "on an ad hoc basis . . . sort of run from the seat of the pants." Said Umstattd, "We would get an idea of a type of machine tool that would save us money. We would investigate it. If it looked good we would buy it. We would do the same thing with furnaces . . . [and] with different parts of manufacturing. It was not a highly organized division." There were, however, some advantages in that seeming lack of organization. For example, engineers who worked on bearing design in a particular industry area—automotive, industrial, railroad—were grouped together with the engineers who designed the tooling used to make those new bearings. This made it easier to develop new products and manufacturing processes in an integrated way. Similarly, the fact that the engineering groups were located in the plant made possible a level of shared understanding and cooperation between them and the operating personnel that would be harder to achieve once R&D was moved off-site. The conditions of the 1930s supported much important work on a relatively low budget.[3]

One critical development—high-precision centerless grinding—was a continuation of a program from pre-Depression years. The traditional type of grinding machine, the so-called centertype grinder, worked on a single piece at a time. Precision grinding took place as the piece, secured at the ends and rotated around its centerline, came into contact with a spinning abrasive wheel. The process itself was fast, but loading and properly positioning each piece was time consuming. In contrast, centerless grinders worked on a continuous stream of pieces, which were not secured and rotated individually, but were moved through the machine between the grinding wheel and a second, regulating wheel. In the mid-1920s, the Cincinnati Milling Machine Company had acquired the patents controlling centerless grinding and had begun to develop and promote the new technology. Frederick A. Geier, principal owner and long-time president of Cincinnati Milling, was a close friend of H. H., and Timken was an early customer for centerless grinding machines. Further development was required, however, to make it a high-precision process. The action of the two wheels together tended to form lobes on the pieces—rounded protrusions no more than .001 inch but still sufficient to make the part unacceptable for precision applications. During the early 1930s, Timken engineers developed new tooling for the Cincinnati grinders and fine-tuned the process so as to solve the lobing problem. Gradually Timken's tool shop modified all of the company's Cincinnati grinders to include this improvement.[4]

The importance of this innovation was immense. The burnishing process that Timken had developed in 1917 had enabled it to produce automotive bearings to acceptable tolerances without grinding. As a result, it reduced its prices and won its first large contract with Ford. With the new centerless technology, the company returned to grinding the outer cup surfaces of these mass-produced bearings. It was able to keep its production volumes high and its costs low, while significantly raising the level of precision on the critical outside dimension, an improvement that raised both the quality and performance of the final product. Developing this technology early was good for the company and its customers, of course. And, when war came, it was very good for the country. Cincinnati Milling also solved the problem of lobing, and centerless grinding became the norm throughout the bearing industry in the course of World War II. But, according to

Timken Products on Land and Sea and in the Air— The Early Years

Cincinnati's chairman and Fred Geier's grandson, James A. D. Geier, "we liked [Timken's] solution better than ours." Cincinnati could have judged only from the output, however, as (personal friendship notwithstanding) Timken maintained the strictest secrecy around its proprietary machine modifications.[5]

Another important development to come out of the Depression years was the Assel Elongator, an improved tube mill developed by Walter Assel, chief engineer of Timken's steel division. The existing process for making high-quality tubing had three basic steps, beginning with the piercing of a round steel billet. In the second step, the pierced billet was passed through a rolling mill. As it moved through the mill, the hollow center was forced over a steel plug so that the tube's walls were shaped to the thickness of the space between the plug and the rolls. This was a time-consuming step. It required up to six passes through the mill to get the wall close to the proper size, and the plug had to be replaced for every pass. It was also not a very precise process, so there was considerable scrap associated with the third step, machining to final dimensions. There was also room to improve the quality of the product—to make the wall thickness more precise, the tubing straighter and more perfectly round. When the steel business fell off drastically in the early 1930s, Timken had both the time and the incentive to work on improving this process. Assel conceived the idea for a new rolling mill that pulled the pierced billets over a long bar, or mandrel, using three rolls instead of the normal two. This had the effect of moving the tube through the mill in a spiral motion. At the midpoint on the rolls was a sharp hump. As the billet passed over that point, both the thickness of the walls and the diameter of the tube were compressed, the metal flowing out toward the ends (hence, the elongation effect).[6]

As the entire company was under strict orders to keep costs down, Assel was hard put to demonstrate his design to the steel company's management so that development could proceed. His solution was a paragon of low-cost prototyping. As William Umstattd recalled, "We experimented on a wooden model of a mill, and instead of using steel, which of course was impossible on a wooden mill, we used a putty sort of substance that performed pretty much like hot steel." The experiment proved the concept. Timken's Wooster tube mill was redesigned around the Assel Elongator and opened in 1937 as the "Assel Mill." There proved to be many benefits to the innovation. It was faster, requiring fewer passes through the mill. The tubing required far less final machining, both because the walls were produced to tighter tolerances and because the rotating motion in the mill produced a better finish. It was more concentric and straighter. The new process was also more versatile and could produce tubing down to quite small dimensions. After World War II it would become the standard technology for making seamless tubing, and Timken's steel division would greatly expand its sales of that product.[7]

The division already had a strong record of innovation from the 1920s. In 1921 it had developed a test (the McQuaid Ehn test) for evaluating the grain size of steel after carburizing that had led to greater understanding of how to eliminate soft spots in finished products by controlling the alloy's microstructure. A related breakthrough in 1924 was the discovery that a small amount of aluminum added to molten steel controlled the state of deoxidation and also provided a more fine-grained microstructure and a tougher steel. Timken was the first steel company to guarantee supplies of this fine-grained steel on a commercial basis. In 1927, it had developed the proper piercing and annealing procedures to produce seamless tubing in the alloy used for ball bearing races and had become the only domestic supplier of this material to the U.S. ball bearing industry.[8]

In 1928 a German metallurgist, Martin Fleischmann, joined Timken as the head of its metallographic laboratory and research program. The following year the company established a joint program of alloy development with the University of Michigan. This was just the kind of relatively inexpensive, longer-term R&D work that was most sustainable during the Depression. The long-term benefit to Timken would be immense: the company emerged from the economic crisis with an array of higher value-added steel products that would open new markets and make the business more profitable.[9]

A number of important innovations resulted, which further illustrate the crucial role of materials in the advancement of other technologies. One part of the program was aimed at developing alloys that included graphite, an addition that enhanced resistance to wear and sliding friction, in particular for applications in

Left: *Martin Fleischmann's work with steel alloys resulted in many new developments, including the 16-25-6 chrome-nickel-molybdenum alloy (Super Steel) used in aircraft engines during and after World War II.*

Right: *Chief engineer Walter Assel pioneered a new rolling process for tubes (the Assel Mill) that became the standard technology for making seamless tubing after World War II.*

machine tools. Out of this came a series of Timken graphitic steels, the first appearing in 1931. Another effort was aimed at developing high-strength alloys that performed well at high temperatures for applications in oil refining, chemical processing, and steam-power generation. The first of these, a chromium-molybdenum alloy, appeared in 1931, with others to follow. Timken's continuing work on high-temperature materials led in the mid-1930s to development of a nickel-chromium-molybdenum corrosion-resistant alloy, patented by Fleischmann. The new material was able to maintain its strength and resist corrosion in a broad range of high-temperature applications. This work would become very significant in the early years of World War II. It provided the foundation for the development of a related alloy, 16-25-6 (Super Steel), which could withstand the intense heat inside turbocharged engines flying at high altitudes. This improvement enabled Allied bombers and fighter planes to fly above the range of German antiaircraft guns and thereby made possible the bombing raids deep into enemy territory that conferred a critical advantage in the final stages of the war. Alloy 16-25-6 was also an essential material in the development of turbojet engines in the postwar era.[10]

Dramatic innovations like centerless grinding, Super Steel, and the Assel Mill made the 1930s an important period in Timken's technical history. Yet it was also important as a time when the company's capacity for steady, incremental improvement of its processes and products expanded significantly. In the Depression crisis, Timken reduced its advertising department from fourteen people down to four in 1932. By 1936, the advertising staff was still only ten people. This was in contrast to staffing of technical departments, which recovered quickly and rose after 1934. By the end of 1936 the total number of Timken employees exceeded the 1929 high by 7 percent, while employment in seven engineering groups (excluding sales engineering, which also grew) rose by nearly 50 percent, from 78 to 116. Research—by which was meant metallurgical research—was nonexistent as a distinct department in 1929, but by 1936 it had a staff of 15. Many of those new hires were trained chemists and metallurgists, as Timken, like numerous other technology-driven companies, took advantage of the favorable hiring conditions created by the closing of some three hundred corporate research and development laboratories. In the same period, Timken's chemical and metallurgical laboratories grew from 13 to 32 people.[11]

When Martin Fleischmann joined Timken in 1928, he had been unhappily surprised by the state of its research facilities and staff. "You could count the people on the fingers of one hand," he recalled. "There was a microscope but nobody knew how to run it. And they gave me a corner up there in the bearing factory fenced in with chicken wire and that was my laboratory. That was it!" In 1929, the company built a metallurgical laboratory next to the Canton steel mill, on Harrison Avenue, but its staff was cut back during the worst years of the Depression. Fleischmann worked without an assistant for a number of years. By the late 1930s, though, all this had changed dramatically. The research laboratory was well staffed and equipped. It included experimental furnaces for alloying and heat treatment, apparatus for studying the problems of gas and inclusions in molten metal, and an elaborate piece of equipment for determining the corrosion resistance of different alloy compositions under varying conditions.[12]

Another important expansion of facilities was the movement of the product-testing group, in August 1937, into a large new laboratory across from the main plant and offices on Dueber Avenue. Many of the machines in the new facility were used to determine bearing life, in most cases by running them to the point of destruction. One tester, specially built to handle bearings up to 24 inches in external diameter, used hydraulic rams to apply pressure simulating up to 500,000 pounds of radial load and 200,000 pounds of thrust load. The enlargement of the bearing-life-testing program had great long-term significance. It was originally conceived as a quality audit, to monitor the performance of Timken bearings. As it continued over the years, however, the program accumulated an invaluable body of information. It provided empirical data to substantiate Timken's claim to leadership in tapered roller bearing technology and to support its continuing drive to expand applications. And it laid the basis for the understanding of the factors contributing to bearing performance that made periodic increases in bearing ratings possible. In the late 1970s, the life-testing program would raise a warning that the steady improvement in bearing performance had stalled, and it would point the way to the changes required to keep Timken bearings competitive.[13]

Another significant aspect of the testing laboratory was its focus on evaluating the products of Timken's customers together with its own bearings—a significant extension of the services provided by sales and application engineers that would expand in the postwar era. The 1930s expansion included fatigue-testing machines for auto and railroad axles. The laboratory's director, Oscar Horger, was a former student of Stephen Timoshenko, the leading international authority in the field of materials strength. The new laboratory received considerable attention in automotive, steel, and railroad trade journals, both on account of its array of advanced devices and because of the anticipation that the equipment would yield information of broad interest in those industries. It had advanced photographic equipment, some of which could produce images up to 5,000X magnification, to aid the study of stresses within metals. The laboratory also had a profilograph, for close analysis of external surface characteristics, and a device developed specifically for testing the quietness of bearings.[14]

In one sense, all of those investments in technical capabilities merely continued a trend of corporate development that had begun in the company's first decade, when H. H. Timken hired Herbert Alden, and W. R. set out to find salesmen who could help automakers design Timken bearings into their cars. It could also be said that the company's approach to developing its industrial markets in the 1920s prefigured the enhancements of the Depression era. Yet the 1930s were distinctive and important for a number of reasons. The buildup of technical personnel and facilities began a shift in the management culture from one that had always valued technical strength to one in which technical values predominated—an engineering culture. The advances made in the 1930s, particularly in process technologies, would have long-term benefits. Most striking, however, would be the way in which the company's enhanced capabilities and knowledge base were deployed during World War II. Timken's ability to innovate quickly in the crisis, across the full range of its technologies, to a great extent defined its wartime experience and further embedded the commitment to technical excellence in its sense of identity. What happened at Timken in the 1930s and 1940s was, to be sure, part of a broad pattern within U.S. industry, and the nation as a whole embraced science and technology in the aftermath of the war. Yet, building on an already strong tradition, this experience had deep and long-lasting effects on the company.[15]

Timken at War

Despite the ideological divisions of the 1930s, the Roosevelt government and the business community formed a successful partnership in waging World War II. From the outbreak of war in Europe, in September 1939, to the December 1941 bombing of Pearl Harbor, the nation's preparations for the likelihood of war were constrained by a strong public desire to stay out of the conflict. In contrast, the enemies it would face had been building up their military strength for nearly a decade. Yet, in the four years following Pearl Harbor, U.S. industrial output doubled and, diverted to military production, transformed the United States into a military superpower. The speed with which the economy was mobilized was astounding to allies and enemies alike. In 1942, U.S. production of planes and tanks was roughly twice that of Germany and Japan combined; its output of heavy guns was six times larger. "Production on this scale made Allied victory a possibility," notes one historian, "though it did not make victory in any sense automatic."[16]

Nor was it "automatic" that U.S. industry would be mobilized so effectively and close the weapons gap so quickly. An important success factor was the extent to which the government enlisted business executives to help plan and supervise wartime production. In January 1942, GM president William S. Knudsen, whom Roosevelt appointed to head the Office of Production Management (predecessor to the War Production Board), gathered a group of corporate leaders, "read out a long list of military products and simply asked for volunteers to produce them." Given the urgency of the moment, the government had little choice but to rely on the business community, and particularly on the nation's leading manufacturing firms. The result was a very practical approach in which private industry was to a great extent allowed to go about getting the job done in its own way. This was a distinctively American approach, in keeping with the established pattern of business-government relations, the New Deal notwithstanding. And it proved effective. It compared favorably—more and more so as the war progressed—with the highly bureaucratic and militarized command economy of Hitler's Germany, which had seemed to enjoy an overwhelming lead when the war began.[17]

Timken's experience well illustrates not only how the crisis galvanized U.S. industry, but also how industry went about mobilizing its resources, particularly its human resources, to turn in an extraordinary performance. At H. H. Timken's urging, the company had gotten an early start on increasing the output of its existing bearing plants and reorienting its bearing production to fit wartime needs. This involved staffing up the plants to enable them to run continuously. Timken hired nearly 3,000 new men in 1939, and after the draft got under way in 1940, it began hiring women. Only a limited amount of new building was feasible, but Timken made a large investment in equipment. On the steel side, there were expansions of existing furnaces and the addition of an 85-ton electric furnace. Timken added many new machine tools in its bearing plants. It also refitted existing equipment for different uses, in particular to effect the necessary change

Elnora Harrisberger (known as "Shorty") came to Timken to help the war effort in 1943 and stayed for thirty-three years. Her daughter worked as a draftswoman in the 1950s, and her grandson currently is a diesel mechanic at the company.

from automotive bearings to the larger bearings required for trucks. Over the course of the war, the company's ability to adapt existing machine tools to new uses would prove to be one of its most valuable assets.

Indeed, Timken's strong organizational capabilities greatly expanded the range of its accomplishments. Before the United States entered the war, much of its war-related work aimed at developing a variety of products, beyond bearings, that required and could benefit from the same metallurgical, engineering, and manufacturing know-how as its standard products. Though Timken over the years chose not to diversify its product line as a business proposition, its wartime experience clearly suggests what the organization could have done if it had taken that route. Some of the company's first government contracts, taken in late 1939, were for production of gears and cams. During 1940 and 1941, Timken manufactured ammunition in various sizes for the U.S. Army and Navy. Making products such as 37-millimeter armor-piercing shells required not only the adaptation of bearing-making machinery and development of production processes but, more fundamentally, sufficient knowledge of hardening metals to produce effective projectiles. It also required organizing and training production personnel to turn out a quality product in high volume. When the Army defined the need for these products—two years before the government would build new, dedicated ammunition plants—it was able to call on Timken, because Timken had already developed those capabilities.[18]

In the most dramatic of such undertakings, the making of gun barrels for cannons out of seamless tubing, the company took the initiative. After the start-up of ammunition production, Timken began experimenting in its tube mill to see if the idea was workable. If so, they believed the process could be a significant improvement over the standard methods, forging or centrifugal casting, which were quite slow. Henry Timken—H. H.'s eldest son, now both chairman and vice president of the company—took the lead in pushing this project and promoting it in Washington. With the approval of the U.S. Ordnance Department, the company added new heat-treat furnaces and quench tanks and produced 100 tubes for testing by the Army and Navy. A persistent problem with cannons was that the ammunition could explode inside the barrel, and when it did the barrel tended to split open, releasing flying shrapnel and usually killing the gun crew. Though Timken's material passed the initial tests, the military remained skeptical, fearful that seamless tubes would burst open even more readily. The company disputed that assumption, and at its urging, the Ordnance Department requested three more gun barrels, to be machined and assembled into cannons and tested in operation. Then, Henry Timken and William Umstattd went to the proving ground and fired the cannons themselves. These new tests demonstrated that barrels made from seamless tubing were far stronger and more durable than conventional barrels. They could withstand more than 7,000 rounds of firing before showing signs of wear, compared to the normal life of several hundred rounds from cast or forged barrels.[19]

Still, the Army was not willing to place an order. Not until Monday morning, December 8, 1941—the day after the bombing of Pearl Harbor—did Timken get a request to manufacture gun barrels. The government bought a vacant factory building in Canton and contracted Timken to handle engineering and management. By that time there were fully assembled tanks sitting in parking lots in Washington, D.C., waiting for guns. Not wanting to profit from the nation's wartime need, Henry Timken sought a contract to supply the gun barrels at no cost. That was unacceptable to the government, so they agreed on a price of 30¢ each. Within just four months, the Timken Ordnance Company plant would be in operation, with the capacity to produce 6,000 gun barrels per month. This was at a time when it took a full year to produce a single forging press for gun barrels. The new Timken plant was innovative, an early experiment with automation. Once the barrel lengths were cut from material sent from the tube mill, a handle was welded onto the end of each so that it could be moved by overhead equipment through the steps of heat treatment, straightening, and cleaning.[20]

In addition, Timken, with the assistance of the Carnegie Institute of Technology, adopted statistical process control (SPC) in order to reduce the tremendous effort that was going into testing every gun barrel on both ends. SPC was based on methods of statistical sampling and theories about the variability of systems that emerged in mathematics in the 1920s. It was first proposed as an approach to quality control in manufacturing by Bell Laboratories researcher Walter Shewhart and was tried out in AT&T's manufacturing unit, Western Electric, in the late 1920s. Shewhart's ideas were brought to wider attention and further developed by a protégé, W. Edwards Deming. Trained in mathematics and physics at Yale, Deming was a student of Shewhart and a leading English statistician, Ronald A. Fisher. In the late 1930s Deming taught a widely attended evening course on statistics at the Graduate School of Agriculture in Washington, D.C. He introduced the U.S. federal government to SPC as an advisor to the Census Bureau in 1940. During World War II, Deming assisted the Statistical Research Group of Columbia University, which was consulting to the government on ways to improve the manufacture of war materiel. In that role, he was instrumental in designing a course on SPC that was taught to thousands of engineers around the country between 1942 and 1945. Many of the men who took that course began to introduce SPC into their companies' operations and would continue the experiment in the postwar years. Deming took the technique to Japan in 1947 when he was commissioned to help the U.S. occupation government conduct a census. SPC would

Timken pioneered the use of seamless tubing for gun barrels during World War II and developed high-temperature alloys for critical aircraft engine parts. Timken bearings went into all types of fighting machines. For the first time, U.S. Timken made ball bearings—briefly—for U.S. and British antiaircraft guns.

become the foundation of the quality revolution in Japan in the 1950s, just as U.S. manufacturers abandoned the technique and reverted to piece-by-piece inspection for quality.[21]

In the course of the war, Timken Ordnance Company produced more than 100,000 gun barrels. Equally important, at a time when the machine-tool industry was nearly overwhelmed but the nation's tube mills had excess capacity, Timken had proven the process and shown the way for other producers of seamless tubing to make the conversion. This was just the kind of breakthrough that gave the United States its overwhelming strength in war materiel. By 1943, the Allies would have a four-to-one advantage over the Axis powers in heavy guns.[22]

Of course, Timken's greatest contribution to the war effort was in the supply of bearings—a product far less visible but no less essential than gun barrels. Similarly, the company's technical achievements in this field, though less dramatic, were hardly less significant. The strength of Timken's process and product engineering organizations enabled it to respond to wartime needs in a way that few, if any, other bearing companies could match. Sales and product engineers who had worked with automotive or industrial customers now collaborated with military engineers and their contractors to develop bearings for a wide range of new applications. Once a new bearing was specified, it was usually necessary to redesign and rebuild existing machine tools to make it. Timken did all of this on urgent schedules, which it could not have met—or exceeded, as it often did—without the strong in-house technical resources that had been built up in the 1930s.

Much the same could be said for Timken's steel division. Timken contributed a number of significant new alloys to the war effort. The most dramatic was alloy 16-25-6, developed for the gas-driven turbo-supercharger that gave the United States its advantage in high-altitude flight. The company produced more than 300,000 supercharger wheels during the war. In addition, it developed—typically on very short notice—improved materials for ball bearings and many aircraft engine parts, including piston pins, propeller hubs, and crankshaft bearings. Its graphitic steels were critically important to the wartime machine-tool industry, its high-temperature alloys essential to the production of synthetic rubber and high-octane gasoline for aircraft. And, equally significant, Timken increased its steel production to wartime levels without building new plants, mainly by making improvements to existing equipment and operating processes. For example, new refractory materials adopted for furnace linings held up longer and so reduced the amount of downtime required for furnace relinings. Equipment that permitted closer regulation of the arc in the electric furnaces made the basic steel-making process more efficient. Timken's metallurgical laboratory developed a direct-reading spectrometer capable of providing on-the-spot analyses of the elements in a heat of molten steel—a significant step forward in process control, hence in overall productivity. Those kinds of improvements were replicated in the rolling mill, the blooming mill, and the piercing mill. They made it possible for Timken to be the largest supplier of steel to the U.S. bearing industry and also to send steel abroad for the ball bearing industries of Britain and Russia.[23]

Timken's tapered roller bearings went to war on all types of aircraft, tanks, half-tracks, tankers, destroyers, and submarines, as well as on the amphibious tank carriers used in the Normandy invasion in 1944. One important application was in the mountings of mobile guns, which required that the guns be able to rotate and change elevation smoothly even on fast-moving trucks, tanks, or ships. Another was in machine tools, many of which had to be made extra large to produce the weapons of war. These required larger, but still ultra-high-precision, bearings in order to do the work effectively. Ball bearings were in short supply from the earliest days of the war, so in some cases the charge to Timken was to design a tapered roller bearing that could serve as a replacement. In two cases the company also undertook to make ball bearings. Immediately following the bombing of Pearl Harbor, the Army defined an urgent need for antiaircraft guns to defend the nation on its home soil. It prevailed upon Timken to make ball bearings for these guns rather than take the time to redesign for tapered roller bearings. Timken did so and along the way improved the bearing by substituting a steel cage for the standard bronze—an alloy of copper, tin, and zinc, all of which were critical materials during wartime. In addition, early in the war Timken made a large number of annular ball bearings in order to help relieve a severe shortage in Britain.[24]

While the need for rapid development of new applications and products challenged Timken's technical organizations, the manufacturing challenge was to keep production up to the highest possible level of output and quality despite the disruptions of a wartime economy. The largest single application of Timken bearings, as in peacetime, was in motor vehicles. The Army's favorite vehicle, the jeep, was designed to take 24 Timken bearings, and some 660,000 jeeps were produced for World War II. Trucks, of which some 2.5 million were produced in the war years, used 20 to 48 tapered roller bearings each, most of them supplied by Timken. By early 1943, the company was producing as many as 2 million truck bearings per month. Output at that level was one of the factors that made it possible for the U.S. Army to have the highly motorized and mobile fighting force that it wanted.[25]

The wartime demands of the aircraft and shipping industries were substantial as well. According to figures supplied by Timken to the U.S. government, a 4-engine bomber used 162 Timken bearings, a medium-sized tank 72, a large tank 100, a scout car 30, and an antiaircraft gun 28. By 1943, the company's annual production measured in number of bearings was more than twice what it had been in 1937. The average bearing weighed 60 percent more, reflecting the shift from cars to trucks and other applications that tended to be heavier and more intricate in design. In stark testimony to the importance of bearings to the war effort, the Allied air forces made the German bearing industry a top-priority bombing target, along with oil and aircraft. Between October 1943 and July 1944, the key industrial city of Schweinfurt suffered three devastating attacks.[26]

On the Home Front

To produce at the level required called for expansion of the bearing plants, expansion that had to take place outside of the Canton area because of the tight labor market within it. Local companies, such as Diebold, Republic Steel, Hercules Motor, and Canton Drop Forge, plus a large new government plant for naval ordnance that was run by Westinghouse, were all operating at peak levels. In 1942,

U.S. soldiers visit a Timken plant. As in most U.S. factories during World War II, women workers kept Timken plants running.

Timken, on behalf of the Defense Plant Corporation, took over a steel mill in Newton Falls, Ohio, that had been closed during the Depression. It recalled many of the men who had been laid off and began to run the plant as a finishing operation for some of its non-bearing steel products, including gun barrels. The next year, Timken on its own started up a similar operation for bearings in Zanesville, Ohio, a town that had a large pottery industry, idled as nonessential during wartime. In Columbus, the Defense Plant Corporation built an addition to Timken's bearing plant that roughly doubled its size.[27]

Yet the real solution to the problem of achieving the necessary levels of production for war, for Timken as for all manufacturers, lay in going outside the usual pool of labor. Even before the United States entered the war, the company began hiring women and calling back some older men who had retired. By the end of 1940, more than half the employees at the drafting tables of Timken's engineering department were women. As in so many industries, however, women would predominate in many departments by the war's end. "They were running everything," noted one employee of Timken Ordnance Company. In downtown Canton, Timken fitted a vacant car showroom as a small factory that employed people, mostly women, who could work only part-time. Timken made ammunition in a plant on Savannah Avenue in Canton that had been the site of bearing manufacture by Gilliam, the company it had acquired in 1925. The company staffed the midnight shift in that plant entirely with African-Americans—women on the plant floor and four young black men in training to be supervisors—assigning one of its most experienced supervisors, Robert Sisson, to train them. With strategies such as this, Timken, which sent more than 5,000 men into the armed forces, increased its total workforce from 8,000 to 18,000 between 1939 and 1944.[28]

H. H. Timken had more than once made the claim that his company was an "anti-friction organization." But following on the changes of the late 1930s, the steps required to meet wartime production schedules could hardly be expected to take place without some conflict and disruption. Within the company, as in the nation as a whole, the union movement gained momentum during these years. In July 1942, a companywide ballot produced an overwhelming majority vote in favor of the CIO as exclusive bargaining agent for Timken employees. Once the United States entered the war, the national leaders of the AFL and CIO had pledged not to strike and to keep their members in line. But the tight labor market, along with the rising assertiveness of the nation's working men and women, made that promise difficult to keep.[29]

The unusual circumstances created some new issues between labor and management, many of them related to hiring women. For example, the union pressed Timken to give preference in hiring to the wives of Timken employees who left to join the armed forces, and it tried to ensure that women who had built up some seniority got opportunities to move into higher-paying positions when those opened up, in preference to men who might be hired in from the outside. When some supervisors removed the Coke machines in their departments after noticing that women tended to use the bathrooms more than men, the union helped push to have them reinstated. Racial tensions on the plant floor placed the CIO on the other side of the fence, however. Nationwide, race relations were coming under new pressures, as the demand for labor brought black and white Americans into closer contact than ever before. Timken plant managers usually avoided conflicts by keeping black employees in low-skill jobs. When Bob Sisson wanted to take Paul Edwards—the brightest young African-American from the midnight shift at Savannah Avenue—with him to his next assignment, his superiors blocked him from doing so. Edwards had to leave Timken to find an opportunity equal to his capabilities. In 1943, 600 machine operators at the Gambrinus bearing plant staged a wildcat strike to protest the promotion of 27 black men to machine jobs. This strike was condemned by the CIO, and its leader was expelled by the Golden Lodge, Timken's chapter of the United Steelworkers of America. When the company fired the strike leader, at the union's request, there was another brief wildcat strike, but the promoted machine operators kept their jobs. Timken, like the rest of American business, would have to struggle for decades to come to terms with the issues created by women and racial minorities in the workplace.[30]

For the most part, though, the topics that divided labor from management were standard fare—a myriad of specific grievances against the way that hirings, firings, assignments, promotions, and pay were handled by foremen and supervisors on the plant floor. Across the nation there were nearly five thousand strikes in 1944 alone. At Timken, in the thirty-month period from Pearl Harbor to D-Day, there were thirty-four work stoppages that collectively cost nearly 400,000 hours of lost working time. Most of these were small-scale, local events. For example, a one-day walkout in the Canton steel mill in 1943 was precipitated by claims that schedule changes aimed at instituting a forty-eight-hour workweek, as mandated by the War Manpower Commission, threatened to downgrade some workers. The most serious strikes came in June and July of 1944. The first began as a localized walkout over hiring issues in Canton but quickly spread to Columbus and ultimately took 1,200 out on strike. This strike, which took place as the D-Day invasion was unfolding in France, evoked much public criticism along with some sympathy for the participants. It ended when the striking workers voted to return, in response to a back-to-work order from the War Labor Board and pleas from local and regional CIO leaders. The second strike, just two weeks later, took some 9,000 people in Canton and Columbus out of work for five days (a loss of some 360,000 hours) over the issue of "accumulated grievances" and the lack of a process for timely resolution. In this case, in addition to orders and pleas, the CIO leadership agreed to request that the War Labor Board place an arbitrator on site, and thus the walkout ended.[31]

Overall, these labor-management conflicts had little impact on Timken's ability to fulfill its wartime contracts. The real story of the company's war effort lay in the contributions made at every level in every department and the impressive results they obtained. Nevertheless, both elements of the wartime experience—the pride of collective achievement and the sense of divided interests—would carry forward into the postwar years.

British Timken in Wartime

The experiences of the Timken companies in Britain and France were shaped by the unique circumstances in each country but also, like those of U.S. Timken, by the tremendous military need for bearings. World War II brought destruction and hardships to Britain that were quite unknown in the United States. Yet Britain, with a much smaller economy, also outproduced Germany in most types of weapons in the early years of the war.[32] British Timken played an important role in that wartime production and, like its U.S. associate firm, expanded considerably in response to the increased demand for Timken bearings.

The British Timken factory in Aston, a highly industrialized section of Birmingham, was situated along a canal that served as a sort of road map for German bombers. Raymond Tuckey, assistant plant manager, recalled nine direct hits on the factory. One was to the furnace in the heat-treatment department. Miraculously, no one was killed, but, said Tuckey, "the chaos was fantastic." The disruption of production at British Timken quickly reached a crisis stage. By that time, 1940, there was a general program for dispersal of industry away from centers such as Birmingham. The war agency overseeing bearings arranged for about one-third of British Timken's production to be moved to a small plant in Coalville, in Leicestershire, and for another heat-treatment shop in Bilston. At about the same time, British Timken took over Fischer Bearings Company, Ltd., a subsidiary of the German ball bearing manufacturer, FAG, that had become confiscated property at the start of the war. In 1941, partly because of continued bombing in Aston, but mainly because of the growing demand for its products, British Timken started construction of a new plant in the Midlands, between Birmingham and London, in the town of Duston. Production of smaller-sized bearings started up at Duston in 1942, before the building was even completed.[33]

Michael Dewar was in the United States for much of the war. In July 1940, well before U.S. industry had begun to change over to production of war materiel, he served as head of a delegation charged with buying tanks. His order for 3,000 tanks from six different suppliers helped launch development of what would become the Sherman tank. Subsequently, he headed the British purchasing and supply missions and remained in the United States through 1942. Beginning in 1940, John Pascoe effectively ran British Timken as its managing director. Pascoe had graduated from Cambridge University with a B.A. in mechanical science and had served in World War I. He had been through an apprenticeship program at Leeds Forge, where Dewar was managing director in the early 1920s. In 1930, he had joined British Timken as director of finance. While Dewar would remain chairman of British Timken until his death in 1950, he lived in London much of the time and left managerial responsibility to Pascoe.[34]

Living conditions were grim in Britain in the first few years after the war. Rationing of clothing and food lasted throughout the 1940s. Few homes had central heating, and there was an acute shortage of housing in the Midlands, due to the destruction wrought by German bombing raids. Timken president William

Umstattd paid a visit in 1945, which must have been memorable, as he took his own supply of cheese, eggs, and chocolate. A more lasting memory at British Timken was that of the many parcels of food sent over from Canton. In the postwar years, the company became the center of its employees' lives, and despite the hardships, a buoyant mood prevailed. Recalled E. R. (Ron) Knapp, later managing director of British Timken, "If you survived the war . . . you were alive and kicking. It was a great place, and we didn't have much, so what we had we were going to enjoy."[35]

Those years saw the beginning of the British Timken Show. The first, in 1945, was really a small agricultural fair, which featured a competition among gardeners cultivating plots on the grounds of the Duston factory. It was the brainchild of Mary Finch, the factory's "labour manager" (director of personnel). In 1946, the show expanded to include displays of Timken bearings and bearing-equipped agricultural machinery, a dog show, livestock competition, equestrian events, a boxing match, and an acrobatic exhibition. Some 3,000 people— mostly employees and their families—attended, and the proceeds went to the District Nursing Association. In the 1950s, John Pascoe developed the annual British Timken Show into a three-day occasion of national importance.[36]

By that time, as decreed by the U.S. courts, Pascoe and British Timken would be locked in competition with U.S. Timken for a share of the expanding markets of postwar Europe. In the prewar years, British Timken had developed many of the same organizational capabilities as Timken in the United States—for example, sales engineering and product development. Having emerged from the war considerably enlarged by the addition of the Duston plant, it would continue to grow rapidly in the postwar era and become a formidable competitor.

Timken France under Occupation

Timken France, by contrast, was weakened, not strengthened, by its wartime experience, which was traumatic in the extreme. An offshoot of British Timken, it remained dependent on the parent company for technical direction and assistance in the prewar years. Its machinery all came from Britain, often secondhand out of Aston. Bearing designs came from British Timken's design unit (often indirectly from Canton), though Timken France made its automotive bearings in metric sizes, converting the British designs and machining its tools to metric dimensions in-house. Its primary market was automotive in the prewar years, and truck bearings made up a large, profitable segment.[37]

On the eve of World War II, Timken France was a company of about 300 employees producing slightly over 500,000 bearings per year—five times its output when it had started production in 1929. The factory, located directly on the

Aulagnier wharf on the River Seine, had also expanded greatly during that time, taking over a number of smaller adjacent factories. Hubert Adrien Hamilton, an Englishman, succeeded the original managing director, Maurice de Beauvivier, in 1937. Charles Nouhaud was in charge of the metallurgical laboratory, the heat-treatment plant, maintenance, and quality control. Early in 1940, when the threat posed to France by Nazi aggression had become clear, the French ministry of war requested Timken France to prepare a second factory farther away from the German border, in the Atlantic port city of Bordeaux, to produce bearings for military needs. This was to be a small operation, with grinding machines only, to finish and assemble bearings from parts shipped from Britain and the United States. Hamilton arranged for a site in a small, empty factory on the outskirts of the city; Nouhaud and one of the factory foremen, Yves Chapotot, went to Bordeaux to ready the site.[38]

The German blitzkrieg—five weeks from the invasion of France to the fall of Paris and capitulation of the French government—made those plans irrelevant. In mid-May, when it began, Timken France received orders to move men and machines immediately. Some 30 men went to Bordeaux, but the chaos of the general evacuation of Paris made moving grinding machines impossible. The French government declared Paris an open city in order to prevent its being destroyed. Just days before the Germans entered the city, Hamilton called Nouhaud, Chapotot, and some others back to do what they could to make the Asnières factory unusable. Then he fled to Bordeaux and, shortly thereafter, to Portugal and on to the United States, in order to avoid being taken prisoner because of his British citizenship. In Asnières, Nouhaud and the others removed critical parts from the most essential machines and hid them in the double-bottomed quench-hardening trays in the heat-treatment shop. "On the very night [June 14] that the German troops were entering Paris by the north," he recalled, "we were leaving by the west with our little truck." On June 17, 1940, France signed an armistice with the German Reich. The nation was divided: Germany occupied the north and reclaimed the northeastern border region of Alsace-Lorraine that it had lost in World War I; Marshal Henri Pétain, a hero of that earlier war, became head of a puppet French government in the south, based in Vichy in the region of Auvergne. Two million French soldiers were sent to Germany as laborers.[39]

The choice open to Timken France's personnel was stark. Said Nouhaud, "Anyone unable to find work in France could keep from starving only by going to work in Germany." They left Bordeaux and returned to Paris, planning to retrieve the hidden machine parts and start up production once again at Asnières. From that time until the liberation of Paris in August 1944, Nouhaud, Chapotot, and other managers—Monsieur Jouve, the head of personnel; Monsieur Gamet, head of sales; and the head of manufacturing, Monsieur Cognard—struggled to keep the plant running. They also tried as much as possible to protect themselves and others from arrest or conscription. There were many crises, the first of which was the threat that the entire plant would be confiscated if it was identified as British owned. In one harrowing night, they gathered up all the records and correspondence written in English or showing any connection to British Timken and sealed them up in an alcove in the factory's cellar. Later, when a burst sewer pipe flooded the space, there would be other frantic nights of work to rescue the documents, clean and dry them, reroute the pipe, and seal the papers up in their hiding place again, all without attracting the notice of other employees, some of whom they feared were informers. A sort of ongoing crisis for the factory's management was to convince the German commandant overseeing Timken France that all of the men working there were absolutely essential and could not be taken for labor in Germany. It was a fine line to tread, between protecting the younger men who were selected and risking endangering the entire plant by arguing too forcefully on their behalf. Nouhaud said, "The officer would get angry and often end up saying, 'OK, fine, we'll just close the factory and send everyone to Germany.' With a stone in our hearts, we had to avoid the worst by agreeing to let one or two people go who did not have any dependents." More horrible still, they had to witness the arrest of a German-speaking woman they had hired to work part-time as a secretary to the commandant, because, after two years there, she was identified by an informant as being Jewish. The woman disappeared. Jouve, the personnel officer, was arrested and sent to prison for several months for his failure to implement the law barring Jews from employment.[40]

Through it all, they had to keep up production in the plant if they were to avoid being shipped to the German labor camps or forced to join the German army. Yet that was often difficult and also involved risks on occasion. The saving grace was the critical importance of the company's product. Early on, Timken France was threatened with having to shut down because of steel shortages. But Citroën, then producing trucks for the German army, intervened through its own German officer. From that point on, he saw to it that Timken France had its steel, with no questions asked about its ties to Britain or the United States. "Only one thing mattered to him—produce for Citroën so as not to halt its production, for which he was responsible," explained Nouhaud. Most often, what he obtained for Timken was ball bearing steel, which was difficult to machine into tapered cups, cones, and rollers. It slowed production but was suitable for standard bearings. Some specialty alloys for other bearings Timken France obtained by itself on the black market. On one occasion, when such steels were requisitioned to be sent to German factories, Nouhaud and Chapotot, "always working at night," buried a good portion of their raw materials in a nearby empty lot. Nouhaud was convinced that the German officer had been informed of their action. "We often had that impression," he said, "and I really was concerned, but he did not press the point. Maybe he thought it was in his interest, too, to keep our machines running."[41]

During the war a number of bearing factories around Paris were bombed by Allied aircraft, including two belonging to SKF. "Everyone thought our turn was coming and fear took hold," recalled Nouhaud. "Still, only a few people took off for the countryside. People were more afraid of working in Germany than they were of the bombings." In this case, they hoped to be spared because of the British and U.S. connection. The attack on the Timken France factory did not come from the air, however. Rather, a team of French Resistance fighters managed to sneak past the German guards on the wharf, overpower the watchman and the night-shift crew in the heat-treatment department, and place ten bombs on machines around the plant. Nouhaud reflected that they did not understand the workings of the factory enough to place the bombs where they would be the most disruptive, but in fact the placement served two good ends: the plant could return to operation within a few weeks, so the jobs were not lost, yet production was considerably slowed down by the damage. "The Resistance fighters' goal had been in large part achieved," he said. "We owed them a great debt."[42]

The liberation of Paris swept away the dangers of the German occupation but ushered in a period of intense social conflict and political turmoil. General Charles de Gaulle established a provisional government but was powerless to prevent a widespread breakdown of authority, which unleashed forces that had been building for five years. As described by a biographer of de Gaulle, "a kind of hidden civil war was going on. Old scores were being settled with a vengeance between the *résistants* and the collaborationists, and many personal vendettas as well. But at the bottom line, it was a struggle for local power between the communists and the Gaullists." Within companies, including Timken France, managers in particular came under attack for having been too cooperative with the Germans. Monsieur Luc, who had replaced Jouve as personnel director, was arrested and put in prison, to be tried for treason. With legal assistance provided by British Timken, Luc won release, but the organization remained deeply divided. Much to the relief of Charles Nouhaud, British Timken in 1944 sent a new general manager, Bernard Riley. That step helped to defuse the situation by focusing attention on the continuing war in Europe. Riley "met with the workers' committee," recalled Nouhaud. "He ignored any questions that did not have to do with production. The immediate goal was to 'produce to win.'"[43]

In the postwar years, however, the situation in France would remain tumultuous and divisive. De Gaulle's government included representatives of many political parties and enacted a liberal socialist agenda, including nationalizing banks, the electric, gas, and coal industries, and two of Timken France's important customers, Renault and the truck manufacturer, Berliet. Yet the governing coalition was an uneasy one for the conservative de Gaulle. Most unruly and demanding were the Communists, who emerged in national elections as the strongest political party and began to push a more radical agenda. With his personal popularity and influence diminished, and in the face of continuing factionalism, de Gaulle resigned from office in 1946. Before he returned to power in 1958, there would be twenty-four successive governments.[44]

Timken France was not immune to the disruptions of the era. William Umstattd visited Asnières frequently in the postwar years and was convinced that the men on the plant floor had simply become accustomed to slowing down production during the war as a form of sabotage and continued to do so afterward as an expression of lingering mistrust and resentment against management. "There was a great deal of hatred among the Frenchmen, one against the other," he said, "and it took a great deal of time to get that straightened out."[45]

After the war, Timken France began to develop some of the capabilities necessary to expand its business. British Timken sent Robert de Beauvivier, the son of the first managing director of Timken France, to establish an application engineering department. Trained in Canton, he became a strong link to the U.S. company. Bernard Riley also helped to foster closer ties there, and Umstattd visited twice a year through the 1950s. While the antitrust decision precluded discussion of markets or prices, it allowed technical cooperation, and a good deal of that developed. Much of the machinery shipped to France under the Marshall Plan came equipped with Timken bearings, as did a large order of locomotives purchased in the United States by the French national railroad company, SNCF. Timken France had never had a service department but seized the opportunity to develop one, with an eye on the replacement market. Once markets opened up for railroad bearings, rolling mill bearings, and precision bearings for machine tools—none of which Timken France could produce commercially—it purchased them from U.S. Timken for resale to French customers.[46]

Entering the Postwar Era

Timken in the United States did not face the same kinds of hurdles in returning to peacetime as its British and French affiliates, but the immediate postwar years were nevertheless unsettled and full of anxiety and conflict. Indeed, disruptions began even before the end of the war, as the tide started to turn in Europe and the tight labor market induced many industrial workers to move from job to job, following higher pay. It was that pattern that prompted Timken to institute a policy against rehiring anyone who quit the company, a policy that would remain in effect until the 1990s. Once victory was secure, the process of reconverting the economy caused widespread, if temporary, unemployment and price inflation. The government abruptly canceled its contracts for war material and began disposing of the plants it had helped to build. Manufacturing companies everywhere laid off most of the women they had hired in the emergency and set up programs to reintegrate thousands of returning soldiers. As these events played out, most people fully expected there to be a severe postwar recession as there had been in 1920–21.[47]

The fall of 1945 and the early months of 1946 brought a strike wave of unprecedented proportions: 200,000 autoworkers struck GM for one hundred days; 300,000 meat packers, 180,000 electrical workers, and 750,000 steel workers followed suit. Timken, whose wartime employment peaked at 18,000 in 1944, was swept up in this wave of labor-management confrontation. The War Labor Relations Board had appointed an arbitrator in the summer of 1945. Under that regime, relations between the company and the union remained difficult but peaceful until October. Then a strike erupted over changes in work schedules made without union consent. That walkout, lasting thirty-three days, was Timken's longest to date—a record that fell just two months later, when the nationwide United Steelworkers strike idled 14,000 Timken employees for eighteen weeks. The outcome of these events at Timken was much as it was across U.S. industry: the company granted wage increases and additional fringe benefits but staunchly resisted union encroachments on its "right to manage." In the nation at large, public opinion in this period increasingly accepted corporate resistance to unions. The war experience had largely moderated the antibusiness sentiment of the 1930s, and as the postwar world became increasingly polarized, rising anticommunism began to change the way many people, both inside and outside the union movement, viewed its goals. Those shifts were codified in 1947 by the passage of the Taft-Hartley Act, which offset many provisions of the Wagner Act of a decade before—for example, by defining "management rights" as a counterweight to "union rights," and "unfair labor practices" as distinct from "unfair management practices"—as well as making it easier for working people to stay out of unions if they wanted.[48]

This changing environment provided the context in which Timken and the Golden Lodge settled down to the task of forging a workable adversarial relationship. Commenting on six months' experience with the two sides, Timken's arbitrator had written in January 1945 that neither the union nor management was terribly skilled at handling grievances, and as a result most plant-floor employees had little trust in the process. That would have to change if strikes were to be avoided, as officials on both sides sincerely wished.[49]

The strikes of 1945–46, 1959, and 1968 reflected the sentiments and issues of industrial America. As Timken management's and the union's skills at negotiating and handling grievances improved, contract talks were increasingly based on facts rather than emotions.

Timken in the postwar era would also have to change the way it dealt with its British and French affiliate companies. The antitrust litigation that forced that issue was launched in 1946 by the U.S. Department of Justice, which had been invigorated by the "trustbusters" who came in with the New Deal. Timken was only one of many large companies, including General Electric and Aluminum Company of America, that were challenged in the courts in the late 1930s and 1940s. The case had its origin in a separate, price-fixing case against the U.S. ball bearing industry that began during World War II. Timken was not named in that suit, but, partly because it had produced ball bearings for export in the early years of the war, it received a subpoena for documents on bearing prices. The war was on and the company was running flat out. Timken responded that it would either contest the subpoena or the Justice Department could send its own employees to Canton to search for the documents. The Justice Department obliged, and, after presenting its evidence to a grand jury in the ball bearing case, it launched a separate suit against Timken based on agreements it had found between U.S. Timken, British Timken, and Timken France dating back to 1928. Those agreements covered the licensing of the Timken trademark and were patterned on Timken's original patent licensing agreement with Electric & Ordnance Accessories. They delineated separate market territories—the British Empire and most of Europe to British Timken; France to French Timken; and the rest of the world, except Russia, to U.S. Timken. Russia was agreed on as a joint territory between British and U.S. Timken, with prices to be negotiated. The Justice Department charged that these were anticompetitive arrangements among independent companies, the effect of which was to eliminate price competition in international bearing markets.[50]

The U.S. District Court in Cleveland heard Timken's case in 1948 and found the company in violation of antitrust laws. Early in 1950, the court ordered Timken to divest its stock in British Timken and Timken France and to cancel all licensing agreements in effect. Timken appealed that decision to the U.S. Supreme Court, and the court agreed to hear the case in November 1950. In December, Michael Dewar died unexpectedly from a heart attack, leaving Timken, per agreement, with the option to buy all of Dewar's shares in the British and French companies. Timken exercised that option as a means of gaining greater control over the situation: if it was forced to sell, at least it could prevent the companies from falling into the hands of a competitor. Thus, in April 1951, Timken became full owner of Timken France and 52 percent owner of British Timken. Just two weeks later, the case was argued before the Supreme Court.[51]

The court upheld the original injunction against the licensing agreements but overturned the lower court's divestiture order on the grounds that the violation stemmed only from the terms of the agreements and not from the basic association with foreign companies. "Such business arrangements," the court stated, "should not be destroyed unless necessary to do away with the prohibited evil." This partial victory left Timken in the awkward position of having to compete actively with British Timken and Timken France—and facing criminal charges if it failed to do so—while at the same time having to uphold its rights and responsibilities as full or majority owners. That was the basis on which it would conduct business internationally for most of the 1950s. Yet the government, in making its case against the licensing agreements, had left the door open to a resolution. It had suggested that Timken could have legally controlled British and French pricing and sales if it had run its affiliates as integrated divisions of the parent firm and not as separate entities in which it merely owned stock. Timken would take that opening to establish its international operations on a new footing in the late 1950s.[52]

Postwar Prospects

Timken had emerged from the era of depression and war in a seemingly unassailable competitive position, a fact that had figured into the government's argument against it. In the United States, the company held 80 percent of the domestic market for tapered roller bearings and 25 percent of the total anti-friction bearing market. Timken increased its productive capacity after the war by buying the Defense Plant Corporation's facility in Columbus and continuing its assembly and finishing operations in Zanesville. In 1948 its revenues were three times what they had been in 1939 ($120 million versus $40 million). Moreover, the opportunities for further growth were clearly in view by the late 1940s. The U.S. economy was getting into full postwar swing—the automotive industry was back to peacetime production levels by 1949—and the supply of bearings worldwide was tight, in part because of the near total destruction of Germany's bearing factories.

The changes in the business environment emanating from the Depression and World War II formed a sharp break with the past—a discontinuity—that had wide-ranging implications. In contrast, the changes at Timken represented, for the most part, an acceleration of trends already in motion. Notable exceptions were in the company's relationships with its plant-floor employees and associate companies abroad. Yet in other areas—leadership style, corporate strategy, corporate culture, organizational capabilities, competitive strength—The Timken Roller Bearing Company of 1949 was largely as it had been in 1929, only more so. After fifty years of company life, the vision and values of H. H. Timken and, through him, Henry Timken, were pervasive and powerful. Timken's automated high-volume production bearing plant at Bucyrus, Ohio, opened in 1953, was an early sign of what the company would be able to accomplish in the postwar era.

Timken at Midcentury:
The Umstattd Era

*F*rom its founding through World War II, The Timken Roller Bearing Company followed a path of development quite similar in its broad outlines to most large, successful U.S. industrial firms. It invested in essential technologies and organizational capabilities, built up profitable markets, and created management functions to control operations and to plan and execute the steps required for continued growth. Like other manufacturing companies, it expanded dramatically during the war. (See Table 6.1.) At war's end it stood on the brink of tremendous potential growth as the U.S. economy entered its postwar boom and the work of rebuilding Europe began.

Going forward, however, the path of Timken's evolution would diverge from the mainstream of corporate America in significant ways. Beginning in the late 1940s, the majority of leading industrial firms decentralized management. They created self-contained divisions along product or geographical lines, both to accommodate wartime expansion and to facilitate continued growth in the postwar era. A related development was the widespread adoption of diversification strategies. These built on established organizational capabilities or (beginning in the 1960s) used acquisitions to open up new avenues for growth.[1]

TABLE 6.1

The Timken Company Comparative Financial Data, 1940–1949 (in Thousands of Dollars, except per Share Data)

	1940	1941	1942	1943	1944	1945	1946	1947	1948	1949
Net sales	$59,100	$90,000	$101,200	$108,700	$112,700	$89,300	$80,500	$107,800	$120,500	$99,438
Net income	8,995	9,477	6,475	6,429	6,294	5,380	5,502	11,124	13,205	3,531
Total assets	$56,376	$58,219	$74,724	$63,562	$65,195	$64,586	$69,593	$73,950	$78,897	$72,983
Total capital and earnings invested in the business	41,694	44,220	45,933	47,614	49,065	49,602	53,288	57,148	63,088	62,558
Return on sales	15.2%	10.5%	6.4%	5.9%	5.6%	6.0%	6.8%	10.3%	11.0%	3.6%
Return on assets	16.0	16.3	8.7	10.1	9.7	8.3	7.9	15.0	16.7	4.8
Return on capital and earnings	21.6	21.4	14.1	13.5	12.8	10.8	10.3	19.5	20.9	5.6
Earnings per share	$3.72	$3.92	$2.68	$2.65	$2.60	$2.22	$2.27	$4.59	$5.45	$1.46
Dividends per share	3.50	3.50	2.00	2.00	2.00	2.00	1.88	3.00	3.00	2.75
Number of employees										13,743
Number of shareholders										19,583

Sources: The Timken Roller Bearing Company Annual Reports, 1940–49; 1953; and C. L. Van Horn to G. L. Deal (February 3, 1960), in The Timken Company archives.
Note: Net sales 1940–1948 are rounded to the nearest $100,000.

Timken was different. It would continue into the 1980s to manage its two businesses as well as its international operations within the confines of a central-ized functional organization. Most important, it would remain tightly focused on its core products, tapered roller bearings and alloy steel bars and seamless tubing. The company certainly did not lack the capabilities or financial resources to launch new lines of business in the postwar years. Yet its commitment to the Timken bearing was, if anything, stronger than ever.[2]

In the 1950s, Timken expanded its share of the U.S. automotive market by developing—at its Bucyrus, Ohio, plant—automated production technologies for higher-volume, lower-cost manufacturing, and by convincing automakers to ac-cept standardized bearing sizes at reduced prices. That initiative made the com-pany the largest domestic bearing producer by the end of the decade. At the same time, Timken's sustained investment in product and process improvements, despite economic ups and downs, gave its bearings and steel a competitive edge they would hold into the late 1970s. Timken also continued its push to expand railroad and industrial applications for its bearings and opened new markets for its seamless tubing. It substituted diversity of customers for diversification as a strategy in order to avoid the constraints of dependence on a single industry or sector. Finally, U.S. Timken moved aggressively into international markets, driven in part by the court order to compete with its associate Timken companies, but also lured by new opportunities for growth as its largest U.S. customers ex-panded abroad. By 1959, British Timken and Timken France would be fully con-solidated operating units. There would also be new Timken bearing plants in Canada, Australia, and Brazil as well as a network of agents and distributors cir-cling the globe. It was, in short, a pivotal decade. Timken's postwar strategy fol-lowed a path that clearly diverged from the dominant pattern for large companies in core industries.

It would be hard to explain that divergence without reference to the com-pany's historic sense of purpose and the corporate culture that sustained it. Con-versely, close examination of the culture suggests that any other course was highly unlikely, if not simply out of the question. The active leadership of Timken family members—H. H. Timken's sons, H. H. (Henry) Timken, Jr., and William R. (Bob) Timken—provided continuity of owner-management and helped to keep the family's values and mission alive. Yet beyond that, by mid-century Timken had a cohesive management culture in which those values were widely shared and the sense of mission was clear-cut and strong. That develop-ment must be attributed primarily to William Umstattd. In the fifteen years of his presidency up to the company's fiftieth anniversary in 1949, he presided over its growth from 5,000 to nearly 14,000 people. His imprint was on the structures, the programs and policies, and the governing philosophies that had shaped the organization as it grew.

Umstattd was at the height of his career in the 1950s. He played a central role in forging a long-term strategy based on the Bucyrus innovations and in launching U.S. Timken into postwar markets at home and abroad. The next two chapters will examine those aspects of the Umstattd era. This one looks more closely at the organization and its culture, which shaped the company's strategic goals and also its ability to achieve them.

Timken at Fifty

The Timken Roller Bearing Company celebrated its birthday in June 1949 with an enormous open house. Everything about this celebration was on a scale befitting an enterprise that reckoned it had produced in its corporate lifetime roughly 1 billion bearings, "ranging in weight from two ounces to 9,068 pounds." Timken had nine North American plants: seven in Ohio, including both bearing and steel facilities; a bearing factory in St. Thomas, Ontario, opened in 1946; and a rock-bit factory in Colorado Springs, opened in 1948. Over a period of two weeks they collectively received more than 82,000 visitors.[3]

In 1932, Timken introduced its third product, the removable rock bit made from Timken steel. In 1948, the company opened a new plant in Colorado Springs, Colorado, dedicated solely to making rock bits for drilling equipment. The rock-bit business remained a division of the company until 1986.

Celebrating their company's heritage in 1949, derby-hatted workers with handlebar mustaches demonstrated bearing-making processes during the company's earliest years.

In Canton during the company's fiftieth anniversary events, six $100 cash prizes were given for guessing the weight of this glass case containing 58,179 silver dollars, the amount of federal taxes the company paid daily.

Miss Josephine Murphy had the most years of service at the company's fiftieth anniversary celebration in 1949. She began in 1900 as W. R. Timken's assistant in St. Louis and moved with the company to Canton. A colorful figure in the community, she handled much of the administration in the early years, including purchasing, taking customer orders, and billing.

The Canton open house was an eight-day event, beginning with visits by customers and reporters on the first two days. The complete tour of the Canton and Gambrinus steel and bearing plants took three to four hours, including bus transportation between the two sites. Timken employees served as greeters and guides, wearing matching outfits: dark trousers or skirts with white shirts; a dark bow tie for the men; an orchid corsage for the women. Foremen and supervisors were on hand to explain operations in the different departments. On the refreshment stop at the Timken Recreation Field, the company served 61,000 bottles of milk, 120,000 bottles of root beer and Coke, and over 150,000 cups of ice cream. Every visitor received a copy of the anniversary edition of the company magazine, the *Timken Trading Post,* that chronicled the company's rise from Henry Timken's days as a carriage maker and inventor. Two large tents held fifty automobiles ranging from a steam-powered 1900 Locomobile to late-model Fords fully equipped with Timken bearings. The company also mounted an exhibit that showed what a bearing factory might have looked like in 1899. It included a blacksmith's forge, a small steam engine, an old-style drill press that manufactured the bearing parts, and an assembly line, in which bearings were put together by hand. All the men working in this "miniature plant" wore derby hats, and most sported handlebar mustaches.[4]

Yet, undoubtedly, what attracted so many people to visit Timken and look the company over was not its venerable age but what it had become. In every one of its plant communities, Timken was the largest industrial employer. It was also a firm with a national reputation: an important producer of alloy steel; the leading manufacturer of tapered roller bearings in the world; and the second largest U.S. bearing manufacturer, after GM's New Departure-Hyatt division. It had the capacity to produce 600,000 tons of alloy steel per year and 48 million bearings. For local residents as well as family members of Timken employees, the open house provided a fascinating, close-up view of manufacturing on a large scale. Taking the Canton-Gambrinus tour involved a lot of walking in hot summer weather, noted one local reporter, but the visitor would be "repaid amply by the insight he gets into the complex, precision operations which furnish about one-third of Canton's industrial employment."[5]

Timken maintained a high profile in those days. Anyone who read the *Saturday Evening Post, Newsweek,* or *Business Week* would have recognized the company's name from its advertising and might have known not only what a Timken bearing looked like, but also many of its applications. The company's struggles with its union in the immediate postwar years, part of a larger conflict taking place nationwide, had been reported extensively in local papers. Since that time, Timken had broadcast a weekly radio program in Canton—with printed transcripts made widely available in other plant communities—in which division managers and department heads described their organizations and how they contributed to the larger enterprise. Each page of the souvenir edition (and every edition) of the *Timken Trading Post* carried a tag line—"The right to work shall not be abridged or made impotent." This signaled Timken's firm determination to resist the union's demand for a closed shop. Large signs, prominently placed throughout the plant, reminded visitors and employees, "Taxes are pretty high." One of the most popular exhibits at the Canton open house was a glass container filled with 58,179 silver dollars, the amount the company paid in federal taxes per day. Timken gave away six $100 prizes for the closest guess of the weight of the coins. Those anti-union and antigovernment positions were as much a part of Timken's corporate identity as its products. They reinforced the divisions between management and the unionized workforce, even as the celebration of the company's past and its achievements brought people together.[6]

Those fundamental tensions were central to the character of the large, complex organization that Timken had become, and they are clearly reflected in company literature. Communications that attempted to give people a sense of community and common purpose simultaneously reinforced the company's highly departmentalized and hierarchical structure. For example, Timken's weekly radio broadcasts, bound each year into a volume titled *The State of the Company*, spoke to a variety of audiences, but mainly its own personnel. "We wanted our men and women," said the foreword to the volume, "to comprehend the interdependence of all our functions and departments and of each of us to all the others, in no matter how seemingly small a capacity." At about the same time, from January 1947 into the early 1950s, the *Timken Trading Post* ran a series of articles with a similar intent. Each article featured one department of the company and its managers, including numerous photographs of operations. This magazine, as its name suggests, had started out in 1942 as a listing of classified ads. But by 1946, it had transformed itself into a full-fledged employee magazine, which gave a human face and a sense of community to work life at Timken by announcing engagements, marriages, births, promotions, and company sporting news. On the one hand, these publications reinforced the hierarchical order of the organization by focusing predominantly on management personalities and concerns, and by providing a conduit through which top managers could transmit information and values. On the other, they worked against the depersonalizing forces inherent in a large industrial corporation, in which the men at the top could hardly be expected to know even the foremen, much less the employees on the shop floor.[7]

Organization and Culture in the Plants

Roughly 10,000 people worked in Timken's main offices and plants in Canton and nearby Gambrinus. The large-scale batch processes used to make Timken bearings and steel created many subdivisions within the workforce. By the late 1940s, facilities at the two locations had been organized to be complementary, and their tasks were divided with almost military rigor. The Canton steel mill, for the most part, handled the upstream steps of steel making, producing ingots, blooms, billets, and pierced rounds for further processing. At Gambrinus, those materials were forged, rolled, or drawn, then finished into seamless tubing for bearings as well as tool steel and many other products for sale on the outside. Conversely, the Gambrinus bearing departments covered the first steps of bearing manufacture, the Canton departments the later steps. For instance, all green machining was situated together in two departments at Gambrinus: Departments 60 and 61 included, respectively, 136 multiple-spindle and 307 single-spindle automatic screw machines that produced cups and cones from Timken seamless tubing. The wire-drawing and header operations (roller header machines cut slugs from wire and formed them into tapered rollers by punching them into a die) were likewise consolidated in a single building at Gambrinus. So was heat treatment, which handled the carburizing and case hardening of bearing components. Grinding operations were consolidated in the Canton factory. The main grinding room held 327 machines and employed 815 people, all organized into departments. These were face grinding, inner diameter (I.D.) grinding, outer diameter (O.D.) grinding, rib grinding, crosshatching, and honing, although within the company many departments were called more often by number than by name. The Canton plant also housed roller grinding, cage making, bearing assembly, and a multitude of inspection departments. Supporting the production departments in both plants were groups such as shipping and receiving, machine repair, tool making, tool inspection, maintenance, safety, and sanitation. Many of those were further subdivided by specific skills and tasks—electricians, pipe fitters, carpenters, painters, etc. Altogether there were nearly eighty distinct functional groups engaged in producing steel and bearings.[8]

The people who worked in those departments were ethnically diverse, reflecting Canton's population, which had received many different immigrant groups around the turn of the twentieth century. One crew in the bloom surface department, for example, included Stavros (Steve) Demetrakis, Diego Gonzales, Peter Wuletich, and Theodore Zampetos. African-Americans remained segregated and suffered discrimination within Timken, as in most of American society at that time. Some tenacious black employees were able to advance. William Powell, who started as a cleaner of spittoons in the 1930s, when "black was the lowest there was," became a security guard after returning to Timken as a World War II veteran. But for the most part, African-Americans remained in menial jobs. They were the chip handlers in the machine rooms, the heavy lifters in the labor department, and the sweepers of sawdust—about 100 pounds of which was spread on the shop floors every day to absorb oil—in the sanitation department. They did not take part in company athletic leagues (and were banned from Canton's public golf courses), but in Columbus, Timken sponsored a softball team in the area Negro league.[9]

William Powell returned to Timken after World War II and became the company's first African-American security guard. A lover of golf, he and his wife built their own course in 1948 when he grew weary of discrimination at local courses. The Powell family continues to operate the Clearview Golf Club in East Canton, Ohio. From left are daughter Renee, wife Marcella, William, and son Lawrence. Renee played on the LPGA tour from 1967 to 1980.

For most 1950s company men, softball played a large part in the Timken culture. In 1948 the company had built a 60-acre recreation park between Canton and Gambrinus that included tennis courts, a skating and fishing pond, a picnic area and playground, two baseball diamonds, and seven softball fields. Columbus got a similar, though somewhat smaller park at about the same time. Timken softballers played against other company teams, but most important was the intramural league. Like everything else, this part of company life was departmentalized. Hence, this typical *Trading Post* report of results: "Tool Room had a 7-1 lead in the last inning when Screw Machine put across seven runs to take a thriller, 8-7." The high points of the season were the contests between the champs of Canton, Gambrinus, Columbus, and Wooster. More than one factory manager was suspected of preventing the transfer of a promising young man who happened to be a good player. Timken also had company baseball teams, Little League teams, a golf league and, in the winter, bowling and basketball leagues. It employed a full-time recreation director. "You could go on a Saturday and see 1,000 people at the recreation center," recalled one employee.[10]

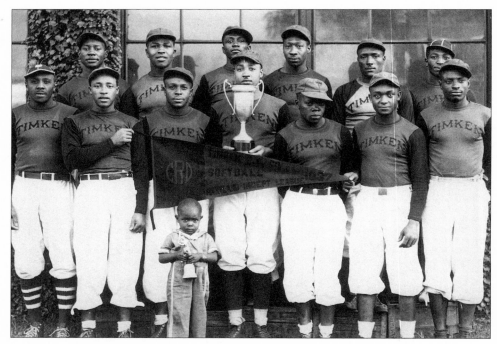

In the 1930s, Timken sponsored a softball team in the Columbus area's Negro League. The team won the pennant in 1937.

In its emphasis on men's sports, and in other ways, the *Trading Post* documented a factory culture that was overwhelmingly male. But in fact, quite a few women worked for Timken in the 1950s. (A section of the magazine offering fashion tips, decorating ideas, and recipes, titled "Feminine Fancies," apparently spoke to their interests.) As in all U.S. manufacturing firms, women who had taken on men's jobs during World War II were displaced at war's end. However, women continued to work in metallurgical and testing laboratories and at the drafting boards of engineering departments, as well as in offices throughout the company. They assembled bearings, and they played an especially large part in inspection and quality control, which involved checking by eye and by gauge literally every cup, cone, and roller that went into Timken's bearings. While there were few, if any, opportunities for advancement in those jobs, the company was solicitous of its female workers in a way that working women of later generations might envy. It employed, full-time, a kind of women's social worker, who helped solve problems both on and off the job, including child-care problems, that made it difficult for women to keep up attendance and work effectively.[11]

In various ways, company policies and practices promoted a positive sense of community and corporate identity. The Timken Roller Bearing Charitable Trust, a corporate philanthropic organization formed in the 1940s, supported local causes in Canton and other Timken plant cities. Though separate, the family's philanthropy through the Timken Foundation naturally brought goodwill to the company as well. In 1945, Timken got a good deal of publicity—including a visit from the nation's most famous sightless person, Helen Keller—for developing a sound-based gauging apparatus for cups and cones that provided employment for the blind. (Since Keller was deaf as well as blind, she could only feel the vibrations by placing her hand on the machine's amplifier.) But once the fanfare died down, the handicapped workers remained on the scene and became a permanent part of Timken's bearing plants. They wore red caps so that coworkers could easily locate and guide them to safety in case of fire.[12]

As early as 1918, Timken (along with many other manufacturing companies) had done away with its apprentice system for training shop-floor personnel and had created a "factory training school" to teach "the proper operation of machinery." By the 1950s, the company's employee job training department supplemented hands-on work with slide lectures, movies, and an array of printed materials. Those provided a general orientation to the company, as well as training at a given task or on a particular machine. They also showed why the job had to be done in a certain way and how it fit into the work of the plant as a whole. There was also a well-publicized employee suggestion program that had been put in place under H. H. Timken. The first award—$1—had been given in 1924. By the 1950s people won $15 for each idea that was put to use, and annual grand prize winners received $2,000. Some $30,000 was awarded annually in this program in the early 1950s. By such methods, the company cultivated loyalty and commitment to a common cause. There were some bread-and-butter benefits to working at Timken as well. The company had always paid relatively high wages, and, as throughout U.S. industry, pay scales rose steadily during the late 1940s and 1950s with the negotiation of successive union contracts. The same negotiations brought hourly employees health insurance and a pension plan similar to what was provided for salaried personnel.[13]

As much as it resisted and maligned its union, the company was ultimately a beneficiary of the union's gains, since they helped to create an environment in which people could feel good about devoting a full working life to the company's interests. In fact, there were many families with multiple generations working at

The company's efforts to accommodate blind workers were recognized in 1945 with a visit by the renowned Helen Keller. Although deaf and blind, she could feel the vibrations from a sound-based, cup- and cone-gauging mechanism developed by Timken engineers. Standing by were (from left) company president William Umstattd, Frederick Crawford (president of Thompson Products, forerunner of today's TRW Inc.), Capt. John Paul Moriarty (the first Timken employee blinded during World War II), and Dept. 81's blind gauger George Corbett.

The company received at least two national citations in the 1950s for its employment of the handi-capped: the Blinded Veterans Association Employer of the Year Award in 1952, and a Commendation from the President's Committee on Employment of the Physically Handicapped in 1956.

Timken, who were regularly featured in the *Trading Post*. A favorite photo arrangement depicted a father explaining some aspect of his work to his son or sons. The sense of long-term mutual commitment was further enhanced by the magazine's practice of regularly noting people's length of employment, for example: "Frank Peterson, I.D. cone grinder, Dept. 73, Canton bearing factory, a 31-year man, is shown with his two sons, Donald, of the Millwright Crew, and Harold, an O.D. cone grinder in Dept. 73."[14] Timken's leaders greatly valued such visible signs of the positive aspects of the company culture, and rightly so, since they helped to make its vast organization an effective production unit.

Although there was much about the organization that contributed to cohesiveness and good feeling, there were also deeply ingrained rigidities that loomed as obstacles to labor-related gains in productivity. The suggestion system aside, Timken's shop-floor employees were undeniably on the controlled end of the command-and-control continuum. This fact was, if anything, reinforced by the incentive pay program instituted shortly after World War II. A man running a grinder, for example, could earn a bonus on top of his hourly wage by producing the maximum number of defect-free pieces for which his machine was rated. If he produced more than that, he did not get an additional bonus, on the assumption that he would have had to sacrifice quality to get that result. But, noted Bob Sisson, who supervised a green-machining department at Gambrinus in this era and had operated the machines himself, "The average man at that time didn't have to work on a piece of machinery too many moons until he knew a few shortcuts." It became common practice under the incentive pay system to string extra pieces on a wire and sink them in the oil in the sump of the machine, to be brought out and added when necessary to make the quota. Sisson took care to give a couple of days' advance notice when a thorough cleaning would require emptying the sumps of oil, but most department supervisors did not.[15]

Outsmarting the incentive pay system was one way skilled machine operators gained a degree of leverage on their working conditions. In another instance, they resisted an early cross-training initiative that would have increased productivity but also given management greater flexibility and control. Umstattd recalled his frustration at the apparent narrowness of training and lack of flexibility among shop-floor personnel during the war when labor was tight and schedules were pressing. When some machine operators were out because of illness—or a wildcat strike—it had proved impossible to get others to take their places, he recalled, "because [for example] the internal cone grinder for some reason or other would not grind the external cones or cups." Initially, he and the manager of the Canton bearing factory, Herchel Richey, tried setting up a few machines in an area of the Canton plant and training some men to be "universal workers" who would be able to fill in for absentees on a variety of machines. When that effort failed, because "people were too set in their ideas," they tried moving the training facility to a plant in Cleveland that Timken had rented for war work. There the machines and operators were organized in groups, each group encompassing all the steps involved in making a finished cup or cone, with productivity measured as the output of the group as a whole. The change acknowledged the barriers to job switching built into Timken's compensation system, which rewarded the individual who cultivated expertise on a particular machine by granting bonuses for optimum output. That experiment also fell short of expectations, however. Umstattd and Richey abandoned the idea for the duration of the war. "We had the same workmen up there that we had used in Canton," Umstattd noted, "and we . . . sold ourselves on the idea that it couldn't be done." [16]

Later, when Timken began to develop its automated high-volume plant, it would sidestep what it took to be an ingrained resistance to change by placing the factory in the rural town of Bucyrus, "where people didn't know how to grind an I.D. cup, an I.D. cone, an O.D. cup, an O.D. cone, and we could teach them how to do more or less universal work." But such power struggles between management and labor were as much a part of the highly evolved factory system as its massive scale and output. Once Timken began to feel the full force of global competition, in the early 1980s, the pressure would build to reexamine and change those fundamental aspects of the organization and culture that nurtured them. [17]

Of course, Timken's management structure and culture had their own rigidities that, to a great extent, mirrored those that held sway on the factory floor. Functional divisions marked out spheres of activity and influence that allowed departments to operate like so many fiefdoms. Multiple layers of authority further limited individual responsibility and increased the distance between the men at the top, who were in a position to have a broad view of the company and its position, and those who most affected its day-to-day operation. When Timken began to reshape itself to compete in a worldwide economy, those characteristics would also be viewed as obstacles to necessary change. As a result, some of the sharpest reductions in personnel would come in the managerial ranks.

The Managerial Hierarchy

In the 1950s, though, Timken was building its managerial hierarchy and cultivating loyalty and commitment in its salaried staff by creating a ladder of opportunity. The *Trading Post* exuded the spirit of upward mobility. Scores of articles referred to Timken's mandatory retirement age of sixty-five and its "strict policy of promoting from within." That policy, combined with extensive training

Herchel Richey embodied the company's belief in the ability of its people to excel within the organization through hard work and a willingness to learn. With only an eighth-grade education, he began learning the machinist trade as an apprentice, rose to factory manager of the bearing and rock-bit divisions, and later became vice president.

programs, worked to move promising young people up through the organization. William Umstattd was the prime example, but the magazine ran monthly features for nearly two years, in 1951–52, on others who had started at a low level and risen within the system. Of the 60 men featured, Herchel Richey ("a 33-year man") held the highest position: factory manager of the bearing and rock-bit divisions and next in line to be vice president of manufacturing. Richey, the *Trading Post* confided, had only graduated from the eighth grade "on his promise that he would not go on to high school (his grades were exceedingly low)." A machinist apprenticeship had given him his start in a career, and because of his experience he took a special interest "in helping the boys who do not go to college" make careers of their own at Timken.[18]

The road to the upper levels of line management began with the company's apprenticeship and supervisory training programs. The apprenticeship program had been organized in the mid-1930s by Joseph Arthur, director of industrial education in the 1950s. Each year it took in about 45 high-school graduates with good grades and strong math skills and then gave them three to four years of practical training, combined with classroom education. Every apprentice was trained in a specialty—master machinist, electrician, tool and gauge inspector, among others—and was attached to a particular Timken department. At graduation, each received an elaborate wooden toolbox with an engraved silver nameplate. The gift, and the program, made a good corporate investment: 80 percent of apprentice graduates stayed to make careers at Timken; and roughly 40 percent joined the management ranks.[19]

The supervisory training program accepted apprentice graduates, college graduates, "and other carefully selected persons who demonstrate good judgment, discretion and common sense"—an opening for men who started out on the factory floor. The program included classes on management principles and the "technical aspects" of the company's business, "self-improvement courses" in basic business skills and disciplines, and project assignments, in which the trainee had "to study a situation, plan an approach and, if approved, perhaps execute the plan." Those who moved along according to schedule could expect annual raises in salary.[20]

In the steel and tube division, a college degree in metallurgy or engineering was a prerequisite for the supervisory training program. And it was much more informal, involving two years of on-the-job training, after which the graduate immediately became a foreman. Self-improvement courses were optional. In fact, the pattern of success without the advantages of education, celebrated by the *Trading Post,* did not really apply to the steel business. John E. Fick, the division's vice president in the 1950s, was a metallurgical engineer who had started out in the research laboratory in the 1920s. His successor, E. S. (Sarge) Hoopes, Jr., came to Timken with an MBA degree from Harvard. The ladder of opportunity started in a different place in the steel division, but it was still a ladder.[21]

The rule of promotion from within dictated that every division hire only entry-level personnel and maintain substantial training programs. In engineering fields, however, the need for internal development was even greater because of the nationwide shortage of engineers. By one estimate, noted the *Trading Post,* U.S. colleges in 1955 graduated fewer than 60 percent of the new engineers that industry needed. Timken hired as many engineering graduates as it could. Mechanical engineers who looked presentable, were well spoken, showed "a genuine interest in people," and were willing to travel found jobs in the bearing sales departments, where they typically spent three more years in training. Steel sales hired metallurgical engineers and developed them the same way. The engineering division gave its college-educated trainees a two- to four-year course inside the company. It also encouraged them to take postgraduate courses on the outside, to participate in technical societies, and to study for the state licensing exam. For a select group, the company provided a broader program aimed at preparing them for special assignments or executive positions.[22]

In addition, to address the shortage of engineers, Timken selected a handful of promising high-school graduates each year to participate in programs that combined on-the-job training with college education at Georgia Tech, the University of Cincinnati, or Tri-State College in Angola, Indiana. Another program trained young draftsmen and draftswomen in a six-year course that included outside instruction in college-level mathematics. In describing that program the *Trading Post* indicated that starting salaries for women would be "at the level of high school female graduates"—i.e., lower than for men—but that raises could be expected "based on merit" and that they would have "the same opportunity for advancement as the men." In the 1950s, 25 out of 100 draftspersons were women.[23]

As people moved higher up the ladder at Timken, outside education became more important. Financial trainees needed not only a college degree but above-average grades. Most, said the *Trading Post,* had majored in accounting, finance, or business administration, but a liberal arts degree was not a disqualification. While in the four-year training program, they were expected to take graduate-level accounting courses on their own time, and subsequently the company paid full tuition and expenses for those who wished to pursue a law degree in a program of evening classes at Canton's William McKinley School of Law until it closed, and afterward at a law school in nearby Akron.[24]

In fact, the system of promotion from within led the company to support an array of opportunities for continuing education. Supervisory personnel in manufacturing departments took outside courses in finance and business administration to prepare them for taking on wider responsibilities. Beginning in the late 1950s, Timken sent numerous rising executives to management education programs at Harvard Business School and elsewhere. But, for those who wanted it, continuing education was available at all levels and was a route to advancement. For example, it was a path open to the many women who staffed Timken's offices in clerical and secretarial positions. The industrial education department provided information and counseling on continuing education, sent people to service schools and classes conducted by its equipment suppliers, arranged informational courses and refresher courses on specific topics, and conducted college courses at company plants. In sum, the management ladder at Timken was infused with the reality as well as the rhetoric of opportunity. It provided many paths to advancement, and annual salary increases, to men (and, in a more limited way, to women) who worked hard and performed their duties satisfactorily.[25]

Timken's organization resembled the majority of large U.S. industrial firms. "If a classic form could be characterized," wrote Michael Useem, a professor of sociology and management, "it was of a functionally defined hierarchy, with managers arrayed in tall lines of authority presiding over narrow spans of control."[26] Within this hierarchy resided the organizational capabilities essential to Timken's success and also many of the cultural traits that defined the firm at midcentury and would help to determine its future course.

Management Culture

In some ways Timken's culture was pretty typical for the era; in others, far from it. As in most similarly organized companies, the hierarchical order and extreme departmentalization of Timken's management gave rise to status and turf consciousness. Jim Nickas, an estimating engineer who had to work with most of the department heads in order to calculate the cost of the company's products, called them "bulls of the woods"—an allusion to a popular comic strip of the 1950s. They could be overbearing and uncooperative. Those tendencies were reinforced by aspects of the all-male culture, including a lot of practical jokes and some hazing, fueled by a good deal of social drinking in off hours. On the other hand, the system of in-house education and promotion from within fostered a strong sense of shared values and corporate identity. Divorce was frowned upon, and a man could be fired for getting caught in an extramarital relationship. No one bought General Motors cars because they used New Departure-Hyatt, not Timken, bearings. And, lest anyone get too overblown an idea of his own importance, all executives, up through the ranks to the chairman of the board, punched in and out on a time clock every day, just like the folks on the factory floor.[27]

One distinctive aspect of the company's culture that was extremely advantageous, however, was an unusually high level of integration and cooperation between Timken's engineering and development groups and its manufacturing departments. Within the engineering organization, bearing design and tool engineering were combined in a single group, and between engineering and operations there was a level of communication that fostered a mode of development in which questions of manufacturability were considered from the beginning. Said product engineer Jack Richey (Herchel Richey's nephew), "I know that as I worked in the engineering department, I found out that when I had a problem, if I went to the guy that made the piece, he could tell me." In the 1950s, Bob Sisson, plant superintendent at Gambrinus, had an arrangement with Walter Green, who ran Timken's process research and development organization, to exchange personnel from time to time so that machine operators from the plant received training on new equipment and those from the research group kept in touch with operating equipment and routines. Such patterns and attitudes gave Timken a leg up on most functionally organized companies in the critical area of linked process and product development. At the same time, the ongoing relationships with customers maintained by Timken sales engineers helped to set the direction of technical programs and infused the engineering culture with a strong customer orientation.[28]

There were jealousies between departments, of course, but the great cultural divide was between steel and bearings. In many ways it was as if they were two completely separate companies. The businesses of steel making and precision manufacturing were quite different to begin with, the operating managers of the two divisions were different—one group college educated, the other not—and there was no love lost between them. One purpose of the *Trading Post*'s series of articles on the people and work of Timken's various departments was to make "the steel side" and "the bearing side" of the organization better acquainted with, and perhaps a little more appreciative of, each other. George Deal, who observed the situation from the secretary-treasurer's office, explained: "At all times, that steel mill was secondary to the bearing factory. It was, in effect, a captive steel mill, and the steel people didn't like that worth a damn."[29]

One can speculate that things might have been quite different if Mark Lothrop had served a longer term as president, or if Fred Griffiths had succeeded as head of Timken's steel business when it was organized as a subsidiary company. But once it returned to divisional status under Umstattd, it became part of an organization that was a bearing company first and foremost. The intracompany exchange rate gave the bearing division its seamless tubing at cost. It also enjoyed first claim on capacity. Overall, just 30 to 35 percent of steel output went into Timken bearings. But when a major customer like Ford made an urgent request for 10,000 extra bearings, the steel division would have to push all other work aside to produce the required materials. "That's why the steel people would say they felt like second-rate citizens," Deal said. "That was tough," concurred Ralph Shipley, superintendent of the Canton steel and tube plant, who became head of the division in the 1970s. "Our biggest problem," Shipley said, "was that we weren't big enough." In the postwar decades, Timken would expand its melting capacity as far as it could within the space constraints of its site in Canton, but that growth was overshadowed by the much greater expansion of bearing capacity. The steel business would not begin to realize its full economic potential until the completion of the Faircrest plant at a new site in the mid-1980s.[30]

The level of ill will between steel and bearings was at times intense. What held it all together was the overriding sense of Timken's position of leadership in both its industries. The pattern of recruitment and training that had prevailed since the late 1930s had made the management culture overwhelmingly an engineering culture that placed a high value on process as well as product innovation. Ultimately, the fact that the two businesses shared the Timken name counted for more than the jealousies that divided them.

The company was the seventeenth largest U.S. steel producer and the fourth largest producer of alloy steels. Yet, with a program of metallurgical research dating back to 1913, Timken's influence in the fields of electric-furnace steel and specialty alloys far exceeded its size. Martin Fleischmann and Walter Assel attained worldwide reputations in the postwar years, as Timken alloy 16-25-6 became a mainstay of jet-engine manufacture and the Assel mill became the dominant technology for making seamless tubing. (SKF built an Assel mill at its Hofors steelworks in the 1950s.) Timken also had a number of Ph.D. metallurgists who were prominent in their fields of specialization. One important application of seamless tubing was pressure tubing for power plants, and Timken's Dr. Claude L. Clark was the leading U.S. authority on high-temperature metallurgy and corrosion. His

Digest of Steels for High-Temperature Applications, published by Timken in the 1950s, remains a standard reference work today. Dr. E. S. Rowland was a widely published expert on the hardening and hardenability of steels.[31]

Those men came out of the metallurgy program of the University of Michigan, where the company had maintained a collaborative relationship for many years. On the bearing side, Oscar Horger, the authority on testing metals and chief engineer for railroad bearings, was likewise a Michigan Ph.D. Samuel M. Weckstein, an engineer who succeeded Louis Klinedinst as head of the industrial bearing division, was well known in the steel industry for his leadership in developing the use of Timken bearings for many steel-mill applications. Whatever the internal dynamics, within the larger technical community Timken steel and bearing personnel clearly moved in similar circles and stood on an equal footing.[32]

Both sides of the business had sales engineers in the field with links to strong internal engineering groups, a structure that facilitated the development of new applications for seamless tubing just as it did for bearings. In the postwar years, the steel division made great strides in developing new markets for mechanical tubing—seamless tubing used to make metal parts, including not only bearing races, but also gears, drill collars, couplings, and many other items. Timken's product was well suited for mechanical tubing because it was produced to close tolerances, which was important for minimizing scrap in the processes of the parts producers. Timken's technical staff supported customers in developing new designs, just as it did on the bearing side. Tubing for the annular gears used in automatic transmissions, rapidly adopted by the automotive industry in the postwar years, became one of the largest markets for Timken steel. James W. Pilz, a Detroit-based sales engineer for bearings who later became corporate executive vice president and a director, recalled that Timken's steel business was selling to many of the same customers as he was. Chrysler, for example, bought tubing for gears and forging bar for pinions, as well as bearings. He was aware of some frustration among steel personnel—"They were thinking that we were a bearing company and here they were in steel"—but his main impression was one of cooperation. "Even though it wasn't formal," said Pilz, "the people that were calling on the same accounts would get together and compare notes to find out if there was something we should work on together that would help us to beat the competition by going with the steel and bearing combination."[33]

The company's sustained investment in its technologies and technical organizations both reflected and fostered the engineering culture. A generous share of this investment went to the steel side of the business. In an expansion of steel capacity in the early 1950s—a response to the Korean War—Timken replaced its open-hearth furnaces with electric furnaces in order to focus entirely on the higher grades of steel required for bearings and other demanding applications. In the process, its steel-making organization made a number of innovations, including the first application of electromagnetic induction stirring to a large electric furnace, and the adaptation from the ceramics industry of a tunnel-type furnace for thermal treatment that reduced gas consumption and increased production. To improve the quality of its product, it also adopted slow-cooling furnaces that produced metallurgical structures better adapted to machining operations both for bearings and for automotive transmission gears. Finally, a new rotary sizer made it possible to produce a wider range of tubing sizes with greater precision. Those capital investments were balanced by investments in knowledge creation, publicly recognized in 1954 by the American Society for Metals, which gave William Umstattd its Medal for the Advancement of Research.[34]

On the bearing side, Timken had created a centralized organization for process research and development during World War II. The division of development and research was headed by Walter F. Green and Herbert C. Edwards and was located in the old Gilliam plant on Savannah Avenue that had recently been vacated as Timken wound up its contract for making ammunition. For the roughly twenty years of its existence, the division would be known familiarly as "Savannah Avenue." In setting it up, Timken anticipated that its automotive customers, having manufactured aircraft engine parts during the war and become accustomed to working with much closer tolerances, would raise the bar for its suppliers once the war ended. Its own extensive product-testing program had pointed in the same direction, demonstrating the close relationship between "accuracy of manufacture" and bearing life. Based on those indications, the process development group had come up with a research agenda that included projects on surface finish, manufacturing tolerances, bearing geometry, improved materials for cages, and more accurate gauges for inspection and quality control. As in the steel division, that work provided guidance for the equipment investments of the 1950s.[35]

In 1957, Timken announced an across-the-board increase of 10 percent or more in bearing capacity ratings. The revision meant that smaller, hence lighter-weight and less costly, bearings could be used in many existing applications and that the range of applications could be expanded. It was not the first increase in ratings by any means, but it reflected the continuing improvement in bearing performance that depended on a number of factors, such as cleaner steel, smoother surfaces, more precise angles, and new bearing geometry. (See Evolution of the Timken Tapered Roller Bearing on pages 90–92.) One particularly important design change that underlay the ratings increase of this era was crowned rollers, which were slightly convex on the long sides. Under heavy loads, those "crowns" flattened out to the exact taper that was needed for true rolling motion. Such improvements in design went hand in hand with process improvements to make the Timken bearing more competitive, particularly against other types of anti-friction bearings. It all reflected well on the work of Timken's technical community.[36]

The fact that virtually all of the company's domestic bearing competitors relied on Timken steel, and that the likes of Chrysler and Ford remained steel customers even though they sometimes had to wait for delivery, was testimony to the quality of Timken products. On the bearing side, the company was a powerful presence in the industry. Timken performed miracles to deliver bearings to Ford, but it also on occasion went to the brink of stopping shipments rather than submit to Ford's demand for a price reduction—and won its case. There was really no competitor in the domestic market that could step into its shoes in those days. Timken's management acknowledged the central role of its technical organizations in that success by launching, in 1957, a major construction program of three new buildings to provide expanded quarters for product engineering, metallurgical research, and the physical testing laboratory.[37]

Everything about the way the company was run indicated that the engineering culture was as strong at the top of the hierarchy as down in the ranks. The Timken brothers, like Umstattd, viewed the firm as a bearing company. But, again like him, they also viewed steel making as an integral part of the business and critical to its success. Henry Timken's particular interest in steel and its technology gave the division a special status that meant a great deal to its personnel. More generally, the active leadership of both Bob and Henry Timken sustained the sense of mission embodied in the Timken name that was the real antidote to poisonous divisional jealousies.

The Personalities at the Top

Henry Timken—chairman of the board of directors from 1940 until 1968—started his work for the company in the steel mill and in steel sales. He remained particularly interested in that side of the business, but he was fascinated by all of the company's technology and manufacturing operations. Jim Pilz recalled the occasions when Henry accompanied him on sales calls. Said Pilz, "He wanted to pore over the blueprint and see what the latest design was, to understand our role in it." And Henry would always want to call on the customer's engineering departments, not just purchasing. "He was intrigued with technology, whether or not we were a part of it. Anything that was new on the technology side . . . Henry Timken wanted to be there." That attitude helped to shape the company's sustained commitment to improvement of its process technologies. Estimating engineer Jim Nickas, whom Henry frequently called upon to work on development projects, characterized the Timken approach: "It wasn't just sitting there and saying, 'Well, with the machines we have, we can do this.' We would say, 'Well, we can buy a new machine, and we could do a lot better.'"[38]

Henry regularly attended machine-tool shows and often spotted new equip-ment that he wanted to try out in the factory. He was a "genius of a mechanic," recalled Bob Sisson. Once, at a Chicago show, he and Sisson both noticed a large machine of a new design that National Machinery Company called a transfer ma-chine. It had five separate precision dies and could move a piece automatically from one to the next, rapidly performing a series of operations it normally took several different machines to execute. Henry and Sisson calculated that the trans-fer machine could be used to make large rollers and could double the output of the incumbent machine. Henry quickly determined that he wanted to buy one, and after Sisson spent a year of development work with National Machinery, he got one.[39]

Henry was comfortable in asserting his prerogatives, and he could be gruff and intimidating to men he did not know. Yet he endeared himself to those he worked with by his modest personal style, which belied his considerable wealth and his position as chairman of the board. Once, when his station wagon stalled at the main gate to Timken's Gambrinus plant, he blocked the entrance for a half-hour while, with the hood up, he tried to figure out the problem. On a visit to National Machinery in Tiffin, Ohio, Sisson recalled, Henry sat down to lunch, took his jacket off and revealed a hole in the elbow of his shirt. Occasionally he could also be caught with mismatched socks. And he was not above using some "choice shop language" to get a point across. The other side of the coin, how-ever, was a fierce reluctance to play the public role of the corporate top execu-tive. Henry would represent the company in any working meeting, but never on a ceremonial occasion. When voted Canton's man of the year, he flatly refused to accept the honor and went out of town, leaving his brother Bob to stand in his place.[40]

Bob Timken complemented his older brother well. Where Henry's strengths and interests were technical, his were financial. People swore Bob's slide rule was faster than any calculator. He would be the one to say, when Henry and the oth-ers got excited about a new product or process, "Yes, but will it make money?" Bob's responsibilities as vice president were not formally specified. He put in a lot of time on the company's antitrust case, and he reviewed all financial reports. "Bob Timken had a gift for figures," recalled George Deal. "He had an uncanny ability to find a mistake . . . and that served a good function." Although he was very well read and well informed, and a lively conversationalist with close friends, with most people Bob was uncommunicative in the extreme. In the late 1930s, Charley Brower, charged by H. H. with overseeing his son's training, had a tough time reporting on how it was going. "I personally feel that Bob is accomplishing a real knowledge of our activities and is highly interested in his work," Brower wrote. "[But] it is hard to get any reactions from Bob, as you know."[41]

Once he settled in, Bob did not venture out of his office much, though his door was always open. He no more liked to participate in public ceremonies than his brother, but he had a highly developed sense of duty. Bob would give the obligatory speech to a group of Timken managers, or even to a public gathering, but always kept it short—three minutes or less. He particularly disliked entertaining customers and was known to hide out in the tap room of his country club playing gin rummy with his cronies in order to avoid doing so. But when he had to, he provided the public face for both the company and the Timken Foundation.[42]

Each of the Timken brothers brought his own particular talents to bear in the service of the company. Undoubtedly, though, their most important role was to provide the continuity of family engagement, both because the family and foundation still owned 25 percent of the stock and because, while Timken had grown dramatically, it still felt like a family firm—in a good sense—to most people working in it. As in H. H.'s day, the women of the Timken family played no formal role in the company, though they naturally participated in the social life required of all business leaders. (On one occasion, when the social obligations on an overseas trip became excessive, Henry's wife, Louise Blyth Timken, threatened Umstattd that she would demand to be paid if it happened again.) The Timken brothers endeared themselves to many by spurning the mansion in which they had grown up—they gave it to Mercy Hospital in 1950—to live in the same neighborhoods as other company executives. Bob and his wife, Mary Jackson Timken, raised their children to view the company with a sense of responsibility rather than privilege.[43]

Still, Henry and Bob behaved like grandsons of the founder in a variety of ways. They punched a time clock like everyone else when in Canton but vacationed far more liberally than the average Timken executive. Though the company maintained spartan executive offices, it always had the most modern aircraft available for corporate travel, thanks to Henry's passion for flying. Henry had a heart attack in 1952, at the age of forty-six. After that, he spent a lot more time away from the company, on hunting trips to Africa and Europe, and particularly at a beloved cattle ranch in Arizona.[44]

The brothers were also comfortable, as H. H. Timken had been, in giving family members employment and some special treatment. (H. H. had found numerous jobs in the firm for his cousin Ed Heinzelman. When Heinzelman years later complained of not having advanced further within the company, H. H. wrote, "I do not know why you did not develop into one of our strong men here. There has never been any favorites played with our employees, with the possible exception of yourself.") In the late 1940s and 1950s, a cousin, Ring Drummond, was Henry's frequent companion around the plants. Drummond had a chemistry degree from the California Institute of Technology and was a talented inventor. Among other things, the gauging mechanism for the blind was his creation. He was also a free spirit and something of a prankster. With no formal responsibilities (one of his titles was Methods Analyst, but it had no job description), Drummond pursued projects that interested him and thought little of ignoring established procedures or spheres of authority when commandeering personnel and materials to get them done. His presence—sometimes with Bob's sons in tow—contributed to the family feeling about the place.[45]

To people who worked at Timken, there was no question about who was running the company. H. H. had made Bill Umstattd president in 1934, and he had been the boss since then. Many saw Henry and Bob as mere boys compared to the imposing Umstattd—Bob was thirty and Henry thirty-four when their father died. At that time, with World War II looming, said Bob, "If we hadn't had Umstattd on our side, we might have been in real trouble." Those who assumed that Umstattd himself viewed, or treated, the Timken brothers as boys were mistaken, however. From the start, when the inner circle of top management included Louis Klinedinst and Charley Brower, with A. C. Ernst as a trusted outside advisor, decisions were made by consensus. Umstattd "didn't depend on other people's ideas," said Bob, "he thought them up himself. He was an originator of things." But he also sought input from others: "Bill Umstattd was never dictatorial. He was quite willing to listen, even to criticism." By the 1950s, Klinedinst, Brower, and Ernst were no longer on the scene, but the inner circle, now reduced to three, still worked in the same way. No actions were taken except by consensus.[46]

Umstattd derived great strength from the fundamental agreement on principles and policies achieved through that working relationship and the support he received from the Timken brothers as a result—usually behind the scenes, but publicly when necessary, as in a number of emotional confrontations over union contracts. The Timkens made it impossible for critics to portray the company's president as an interloper, largely responsible for the deterioration in labor relations that had occurred since H. H. Timken's day. In other ways as well, Henry and Bob threw the weight of the family name and all it stood for behind him. Of course, the steady commitment of keeping the family wealth tied up in the company was a tacit form of support of inestimable value. All of those things maintained a solid foundation for Umstattd's leadership.[47]

"Uncle Bill"

Bill Umstattd was a walk-around manager if ever there was one. That is what Timken employees invariably mention first when describing him. Every morning around 6:30 he would be in a bearing plant or a steel mill, marching through, looking things over. "He was about six feet or six feet one inch tall," recalled product engineer Jack Richey, "but when he walked through the factory, he looked about seven feet." Because he was such a familiar figure, many people referred to him as "Uncle Bill." Over the course of a day, Umstattd spent

William E. Umstattd
Timken president from 1934 to 1959

about as much time making the rounds of different departments as he did in his office. In the steel mill, said Ralph Shipley, "he wouldn't come out to give orders; he just came out to be friendly." In the engineering departments, he liked to ask questions about new materials, or designs, or ongoing projects. In the bearing plants, however, he rarely passed through without noticing something worth a comment or a question. "He was a factory man from the ground up," said Bob Sisson. "He always was sharp. He could see things that needed to be done, usually to the physical establishment." If he had to speak to a foreman about water or a spilled tray of cups or cones on the floor, he was stern and peremptory: "Young man, I don't know how you're going to get rid of it, but get rid of it!" "He ran [the company] with an iron hand," said George Deal. Umstattd came down hard on anyone he thought was "feeding him a line," and if a man balked at a tough assignment, he would likely be told to do the job or be replaced by someone who would. At the same time, someone Umstattd knew well and trusted could disagree with him and get away with it.[48]

Umstattd was a self-educated man who read a great deal and kept a dictionary at hand in his office. He was deeply committed to Timken's policy of promotion from within and a great believer in lifelong self-improvement. He built up the program to send Timken executives to advanced management training; but he also arranged a course for them in Canton on etiquette, for example the proper use of tableware. Umstattd had joined Timken as a young man and had modeled himself on George Obermier, his mentor, and on H. H. Timken. Like them, he was always polite, correct, and reserved—a man of few words, intimidating to many people. He had a good sense of humor, though, a saving grace for such a stern personality. He also had a thoughtful and generous private side that made him the first person to visit a Timken employee or close friend who landed in the hospital. He was, in short, a man of contrasts. In the winter, Umstattd was known to keep a heater under his desk and open the window to make his office so cold that subordinates coming to speak to him would keep their business short. On the other hand, during a bitter strike in the middle of winter, he opened the gates of the Canton plant so that the pickets, including some who had publicly vilified him, could take coal to heat their homes.[49]

In one respect, however, Umstattd was perfectly consistent. That was in his devotion to the company and to preserving what he deemed its essential characteristics. Most basic, perhaps, was the ethical standard that dictated the company must always be as good as its word. The story from H. H. Timken's day that conveyed this principle involved the bid on an early contract for bearing-equipped axles. H. H. and W. R. had failed to include the cost of wheels, which were part of the order. They absorbed the cost and completed the contract, losing a lot of money they could barely afford, but gaining a reputation for honorable dealings. Umstattd had a similar story of his own. During the Depression, a bearing Timken had developed for mine cars proved to have a faulty collar: it held the bearing on the axle but failed to keep it aligned and tight. The replacement cost was substantial, but, said Umstattd, "We assumed that whole cost and as a consequence we got perhaps 98 percent of the mine car business in the U.S." Going forward, he insisted that Timken should always bear the cost of fixing not only its own mistakes but also mistakes its customers made, if it could have advised them better. Another firm rule: if the company quoted a price on a bearing for a particular application, that was the price for all buyers. Timken gave volume discounts but did not cut special deals. Customers, suppliers, and union leaders could all testify to the fact that Umstattd and Timken were hard-nosed but always straight in their dealings.[50]

Other characteristics of the way H. H. Timken did business—sustained capital investment combined with avoidance of debt—became fundamental tenets of operation in the Umstattd era. Of course, H. H. had used bank loans in the 1920s when necessary, but the company had sweated out the repayment during the 1920–21 depression. The experience of seeing many companies fail in the Great Depression because of indebtedness had settled Timken firmly on the policy of maintaining cash reserves and spurning borrowing. Said George Deal, "We never borrowed a dime from anybody. The bankers would come in here and just almost beg to loan us some money. We'd say, 'Thank you but we have no need for it.'" This policy drew attention in mid-1958, when the company announced a $51-million program for new plant and equipment in the midst of a recession that had industry generally cutting capital spending by some 17 percent. Though Timken's revenues and forecasts were down, the company had a large cash reserve because the year before it had raised $19 million by issuing and selling nearly 500,000 shares of new common stock. Apparently, even dilution of ownership was preferable to incurring debt in the corporate mindset of the time.[51]

As freely as money was spent on new machinery, however, it was begrudged to office furnishings. Although sales grew by a factor of twelve and earnings by a factor of nine under his leadership, Umstattd scorned the idea of outfitting executive offices as many would have thought appropriate to a company Timken's size. They were virtually as they had been remodeled by H. H. in the early 1930s, with dark wood paneling (folks in the plant called the area "mahogany row"), but only halfway up the walls, because the top half was all glass. H. H. had adopted that design, he said, because "one of the most intelligent rich men I ever knew advised me . . . that if some day some adventuress came in to see me in an entirely closed-in private office a beautiful opportunity would arise for a blackmail case."[52]

To be sure, there was a reasonable business rationale for a modest corporate style—it would be more difficult to hold the line against requests for price reductions from the likes of Ford and Chrysler if money was spent on visible executive perks. But Timken's practice seemed a bit extreme to most observers. Frederick C. Crawford, president of auto parts supplier Thompson Products, Inc., and later TRW, remembered his first visit to the executive offices—to all appearances merely a glassed-in section of the Canton bearing plant. "I said, 'Bill, this is a very humble spot for the fellow making so damn much money.' They were very profitable then. And Umstattd said, 'Well, Mr. Timken used to say that's why we're making money.'"[53]

Finally, William Umstattd was fanatical about the Timken bearing. He raised the competition between tapered roller bearings and ball bearings to something like a holy war. "Ball bearings was a dirty word within The Timken Company," recalled Jim Nickas. "We didn't want to be working around someone and hear him even talk about ball bearings." Every piece of equipment that came into the plants, down to the printing press that stamped the sales motto of that era ("Timken bearings roll the load") on packing boxes and crates, had to come equipped or be refitted with Timken bearings on its moving parts. Umstattd was mortified the day that the president of Daimler-Benz ribbed him about his cane, which had a tripod base attached by a rickety ball-and-socket joint. After that, he had a new cane made in-house, something more fitting for the president of Timken, with a specially designed tapered roller bearing at the joint.[54]

Henry and Bob Timken shared those values. As major stockholders and board members, they had to approve the company's capital expenditures and financial policies, of course, and they fully supported the spartan corporate style. Indeed, Henry resisted any remodeling or redecorating of his office long after others had gotten new curtains and furniture. He also used his father's desk for many years, refusing to get it refinished to remove the many cigarette burns that were testimony to H. H.'s heavy habit. When Bob Timken, an avid sailor, bought a new yacht that had ball bearings on the steering-gear pulleys, a Timken engineer had to go to work with the designer on a substitution of tapered roller bearings. When it turned out this would hold up delivery of the boat, Bob said some other bearing would be okay, for example, needle bearings—anything but ball bearings.[55]

In one major respect, however, Umstattd differed dramatically from all the Timkens. That was in the way he took to, and enjoyed, having a public persona as president of an important industrial corporation. The company's tough stand against key labor union demands made him a lightning rod for attacks from that quarter, and Bill Umstattd gave as good as he got. In politics he was an unabashed conservative in an ideological age and became a spokesman for the cause in his speeches and through corporate advertising. For that, as well as for his leadership of The Timken Roller Bearing Company through a period of strong profitability and growth, he was well known and respected within the business community.

Politics and Labor

When he first became president, Umstattd had little experience with public appearances or public speaking. In the 1930s, the company had kept a low profile, to the point of being isolated. But when it began to have labor troubles in the 1940s, Umstattd decided to make Timken better known in the community. In addition to the radio broadcasts, he began to host luncheons for local businessmen, professionals, and civic leaders, and to give speeches on those occasions. "He started to give talks and he loved it," George Deal recalled. "He would give a talk to anybody. He was very intelligent. Everybody was anxious to hear Bill Umstattd." Beyond mere enjoyment, however, there was a sense of mission in his new public role. "Twenty years ago a manufacturer would not have been put in the position of having to defend private enterprise," Umstattd noted to a crowd of three hundred in February 1949, "but today we must defend it vigorously because it is being attacked in all quarters of the globe."[56]

Umstattd also began to gain a reputation in the business community because of his handling of relations with the United Steelworkers, which represented the majority of Timken's employees in the 1950s. When the Canton plants were first unionized in the late 1930s, he had personally negotiated with the USW, and he remained closely involved in labor policy after setting up a director of labor relations in the 1940s. The USW's I. W. Abel, Harry Mayfield from Columbus, and Abel's successor in the district, John S. Johns, were formidable opponents. On a personal level, the two sides respected each other as hard-nosed but honest, worthy opponents whose word could be trusted. Publicly, they waged a bitter war of propaganda, in which each attacked the other in the strongest possible terms.

The tone was captured, if not set, by a 1947 *Life* magazine feature on labor relations "in the industrial heart of America." Written by John Dos Passos, a well-known novelist and author of widely read books of commentary on the national scene, the piece included a thinly disguised section on Canton and Timken that portrayed Umstattd as a shrewd climber "who made himself indispensable to the old man" and ended up "in the old man's shoes." H. H. Timken had been a boss who "knew everybody who worked for him and everybody knew him." In contrast, Dos Passos said of Umstattd, quoting one of the working men he interviewed, "'This guy stalks through the plant straight as a ramrod looking like a Prussian general, never speaks to an employe [sic] except maybe to bawl out a foreman because the sweepers aren't keeping up with the litter on the floor of the shop. A regular Nazi. . .'"[57] Those were harsh terms in 1947. Not long after the article was published, Umstattd's older son, William Jr., died from the effects of being held in a prison camp during World War II. Umstattd was justifiably enraged by the *Life* article.

Yet the whole debate was highly charged, and he was deeply involved in it. He frequently portrayed union leaders as manipulating the rank and file to serve their own ambitions and labeled them as outright communists, if not tools of the Soviet Union in its effort to win the war of economic systems. Timken did a lot of political advertising. A major theme was the evil of inflation, driven by wage increases not supported by increased productivity and inevitably followed by price increases. One ad that ran over a period of several years in local newspapers and national publications, such as *U.S. News and World Report* and the *Wall Street Journal,* included sketched portraits of Lenin and Stalin with a quotation in bold letters: "We shall force the United States to *spend* itself into destruction." At the bottom was the trademark tag line: "The right to work shall not be abridged or made impotent." Another series of ads took on the right-to-work issue directly. It defended the freedom to choose whether or not to join a union as "a basic American right." In 1958 Timken moved from words to action, playing a highly visible role in an unsuccessful petition drive for a constitutional amendment to make Ohio a right-to-work state.[58]

In addition, the company ran many advertisements aimed at raising public consciousness of what Umstattd called "confiscatory taxes and reckless spending by Government." The Washington bureaucrat was portrayed as a villain in a series that complained about money appropriated for "local improvements" that "melts away in Washington before it ever gets back home." Harsher still was Timken's criticism of the U.S. Justice Department. Its antitrust suits—which, stated one ad, too many companies settled by paying a fine in order to avoid costly and time-consuming litigation—amounted to "legalized racketeering."[59]

On one level, Timken's advertising campaign must be seen as part of a broad phenomenon, the widespread reaction by U.S. businessmen to the dramatic changes emanating from the New Deal. But the effect within the company was to maintain the polarization that had developed during the political contests of the 1930s. Naturally, the union countered Timken's advertising program. In Columbus, in 1950, the CIO launched a weekly radio show, called "Background for Thinking," that tackled Timken's advertisements head-on and decried its "desperate attempt to instill fear in the minds of workers and to bring discredit upon our federal government and the Congress of Industrial Organizations." In Canton the USW's *Golden Lodge News* countered the company's accusations of Soviet influence with charges of "Gestapo tactics" and "sweatshop" conditions in Timken plants. On a couple of occasions the USW called for boycotts of the company's products. Umstattd personally addressed every single union charge, as well as many issues of his own choosing, in a monthly page-long statement in the *Trading Post,* titled "Memo from the President."[60]

Although the vast majority of the men running large U.S. corporations was ideologically and practically opposed to labor unionism, few involved themselves in labor relations to the extent that Umstattd did. In the early days when he handled union negotiations himself, he established a style of managing contract talks that became a permanent feature at Timken. He insisted that all negotiations take place only during business hours. The company timed the meetings with a clock that rang at starting times, breaks, and the end of the day. No Timken negotiator was going to get worn down, perhaps to the point of giving in on minor issues that could add up to a major concession, by a meeting that dragged on into the night. The company employed a court stenographer for every meeting and posted transcripts in its employment office so that anyone could read exactly what had been said. The time off and the transcripts also enabled Umstattd and other top managers to give direction to the company's representatives.[61]

Those ground rules, strictly enforced, made it easier for Timken to keep a tight rein on the process of negotiation. The situation within the USW also on occasion worked to its advantage. The major steel producers bargained as a group with the union. Then the national organization put a good deal of pressure on locals in the rest of the industry to accept that so-called pattern contract. Timken could put the local in a tough position by offering a better economic package than the pattern contract. For example, in 1949 the company was willing to extend to its hourly employees the combination of a contributory pension plan and a fully paid health insurance plan then in place for salaried personnel. The union was forced to press for a fully paid pension plan patterned on one granted by Bethlehem Steel and others after a massive strike that had idled some 500,000 steelworkers. After its own extended strike, the company accepted the Bethlehem plan. But in order to get that concession, the union had to agree to a contributory health insurance plan and an overall package that, they were forced to admit, was inferior to what Timken had originally offered. Such situations bolstered one of management's most fundamental arguments against the union—that its leadership was primarily interested in "unionism on a national basis," while the company was interested "only in our own people."[62]

Timken's focus in all its dealings with the union was on preserving its "right to manage." Following the prolonged 1946 strike, the company had won a "reserved rights contract," the essence of which was that management maintained all existing rights and powers unless specifically limited by future contracts. That placed it in a strong position going into negotiations. Most years in the 1950s, Timken succeeded in keeping the focus on wages, vacations, paid holidays, and the like. It haggled over dollars and cents up until the final days before contracts were due to expire, then granted all that was requested in that area in return for concessions on right-to-manage issues. By meeting or exceeding the financial provisions of the pattern contracts, it maintained many management prerogatives that Big Steel gave up, such as the right to make temporary assignments and the right to discipline for absenteeism without intervention from the union.[63] On two occasions, in 1952 and 1959, Timken took strikes rather than submit to union demands. In 1952 the issues were seniority (how it would be used in filling openings) and the closed, or union shop. In a union shop, all of the workers had to belong to the union. The USW won a "modified union shop" from Big Steel, which provided that new hires would have an opportunity to resign from the union within their first thirty days of employment. Timken resisted that plan mainly because it would have required existing non-union employees to join. After a thirty-three-day strike it accepted the modified union shop but with provisions that non-union employees could not be forced into the union, and that members could have an opportunity to leave the union within a specified ten-day period at the end of each contract period. The company's resistance to the union shop, combined with its aggressive efforts in the war of words, had the desired effect: in the first four years of the modified union shop, according to the estimate of the *Golden Lodge,* 42 percent of new employees elected not to remain in the union beyond the initial sign-up period.[64]

Umstattd's approach to dealing with the USW largely succeeded in fending off the incursions of the union into management's domain. Yet the ideological contest he waged with such vigor left a legacy of mutual hostility between Timken's management and its unionized workforce that fed on passions inflamed by heated rhetoric and spilled over into violence during strikes. The heightened atmosphere of distrust contributed to the strain of authoritarianism developing within the culture of the managerial hierarchy and raised a further barrier to communication and cooperation between supervisors and shop-floor personnel. Overcoming that legacy would be one of the biggest challenges facing Timken in the 1980s in its drive to remain competitive in a global economy.

However, the threat of serious competition from abroad was barely on the horizon in the 1950s. The decade saw economic expansion and retraction linked to the Korean War and later to a recession in 1958. But in general the 1950s began a period of solid growth at home and abroad that continued for nearly twenty years. The outstanding success of the Bucyrus plant contributed additional momentum to Timken's growth.

FOCUS CHAPTER

Bucyrus

Timken Company lore places Henry Timken (H. H. Timken, Jr.) and vice president for engineering Albert Bergstrom on a train from Detroit to Canton in February 1947—possibly returning from a meeting with Ford—when Bergstrom sketched a diagram of an automated continuous cup line on a tablecloth. Within three years, the company would have a pilot line in operation, located 90 miles west of Canton in Bucyrus, Ohio. By 1953, the output of a full-scale plant—with five cup lines and six cone lines, and using cages and rollers supplied from Canton and Columbus—would be 30 million fully assembled bearings per year. That was well over half the combined annual production of Timken's other plants. Bucyrus, and "the Bucyrus concept" that evolved out of it, would govern the company's strategy for thirty years.

Bucyrus was a product of its time. Shortly after World War II, there was a wave of excitement in the technical and business communities about "automation." The term was first used in 1946 by a Ford vice president to describe the workings of a new Ford engine plant, and it was rapidly popularized after appearing in a 1948 article in *American Machinist*. The basic elements of automated production were far from new. In the words of historian Carroll Pursell, it involved "machines to do the actual production of goods, other machines to move the workpiece between the production machines, and some control system to regulate the whole process." Computers, a wartime development, would provide the ultimate control system. They were first adopted in the late 1950s in the oil refining and chemical industries as well as in some other continuous process industries. But automation proceeded initially in the metalworking industries on the basis of long-established technologies for governing machine operations, such as hydraulic and electromechanical actuators, mechanical stops, and cams—irregularly shaped wheels mounted on rotating shafts that, as the shafts turned, controlled the motion of contacting parts. Such devices had been used on machine tools since the end of the Civil War to render at least part of their operations automatic. Transfer machinery, first used by Waltham Watch Company in 1888, had been the key to Henry Ford's achievement of true mass production with the introduction of the moving assembly line in 1913. It was widely used by automakers by the 1930s.[1]

What was new about the postwar concept of automation was the idea of bringing "self-acting" machine tools, transfer mechanisms, and controls together in a production system that both maximized output and minimized labor. In 1920, A. O. Smith Company of Milwaukee had pioneered such a system for production of automobile frames, but that remained a solitary example of the potential in automation. In the auto supply industry, where the volume requirements were high, metal fabricators like Timken had stuck with batch methods and obtained volume output by assembling huge departments of special-purpose machine tools. But the engineering and production achievements made during the war created a new sense of what was technically possible. It was matched in the late 1940s by growing confidence that markets would expand in the postwar economy—as indeed they did, under the influence of government programs (both military and civilian) and consumer spending fueled by the pent-up demand and high savings rates of the war years. Also, undeniably, the union gains of the late 1930s and the widespread strikes of the immediate postwar years prompted industry leaders to try to gain greater management control over production through technology. All of those factors contributed to the enthusiasm for automation, and provided the context in which Timken developed the Bucyrus plant.[2]

At the same time, many streams of prior development within the company came together to shape its decision on automation and make Bucyrus possible. Notwithstanding the early example of A. O. Smith and Ford's engine-plant leadership, it was risky to attempt to build a fully automated plant for a precision, heat-treated product such as the anti-friction bearing. Timken was near the forefront of automation within the metalworking industries and was the first bearing producer in the world to achieve a continuous process from green machining up to bearing assembly. The company's ready embrace of the concept of automation, and its ultimate success in achieving it, could not be explained without reference to the leadership of Henry Timken and others who were committed to keeping Timken on the forward edge of development in its process technologies, and more broadly to the strength of its engineering capabilities and culture.

Timken had had striking success at the Timken Ordnance Company plant in moving the workpieces (in that case, large gun-barrel tubes) from station to station via an overhead conveyor system. Henry Timken had been deeply engaged in the project. He had spent much of his time in the plant, sometimes running the equipment himself. That experience undoubtedly opened the door for the design of a bearing plant on similar principles.[3]

The impetus for development of automated production technologies also came, in part, from Timken's division of development and research—Savannah Avenue. The committee that oversaw its formation in October 1943 had included Henry Timken, Al Bergstrom, and Albert M. Donze, vice president for manufacturing. Until then, the company had maintained a number of separate process engineering groups, located in several different plants. This situation, the committee noted, was "unsatisfactory" because experimental work was "not entirely segregated from production work," and because it could not easily be coordinated. Another consideration, however, was secrecy. Much of the work, said the committee, "is expected to be of a patentable nature or of a nature that should be safeguarded as trade secrets." Access to the Savannah Avenue facility would be strictly limited, and the mechanics and machine operators recruited from the plants to work there were to be placed on salary, with full benefits, in order to secure their loyalty and forestall the possibility of their being hired away by competitors.[4] H. H. Timken had always viewed innovation in manufacturing processes as a valuable competitive weapon. His successors did, too, and they looked ahead to the likelihood that competition would be intense in the postwar world.

The work conducted at Savannah Avenue would have wide-ranging effects, but two related developments, in particular, paved the way to Bucyrus. The first of those was an advance, not in technology, but in understanding the economics of production. It came from a program that, reminiscent of Frederick W. Taylor's "scientific management" studies in the early 1900s, aimed at establishing maximum production levels on different machines in order to set incentive bonus rates. (Another reason to enhance the status of machine operators at Savannah Avenue was to encourage them to put their best efforts into this task.) Once the company began to get reliable data on the subject, it began calculating its production costs as a function of the cost of running the machine (capital cost, electricity, labor, overhead) divided by the number of pieces produced per hour. Those calculations made it readily apparent that Timken could make significant cost reductions by producing fewer bearing sizes in much larger quantities, particularly in automotive bearings, where the volume was potentially quite large.[5]

H. H. Timken had, of course, understood the economics of volume production. By 1915, he had determined that the future success of the company depended on securing its business with the major auto manufacturers by operating on the principle of "large volume based on a small profit." Yet, for decades—as was common in oligopolistic, capital-intensive industries in the United States— Timken had maintained its share of the automotive market without significant price competition. It had an estimating department that figured production costs for new bearing designs, and it had methods of calculating costs for purposes of accounting and financial reporting. But, in a pattern that was widespread in U.S. industry, Timken had long since given up close examination of the costs of its standard bearings and had been operating profitably without it. The information on the hourly cost of running each machine was therefore an eye opener. It laid a new foundation for cost estimating and pricing of new bearing designs and of bearings produced in small numbers for industrial customers, and it prompted reexamination of the automotive bearing business.[6]

One outcome of Timken's working closely with its automotive customers over the years had been that each customer was buying bearings designed specifically for its cars. (The policy of limiting designs and sizes that H. H. and W. R. Timken had maintained in the company's first decade had apparently given way as more and more of its business came in large orders from the major automakers.) The automobiles that went into production at the end of World War II called for about 40 different sizes of Timken bearings. The company's improved grasp of its unit costs provided the basis for approaching its automotive customers with a proposal to standardize on a much smaller range of sizes, which would be priced significantly lower through high-volume production. Standardization would become a central element of the Bucyrus concept.[7]

Another important development to come out of Savannah Avenue—tungsten-carbide tooling—offered a potential breakthrough in machine productivity that would make the terms of Timken's proposal on standardization truly attractive to its customers. Tungsten carbide is an extremely hard compound of carbon and the metallic element tungsten. It was introduced to U.S. industry as a material for cutting tools by the German steel maker Krupp in the late 1920s and, having undergone further development, became widely used in the automotive industry by the mid-1930s. Much more costly than tool steel, tungsten carbide was economical for mass-production systems because it offered longer tool life and much improved performance. When the master machinists at Savannah Avenue experimented on machines with tungsten-carbide cutting surfaces, the results were dramatic. A

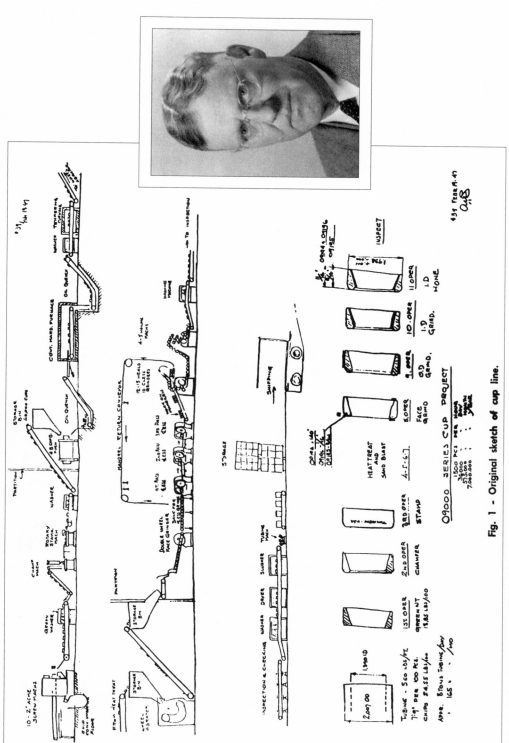

Fig. 1 – Original sketch of cup line.

This sketch drawn on a paper tablecloth in 1947 by Albert Bergstrom (pictured right), vice president of engineering, established the concept of automated, high-volume bearing production pioneered at Bucyrus.

single-spindle screw machine set up to cut lengths of seamless tubing into cups or cones produced eight times more per hour than the same machine with a cutting edge made of steel. It also made cuts with greater precision, producing far less scrap in the process.

Thus, by 1946, the work at Savannah Avenue had given the company an economic analysis that pointed toward high-volume production and the technology to make it successful. Timken's automotive customers responded positively to its proposal to sell them lower-priced bearings in a limited number of standardized sizes, and the company determined to proceed with development. It was at that stage that Henry Timken and Al Bergstrom sat down to brainstorm the layout of an automated plant and a conveyor system that would move material continuously from the first cut of seamless tubing to the packaging of finished bearings.[8]

The ideas behind Umstattd's wartime experiments in retraining machine operators and reorganizing their work resurfaced as plans progressed for a pilot facility. By Umstattd's own account, he was the one who pressed for a nonindustrial location in discussions with Henry Timken, Bergstrom, and Herchel Richey. But it is likely that everyone in management was thinking along similar lines. They wanted to hire young men off the farm and train them as Umstattd envisioned, to run screw machines, grinders, honing machines, and assembly machines, all equally well, and to work in groups with responsibility for overall output, not just the production of a single machine. Here again there was an element of Taylorism—Taylor also had had the idea of hiring and training unskilled workers in order to implement new operating practices. On the other hand, in its elements of cross-training and teamwork, the plan anticipated the much more worker-friendly (and empowering) management trends of the 1980s and 1990s.[9]

Another important consideration for Umstattd, Henry Timken, and the others was the desire to move to a non-union environment. They believed that there was enough of the small businessman in most farmers that the ethos of the community, and therefore of the new plant, would be resistant to unions. Bucyrus was a relatively small town, somewhat over 12,000 in population, surrounded by farmland. It had a few other industrial companies (including a rubber company that was unionized), but Timken would be the major employer. Finally, Bucyrus was strategically located. It was about halfway between Canton and Detroit on a major east-west highway and a railroad line. It was also far enough from Canton to comply with the U.S. government's post–World War II request that Timken build any future bearing plants outside the radius of destruction of an atomic bomb (calculated to be 60 miles) so that in the event of war no more than one plant could be destroyed by a single hit. On many counts, Bucyrus fit the bill for the proposed automated plant.[10]

With all the elements of the Bucyrus concept in place—standardization, automation, and a fresh start on industrial relations—Timken's engineering organizations mobilized to make that concept a reality. One essential step was to establish which bearing sizes should be offered as "standard." At Bergstrom's urging, Timken's product engineers attempted to go beyond simply selecting from existing bearings to new designs that would offer improvements across a range of applications beyond the automotive industry. The first such new design was for front-wheel bearings, the most common automotive application. Recalled Timken product engineer Jack Richey, "We just cut them down as small as we could on the O.D. and as narrow as we could." As the project moved forward, the design evolved, so that eventually the new front-wheel bearings, though smaller and lighter weight than the previous design, could carry greater loads. They were also designed so that the surrounding parts could be simpler and more compact, hence less expensive for automakers to manufacture. In all, Timken designated 13 different bearing sizes for high-volume production.[11]

Another critical part of the program was development of the high-volume production equipment needed to achieve the goals set for the plant. The machines that Timken wanted could not be bought: its need for fast, economical production dictated relatively simple, single-purpose equipment, while the trend in the machine-tool industry had for many years been toward larger, more complex and versatile machines. In addition, continuous flow required numerous changes in the mechanisms for feeding each workpiece into each machine, positioning it, and controlling its exit as it moved on to the next step. Timken worked closely with ten different machine-tool and equipment suppliers, funding their research and development costs as well as its own, in order to get what it needed. Where machines were specially designed, the engineers at Savannah Avenue made wooden models first, then prototypes that could be tested fully and revised before the equipment was ordered in quantity and placed on a production line. Much of this development took place at a pilot facility in Bucyrus, a building purchased from Smith Tool and Engineering Company, which was moving to Cleveland. Timken took over the plant, hired a few of Smith's employees, and moved part of its Savannah Avenue staff there in January 1948. An experimental cup line would be the means by which it developed and proved the Bucyrus concept. The pilot plant produced its first cups in June, but not until early 1950 was all the new equipment fully developed, installed, and sufficiently proven for the company to commit to investing in a full-scale plant.[12]

The steps involved in developing the single-spindle screw machines that handled the first step of green machining were representative of the kind of problem solving needed to get the Bucyrus plant up and running. One question that arose early was whether it would be possible to start the process with seamless tubing that had been hot-rolled only, not finished to exact dimensions by an additional step of cold-rolling. To do so would save $2 to $4 per tube. The challenge was to adapt the screw machine to be able to position each tube correctly for cutting, even though the outside diameters of the tubes could vary as much as 0.06

inches. On standard machines, hot-rolled tubing was positioned by hand. For the Bucyrus plant, Timken and the three suppliers working with it on screw machines adapted a kind of washer, called a Belleville spring, that enabled a positioning device to maintain constant pressure over a range of tube sizes. The need to keep machine downtime to an absolute minimum—an essential element of continuous processing—dictated another important design feature. This involved placing the cutting tools in tool holders that could be fitted easily into the proper position in the machine. Multiple sets of these assemblies, all interchangeable, allowed the plant to keep preground, preset tools always at the ready for tool changes with virtually no downtime. With the tool holders, it was also possible to design for quick, easy adjustments of tool position when setting up for a different-sized part. And the design permitted timely, scheduled tool changes that averted the possibility of dull tools causing loss of precision—a quality-control method borrowed from the manufacturers of aircraft engines.[13]

In order to realize the productivity opportunities made possible by tungsten-carbide cutting tools, Timken's engineers needed to come up with a way to handle the cut-off chips. If not removed, they could build up and jam the machine, causing serious tool damage. Part of the solution was to use two cutting tools. A breakdown tool made the first rough cut; a second, finishing tool cut the parts to close tolerance. The interaction between the two allowed the chips to fall down, out of the tools' working area. Specially designed chip breakers reduced them in size, and chips, plus coolant, then flowed out through a hole in the machine's base into a sluiceway. A pick-off device caught the finished piece and placed it on a conveyor to move on to the next step. Below, chips and coolant were separated, the coolant to recirculate and the chips to be sent back to the Canton steel mill and remelted. That recycling system was an original design from Savannah Avenue.[14]

In addition to cutting tools, each screw machine had tools for boring, turning, and forming—four separate tool mountings on each machine for all the steps involved in shaping a cup or cone. Another Timken innovation was the system of cams that controlled the movement of the tools and returned them quickly, once each piece was finished, back into position to start a new piece. That system alone, Timken calculated, increased the productivity of each machine by as much as 30 percent. Grinding machines, honing machines, automatic gauging machines, wrapping and packing machines all received the same kind of attention.[15]

Another critical area of innovation was heat treatment. Entirely new equipment and methods were required to convert a batch process involving multiple heating and cooling steps into a continuous flow. Timken's heat-treat specialist, Leo Everitt, worked closely with its principal contractor in this field, Surface Combustion Corporation of Toledo, Ohio, to devise solutions to the many technical problems this posed. Five furnace lines, including 22 furnaces, handled the carburizing, case hardening, and tempering of cups and cones in various sizes. The all-important control system used microswitches and in some places photoelectric eyes to keep the pieces moving smoothly, and automatically, through the line. It was, said Everitt and O. E. Cullen, chief metallurgist for Surface Combustion, a "push-button heat treat operation." It could be run by five machine attendants, whose responsibilities included sampling and testing, watching warning lights, and monitoring control instruments.[16]

Because the furnaces had to run continuously to operate economically, and because the rest of the plant ran on a five-day week, an important aspect of the conveyor system that moved material through the plant was buffering or "product banking." Green-machined pieces accumulated in storage bins on the front end of the heat-treatment lines at the end of the week. By Monday, the bins on the discharge end were full of heat-treated cups and cones. Buffering at various spots in the plant, either in bins or spiral storage devices, protected the flow against disruptions and made it possible to change over routinely from one size bearing to another without having to stop the entire line. Timken called the bearings made at Bucyrus "Green Light" bearings to signify that the lines were always running.[17]

In March 1950, Timken pronounced its pilot a success and announced that it would build a full-scale production plant in Bucyrus. The company bought an 87-acre tract of land just outside the town limits from a local farmer, Austin C. Yaussey. The town and county joined forces to supply sewer and water links to the site. Following a ceremonial exchange of check and deed in the Yaussey farmhouse kitchen, some 40 local officials and businessmen joined Timken executives in a banquet to celebrate the coming of a new $4,000,000 plant that was to employ roughly 600 people. The facility was built in two stages. The first building, with five cup lines, became operational in mid-1951; the second, with six cone lines, came on line in early 1953.[18]

In 1956, Timken opened a second facility next to the plant, the Bucyrus Distribution Center. This was another ambitious undertaking for its time, a consolidation of product distribution for all of Timken's U.S. bearing plants. The company's customers were beginning to implement closer inventory controls, and they wanted Timken's shipping dates to be coordinated with their production schedules—a foretaste of just-in-time delivery. As long as each plant had its own shipping department, it would be difficult for the company to meet that customer need. One of the main ideas behind the distribution center was Henry Timken's: a proposal to store items randomly, rather than grouped by part number, in order to minimize the amount of warehouse space required. Computerization was the key to making this work. Stock came into the center during the day and was moved by conveyor to its storage place, the location of each piece recorded on punched cards. The day shift also drew up shipping orders and recorded those on cards as well. The midnight shift pulled the stock and sent it to the packing area to be shipped the following day. Integrated data processing allowed records to be linked and reports to be generated with a minimum of manual effort. An IBM 650 computer that filled an entire room at the Canton plant processed the cards and controlled all the inventory and shipping. One former employee recalled that the distribution center "was set up to receive at one end and plug through the process—just like a manufacturing plant." By 1957 it was handling more than 10 million pieces per month.[19]

The location in Bucyrus provided the kind of clean slate for training personnel that Umstattd, Herchel Richey, and other Timken executives had hoped for. The pilot line employed about 30 people, including 7 women. About 400 people worked at the Bucyrus plant in the early 1950s; with the shipping center, it would have 700 employees by 1957. They came largely from Bucyrus and the surrounding area, and a great many were World War II veterans. Most had completed high school, some had attended college, and all had taken and passed a mechanical aptitude test. Only the plant manager, Russell P. Fowler, and the superintendent, Edward Barwick, had any prior experience in making bearings. Glenn Wilson, who hired on in 1949 and became a supervisor in machine repair, recalled that it was the engineers from Savannah Avenue—the men who had designed the machines and the continuous line—who provided the training in the early years.[20]

Within the bearing plant, machine attendants, maintenance personnel, and foremen all received broad training that enabled them to work in any area of the operation. A machinist or maintenance man, for example, learned to handle millwright duties, machine repair, plumbing, and electrical repairs. Practically everyone in the plant rotated through different jobs on a regular basis. Timken got the "universal workers" that Umstattd had wanted, by selection and training and by changing the nature of the work. These were machine attendants, no longer machine operators. To engender the proper respect for the equipment, Timken labeled each machine prominently with the amount it had cost. A motto engraved on a plaque in the front office of the Bucyrus plant captured the pervasive engineering ethos: "You can't build today's products with yesterday's machines and be in business tomorrow."[21]

In the automated plant, machines reigned supreme, but they created jobs for humans that were better in many respects than those in conventional plants, beginning with broader training and less routinized tasks. Each production line was divided into groups, and bonus incentives were awarded by group, based on the number of pieces produced. While there were some fourteen levels of basic compensation, every hourly worker in the plant received a bonus on the same principles. In the 1950s, bonuses were typically 20 to 30 percent of base pay. Timken paid the highest wages in the area by a good margin. (In order to minimize the resentment that caused among local employers, the company adopted a policy of refusing to hire anyone away from another employer.) People at Bucyrus understood that the company's desire to keep the plant non-union was largely responsible for the high wages and innovative policies from which they were benefiting. Yet that did nothing to undermine the goodwill engendered by its desirable working environment. Moreover, there was a strong family feeling, which the company cultivated much as it did in Canton with recreational events, particularly sports competitions. Numerous families had more than one member working in the plant, and in general people knew each other and got along well. Within the plant there was the sense that everyone in the area who wanted an industrial job wanted to work for Timken. One of the lucky ones said, "You had to almost know somebody who knew somebody to get in." Despite numerous organizing drives, the Bucyrus plant would remain non-union.[22]

Timken kept its Bucyrus operations secret for quite a while. A meeting of sales representatives held there in 1955 was the first time anyone had seen the inside except the plant's employees and a small number of engineers and top executives. After that, the company began inviting some of its customers for tours. In September 1957, though, it threw off the wraps completely, issuing an invitation to magazine and newspaper editors from major U.S. cities and Europe to visit Bucyrus at Timken's expense and to tour the plant, taking whatever pictures and asking whatever questions they wanted.[23]

The event that precipitated Timken's publicity effort was unexpected. It was the publication in *American Machinist,* in January 1957, of an admiring article on a Soviet automated bearing factory that produced 1.5 million bearings per year, 40 percent of them tapered roller bearings. The piece described features similar to those of the Bucyrus plant, including continuous heat treatment, tungsten-carbide tooling, centerless grinding, tool holders, chip breakers, and automatic gauging. According to its author (the London editor of *American Machinist),* the article, with extensive photographs, provided a corrective to the "serious underestimation" of Soviet technical capabilities by the West. The magazine touted it as "the first detailed report to appear anywhere on the manufacture of bearings without use of a single operator."[24]

The challenge would have been difficult for Timken to pass up under any circumstances. At the end of the war in 1945, Umstattd, Bergstrom, and Oscar Horger, chief of Timken's railroad division, had traveled to Moscow with the expectation of selling bearings and advising the Soviet government on the manufacture of tapered roller bearings. They had made no sales but had come away with an awareness of Soviet plans for rapid recovery, modernization, and postwar production, including production of bearings, on an unprecedented scale. With the coming of the Cold War, Timken management had become strongly and outspokenly anticommunist. Given the nature of its political advertising, the company could hardly have declined to answer the claims made for the Soviet achievement, which was really dwarfed by what it had done at Bucyrus.[25]

The Timken plant was built on a much larger scale and was more flexible, with an output of 30 million bearings per year in 14 sizes versus the 1.5 million bearings per year produced in the Soviet plant in one size of ball bearings and one size of tapered roller bearings. Based on data in the *American Machinist* article, Timken calculated that the Moscow plant was producing 35 bearings per plant employee, per eight-hour shift. The comparative number for Bucyrus was 192. Finally, while the Soviet technology was similar in many respects, it did not include green machining (its process started with blanks manufactured elsewhere), an area that, as described, required some of Timken's most inventive problem solving.[26]

But it made sense to start publicizing Bucyrus for other reasons as well. By 1957, Timken felt confident that it would be difficult for competitors to copy its achievement. Other U.S. bearing manufacturers had automated portions of the production process. In 1948, GM's New Departure division had installed conveyors to move pieces between machines and through inspection and packing in its

Timken shared its Bucyrus innovations with the world in 1957 through press conferences and plant tours. For cone production, a system of conveyors, chutes, and elevators ensures a continuous flow of product through the various machine operations. The plant's annual production capacity was 33 million cups and 27 million cones. By 1998, the plant was producing 76 million cups and 66 million cones annually.

In 1992, Industry Week *magazine named the Bucyrus plant one of America's Best Plants. The award recognized the plant's leadership in developing self-directed work teams, superior problem-solving programs, and an innovative process for implementing improvement ideas. Peter Ashton, executive vice president and president—bearings, spoke to Timken employees at the event.*

Sandusky, Ohio, plant, which could produce 18 million bearings a year. Bower, by that time a division of Federal-Mogul Corporation, had a heat-treating line for cups, cones, and rollers. Yet there was nothing out there that compared to Bucyrus. "We have gained a big lead over our competitors and expect to keep it," William Umstattd told the press. Timken was selling bearings produced at Bucyrus for 15 percent less than comparable sizes produced in its other plants. As the editors of the nation's trade journals toured the plant, engineers at Savannah Avenue were working on further improvements aimed at increasing that differential to 25 percent. Green Light bearing sizes had been widely adopted for the 1958 model year in the automotive industry, and Timken sales engineers were beginning to talk to their industrial customers about using them. The formal unveiling of the plant supported that sales initiative.[27]

There was likely another intended audience for the Bucyrus publicity, in addition to customers and the technical community—Timken's employees. As exciting as the idea of automation was to engineers and business executives, it was appalling to many industrial workers and their advocates. To them, visions such as "a plant which could make most of the roller bearings for the entire automotive industry . . . without human hands touching the product in any of the operations" bespoke unemployment, not progress. Such fears were fed by the reality of significant job losses in the industries that had automated most completely and rapidly, such as oil refining. By the mid-1950s there was criticism from many quarters of the potential dehumanizing effects of automation. The response from industry in general was to point to the improved working conditions for those employed in automated plants, and that was a central theme in Timken's presentation of its new plant.[28]

Thus emerged the Bucyrus concept, with its three key principles. They were "[1] selling customers on the advantages of standardizing their bearing applications to bearing sizes adapted to high production; [2] the subsequent production of those bearings at unprecedented production rates, in [3] as nearly an ideal industrial environment for employees as possible." This was not empty rhetoric. Rather, it was Timken's response to the dramatic changes it faced in the postwar economy. The pattern established at Bucyrus of locating in a small town where it could become the largest employer and could hire and train its personnel from the ground up, with the expectation of keeping the plant non-union, became a formula for future expansion. High-volume production of standardized bearings formed the centerpiece of a strategy for profitable growth, both at home and abroad. (The Bucyrus concept went to British Timken in the 1950s.) In pursuit of that strategy, Timken continued to invest in refining the technology developed for Bucyrus and in applying it, where feasible, in other bearing plants. Those investments served the company well through the 1970s, as it struggled both to meet the seemingly limitless demand for bearings in the postwar economy and to retain its position of leadership in an increasingly competitive industry.[29]

Timken Bearings on a Roll: Expansion of Markets at Home and Abroad

*T*he 1950s was an up-and-down decade for the U.S. economy. Early in the decade the Korean War drove a new buildup of productive capacity, which prompted Timken to expand its electric-furnace steel-making capacity. After the new furnaces came on line in 1952, the monthly output of its melt shop reached 55,000 tons (peak monthly production during World War II had been 48,000 tons). Related increases in downstream capacity included a new Assel tube mill at Canton and a new rolling mill and annealing furnace at Gambrinus. Timken also had to add new machinery in its bearing plants to increase, once again, its production of larger bearings for trucks and other military equipment. The demobilization from the Korean conflict, beginning in the summer of 1953, idled some of this new capacity and most of the employees that had been taken on in the wartime expansion program. However, by late 1955, Timken would again be planning to expand its steel and bearing plants in order to keep pace with its growing business.[1]

In the bearing business, the company's success with Bucyrus and its introduction of some important new products drove longer-term market growth. Like many other U.S. companies, Timken moved aggressively in the 1950s to meet

211

demand by setting up manufacturing facilities abroad. To a great extent it was pulled into international markets by its big customers—Caterpillar in construction equipment, John Deere in agricultural machinery, Eaton and Dana in automotive parts, and the auto companies themselves—all of which were establishing or expanding manufacturing facilities on a worldwide basis. But for Timken, there was an important difference. Unlike most firms going international, Timken was operating under the court order issued in its antitrust case, and was therefore competing in many markets against Timken bearings produced by its own affiliate companies. The competition, especially from British Timken, was fierce. Only at the end of the decade would it resolve that problem by consolidating and running Timken France and British Timken as divisions.

New Products in the 1950s

Timken's technical organizations, strengthened and energized by continuing investments during the 1950s, helped to drive the expansion of markets in the postwar era. In 1951, Timken opened a new facility dedicated to producing precision bearings. Much like Bucyrus, this development came out of work undertaken at Savannah Avenue, combining new machine-tool technology and an innovative approach to training machine operators. It began with an experimental plant in the rural town of Zoarville, Ohio, south of Canton, and then moved into a purchased building in nearby New Philadelphia. Previously, the Canton plant had manufactured two grades of precision bearings. These were regular bearing sizes specially ground to have exceptionally close tolerances. Number 3 bearings were guaranteed to be within 0.0003 inches of specified dimensions, Number 0 bearings within 0.00015, that is, twice as precise. New Philadelphia produced those two grades plus a 00 bearing that doubled the precision again, with tolerances guaranteed to 0.000075 inches. The 00 bearing, and the greater capacity to produce standard precision bearings, made it possible for Timken to expand its machine-tool market. The company built the New Philadelphia plant in anticipation that that industry would grow rapidly after the war, as the United States reconverted to a peacetime economy and the reconstruction of Europe began.[2]

Undoubtedly, the era's most significant new product was the All-Purpose (AP™) bearing for rail freight cars. This was the one major market for bearings that Timken had yet to crack, and it was a large one, with some 1.8 million freight cars in the United States alone. Timken bearings had found their way onto most passenger trains and locomotives. But the company still had not overcome the resistance of railroad executives to making a significant investment in lowering the operating costs of rolling stock, since they would have to share the return on that investment with their competitors as their freight cars traveled North America's far-flung rail system.

The AP™ (All-Purpose) bearing is a self-contained, preassembled and prelubricated, two-row bearing that was designed specifically to support the wheels on railway cars. Its introduction in 1954 permitted a simple conversion of existing railroad axles from plain bearings to tapered roller bearings. A 1958 Timken freight car economic study calculated annual savings to the railroad industry of about $288 million with the AP bearing. This bearing has replaced every plain bearing previously used in that application.

In an outstanding example of linked product and process development, the AP bearing solved that problem by reducing installation costs to the point that it made sense for all railroad lines to adopt anti-friction bearings. Central to Timken's strategy for developing this product was standardization. Timken product engineer Clifford Eastburg developed a basic design for the AP bearing that, produced in a range of sizes, was adaptable to all types of rail cars. It included two cone-and-roller assemblies inside a single large cup, which formed a housing that was sealed on both ends to create a self-contained unit. The design eliminated the need for the standard bearing housing, or journal box, which had been an expensive part to build and maintain on the axle. It also permitted railroad companies to retrofit existing freight cars, a major advantage. Most important, the AP bearing was introduced at a reasonable price. Another Timken engineer, Harley Urbach, was responsible for developing the manufacturing process. When the bearing design first emerged and its production cost was calculated, Al Bergstrom decreed that 25 to 30 percent of that cost had to be taken out for the new product to succeed. Since a number of the bearing-housing parts were made outside, this required not only reducing Timken's manufacturing costs but working with suppliers to reduce their costs as well. The effort was successful, however, and in August 1954, the first AP-bearing-equipped cars—eighteen 70-ton covered hopper cars on the Atlantic Coast Line Railroad, based in Waycross, Georgia—were put into service.[3]

In the long run, however, Urbach recognized that one of the greatest advantages of the design standardization achieved with the AP bearing was its suitability for high-volume production in the Bucyrus mode. In November 1955, Timken announced that it would build a new facility for producing railroad bearings at its Columbus plant. Bucyrus had taken over a large portion of the work on automotive and farm-equipment bearings formerly manufactured at Columbus,

In 1963, Bob Timken (left) and Henry Timken celebrated with employees the production of the one-millionth AP bearing at the company's Columbus, Ohio, plant.

and (as Umstattd pointed out in an interview) the workforce at Columbus had shown a willingness to be flexible in adapting to the new mode of production. Timken mounted another development project with its equipment suppliers, to apply innovations made for Bucyrus to machines that could produce the much larger double-row, double-cup AP bearings. The new facility came on line in early 1958, producing bearings at roughly ten times the rate of the Canton plant. Since Timken maintained the original price of the AP bearing, it became one of the company's most profitable products. Said estimating engineer Jim Nickas, "That's when I started buying stock in the company."[4]

The new railroad bearing took off somewhat slowly, as a few rail companies tried it first on freight routes that did not cross system lines. But AP bearings quickly demonstrated their advantages. The chief one was the virtual elimination of "hot boxes," or fires in journal boxes caused by overheating on the axle, which ignited the oil-soaked cotton cloth that served to lubricate plain bearings. When hot-box fires erupted, trains had to stop and sideline the affected cars, causing expensive delays. As most rail freight lines had converted to diesel engines in the late 1940s, longer, faster-running trains had become possible and promised to make trains more competitive against trucking lines. Hot boxes became the major impediment to realizing those gains, and eliminating the problem could have dramatic effects. For example, trains bringing livestock into Chicago from the West could make the run fast enough to eliminate the need for a rest stop that required unloading all the cattle or pigs for feeding and watering. The western lines, the Santa Fe and the Northern Pacific, were some of the first to begin conversion to "roller freight." By the late 1950s, Timken was receiving large orders for the AP bearing. It doubled capacity at Columbus in 1962, and the following year celebrated production of the millionth AP bearing with a ceremony and announcement of a 5-percent price reduction on two of the most common sizes. Columbus would produce the two-millionth bearing less than three years later.[5]

Company president Herbert Markley (center) attended the ceremony honoring Clifford Eastburg (left) and Harley Urbach with the Elmer A. Sperry Award in 1977. The award recognized the AP bearing's significant contributions to railroad and industrial applications. The award also cited the company's railroad engineering department.

In the 1950s, conversion to roller freight meant, for the most part, buying new cars equipped with AP bearings, but eventually the railroad lines began to retrofit their rolling stock on a large scale. Timken helped to speed the process by sharing the AP bearing design with its competitors, a step that betokened its strong position in the market. (In the 1960s, Timken's chief engineer in the railroad bearing division, Oscar Horger, would defect to Brenco, a manufacturer of plain bearings for the railroad industry that went on to become the leading competitor for AP bearings.) The AP also became one of the company's most successful export products. By the early 1960s, Timken would have 60 percent of a domestic market that was estimated to be worth $30 million a year and still growing—just half of the U.S. freight-car fleet would be running on tapered roller bearings by 1976. The impact on the bearing business was significant, in particular because it further decreased the company's dependence on the automotive market. Of course, the AP bearing also had a dramatic impact on railroads. In 1977, Eastburg and Urbach received international recognition for their contribution to the transportation industry with the Elmer A. Sperry Award of the American Society of Mechanical Engineers. One of the most prestigious engineering prizes, the award honored Sperry, inventor of the navigational gyroscope, and had been won in prior years by the likes of Igor Sikorsky, for the helicopter, and Geoffrey de Havilland and Frank Halford, for jet aircraft.[6]

The Bucyrus Concept as Corporate Strategy

To some extent, the formula for success with the AP bearing was traditional. Early on, H. H. and W. R. Timken had established the capability to engineer specific applications to create new markets for tapered roller bearings. H. H. had set the pattern of investing in manufacturing processes so that Timken bearings could compete on both quality and price. Large-scale, low-cost production had helped the company to win and keep the lion's share of Ford's business during a period of dramatic auto-industry growth. Yet, in the context of the booming postwar economy, the shift from batch to automated high-volume production at Bucyrus was a change of large magnitude that opened up market vistas unimaginable just ten years before.

As a first mover with the Bucyrus concept for automotive and then railroad bearings, Timken gained a clear lead over the rest of the industry in the 1950s. It became the largest bearing maker and consistently one of the most profitable. All of its investments in new facilities and equipment were financed from earnings. At the same time, its decade averages for return on sales (9 percent) and return on equity (15.8 percent) were at levels, as *Forbes* magazine noted, "rarely seen in companies that live and die by the orders of capital goods makers."[7] (See Table 7.1.)

Understandably, Umstattd's long-term strategy for the company focused on sustaining the drive as long as possible. Timken began to push for standardization in more industries—construction equipment, farm equipment, and industrial trucks in the late 1950s. At the same time, it began to introduce machine-tool technology developed for Bucyrus into the Canton and Gambrinus bearing factories, to set up some dedicated lines for specific products, and to capture as many of the economies of long runs as possible. That was one of the major items in the spending program financed by the sale of stock in 1957.[8]

Competition for domestic markets was heating up in the late 1950s. Federal-Mogul-Bower, the second largest producer of tapered roller bearings, was growing at a good rate, although Timken was growing faster and remained more than twice as large as Bower in terms of revenue. GM's New Departure-Hyatt division had begun making tapered roller bearings for automotive and industrial applications after the war. In the railroad market it had competed with a cylindrical roller bearing but switched to making the AP in the late 1950s. In 1955, SKF's U.S. subsidiary, SKF Industries, also entered the field with the acquisition of Tyson Bearing Company, a maker of tapered roller bearings located virtually next door to Timken, in Massillon, Ohio. It had been formed in 1929 by Frank Tyson, a mechanical engineer and inventor who had patented a cageless tapered roller bearing. Tyson had gotten the idea for his invention while working for Timken in 1915–1919, helping to install new machine tools for World War I production. The Tyson plant was small, with just 300 employees, but SKF Industries almost immediately began investing to expand the operation, broaden the range of bearings produced, and improve quality.[9]

In short, the time was long since past when Timken had the field to itself. In earlier days, H. H. and W. R. had taken it for granted that, if their ball bearing competitors ventured into tapered roller bearings, they would have to move to producing a general line of bearings in response. But that idea was anathema in the Timken organization of the 1950s. Henry and Bob Timken and Umstattd fully expected the company to maintain its leadership position by continuing to do what it had always done—making Timken bearings better and cheaper than other tapered roller bearings, and continuing to capture new markets from competing types. To be sure, they could have grown the company more rapidly by producing a general line of bearings—just as they could have done so by diversifying into related lines of business or using debt to leverage their assets and invest in new plants and equipment at higher rates. Such steps would have brought Timken

TABLE 7.1

The Timken Company Comparative Financial Data, 1950–1959 (in Thousands of Dollars, except per Share Data)

	1950	1951	1952	1953	1954	1955	1956	1957	1958	1959
Net sales	$144,055	$188,656	$169,633	$178,165	$135,551	$196,054	$214,475	$205,242	$155,187	$262,093
Net income	15,403	14,068	10,597	10,856	10,658	22,100	21,790	20,746	11,171	29,856
Total assets	$88,824	$104,495	$114,757	$112,397	$107,616	$121,340	$139,289	$164,896	$167,018	$227,018
Long-term bank loans										18,000
Total capital and earnings invested in the business	69,486	76,290	79,622	88,214	91,608	104,023	116,127	144,276	146,747	163,289
Return on sales	10.7%	7.5%	6.2%	6.1%	7.9%	11.3%	10.2%	10.1%	7.2%	11.4%
Return on assets	17.3	13.5	9.2	9.7	9.9	18.2	15.6	12.6	6.7	13.2
Return on capital and earnings	22.2	18.4	13.3	12.3	11.6	21.2	18.8	14.4	7.6	18.3
Earnings per share	$3.18	$2.90	$2.19	$2.24	$2.20	$4.56	$4.50	$3.89	$2.10	$5.60
Dividends per share	1.75	1.50	1.50	1.50	1.50	2.00	2.00	2.25	2.00	2.40
Number of employees	17,563	17,934	17,584	14,690	14,305	15,012	14,974	13,778	13,805	20,594
Number of shareholders	19,686	20,403	20,610	20,535	21,108	20,652	19,764	22,674	23,151	23,127

Source: The Timken Roller Bearing Company Annual Reports, 1950–1959.

Note: Per share data adjusted for 2-for-1 stock split in 1957.

more in line with prevailing U.S.-industry trends. Yet they were unthinkable in the context of deeply engrained company values and a sense of corporate purpose focused more tightly than ever on the Timken bearing.

Looking ahead, technical superiority in both products and processes would become an even stronger imperative once the drive for standardization began to succeed. By the 1960s, all makers of inch-sized tapered roller bearings would be standardized on Timken's bearing dimensions and using its part numbers. That situation held the seeds of future problems, but thanks largely to the technology developed at Bucyrus, Timken would retain an edge in quality and price through the 1970s.

At any rate, by the end of the 1950s, Timken's view of its potential markets looked well beyond the borders of the United States. It was busy planning manufacturing plants in Australia and Brazil, setting up a worldwide network of agents and distributors, and consolidating its affiliate companies in Britain and France. As focused as he was on building a competitive strategy on the Bucyrus concept, Umstattd had become equally determined to make Timken an international force.

U.S. Timken in the International Arena

A mix of powerful forces pulled Timken overseas in the post–World War II era. The company had established a sales and service subsidiary in Canada in 1922. But aside from that, exports from U.S. Timken were so negligible in the prewar years that all of the company's foreign sales were handled by Umstattd's personal secretary. The disruptions caused by the war began to change that situation even before V-J Day. The experience of wartime shortages prompted the company's Canadian customers to want a domestic supply of essential bearings. They encouraged Timken to begin manufacturing in Canada, and in 1944 it agreed to do so. Two years later a new Timken plant opened in St. Thomas, a hub of truck and railway transportation in the industrialized southwestern region of Ontario, just north of Lake Erie and halfway between the auto manufacturing centers of St. Catharines (near Buffalo) and Windsor (near Detroit). Timken had chosen St. Thomas after looking at some thirty Canadian cities. It had a profile somewhat similar to that of Bucyrus, with a population of 18,000 employed by the railroads and in light industry and farming.[10]

Also in 1944, Timken created a sales subsidiary in São Paulo, Brazil, The Timken Roller Bearing Company of South America. In that region the United States had long been viewed as an imperialist aggressor, not a trading partner. That situation began to change, however, with the break in established links to Europe caused by the war and its aftermath on the European continent. Jules A. Moreland, a district sales manager for Timken's railway division, went to São Paulo as general manager. One of his first big sales was to the government of Argentina: bearings for 210 diesel locomotives for its national railroad. In 1945, Timken formed what it called The Foreign Division, under the direction of Howard C. Sauer. Sauer's charge was mainly to expedite shipments to Latin America and to serve as a liaison between U.S. Timken, British Timken, and Timken France.[11]

In 1946, Timken established Canadian Timken Limited in response to customer and government requests for a local supply of Timken bearings. Today, the plant serves customers throughout North America and abroad.

The 1951 antitrust decision that directed Timken to compete with its associate companies abroad or find itself in violation of federal law spurred the company to work harder to build overseas markets. Sauer began to travel extensively around the world to set up relationships with distributors in countries where British Timken and Timken France had been selling for some time. In addition, Timken hired a Swiss national, Erich Fischer, as a consultant and agent to help it set up sales operations in Europe. Fischer had been an exchange student in the United States in the 1930s, had married an American, and had attended Harvard Business School immediately after World War II. Recognizing that many established business relationships between the United States and Europe had been severed by the war, he set out to develop a business selling U.S.-made steel abroad. His uncle, a metallurgist, recommended that he approach Timken, and he did so by letter in late 1947. Howard Sauer hired him. Beginning in 1948, Fischer sold Timken seamless tubing and bar steel, on commission, to European bearing and auto manufacturers and a variety of other industries. Once or twice a year he visited Canton, and he got to know Umstattd and the Timken brothers well. In 1951, faced with the need to mount, in Fischer's words, "a crash program to comply with the court's decree," Umstattd turned to him. Fischer undertook to sell bearings and to create a distribution network and sales organization in Europe.[12]

Like Sauer, he worked on setting up relationships with distributors in different countries, beginning with Antonopoulos Brothers in Athens, Greece. By 1955, in addition to 20 Latin American sales representatives, Timken had 36 agents in cities around the world, including Hong Kong, Teheran, Stockholm, and Johannesburg. The company brought all of these men together in Canton for a five-day meeting, with extensive plant tours (including the then top-secret Bucyrus plant) and presentations about the company and about Timken bearings and their applications. This was its first international sales conference. At the second such meeting, held in Zurich in 1957, Timken executives met with 63 distributors from 27 countries in Europe, Africa, and the Middle East.[13]

One of the more subtle and difficult points to get across at those meetings was the explanation of why agents could not handle the products of British Timken and Timken France as well as those of U.S. Timken. To non-Americans, the court-ordered competition between affiliated companies whose products all bore the same trademark was incomprehensible and a bit ridiculous. But to the officers of U.S. Timken, who faced criminal charges if found in violation of the court order, it was serious business indeed.

It was not just the court's ruling that sent U.S. Timken abroad, however. It was also the growing importance of the international market. By the mid-1950s, the post–World War II recovery of the industrialized European economies was in full swing, and much of the rest of the world was striving, with encouragement and assistance from the United States, to industrialize as quickly as possible. International agreements at the end of the war had created mechanisms, such as the International Monetary Fund, the World Bank, and the General Agreement on Tariffs and Trade, to support economic development and trade worldwide. The Cold War, in a variety of ways, provided additional impetus for political cooperation and increasing economic interdependence among noncommunist nations. Out of those factors arose an unprecedented opportunity for U.S. industry to expand abroad. Rather quickly, many U.S. companies that dominated their home markets and had been accustomed to exporting their products discovered that they could compete far more effectively for a share of expanding international markets by producing in the regions where they sought to do business. Between 1955 and 1970, the postwar boom years in America, direct overseas investment by U.S. multinational corporations would grow faster than the U.S. economy as a whole. And the leading multinationals included many of the manufacturing firms—automakers such as Ford and GM, machinery and equipment producers such as Caterpillar, John Deere, and Dana Corporation—that were U.S. Timken's largest customers.[14]

One of the large customers for Timken bearings that helped to draw the company into international markets was Rockwell Spring and Axle, a successor company to Timken-Detroit Axle. In 1940, Willard and Walter Rockwell had become, respectively, chairman and president of Timken-Detroit. The Timken family, still the major shareholder, was represented on the board by Henry and Bob. In the meantime, however, Willard Rockwell had also become president of Standard Steel Spring Company, another auto parts maker. Beginning in 1936, he had built it up through acquisitions into a large producer of parts for automobiles, trucks, and farm equipment. In 1953 the two companies, Timken-Detroit and Standard Steel Spring, merged to create Rockwell Spring and Axle, with 21 plants in nine states. By 1958, when it renamed itself Rockwell Standard, it had diversified into a much broader line of automotive parts, for example valves, and was expanding aggressively on a worldwide scale. While Timken-Detroit disappeared after forty-four years in business, the Timken family's investment was converted into a large stake in a firm that would transform itself through subsequent mergers into one of the giants of U.S. industry, Rockwell International. From the mid-1950s onward, it was the movement of such dynamic U.S. companies abroad more than anything else that focused the attention of the men in Canton on markets outside the United States.[15]

Umstattd began to travel a good bit in the postwar years. A man who took pleasure in familiar comforts—he was a big consumer of Coca-Cola and insisted on having a Manhattan cocktail every evening—he also greatly enjoyed meeting people and visiting new places. The more he saw of the world, the more opportunity he saw there for Timken. Bob Timken once quipped, "Every place you go, we start up a plant. I'll have to keep you home or we'll run out of money." Traveling through Europe with Erich Fischer in the mid-1950s, Umstattd decided that U.S. Timken should establish a sales company in Germany. British Timken had a strong organization there (still led by Max Wrba), while SKF and FAG had built new plants since the war and were also strong. The market was so tight, in fact, that it was at first impossible to find a large distributor to handle U.S. Timken bearings. So, over strenuous objections and threats of all-out competition from John Pascoe, Umstattd created Timken Rollenlager GmbH in September 1956. This unit was originally located in Cologne, where Ford had a manufacturing plant. But German Ford preferred to use German bearings and never became a good Timken customer. Within less than a year, Timken Rollenlager moved to Düsseldorf. The organization also struggled to establish management leadership. Umstattd tapped Fred Reiser, Jr., a sales manager for industrial bearings in Cincinnati, to be general manager in Germany. But Reiser had difficulty functioning in an unfamiliar culture so far from his home base, and in 1958 he was succeeded by William E. Judy. Judy had served in the U.S. Army during World War II and was conversant in German. A professional engineer, he had joined Timken as a trainee in the metallurgical laboratory and was working as a steel sales engineer when he was chosen for the job in Germany. He would remain as general manager of Timken Rollenlager until 1965.[16]

Initially, most of the available business in Germany was for large bearings for steel rolling mills, essentially spare parts for American-made mills that had been sent to Germany under the Marshall Plan. Erich Fischer hired a cadre of European engineers, who then trained in Canton to become Timken sales engineers. Those men—Claude Perret, Henry Altorfer, Rudi Knoell, and Jürgen Knauer—became the core of U.S. Timken's European sales force. As in the United States, the strength of the organization lay in the technical support it provided, in both sales and service. This support quickly gained Timken Rollenlager a good reputation in Germany. But there were frustrations, as Henry Altorfer recalled, because once the engineering on a new application had been done (and sent back to Canton for approval), the sale often went to British Timken, whose prices were lower: "U.S. Timken did all the engineering and British Timken all the selling," said Altorfer. Before long, though, Timken Rollenlager made inroads into the German machine-tool industry and also gained a good long-term customer in Zahnradfabrik Friedrichshafen, which used large bearings for the gearboxes it produced for trucks and tractors. By the end of the decade, Timken would begin to gain a foothold in the German automotive industry.[17]

In the first few months of 1957, Umstattd set out on a round-the-world business trip—one of the ones that resulted in a new plant. An early stop was Australia, where British Timken had something of a lock on the market by virtue of its holding all the available import licenses for tapered roller bearings. Umstattd went over to see what he could do about that situation. He took along Elmer Sweitzer, manager of the Zanesville plant, and Edgerly Austin, the recently retired general manager of automotive sales. They received a warm welcome. Much like Canada, Australia had suffered wartime disruptions of bearing imports and was eager to have a domestic supply. In addition, many of Timken's important U.S. customers—Ford, GM, International Harvester, John Deere, Massey Ferguson— were manufacturing in Australia and were also interested in securing a local source of bearings. Personnel from International Harvester there helped Umstattd with the task of finding a good plant location, and by the time he left, the decision was largely made to build a factory in Ballarat, Victoria, a city of about 50,000 located some 65 miles west of Melbourne. Australia's largest inland city, Ballarat had been a gold-mining town in the nineteenth century, but by the 1950s had considerable industrial development with some 300 manufacturing plants in a diversified range of industries.[18]

Once Umstattd had moved along in his travels, Herbert Markley implemented the decision to initiate manufacturing in Australia. Markley had started with Timken as an accountant trainee in 1938 and had been selected by Umstattd to be assistant to the president in 1956. In the spring of 1958, he would become

As in postwar Canada, manufacturers in Australia were looking for a local bearing supplier. In 1958, Australian Timken Proprietary Limited began production with 18 employees. For many years it was Australia's only anti-friction bearing manufacturer. A "25-Year Club" plaque at the plant honors employees who have achieved twenty-five years of continuous service to the company.

vice president, with responsibility for all of the company's overseas operations. Markley had a new subsidiary, Australian Timken Proprietary Limited, in place by the fall of 1957, with construction of the Ballarat plant in progress. In less than a year, Australian Timken began producing bearings on a limited scale. Initial plans called for building up to about 1 million bearings per year for the Australian and New Zealand markets, but in the long term Timken envisioned expanding the Ballarat plant to produce for wider markets, for example in Indonesia, Malaysia, and India. The company installed U.S. managers at the outset—Elmer Sweitzer and Walter Jehu, who came out of the industrial bearings sales organization. But in the spring of 1957 Markley had hired three Australians and sent them to Canton for several months of training, so they could return and help get the plant up and running. One of those men, hired as secretary-treasurer of Australian Timken, was William J. C. North. North would become managing director in 1963 and remain in that position until 1985.[19]

By 1959, construction was under way on another new plant in São Paulo, Brazil, which aimed to produce 2.25 million bearings per year for Latin America. Brazil was developing rapidly and had attracted many of the same U.S. companies that were setting up manufacturing operations in other parts of the world. The Brazilian government had decreed that cars, trucks, and other equipment produced in Brazil had to use mostly domestic-made parts, a measure that also prompted SKF to build a bearing plant in Brazil in 1959. (SKF's history notes there were "no fewer than 12 truck manufacturers" in Brazil at that time.) Timken complied with the domestic-content decree as much as possible in building and equipping its plant, but it shipped steel from Canton until, after some struggle, it was able to develop a supply of the quality material it needed. In 1960, the company formed a new subsidiary in Brazil, Timken do Brasil, to handle bearing manufacture as well as sales and service. Its plant in São Paulo came on line in 1961.[20]

In 1985, Timken do Brasil, the company's sixth international bearing manufacturing facility, celebrated its twenty-fifth year in operation. A giant cake was the centerpiece of its open-house festivities. The plant has grown from 100 workers in 1960 to an enterprise of 450 people who produce about 1.2 million cups and cones per month.

Thus, considerable momentum was building behind Timken's international expansion by the end of the 1950s. That would increase manyfold once U.S. Timken consolidated Timken France and British Timken and started construction of a new plant in Colmar, France, near the center of the emerging European Common Market. British Timken was an organization with culture and capabilities largely similar to those of the U.S. firm, but one with a proud tradition as an independent company and a recent history of fierce competition with its parent.

British Timken in the 1950s

British Timken, Ltd., was a dynamic, growing enterprise and a formidable competitor for its majority owner, U.S. Timken. The transition from Michael Dewar to John Pascoe brought leadership to the company that was autocratic and rather grandiose in style, but solid in substance. In the 1950s, British Timken's workforce grew from under 2,000 to about 4,700. It was the largest employer in the county of Northampton, and its presence there expanded in 1954 with the building of a second factory in Daventry, just a few miles from Duston. Its output grew by 60 percent, from 8 million to 12.8 million bearings per year, while its annual revenues more than doubled, from just under £5 million to more than £11 million. Just as important, though intangible, the company gained a wide reputation as one of Britain's preeminent industrial firms.[21]

In organization and culture, British Timken had many similarities to its U.S. parent, but all with a distinctive British twist. It had, for example, an apprentice-ship program that was both like and unlike the system in Canton. This took shape rapidly in the postwar years, in response to an acute shortage of skilled labor. As the company expanded, and particularly after the Daventry plant was built, it was increasingly difficult to find people with the appropriate level of technical train-ing. Northampton had traditionally been the center of the shoe industry, which had not required the kind of education and skills essential to the manufacture of bearings. British Timken's solution was to start a training program. At that time, children were not legally required to attend school past age fourteen, and many young men who had suffered loss or hardship during the war were eager to start making their way in the world. British Timken attracted those "school leavers" with a five-year apprenticeship leading to a secure job and possibly to consider-able advancement. A government policy that gave tax rebates to engineering com-panies with structured apprenticeship programs helped the company follow through on this plan. With some justification, British Timken saw itself as part of the larger educational system. The salary was small, but benefits included free uni-forms, subsidized lunches, paid summer vacations, and time off to attend outside courses. The company sent detailed progress reports to the parents of its younger apprentices and held the occasional open house.[22]

At fifteen, young men could start at British Timken as craft apprentices. They trained for certification to work in machine-tool repair, or in the tool room or de-velopment machine shop. The company looked on graduates of this program as good candidates for production supervisory jobs, and it opened the door for the most talented among them to move into higher levels of training. The program for technician apprentices accepted young men, and occasionally young women, who had passed the O-level examinations (usually taken at age sixteen) in four subjects, including mathematics, English, and science. Technician apprentices studied to become draftspersons or technicians in one of the many technical de-partments, but they were also supported in studying to become certified in me-chanical engineering and could hope to go on to a variety of engineering and management positions. For those who passed the A-level examinations required for attending a college or university, British Timken offered student apprenticeships

British Timken's apprenticeship program, critical to building its organizational capabilities in the years after World War II, continues today. In 1996, Kay Sketchley (foreground) became the first woman in the United Kingdom to achieve Level 3 qualification in electrical engineering maintenance.

and commercial apprenticeships, which combined on-the-job training with formal education and led to higher-level technical jobs and positions in accounting and management. Finally, graduate apprenticeships were shorter programs for those with degrees in hand. It was at that level that most sales engineers entered the company. According to Ron Knapp, who joined British Timken as an engineer trainee at the end of the war and later became managing director, the program was "by far and away the best apprentice scheme" in the area, and many companies tried to hire away its graduates. Another graduate of the program, Peter Ashton, went on to become head of Timken's worldwide bearing business in the 1980s.[23]

Thus, much as in U.S. Timken, the extensive training program was a wide road to advancement. It was also part of a clearly defined hierarchy with a strong and colorful personality at the top. Frederick John Pascoe was a short man but a forceful presence in any setting, with intense eyes and upright posture. He became Sir John Pascoe in January 1957, and he clearly liked the trappings of corporate leadership. At British Timken headquarters, at the Duston plant, he had a large office—visitors from Canton noted that it was larger than the offices of Bob and Henry Timken and Umstattd combined. It was a long room with walnut paneling and a marble fireplace, and Pascoe's desk, placed at one end, was on a raised platform. Company personnel who had business with him were generally required to stand in his presence, and smoking was forbidden, though he himself smoked. Eating arrangements just as clearly reflected his sense of order. Senior managers ate in the Number 1 Dining Room, but by invitation only. Pascoe sat at the head of a long table. There were three courses for lunch and full service. Duston also had a Number 2 Dining Room, somewhat less formal, for senior staff, as well as a staff dining room, and a works canteen.[24]

For advice, Pascoe tended to rely on a small group of men who were directors but not employees of British Timken, including his son-in-law, John Eden, who was then a Member of Parliament and served with Pascoe on a number of corporate boards. Within the organization, he surrounded himself with people who were capable but not the sort to challenge his opinions. His second-in-command in the 1950s, Stephen Bennett, for example, was uniformly respectful and quiet in Pascoe's presence but became a strong (though far less formal and more flexible) leader in his own right as managing director in the 1960s. One of the few men who would go up against Pascoe directly was David McNicoll, long-time manager of the Aston plant who transferred to Duston as chief engineer when Aston closed in the late 1950s. From the 1930s well into the 1960s, McNicoll played a leading role in many areas of company life, from product design to labor relations.[25]

For all the formality at the top, or perhaps because of it, a strong sense of family pervaded British Timken in the 1950s. With so many young people in the factories, there was a lot of joking around. One favorite sport involved the daily ceremony of tea breaks, where mugs, all labeled with names, went by conveyor to be filled and then returned to their owners—some of whom found their mugs had been nailed to the conveyor. A popular prank in the screw-machine department, when a man had to lean in to change a tool, was to pull the top of the machine down, effectively covering him with oil—and in those days the machines ran on whale oil. Ron Knapp, more than once a victim of that trick, vowed that if he ever rose to a position of authority, he would see to it that the company "switched from bloody whale oil." And he did.[26]

Athletic competition was a central part of British Timken's culture, even more than it was in Ohio. Both the Duston and Daventry plants were situated on substantial acreage, and some of this land was developed into a football (soccer) field, with stands and floodlights, tennis courts, a cricket pitch, a bowls pitch, rifle and archery ranges, and a well-stocked lake for fishing, John Pascoe's favorite sport. Although football and cricket were the two sports most associated with British Timken, it also had Ping-Pong and chess teams, an interdepartmental snooker league, and a baseball team in the 1950s. At the Daventry plant there was a large indoor Sports and Social Club that was the site of a wide variety of club activities and entertainment. Pascoe was vice president of the English Schools Cricket Association and manager of the football team of the nearby town of Kettering. The company financially supported a number of local sporting teams, lending its facilities and providing off-season employment for professional players, more than one of whom became effective celebrity salesmen for Timken bearings. Some British Timken managers were outstanding athletes: Ron Knapp had played rugby at Cambridge University and was a member of the Welsh national team; Raymond Tuckey, general manager for sales, was a Wimbledon champion in doubles tennis.[27]

In the 1950s, Pascoe developed the annual British Timken show into a three-day sporting event of national importance. He invited Britain's best runners to compete in its track meet. The horse competitions, both dressage and jumping, attracted Olympic riders. (Pascoe's wife and daughter were both excellent riders.) Trotting races were included after British Timken built a track on land connected to its plant. The event hosted 30,000 in 1957. Famous people sometimes attended: the Duke of Wellington opened the new British Timken running track in 1954. Calouste Sarkis Gulbenkian, the wealthy oil entrepreneur known popularly as "Mr. Five Percent," adorned with an orchid in his lapel, liked to drive a fancy phaeton in the carriage parade. But the show was most important to the company as a way of entertaining customers and cementing good public relations in the county of Northampton.[28]

All the athletic competition and company-centered social events of course provided other outlets for high spirits and helped to pull people together. For the coronation of Queen Elizabeth II in June 1953, British Timken organized a television projection of the ceremony in Westminster Abbey and in the evening

Courtesy of Northamptonshire Evening Telegram.

British Timken employees warmly greeted H.R.H. Princess Anne in 1971 for a tour of the Duston plant. Escorted on the walkway by managing director Stephen Bennett, she returned that evening to Buckingham Palace in a helicopter—equipped with 36 Timken bearings.

sponsored dancing on the green and a big fireworks display. Workers on the shop floor were all unionized, but annual pay negotiations went smoothly and there were no strikes in the 1950s, with disputes and disciplinary matters settled according to strict procedures. When there was a temporary slowdown in business, hourly employees were not laid off but were set to work clearing rocks from the fields or otherwise improving the plant property. As in Canton, men at all levels of the company made long careers there.[29]

Wages and salaries were low at British Timken in the 1950s, certainly compared to prevailing U.S. pay rates. But the relatively low cost of labor was one of the things that gave its products an advantage in international markets. The 1949 devaluation of the pound sterling gave an additional boost to British exports, as the pound lost 30 percent of its value relative to the U.S. dollar, falling to $2.80 per pound. Those factors helped put British Timken in a good position to compete worldwide with U.S. Timken, as dictated by the U.S. Supreme Court, while its markets in Britain expanded rapidly.[30]

British Timken Products

British Timken produced many bearings identical to those of U.S. Timken, but it also made some unique products developed specifically for its own customers by the design team under Dave McNicoll at the Aston plant. The most notable of those was a propeller-blade root bearing produced for Rotol, a propeller company formed as a joint venture between Rolls Royce and British Aerospace. This was one of many Timken bearings developed in collaboration with the British aircraft industry. A highly successful British aircraft, the Vickers "Viscount" passenger plane, used 20 Timken bearings on its propellers and landing wheels. British Timken bearings were also widely used in helicopter applications—in gearboxes and on the main rotor shafts, on which the full weight of the aircraft was carried in flight. While technically successful, none of those aircraft bearings developed into major product lines, because the British aircraft industry itself remained small, failing to expand into international markets. Another unique Aston product was railroad journal boxes. In the prewar era, these had been made in the shop that produced industrial bearings, merely as a sideline to railroad bearings. After the war, however, the entire shop, furnished with new machines, was turned over to production of journal boxes of all types, and they became an important product for British Timken in the 1950s.[31]

British Timken closed the Aston plant in 1958. Some time before, it had determined it could not hope to increase production in the old factory, which was in a depressed part of Birmingham, a city badly damaged by bombs during the war. The Daventry plant had already taken over production of very large bearings for applications such as steel-rolling mills, large machine tools, and weapons.

Three years later it took over making aircraft bearings as well. However, most of the pressure to expand production fell on Duston, which trebled in floor space between 1945 and 1959.

One of the things that made such rapid expansion possible was the technical support that came from Canton. Many of the specialized machines developed for U.S. Timken by its machine-tool suppliers, and much of the process research conducted at Savannah Avenue, were transferred to British Timken as it ordered new equipment directly from the United States. While the antitrust decision had strictly forbidden contact on commercial matters, or any discussion of prices, it had placed no restriction on technical collaboration. Rather, it was understood by all that U.S. Timken had a stake in ensuring that products sold under the Timken name—often as replacements for products made in Ohio—conformed to all the specifications of the trademark. The necessary technical communication was handled through a British Timken office established in Canton in 1952, staffed on six-month rotations by British Timken engineers who held the title Technical Liaison Officer. Since requests for information tended to come no more than a few times each week, the posting provided an excellent learning experience, and the arrangement forged some solid bonds between technical organizations.[32]

As part of this large-scale transfer of technology, the Bucyrus concept came to British Timken in 1953. Dubbed the N.B. (for New Building), it took shape at the Duston plant as a sort of factory within a factory—extremely secret, surrounded by a high fence with barbed wire at the top and a guarded gate with limited entry. (At that time, the Bucyrus, Ohio, plant was still shrouded in secrecy as well.) The N.B., designed for output of 5 million bearings per year, was much smaller than Bucyrus, but British Timken had good success with standardized bearings, both in its domestic market and overseas. For example in Australia, it was the sole supplier to Ford in the mid- to late 1950s.[33]

In general, as many of the leading U.S. manufacturing firms expanded their investments and alliances in British industry, British companies benefited from the relatively large investments in research and development that those firms had been making for many years. British Timken was no exception. The push of technology from Canton was strong, in both products and processes, and it helped to confer an advantage over British and other European competitors. Yet the transfer could not have been as swift and successful as it was without British Timken's in-house technical capabilities.[34]

Those capabilities included a sales engineering function that operated much as it did in U.S. Timken. In Britain and continental Europe, SKF had become a serious competitor in tapered roller bearings. As in the United States, most automakers in Britain wanted two sources of supply, and SKF had stepped in to provide an alternative. Its bearings were invariably lower in price, so the job of the Timken sales engineer was to convince the customer why he should pay a little more. British Timken salesmen were fully familiar with the frustration of designing an application only to have the sale go to the competitor. Said Raymond Tuckey, echoing his U.S. Timken counterparts, "They were quite happy for us to do the engineering and get the customer to adapt his design to take a Timken bearing . . . then come along and sell it to them 10 percent cheaper."[35]

The bearing design department continued to develop new products for its own markets, though it was increasingly influenced by the drive for standardization coming from Canton. In 1957, British Timken built the so-called East Works at Daventry to house a highly automated line for producing railroad bearings similar to the line designed for the AP bearing at Columbus. The machinery was modified, however, to make a bearing specifically designed for British Rail Company, with some changes made to save money on high-strength steel, an expensive material in Britain at that time. Unfortunately, British Rail canceled its program not long after the East Works was built, and without it the British Timken bearing was not able to compete with the AP. The company retooled the plant and switched over to producing the American-designed railway bearing.[36]

Thus, for a variety of internal and external reasons, British Timken was becoming more Americanized in its products and processes well before the thought of consolidation took hold in Canton. To many people in the company, the edict of the U.S. Supreme Court simply defied logic—as, indeed, did much of U.S. antitrust law in the eyes of many British observers of the time. "It was quite incredible," recalled Dennis Ashton, manager of the Daventry plant in the 1950s. "You were selling the same product, which had to be guaranteed to be identical, yet you were competing with one another." Still, British Timken happily charted an independent course when it saw fit, even when that diverged from the accepted wisdom in the U.S. company. And, forced to compete, it did so quite effectively.[37]

Going Its Own Way

Hindsight makes two British Timken initiatives—statistical process control and precision ball bearings—seem particularly significant. Both placed the company on the forward edge of important industry trends. Yet U.S. Timken abruptly terminated both following the consolidation, only to take them up again decades later when their value was fully proven by outside events.

U.S. Timken had first instituted SPC at the gun-barrel factory of Timken Ordnance Company during World War II. In the immediate postwar years, under Robert Wagenalls, chief of inspection, the methodology spread into the green-machining and grinding departments of the bearing plants. SPC involved sampling at regular intervals—taking a handful of pieces coming off a machine, gauging them, calculating the average dimensions, and graphing the result. When the graph showed the dimensions beginning to get outside an acceptable limit of variation, the machine was stopped and the problem corrected. The purpose of the charts, explained the *Timken Trading Post* in 1952, was "to help the operator and the control inspectors to control the quality of the product directly at the machine." SPC did not eliminate the need for inspection. For example, visual inspection was still required to catch surface flaws and other observable defects, and Timken would always gauge every bearing on the most critical dimensions—the bore size of the cone, and the cup O.D. But control of the process ensured a baseline of dimensional accuracy that raised the overall quality of machine output and took a great deal of pressure off the inspection program.[38]

That idea had a strong appeal at British Timken, which was having a tough time building its staff fast enough to keep up with expanding production. Controlling the manufacturing process to reduce the effort required for inspection was a way to avoid having to build a vast inspection organization. In contrast—along with every other American company that had experimented with it, including the pioneer, AT&T—U.S. Timken abandoned SPC in the 1950s. At U.S. Timken, the pressure to increase output focused attention on the time it took for machine operators to take and gauge samples and record the results. That was one consideration in the decision to discontinue SPC. Yet a fundamental aspect of SPC was that it increased the responsibility and control of the machine operator. That was a development which, amid the excitement over automation and all it portended, clearly went against the dominant trend of thinking about manufacturing processes.[39]

But British Timken persisted. When some young engineers returned from a stint in Canton excited by the experiments with SPC, they convinced Pascoe to allow them to pursue it. They had the full support of assistant general manager Stephen Bennett, who had graduated with top honors in mathematics from Cambridge University. In 1952, 16 engineers from British Timken and Fischer Bearings Company, along with a lone representative from Timken France—Charlie Nouhaud—took a two-week course from a British expert in the field, M. J. Mulroney, a lecturer in statistics at Leicester College of Technology. Mulroney then came to speak at Duston, and subsequently, the company sent its shop foremen to his course. In mid-1954, instructors began teaching the course on-site at Duston, so that eventually every person in the inspection department was trained in the new method. The inspectors then began conducting the sampling, making the charts, and working with the machine operators to keep their equipment in control. This staged approach helped to break down resistance among the ranks of men who were comfortable with gauges but quite uncomfortable with statistical concepts. "In this manner," joked the company magazine, the course "was given guinea-pig style to . . . the martyred few— they suffered that others might learn." Eventually, tough as it was, British Timken implemented statistical process control throughout its plants.[40]

At Christmas in 1947, The Timken Roller Bearing Company sent to each of its British Timken and Timken France employees a gift box of assorted foods. Here, at the Fischer Bearings Company, posters of gratitude graced factory doors. During World War II, British Timken took over Fischer, a German ball bearing maker in Wolverhampton, England, and subsequently bought the operation, only to sell it in 1959. The plant changed hands twice more before Timken bought its aerospace bearings unit in 1997.

By 1960, when U.S. Timken began to exercise more active control over British operations, SPC was long gone from its own plants. Its main concern was to regularize operations across all Timken locations as quickly as possible. Ron Knapp, the company's first "statistical officer," recalled, "When the Americans came, they said 'Chuck all those bloody charts away. That's a lot of nonsense.'" Looking back, from his perspective, the decision was "deplorable. . . . We were twenty years ahead." Of course, it would have been harder to see that at the time. British Timken promptly conformed to the order from Canton.[41]

Likewise, the British company sold its ball bearing subsidiary before the end of 1959. British Timken had assumed oversight of Fischer Bearings in 1940 at the government's request, but at war's end it bought Fischer from the government, and in the 1950s Pascoe set out to effect a proper merger. Fischer made ball bearings and straight roller bearings in two factories near Birmingham, at Wolverhampton and Hednesford. A large customer, Rolls Royce, used Fischer bearings in its jet and piston engines, as well as in its cars. The company also produced a variety of bearings for the machine-tool industry. Another significant product was miniature bearings, still under development in the 1950s. During World War II, Pascoe had responded to an urgent request from the British Ministry of Aircraft Production to produce bearings of just one-eighth-inch bore with one-sixteenth-inch balls, which were needed for small pumps used in de-icing the wings of combat aircraft. Fischer had succeeded in developing the bearing and had named it in Pascoe's honor, the FJP.1. In the immediate postwar years, Fischer had an uphill battle to develop both manufacturing methods and a commercial market for miniature bearings. But with British Timken's encouragement and support, it got in on the ground floor of what would become one of the more significant growth markets for anti-friction bearings.[41]

From the vantage point of the 1990s, John Pascoe's support of improved methods of quality control and his move into a high-end niche for precision bearings look like the actions of a dynamic and foresighted corporate executive. Yet his all-out competition with U.S. Timken in international markets, which people in his own organization could clearly see was, in the long run, detrimental to the Timken trademark, seems to have been driven by pride as much as anything—both personal pride and pride in British Timken and its long tradition as an independent company. In addition to the advantages conferred by relatively low wages and weak currency, it had a considerable head start over Canton in the development of international markets. Those factors made it a formidable competitor.

Although the British Empire did not survive in a formal sense much beyond the end of World War II, commercial ties and loyalties built up over the years remained largely in place. British Timken had established a sales company in South Africa in 1932 and had succeeded in developing a market there, especially for railroad bearings. In the postwar period, South African Railways specified Timken bearings when it made a large order for new locomotives and passenger cars. To help fulfill such orders, British Timken in 1951 established a plant for grinding and assembling bearings and fabricating journal boxes in Benoni, Transvaal. India was another established market for railroad bearings, and British Timken also had a solid lead in Australia and New Zealand, where it secured the large order from Ford and also sold bearings for railroads, rolling mills, and mine cars. The company had long had a network of distributors and had done well in the replacement market in Europe. In 1953, it appointed 14 new distributors in West Germany, the Middle East, the Belgian Congo, the Philippines, Central America, and the Caribbean. British Timken even went after the North American market in the 1950s, setting up a small plant in Toronto to service Rotol bearings and a sales office in Montreal, which made some forays into the United States.[43]

The competition was most intense in Europe, however. In Paris there were three separate Timken agents with shop sites on the west bank of the Seine. Customers would frequently be talking to all three for a particular application. All were selling Timken bearings, with the same part number. But, said British Timken's Ron Knapp, "If you were sensible you bought an American one." That was because of materials: Timken France used all through-hardened steel; British Timken had case-hardened cups and cones, but used chrome steel; while U.S. Timken used nickel-molybdenum steel, all case hardened, except in the rollers of the smallest bearings. Of course, customers used their own criteria, so U.S. Timken did not always carry the day. George Bentley, who would later become

British Timken's chief engineer, handled one big sale of rolling-mill bearings to Voest, in Linz, Austria. U.S. Timken sent over Sam Weckstein, long-time head of its industrial bearing engineering division, to make its case. Timken France had a representative there as well. But Bentley walked off with the business. "Sam Weckstein was furious," he recalled.[44]

Management in Canton was utterly frustrated by the "cutthroat competition" that was hampering its entry into key European markets. An independent British Timken had become a roadblock to its plans for international expansion. Ultimately, however, Timken was able to resolve this problem, by following the course spelled out by the U.S. Justice Department and the Supreme Court—consolidating its associate companies and running them as divisions, from Canton.[45]

Consolidation, 1958–1959

This change in direction was precipitated by Timken France, when it took on a contract to sell bearings to communist China. The U.S. government urged Timken to stop the sale, but the court order from the antitrust case prevented it from exerting that kind of control. The situation prompted a review of the arguments in the case, which clearly indicated that Timken could legally control the operations of a foreign enterprise if it were a division of the U.S. parent firm and not a separate corporate identity in which Timken merely owned stock (albeit 100 percent of the stock). Timken proposed to the government that it be allowed to dissolve the original French company—La Société Anonyme Française Timken—absorb its assets, and run the business directly. The U.S. Justice Department agreed to that resolution of the problem, and early in 1958 a newly reconstituted Timken France came into being.[46]

The timing of this development was portentous. In 1957, the Treaty of Rome had created the European Economic Community, including West Germany, France, Italy, Belgium, Luxembourg, and the Netherlands. By agreement, tariffs on goods exchanged among those countries were to be phased out over a period of years. The vision of a more unified market promised significant new opportunities for U.S. multinational firms, which were generally welcomed—though not without ambivalence—as contributors to the continuing resurgence of the European economies. The old Timken France, with its factory in Asnières, simply was not up to the challenges the new European market presented. Indeed, through the 1950s, though the plant was producing all-out and importing bearings from both U.S. and British Timken, it still could not keep up with market demand. The situation was so bad it created openings for other companies to step into the breach. La Précision Industrielle, founded by a former Timken

France sales manager, Monsieur Gamet, found a niche in precision tapered roller bearings. A ball bearing manufacturer, Société Nouvelle de Roulements (SNR), entered the tapered roller bearing field in the 1950s and would later become a substantial competitor.[47]

U.S. Timken was determined to act quickly to find a new plant location. It was constrained from expanding in Asnières by restrictions imposed by the French government in an effort to move industry out of metropolitan Paris. At the same time, because Asnières was a stronghold of the Communist party and the workforce in the plant remained highly politicized—there were a number of strikes in the 1950s—the Timken brothers and Umstattd were unwilling to invest further capital there. They were skeptical, in fact, of the wisdom of remaining in France at all, largely because of the continuing political strength of the Communists, who won about 20 percent of the vote in every national election through the decade. That was a big concern in Canton, where West Germany—in the midst of a long period of political stability under the moderate conservative Konrad Adenauer—had begun to look more appealing.[48]

Bernard Riley and Charlie Nouhaud determined to take action to shape the decision. With the assistance of John Pascoe, they were able to arrange a meeting in the spring of 1958 with Antoine Pinay, the French minister of finance. Having held on to that position through numerous changes of governments, Pinay was a strong figure in his own realm and was interested in attracting U.S. manufacturing to France. Bob Timken came from Canton for the meeting, Riley also attended, and Nouhaud helped to translate. "Mr. Timken's basic argument against France was the political instability" and the strength of the Communists, recalled Nouhaud. Pinay argued that the Communists had reached the peak of their political strength in France, whereas Germany still had to face the rise of opposition from the left. "We are the ones who are going to have the political stability, believe me," he said. According to Nouhaud, "Mr. Pinay's tone was so persuasive that Mr. Timken was convinced. Mr. Riley was very satisfied and told me that very evening to start looking for a site for the new factory."[49]

There would be much to test Timken's resolve as it proceeded with its plans. An extreme crisis in April and May brought de Gaulle back to power. Officers of the French army were determined to pursue a war in Algeria—a territorial possession of France for more than a century—to suppress an independence movement there. They threatened a coup d'état at home against any government that sought to negotiate a settlement. The French president, René Coty, called on de Gaulle to form a new government, and in early June the National Assembly voted to grant him emergency powers and then adjourned for six months. An appointed committee drafted a new constitution over the summer, one that gave the French president strong powers and a large measure of independence from the legislature. It was overwhelmingly adopted in a national referendum in September. The Gaullist party won nearly half the seats in a new National Assembly in October, and de Gaulle became the president of France in January 1959. Those events ensured political stability, as Pinay had foreseen. But de Gaulle was no great friend to the United States, and he was ambivalent toward the Common Market and the industrialization of France.[50]

Timken went forward with its plan to find a plant location as those events unfolded. It obtained a list of cities that had taken the step of establishing industrial zones, where factories could be built. The company sent letters of inquiry to all, and to those that responded it sent a detailed questionnaire on subjects ranging from the availability of natural gas to power furnaces to the membership of local churches. That step helped to narrow the field, as officials in many locations declined to go to the trouble of answering such specific questions—especially coming from a company that wasn't French. The possibilities were reduced to twenty-two locations. Charles Nouhaud visited most of those along with two men sent from Canton, Harley Urbach, then second-in-command to Bergstrom in the engineering department, and Herb Markley. Wearing heavy boots in defense against the spring mud, the three toured potential sites all over France, though few offered space for industrial development sufficient to Timken's needs.[51]

One site emerged early as a front-runner, the Alsatian city of Colmar. Colmar's location in an established industrial region bordering both Germany and Switzerland gave it some clear advantages. It was near the center of the Common Market, had good road and rail connections, and was just 12 miles from the Rhine River. But Colmar's greatest advantage was the determination and skill of its city leaders in their efforts to bring Timken to town, as a first step toward the economic revitalization of the city and region. Situated on a narrow plain along the Rhine and against the Vosges Mountains, Alsace was one of Europe's best-known wine regions, but it had also long been a center of the textile industry, with leading companies such as Haussmann, Herzog, and Kiener. But those companies were in decline in the 1950s. Colmar had just created its industrial zone as a first step toward addressing that problem, when Timken's inquiry arrived. Much as Charles Dougherty and Canton's board of trade had done to win Timken over in 1901, Colmar's mayor, Joseph Rey, acted decisively to make his city the site of the new French plant.[52]

For a start, Rey and his staff returned their answers to the company's lengthy questionnaire immediately. They worked hard over a weekend to do so, and traveled to Asnières to present themselves and deliver it in person. In late April 1958, the town council voted to give Timken an option on land in a northern section of the city. Discussions with the company proceeded over the next five months, with

Rey and his deputy Edmond Gerrer devoting considerable time to ensuring that Timken's concerns were addressed. Colmar undertook to build a railroad track to connect Timken to the major rail routes, as well as a sizable block of new housing to accommodate future Timken employees. When it became clear that the potential labor pool in the area lacked the technical training required for precision manufacturing, Louis Matler, the director of the regional technical school, added classes on running equipment such as screw machines and grinders—skills never before required by the regional economy. The head of Colmar's chamber of commerce played a critical role in assuaging the fears of other businesses that Timken would hire away their best people. All in all, it was an effective, concerted effort by a strong core group of town leaders committed to the industrial development of the region. Colmar had many of the small-town characteristics that had made Bucyrus attractive. That and the spirit displayed by Mayor Rey and his colleagues were the critical factors in Timken's decision to locate there.[53]

The effort to bring Timken to Colmar did not go unopposed, however. The rise of the Gaullist party during 1958 made resistance to industrialization a viable political position. Mayor Rey had been a centrist party deputy to the National Assembly, and when he ran again for that office in the fall of 1958 (in the midst of the negotiations with Timken), he lost his seat. He and his associates were impressed—and relieved—that Umstattd and the Timkens took the long-term view of events and persisted in their plans despite the political uncertainty surrounding them. The company gave notice in October that it would exercise its option to purchase the tract of land, some 68 acres, that had been offered. It then hired an architect for the new factory and leased an empty textile plant, where it set up facilities to train tool makers and sales engineers. The political storm continued to swirl around it, however, as those plans advanced. The spring of 1959 brought a hotly contested mayoral election in which Rey's opponent, the leading spokesman against the plan for industrialization, was the man whose land had been appropriated by the town for the industrial district and was now being sold to Timken. It was an emotional and "ugly" contest, recalled Edmond Gerrer. Rey won, and in mid-May, Timken purchased the land and broke ground for the new plant. But at the formal opening ceremony in 1961, the mayor was hospitalized with an ulcer.[54]

In the long run, though, he achieved what he had hoped, not just for Colmar but for the region as a whole. Timken was the first big company to establish operations there, but in less than ten years it would be joined by others in various industries, including food processing, aluminum fabrication, paper and cardboard manufacturing, and watch making. Colmar also became a center of technical education, with an expanded technical college, specialized schools for training in retail and photographic as well as textile industries, accelerated programs for training and retraining adults in trades related to the construction and

The friendship between The Timken Company and the people of Colmar has grown steadily since their association began in 1958. In 1995, two Timken retirees, Harrison Kirkbride and Edgar Bealer—American veterans who fought to free Colmar in 1945—brought their wives and joined Timken France in celebrating the city's fiftieth anniversary of liberation. They are flanked by Timken France executives (from left) Maurice Amiel, Lucien Dambrin, and Roger Violy.

metals industries, and a branch of the Conservatoire National des Arts et Métiers, which offered courses toward advanced degrees in economics and engineering. With the higher level of economic activity and expanded tax base, the city was able to restore its historic central city, which had numerous buildings dating back to the Middle Ages.[55]

In 1958, U.S. Timken, emboldened by its successful consolidation of Timken France, set out to acquire the publicly owned shares of British Timken, so that it too could be operated as a division of the U.S. company. This would turn out to be an expensive purchase, as the market price of British Timken shares rose sharply once the intentions of U.S. Timken became known. But Umstattd and Bob and Henry Timken were convinced it was the right move. Looking ahead they anticipated that the European market for Timken bearings would grow faster than the market at home, largely because there was still so much ground to be won from ball bearings. The new plant in Colmar would help Timken make the most of future growth in the European Economic Community, but the all-out competition from British Timken loomed as an obstacle to realizing that potential. Conscious as ever of the need to protect the Timken trademark, they were also eager to end the situation in which British Timken bearings, made with chrome steel, not nickel-molybdenum, were being offered as the equivalent of bearings made in Canton. Once decided, they moved quickly, wanting to act before the U.S. Justice Department had a chance to change its position.[56]

Between William Umstattd and John Pascoe there was mutual respect, but no love lost. The competition of the 1950s only worsened the tensions they felt. Then, when U.S. Timken embarked on its effort to buy the outstanding British Timken shares, Pascoe and the entire board of directors were put in a rather ticklish position. While they supported the buyout, they had a responsibility to represent the interests of all the company's stockholders and thus to get the best price they could for the British shares. Pascoe and others believed that British Timken stock, at about twelve times earnings in late 1958, was seriously undervalued, largely because of the potential for growth in Timken's share of the European bearing market. To raise the price, the board voted a 25 percent stock dividend and, shortly thereafter, a substantial increase in the regular cash dividend. British Timken stock was rising anyway, once U.S. Timken's intentions became public knowledge, but the board's maneuvers doubtless contributed to an overall rise of 16 shillings per share between December 1958 and April 1959, which added a total of $12.8 million to the purchase price. The total cost to Timken, including redemption of some preferred stock, was $31 million. The company had to borrow $25 million to complete the deal.[57]

Whatever their motivation, Pascoe's actions caused a sense of betrayal in Canton. For that reason, among others, it was inevitable that his role would change when British Timken became a division of The Timken Roller Bearing Company. Pascoe relinquished the position of managing director to Stephen Bennett but stayed on as chairman, moving to London as Dewar had done when handing over the reins in the late 1940s. He also was elected a director of U.S. Timken, and he remained in both positions until his death, at age seventy, in 1963. In short, both sides managed the transition with good grace and dignity, though it was clearly understood in the ranks at British Timken that Pascoe had been moved out.

That did little, really, to sour the relationship between the two companies. In most areas, Canton was careful to take its time in imposing its own policies and practices on the British organization. At the same time, it made needed investments in equipment, some of which had become rather rundown under Pascoe's regime. The organizations were similar in many ways. Shared pride in the Timken product and name was a strong bond. The consolidation of the two organizations opened the way for Timken to move ahead at full speed with what had become its main strategic priority—expanding the bearing business on a worldwide scale.

Toward a New Era

William Umstattd stepped down as president on September 1, 1959, having reached the mandatory retirement age of sixty-five. However, after forty years of working for Timken, he was still eager to be engaged in the company's affairs. Henry and Bob Timken, having worked effectively with Umstattd for so long, were just as eager to keep him involved. To permit that, Timken's board of directors organized an executive committee of the board and elected him to serve as its chairman. He would remain in that position until his death in 1973.

William Umstattd was a leader in the Canton community as well as at Timken. In 1971, National Football League Commissioner Pete Rozelle (left) recognized him as the driving force behind Canton's bid to become home to the National Professional Football Hall of Fame, which opened in 1963.

Umstattd had been grooming a presidential successor. Dwight A. Bessmer was trained as a mining engineer and worked as a bearing salesman in the industrial division from 1933 to 1940, when he became Timken's director of purchasing. Umstattd had tapped him in 1951 to be assistant to the president, and he had gone on to become a vice president in 1953 and executive vice president in 1957. Unfortunately, within six months of becoming president, Bessmer developed some health problems that proved to be alcohol-related. Umstattd demanded his resignation. Much against his wishes, Bob Timken then agreed to serve as the company's president. In line with the policy of promotion from within, it was Bob's firm belief that family members should not take the position of president but should leave that open, so that ambitious non-family executives could reasonably aspire to rise to the top. Otherwise, he thought, it would be hard to get and keep good people. He had seen other cases in which family members had monopolized top management positions, to their companies' detriment. It was important, Bob said, that people knew "you don't have to have the Timken name to get the top job." That philosophy notwithstanding, there was really no one else in Timken's management whose career path had prepared him to be president. Bob Timken's "temporary" appointment would last for eight years.[58]

Thus, for most of the 1960s, the top management team would remain much as it had been since the end of World War II. Two future corporate leaders joined the company in 1962: Bob Timken's older son, William R. (Tim) Timken, Jr., and Joseph F. Toot, whom Umstattd identified early as presidential material. Umstattd would play a large role in preparing these two young men to assume their responsibilities. Indeed, Joe Toot later suggested that Umstattd's influence on the company was as great in the 1960s as it had ever been—not in day-to-day decision making but in guiding ideas, particularly for the international business.[59] Corporate strategy would continue to rest on the twin pillars of international expansion and the Bucyrus concept of standardization and high-volume production. The defining organizational and cultural characteristics of the company remained resolutely unchanged.

Competition on an International Scale

In its domestic markets Timken was stronger than ever in the 1960s. Sustained investments in its manufacturing technologies, combined with the success of its drive for standardization in bearing applications across a number of industries—by the mid-1960s it was able to make long production runs on 559 sizes—made it the low-cost producer by a significant margin. Continuing improvements in bearing life and capacity ratings also contributed to making Timken bearings more competitive than ever against other types. This was reflected in a major decision General Motors made in 1964: to switch the front-wheel bearings on its small and medium-sized cars from ball to tapered roller bearings. This landmark decision forced GM's New Departure-Hyatt division to scramble to go into production on the sizes required. Timken already supplied bearings to various GM divisions for other applications. This change opened the door a good bit wider.[1]

That year, Timken shocked the industry by lowering its prices 2 to 8 percent on those high-volume sizes, despite the booming market. Competitors like New Departure-Hyatt and Federal-Mogul-Bower grumbled publicly about having to meet the lower prices, but in Bob Timken's view, that was preferable to having customers grumble that Timken was *too* profitable. Even with the price cuts, the company's after-tax profits averaged nearly 12 percent of sales in the five-year period from 1963 through 1967. (See Table 8.1.) That was higher than any prior year in the post–World War II era—since 1946 the average had been just a little over 8 percent. The 1960s would also be a decade of growth, but not spectacular growth, especially compared to high-profile "growth companies" of the era such as IBM, Xerox, and Litton Industries. Timken did fine compared to other so-called smoke-stack manufacturers. Its compound annual growth in earnings per share from 1956 to 1966 was about 7 percent. That placed it in the top 40 percent of the Fortune 500 list of industrial companies, somewhat below Caterpillar and Ford, but equal to GM and above Federal-Mogul.[2]

U.S. industry as a whole was ascendant. It was growing and profitable at home, with the post–World War II economic boom in full force. Foreign competitors, especially the Japanese, began to make inroads into some domestic markets—including miniature ball bearings—but overall exports remained well ahead of imports. At the same time, the nation's leading firms continued to expand operations internationally and to participate in the growth of a reconstructed Europe and the developing economies in other parts of the world. The spread of U.S. multinational companies proceeded at a strong pace, peaking in 1968, when some 540 manufacturing subsidiaries were organized or purchased abroad.[3] Having moved aggressively into international markets, Timken in the 1960s faced the task of consolidating the expansion of the previous decade and building an effective multinational corporation.

Timken bearings had been manufactured in Britain since 1909 and in France since World War I, but under the direction of British Timken. Corporate management in Canton had little experience in directing overseas operations. The push into international markets in the 1950s brought it to the point of directly managing production and marketing in six countries outside the United States—Canada, Britain, France, Australia, Brazil, and South Africa. Its approach to the task reflected both the strengths and the weaknesses of its organization and culture.

The company continued to operate much as it always had, with strong functional organizations pursuing excellence in the execution of business strategies set in the corporate office. Umstattd's "retirement" notwithstanding, the personnel at the top had not changed. But the next generation of leaders was in training.

The Corporate Office

In the 1960s, Henry and Bob Timken and William Umstattd, who remained actively involved as chairman of the executive committee of the board of directors, continued to set company strategy and make all high-level management

TABLE 8.1

Timken Company Comparative Financial Data, 1960–1969 (in Thousands of Dollars, except per Share Data)

	1960	1961	1962	1963	1964	1965	1966	1967	1968	1969
Net sales	$244,806	$240,001	$277,205	$292,456	$334,406	$375,674	$392,892	$355,056	$351,427	$399,396
Net income	19,181	15,988	25,063	30,956	39,821	48,768	48,537	35,522	34,141	34,692
Total assets	$224,595	$225,776	$234,925	$238,611	$253,521	$291,009	$314,510	$328,147	$353,520	$378,223
Long-term bank loans	18,000	21,875	18,750	6,250						
Total capital and earnings invested in the business	169,685	172,888	185,166	200,141	220,785	247,378	274,925	291,439	306,486	321,973
Return on sales	7.8%	6.7%	9.0%	10.6%	11.9%	13.0%	12.4%	10.0%	9.7%	8.7%
Return on assets	8.5	7.1	10.7	13.0	15.7	16.8	15.4	10.8	9.7	9.2
Return on capital and earnings	11.3	9.2	13.5	15.5	18.0	19.7	17.7	12.2	11.1	10.8
Earnings per share	$1.80	$1.50	$2.35	$2.91	$3.74	$4.58	$4.56	$3.33	$3.20	$3.26
Dividends per share	1.20	1.20	1.20	1.50	1.80	2.00	2.00	1.80	1.80	1.80
Number of employees	19,521	19,909	19,560	18,957	20,469	21,090	21,420	20,567	20,601	22,635
Number of shareholders	24,350	24,003	24,426	23,553	23,881	27,130	30,016	32,100	31,569	32,400

Source: The Timken Roller Bearing Company Annual Reports, 1960–69.

Note: Per share data adjusted for 2-for-1 stock split in 1965.

decisions. The company's 11-member board was composed entirely of insiders: some past and current divisional executives; John M. Timken, brother of Henry and Bob; and, succeeding John Pascoe in 1962, British Timken's Stephen Bennett. There would be no outside members of the board from the early 1930s, when A. C. Ernst stepped down, until 1978. George L. Deal, who had become treasurer (and a member of the board) in 1953 and was vice president for finance from 1964 to 1973, recalled that he had to write the Securities and Exchange Commission more than once to explain Timken's insistence on having such an insider board. "They didn't like it, but there wasn't anything they could do about it," Deal noted. "We were very comfortable, right or wrong, with that kind of organization."[4]

In fact, because of the board's makeup, its role was primarily to give formal approval to decisions that had already been made. "We would hold our annual meetings in [Henry's] office," Deal said. "A couple of us sometimes stood outside the door and just got our heads in. That's how informal a board meeting it was when Henry was running it. . . . [He] was the boss and that was it." For all the informality, as Deal's comment suggests, it was a top-down style of corporate management. Among the three men at the top, there remained the close collegial relationship that had existed for many years. Observed Joe Toot, who would join the corporate office in the late 1960s, "The intensity of their communication was extraordinary."[5]

Executive vice president Herb Markley was a junior member of that inner group. Though he was on a track to be president, Markley had been considered still too narrowly trained and inexperienced for the position in 1960 when Dwight Bessmer resigned. He had joined the company as an accountant trainee in 1938 and had gone to law school as part of that training. During World War II, he had worked in the U.S. Army intelligence service and spent the final months of the war in post-liberation Paris. Through that experience he had developed a love of travel that would serve him, and Timken, in good stead. Because of his legal training, Markley was very involved in the company's antitrust litigation, and he advanced steadily within the corporate office in the postwar years, becoming assistant to the president in 1955. After working closely with Umstattd in that position for three years, Markley became vice president with responsibility for international operations, in which role he handled virtually all the details of setting up the company's new manufacturing operations in Australia, Brazil, and France. As executive vice president in the 1960s, he attended advanced management programs at Harvard Business School and the University of Pennsylvania. Just as important, he received intensive training in the Timken style of management within the tight-knit group that ran the company from its spartan offices on Mahogany Row.[6]

One project of particular importance to top management in the 1960s was the development of the next generation of company leaders—Joe Toot and Tim Timken. (Much like Umstattd in the 1930s, Markley, as president from 1968 to 1979, would help to provide a smooth transition.) Both in their twenties, Timken and Toot joined the company on the same day, September 4, 1962.

At Bob Timken's insistence, their first assignments sent them into the bearing factory to get a sense of the business from the ground up. There they would stay for a couple of years, working as "project men" under the direction of Bob Sisson. He rotated them through the different departments in the factory and took them along on his varied assignments, including troubleshooting at some of Timken's international plants. Bob Timken left it pretty much up to Sisson to design their training program, but he made it clear "they had to get dirty and learn the bearing business."[7]

Sisson took him at his word, insisting, for example, that Joe Toot stay in Department 74 until he could set up the continuous grinding line himself and run it without making too much scrap. "He had to sweat blood to do that. . . ," Sisson said, "but he was really proud of himself when he got the first okay roller out of that line." The tour of duty with Sisson helped Joe and Tim appreciate the skill and know-how that kept things running on the shop floor—in part by enduring some teasing about what a Harvard MBA degree did *not* equip them to do. They also learned to respect the shop-floor culture and spirit. And Sisson was ready to point out how management sometimes got in the way of smooth operations. Looking at the company from his perspective, they saw a number of things that they would later decide to change.[8]

Both young men had attended elite schools. Joe went to Phillips Exeter Academy, Princeton University, and Harvard Business School. Tim, three years younger, was also a Harvard MBA but had gone to a rival prep school, Phillips Academy, in Andover, Massachusetts, and to Stan-

By September 1962, the company's future leaders were on board. Tim Timken's (right) first summer job was shoveling dolomite into steel mill furnaces. Joe Toot had to learn to set up and run a continuous grinding line.

ford University in California. Both were All-American athletes—Timken a collegiate swimmer (who remained a world-class competitor in swimming in the 1990s); Toot, the captain of Princeton's fencing team. It was not until their years at Harvard that they became close friends, but they had known each other all their lives and had similar upbringings in many respects.

Joe was a Canton native, the son of a physician and a nurse. He had taken summer jobs at Republic Steel in Canton and with a construction company, and in both cases, he had been required to become a union member in order to work. He recalled being outraged at being forced to join, on the one hand, but on the other being impressed with a sense of why unions existed in the first place. "I had my first brush with a tyrannical, unfair supervisor when I was working on that construction job," he said, "and I've never forgotten it." While his empathy for the individual factory employee would remain, his distaste for unions would grow stronger under the tutelage of Umstattd and others in the corporate office. Umstattd was Joe Toot's mentor and champion. They knew each other as family friends and hunting companions while Joe was still in school. "We were looking for people with ambition and willingness to work hard," recalled Bob Timken. Umstattd had seen those qualities in his young friend and had recruited him into the company. His intention even then was that Joe should be developed to become president of the company. The fit seemed even more perfect when Joe Toot married Tim's sister, Edith M. Timken, in 1965.[9]

Tim Timken's first summer job with the company, at the age of eighteen—shoveling dolomite into the furnaces—was not something he chose for himself. "It was [my father's] idea, not my idea," Tim noted. "He laid the program out." When he first joined Timken full-time, he drove such a rundown old car that Bob Sisson kidded him about being a bad advertisement for the company. Tim replied, "My dad thinks if it runs, it's still good enough for me." Bob Timken was absolutely insistent that his son should cultivate not only humility, but a sense of duty to the company as preparation for assuming leadership. In fact, he would push his son to take a more active role than he himself had played—for example, by becoming a high-level salesman of bearings and steel. This was one of the ways in which Bob demonstrated his awareness of the changes in the business environment that were placing increasing demands on corporate executives.[10]

The degrees in business administration that Tim and Joe held were important, in Bob Timken's view. He had attended Harvard Business School for one year only but had become a believer in the case method of teaching. "In the old days, I suppose, you didn't look for trained people as much as you do now," he later recalled. But he had encouraged his son to get the training. In the late 1960s, the company would change its recruiting for entry-level management positions to take in more people with advanced degrees. Recalled Bob, "The first time we hired an MBA student other than those two, everybody said, 'They've quit the old policy. They're not promoting from within anymore.' It wasn't really true because we were just hiring people with a little more education." It was his way of professionalizing Timken's management. Subsequently, Bob pushed to get all the company's officers and everyone in a general management position to attend an advanced management course at a recognized business school. That was because, in his view, the group had become too "inbred." In later years, he would insist that any family member who wanted to work in the company should have a graduate degree.[11]

Once they passed through the initial years of training with Sisson, Tim and Joe embarked on a series of assignments that exposed them to different aspects of the company's business, in particular its international operations. After a stint as an assistant to the vice president for sales, Tim went to Colmar in January 1965. After just ten months there, he was called back to Canton to set up a corporate development department, and he joined the board of directors that year. In 1968 he became corporate vice president with responsibility for all domestic operations.

In June 1965, Joe Toot was posted to Düsseldorf as general manager of Timken Rollenlager. During that year, Timken closed its factory in Asnières. It also created a new management entity in Colmar, Timken Europe, to coordinate European sales and manufacturing. In January 1966, Toot moved to Colmar to be deputy managing director of Timken France and Timken Europe. (One of his first assignments was to sell Timken's property back to the city of Asnières.) The next year he too returned to Canton and became vice president for international operations. In 1968, he became corporate vice president, still with responsibility for international operations—the counterpart to Tim Timken on the domestic side. He was elected to the board of directors in 1968. The company's new leadership team had come into being.[12]

Even at the time, Joe Toot later recalled, he felt that those two career paths were carefully thought out and orchestrated by Henry, Bob, and Umstattd, in particular the emphasis on getting out of Canton to gain perspective on the international business. That later became the accepted path for rising Timken executives. Toot and Timken set a high standard for U.S. executives abroad, which became part of the expectations placed on those that followed them. Both spoke French comfortably (Joe had lived in Paris), and both carried the no-frills style and work ethic of Canton with them when they went overseas.

The training that Tim and Joe received, including its heavy emphasis on international business, was clearly intended as a departure for Timken's top management. Yet the approach the company took to developing that business was firmly rooted in the past. It was very much in keeping with the top-down style of management that prevailed in those days. "Remember," said Joe in retrospect, "this was a tightly run ship. . . command and control, few people in charge. All of a sudden it goes all over the world. Well, the style didn't change. The style remained

'Joe, you go find out what they're doing and straighten them out. If it gets too big, call us and we'll give you the help you need.'"[13] The international business would be run from Canton and according to the strategy that had made Timken the clear leader in U.S. markets.

William Umstattd said in 1960: "As I envisage the picture around the world, the United States is definitely tapered roller bearing minded. The rest of the world, to a great extent, is ball bearing minded, or certainly cylindrical roller bearing minded. We are going to change the minds of engineers around the world to the point where they use the best bearing instead of just bearings that are better than a friction bearing." Timken, he anticipated, would use its Bucyrus strategy to penetrate the European automotive market first, and then its industrial markets, with standardized bearings produced at low cost in long production runs.[14]

So confident was Timken in its strategy that when the French automaker, Renault, proposed to sell its bearing subsidiary, Société Nouvelle de Roulements (SNR), Timken declined to buy. It would expand by selling "the best bearing" in the familiar way. In part, the company simply felt constrained by the court order in its antitrust case, which was still in force and barred any collaboration on markets and prices with a separately organized foreign company. But Maurice Amiel, who would lead Timken's European division in the 1980s and 1990s, gave another explanation that must also be considered. "The theory of the company at that time," said Amiel, "was that we were overwhelming in our technology. Everybody was going to recognize it and admit it." In fact, the company's technical strengths—in particular its sales engineering—would serve it well in the effort to build market share in Europe. But other factors, such as strong price competition from established competitors and the predominance of the metric system in European manufacturing, offset that advantage to a great degree, forcing Timken to struggle to gain a foothold, especially in the industrial market. In retrospect, spurning an opportunity for a strategic acquisition would appear to have been a mistake. In the short run, however, having invested to build new plants around the world, the company was focused, not on further expansion, but on consolidating prior growth.[15]

Integration of International Operations

In April 1960, Timken brought the general managers of all its international operations—in Canada, Britain, France, South Africa, Australia, and Brazil—together with the managers of its U.S. plants for ten days of meetings and plant tours in Ohio. The heart of the program was a four-day "working conference" that provided a sort of crash course on the corporate organization and its approach to business. Attendees listened to presentations by nearly 40 speakers

A common practice of Timken top management was to bring together company leaders from around the world to create a unified sense of purpose and ensure understanding of the company's strategies. In 1971, top management was represented by (front row from left) Joe Toot, Herb Markley, Tim Timken, and William Umstattd (retired president).

representing sales, advertising, engineering, operations, administration, and top management. Building one upon the other, they delivered a clear message: there would be strong direction from the center. That was a common pattern for U.S. companies in the first stage of extending operations abroad and an approach that flowed naturally from the deep, functionally organized management structures they had built. The Timken speakers conveyed a sense of why that should be so, as they detailed all that was behind the directives coming from Canton—technical expertise, research, modern business practices and analytical tools, and an evolving computer system, not to mention long years of experience as an industry leader. It was an impressive display of organizational strength, the purpose of which, frankly expressed, was to help managers in the field get comfortable with the level of conformity that was going to be required.[16]

At the same time, to the extent that cooperation and a unified sense of purpose could be achieved by assertion, this session provided that as well. Bob Timken, in an opening talk, stressed the overriding need for a single standard of quality across the company's operations and warned against the danger of "floundering in a morass of international misunderstandings, jealousies and functions that will make it impossible to keep our heads above water." Bill Umstattd wrapped up with a similar message. "We are one family," said Umstattd, "and when a decision is made, let's not say that it is imposed upon us by 'they'. . . . It isn't a question of 'they' or 'us' or 'anyone else.' It is a question of The Timken Roller Bearing Company saying that certain things must be done. Every man whether he is a manager of a small plant, a medium-sized plant or a big plant should enter into the spirit of the decision and say, 'We must do this, not because it was imposed on us by *they,* but because *we* must do it—*we* think it is right, therefore, we must do it.'"[17] This was an ethos well-suited to drive integration, though it did not allow much room for local managers to think creatively or to question decisions made in Canton, even when conditions on the ground suggested the need for modification.

The ultimate goal of integration was to be able to coordinate sales and production on a worldwide basis. The problem had many facets. For example, Timken wanted its sales and service engineering to be consistent across divisions, so that customers with the same need or problem would get the same recommendations, no matter which office they were dealing with. The company also wished to transfer the cost-accounting system developed in Canton to other operations, so that each unit's economics could be compared meaningfully to all others. The objective was to be able to maximize the profitability of the system as a whole by supplying the bearings for each order from the factory that could deliver them most cost-effectively, taking into account manufacturing efficiency, shipping costs, and tariffs. In order to get to that point, the products of all Timken plants had to be interchangeable, and that was a goal with far-reaching implications.

Timken had begun to work toward interchangeability of its U.S.-produced bearings in 1955, in connection with the establishment of the Bucyrus shipping center. Because it pulled together bearings from different plants to fill orders centrally, the shipping center brought to light the fact that there were often significant variations among products having the same part numbers. Most production managers, Timken discovered, had come to view the company's stated tolerances—the acceptable degree of variation from specified dimensions, established by Timken's engineering department—as simply unrealistic. Having been judged unrealistic, they were frequently ignored. "In other instances," noted Joseph Selby, the manager for quality control, "we were making product to different tolerances for one division or one customer than for others, although the two would be identified as the same quality." The introduction of the shipping center meant that bearings were now produced for inventory, not for specific customer orders. The products of all plants had to be fully interchangeable. The divisions took a pragmatic approach to the problem: Manufacturing proposed a new system of tolerances wide enough to be maintainable by all plants under normal operating conditions. After lengthy negotiations with Engineering, the new system became the official standard for the precision of Timken bearings.[18]

Establishing a common standard was only the first step. Each plant had to be equipped with the machines, the tooling, and the gauges required to ensure that level of quality—a costly proposition that would take years to complete. Of the bearing parts, rollers presented the most formidable problems. After the crowned roller (with a slightly bowed shape on the long sides) was shown to make a significant improvement in bearing load-carrying capacities, it had taken more than five years for the company to convert all its U.S. plants to make that design. Now it would have to undertake the conversion on an international scale. Selby said of this effort: "The tooling problems are formidable, and an entirely new concept of gauging is required." In 1960, Selby was responsible for coordinating Timken's push for interchangeability. As he explained to the managers gathered in Canton, the problem of standardized rollers was compounded at British and French Timken because they had traditionally used through-hardened rather than case-hardened steel for those parts. Changing processes meant not only finding a source for the appropriate grade of steel, but also changing the tooling to handle the new material.[19]

Another knotty quality problem lay in gauging for taper. While there were established international sources for size gauges providing an adequate degree of reliability for the company's standard bearings, the available tools for measuring angles were less desirable. Accuracy of gauges was absolutely essential to Timken's system of inspection. It was preserved by regularly checking the gauges the inspectors used against a master, which had to be maintained at a level of precision above the gauges it was measuring. In its own gauge department in Canton, Timken had developed a taper-measuring machine. This it judged superior to the so-called angle slip block—a readily available device that had the necessary accuracy but, in its manner of use, allowed a greater chance for human error. Mike Curtis, the general manager of Timken's control inspection department, and Timken engineer Jack Burness had pushed the development of an improved taper-measuring device. It was so precise it became the U.S. Bureau of Standards' means of measuring taper. As of 1960, Selby explained, the master gauges in all U.S. plants, and for Canadian and Australian Timken, were being sent back to Canton once a year for inspection and reworking. The costs of that practice, including shipping, customs duties, and the value of lost time, were high and would get much higher if Britain, France, and Brazil also were to be serviced in that way.[20] The company faced a tough choice: carry the cost of maintaining a centralized system ("obviously the safest method of doing the job," said Selby); or allow the international plants to make their own taper masters using angle slip blocks. It chose the safe but costly approach. Clearly, quality was one area in which the demands of expanding the business internationally pushed the limits of Timken's established systems. "In a strict sense," Selby said, the goal of having all Timken bearings maintain a single standard of quality worldwide would "never be possible." The company was constantly improving quality with the introduction of new equipment, he explained. "Since it would be physically impossible, for instance, to replace all grinding machines in all plants simultaneously, it is obvious that we shall be making a better product at some plants than at others." What was possible, however, was "to insure that all product is within our published tolerances." That was the goal aimed at and achieved in the 1960s.[21]

Of course, Timken quality had an important materials component. The company judged the nickel-molybdenum steel that had been used in Canton since the 1920s to be one of its greatest competitive assets. Extensive testing had shown case-hardened "nickel-moly" to be stronger and more wear resistant than the chrome steels commonly used for bearings. It also had a manufacturing advantage that contributed to quality: it was much more tolerant of variation in heat-treating and metalworking practices than chrome steels, so the plant could get more consistent results. Added to the choice of alloy were all the process understanding and technology that had been developed by Timken's steel and tube division over the years. The company decided initially that it would not attempt to supply nickel-moly steel to all the international plants from Canton but would provide centralized support for developing local sources of supply. Its approach was to draw up detailed specifications to be provided to potential steel suppliers and to offer technical support to help the suppliers meet them. Still, it was a formidable task to develop steel sources that met Timken standards.[22]

British Timken was in a relatively good position. In the early 1950s, a Birmingham-based company, Tube Investments, had determined to sell into the bearings industry. It had licensed Assel tube-making technology from U.S. Timken, to put in a plant in Desford, Leicester, that had produced tubing for military applications during World War II. With considerable technical support from Canton, the Desford plant had an Assel mill in operation by 1954. It became Tubes, Ltd., a subsidiary of Tube Investments, and was the main source of tubing for the rapidly growing Duston and Daventry plants. Timken became its largest customer. Tubes, Ltd., also sold to Timken France in the 1950s. As the demand for bearings grew, it added a second Assel mill in 1962. It would add a third in 1972, to become the largest tube-making complex of its kind in the world after Timken, which had installed its fourth Assel mill in Canton in 1962. The organization worked closely with British Timken, both to manage its production to meet Timken's needs, and to keep its quality up to Timken's standards. For example, it readily invested in the kind of slow-cool furnace that U.S. Timken advocated for producing the metallurgical structure best suited to bearing manufacture. There was also a strong three-way interaction between British Timken, Tubes, Ltd., and its main steel supplier, Samuel Fox & Company, Ltd. In 1960, British Timken began switching from high-carbon chrome steel to nickel-moly. This was a complicated procedure at the plant, because the two types of steel had to be handled quite differently in heat treatment. During the changeover, when there were both types in the stockyard, they had to be kept rigorously separated to avoid disasters in production. That aside, however, it was a smooth transition.[23]

The situation was more problematic for Timken France. In the early 1960s, its tubing came from Desford and Canton, but the cost of relying completely on imported materials was high. When it had first decided on Colmar as a plant location, Timken had counted on its being quite accessible for steel shipments because of its link to the Rhine River. The Rhine, however, proved uncooperative. It was subject to freezing in winter and low water in summer. In the mid-1960s, Timken began actively looking for a tube supplier located on the European continent. There were by that time a handful of firms operating Assel mills in Europe, one of which, VALTI, was jointly owned by Tube Investments and a French company, Vallourec. Although Tube Investments had undertaken the venture primarily to supply French Timken and create a second source of supply for British Timken, the party that had to be sold was corporate management in Canton. That required, first, a further investment in a slow-cool furnace and, subsequently, convincing Timken's tough-minded metallurgists that the material coming from the French steel supplier, Ugine, would meet their standards. Ultimately, though, VALTI made the grade. British and French Timken would have two sources of supply into the 1990s.[24]

The big push for interchangeable products, which consumed much of the company's energies in the early 1960s, paid off nicely in 1965 when a surge of industrial growth in the United States put Timken under intense pressure to keep up with domestic demand. Over the next two years, the company would import hundreds of thousands of bearings made in British, French, Australian, and Canadian

Timken plants in order to avoid falling short in supplying its U.S. customers. It was an impressive early display of the kind of integration that would be required of all multinational companies in the global economy of the 1990s.[25]

Another successful initiative of the 1960s was the creation, at Colmar, of a strong application engineering department and a training program for sales and application engineers. Claude Perret, who had taken the course at U.S. Timken in the early 1950s, came from Timken Rollenlager, in Düsseldorf, to set up the training program. He was joined by Edward Keim, a veteran from the industrial sales engineering division in Canton. They got under way early in 1960, well before the Colmar plant was in operation. In terms of curriculum, the course they taught was exactly the same as in Canton, but it had to be conducted in several languages. The trainees coming into the program had been hired in Australia, South Africa, Latin America, Britain, France, and Germany—all the centers of Timken's operations except Canada and the United States. The company's official international language was English, and all the engineers hired had to speak it conversationally. But technical concepts required a whole different vocabulary, and there was still much explaining to do in native tongues.[26]

In the 1960s, the program had as many as 40 students. After two years in Colmar, they went to Canton for a final period of training. Because of the extensive travel and the living abroad required of trainees, the company made it an unofficial policy to hire mostly unmarried men—a decision that had some unintended effects. Quite a few of the men found wives in Colmar, so, far from being unattached and happy to travel, they suddenly had reasons to want to stay in France. At the same time, this group of young men from around the world formed bonds of understanding and collegiality that would remain strong over the years as they rose through the ranks in different parts of Timken's international organization. It was largely they who would implement integration of sales and customer support on a worldwide scale.[27]

Timken's strong functional organizations proved themselves well equipped to handle the challenges of coordinating a multinational business at the operational level. The company would find, however, that adapting its business strategy to the realities of international markets posed some unfamiliar and vexing problems.

The Bucyrus Strategy Abroad

Timken's strategy of high-volume, low-cost production of a limited number of bearing sizes, overwhelmingly successful in North America, met with varying levels of success in other parts of the world. The U.S. automotive and equipment manufacturers who were Timken's best customers accounted for a great deal of the market in Australia and Brazil. The manufacturing plants in both countries had Department 36 technology, the modified version of Bucyrus designed to operate economically at lower volumes. Australian Timken grew steadily, focusing exclusively on the small Green Light bearings sold mainly for automotive applications. SKF had a ball bearing plant in Australia and was an established competitor. Federal-Mogul-Bower and a number of Japanese companies sold imported tapered roller bearings. But, except for a brief time in the 1970s, Timken was the only company to manufacture them there. Timken do Brasil struggled against extremely unsettled political and economic conditions in Brazil in the 1960s. It would grow rapidly once those factors came under control.[28]

In South Africa, by contrast, the company's focus was primarily on railroad bearings—the South African Railway was the largest railroad in the world under unified management. There the decade of the 1960s was primarily one of making up lost ground. Just after World War II, the railroad company had specified Timken bearings exclusively on a large new order of locomotives and passenger cars, an order that had been taken and filled by British Timken. Early on it had begun experiencing failures in the journal boxes that were an integral part of British Timken's product. (The plant opened by British Timken at Benoni in 1951 had been put in place to manufacture journal boxes.) The root cause of the failures was a design problem. British Timken's engineers recognized and quickly corrected it, but they did not then communicate clearly to the railroad about the problem or its solution. Over the course of the 1950s, far from expanding the market with the new AP bearing, the company lost the entire South African Railway business.[29]

In 1958, however, British Timken hired Kendall Brooke, a young South African engineer, out of the railroad company's London office. Once Brooke had uncovered the nature of the problem, John Pascoe charged him with the task of regaining the lost customer. Shortly thereafter, British Timken was consolidated with the U.S. company. According to Brooke, management in Canton was at first unimpressed by the South African business, but the large potential market for the AP bearing was appealing. (British Timken had begun producing the AP in 1958.) Brooke continued his campaign, and by 1967, South African Railways had again standardized on Timken bearings. The following year the company committed to building a new factory in Benoni to produce AP bearings. Brooke became managing director of Timken South Africa in 1969, and in the 1970s, with the new plant on line, he succeeded in extending the reach of the AP bearing into Zimbabwe, Zambia, and Mozambique.[30]

In Europe, the situation was far more complicated. To be sure, U.S. companies provided a significant market for Timken bearings, particularly after 1960, as the pace of establishing European manufacturing facilities picked up. Yet that accounted for only a small portion of the total market—a market that was growing dramatically. In the larger arena, the "best bearing" faced entrenched partiality, not only to other types of bearings, but also to metric dimensions. There were strong European competitors making ball, straight roller, and tapered roller bearings, in particular SKF, which had been making its own metric-sized tapered roller bearings since 1924. Those factors did not stop Timken's progress, but they slowed it down.

The company scored a big, early success in the German automotive market. Bill Judy, who was sent to head up Timken Rollenlager in 1958, recalled that the initial marketing approach was straightforward. They composed a form letter on the advantages of "Grün Licht" (Green Light) bearings, sent it to the automakers, and prepared to follow up on responses. The U.S.-made Green Light front-wheel bearings had some clear advantages going into that market. They were smaller than comparable ball bearings and so could save on the weight of the car, and, even coming all the way from Bucyrus, they were advantageously priced. Another strong selling point was the degree to which Timken had penetrated the U.S. automotive market. Recalled Gerhard Reiter, who joined Timken Rollenlager as a sales engineer in 1960, "The American car industry was really the leading car industry. When we came with American references . . . the German design engineers listened."[31]

The extensive data Timken could supply on performance on U.S. cars was a valuable selling aid, and the world of automotive engineering was small enough that there was a fair amount of movement between companies. For all that, the first business came from Borgward and was taken away, not from a ball bearing company, but from British Timken. That proved to be a critically important sale. Although Borgward went out of business in Germany in 1959, the two key men that Timken had sold to moved on to other companies: Karl Monz to BMW and Karl Dziggle to Volkswagen. They helped to open doors, and both of those companies became important customers. The entire German automotive industry would be using Timken front-wheel bearings by the mid-1960s.[32]

In short, the company's technical strength and the reputation of its product provided advantages. But they could not ensure the kind of success it enjoyed in the United States, even within the tapered roller bearing field. Timken was the newcomer, and the competition was well established. In some cases, it would take years for Timken even to get a hearing because of automakers' established relationships with other bearing companies—for example, at Renault, the owner of SNR; and at Fiat in Italy, whose owners, the Agnelli family, also owned RIV, the leading Italian bearing company. In 1965, SKF bought RIV, and the Agnellis became shareholders in the Swedish bearings firm. SKF was growing aggressively through acquisitions and became the largest bearing producer worldwide in the mid-1960s. RIV alone had 10 manufacturing plants in Italy as well as factories in Spain and Argentina. In addition, through the 1960s and 1970s, SKF acquired 5 French companies in specialized areas of the industry.[33]

Yet SKF was only the largest in a large field that included not only the other long-established European firms, FAG, RIV, and SNR, but also many small postwar start-ups and at least one Japanese transplant, NTN. As soon as Timken's Green Light bearings began to make inroads in automotive applications, the strongest of those competitors tooled up to begin producing the same sizes—a move much to the liking of the automakers, who valued having multiple sources of supply. They also began developing their sales and application engineering capabilities, once the value of that kind of customer service was demonstrated.[34]

In that highly competitive environment, pricing, supply, and delivery were all tricky issues, often difficult to handle in a highly centralized way. Top managers in Canton were inexperienced at being the newcomer—and underdog—in the market. There were some difficult lessons to be learned as Colmar struggled unsuccessfully to turn a profit in its early years of operation. Timken had chosen to install a Department 36 line for automotive wheel bearings, mainly on the basis of a large order from Simca, the French automaker in which Chrysler had bought a stake in 1958. Not long after the plant went into production in 1961, a directive came from Canton to raise the price on those bearings, in line with an increase being made in the United States. Jules Moreland, director of sales for Timken France, pressed to have the increase made gradually, but a long-standing Timken policy of selling the same bearing at one price to all customers worked against that. The order was sustained and the Simca business was lost, with SKF stepping into the breach. It would take nearly five years to regain Simca as a customer. In the meantime, the company had to hustle to bring in orders from VW and Mercedes to take up the output from Colmar.[35]

Timken still faced an uphill battle to build the sales required to make a high-volume line profitable. It was a Catch-22: without that volume, Colmar remained a high-cost producer and could not price its bearings competitively. The problem was made worse by the fact that the French plant relied on rollers imported from U.S. Timken, which took the profit on the product, making Colmar's costs appear even higher. In addition, it had some factory problems in the early years. It was one thing to train people to use machines but quite another to develop an organization that could run equipment at production levels, solving problems as they arose. All these factors meant that, where SKF, FAG, and others had tooled up to produce inch-sized tapered roller bearings, they tended to have the advantage on price.[36]

Addressing Colmar's problems with costs and pricing became Joe Toot's first assignment on his posting there in early 1966—and his first big test as a manager. Called back to Canton to give his assessment of the situation, he proposed that

Timken initiate production of rollers at Colmar and that it focus the plant on making a narrower range of bearing sizes, to reduce unit costs. Bob Sisson, by now a troubleshooter with the title General Manager for Manufacturing, succeeded in solving the problems that had been plaguing production. Timken France became profitable in 1967.[37]

Emergence of Timken Europe

Through the 1960s and 1970s, Timken progressively strengthened its organization in Europe to meet the competitive challenges it faced there. Though Canton provided strong direction, with few exceptions Timken chose European executives to run European operations. In particular, it drew on the strength of the British Timken organization, which had considerable experience in managing an international business. After a brief, unsuccessful, experiment with a U.S. plant manager, Paul C. Wiseman, as general manager of Timken France, the company had installed Tony Grainger. Grainger had joined British Timken in 1929 and had been its leading salesman in Europe in the 1950s—and a thorn in the side of U.S. Timken. When the company created Timken Europe in 1965, Grainger became its managing director, retaining his existing position as the head of Timken France.

When originally created, Timken Europe had no legal status, just a charge to coordinate the company's European sales and production. It consisted of Grainger, his deputy managing director, Joe Toot, and Bill Judy, who moved from Timken Rollenlager to Colmar to take responsibility for developing a European sales organization. Almost immediately, however, the company began to consider how to expand its scope and role, and how to make it a legal entity. There were by this time Timken sales engineers living and working in Italy, Spain, and Belgium, although only in France and Germany was it legally established to do business. Without being formally registered in those other countries, Timken could not fully support its employees. Just as important, where it had developed significant business, the company was anxious to have an official presence in order to be able to supply its large customers without being wholly dependent on distributors. Some accounts had simply become too big to handle effectively in that way, and in some countries distributors' commissions were absorbing a significant portion of the revenue from sales.[38]

Timken relied heavily on key distributors—for example, Daniel Doyen in Brussels, Ubel in Amsterdam, Nomo-Kullager in Stockholm, Bianchi Cuscinetti in Milan—to help build its customer base among industrial companies. Maria Luisa Garavaglia Fuchs was a sales representative for Bianchi in the 1960s—one of the very few women in the business of selling bearings. Later a regional manager for Bianchi, she recalled that in 1960, when Jules Moreland first approached Luigi Bianchi to become a distributor, Timken had the reputation in Italy of having a good product but also of being slow on delivery. Bianchi did his own market research before deciding to take Timken on, and once decided, he invested a substantial amount to purchase the stock of bearings his firm would need to supply the market effectively. Timken assisted Bianchi with technical support for selling. For example, Fuchs, who already had an engineering background, took a two-week course from Timken in Colmar. Later the company placed a sales engineer, Armando Pasquale, in Milan. By 1967, the business had expanded enough in Italy that a second sales engineer, Roberto Dotti, went to support Bianchi. Neither man had an office, however. They worked out of their homes and used office space on the distributor's premises. That was a typical situation and one the company wanted to correct.[39]

In 1970, the new Timken Europe came into being as a French company and a wholly owned subsidiary of The Timken Roller Bearing Company. In accordance with the original antitrust decision against it, Timken had to be careful to avoid seeming to create a successor to Timken France, against which it would then have to compete. Timken Europe was therefore chartered as a sales organization only, to buy bearings from Timken France, British Timken, and U.S. Timken for resale on the European continent. It set up offices in Brussels, Milan, and Göteborg, Sweden (SKF's home town). At the same time, the company restructured its relationships with its distributors through a program that phased out the system of commissions and replaced it with one in which the distributor's gross profit came directly from its margin on sales.[40]

The new organization put Timken's European operations on a stronger footing. Yet there remained a nagging issue that hampered its effort to build market share. That was the question of adopting the metric bearing dimensions that had been standardized in Europe by the International Standards Organization (ISO). The company's policy on ISO bearings in particular affected its ability to penetrate nonautomotive markets.

Metric **versus** *Inch-Sized Bearings*

The metric issue had a long history. SKF had played the leading role in standardization in Europe beginning in the mid-1920s, when the ISO's predecessor group, the International Standards Association (ISA), was formed, with its headquarters in Sweden. Timken, in contrast, had not felt the need to establish standard sizes in that era, mainly because it had virtually no competition in its home markets. On the one hand it recognized that standardization on a limited number of sizes was highly desirable from a manufacturing standpoint; but on the other, it had a strong tradition of designing its bearings to the exact needs of each customer. In 1928, SKF's chief engineer, attending professional conferences in New York as a representative of the Swedish Industrial Standardization Committee, had made a direct appeal for U.S. assistance in devising an international standard for tapered roller bearings. However, as Ernest Wooler, then Timken's chief engineer, reported, "We were not particularly interested at that time and the subject was practically dropped."[41]

Back in Europe, though, SKF proceeded with a proposal to standardize on the metric sizes of bearings it was making. By 1931, the ISA was close to adopting that standard, and there was considerable competitive pressure on Timken France and Deutsche Timken to convert from inch sizes to SKF's sizes. On short notice, Wooler decided to attend an ISA conference in Copenhagen, at which the standards were to be decided upon, and he hastily pulled together a plan for making inch-sized tapered roller bearings the international standard. With this plan, he succeeded in temporarily derailing the SKF proposal and placing Timken's proposal under consideration. When Wooler returned home, he refined his proposal, and it was adopted as the U.S. standard by the Society of Automotive Engineers, the American Standards Association, and the Anti-Friction Bearing Manufacturers Association, which was formed in 1933. Ultimately, however, SKF's plan and its metric bearing sizes became the ISA standard. Both Timken France and British Timken began making them, in addition to inch-sized bearings, in the 1930s. They produced substantial numbers of ISA bearings for many different applications during World War II.[42]

The ISA was abolished during the war and succeeded by the ISO at the war's end. At that point, the U.S. bearing industry began to push to have its own standard inch dimensions considered as an international standard for tapered roller bearings. There was a strong technical objection to the ISA (now ISO) standard sizes, because they were based on ball bearing dimensions. That is to say, the ISO system provided a range of ball bearings, straight roller bearings, and tapered roller bearings with exactly the same sized bore (the hole in the middle) and outer dimensions. This system had advantages. One type of bearing could be substituted for another without changing the design of the machine it was going into; and the same tools and gauges could be used for all types of bearings, with significant economies to both manufacturers and customers. But it made for a sub-optimal design for the tapered roller bearing, which could have the same bearing capacity with the same bore and a *smaller* O.D. Moreover, the ISO standard did not allow the customer to optimize his design around specific load requirements—a critical aspect of Timken's approach to selling bearings.[43]

British Timken discontinued making ISO bearings in 1945 because, said sales director Raymond Tuckey, "We decided . . . it was wrong for us to push bearings with the bad characteristics which the ISO bearings have, due to their being designed to bores and O.D.s suitable for ball bearings." With the better-designed, inch-sized bearings and an advantage over its competitors in production capacity, it was possible by 1950, Tuckey said, to "eliminate [ISO bearings] to a very great extent from British industry." French manufacturers retained a strong preference for metric sizes, however, and Timken France continued to make ISO bearings in the postwar era. Inch sizes gained wider acceptance in Europe in the 1950s, as both British and U.S. Timken began selling Green Light bearings. But ISO bearings, made of standard ball bearing steel and sold at relatively low prices, remained strong in the marketplace. In 1960, the ISO acknowledged that reality and recommended two standards for tapered roller bearings, one in inches and one in metric.[44]

The competition became more intense after 1960. According to Tuckey, at that time SKF "started to take tapered roller bearings seriously, whereas previously they had been content to copy Timken bearings and obtain what orders they could through lower prices." In particular, SKF developed some new metric sizes. These abandoned the principle of conforming to ball bearing sizes and were designed along lines more appropriate for tapered roller bearings. However, they followed long-established ISO guidelines for preferred dimensions, which dictated that sizes vary in 5-millimeter increments—for example, 45 millimeters was acceptable, while 46 millimeters was not. This new development hurt Timken, especially in industrial markets. Since that was a field in which plain bearings were still widely used, it offered a significant opportunity for growth if Timken could convince producers to become "tapered roller bearing minded"—as it had on a large scale in the U.S. industrial market. Timken readily developed good customers among U.S. multinationals, including International Harvester, Caterpillar, Allis Chalmers, and Cincinnati Milling Machine, but European manufacturers were largely resistant to working in inch dimensions. By the mid-1960s, with SKF, FAG, and SNR all producing the improved ISO lines and often selling them at prices lower than comparable Timken bearings, even some U.S. subsidiaries and licensees began to switch. In his annual report on Timken Europe operations for 1966, Tony Grainger stated the case plainly: "Particularly with respect to industrial sizes . . . we cannot emphasize too strongly how difficult it is to compete with our inch dimension bearings." As of 1967, even with its significant success in the German automotive industry, Timken reckoned it had captured only 5 percent of the total European anti-friction bearing market and 12 percent of the market for tapered roller bearings.[45]

In that year, the company introduced the J-Line family of bearings in all its markets. This new product line came out of a two-year program aimed at standardizing on a limited number of bearings for high-volume production in size

ranges larger than automotive wheel bearings (the principal Green Light range)—
that is, for other automotive and industrial applications such as farm and construction equipment. It was intended to be, not just a consolidation of existing
products, but an overall improvement in design: "a group of bearings which
would deliver *maximum capacity in a minimum space—employing optimum
bearing sections."* Out of 281 existing bearings came 30 J-Line bearings ranging in
bore size from 50 to 200 millimeters (about 2 to 8 inches). These were designed
so that both the bore and the O.D. dimensions varied in millimeter increments,
and they could be specified either in inch or in metric dimensions. The concept
was that they would thus be "universally acceptable." In introducing J-Line bearings to an international gathering of Timken sales representatives in 1967, vice
president for sales Paul J. Reeves asserted that the company had "taken the 'metric bull' by its 'metric horns' and . . . taken the first giant step forward toward a
'one-worldness' in bearings." Yet Timken was still thinking solely in its own terms,
not in those of the European industrial customers it hoped to win.[46]

The company hoped that the J-Line, through superior design, would eventually displace ISO bearings in comparable sizes, but that was not to be. While
the J-Line family met with some success among European industrial customers, it
did not significantly increase Timken's market share. In 1971, therefore, the company began to work within the committees of the ISO to develop new standard
sizes for tapered roller bearings that better met its technical criteria. In the old ISO
system, the dimensions had been set to allow tapered roller bearings to be interchangeable with ball or straight roller bearings. Timken pushed to have standard
dimensions set "to provide the most efficient and cost effective bearing for any
application." The company largely succeeded in having this "application concept" incorporated into a new set of standard bearing sizes. The result was a new
"master plan" for metric tapered roller bearings—International Standard ISO
355—ratified at the end of 1976. This included the majority of the old ISO bearings, but eliminated those considered to be unsatisfactory designs and added
some new lines of bearings proposed by Timken. Those new bearings (for which
Timken retained the J prefix) were designated by purpose, for example, JP for
machine tools and high-speed applications, JW for high-thrust load applications
such as worm drives.[47]

With the adoption of ISO 355, Timken made a long-term commitment to
metrication of all its products, adopting the following as official policy: "It shall be
the company position that a gradual and careful transition toward full metric capability be pursued in the design, manufacture and marketing of all products in
the future." Of the 475 bearings in the new ISO system, Timken determined it
would produce about 120 to start out and would await development of market demand for other sizes before tooling up to make them. Since the end of the Second

World War, Colmar had been the only plant to produce ISO bearings, but now the company planned to manufacture them at other locations as well if it made sense to do so. In August 1977, it lowered the prices on many ISO bearings produced at Colmar to make them more competitive and determined in earnest to seek a larger share of the European market, which it estimated to be around $200 million per year in the late 1970s.[48]

Despite all these changes, achieving that goal would remain an uphill battle. Timken's competitors in Europe were already tooled up to make a much wider range of ISO 355 bearings. As more European manufacturers began to adopt tapered roller bearings, SKF and FAG got a head start on building the sales that allowed them to move to high-volume production, and they were aggressive in using low pricing to capture market share. Japanese bearing companies also had begun to make their presence felt in Europe and were on the metric standard. Under those conditions, it would be tough to build the demand required to expand the range of ISO bearings produced, and ultimately it would be impossible to establish a position in the industrial market comparable to what Timken held in the United States. In the 1990s, Timken would still be producing about the same number of ISO 355 bearing sizes as it produced in the late 1970s.[49]

Timken thus discovered that technology alone could not ensure the level of success in international markets that it enjoyed in the United States. That would become more true rather than less so as time went on. Still, for highly engineered products such as bearings and specialty steels, strong technology was a necessary, if not sufficient, condition for industry leadership. Timken's sales engineering capability, backed up by its strong technical organization—especially in Canton, but also in Duston and Colmar—enabled it to win key customers and expand its market with new applications and products. It was a historic pattern for Timken, and it continued to serve the company well, particularly in Europe.

Technical Strengths

However the company might struggle with market share and profitability, its reputation as the leader in tapered roller bearings was assured by its work with leading-edge customers. For example, when the first opening came at Volkswagen with a redesign of the Beetle in the early 1960s, VW's chief of chassis design, Albrecht Fischer, worked closely with Timken to make the change from ball bearings on the front axle. There were many reasons for the switch. VW wanted to use a new braking system that put a squeeze on space, but it also wanted to increase the carrying capacity of the trunk in the front of the car. Timken's bearing addressed those needs—it was smaller but would carry a greater load. It was also quieter than what VW had been using, a function of precision in manufacturing. At the same time, the level of technical support that Fischer received through an extended period of design, testing, and comparison to competing bearings helped to make him a long-term customer.[50]

For many years, Volkswagen was the company's largest customer in Europe. In 1997, Timken France received its prestigious quality award, "Qualitaetspreis Formel Q 1997 der Marke Volkswagen." From left are Jon Elsasser, group vice president for Timken bearing operations in Europe; Mrs. Andrea Fuder, purchasing supervisor at Volkswagen; Jean-Claude Carlin, general manager of manufacturing at Colmar; Mr. Stefan Brandes, machine operator, and Mrs. Ursula Gust-Meinhardt, supplies-quality department, at Volkswagen; Jens Goldenbohm, sales engineer at Timken Hannover; and Gerhard Reiter, general manager of automotive sales and marketing for Timken in Europe.

Immediately following the completion of the Beetle project, Fischer moved on to the design of a larger sedan, the 411. In that instance, the collaboration had to be even closer, because VW's manufacturing department aimed to produce the car with robotic assembly. Fischer brought Timken in early to consult on both the engineering and manufacturing goals. That led to one of the first applications for high-volume production of Timken's SET-RIGHT™ mountings, which used a spacer between the two bearings facing each other on either side of the wheel mounting to achieve the proper bearing setting without adjustment by hand. On that solid foundation, the collaboration would continue through design of the VW Golf in the 1970s and subsequent vehicles. For many years, VW was Timken's largest customer in Europe. In the 1990s, shifts in the balance between technical and cost considerations would allow improved ball bearings to win back the front axle, but by that time, Timken would have many more bearings in completely new applications on VW cars, for example, in transmissions.[51]

In 1967, Timken scored another coup with a new product, the UNIT-BEARING™, a preset, nonadjustable bearing with load-carrying characteristics suited in particular for automobile rear wheels. Thomas W. Strouble, the lead design and development engineer for the UNIT-BEARING and later senior vice

The UNIT-BEARING™ was developed specifically for use on the rear axles of automobiles. This single-row bearing offers unique load-carrying characteristics: it is preset and carries heavy radial loads, as well as loads in either thrust direction. More than 100 million have been sold since they were introduced in 1967.

president for technology, recalled that the idea for it came out of discussions between Timken and its automotive customers in Detroit. According to Ralph McKelvey, director of engineering research at that time, the U.S. automakers made it clear that Timken bearings were about to lose the rear-wheel application to ball bearings because of the manufacturing cost of adjusting them. However, the first sale of the UNIT-BEARING was made, not in Detroit, but in SKF's backyard—Göteborg, Sweden—by sales engineers from British Timken. It was to Volvo, a company that had been launched by Sven Wingquist in 1926 and operated as an SKF subsidiary until 1935. Volvo would stick with the UNIT-BEARING for thirty years, using it on its 140-, 240-, 740-, and 940-series passenger cars. In those thirty years, Timken sold over 100 million UNIT-BEARINGs.[52]

Customer support and new product development enabled Timken to expand its markets in a tough competitive environment. Yet what most differentiated Timken and sustained its reputation as an industry leader was the ability of its international cadre of sales engineers to bring to bear the technical resources of the company—in application engineering, service engineering (for example, showing customers how to assemble bearings into their equipment most effectively), product testing, metallurgy, and many other fields critical to bearing performance—on the problems customers faced in advancing their own technologies. Timken's work with French National Railways (SNCF) to develop its high-speed *Train à Grande Vitesse* (TGV) is a case in point. The railway company committed to developing the high-speed train in 1967, with the goal of operating at 200 kilometers per hour in regular service. SNCF engineers knew that improvements in bearings would be critical to its success, but they were not disposed to turn to Timken for assistance. Quite the contrary. SNCF in the 1960s was switching its roller freight from plain bearings to tapered roller bearings, and most of that business went to SKF. European railroad cars were designed to take a bearing inside a cartridge. To use Timken AP bearings, a railway company had to buy the housing separately or redesign its cars, both relatively costly solutions. Those issues with the AP compounded another problem for Timken—the fact that European companies preferred to buy products manufactured within the Common Market. According to Jean Bouley, then assistant director of rolling stock for SNCF, he and his colleagues viewed Timken as strong primarily on freight applications. They favored SKF as better attuned to their goals for passenger trains, and also "more European."[53]

Those attitudes broke down rapidly, however, once Timken got a chance to participate in the TGV program. The first opening came just before that, when Timken France sales engineer Pierre Mazeraud and rail specialist Rudi Lorist committed the company to work with SNCF on development of a cartridge bearing. This brought the engineering groups of the two companies into contact. SNCF gained confidence in Timken, while Timken gained insight into SNCF's technical goals. Early in 1967, Timken's railroad engineering division began work at a test track in Ohio on improvements to bearings that would permit operation at 250 kilometers per hour. Said Bouley, it was a "genius strategy" to start testing at a speed that exceeded SNCF's stated goal. When, later that year, the railway company invited Timken, SKF, and the French bearing maker SNR to start testing bearings for "Le Capitole" at 250 kilometers per hour—"to have a margin over the goal of 200"—Timken already had test data in hand. SNCF was ready to push on beyond 250 by 1970, and Timken was already testing at 300 kilometers per hour. It was another sign, said Bouley, of the company's "strategic foresight." SNCF made its choice of bearing suppliers in 1973, by which time it was Timken that had the inside track.[54]

From that point forward the two companies worked in close collaboration on the technical issues that had to be solved to move from bench testing to actual operation at high speeds. This required on Timken's part an openness to joint inquiry into the weak points of bearings, where failure might occur under the demanding conditions the TGV would impose. A small joint team looked at lubricants, seals, bearing geometry and finishes, and especially steel quality, since bearing failure was known to be correlated to levels of nonmetallic inclusions in the basic material. Bouley remarked that it was "a perfect fit between customer and supplier, because both had the goals of technical excellence." When the TGV Paris-Lyon line went into operation in 1981, SNCF ordered cartridge bearings for 10 locomotives—a small order given the cost of development, but the opening to a market that would grow considerably as the TGV led the way toward the creation of a European network of high-speed trains. SNCF continued to push the technology as it gained experience on the Paris-Lyon line, and Timken continued to push its own technology to keep pace. In 1991, the TGV Atlantique line would begin operating routinely at 300 kilometers per hour.[55]

Another collaboration with far-reaching significance began in the mid-1970s around development of a five-speed passenger-car transmission for British Leyland's Rover 3500 sedan. This was not the first such transmission—the five-speed Morris Maxi preceded it—but the design became the standard for the many that followed. According to David Eley, Rover's chief engineer for rear-wheel-drive transmissions at the time, two key factors dictated that Timken bearings should replace the ball and straight roller bearings commonly used: their longer life expectancy; and their greater capacity relative to size. One of the more significant aspects of this application was that it utilized standard front-wheel bearing sizes—Green Light bearings that Timken could produce in high volume and sell at relatively low prices. To make it happen, however, Eley had to work closely with British Timken's manager for automotive sales, John Hunt, on the technical issues involved. Hunt, in turn, was backed up by the testing laboratory at Duston, which provided extensive data on bearing life under different conditions. A particular challenge with the five-speed gear box was to get the pre-load on the bearings just right, not too much and not too little. This was a manufacturing problem, and Hunt spent many hours working on it at the Rover factory. The Rover 3500 also used the UNIT-BEARING on its rear axle, the first British car to do so. Hunt assisted with that application as well. Said Eley, "We relied very heavily on John for his expertise." In the 1980s, Timken became the sole supplier of tapered roller bearings to Rover. In the 1990s, after British Leyland transformed itself into the Rover Group, it would move ahead of Volkswagen to become the company's largest European customer.[56]

Citizen of the World

Innovation through sales engineering was a part of U.S. Timken's traditional way of doing business that served it well as it expanded in the international arena. The same can be said of some other long-established characteristics. In 1961

The Timken family's International Fund helped restore Colmar's Bartholdi Museum in France. In 1976, Mayor Joseph Rey presented the Timken family with an original model of Auguste Bartholdi's Statue of Liberty, now housed in the Statue of Liberty Museum in New York. Molded and signed by Bartholdi, it was one of only three owned by the Bartholdi Museum. From left are Mayor Rey, Mrs. and Mr. W. R. Timken, and W. R. Timken, Jr.

William Umstattd received the distinction of induction into the French Legion of Honor, an award won by relatively few Americans. (Those few included Thomas Edison, Theodore Roosevelt, and Dwight Eisenhower.) Umstattd was recognized for his service in France during World War I but also for his leading role in developing Timken France after World War II, culminating in the move to Colmar, which opened that year. The award signified the respect the company had earned by its approach to building its international operations.[57]

Going forward that respect would grow, in large part because of the active leadership of the Timken family. Particularly in Europe, their visible role in the company was a critical factor distinguishing it in a positive way from most U.S. multinational corporations. The family carried that advantage further by taking abroad H. H. Timken's philosophy of giving some of its wealth back to those who helped create it. In 1959 Henry, Bob, and John Timken established the Timken International Fund as a vehicle for extending the reach of the family foundation into the company's plant communities abroad. It had the same mission as the Timken

In 1998, W. J. (Jack) Timken, president of the Timken Foundation, visited Carmel Junior College in Jamshedpur, India, where the family Foundation's International Fund donated $140,000 for a building addition. (In India, schools up to grade 12 often are called colleges.) Carmel College focuses primarily on improving education standards in the city of Jamshedpur.

Foundation—to give large capital gifts that might be difficult to raise from other sources and would be likely to have broad impact. Its first gift to Colmar, in 1965, paid for the construction of a large indoor swimming pool. Timken money also helped to restore Colmar's art museum, Unterlinden, and the Bartholdi Museum, former home of Auguste Bartholdi, the sculptor of the Statue of Liberty. The most popular art museum in France outside of Paris, Unterlinden is located in a thirteenth-century convent and houses one of the best-known works of art in Europe, the Issenheim altarpiece of Mathias Grünewald. Those restorations helped to maintain tourism as a vital part of the city's economy.[58]

In Britain, the Nene Foundation, created in 1965, distributed money granted each year by the Timken International Fund. There, as everywhere, public swimming pools were favorite Timken projects, but the donations of the Nene Foundation were spread broadly among hospitals, schools, community centers, libraries, fire departments, and youth clubs. Of H. H. Timken's three sons, Bob was the one to assume the most direct responsibility for the work of the family foundations. In 1977, the Nene Foundation celebrated the milestone of £1 million donated in the communities of Duston and Daventry, and in recognition of his efforts Daventry honored Bob Timken with the key to the city.[59]

The company's image as an enlightened corporate citizen was also enhanced by some good choices about what policies to import from Canton. Its insistence on hiring and training young people and promoting from within, for example, went over well in cultures that valued stability at least as much as upward mobility. In France, Timken also won points for *not* following the practice used at home of laying people off in a downturn, but allowing its French plant managers to reduce the workweek instead. From 1968 through the early 1970s, there were numerous strikes at the Colmar plant, part of a wave of political and labor unrest sparked by student protests in Paris. These strikes were often less about work-related issues than political issues—for example, the Vietnam War—and Timken's U.S. ownership made it a target for such protests. At the outset, the policy of Timken France followed standard practice at Canton: make concessions on wages, but preserve the right to manage. In 1975, however, Maurice Amiel became general manager of Timken France and set out to take a different approach. Amiel had joined the company in 1958, the first hire following the consolidation with U.S. Timken. He had come with degrees in both business and law and since then had completed the Program for Management Development at Harvard Business School and a tour of duty in Canton as executive assistant for international operations. Facing a strike in 1975 and another in 1978, the French management group on the scene refused to grant any concessions but also took the unusual step of sharing financial information with the striking employees. Said Amiel: "We started to open our books to all our people, which was very contrary to The Timken Company philosophy. We told them, 'Don't believe what the unions tell you. These are the books. This is our chart of accounts and we can certify it. This is the money we make. If we don't make money, we can't pay. We'd better all work at getting the company to survive.'" The strategy succeeded—1978 was the last strike at Colmar.[60]

That success with labor relations further cemented the goodwill of the community. While Colmar's leaders, and public opinion generally, had remained supportive of the company throughout, the end of strikes and the building of trust between management and labor made it easier to be unequivocally pleased with its association with Timken. Since the general managers of Timken France had been mostly British (one American excepted), the rise of Amiel, a Frenchman, was also a source of local pride in Colmar and often an advantage in the European community.[61]

In South Africa, too, the company had the good sense to support the local management. There, Kendall Brooke set out to eliminate the apartheid system from the Timken plant as much as possible. On becoming managing director in 1969, he began training some black South African employees as clerks. Initially he had to place partitions in the office to separate black from white clerical staff, but within a year he had people working together. He judged that his most important achievement—"the development of a culture inside of Timken South Africa which made it clear to everybody, particularly our black and white staff, male and female, that there were no second-class citizens." Brooke also hired across racial lines in building up manufacturing personnel, paid strictly according to job classifications, and launched an interracial four-year apprenticeship program. With approval from Canton, he created a fund for housing loans at a token rate of interest and found various ways to assist his black staff members in building or renovating homes where they lived, in the black township of Daveyton. Those initiatives were not directed by U.S. Timken but were strongly encouraged. Said Brooke, they were "an outgrowth of my simple desire to make our operations in South Africa a reflection of the corporation." The success he achieved would allow Timken in good conscience to decline to subscribe to the Sullivan Principles, which bound U.S. corporations doing business in South Africa to submit to annual reviews of their management policies. The company weathered a number of shareholder resolutions protesting that decision, and got consistently high marks from the U.S. State Department when, in the 1980s, it began to review the practices of companies not already signed up to the Sullivan Principles.[62]

Timken South Africa's managing director Kendall Brooke (left) created a company fund to provide housing loans at affordable rates for Timken employees, which helped Rufus Mashile and his family purchase their home in Daveyton. Tim Timken (right) visited the housing development in 1985.

In sum, U.S. Timken's traditional world-view, culture, and mode of operation served it quite well in most instances as it strove to shape an effective multinational organization. In the post–World War II decades—when, in the words of business historian Mira Wilkins, "the American dollar, the American traveler, the American diplomat, and the American businessman [became] ubiquitous" in international set-tings—many U.S. officials and companies abroad gained a reputation for insensi-tivity to local customs and issues, as portrayed in the popular 1959 novel *The Ugly American*.[63] Timken's success in integrating into its plant communities offered a positive contrast to that pattern. In the 1970s and 1980s, its focus would shift from competing to expand its share of international markets to defending its domestic stronghold, as international competitors brought the battle home to the United States. At the same time, after a decade of relatively slow growth in the 1960s, Timken would face the challenges of extremely rapid growth driven by strong worldwide demand for its products.

CHAPTER NINE

Chasing Demand

*I*f Timken was not a high-flying growth company, growth was nevertheless the dominant factor in its organizational life from the mid-1960s through the late 1970s. For both the bearing and steel sides of the business, it was a time of heavy investment, expansion, profitability, and industry leadership. Paradoxically, it was also a time in which the company lost ground to competitors in two key areas—low-cost production and material quality. That trend was not apparent at the time, however, and its worst effects would not be felt until the 1980s.

Largely at the urging of Bob Timken, the company began in the 1960s to undertake some changes of long-term significance. One of the most important was the creation of a centralized research and development organization. At his insistence, the company also began to develop systems and disciplines that brought it more into the mainstream of professionalized management practice. Yet change progressed slowly in many areas—much too slowly, it would appear in retrospect. Timken's management organization and culture in the late 1970s would remain almost as rigid and hierarchical as it had been twenty years before. In some respects, that was by choice. To a great extent, however, the impetus for change was simply overwhelmed by the incessant pressure to keep up with demand.

In the 1980s, Timken would be forced to change dramatically under much more difficult circumstances, but it would have been much further behind without Bob Timken's initiatives. Within the inner circle of leadership in the 1960s, he was the one most attuned to trends in corporate management and most open to considering that Timken might have fallen behind the curve. It was out of such considerations that Timken Research emerged.

Creation of Timken Research

At the end of 1963, Bob Timken appointed a committee to study the company's technical programs. He had determined to build a research center in Canton, removed from the plants, and wanted a proposal for an expanded research agenda and the resources needed to carry it out. His request put the company on the road to establishing a new research and development organization, which in 1966 would take up residence in a new facility in North Canton, 12 miles from the corporate offices on Dueber Avenue.[1] It was also Bob's idea to call the new organization Timken Research, a name that embraced both bearings and steel and invoked the company's long tradition of leadership in its core technologies.[2]

In U.S. industry generally, there had been an upsurge of investment in centralized R&D that was approaching flood tide in the mid-1960s. Inspired by the contributions of science and technology to the winning of World War II, and driven by the ensuing Cold War, the federal government had begun to provide funding for research in both academic and industrial laboratories on a large scale, much of it channeled through the Defense Department and defense-related agencies such as the Atomic Energy Commission and the National Aeronautics and Space Administration (NASA). In that context, many companies that had never before conducted research organized R&D departments and began to compete for government funding. The trend accelerated after the Soviet Union launched Sputnik in 1957. By 1964, NASA's R&D funding (not the largest agency budget by any means) was $1.5 billion, three times larger than it had been in 1956. At the same time, the dramatic commercial achievements of companies that had established R&D laboratories before World War II—such as DuPont in synthetic fibers, AT&T in communications technology, and RCA in television—helped to foster a business environment that favored such investment.[3]

That was the environment in which Bob Timken pushed the company to create Timken Research. NASA had set a research agenda for bearings, in particular in the complex field of tribology—"the science and technology of friction, wear and lubrication"—an area with broad implications for bearing performance. In 1962, SKF opened a centralized research laboratory in King of Prussia, Pennsylvania, to serve its 6 U.S. plants and also to conduct tribological and other research under government contract. Neither Bob nor anyone else in the company's top management intended to rely on government funding. But they were determined that Timken should remain a leader in its industries, and in the 1960s that clearly implied the need for a formal R&D program. When the company looked outside for benchmarks, it studied International Nickel Company, Republic Steel, and Caterpillar Tractor, which had all previously taken steps to centralize R&D and place it in appropriate facilities. Caterpillar's R&D spending was around 5 percent of sales; Timken's averaged less than 1 percent of sales in the years 1961–63. Timken had its long-established R&D programs in metallurgy, process and product engineering, and product testing, but it was clearly time to consider whether those were conceived, directed, and funded well enough to maintain the company's competitiveness over the long term.[4]

At the same time, there were seven distinct technical organizations conducting work at three separate locations. Those were Savannah Avenue and the three facilities built around corporate headquarters in the late 1950s—the Physical Laboratory and Engineering Laboratory opposite the Canton bearing factory on Dueber Avenue, and the Metallurgical Laboratory next to the Canton steel mill on Harrison Avenue. The metallurgical department had two divisions: physical metallurgy, which conducted work related to the properties and performance of bearing materials; and process metallurgy, which concerned itself with steel making. The Physical Laboratory was responsible for the company's large program of physical testing. Engineering was the organization of product and application engineers that had long been divided into three divisions—automotive, industrial, and railroad—each with a chief engineer. Finally, there was the production development division at Savannah Avenue, now called Process Development. Every one of those departments had strong organizational identities and leaders. When the committee began to consider a centralized R&D program, an important part of the task was to determine how best to coordinate those elements and where to locate them.[5]

Its report emerged in March 1964. The committee had looked closely at the programs in place and found much that needed to be improved. Process Development set the internal standard. With 99 full-time personnel, its work was largely protected from the short-term demands of customers and operations. It was by far the best-organized and most generously funded part of the company's technical program. And, said the committee, its work was "concentrated on a well-planned and well-supervised development program." The smashing success of the Bucyrus and Columbus continuous high-production lines, along with all the spinoff improvements throughout Timken's bearing plants, had given this organization solid recognition as an important corporate asset. In the early 1960s, its work focused on further improving the machine-tool technology on which the bearing business depended for its competitiveness, particularly in the areas of grinding and in-process gauging. The division provided a benchmark for what could be achieved by centralizing R&D, focusing on longer-term problems, and providing unified direction, adequate staffing, and consistent funding.[6]

In contrast, the research portion of the programs at the other two R&D locations had limited staff, most of whom were assigned to the work on a part-time basis only. That situation was an artifact of an early decision by H. H. Timken, Jr., made in 1943 at the time the Savannah Avenue process research group was created. Henry insisted that the company should employ only as many researchers as it could afford to support in bad economic times as well as good. He had judged that number to be about 100; hence, the total research staff had been arbitrarily held at that level for twenty years. The creation of Timken Research would have to break that barrier.[7]

The committee also found the metallurgical and engineering research programs to be "suffer[ing] seriously from dilution of effort by the intrusion of customer needs into planned project work." The main work of the metallurgical department was to provide quality control in Timken's steel operations. The engineering organization and the large staff of the Physical Laboratory focused mainly on customer needs, either developing new applications or, often, testing bearing applications in customers' equipment. Those were vital technical functions but different from research into general questions—for example, research into problems such as the causes of fatigue or factors affecting bearing capacity and reliability. The committee recommended that research programs be consolidated, provided with increased staffing and funding, and moved away from the existing laboratories. But it also acknowledged the need to avoid damaging "the present close technical cooperation between research and operating people and other technical groups within the company." Too much isolation, the committee recognized, would be an overcorrection. It further suggested that the production development division be expanded in scope "to become a truly corporate development program," and that it be coordinated with the research programs.[8]

In laying out a research agenda, the committee disavowed any interest in fundamental research (by its terms, work that was disconnected from "the profit motive"). But it defined a need to study some "basic principles" in order to address the technical problems at hand. It proposed programs to study the factors determining performance of both Timken bearings and Timken steel. Another recommendation was for a "well-manned, fairly large scale" research program in new bearing applications, which had traditionally been handled as a function of sales and application engineering. The committee also called for an effort to develop new high-strength steels and new high-temperature and corrosion-resistant steels—the latter a field in which Timken had once been a leader but had since abandoned. Finally, it recommended that Timken could make judicious use of government funding in a few areas of inquiry. The company would move into that realm slowly and in a limited way, working as a subcontractor on some NASA programs in the 1960s. In 1972, Timken would take on its first-ever prime contract for government research—a three-year, $225,000 program for developing ultra-high-speed tapered roller bearings.[9]

Out of the committee's work emerged a centralized organization with two divisions—research, and production development—both under directors reporting to a vice president for engineering and research. (Harley Urbach held the vice-presidential post at the time Timken Research opened in the spring of 1966.) Walter Green, the long-time head of the original production development division, remained in that position but moved his organization from Savannah Avenue into enlarged facilities at the new site. Elbert Rowland, former head of physical metallurgy, became director of the research division, which was initially quite a small organization with two parts, physical metallurgy and engineering research. Some of the personnel and equipment from the Physical Laboratory moved to the research center to form the nucleus of the engineering research group, but the physical testing program remained intact with its established mission and leadership. Engineering—for automotive, industrial, and railroad bearing applications—also remained separate and did not move. Process metallurgy remained part of the large metallurgical division in the laboratory in Canton, under the direction of Daniel J. Girardi, another Michigan Ph.D. who had joined Timken about the same time as Rowland. In short, the centralization was far from complete. And the new research division was dwarfed by the three long-established technical departments, still under the direction of the men who had run them for many years.[10]

The R&D committee assumed that Timken Research would expand in order to execute the program envisioned. It recommended a research staff of 84 people, including 2 chemists, 3 physicists, and 13 metallurgists. But it also anticipated difficulty in hiring so many new people in a tight labor market and cautioned that it might take three to five years to get the program up and running. In fact, the new research division would struggle even longer than that to settle into an effective working relationship with the rest of the company. Although the company had a

tradition of cooperation, both among its various technical organizations and between research and operating departments, that broke down in the early years of
Timken Research. It proved difficult for the upstart organization to get support
from the much stronger and longer-established technical departments, which continued to function as they had always done. And to compound the problem,
Timken Research, in its off-site facility and under orders to maintain strict secrecy,
ended up conducting its work largely in isolation. According to Ralph McKelvey,
who succeeded Urbach as vice president for engineering and research in 1972, the
research organization "just didn't do anything that Engineering wanted done. . . .
Finally, some of us persuaded them to open up a little, and communications became better." McKelvey charged the new director of research, Arthur L. Christenson, with pushing harder to apply the work being done in the laboratory. It also
helped that both Rowland and Girardi retired about the same time. Just as Christenson took over from Rowland, the direction of both physical and process metallurgy came under a new chief metallurgist, C. Philip Weigel.[11]

Thus, while Bob Timken's R&D initiative set the company on a track necessary to sustain its position of technological leadership, the greatest returns on the
investment in Timken Research would not be realized for some years after its creation. Similarly, management changes that he called for in 1968 would have great
significance in the long run but would not happen quickly.

Bob Timken's Mandate

Henry Timken died unexpectedly in March 1968, struck by a heart attack
while at dinner on a business trip in Washington, D.C. He was sixty-one years old.
Following his death, Bob Timken took over as chairman of the company's board
of directors and Herb Markley became president. Tim Timken and Joe Toot became corporate vice presidents, Tim with responsibility for all domestic operations
and Joe for international. Reflecting on that moment, Tim Timken would see it as
a watershed: the start of a move away from "the old company," which seemed to
have changed little since H. H. Timken's day, and toward the "modern" company
that would emerge in the 1980s.

The process of change began when Bob Timken charged the younger generation to take up the reins and introduce the tools of professional management,
such as market research and long-range planning, that had by then become standard in progressively run corporations. Markley, as president, was to preside over
the transition, while Timken and Toot were to implement what they had learned
in business school and in their subsequent years of training at the company. So
there could be no doubt that the transfer of authority was real, Bob Timken told

them to start making decisions and left for a month. From that point until his retirement as chairman in 1975, he disengaged himself from the day-to-day running of the company and limited his role to keeping an eye on finances and serving as a "court of last resort" in decision making by the new top-management team.[12]

The need for change had been building for some time. The growth in demand for bearings in 1964–65 had caught Timken unawares. It had taken every ounce of the company's resources simply to fill its orders. Each year thereafter it added as much capacity as it could and still had to rely heavily on costly overtime to keep up sufficient production. Dealing with that unanticipated demand was "frustrating," said James Pilz, then vice president of sales. His division's efforts had been, by necessity, "devoted primarily to following deliveries and servicing our accounts—with little serious regard for competitive or pricing problems." At the beginning of 1967, it was still a stretch for the company to plan its capital spending more than two years out. Tim Timken, called back to Canton from Colmar in 1965 to help out with the situation, recalled joking that the company determined its capital budget by spending whatever money was "left in the till" at the end of the year. Part of his charge was to produce a five- to ten-year forecast of future sales that would provide the foundation for more informed budgeting. Timken had by that time recognized the issues and had begun to develop the analytical tools it would need to address them. That development would continue, and accelerate, from 1968 forward.[13]

Like so many other things, Timken's management information systems had their origin at Bucyrus. In the early 1950s, George Deal and assistant treasurer Richard Gulling had taken on the task of investigating how the company might benefit from the new technology of computers. They had begun to conceptualize a centralized system for tracking inventory of automotive bearings when the idea of the Bucyrus shipping center arose. Computerization would be essential to its success, and Gulling got the job of developing the order-inventory-scheduling (OIS) system that controlled it. That turned out to be a hellish assignment that nearly cost him his job. There was no ready-made software for such a task, and the mathematicians Gulling hired to do the programming made some serious errors before they finally got it right. He also learned the hard way the necessity of collaborating with end users when designing an information system.[14]

For all that, Timken pushed forward in the 1960s and 1970s to develop some sophisticated programs. After OIS came FIS—factory inventory scheduling, a system that tracked and coordinated the work of all the many discrete departments in the bearing plants. Its purpose was to give the company control over its products from the time a customer placed an order to the time it was delivered. Another homegrown computer application, FIS also had its development problems, not the least of which was its size and complexity: It took eighteen hours to run the daily reports it was designed to produce. It would take years (and the movement from punched cards to terminal entry on the plant floor) to get to the point of having information timely enough to be useful in day-to-day operations. Still, Timken forged ahead to develop ELS: an economic-lot-size approach to scheduling production runs. Kevin Ramsey, who worked with Gulling to develop those systems, recalled that ELS was "way in advance of anything anybody was doing. You just don't make what you have orders for, but you ask yourself, What is economic to me? You make an economic quantity, which may be three times the orders because it is theoretically the most economic quantity to produce." By the 1990s, once Timken and the rest of U.S. industry had adopted more flexible manufacturing systems and the discipline of just-in-time deliveries, the inventory buildup created by the ELS approach would be deemed unacceptable. But in an environment in which the demand for bearings consistently exceeded supply, it was an invaluable tool. ELS could have been imagined only after all the prior work toward inventory control had been done. Subsequently, the company would move on to develop an electronic system for scheduling and tracking customer orders through its steel plants.[15]

The hurdles to creating and then using such systems in a large manufacturing organization were many. They began with the need to get the "knowledge each foreman [had] in his little black production book" into the system in the first place. As in most large corporations, computerization had taken hold first in the accounting function, where data were readily obtained and the concepts and programs for financial control were well established. It was a much more difficult task to apply the tools to manufacturing operations.[16]

A related development, formalized in 1970, was the transformation of the sales function into marketing. The frantic, frustrating period of the mid-1960s had raised awareness of the need to take a more strategic approach to selling. Timken was also feeling the beginning of serious competition in its U.S. markets, both from SKF and from the Japanese. That put pressure on prices in some bearing categories and on margins. James Pilz, then vice president for sales, noted that the shift to the marketing mentality meant learning "to know when to lose an order, how to sell for profit, and how to sell for growth at a profit, when to concentrate for market penetration, and when to concentrate on profit. . . . That is marketing, [and] that is a lot different from selling." It all involved market research and analysis and was tied closely to the effort to improve control over manufacturing schedules and inventory.[17]

The development of information systems and a marketing function were significant and essential changes that, as Bob Timken had wanted, brought the company more in line with broad trends in business administration. But this was no headlong rush to mimic every other professionally managed corporation. The company did not seek the advice of consultants, nor did it start looking outside for high-level managers with the skills or experience it lacked. Timken remained committed to its long-time policy of promoting from within. At Bob's urging, it had begun in 1965 to hire MBAs into its entry-level executive training programs. After 1968, the new top-management team began paying greater attention to the career development of a larger group of rising executives, moving them around within the company, particularly on international assignments, to replicate the kind of preparation for greater responsibility that Joe Toot and Tim Timken had received. As they played an increasingly central role in managing the firm and forged their working partnership, Tim and Joe would continue to place a high priority on the career development of rising corporate executives and would remain personally involved in the process.[18]

In 1970, Timken adopted a more elegant form of its name: The Timken Company. Tim Timken recalled that the change was prompted in part by the growing importance of the steel business. The company wanted to signal its customers that it was committed to being a reliable steel supplier. The new name also symbolically opened the door to diversification beyond tapered roller bearings, though it was an opening Timken would not take for another twenty years.[19] In the short run, the change complemented the broader effort to modernize the firm, still far from complete. In 1973, Tim and Joe advanced to new positions. Joe took on the full field of operational responsibilities as executive vice president. Tim became vice chairman of the board and chairman of its finance committee. He would succeed his father as chairman of the board in 1975.

Timken's president, Herb Markley, championed the expansion of management information systems. He also took great interest in revamping and expanding Timken's educational and training programs in order to give managers throughout the company a higher-level perspective on business issues. The effort culminated in the mid-1970s with a new program designed specifically for the most grassroots level of management—the foremen on the shop floor. This program would evolve in 1979 into the Timken Management Institute. Deeply committed to this effort, Markley sat for hours of interviews that became a six-volume set of videos, entitled "The Development of Management Philosophy and Policy," in which he talked extensively about the company's history. To the majority of employees, said Markley, the "front-line supervisor . . . *is* the company." It was important that such supervisors be able to communicate an understanding of the why and wherefore of its policies.[20]

In fact, even as they worked to change the company, the new generation of leaders became more grounded than ever in its history. Leading up to its seventy-fifth anniversary in 1974, Timken mounted a variety of history projects: long-time employees were interviewed; each department was asked to put together its own history; some manuscripts were written, including a "History for W. E. Umstattd" in 1969. It was through the research connected to those projects that the company rediscovered the 1924 *Forbes* magazine interview with H. H. Timken and, in particular, his quotation of Henry Timken's thoughts on independence: *"If you want to lead in any line you must bring to it independence of thought, unfailing industry, aggression, and indomitable purpose."* Henry Timken's admonition, revived and reinterpreted in a much changed business context, once again became a guiding philosophy. It provided a solid grounding for the course Timken's leaders charted as they went forward and a rationale for all the things they chose *not* to change.[21]

Independence

In an era of increasing governmental regulation and public scrutiny of U.S. corporations, Timken's management vigorously defended the company's independence. That was the pattern, for example, in its refusal to subscribe to the Sullivan Principles governing the conduct of business in South Africa. The Timkens, Markley, and Toot accepted government oversight, but believed that submitting to standards set by a third party was not good corporate governance. In the area of environmental protection Timken, like most U.S. manufacturers, strongly protested the imposition of federal standards, for example on emissions, that created constantly moving targets. But the company had a long tradition of responsibility to its plant communities—it had installed its first bag house to control emissions from the steel mill in the 1930s, and in the 1940s had invested in technology to recapture, clean, and reuse the water its operations required. In keeping with that tradition, it made large investments to meet, and where possible exceed, the standards that were set.[22]

In 1978, the New York Stock Exchange enacted new rules that required listed companies to have at least two outside directors. Although it gave serious consideration to moving to another exchange, Timken's board ultimately decided to add two outside directors at that time. The new directors were Joseph S. Hoover, vice chairman of The Hoover Company, a Canton neighbor, and Robert G. Wingerter, CEO of Libbey-Owens-Ford. Wingerter had worked for twenty-five years in industrial and automotive sales at Timken, but had gone to Rockwell Standard Company in 1963 and had moved to Libbey-Owens-Ford in 1967, when Rockwell Standard merged with North American Aviation to create North American Rockwell (Rockwell International by 1973). Both new directors had considerable experience in international business, and they would remain on the Timken board for ten years. Both were also trusted friends familiar with the company.[23]

Timken Company plants throughout the world have invested millions of dollars to protect the earth's air, water, and land. The company's waste-water treatment and water purification plants (above) are two examples. In Canton, the company recycles 30 million gallons of water each day. The Steel Business recycles the equivalent of 5,600 cars every operating day. In 1997, the company's plant in England recycled 81 tons of cardboard, and Timken France reduced its water usage by 30 percent with a new recirculation system.

Timken has received numerous honors, including Governor's Awards in Ohio and New Hampshire for outstanding achievement in pollution prevention.

Thus, Timken judiciously bowed to pressures to conform in some areas. But in others the company challenged government policies and vigorously pursued its case through the legal system. In the mid-1970s, Timken faced a charge of discrimination in its hiring practices at Bucyrus. It took the government to court, arguing that the racial balance in the plant reflected the population in the city of Bucyrus, and that the company should not be forced to recruit minority employees in another city forty miles away in order to reflect the racial minorities there. A key element of Timken's case was the relationship it had built up with the local community as the largest employer in town since the late 1940s. The company also cited statistics showing that people who worked close to home had better work attendance and more commitment to their jobs. (It did not argue that it wanted to avoid having to recruit in some surrounding cities, where union sentiment was strong, though that was also true.) At Markley's direction, Timken's outside counsel, Robert Rybolt, brought in "the best constitutional lawyer in the country"—Dean Griswold, of Jones, Day in Cleveland, former U.S. solicitor general and Harvard Law School professor—to review its arguments. The final outcome was a landmark decision in Timken's favor.[24]

In what would be a much longer-running battle, Timken set out in the 1970s to obtain relief from the U.S. Treasury Department under existing trade regulations barring importers from "dumping" products in U.S. markets at prices below those in their home markets, plus shipping costs and tariffs. Confronted in the late 1960s by imported Japanese tapered roller bearings priced from 20 to 60 percent below those of U.S. producers, Timken had begun under Herb Markley's direction to put together an antidumping case, which it filed in 1969. Like most others who sought antidumping rulings, however, it came away disappointed. Free trade had been a central element of U.S. foreign policy since the end of World War II, and federal officials tended to be skeptical of companies seeking legal protection against low-priced imported products. Public distrust of large corporations, particularly multinationals, was running high; consumerism was on the rise; and in industry, too, there was opposition to government actions that might tend to increase prices. The first judgment on Timken's complaint, by the U.S. Treasury Department in 1970, went against the company.[25]

Many U.S. companies, especially in industries such as chemicals, electronics, textiles, and apparel, were disillusioned by similar experiences, and responded by moving much of their manufacturing offshore. Characteristically, Timken chose instead to continue its legal battle, appealing the Treasury Department's decision. Said Tim Timken, "We felt it was management's responsibility to fight any illegal actions that would take away the jobs of Timken employees." In 1972, Herb Markley again brought in the leading practitioner in this area of law, Eugene L. Stewart. Stewart had been working on import injury cases since the early 1950s. He had, for example, worked with the glass industry, and he was recommended to Timken by Bob Wingerter at Libbey-Owens-Ford. Under Stewart's direction, the company undertook the tedious task of gathering detailed information comparing prices on bearings in the Japanese market to prices of imports to the United States.[26] In 1973, Timken filed a new antidumping petition with the Treasury Department. So important was this case that Markley selected Joe Toot to be the company's witness, a responsibility that entailed a heavy commitment of time. But the effort paid off: in 1974 Timken won a judgment that Japanese pricing did, in fact, amount to dumping. Timken had to sue the Secretary of the Treasury in 1976 to secure enforcement of that ruling, but ultimately the U.S. International Trade Commission placed antidumping duties on tapered roller bearings under four inches in outer diameter. That helped to protect an important segment of Timken's market. The U.S. ball bearing industry, in contrast, was decimated by Japanese competition.[27]

If Timken's antidumping crusade set it apart from the mainstream of U.S. industry, the distinctiveness of its corporate culture was even more striking. In the late 1950s, Timken management had been characterized as "staid" by the financial press. By the 1970s, it was more out of step than ever. In the area of finance, the shared wisdom of executives (not to mention consultants) heavily favored using leverage to finance growth. Inflation and the tax code rewarded the use of debt. But, with the minor exception of some bonds to pay for mandated environmental protection measures, Timken continued to avoid borrowing. When questioned about this point, Herb Markley explained, "In Timken's view a company that relies on lenders for capital must accept direction from the outside sources. Timken doesn't want that. The company cherishes its independence." Management still declined to make presentations to stock analysts in New York, in part out of concern that the information would help its competitors. Said George Deal, "We were still very stingy about giving out information."[28]

Moreover, in the midst of sweeping cultural changes in the nation at large, Timken's management remained overwhelmingly male, conservative in culture and politics, and highly authoritarian. William Umstattd's spirit and style were firmly imprinted on the corporate leaders that had developed under his tutelage. Herb Markley had modeled himself on his mentor, including walking through the plants as much as he could. Committed to hands-on management and the austere style that had always characterized the company, he shared a secretary and eschewed the help of an assistant at a time when Timken was approaching $1 billion in revenues. From Umstattd he said he had learned that a leader should listen to other people's ideas and tolerate their mistakes, within limits. Yet individuals who had occasionally questioned an order from Umstattd found that doing so with Markley was "a no-no." In a large organization, Markley believed, it was necessary to be a disciplinarian as well as a leader. "You can't expect to be loved," he counseled Timken foremen. "It is more important to be respected for being fair and firm."[29]

Those values, maintained consistently at the top, continued to infuse the entire organization with the ethos of command-and-control. Routine executive meetings were invariably white-knuckle affairs for the vice presidents. An experienced design engineer who questioned the concept of a new product coming down from management could expect to be told by the vice president of engineering, "You will design the bearing or you will pack up your stuff and get out of here." Working in the Canton bearing plant, said one long-term machine operator, was like being "under military rule."[30]

In short, while the company initiated some important management changes in response to Bob Timken's mandate, there was much that did not change. The willingness to defy conventional wisdom and practice in the name of independence served Timken well in many ways. But it also supported a degree of insularity that hindered changes in key areas, such as management structure and culture, that were needed to prepare Timken fully for the rigors of all-out global competition. That realization would hit hard in the 1980s. In the meantime, the change effort was largely overshadowed by the need to respond to the continuing growth in demand for Timken bearings and steel.

Chasing Demand—Bearings

The 1970s was a period when demand for bearings and competition among bearing manufacturers both intensified. Timken met those challenges mainly by expanding its capacity in automated high-volume plants on the Bucyrus model. Its most significant investment in competitive terms was a new plant in Gaffney, South Carolina. The plant came on line in 1971—the first major capital investment decision to result from the company's recently developed capability in sales forecasting and capacity planning.[31]

Gaffney was Bucyrus on a large scale. Built on nearly 190 acres of what was once a horse farm, it had some 570,000 square feet of floor space versus 180,000 at Bucyrus. It was intended to employ more than 1,000 workers versus 700 at Bucyrus. Designed on the Bucyrus pattern, it was an ultra-high-volume facility for Green Light bearings. Gaffney repeated the Bucyrus pattern of placing a new plant in a rural, non-union environment. It was, in addition, part of a trend among U.S. companies in the 1970s, which were moving production facilities south as a strategy for dealing with rising labor costs. According to Tim Timken, the move also reflected a desire not to have "all our eggs in one basket"—this would be the first

Right: *In 1969, corporate vice president Tim Timken (left), president Herb Markley (center), and South Carolina's development director Bob Kirby broke ground for the first U.S. plant outside Ohio, in Gaffney.*

Below: *Start-up began in 1971 when Governor John West (center) joined Markley and chairman Bob Timken in the ribbon-cutting ceremony. The plant has earned numerous awards for excellence in manufacturing, including the prestigious Shingo Prize in 1994.*

U.S. Timken plant built outside Ohio. The Gaffney decision was made in the late 1960s. It was a bold initiative to end the game of constant catch-up the company had been playing with smaller additions to Bucyrus, and, at the same time, to be more aggressive in pursuing growth. But in the long run it proved to be one of the best defensive moves Timken could have made. With Bucyrus and Gaffney together, the company's position became unassailable in the field of small, low-cost bearings—an area in which the Japanese routed the U.S. ball bearing industry.[32]

Four companies jointly controlled 90 percent of the Japanese bearing industry and exported to other countries: Koyo Seiko; Nippon Seiko (NSK); Toyo Bearing Manufacturing Company (NTN); and Fujikoshi (Nachi). NSK, the oldest, was established in 1916. All had been built up significantly since World War II under the protectionist trade policies of the Japanese government. When they had first shown up in U.S. markets in the early 1960s, U.S. bearing manufacturers had largely discounted them as serious competitors because of early quality problems and lengthy delays in delivery. They proved competitive in the long run, however, especially on price. Japanese producers focused on smaller-sized bearings that could be manufactured in volume at low cost and did not require sales engineering, and they were willing to sacrifice profit in order to penetrate new markets. Between 1964 and 1968, they captured a large proportion of the U.S. market for miniature ball bearings—between 40 and 50 percent by some estimates.[33]

After 1970, their progress in that field was slowed by a government ruling that all bearings used in defense applications had to be produced in North America, a policy aimed at preserving a domestic industry vital to national security. There was no such protection, though, for "commodity" bearings—the small, high-volume ball bearings that went into household appliances, which Japanese makers sold at 30 to 40 percent below U.S. prices for most of the 1970s. Between 1968 and 1973, the Japanese share of the total bearing market in the United States doubled, from 8 to 16 percent, but in that segment it surged to 60 percent. The ball bearing industry received some relief in the mid-1970s from higher tariffs placed on Japanese bearings in response to complaints of dumping. With demand still high, U.S. producers of small ball bearings remained alive, but they did not invest to make their high-volume plants competitive, choosing instead to focus on larger-sized bearings where margins were higher and competition less intense. By 1979, several former industry leaders, including GM's New Departure-Hyatt and SKF Industries, would concede the commodity ball bearing market to Japanese competitors.[34]

In Timken's segment of the industry, the story could hardly have been more different. There the Japanese followed much the same strategy, focusing on small, high-volume sizes of tapered roller bearings. And there they hit a wall. By 1971, they had captured about 1 percent of the market; ten years later they would have no more than 9 percent. In 1979, Koyo Seiko, which had begun producing bearings in the United States, abandoned the most competitive sizes for automotive applications.[35] In 1974, Timken took the competition home to Japan, establishing a sales subsidiary, Nihon Timken K. K., and undertaking to begin training Japanese sales engineers in Canton. It would be quite a few years before the initiative began to bear fruit, but it was an important move at the time, for symbolic as well as practical reasons. Similarly, the company's stand against illegal dumping betokened its determination not to cede any market share without a fight.

The brutal price competition and a declining market share drove Federal-Mogul's Bower division—one of Timken's oldest competitors—out of the business of making automotive bearings by 1971. NTN would ultimately acquire Bower, but Timken got most of the business it had given up. Coincidentally with the announcement of Bower's exit, Volkswagen announced it would go to Timken for all of the front-wheel bearings for its U.S.-produced cars, a contract that started at 10,000 bearings per month. Timken could win—and handle—the additional business because it had built the Gaffney plant.[36]

The surge in demand of the 1970s thus came partly through the attrition of competitors that could not meet the increased competition in the market for small bearings. Timken also developed a number of new bearing products that helped to expand the market. For the railroad industry it introduced the XP™ (Xtended Performance) bearing in 1972. Through a combination of improved seals, more effective lubrication, and finer finishes on bearing parts, it was rated to last for 600,000 miles of service or ten years without reconditioning or even lubrication, with a savings of $200 to $1,000 in maintenance costs per car during that time. The Hydra-Rib™ bearing, introduced in the early 1970s, improved control of low-level vibration or "chatter" in machine tools, which limited precision. At the same time, Timken offered the services of a computer program it had developed to analyze all the factors related to chatter that affected proper bearing selection. An important product in the automotive field was the UNIPAC™ bearing, introduced in 1979. Like the SET-RIGHT mounting and the UNIT-BEARING, the UNIPAC bearing reduced automakers' assembly costs by eliminating the need for adjustment of the bearings. It combined two cone-and-roller assemblies within a double cup, all preset, prelubricated, and sealed so that it could be installed quickly in the manufacturing process.[37]

But the phenomenon of demand was broader than that. In 1974—"the infamous summer of 1974," according to Joseph M. Bruening, president of Timken's largest distributor, Bearings, Inc.—there was an acute worldwide shortage of bearings in the middle range of sizes used for many industrial applications. As Tim Timken recalled, that was the point at which he and Joe Toot really began to feel both the pressure and the opportunity that the market presented. They became

The Hydra-Rib™ bearing is a self-contained tapered roller bearing introduced in 1972 to maintain optimum preload in machine-tool spindles. It has a floating outer-race rib, positioned by hydraulic or pneumatic pressure, in contact with the large roller ends, instead of the usual fixed inner-race rib. It has improved the cutting accuracy of machine-tool spindles by 60 percent.

The UNIPAC™ bearing is a two-row tapered roller bearing, supplied as a maintenance-free, preset, prelubricated and sealed package, originally designed for passenger-car wheels. It simplified significantly the mounting and assembly of automotive wheel bearings, which in turn reduced customers' costs. Introduced in 1979, it was the first in a series of new package-type bearings that include UNIPAC-PLUS™, SENSOR-PAC™, and PINION-PAC™ bearings.

much more focused on growth—on expanding capacity but also on pushing output to take full advantage of the demand situation. They began to pay attention to asset turnover, the ratio of sales to assets. It had averaged under 0.70 from the mid-1960s forward, but rose steadily after 1974 to 0.94 in 1979.[38]

They also paid attention to what their major U.S. customers, for example, Caterpillar, were saying about supply (as paraphrased by Tim Timken): "We're going flat out and adding millions of square feet of manufacturing space. If you don't come with us, your competitive position is going to be severely eroded." It would be very bad for the company in the long run if its major customers came to feel they had run into a blind alley of shortages. Said Timken, "We felt, as an extension of our philosophy of focus, that we had a special calling to make sure there was adequate tapered roller bearing capacity." That calling led the company to build an ultramodern, high-volume facility for midsized bearings, in Lincolnton, North Carolina. It came on line in 1979.[39]

Although Timken succeeded in staying on top of the U.S. bearing business, grew steadily in size, and was profitable through the 1970s, it nevertheless struggled in a harsh economic climate. That was the era of "stagflation"—high inflation with high unemployment and low growth, punctuated by oil crises in 1973 and 1975. Like other manufacturers, the company raised prices a number of times, but it still suffered shrinking profit margins. (Corporate operating income had averaged 20 percent of sales through the 1960s but trended downward

The Lincolnton plant in North Carolina relies on highly automated material-handling equipment and computerized shop-floor management systems to achieve medium-volume, low-cost production of bearings for heavy-duty applications. Steve Fredell and Ressie Jefferies help maintain this robot and control manufacturing processes.

steadily in the 1970s, averaging just 15 percent of sales.) The stiff competition in small, high-volume bearings added to the pain by keeping prices low in the field in which the company was most cost-competitive. By 1978, when annual sales surpassed $1 billion, bearings accounted for 71 percent of revenues, but steel and bearing profits were about equal.[40]

Conditions in the 1970s were tougher still for Timken's divisions in Europe. High demand, inflation, and strong price competition were all factors there, as in the United States. But there was the added complication of fluctuations in exchange rates among European currencies, which were difficult to predict and which had significant impact on the competitiveness of producers in different countries. The competition in tapered roller bearings was also much stronger. In 1970, SKF launched a broad program to modernize its plants and rationalize its worldwide operations (excluding the United States, where antitrust law prohibited it prior to the 1980s). FAG did much the same on a smaller scale. Those investments made them more competitive than ever on price. British Timken continued as the leader in its domestic markets, for much the same reasons that U.S. Timken did on its home turf. But Timken France, a much smaller organization, was not as strong relative to the competition on the European continent. It was profitable in the 1970s, helped along by a weak French currency, but still had difficulty generating enough sales and income to pay for needed capital investments. There was no expansion of capacity at Colmar for roughly a decade, from 1964 to 1973. Timken France lost some business in those years because of delivery problems and inability to meet demand.[41]

In 1973, with Britain joining the Common Market, British Timken likewise joined Timken Europe. The challenge was then to create a unified management group for what had grown up as three quite separate organizations—British Timken, Timken France, and Timken Rollenlager—and to devise a longer-term plan to rationalize production and expand the company's presence in Europe by 1980. Progress would be slow on the organizational front through the 1970s, but Timken took a number of steps that greatly strengthened its position in the European market. In particular, it committed to building at Colmar a fully continuous Bucyrus-type line for automotive bearings and, subsequently, new heat-treat, roller-grinding, and cold-forming facilities. The net effect of those investments would be to double the plant's capacity from 15 to 30 million bearings per year.[42]

Near the end of the decade, Timken undertook a rationalization program of its own. In creating Timken Europe, it had left an opening for customers and distributors to order direct from the French, British, or U.S. manufacturing units, which had significant variations in costs and priced bearings accordingly within their home markets. Each unit individually maintained Timken's long-established policy of charging all customers the same price for the same bearings (apart from volume discounts). But with no adjustment for international cost and price differences, the system had the effect of setting up a competition among the three. Under the circumstances, customers naturally always tried to order from the source with the best price. The situation was harmful to Timken France, in particular, but bad for business overall. The solution was the Timken Europa Distribution Center. Located in Haan, Germany, near Düsseldorf, Timken Europa opened in early 1979. With a large, highly automated and computerized facility for stocking inventory and filling orders, the new center unified both distribution and pricing of Timken bearings, regardless of manufacturing source. Combined with the investments in Colmar and the movement toward a more integrated organization, it helped to place the company on a firmer footing in the European marketplace.[43]

Many U.S. corporations cut back on capital spending as tough economic conditions squeezed profit margins. But Timken, in growth mode, took the opposite course. The Haan distribution center was only one project in a $500-million, five-year capital investment program launched in 1977. The new Lincolnton plant was another. Other big-ticket items included new piercing and rolling mills in the company's steel operations. Those were part of a long stream of investments in steel-making equipment that enabled the steel side of the business to keep pace with the growth in demand it faced in the postwar era.

Chasing Demand: Timken Steel

In fact, practically every year from the late 1950s through the 1970s, Timken put some major new piece of equipment into operation in its steel plants in Canton and Gambrinus. The main driver for all that investment was the bearing business. James K. Preston, who joined the company as a steel supervisory trainee in 1952 and became the first general manager of the Faircrest steel plant in the 1980s, observed: "The reason for the steel plant to be there was because of the bearings. If we didn't remember that, we were in trouble."[44]

Yet the economics of steel making dictated that Timken needed much more capacity than its bearing division required. From the 1930s onward, therefore, Timken sold 60 to 70 percent of its steel to outside customers. The steel division's ability to develop profitable new products and applications was an important factor in the company's overall success. Indeed, H. H. Timken's bold move to gain a competitive advantage for Timken bearings by integrating backward into steel production could not have succeeded over the long run without it. Being a "captive" of the bearing business shaped—and limited—the markets that the steel division pursued. But the relationship also created some differentiated capabilities and products (mechanical tubing in particular) that gave Timken steel a competitive advantage in *its* industry. The pressures upon it to expand output in the 1960s and 1970s thus came not only from growth in the market for Timken bearings but also from increased demand for its other steel products.

Vacuum-arc remelting is an example of a technology that Timken first adopted to obtain a higher quality of steel for bearings and that later led the company into other markets. It is a refinement step that further removes gas and inclusions from electric-furnace steel. The company installed a vacuum-arc furnace in 1958 and was able to produce cleaner, higher-strength steel as a result. In the end, few Timken bearings were produced using vacuum-arc steel because it was judged too expensive. But the material opened new markets for Timken steel in the aerospace industry, for example, in airplane landing gears and helicopter parts. The demand became so great in the mid-1960s, as a result of the Vietnam War, that the company installed a second vacuum-arc furnace in 1969. Similarly, Timken installed its first vacuum degassing unit in 1964 and found a large enough market for degassed steel to add another the following year.[45]

That was a common pattern for adoption of new steel-making technologies: in the quest to develop improved materials for Timken bearings, the steel division investigated promising new processes as they appeared in the industry. Even when they proved not to be critical to bearing manufacture, Timken steel often entered new markets as a result. One of the company's most pioneering innovations in steel making—its early introduction of continuous casting—followed the same general pattern. In that case, however, the attraction of the new technology was its potential to reduce cost, and the initiative for its adoption came, not from the division, but from Henry Timken in the corporate office. Continuous casting was an alternative to ingot casting that offered high productivity with greatly reduced capital and operating costs. (The efficiency of continuous casting later became evident when minimills using this technology destabilized the U.S. basic steel industry, beginning in the 1980s.) It had been adopted widely in Europe and Britain by the early 1960s. In fact, British Timken had the first experience with continuous casting when it worked closely with United Steel Companies, Ltd., in an effort to develop bearing applications for steel from United Steel's experimental caster. But in 1964, when steel-division executives went to Germany to investigate the process, only one company in North America, Atlas Steels Ltd. of Canada, was using a caster for alloy steels.[46]

Nowhere in the world had the process been employed for bearing-grade steels. George T. Matthews, Timken's first "continuous casting metallurgist," recalled that casters had a bad reputation for problems with high levels of nonmetallic inclusions. Yet by eliminating several steps that produced waste in the casting and handling of ingots, it promised to increase yields from 75 percent to between 90 and

95 percent. According to Matthews, the German company, Concast, from which Timken purchased its machine in 1965, "guaranteed" it could be used successfully for bearing steels. But, he said, "there was great concern among the technical people on the steel side about whether we were going to be able to pull this off." Henry Timken simply believed that his company could produce bearing steels with a caster if it set out to do so. And set out it did.[47]

The caster went into a new building next to Timken's Harrison Avenue melt shop, and the development team attempted its first cast in December 1968. It took two more years to bring the new caster on line, during which time there were many technical challenges to be overcome. For example, the process had never before been used with molten steel deoxidized by the addition of aluminum, as was standard practice in Timken's melt shop. The company was the first to produce such steels with a caster. But ultimately the steel division could not solve the problem of inclusions. As a result, the metal coming out of the caster lacked properties that were required for an application as demanding as bearings. To obtain them it was necessary to use reduction methods such as rolling. The machine that Timken had installed produced blooms of roughly 9-by-12 inches, and the necessary reductions meant that the finished sizes were considerably smaller. Within the company, the uses were limited to producing wire for making rollers and the races of some very small bearings.[48]

Sarge Hoopes, vice president for steel in the 1960s, asked the metallurgical division to develop outside markets for continuously cast steel. Timken succeeded in doing that by starting out with an application somewhat less demanding than bearings—bar steel for gears. There remained a great deal of skepticism in the industry about the quality of material that continuous casting could produce. Timken was able to clean up its process to the extent of eliminating large-sized inclusions, and it also offered substantial discounts to customers ordering continuously cast gear steel. Those steps enabled it to get a foothold in the market. Once it qualified its bar steel for that application, Timken began making seamless tubing from billets off the caster. It took five years, but ultimately the steel division succeeded in opening one of its largest applications for mechanical tubing, automatic transmissions, to steel from the caster.[49]

Henry Timken died in 1968, before those successes were achieved. The ambitious goals he had set for the company in continuous casting proved unattainable in the short run, but in the 1990s, technical advances would enable large-cross-section casters to produce steel that approached the cleanness obtainable in the best ingot technologies (which had also improved considerably by then). His initiative had put Timken on the leading edge of one of the most significant twentieth-century manufacturing innovations.

Timken's steel business fell off with the industry as a whole in the early 1970s, as the United States pulled out of the Vietnam War. But it picked up again dramatically following the first oil crisis of the decade, in 1973—an embargo imposed by the Arab oil-producing nations on shipments to Japan, Western Europe, and the United States in retaliation for their support of Israel in the Yom Kippur War. Timken had developed a number of new applications for mechanical tubing in the oil industry, such as couplings for oil pipe and a collar that was placed just above the drill bit in oil-well drilling equipment. It was the only producer capable of making the thick-walled material required to withstand the pressures involved, particularly in directional (i.e., not vertical) drilling. As the U.S. oil industry went all out to discover and develop new domestic resources, this became a large and quite profitable market for Timken steel. Another important new application of the 1970s was heavy-wall, high-pressure tubing for the chemical industry, a product with a highly polished inner surface for use in the manufacture of polyethylene packaging materials. In addition, Timken Research produced a number of new high-temperature corrosion-resistant alloys for applications such as the main shaft in aircraft engines as well as a series of weldable high-strength alloys. That represented a significant revival of alloy development, which had been largely dormant in the postwar era.[50]

As those examples suggest, one of Timken Steel's greatest strengths was its ability to adjust to changing market conditions by developing new applications. Its sales engineering function, backed up by strong internal technical organizations, gave it that capability. And, with the Timken bearing business as its single largest customer, it never became overly dependent on any outside market. Its flexibility was part of what made Timken a strong competitor in the steel industry.[51]

To keep up with the demand from both internal and external customers, the steel division added four new electric furnaces between 1963 and 1971 and renovated those that were not replaced. It also added and improved downstream equipment. Timken's fourth Assel tube mill came on line in 1962. From the mid-1970s onward, however, there was intense pressure on output exerted indirectly by the strong demand for bearings. (Timken also supplied steel to most other U.S. bearing manufacturers.) In 1975, Timken acquired Latrobe Steel Company. This would prove to be a development of great strategic significance in the long term. But Timken made the acquisition mainly in an effort to add critical capacity.

Acquisition of Latrobe Steel Company

Bob Timken clearly recalled the thinking that led him to suggest making an overture to Latrobe. The company was buying small roller wire from its Canton neighbor, Republic Steel, and Republic was planning to cut off its supply. The steel division estimated it would take about $25 million to build the kind of large automated rolling mill required to produce roller wire cost-effectively. "At that point," said Bob, "we looked around to see if anyone had such a mill." Latrobe did have the mill and was running it at only about 50 percent capacity. In 1975, Timken acquired the company in an exchange of stock valued at about $16.5 million. "It saved us the $25 million," Bob said. "The real reason we acquired Latrobe was to get the benefit of that wire mill."[52]

Timken gained much more than a rolling mill, however, as Bob fully appreciated. Latrobe Steel had a tradition of leadership in its segment of the specialty steel industry similar to the company's own. Latrobe's investment in the state-of-the-art rolling mill had much to do with bringing it to the point of being acquired in the mid-1970s. But that aggressiveness, too, was in the Timken mold.

Charles Guttzeit   *Marcus W. Saxman*   *Marshall Schober*

Cofounders Charles Guttzeit and Marcus Saxman started Latrobe Electric Steel Company in 1913 with a single 6-ton, electric-arc furnace. Today, Latrobe melts 132 million pounds of specialty steels per year in more than 300 grades. Marshall Schober served as president from 1971 to 1986 and was the key figure in negotiating the successful acquisition by Timken.

The company had been founded as Latrobe Electric Steel Company in March 1913, by Charles W. Guttzeit and Marcus W. Saxman. Guttzeit was a colorful character. Born in Shanghai, China, the son of a German army general and an upper-class Chinese woman, he had been a ship's captain, a gold prospector, and an inventor before joining a New Jersey steel company. There he got the idea to create a new steel-making concern relying entirely on electric-furnace technology. At that time there were only about ten electric-arc furnaces making steel in the United States. (Timken would start its steel operations in 1916.) Guttzeit went to

Latrobe, in western Pennsylvania—the heartland of coal mining and steel making—to find financial backing for his venture. He joined forces with Saxman, a Latrobe businessman whose family had established itself in the coal industry in the 1850s. Saxman raised the starting capital and became president of the new company, which began operations with a single 6-ton electric-arc furnace. Guttzeit was its first general manager.[53]

His original idea was to focus on producing steel castings of an alloy with high manganese content, for hardness and durability. By 1915, however, Latrobe had identified a large new market in tool steel. That was an application, much like bearings, in which performance was largely dependent on material quality, and electric-furnace steel offered significant advantages. World War I was in progress in Europe, and there was great demand for materials to build machine tools for the manufacture of war materiel. Between 1916 and 1918 Latrobe added two additional electric furnaces, rolling mills, forging hammers, and heat-treatment equipment to help meet wartime needs.[54]

In 1919, the company established a metallurgical laboratory and hired David J. Giles to organize a research department. Giles's organization made a number of contributions to the industry, for example, in the testing of tool steels. Over the years, it also developed numerous significant new products for Latrobe. Those products, in addition to its standard tool steels, helped the company to weather the Depression with only one losing year and to sustain its technical program through the 1930s, as Timken did.[55]

Much like Timken, Latrobe was able to respond to the World War II crisis with greatly increased output and to use its strong technical capabilities to make some significant innovations in the early postwar years. In the late 1930s, it had developed a low-tungsten alloy for high-speed tool steels, an innovation that took on great importance during the war, when the United States was cut off from its major sources of tungsten in China and Korea. Latrobe also made a major breakthrough on a long-standing problem in tool steels. That was segregation—the separation of an essential alloying element into particles in the metal, which weakened it and made it wear more rapidly. The company introduced a line of Desegatized™ steel in 1946 that set a new standard for tool-steel quality.[56]

In the postwar era, Latrobe continued to differentiate itself through the introduction of improved tool steels. Free-machining steel (1950) contained a small amount of sulfur that caused chips to break away cleanly as the steel was machined to make cutting tools, ensuring that the tools would have a smooth surface. Nondeforming high-speed tool steel (1956) was a line of heat-treatable high-strength alloys sold in forgings, which resisted distortions of shape during heat treatment, so that the tools made from the forgings maintained close tolerances on size dimensions.[57]

Latrobe took up vacuum-arc remelting technology about the same time as Timken, in the late 1950s. Between 1957 and 1962 it installed four commercial-sized vacuum-arc remelt furnaces and doubled its spending for research to support the new line of business. As a result, Latrobe became one of the two largest producers of vacuum-arc remelted steels, second only to Republic Steel. Combined with its tool steels, those high-performance materials, sold mainly for aerospace applications, made Latrobe one of the fastest-growing and most profitable companies in the U.S. specialty steel industry. The company also expanded its sales into international markets. In 1964, Latrobe established three small divisions in related lines. Cast Masters, with facilities in both Latrobe and Racine, Wisconsin, specialized in precision casting of steel products such as forging dies and molds for plastics. Special Products manufactured heat-treated parts for customers in various industries. Koncor Industries, in Wauseon, Ohio, near Toledo, was both a distributor and a finisher of Latrobe's tool-steel products—an outpost of the company established to provide value-added products and services to its machine-tool customers.[58]

Marcus W. Saxman III, grandson of the founder, became president of Latrobe in 1966. Looking at forecasts of strong growth in demand for the company's products into the 1970s, he committed that year to an $18.5-million expansion of facilities, the centerpiece of which was a large new rolling mill. With the steady expansion of its melting facilities—its seventh vacuum-arc furnace would come on line in 1968—Latrobe's downstream equipment had become outdated and was running at full capacity. Although the new mill would add much more capacity than needed in the short run, it represented an opportunity for Latrobe to expand its line of rolled products. The company had previously financed all of its expansion internally, but it had to borrow to complete this program. By the time the new rolling mill came on line in 1968, Latrobe was carrying nearly $16 million in debt, an amount that loomed large compared to its total shareholders' equity of just $26 million.[59]

It was a bold investment unfortunately timed. Latrobe's revenues rose by 17 percent in 1969, from $46 million to $54 million, but its net income fell by nearly 70 percent. Some of the pressures on profits were related to delays—including a fifty-four-day strike—in bringing the new downstream facilities on line. But there was also pressure from longer-term problems: inflationary pressures on the cost of raw materials and interest payments on its debt. Those conditions set the company up for two years of net losses in 1970 and 1971, as the U.S. economy entered the post–Vietnam War recession and the specialty steel industry began to feel the impact of intensifying global competition. (By Saxman's calculation, low-priced imports captured some 30 percent of the market for high-speed tool steel in 1970.) With its solid fundamentals, Latrobe revived with the economy and was running close to capacity by June 1974, when it attracted the attention of acquisition-minded Eastmet Corporation. The company had paid no dividends for several years and its stock price was down. All of that made it a very attractive takeover target.[60]

Marshall Schober had become Latrobe's president in 1971. He recalled learning of Eastmet's tender offer from Latrobe's treasurer, Joseph R. Gregg, who interrupted a meeting to tell him the company's stock had stopped trading on the New York Stock Exchange. By late afternoon, Schober had arranged to fly in all of Latrobe's directors for an emergency meeting, and by the next day the company had spoken to every holder of more than 500 shares of stock. But the tender offer, he realized, was an attractive one—$11 per share for stock that had been trading around $6. The company filed several lawsuits to slow Eastmet down, but it had little reason to feel confident that a majority of its shareholders would decline the tender offer.[61]

Over the next four weeks, Eastmet worked to put together a large enough block of stock to effect the takeover. It was during that time that Bob Timken, having read about the hostile takeover attempt, suggested approaching Latrobe with an offer to play the white knight by making a friendly acquisition. This Timken did through a third party, Davitt Bell, chairman of Edgewater Steel, a Timken customer and supplier. Schober and other officers and directors were determined to resist Eastmet, a company that had grown rapidly by acquisitions. They believed Eastmet was mainly interested in Latrobe's new rolling mill and was likely to sell off its other assets piecemeal. On the other hand, they also wanted to go it on their own, if possible, and they succeeded in the end, mainly because key members of the Saxman family rejected the deal. But, Schober observed, in an era of industry consolidation, "You can't be too successful, and you can't be too unsuccessful. Either way, you lose." Latrobe had fought off Eastmet, but it was now "in the sights of every gunslinger on Wall Street." When Herb Markley approached him at a business gathering in New York and renewed Timken's expression of interest, Schober was ready to move forward with plans for a friendly takeover.[62]

In the fall of 1974, Timken sent over some steel billets from Canton to be processed into roller wire in Latrobe's new rolling mill, the newest and most advanced such mill in the specialty steel industry. Latrobe's mill had 20 mill stands set up sequentially to convert steel billets 7 inches square and 15 feet long into round rods, bar, and wire as small as 0.22 inches in diameter. It had the horsepower to handle the most difficult alloys and was designed for quick changes in setup, for the flexibility to run small as well as large orders cost-effectively. This was the equipment that Timken had its eye on. When the material it produced checked out for quality, the companies proceeded with their negotiations. By January 1975, they had agreed on a merger that gave Latrobe's shareholders about $13 per share in Timken stock.[63]

Schober could feel good about the deal he had made for the company. Timken chose not to make Latrobe a division, but organized it as a wholly owned subsidiary and kept its management largely intact. "Normally, when anybody new comes in, they tear the place apart. We were very careful not to do that," said Bob Timken. Schober reported directly to Joe Toot, then executive vice president, and Toot made weekly trips to Latrobe for a few years. The relationship was not without its struggles. Toot pushed for higher standards of performance and participated in "big decisions," but did not impose Timken's bureaucracy on an organization used to operating without it. Schober stood his ground when challenged on key issues, such as pricing, but in general was ready to adapt to Timken's way of doing things and found Toot a good teacher.[64]

The takeover was more fraught with anxiety for Latrobe's unionized hourly workforce and the community. The city had experienced other mergers in which new corporate owners from out of town had decimated the local businesses. The fact that, in 1975, the Timken Foundation committed $50,000 to renovations of Latrobe's hospital allayed those fears to a great extent, and the family foundation continued to invest in community projects each year thereafter. Thus it became clear that the Timkens would continue the strong tradition of philanthropy and community leadership established over generations by the Saxman family.[65]

The concerns of Latrobe's employees were not put to rest so easily. Timken's reputation for tough dealings with the United Steelworkers preceded it. Latrobe's contract with the USW came up for renewal in August 1977. "I told my people we'd have a six-month strike in 1977," said the union's district director James N. Coyne, "based on Timken's way of doing things." Marshall Schober had similarly prepared Timken. "There was going to be a fight, I don't care what happened," he recalled. "We could have offered them the moon, but there was going to be a fight."[66]

Latrobe had been unionized since 1937 and had had no strikes from that point into the 1960s. Over the years, the company had basically accepted the pattern contracts coming down from Big Steel. Now, guided by Timken, it pushed for changes in work rules, scheduling, and procedures for handling grievances that aimed at restoring much of the management control it had given up. According to Coyne, the demands amounted to "the right to unilaterally eliminate long-standing customs, practices, and understandings." Said another union official, "They are trying to take away the gains won over forty years of fighting." Latrobe and Timken took the position that the changes were necessary "to achieve operating efficiency." Those were battle lines that would be drawn in company after company from the late 1970s onward. In fact, there were no fewer than eight strikes in western Pennsylvania in 1977–78, as other small steel producers and suppliers that, like Latrobe, had long followed the USW pattern contracts attempted to break out of the pattern either on pay or work rules.[67]

With such fundamental issues at stake, the Latrobe strike was long and bitter. More than six months into it, the union membership voted down by 1,080 to 1 a new contract that granted wage concessions but stuck with the work-rule changes. Three months later, there were enough concessions on both sides for a contract to be signed and accepted by a majority of the union members. Latrobe got its revised work rules, however, which eventually allowed it to operate with

On the heels of a recession, the company in 1992 improved Latrobe's ability to compete by investing $40 million in a new precision forging facility. During start-up, Latrobe's Greg Glova (left) showed president Joe Toot the facility.

a workforce 26 percent smaller than before. As an independent company, Schober observed, Latrobe would have found it impossible to sustain a long strike and win such changes—essential changes that other steel companies would make later, when the industry was under even greater competitive pressure. Latrobe began running profitably within months after the end of the strike, and, going forward, Timken balanced its tough stand on work rules with substantial investments that helped to keep its subsidiary competitive. In 1980 it launched a program that put more than $40 million into new plant and equipment over the next few years.[68]

In addition to the contribution of its rolling mill, Latrobe helped to relieve the pressure on steel output by taking over Timken's business in vacuum-arc remelted steels. The Canton steel mill was able to remove that equipment to make room for additional melting capacity. In 1977, Canton added another large electric furnace. But the company had reached the point where adding new furnaces could no longer solve its capacity issues, because the downstream equipment simply could not handle more throughput. As it was, the Harrison steel shop was "a logistics nightmare," said George Matthews. By the end of the decade Timken was obliged to consider building a new steel plant at a new location. That consideration was part of a broader effort to prepare the company for what was clearly going to be a tougher competitive environment in the 1980s.[69]

Toward the 1980s

The decade of the 1970s presented numerous challenges. But it was also a time of heady accomplishment pervaded by the sense that Timken was the clear leader in its chosen fields. On the bearing side, it held its own against Japanese competition and gained market share against major U.S. rivals. On the steel side, it opened up significant new applications for mechanical tubing, particularly in the oil industry, where it was the sole supplier for critical parts made out of thick-walled tubing. And the company grew steadily and profitably throughout the decade, despite losses at Latrobe in 1977 and 1978 resulting from its long strike. (See Table 9.1.) Between 1969 and 1979, Timken's revenues increased at a compound annual rate of 12 percent, its net income at a rate of 11 percent. That compared to just 4 percent growth in revenues and 2 percent in net income for the decade before.

In the corporate office, those results could be, and were, compared favorably to the performance of Timken's competitors. SKF was the leading bearing producer worldwide and the company most like Timken, manufacturing both bearings and steel. It was about three times larger in total revenues, but it had not grown as fast as Timken in the 1970s—SKF's compound annual growth in revenues was 10 percent. Nor had it been as profitable. (See Figure 9.1.) Timken averaged an 8 percent return on sales through the 1970s, versus 2.6 percent for SKF. The Japanese companies and the German bearing maker FAG placed a relatively low priority on profitability, and so were not comparable on financial performance. Direct comparisons could not be made for the company's major U.S. bearing competitors, because they were all part of larger companies—Bower was a division of Federal-Mogul; New Departure-Hyatt was a division of

TABLE 9.1

The Timken Company Comparative Financial Data, 1970–1979 (in Thousands of Dollars, except per Share Data)

	1970	1971	1972	1973	1974	1975	1976	1977	1978	1979
Net sales	$389,195	$410,613	$470,758	$567,471	$665,492	$804,491	$884,427	$974,352	$1,105,818	$1,282,069
Net income	28,615	38,117	42,308	53,020	52,932	61,323	60,888	74,441	88,639	102,131
Total assets	$389,645	$420,662	$440,716	$494,077	$541,491	$655,208	$716,212	$779,492	$863,308	$942,912
Long-term obligations						18,936	29,456	28,129	30,186	28,906
Total capital and earnings invested in the business	331,626	350,502	372,776	402,253	432,170	499,569	536,314	579,538	628,969	705,859
Return on sales	7.4%	9.3%	9.0%	9.3%	8.0%	7.6%	6.9%	7.6%	8.0%	8.0%
Return on assets	7.3	9.1	9.6	10.7	9.8	9.4	8.5	9.5	10.3	10.8
Return on capital and earnings	8.6	10.9	11.3	13.2	12.2	12.3	11.4	12.8	14.1	14.5
Earnings per share	$2.69	$3.58	$3.97	$4.98	$5.01	$5.49	$5.45	$6.66	$8.04	$9.14
Dividends per share	1.80	1.80	1.87	2.00	2.00	2.10	2.20	2.60	3.00	3.25
Number of employees	20,984	19,984	20,584	21,885	22,196	22,609	22,914	23,089	23,268	23,772
Number of shareholders	33,875	31,261	30,700	29,372	29,728	31,638	29,109	27,481	26,559	25,864

Source: The Timken Company Annual Reports, 1970–79.

Note: Data from 1975 forward reflects 1975 acquisition of Latrobe Steel Company.

GM; and Torrington, a producer of needle roller bearings that had moved strongly into tapered roller bearings in the 1960s, was a division of Ingersoll-Rand. Still, there was nothing going on in the industry to cause Timken's executives to doubt that their company was both the market leader in its chosen field and the best-performing bearing company in the world.[70]

On the other hand, there was some evidence to suggest that Timken would have to take steps to preserve its leadership position. The deterioration of operating margins pointed to the need to reduce costs. A far more troubling piece of information had to do with bearing performance. The steady increase in bearing ratings, which had continued through the 1960s, was the bedrock of Timken's competitive strength. But when the marketing department asked for a ratings increase in the early 1970s—the most recent had been in 1967—it came away disappointed. The evidence from the company's bearing-life-testing program indicated that it had reached a plateau.[71]

That finding spurred Timken Research to launch an effort to determine the factors influencing those bearing-life test results. The two researchers assigned to the case, Jack D. Stover and Ronald L. Widner, each brought to the assignment the

FIGURE 9.1

**Timken and SKF
Return on Sales 1968–1981**

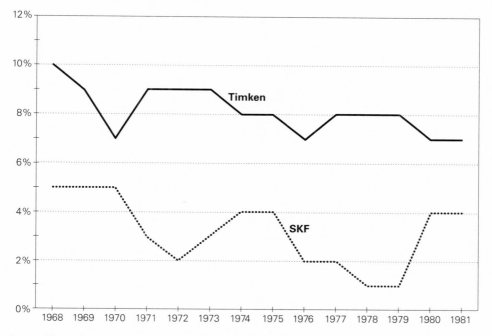

Sources: The Timken Company and SKF Annual Reports, 1968–81.

advantage of having worked on both bearing and steel problems. In addition, they had a powerful research tool, ultrasonic inspection, which had been in use for quality control in the steel plant since the early 1960s. In a laboratory setting, with advanced ultrasonic equipment for detection of nonmetallic inclusions in steel, they established a clear correlation between clean steel and bearing-life performance. Those results indicated that the next increase in bearing ratings would require a reduction in the level of inclusions in Timken steel. Confirming evidence came through the analysis of life tests run routinely on bearings from all Timken plants. In the early 1970s, Timken was getting cleaner steel from its European suppliers and demonstrating better results in life tests on bearings from British Timken and Timken France.[72]

The message was not one the company was eager to hear. That was especially true of the steel division—Jack Stover recalled the harassment he received from steel executives at the company's monthly management dinners. But top management, too, was reluctant to accept the import of the research findings. Charles H. West, Timken's chief engineer for industrial bearings, arranged for Widner and Stover to present their material to the executive team. The issue of clean steel was especially important to him, because it posed the greatest problems for larger-sized bearings. West and his assistant chief engineer, Robert L. Leibensperger—who had come out of Timken Research to help apply some of the work done there—determined to push for an increase in research funding to address the problem systematically. They had to go back more than once before the issue received serious attention. With all the usual indicators of success so strong, it was simply difficult to make the case that the Timken bearing was no longer way ahead of the competition.[73]

In the end, however, the evidence prevailed. Timken launched a clean-steel program, bringing all of its existing knowledge and know-how to bear on the problem. Coincidentally, Tom Strouble recalled, Herb Markley, Tim, and Joe had become convinced by evidence that companies that invested in research tended to perform well financially. In 1978, they commissioned Strouble to lead a task force to study the issue. Within just a few months, that committee came back with some strong recommendations for expanding the research program and refocusing it to place greater emphasis on theoretical problems. "There is no question," reported the committee, "that we have allowed the pendulum to swing too far toward less sophisticated programs which show short term returns at the expense of a longer term technology base." One sign of the change was the fact that Timken no longer could claim to have the leading experts in fields of critical importance to its businesses. "These 'experts' are the foundation of our technology base and are as necessary a part of the R&D team as the innovators, creators, doers, and administrators." Without them, the committee suggested, the program would be restricted to "more of the same."[74]

Major agenda items set forth by the committee for an enlarged R&D organization were to identify the company's long-term technical needs and opportunities, to provide support to steel operations comparable to that given to bearings, and to increase new product introductions in both bearings and steel. However, of the nine high-priority issues to be addressed, six focused on reducing manufacturing costs of both steel and bearings—a clear indication of the pressing need in that area. One of Tim Timken's concerns in the late 1970s was that much of the company's equipment was relatively old and did not have state-of-the-art electronic controls. He supported an increase in research funding as a way to move Timken faster in that direction.[75]

Near the end of 1978, the company announced it would double the size of its central R&D organization and facilities. In contrast to the era in which Timken Research was created, this expansion came at a time of deep disenchantment with R&D in corporate America. R&D spending, both public and private, had trended steadily downward from the late 1960s on. Concurrently, U.S. corporations turned in increasing numbers to diversification as a hedge against business cycles and a vehicle for growth. Even many technology-based companies followed this trend, buying into industries with unrelated technologies and even into nontechnological industries such as financial services.[76]

Timken's commitment to a significantly higher level of R&D spending in that environment highlighted the different path it had chosen in focusing so narrowly on tapered roller bearings and specialty steel. It simply had to maintain leadership in its products and processes for the strategy to succeed. That was the basic premise that had guided investment decisions since H. H. Timken's day. In fact, the situation in which the company found itself in the late 1970s was in some ways parallel to what H. H. had faced in the early 1920s. Having won the business of Ford Motor Company in 1918, Timken had been largely consumed with maintaining the levels of output required to handle it. Its processes had slipped some on quality, and it had allowed its competitors to get ahead in technology. "We were too prosperous," H. H. had said of that time, "and getting dead on our feet." The executives of the 1970s had likewise fallen prey to some of the perils of success.[77]

But there was a big difference in the size of the problem the company confronted. In the 1920s, U.S. industry, and the automotive industry in particular, was in the midst of a period of rapid growth. In contrast, the 1980s would bring an extended worldwide recession leading into an era of chronic oversupply that would devastate many of the company's major customers. The competitive landscape had been transformed by globalization, and performance standards for bearings and steel had increased dramatically. The world had changed. The penalties for falling behind the curve—even a little bit—would be greater. And it would be harder to catch up.

Those were the challenges faced by the new executive team of Tim Timken and Joe Toot. Joe succeeded Herb Markley as president near the end of 1979, though, in the Umstattd tradition, Markley stayed on to serve as chairman of the executive committee of the board of directors.[78] Like Umstattd, over the course of his Timken career he had gained wide respect in the business community. At the time of his retirement, Markley was serving a term as chairman of the board of the National Association of Manufacturers, the culmination of a long-term active participation in that organization. His other major commitment was to education. He served on various advisory boards at Miami University of Ohio and Case Western Reserve University, spoke to many college audiences, received numerous honorary degrees, and in 1976 spent a week at each of five different colleges as a Woodrow Wilson Visiting Fellow. In the Umstattd mold, Markley was also active in a broad range of community and civic organizations and a frequent public speaker.

As Joe took over, the company was moving forward with a broad-ranging assessment of both the opportunities and the challenges facing its steel business. That effort had arisen from the need to consider a major capacity expansion, but it had taken on additional significance in light of the research findings on bearing-life performance. The assessment would lead to a surprising result—in 1981, Timken would commit to building a large new steel plant in Ohio, the first to be built in the United States since 1962. Though fully consistent with a long stream of strategic thinking, that decision was surely the most momentous since H. H. Timken entered the steel business in the first place. It would seem even more so after 1982, when the company sustained its commitment in the face of its first unprofitable year since the Depression and a competitive environment more brutal than anything imagined in the 1970s.

Faircrest

*T*he building of the Faircrest steel plant was a transforming event. The investment was essential to make both Timken steel and bearings competitive in quality and cost. But the risk was enormous. The new plant's $500-million price tag represented nearly two-thirds of the company's total equity in 1981 when it made the commitment, and there would be no return on the investment until the plant was up and running. As Timken poured money into Faircrest through the early 1980s, the U.S. economy went into a deep recession, with a number of its core industries in dire straits. A strong U.S. dollar relative to other currencies added to the pain, making U.S. manufactured goods less price competitive in both domestic and world markets. The automotive industry ceded its position as number one in the world to the Japanese, while the large, integrated steel producers, with more than half their capacity idled, gave up trying to compete with superior and lower-priced Japanese steel and began diversifying into oil, chemicals, and financial services. In that environment, Timken's dramatic move to secure a leadership position in its core businesses was a defining act. Both symbolically and realistically, the future of the company was riding on it. Moreover, while the decision to build Faircrest was firmly grounded in Timken's long-standing tradition of strategic focus and investment in new technology, the decision-making process was the starting point for changes that would ripple through the organization, affecting structure, strategy, and ultimately corporate culture.

In 1978, when the company began to consider the related questions of steel-making capacity and steel quality, it was still largely consumed with the task of keeping up with demand for Timken bearings and mechanical tubing. The Lincolnton bearing plant was under construction—the second plant in less than a decade to spring from a corporate strategy emphasizing high-volume production of standardized bearings. That strategy had developed out of Bucyrus in the 1950s, and it remained largely unexamined despite some fundamental underlying changes in the business environment. The organizational development that Bob Timken had called for in 1968 was proceeding, but slowly. It would be some years before efforts to recruit MBAs into entry-level management positions and to provide broader exposure to those advancing within the executive ranks began to have an impact. In the meantime, Timken's functionally organized managerial hierarchy, though strong on execution of the familiar strategy, was ill equipped to formulate a new one and was bogged down in creeping bureaucracy. The company's engineering culture supported incremental improvement of manufacturing processes but had become too insular to perceive that some competitors' processes were altogether better. The command-and-control style of operations management was a barrier to process innovation and improved productivity. In retrospect, Tim Timken and Joe Toot would look back on the 1970s as a period in which, for all those reasons, the company lost ground to world competitors on both cost and quality. They would judge that organizational change had been too slow and that they had stayed too long with the strategic emphasis on standardized bearings. Those problems were not readily apparent at the time, however, largely because of the company's continuing strength in markets characterized by high demand.[1]

Yet Timken's young top-management team knew that they wanted to start doing some things differently. As director of corporate development in 1967, Tim had formed a department of market research to gain a better understanding of the company's markets and competitors. The next year he had drafted John Schubach into the department to work on developing some new analytical tools for decision making. Schubach had grown up in Canton and knew both Tim and Joe personally. He had started working for Timken in 1956 as a summer job while attending engineering school, and had joined full-time in industrial sales engineering in 1963. He left for two years to get an MBA at Harvard and then returned in 1966 to work in the engineering department, where he helped replace mechanical calculators with computers better able to perform the elaborate calculations required for designing bearings. In 1968, Schubach worked with Tim on an exercise to develop a complex probabilistic model of factors such as market demand, operating economics, and material costs, as an aid to making an investment decision on a new furnace for vacuum remelted steel. Ultimately, they decided the methodology was too elaborate, but the basic concept of analyzing critical factors remained part of the company's planning function thereafter.[2]

The analysis would have to be rigorous for a decision as important as a major increase in steel-making capacity. Joe and Tim were determined that it should begin with a thorough investigation of what was going on in the steel industry worldwide. They agreed at the outset that they would not consider any proposal for new capacity that did not promise to "improve quality substantially and lower costs dramatically."[3]

Yet putting together a team to conduct the kind of study they wanted posed a problem. Timken's insularity was, if anything, greater on the steel side than on the bearing side of the company. The company had a tradition of technological leadership in the domestic steel industry, including most recently its early implementation of continuous casting. But it had not attempted to compete in international markets, and through the 1970s the specialty steel segment of the industry in which Timken operated remained largely free from the pressure of Japanese and European imports. Within the segment, the company's steel division was even less bothered by competition than most. Timken's bearing plants claimed a large share of its output, and there was typically much higher demand for the remainder than it could possibly fill. Margins were high, and the business was very profitable—more profitable than bearings in the late 1970s, although the calculation was complicated by the fact that there was not a separate income statement for the steel business. As far as the research findings about steel quality and bearing life were concerned, the steel-division attitude was standoffish. According to Jim Preston, future general manager of the Faircrest plant, "If there was a problem with the bearings and they weren't performing the way they thought they should have, we thought it was somebody else's fault, not ours." As to the need for capacity expansion, the senior managers of the division were steeped in the historic resentment over being second-class citizens within the company, and they were tired of seeing the lion's share of capital investments going into the bearing plants. Predisposed to favoring the idea of adding new capacity, they had little use for the kind of painstaking market and industry analysis that interested Tim Timken. They were not, Tim and Joe decided, the best candidates to take a fresh, objective look at the business and its future prospects.[4]

Indeed, their goal was to use the occasion to develop a model for future strategic decision making. They determined that the process should be focused outward—on customers, competitors, and the economic environment. At the same time, it should integrate the perspectives of key internal constituencies—engineering, manufacturing, and marketing. Timken's old process, fragmented by its functional organization and constrained by its traditional corporate culture, met neither of those criteria. Tim and Joe therefore determined to work outside existing channels.

They charged John Schubach to lead a team to study the steel industry and the question of a capacity expansion. Since his stint in corporate development, Schubach had worked with Jim Pilz in both marketing and international divisions. He was shortly joined by William Hudson, Timken's chief cost accountant. Subsequently, Tim and Joe added Bill Bowling on a half-time basis. Bowling was another 1960s hire who had come to Timken with both an engineering degree and an MBA, and he had done a tour of duty in the management of Timken Europe. He also had the distinction of having worked in both the bearing and steel divisions. A down-to-earth man, he was by his own admission more interested in the human aspects of managing a business than in strategy. But he had the correct training, an approved career track, and the open-mindedness of a relative newcomer to the company. The team's charge was to start "with a clean sheet of paper"—to talk to customers and to find out what competitors were doing before even beginning to look at the question of Timken's capacity needs. Every week the team was to meet with Tim and Joe and report on its progress.[5]

The team expanded during 1979 when it came time to visit other steel companies: Ray Bloom, from Timken Research; Lars Djupedal, from steel engineering; George Matthews, process metallurgist; and Jim Preston, then head of the Canton melt shop, all joined at that point. They began by visiting other U.S. steel makers, where they saw nothing that was new to them. When they headed to Europe, however, the benchmarking exercise became a classic learning experience, which one U. S. company after another would replicate in the 1980s. Bowling spoke for the steel personnel: "I think we went out with the idea that this was a waste of time—we already knew everything anyway." Once out in the world, though, they found not only new technology, but new ways of working and strikingly superior results, particularly in Germany. As Jim Preston recalled, "We told [the German plant personnel] that we were very impressed with how well they were doing. What they said to us was, 'We think we are doing pretty well. We think, in fact, that we are almost as good as the Japanese.'" Said Preston, "We decided that if *they* were impressed by the Japanese, we had better get ourselves to Japan."[6]

Once there, said Bowling, it was "culture shock" to see what was an eight-hour task for Timken—making a heat of steel—completed in one hour. "We went there knowing we had to improve; we just didn't know how much." But, they assured themselves, "Anything that is made that fast can't be good." George Matthews, the team's metallurgist, was skeptical of Japanese practices when he learned that they used ten-to-one reduction ratios for the most demanding automotive applications of mechanical tubing. Of course, Timken knew that reduction improved the properties of the metal. But such a high reduction rate seemed extreme. Timken was successfully using ratios of four- or six-to-one for similar applications. Said John Schubach, "We thought that these Japanese didn't know what the hell they were doing."[7]

Nevertheless, the company had contracted with the Japanese steel maker Sumitomo Metal Industries for a feasibility study of a new plant. The serious learning began when Sumitomo supplied samples of Japanese-made steel for evaluation. "It was an eye-opener," George Matthews recalled. Ultrasonic inspection for inclusions revealed that the bearing steels, made faster and more cheaply than Timken's, were unquestionably cleaner. Moreover, as the team gradually recognized, the Japanese were taking higher reductions for superior performance because their customers were demanding it. Recalled Schubach, "It was at that time that we began to see clearly that we were in a little bit of trouble on steel performance . . . that is, the steel performance characteristics going into our bearings and their effect on bearing performance." It was now apparent to all that the investment under consideration involved a great deal more than steel-making capacity—it touched upon the competitiveness of the company as a whole.[8]

To proceed from that point, Tim and Joe took another uncharacteristic step. During 1979 Timken had commissioned a second outside study, an analysis of capacity needs by Dravo Engineers and Constructors of Pittsburgh, Pennsylvania. Now, Timken began working closely with Dravo on an intensive planning exercise, scouring the worldwide steel industry to determine the best steel-making technologies and practices. Three innovations were especially significant: ultra-high-power electric-arc furnaces; ladle refining; and bottom pouring of ingots. Since 1916, Timken had been melting, alloying, and refining steel in the furnace. The new best practice for producing clean steel used the furnace for melting only, covering the molten metal in the furnace with a layer of slag, oxidizing the bath with gaseous oxygen to reduce carbon and phosphorous, and superheating the bath for refining. At a separate station, state-of-the-art refining equipment utilized a sealed-to-the-ladle system that allowed arc heating, vacuum degassing, and stirring. Bottom pouring of ingots—that is, filling the molds from the bottom up—made it possible to shroud the ingot molds in argon gas to keep out oxygen and maintain steel cleanness. Timken had used bottom pouring in its steel mill in the 1940s but, along with the rest of the U.S. steel industry, had abandoned it because it was judged too labor intensive and time consuming—even though top pouring necessitated an extra "conditioning" step to improve surface quality. "How we ever got lulled into that is beyond me,"

George Matthews said. Those technologies and practices in combination were what enabled European and Japanese steel makers to produce cleaner steel in a fraction of the time.[9]

Between the spring of 1980 and the end of January 1981, a concrete vision of the new Timken steel plant took shape. The electric furnace would be German; the ladle refiner a U.S. design, but with French technology added; the bottom-pouring technology Japanese; the rolling mill German with U.S. technology; the transformer Finnish; the inspection system Norwegian. All those decisions were guided by Timken's determination to aim for "the leading edge of proven technology."[10]

There were four particularly tough decisions to be made in this phase of planning. The first concerned capacity: how big should the new plant be? With some projections for future demand for bearings and alloy steels that would turn out to be overly optimistic, the team proposed increasing Timken's current capacity by 50 percent, from 1 million ingot tons annually to 1.5 million. This was to be achieved with a single 170-ton electric-arc furnace. The plant would be laid out, however, to add three additional furnaces, boosting its capacity to 2 million tons in future phases of development.[11]

A second critical decision was largely technical but related to the question of capacity: should they install a continuous caster or use ingot technology? In a perverse way, this was partly a question of image. Continuous casting offered the possibility of achieving higher-volume output at lower cost, through savings in labor and energy. With the sweeping advance of minimills in the world steel industry since the early 1960s, ingot casting had come to be regarded in many quarters as outdated—"a buggy-whip technology." Timken had been out in front in the U.S. industry in adopting continuous casting. Yet neither it nor any other steel maker had succeeded in developing the technology to produce material comparable to ingot-cast steel in quality, particularly in cleanness, with the improvements made through Japanese ladle-refining and bottom-pouring techniques. On the other hand, continuous casting had advanced considerably since the late 1960s—Sumitomo was producing steel with a jumbo caster that approached the quality of ingot-cast material, though not consistently. Theoretically, it could be developed to produce as clean a steel as ingot casting.[12]

This time around, however, Timken avoided the temptation to assume it could succeed by throwing its formidable technical resources at the problem. Business considerations prevailed: Timken bearings required the very best steel, not just close to the best; and the company judged the technical risk to be too great. With just the one furnace, it would at any rate be difficult to realize the full economies of a continuous caster without a loss of flexibility in product mix. The plant would be laid out so that a caster could be installed when additional furnaces were added and the technology improved.[13]

The other two key issues to be decided were also interrelated: the location of the plant, and the operating principles on which it would be run. For the feasibility study, Dravo evaluated two locations. One was the so-called Gambrinus Farm Site, 450 acres on Faircrest Street in Perry Township, adjacent to Timken's existing Gambrinus steel plant. The other was called "Site X," assumed to be remote from other Timken facilities and in a non-union environment. The local site was attractive for many reasons, but particularly because a large portion of the new plant's output would be intended for making tubing, and it would be near Timken's existing tube mills. A distant facility would be more expensive to operate because of transportation costs and somewhat more expensive to build, without the infrastructure already in place in Canton.[14]

As Timken had learned from its observation of Japanese steel operations, however, some of the greatest gains to be made in both productivity and product quality came from the way work was organized and the human relations environment in the plant. Cross-training, teamwork, and decision-making responsibility on the shop floor were all important parts of the mix. Joe Toot was especially focused on this set of issues. As John Schubach recalled, when the engineers' attention drifted away from the "soft" issues, Joe would bring them back. Said Schubach, "He was always saying things like, 'We have to find a different way to run this place. We have to build into it the ability to experiment and do new things.'"[15]

Since the 1940s, when Umstattd had first begun to envision Bucyrus, the company's approach to innovation in working relations had been to place new plants in largely rural locations, where Timken could try to avoid union hassles and train a more flexible workforce. That tradition made Site X an appealing alternative to the Canton-Gambrinus area, where the company would be forced to deal with the United Steelworkers. On the other hand, for the high-technology plant that was planned, a skilled and experienced pool of labor would be a distinct advantage. Added to the other positive aspects of remaining local, it made the decision on location extremely difficult. Of the four key questions, it was the one that could not be decided by the end of the feasibility study.[16]

On a Saturday morning in early 1981, Tim Timken called together the company's management committee to review the results of the study and make a decision on whether to proceed. Finally, he put a direct question to each man in the room: "Okay, it's your company, you say what you would do with this decision." It was the consensus of the group that the plant should be built. Indeed, the feasibility study had made the choice seem rather clear-cut. In Bill Bowling's words: "[We] recognized the fact that this might not be a question of, 'Well, we'll stay small in the steel industry.' It was 'Either you do this, or you are not going to be in the steel industry, and then you will be dependent on outsiders for your bearing steel.'" Still, it was a $500-million decision. Tim concluded, "It's a big risk. But if we take it, there will be nobody in a better position to be in the business." Timken announced in April 1981 that it would build a new steel mill.[17]

The next step was to reach a firm decision on location. Dravo undertook a more specific study of potential sites outside of Ohio. By August 1981, it had developed two other strong possibilities, in Tennessee and Kentucky. In the meantime, Timken began negotiating with the USW to obtain, if possible, the flexibility it needed to run the new plant as it wished to do. The company wanted to be able to recruit from the ranks of current employees on the basis of technical and team-related capabilities, not seniority, and to hire from the outside if necessary. It sought to redefine and reduce steel-mill job classifications from 80 to 27 and to be free to reassign people within the plant without the union's interference. It asked for a contract provision prohibiting the union from calling a strike at the plant for ten years following the start of construction. Finally, Timken sought some pay concessions—lower-than-normal starting wages for the first three months on the job in all its unionized plants, and a reduction in incentive pay for 250 employees at its Canton rolling mills.[18]

In the fall of 1981, the negotiations moved toward a union vote on a special contract allowing those terms for the new Timken steel plant. The national economy, and the steel industry in particular, were in the grip of a deepening recession; unemployment in Canton was at 10.7 percent. The threat of Site X hanging over it, the union membership was disposed to accepting the deal. But, in a major tactical blunder, the USW scheduled the vote for the Sunday afternoon in October that the Cleveland Browns were playing their archrival, the Pittsburgh Steelers. It was a glorious fall day—perfect weather for all types of recreation—and only about 40 percent of those eligible to vote showed up. The contract was narrowly defeated. Timken agreed to postpone its decision until a second vote could be taken, two weeks later. Tim Timken stated publicly that the plant would not be built in Canton if the contract was voted down. At the same time, though, the company agreed to remove the clause cutting incentive pay at existing plants, which had occasioned many of the negative votes. The contract was overwhelmingly approved, and Timken made its firm commitment to what would be known as the Faircrest plant.[19]

In late 1981, Joe and Tim added to the original study team, creating a steel project team. They recruited a group of about 25 engineers and human-resources personnel from around the company—once again looking outside the steel division for some new thinking. Timken had determined to hire Dravo as the prime contractor for construction, and the new team's charge was to work with Dravo on the detailed planning and implementation stages of the construction project. Many of the project team members would be part of the management group at Faircrest once it was

Many, including some in Timken management, questioned the wisdom of building the sprawling Faircrest steel plant in 1982–85 during the steel industry's severe recession. One publication even dubbed it "Timken's Folly." Yet the investment proved critical to maintaining the company's leadership in both bearings and steel.

built. Bill Bowling was project team leader. As the project moved forward, he would meet weekly with Joe to consider upcoming issues and review progress. In addition, Joe took personal responsibility for establishing the performance criteria for Dravo and the project management procedures under which they would interface with the Timken team. Recalled John Schubach, "He set up the process by which the presidents of all our major suppliers were personally on the hook for making sure that they were going to perform to our expectations."[20]

Like Umstattd and Markley before him, Joe Toot was a president who kept close control over those aspects of the business he judged to be most significant, and this was arguably the most significant undertaking since the company had integrated into steel making in 1916. Unlike that episode, however, there would be no false starts, largely because of Joe's drive to get things done right the first time. It was a new experience for Dravo, an organization accustomed to providing "turnkey" manufacturing facilities for the steel industry—handling all the work from planning through construction on its own and simply handing over the completed plant to the owner. Timken would get extraordinary performance from Dravo and, in the process, learn a great deal about how to work effectively with its suppliers.[21]

In 1982, events severely tested the company's commitment to the Faircrest project. It had broken ground and begun construction in the spring, but by fall Timken was headed for its first after-tax loss since 1932. Worldwide manufacturing was in deep recession, and the demand for both bearings and steel had dropped off precipitously. Prospects for 1983 were no better: Timken would eke out a profit, but its revenues would fall below $1 billion for the first time since 1978. Hundreds of people laid off from both steel and bearings plants faced grim prospects. By this time the Faircrest site had been cleared and the company had invested more than $70 million in the project. Tim and Joe calculated it was probably the last point at which they could reasonably abandon it altogether. Bob Timken was opposed to continuing, and, though retired as chairman, he remained an influential member of the board. To him the company was still a bearing manufacturer first and foremost. He was concerned that the investment would sink the bearing business. But Tim and Joe were determined to proceed. "It took a lot of convincing to get my father to go along," Tim recalled. In that instance, all the research and analysis that had gone into the decision in the first place paid off. Said Tim, "I had the facts. That was the only way you could deal with my father."[22]

The Faircrest project would proceed, but at a slower pace. It had been on a fast track, to be completed in late 1984, and was now extended for a year, in order to spread the cost over a longer period. At the same time, however, Timken pushed to upgrade its existing steel-making technology, investing $92 million in a modernization of the Harrison Avenue steel plant that included implementation of ladle refining and bottom pouring. The company's traditional financial conservatism helped it a good deal in that situation. Because of its strong balance sheet, Timken was able to proceed with large-scale capital improvements at a time when others were not. Indeed, the building of the Faircrest plant brought the company a level of public attention quite rare in its hundred-year history, not the least of which was a visit by U.S. President Ronald Reagan to the partially completed plant in September 1984. Reagan lauded Timken for its investment in the midst of the continuing recession in the steel industry, when others were closing plants and consolidating, not building. A staunch Republican Party supporter, Tim Timken returned the favor by suggesting that provisions for accelerated depreciation and investment tax credits included in the President's 1981 tax-reform legislation had helped to make the investment possible.[23]

In September 1984, President Ronald Reagan toured the Faircrest plant under construction and said, "I've seen the future." Chairman Tim Timken led the President to the podium to speak to a large crowd of Timken associates.

The company had learned some time before that investing during a recession could bring real advantages. As William Umstattd had told *Business Week* back in 1958, he liked to purchase new equipment in a slow economy, not because he hoped to pay less, but because he expected to get "a lot better service."[24] In just that way, the recession of the 1980s brought a bit of serendipity to the Faircrest project, with dramatic results.

At the time of the feasibility study, there was not much advanced control technology in steel making. Out of a total estimated budget of $500 million, the study team allocated only about $5 million for computers and software. One piece of equipment, however, did have such technology—the electric-arc furnace that Timken proposed to buy from Krupp Stahltechnik GmbH. Its brand-new computer controls were the result of an extensive research program at Krupp funded by the German government. As Bill Bowling recalled, "We kept thinking to ourselves, 'Why shouldn't we do that with the rest of the steel mill equipment?'" Because of the worldwide recession, when the steel project team decided to pursue the idea, they were readily able to find equipment builders willing to cooperate and do the necessary research to develop what was, in effect, the next generation of steel-making equipment, with process-control capabilities. Bowling reflected on the fortuitous timing: "In retrospect, you say it took a lot of guts to build a steel mill in the middle of a major recession. Well, if we had built it much earlier, we would have built the last dinosaur."[25]

In 1994, the Faircrest plant won 33 Metalproducing's Top Operations and Plants Award and Industry Week magazine's America's Best Plants Award. President and CEO Joe Toot, a major force in shaping the plant's direction, stands in the billet mill control booth while associate Frank Garcia operates one of the most advanced computer control systems in the steel industry.

The control technology on the equipment was, however, only part of the ultimate computerization program developed for Faircrest. Timken mostly had had to go abroad for state-of-the-art hardware, but in software, the United States was the world leader. By bringing the two together, the company got a long lead on the rest of the steel industry. "Our central idea," Joe recalled, "was to build a facility that could be improved continuously. We were spending so much we had to get larger returns." The team envisioned software as the means to achieve that goal, by providing the data that would make it possible to improve process efficiency and product quality simultaneously. Timken bought control software from outside suppliers but handled the integration of programs in-house in order to keep the total plant operating system proprietary. Another factor critical to success, said Joe: they again looked companywide and assigned software development to "very young people, around twenty-five years old, who were skilled in the latest and best" programming techniques.[26]

Of course, the company had experience in developing complex computer systems to schedule and coordinate production, but the Faircrest system went much further than anything it had done before in collecting, and especially in linking, data from every department on all levels. So, for example, if a mid-process check of molten metal showed that the chemistry of an alloy was not precisely what the customer ordered, the analysis could be sent from the computer of the metallurgical laboratory to the plant-level computer. That computer could scan future orders for an exact match, and if one was found, it could update the process-control computers throughout the plant so that the new order could be run to the proper customer specifications. By the mid-1980s, when Faircrest came on line, quite a few U.S. companies were using computers and creating large databases, but very few were beginning to integrate information systems in such a powerful way. After a decade in operation, the plant would exceed Joe's and Tim's hopes for continuous improvement, based in no small measure on the success achieved in that area.[27]

There were other exciting technologies at Faircrest. One of those was a continuous heat-treatment line. It incorporated a Timken-patented system for quenching tubing both inside and outside, either simultaneously or independently, a level of control that enhanced the company's ability to give customers the precise properties specified and to produce tubing with better properties overall. It also had improved temperature control at all stages and a variety of energy-saving aspects. Controlled jointly by two interactive computer systems—one to store the processing information for each job and one to govern the equipment at each step of the process path—the entire line, including two furnaces (an austenitizing furnace and a tempering furnace), a quenching unit, a straightening unit, cooling bed, and saw (to cut finished lengths), could be run by just four people.[28]

Yet for Timken, cutting-edge technologies were far less revolutionary than the new operating philosophy embodied in the Faircrest plant. That philosophy took shape over the course of the project, in parallel with the engineering and construction. Jim Preston noted that Joe Toot was the "cheerleader" for doing things differently. His support from above opened up the possibilities completely. "We just had a wonderful time . . . looking back at what our previous experience had been and asking, 'Why do we need to do things this way?'" But it was also challenging. Part of the steel project team was a human resources group charged with designing the essential training programs for supervisory and operating personnel. Teamwork was a central concept: people would be trained to work together in areas, taking responsibility for a variety of tasks and often making decisions that traditionally had been in the hands of senior management. What the project team found was that it was relatively easy to enunciate such a principle and quite difficult to put it into practice after long years of experience in a hierarchical organization with top-down control. For one thing, the team itself had much more autonomy and responsibility than most of its members had ever had before, and it took some time before they became comfortable with it. It took a great deal of work—for example, role playing with videotape feedback—just to develop concrete ideas about how supervisors should interact with the people they were supervising. They knew they had to give up the old combative style. They also had to replace it with new ways of exercising authority.[29]

The cultural change gained a momentum of its own as the plant neared completion and the management group began hiring and training hourly personnel, 80 percent of whom came from Timken's existing steel plants. In one important respect, the pioneer workforce at Faircrest was self-selecting—anyone who wanted to apply for a job there had to take a four-hour aptitude test and submit to psychological evaluations for characteristics such as initiative and the capability for teamwork. Beyond that, it took a thick skin to handle the hostility that came from many of the steelworkers who stayed behind. There was considerable skepticism about the idea that there would be true collaboration between management and labor, and also scorn for people who signed on to work under a contract that had granted significant concessions to the company—even though a large majority had voted to accept that contract. Those feelings were expressed in the local nickname for the plant: "Fairy-crest." But the incentives were strong, beginning with the most basic desire to have a job. To Canton steelworkers, many of whom had been laid off for several years, the recession of the early 1980s felt a lot like a full-fledged depression with no end in sight. It was impossible not to be impressed with the investment the company was making. "I was not a fan of President Reagan, but I did come out for his visit, just to see what was going on," said one steelworker. "From that point on, I've always felt that this place was going to be the future of the company." With a state-of-the-art steel mill, it looked like the future could include a secure job and, if the company's promises proved true, an opportunity to be part of something truly exciting.[30]

In fact, though not everything went smoothly by any means, there proved to be a genuine commitment to doing things differently at Faircrest. Early on, the steel project team had sent eight of its members for extended process-control training—one to each of its key equipment suppliers. Once back at Timken, each individual was responsible for writing the training manual for that equipment.

When it came time to train the equipment operators, the team decided that the operators should have a similar chance to visit Timken's suppliers and experience best practices firsthand. It was culture shock again when the corporate personnel office objected to sending hourly workers off where there would be no time clocks to punch in and out. "It just showed what kind of isolated, little-company mentality we had," Bowling recalled. "Here you spend half a billion dollars, and you can't trust hourly employees without a time card." The episode clearly showed how far the team had moved from the company's traditional mindset. There would be no time clocks at Faircrest, just electronic record keeping of hours worked, for the practical need to calculate pay, "as opposed to wanting to control [people], which was coming through loud and clear back then." The plant also adopted the term "associates" to apply to all who worked there, further laying to rest, at least symbolically, the old hierarchy of management and labor.[31]

Of course, the most important differences in the long run were in the day-to-day operation of the plant. Once they got out to Faircrest, the hourly personnel discovered that, in fact, they were able to have a real say in how the steel mill should be run. "That's where the ownership came from," said one. "You felt like you were part of the whole plan instead of just a clock number."[32] For example, it was a team of salaried and hourly associates that developed the performance pay plan for hourly compensation at Faircrest. The team determined that bonuses should be based on the performance of the entire plant on five factors critical to success—quality; investment utilization; labor efficiency; energy efficiency; and parts, supplies, and services. It was a formula to reward both teamwork and continuous improvement—a significant departure from incentive programs of the past.

The changes were positive for plant managers as well. As Jim Preston recalled, the opportunity to do things in new ways was exciting, but the pressure was intense. "There were a lot of us who had our hearts in our throats plenty of times. We knew we had to hit the ground running with quality better than anything we had seen up to that time." Having everyone contributing fully made that possible. For example, it was a suggestion from maintenance mechanic Larry Blackburn in a team meeting that prompted an experiment with quenching hot ingots in water before moving them to the soaking pits and then to the rolling mill. That proved to be the solution to a long-standing problem with surface quality in some of Timken's most important bearing-grade alloys. It would never have been considered by an experienced Timken steel-mill manager, said Preston, because they had long before judged it to be too expensive. But it was far less expensive than cleaning up surfaces after the fact, and it was a critical step in making Timken steel competitive in both cost and quality.[33]

In 1995, then executive vice president and president of the Steel Business Charles H. West congratulated scrap loader Mark Piatt, one of the earliest Faircrest associates, at the tenth anniversary celebration. In the 1990s, Faircrest raised production from its designed capacity of 550,000 tons per year to 870,000 with no major additional capital investment.

Once Faircrest became operational, it soon became apparent that the project was an enormous success. The plant came on line on August 5, 1985, a date that had been set two years before. Timken and Dravo had kept to an aggressive schedule and had come in $50 million under budget. And, at Joe Toot's urging, the objective of first-time quality had been fulfilled: out of nearly four million hours of construction work that went into Faircrest, only eleven hundred were spent on work that had to be redone. The first heat of the furnace produced salable metal, and in more than 3,000 heats made in the first two years, only three at the very beginning had to be scrapped because of improper chemistry. In Joe's words, the Faircrest project was a landmark of "extraordinary expectations and achievement." It became the benchmark for the entire company in the 1990s.[34]

The operating economics of the Faircrest plant put it in a league of its own within the industry, producing steel at less than two hours of labor per ingot ton versus an industry average of nearly seven hours. The continuous heat-treat facility enabled Timken to market tubing and bar steel with superior properties at no additional cost. In addition, because Faircrest had been built to produce billets all the way up to 12 inches square—sufficient for the largest size of seamless tubing for Timken bearings—the company was able to enter a new market, large steel bars. Those were essential for applications such as forged crankshafts for large diesel engines made by Cummins, Mack, and Caterpillar. Just as the company's unique investment in tube-making capacity had made it the leader in mechanical tubing, the large-scale mill installed at Faircrest would make it number one in the world market for large bars.[35]

Even more important for the company as a whole was the impact of improvements in steel quality on the performance capabilities of Timken bearings. Even before Faircrest came on line, the investments in new technology for the

Harrison Avenue steel plant had raised steel quality enough to permit an increase in bearing ratings in 1982. A second ratings increase in November 1986 ranged from 11 percent on small bearings (under 18 centimeters) to 35 percent on larger bearings—an increase of 25 percent in load-carrying capacity betokened an increase of more than 100 percent in bearing life. Chuck West, as chief engineer for industrial bearings, had led the effort in the late 1970s to get the company to recognize the need for improvement in steel quality and became Timken's executive vice president for steel in 1986. Said West, "We took material out as the controlling factor in bearing performance."[36]

Faircrest became a shining example, in the steel industry and beyond, of what could be achieved through timely investment in new technology, enlightened leadership, and an empowered workforce. Its impact on the company was considerable. In terms of its strategic thinking, Timken had begun to change itself from a vertically integrated bearing manufacturer into a "worldwide leader in bearings and steel." That change would be given concrete expression in 1986 with a reorganization of the company that replaced functional divisions with two new business units, Bearings and Steel. To support the businesses and formalize the kind of decision-making process that had led to Faircrest, Timken established a corporate office of strategic management, with John Schubach as its vice president. And, over the longer term, it would undertake the more difficult task of companywide cultural change, urged on by an impressive performance of continuous improvement at Faircrest. In the 1980s, some harsh economic and competitive realities would force Timken to reevaluate most aspects of its traditional way of doing business. The experience gained in the planning, building, and operation of Faircrest would point the way toward many of the changes it needed to make.

Crisis and Transition: The Challenge of Global Competition

*T*he early 1980s ushered in some painful times for U.S.-based industrial firms, and Timken was no exception. In the wake of back-to-back recessions in 1979 and 1981–82, the market pattern that had prevailed since the beginning of World War II, in which demand for Timken bearings consistently exceeded supply, came to an end. Competition intensified dramatically, with offshore producers led by the Japanese penetrating U.S. markets as never before, assisted by the dramatic rise in the value of the dollar. Those conditions hurt Timken by weakening its U.S. customers. And they exerted pressure at the two points of weakness that had developed in the 1970s—its relatively high production and overhead costs, and its loss of clear leadership in bearing quality. The new Faircrest steel plant, after coming on line in late 1985, would play the major role in solving the latter problem, while the struggle to reduce costs significantly would continue into the 1990s.

In the meantime, however, there were some chastening experiences for a company accustomed to having "the best bearing" and to being the most profitable in the industry. Timken's operating margins, which had trended downward through the 1970s, plunged in 1982, producing its first after-tax loss since 1932.

With the continuation of oversupply and fierce worldwide competition in the bearing industry, there would be no quick bouncing back. Instead, the company felt the sting of disappointing financial results through the decade and beyond: operating losses in 1985, 1986, and 1991, and after-tax losses in 1985, 1991, and 1993. (See Figure 10.1 and Table 10.1.) Its compound annual sales growth for 1979–89 was under 2 percent, versus more than 12 percent in the decade before. No longer the most profitable bearing company, Timken was outstripped by SKF. (See Figure 10.2.)[1]

Timken's sustained program of investment leading up to the 1980s enabled it to remain competitive—between 1960 and 1980, its annual capital expenditures averaged 7.6 percent of sales, compared to an average of 3.5 percent for U.S. industry as a whole. That, plus its underlying financial strength and the large block of stock (19 percent) owned by the Timken Foundation and the family, spared it from the worst that the era dealt many U.S. corporations. The company remained strong while many steel competitors and a number of bearing companies failed. Yet, within the organization, the loss of industry leadership felt very much like a threat to

FIGURE 10.1

**Timken Operating Margins
1950–1996**

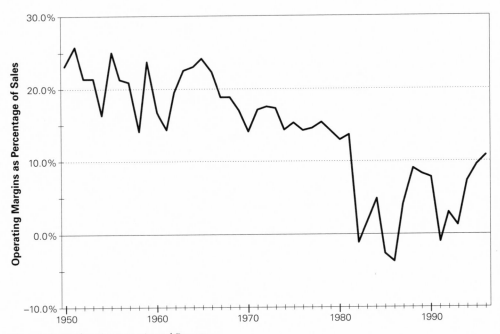

Source: The Timken Company Annual Reports

TABLE 10.1

The Timken Company Comparative Financial Data, 1980–1989 (in Thousands of Dollars, except per Share Data)

	1980	1981	1982	1983	1984	1985	1986	1987	1988	1989
Net sales	$1,338,499	$1,427,158	$1,014,361	$937,320	$1,149,908	$1,090,674	$1,058,055	$1,230,258	$1,554,143	$1,532,962
Net income	92,632	101,115	(3,001)	530	46,057	(3,903)	2,736	10,319	65,912	55,345
Total assets	$1,028,443	$1,101,431	$1,014,760	$1,107,727	$1,279,124	$1,375,419	$1,403,529	$1,466,634	$1,593,031	$1,565,961
Long-term debt	28,345	26,341	25,037	49,844	90,190	159,559	159,496	159,126	158,485	48,188
Total capital and earnings invested in the business	762,767	822,570	789,177	776,574	789,871	789,281	806,622	923,093	973,716	1,064,804
Return on sales	6.9%	7.1%	(0.3)%	0.1%	4.0%	(0.4)%	0.3%	0.8%	4.2%	3.6%
Return on assets	9.0	9.2	(0.3)	0.0	3.6	(0.3)	0.2	0.7	4.1	3.5
Return on capital and earnings	12.1	12.3	(0.4)	0.1	5.8	(0.5)	0.3	1.1	6.8	5.2
Earnings per share	$4.13	$4.51	($0.14)	$0.03	$1.96	($0.16)	$0.11	$0.39	$2.34	$1.88
Dividends per share	1.63	1.70	1.50	0.90	1.00	0.90	0.50	0.50	0.70	0.92
Number of employees	22,218	20,920	15,520	17,764	19,313	17,561	16,565	16,721	18,050	17,248
Number of shareholders	24,432	30,048	29,909	28,035	26,958	26,136	23,186	22,470	21,184	22,445

Source: The Timken Company Annual Reports, 1980–89.

Note: Per share data adjusted for 2-for-1 stock split in 1988.

Timken's survival. The company maintained its commitment to expand Timken Research and to build Faircrest—both steps considered necessary to restore its leading edge in bearing quality. But in every other respect, said Tim Timken, "we went into a bunker mentality." That mindset held its grip to the end of the 1980s.[2]

Tim Timken and Joe Toot, in their mid-forties in 1982, had come of age as corporate leaders in a very different environment. Both were deeply grounded in the management concepts and style of the generation that preceded them. Now they faced problems their predecessors had hardly imagined, much less experienced. Herb Markley retired from the board of directors during 1982 and died in March 1983. Bob Timken, then in his seventies, remained on the board and was a source of moral support. "When things got really grim," Tim recalled, "I would talk to him. He always had an optimistic view and reminded me that the world wouldn't come to an end." Tim's younger brother, Ward J. (Jack) Timken added to the family presence. After graduation from the University of Arizona, Jack had begun his Timken career in 1968 as his uncle Henry had done, on the steel side of the business. He had joined the board of directors in 1971. In 1977, Jack left

FIGURE 10.2

**Timken and SKF
Return on Sales, 1979–1989**

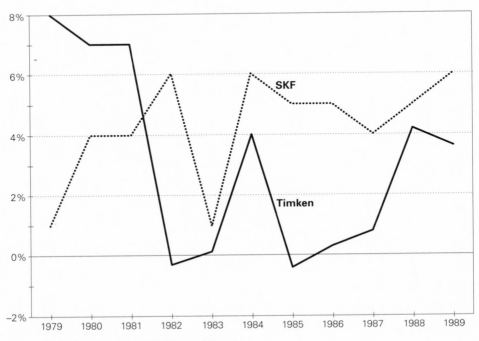

Source: The Timken Company and SKF Annual Reports

steel operations to become director of corporate development, and in 1985, after completing a master's degree in management science at the Stanford Graduate School of Business, he moved to director for human resource development. In 1992 he would become a corporate vice president. Jack's involvement continued a strong tradition of family commitment and provided stability in a difficult period.[3] But in the end the responsibility for steering the company back to its leadership position in the industry rested squarely and heavily on Tim and Joe.

Theirs was a partnership based on similar backgrounds, shared values, and some complementary strengths. Intensely analytical and concerned with process, Joe willingly immersed himself in the details of critical issues and projects, Faircrest being the most obvious example. Tim, by his own account less of a "perfectionist" about process and details, was comfortable with the responsibility for maintaining focus on the big picture. "This is an agreed-upon role that fits our personalities," said Tim. "He's more in the trees, chopping them down, and I'm looking at the forest trying to figure out whether or not we should chop the trees down." The metaphor was apt for some of the tough decisions they had to make and enact. With a close working relationship, they made all major decisions together and, like other Timken top-management teams over the years, they worked out effective methods for reaching agreement. For the most part, their differences were ones of emphasis, concerning the urgency of a particular issue rather than its substance. There was a positive side to that, as Tim explained: "When he gets uptight over something, it doesn't bother me. Some of the things that bother me, don't bother him. So, we reinforce each other pretty well when we are down. We don't get down over the same things." At the most trying moments, both men believed, their common background in competitive sports provided the mental conditioning that enabled them to persevere. "We just didn't know how to say 'Uncle,'" said Joe. "We never did."[4]

Their perseverance through the 1980s crisis would prompt a reassessment of nearly every facet of the company's strategy, structure, and culture. Emerging from this process, Timken, at its core, would remain much the same company that it had always been. Yet it would successfully leave behind many of those aspects of the corporate culture that had rigidified since the 1950s. In particular, it would begin to open up to outside influences. Continuing into the 1990s, the changes initiated as a result would alter Timken in fundamental and positive ways.

Into the Bunker

Timken's problems occurred within the context of a larger crisis that gripped U.S. industry and, in particular, the industrial heartland of the Midwest. The conditions that had made the United States the preeminent industrial power in the post–World War II world had changed fundamentally. Most important, beginning in the mid-1960s, industry as a whole in both West Germany and Japan had achieved higher rates of growth in productivity than U.S. industry, in part through higher levels of capital investment and spending for R&D. In 1977 those nations surpassed the United States in productivity, measured in output per hour. That shift undermined the competitiveness of U.S.-made products, both abroad and, increasingly, at home, as European and Asian manufacturers began to focus on capturing a larger share of the huge American market. For the first time since the 1890s, the United States began in 1971 to import more than it exported. (That was in part because of dependence on foreign oil, but Europe and Japan, even more dependent on imported oil, strengthened their export/import balances at the same time.) The nation remained a net exporter of manufactured goods most years until 1982, but that positive overall balance belied the deep penetration of imported products into many industrial sectors, including core industries such as automobiles, steel, and machine tools. The situation became dire in the early 1980s. Steps taken by the United States and other governments to bring inflation under control triggered the worst economic recession since the 1930s. After decades of high demand and steady industrial expansion on a worldwide scale, most manufactured products were suddenly in a severe state of oversupply. In addition, from late 1980 through early 1985, the value of the U.S. dollar rose steadily relative to other currencies. That put U.S.-made goods at a significant disadvantage just at the time when shrinking demand made competition fiercer than ever. The problem of the strong dollar went away (in fact reversed itself) for several years after 1985. But the problems of oversupply and global competition remained.[5]

The weight of those problems fell disproportionately on the Midwest (including Ohio, Illinois, Indiana, Michigan, and Wisconsin), where heavy manufacturing of durable goods such as fabricated metal products, machinery, and transportation equipment predominated. Led by the automotive industry, the region had begun to lose the competitive battle in international and domestic markets in the late 1970s, and it suffered dire consequences when recession struck. Companies closed uncompetitive Midwestern plants, many permanently. By 1983, the region lost roughly one-fourth of the manufacturing jobs it had had in 1969, experiencing a much greater drop in the early 1980s than did the nation as a whole. Per capita income, which had run above the national norm through the 1970s, fell below it by 1981; and between 1980 and 1986, the region's population shrank by more than 200,000 people per year (more than 400,000 in the worst year, 1982) as industrial workers left to seek employment in other regions.[6]

Timken had moved to Canton in 1901 precisely because of the growing concentration of manufacturing in the region. Its durable goods producers were the company's major customers for both bearings and steel. In the early 1980s, Timken lost a good portion of its domestic customer base. The general crisis in manufacturing had a great deal to do with the air of crisis within the company.

Yet Timken had its own competitive issues. In the early 1980s, the company had to cut its prices on the most widely used bearing sizes by 25 percent in order to hold market share against the four Japanese companies exporting to the United States—NSK, Koyo Seiko, NTN, and Nachi-Fujikoshi. It was a common pattern for Japanese manufacturers to enter an industry at the low end of a product line, then move up. That is what they did in tapered roller bearings. Ironically, Timken's great success with its program of standardization helped to make such a strategy feasible. By the 1980s, recalled Jim Pilz, executive vice president in those years, "standardization was so complete that it was easy for a company to come in and compete against us." Timken sizes and part numbers had become the industry standard, so there was literally no risk to a producer in tooling up to make a new bearing—which the Japanese did, beginning with a limited number of large-volume sizes. Said Pilz, "First they would make them for service, then they would get their quality up and go in and get an order for production. Pretty soon, we had new competition on the bearing standardization that we had pioneered."[7]

There were other strong competitors in the U.S. market, however, in particular SKF. Its rationalization program, begun in the 1970s, was well along by the early 1980s. Over the course of ten years, SKF had closed six plants (four of them in Europe), reduced its workforce by 20,000, more than a third of the total, and reduced the part numbers it was producing from 50,000 down to 18,000. (By contrast, Timken, making tapered roller bearings only, was producing 26,000 part numbers in 1981.) The SKF plants that remained produced a smaller range of products in longer production runs. Those changes made SKF as competitive as any bearing manufacturer. By 1982, it had managed to curtail Japan's market share in Europe at less than 10 percent and to maintain its own share of the worldwide bearings market at 24 percent—equal to the combined share of the four leading Japanese producers. Initially, SKF was barred by antitrust law from including its U.S. affiliate, SKF Industries, in the worldwide rationalization program. That barrier came down, however, with the more relaxed approach to antitrust enforcement that came in with the administration of Ronald Reagan in 1980. Thereafter, SKF launched a concerted effort to expand its less-than-10-percent share of the U.S. bearings market, initially by importing bearings from its European plants and later by building new plants in the United States.[8]

Those strong competitors brought home the reality of the problems that Timken faced in bearing production costs and product quality. The importance of Faircrest as a source of low-cost, high-quality steel took on new dimensions. But the plant would not come on line for some time, and meanwhile other problems needed to be addressed. Material quality was an issue in the early 1980s primarily for larger-sized industrial bearings. For the company's smaller, high-volume automotive bearings, quality issues were more related to control of manufacturing processes. Japanese practices that had evolved from the adoption of statistical process control in the 1940s simply yielded a higher level of product quality at a lower cost than U.S. systems that still relied on piece-by-piece inspection—SPC kept processes in control and so produced fewer defective parts in the first place. Beginning in 1979 with the Nashua Corporation, a small manufacturer of office and computer products, followed by Ford in 1980, U.S. industrial companies began adopting SPC and many of the related operating principles advocated by W. Edwards Deming. Timken joined that trend in 1981, appointing James Doebereiner director of quality advancement to lead the effort. By 1983, SPC systems were in place on the high-volume lines at Bucyrus, Gaffney, and Columbus. Within two more years, the company implemented electronic SPC and began to extend the system to Colmar and the continuous line at British Timken.[9]

Timken was swept along in those changes by the "quality revolution" in U.S. manufacturing. Its customers were themselves under heavy pressure to improve quality and reduce costs. They wanted to do away with their own inspection systems, which had screened parts coming into their plants from suppliers, on the assumption that a small percentage of defects was inevitable. By 1986, customers were talking about "zero-defect performance" and requiring suppliers like Timken to certify the quality of their products. The use of SPC was an absolute prerequisite for certification, but it was no longer sufficient. Timken had also to provide documentation of its "quality systems" to verify that machine operators were directly involved in controlling processes, that SPC data were regularly audited to ensure their validity, and that plant managers were themselves using the data to prevent problems and improve process control over the long run. British and European customers, though a year or two behind, were by that time beginning to make similar demands. By opening Timken's plants to outside evaluation, the certification process helped to speed along its conversion to quality techniques.[10]

For example, when GM's Detroit Diesel Allison division sought to identify parts suppliers for a new engine, its engineers came on site. They evaluated equipment, gauges, and processes as well as how employees were trained, how Timken checked its own incoming materials, and how it ensured traceability—so that a defective part could be traced back to the machine that produced it and the problem corrected. Timken's quality systems became more rigorous as a result. In 1989 the bearing business was a finalist for the prestigious Malcolm Baldrige National Quality Award, and from the late 1980s on it would win hundreds of customer quality awards each year.[11]

Yet, while quality measures were essential to maintain competitiveness, they did not confer any particular advantage. A purchasing agent from the transmission division of Eaton Corporation, who was buying $60 million worth of bearings a year, was quoted in *Industry Week* as saying that "with reputable companies, the quality is pretty much equal around the world." Therefore, in many sizes of

Above: *Since the mid-1980s, The Timken Company has earned thousands of customer quality awards. In 1993, Ford Motor Company presented to Timken its Total Quality Excellence (TQE) Award, recognizing "superior performance and commitment to continuous improvement in all aspects of business." From left are Ford's chairman and CEO Alex Trotman, chairman Tim Timken, and Ford's then vice president of purchasing, Norm Ehlers.*

Right: *Admirers of all ages came to Timken plants, where associates and their families celebrated receiving the TQE Award. Five-year-old Sarah is the daughter of Bucyrus bearing plant associate Daniel Leonhardt.*

The Platinum Pentastar is Chrysler Corporation's highest supplier award and recognizes excellence in manufacturing and service, including quality, technology, cost reduction, and delivery. In 1997, Bob Leibensperger (right) and Bill Bowling, then executive vice presidents of the company and presidents of Bearings and Steel, respectively, accepted the award on behalf of the company.

bearings, price was the determining factor, and the competition on price was withering. Imported bearings, nearly 50 percent of them from Japan, were selling at steep discounts—50 percent below U.S. prices in extreme cases. They made deep inroads into the U.S. market, reaching 60 percent in ball bearings and 20 percent in roller bearings by the end of 1986. Timken lost substantial sales and had to make deep cuts in its prices on the most competitive sizes.[12]

The industry as a whole was hard hit—six of fifty U.S. bearing plants were closed or sold, and between 1980 and 1984 alone some 13,000 jobs were lost. Timken laid off 2,000 hourly employees in 1982 and 1983 and reduced salaries by 6 percent across the board in 1984. In August 1985, amid continuing layoffs, Joe Toot announced that the company would cut its salaried staff by 500. That was followed in January 1986 by permanent salary reductions of 10 percent for all officers and 8 percent for others, with future raises to be merit pay only. In December 1986, facing the company's worst-ever operating loss, Joe and Tim decided to close the Columbus bearing plant. The AP bearing plant would remain, but the rest of Columbus operations would phase out and shut down entirely by 1989.[13]

Timken's leaders remained committed to investments essential to improving the company's competitiveness. R&D expenditures rose steadily, both in absolute terms and in relation to revenues: from $14 million (0.7 percent of sales) in 1978, to $35 million (3 percent of sales) in 1986. The latter percentage was comparable to the amount spent by technology leaders in manufacturing, such as TRW, General Dynamics, and General Electric, and was far above the level of the steel industry, in which R&D spending averaged about 0.5 percent of sales in the 1980s. In addition, Timken invested heavily in computer technology. It linked its offices worldwide with personal computers and intelligent terminals, and it developed new, more powerful information systems to schedule and coordinate manufacturing that placed terminals for data entry and retrieval right on the factory floor. The company was also hiring and training personnel at Faircrest in 1984 and 1985. But it cut all other spending to the bone.[14]

Joe and Tim believed the steps they had taken would eventually return Timken to a position of leadership. Meanwhile, they were still largely in a survival mode. The year 1986 brought the company's largest ever operating loss and its lowest stock prices in a decade. (See Appendix B.) The fourth quarter was "sheer hell," recalled Tim. "I think we wondered a little bit at that time whether we could remain independent." In December, the board of directors declared a special dividend of one shareholder right for each share of Timken common stock. Each right, exercisable in the event of a takeover attempt, permitted the owner to buy a share of newly issued stock for $135. With the large stake controlled by the Timken family and additional shares owned by non-family officers and directors, the company could feel reasonably secure. But it was an action that expressed the deep concern of the time.[15]

Restructuring

Another initiative of 1986 that would be beneficial in the long run but was initially quite painful was the restructuring of the company into business units. Announced in December 1985, it was to be completed by February 1, 1986. In reality, it rolled out over much of the year, right along with salary cuts and staff reductions. Virtually everyone ended up reporting to someone new. As one outside observer described it: "Layer by layer, managers were promoted, demoted, retired, or reassigned. . . . Disruptions were inevitable as individuals, departments, plants, and even whole divisions waited to see for whom they would be working."[16] For an organization that had evolved along a familiar path for some forty years, the changes were wrenching.

By the mid-1980s, however, most large corporations with multiple lines of business and international operations had already taken the step of replacing functional organizations with business units. By design in a functional organization, only a very few people at the top had a view of the business that embraced marketing, manufacturing, engineering, and R&D, combined with a grasp of the company's financial position. The senior managers of each division were primarily focused on achieving excellence within their own functions. The setup had served Timken well for a long time and, in particular, had supported the policy of sustained investment in manufacturing and research in a way that business units, competing for corporate funds and more driven toward financial performance, might not have. But, even in a company with only two major lines of business, functional divisions made it difficult to respond effectively—and quickly—to the challenges posed by an environment of oversupply and strong competition. Moreover, Timken had simply become too big to depend on just two men at the top for business planning and strategic thinking.

No one understood that better than the two men at the top in the 1980s. In setting up the decision-making process that led to Faircrest, Tim and Joe had opened the door to managing the steel division as a distinct business. They had also raised the standard for strategic planning. And, by structuring the team as they did—bypassing the existing divisional leadership—they had implicitly set aside the functional organization as inadequate to the task. Those were all significant departures in a tradition-bound company, and they laid the foundation for the larger changes that followed.

Most significant of all, however, was the opening up to ideas and influences from the outside. That had really begun in the mid-1970s with the dawning recognition that Timken had been surpassed in some critical areas of product quality. In the late 1970s, Herb Markley had taken the first step by bringing in the industrial engineering firm of Alexander Proudfoot. As Joe Toot recalled, it was a wake-up call to learn from Proudfoot that Timken did not have all of the best manufacturing practices. That was followed by the worldwide benchmarking exercise for Faircrest and the collaboration with leading-edge consultants in developing plans for the new plant. Before, said Tim Timken, the feeling had been that "if you had to rely on consultants, you didn't know what you were doing." Now, he and Joe had stood that idea on its head. They wanted to collaborate with outsiders who could, in Joe's words, "show us what the best practice among leadership firms really was."[17]

That was their purpose in working with McKinsey & Company on the corporate reorganization. Tim and Joe knew how they wanted to restructure the firm; Timken sold its rock-bit division, which accounted for less than 1 percent of its annual sales, and it reorganized into two new business units, Bearings and Steel. At Joe's urging, with the goal of maintaining Timken's functional excellence, the restructuring also created four "corporate centers": finance; personnel administration and logistics; technology; and strategic management. McKinsey's role was to help Timken implement those changes. Its approach was straightforward: get the senior people in each unit in place, then move downward layer by layer, allowing the managers at each level to participate in designing their organizations and selecting the personnel who would report to them.[18]

Yet from McKinsey also came the message that not just the structure but the culture of management had to change if the reorganization was to achieve its goal of improving the company's performance. The consultants brought an analytical approach to thinking about that problem. This was the McKinsey 7S Framework, which included "hard" factors—strategy, structure, skills, systems, and staff—but also critical "soft" factors—style and, most important, shared values. In the business bestseller, *In Search of Excellence* (1984), Thomas J. Peters and Robert H. Waterman, Jr., who originated the 7S Framework, noted that one of its main contributions was "to remind the world of professional managers that 'soft is hard'"— that is, that cultural factors are at least as critical to success as strategy and structure.[19] The course of change at Timken from 1986 into the 1990s would prove that point conclusively.

In the short run, McKinsey played a key role in selling the idea of change to the new senior management team. Said John Schubach, "McKinsey understood that it was as important to build an understanding—a case for needing the change, an understanding of what the change should be—as it was to get the boxes right." Peter Ashton, who became executive vice president for the bearing business, expressed the understanding that emerged: "The thought was 'we just don't behave like businessmen. We're all engineers around here.' So, by reorganizing into businesses and forcing the business planning activities to become big issues, not little issues, we would begin to behave in a more entrepreneurial way."[20]

Most important, McKinsey pushed to change the top-down approach to management that was deeply embedded in Timken's culture—from the top down. Said Chuck West, executive vice president for steel, "As [McKinsey] spent time with our whole organization, looking for strengths and weaknesses—what was good in the way of performance, what was standing in the way—senior management style was clearly an obstacle and was handled very well, I think. From that time forward, the chairman's role was very different, the president's role very different, and the responsibility on out through the rest of us was very different from what it was before. I would say issues of style were just as important as formal organization, if not more important." Those issues would remain even after the disruptions of the reorganization died down. As McKinsey's lead consultant, James Bennett, remarked, "A less hierarchical organization was a special challenge." Thus, it would be some years before Timken realized the full benefits of its restructuring.[21]

Moreover, along with the turmoil in the ranks of management, the period of restructuring brought a new low in relations between the company and its unionized hourly employees in Canton, Columbus, and Wooster. The 1960s and 1970s had been an era of labor peace marked by a single strike in 1968, in which the USW, after holding out for seven weeks, won an economic package that went beyond the gains made in the steel industry generally and was hailed by District Director John S. Johns as the "best ever" contract negotiated by the union. Contracts in the 1970s had brought further financial gains. In addition, the USW negotiated the end of the modified union shop provision that, since 1952, had permitted hourly employees to get out of union membership if they wanted to. Only a small proportion had ever done so, but it was a significant symbolic change when Timken's unionized Ohio plants became a closed shop. In that era of chasing demand, with all the plants running flat out and mandatory overtime (instituted in the early 1970s), getting a little time off was much more of a concern than wages and benefits.[22]

Yet Timken's relationship to the unionized workforce in Ohio was not an easy one. At the company's non-union plants, it had created the position of manager of employee relations following a close call at Bucyrus in 1977, in which a United Auto Workers unionizing drive went to a vote and the union polled 40 percent. The new function improved communications between plant management and shop-floor employees, providing a mechanism for problem review and generally helping to build trust. But it had not extended to the unionized plants. There, the rigid, adversarial relationship between Timken and the USW still infused the broader relation between management and the hourly workforce, to be converted into outright hostility in the harsh economic conditions of the 1980s.[23]

The Faircrest contract had been negotiated in 1981 amid a general air of crisis in U.S. industry, when Timken's proposed steel expansion stood out like a beacon in a sea of layoffs and plant closings. Harry Mayfield, by that time chief USW negotiator for the district, said the union was convinced that, if Timken built its new mill in the South, it would only be a matter of time before all its Ohio plants were closed. At the time of the next regular contract negotiation in 1983, there were roughly 2,000 Timken hourly employees laid off in the Canton area, some of whom had been out of work for twenty months. The steel industry as a whole was in crisis, and the USW had granted wage concessions to Big Steel. Leading up to the negotiation, the company mounted a large-scale communications campaign, called "Our War on Competition." The campaign talked about Timken's loss of market share and the need for everyone to help make it more competitive. Said one observer of this program, "Although employees clearly perceived the attempt to soften them up before negotiations, they were impressed that the company was, for the first time, attempting to reach them directly." Nearly 5,000 union members voted by a 2-to-1 margin to accept the concessionary contract.[24]

But when the contract came up for renewal in 1986, the mood was dramatically different. Most people had assumed in 1983 that the crisis, and the need for wage concessions, would be short-lived. Timken instead put forward a contract with cuts in both pay and health benefits. In the interim, communications had not really improved. So, despite the cuts being made at the management level, there was little goodwill to fall back on when union members expressed skepticism over the need for further concessions. Rumors raged: that Timken was shifting work to non-union plants, or plants abroad; that it was being sold to the Japanese; that the losses it reported were "really the result of accounting gymnastics." After voting down by overwhelming margins both the company's first contract proposal and a second, modified but still concessionary one, union members went out on strike. Before the second vote, I. W. Abel, now retired as USW International president, came to speak in Canton to rally the troops. Labor had to stand firm, Abel argued, or working people would find themselves "in an era like that of the Great Depression of the 1930s." And, in a return to the hostile tone of the days when Abel himself had squared off against Umstattd, the *Golden Lodge News* abandoned its general attacks on management to vilify individual company leaders. In particular it singled out Joe Toot, whose recent divorce from Edith Timken became the subject of posters on the picket line. Said one striking Timken employee to the press, "They'll win. They always have. But it's not only the money. It's not only the benefits. It's the morale. They've got a serious morale problem."[25]

Timken continued to struggle with that morale problem through the 1980s. After a thirty-day strike, the union and the company reached a compromise. But there would be another long strike in 1989 over the company's effort, amid layoffs due to a weak market in steel, to reduce pension obligations and freeze cost-of-living adjustments to wages. During this period, the impressive results at

Faircrest provided clear evidence of the gains to be made from more open and collaborative relationships in the plant. In the ranks of both management and labor, however, there was a sense that Faircrest was a world apart and not a realistic example for the rest of the company. That was a valid assessment of the situation in the 1980s. In fact, it was not until the 1990s, when the cultural changes initiated with the restructuring began to take hold and the lines of communication really opened up—when Tim and Joe determined to push the company to the next level of alignment with worldwide best practices in management—that the advances made at Faircrest could begin to spread more widely.[26]

Upturn

In the meantime, the company's fortunes turned upward from the low point of 1986. One positive development late that year was Timken's success in a new round of legal action against dumping by bearing importers. The antidumping protest had become a personal crusade for Joe Toot; it was an area in which his passion for detail served the company particularly well. He had been involved as a corporate vice president in the early 1970s, and had worked closely with Markley on the issue. "It was a matter of crucial significance," said Joe. "We were determined to beat the Japanese with the force of law—which they were breaking—as well as with cost reductions and quality improvements." Timken's efforts had been successful in the 1970s, but the decision only covered bearings up to four inches in outer diameter and applied only to Japanese importers. Now the problem extended over a wider range of bearing sizes and sources.[27]

By this time, with U.S. industry having lost its once commanding lead in key segments such as steel, autos, and consumer electronics, many government officials looked somewhat differently on the problem of foreign competition than they had in the 1970s. The U.S. Congress, traditionally more disposed than the executive branch to enforce antidumping regulations, had become concerned about the threat to the domestic bearing industry. It had directed the Department of Defense to study the problem, and that had resulted in a new "buy American" order for the military and a fresh investigation of dumping. In 1985, the International Trade Commission (ITC) started hearings on possible dumping infractions, at which Joe testified. Tim provided indirect support, taking advantage of his position as a major Republican party activist and donor to speak directly to Republican congressmen and officials of Ronald Reagan's administration—including the president himself—of his concerns about the future of U.S. manufacturing. But the wheels of government ground slowly. Neither Tim nor Joe was disposed to sitting still and waiting to be "rescued."[28]

In August 1986 the company filed an antidumping petition against tapered roller bearing imports from Japan, Italy, Yugoslavia, Romania, Hungary, and China. Its complaint went both to the ITC, which had responsibility for determining if dumping had unfairly injured U.S. bearing makers, and to the Department of Commerce, which had the power to establish dumping "margins"— the difference between the current selling price and the fair price as determined by the department. To prepare its case, Timken got sworn affidavits from hundreds of its sales managers around the country that detailed their experiences with unfair pricing. Timken Research developed computer models on bearing-life comparisons. And, said *Timken* magazine, "company employees around the world gathered information about the costs of bearings, steel, utilities and raw materials for use in developing the cases."[29]

As in the 1970s, Joe Toot was the witness who presented the company's side of the issue, and Eugene Stewart again provided legal expertise. Now, however, a team of seven Timken executives worked closely with them to prepare Joe's arguments and responses to potential questions on cross-examination. The preparation was intense. In mock sessions in Timken's boardroom, John Schubach played devil's advocate, doing his best to counter the company's case—said Stewart, he was a "formidable foe" in that forum. Then, recalled Stewart, Joe Toot "holed up" in a Washington, D.C., hotel room to study for his presentation. By the time of the hearing, he knew his material so well that he could deliver his testimony extemporaneously. It was a pitched battle. A number of bearing distributors and customers testified on the other side of the issue. But Timken won its case. The ITC found that injurious dumping had occurred in every instance, and the Department of Commerce levied substantial margins.[30]

That proved to be an effective deterrent to underpricing of imports, though it also served to hasten the movement of Japanese bearing makers to build plants in the United States. The competition would still be intense. But that was okay, Joe Toot believed, as long as there was "a level playing field." Timken won similar judgments in Canada and Australia, though it did not succeed in winning antidumping complaints made on behalf of its steel business. The antidumping victory in bearings had an immediate practical impact: by the end of 1987 both prices and Timken's market share were up. It was not, of course, a long-term answer to the competitive challenges that the company faced. But by 1987, such answers were beginning to come from other directions.[31]

Most dramatic was the impact of Faircrest steel. "We saw, when we started production, just how good this stuff really was," said George Matthews. "It was an eye-opener." In fact, Faircrest's air-melted steel proved to be as clean as vacuum-arc remelted steels. Timken began marketing it in 1986 under the trademark "Para-premium" steel, for which it obtained a new classification from the American

Society for Testing Metals. Produced in high volume at low cost, Timken Parapremium steel offered higher material strength at competitive prices, a significant advantage in many of the established applications for mechanical tubing—crankshafts, gears, pinions, oil-drilling equipment, and, of course, bearings. Going forward, it would help Timken to gain a strong position in new markets, in particular large bars.[32]

The dramatic increase in bearing ratings that came from cleaner steel also began to translate into significant market advantages after 1986. "In a very real sense," stated Timken's annual report of that year, "our new technologies offer a challenge to customers whose ingenuity will enable them to design smaller, lighter and stronger parts." Within a few years, that "challenge" was articulated more forcefully with the term "power density"—"the ability of steel parts, such

Displayed at Timken Research in Canton, this transaxle used in Chrysler minivans contains six P900™ bearings. The power density concept, along with associated improvements in gear-steel alloys and lubricants, allowed an increase in horsepower from 75 to 224 and a 250 percent life improvement. From left, Timken Research directors Ravi Bhatia and Ronald Widner were two of many working with executive vice president, COO, and president — bearings Bob Leibensperger to develop the concept.

as bearings and gears, to handle larger loads while taking up less space." Developed at Timken Research under the leadership of Bob Leibensperger, who became vice president for technology in 1986, the concept of power density captured the essence of the competitive advantage Timken had gained through Faircrest. Customers could redesign their own equipment around higher performance with the same-sized bearing, or, depending on their priorities, a smaller, lighter-weight bearing providing the same performance. In presenting that kind of opportunity, the power density principle increased the significance of one of

Timken's greatest and most differentiating organizational strengths, its sales engineering function, through which the full range of the company's technical resources was brought to bear on its customers' problems. Leibensperger recalled that in the 1980s, everyone was so caught up on the issue of price it took a lot of convincing to put across "the philosophy of selling value"—even though that philosophy had deep roots in Timken's past. But in the 1990s, the "value proposition" would become the basis for forging stronger relationships with key customers, for example Chrysler, which came to rely on Timken for its organizational resources as well as its bearings and steel.[33]

Thus, it was not just clean steel that enabled Timken to regain its technological leadership in the late 1980s. Its aggressive move to computerization had an impact on both products and processes. And the expanded program of R&D contributed new bearing products and, equally important, enhanced understanding of the factors controlling bearing performance. For example, in the Performance-900™ (P900) series, introduced in 1988, Timken used an "advanced numerical technique" to make the geometric profile of the bearing races exactly suited to provide the best distribution of stresses and the longest bearing life in a particular application. It took into account not only loads and stresses, but also environmental factors such as lubrication and operating temperatures. A companion to the new product was SELECT-A-NALYSIS™—a computerized system for evaluating the factors determining bearing selection for a specific application. It was a tool developed for use by Timken engineers, but the company made it available on line to many of its customers. Computerization, applied to manufacturing and gauging, played an important role in the development of a new line of ultra-precision bearings produced at New Philadelphia. Timken also was beginning to adapt electronic sensors and controls to produce a line of "intelligent" bearings. For example, Leibensperger had developed a new version of the Hydra-Rib bearing with the capability to make adjustments for changes in temperature or hydraulic pressure, for applications in printing presses and industrial robots.[34]

There were parallels to those kinds of innovations in the steel business. Timken's R&D program and steel sales engineering enabled both Timken and Latrobe to develop new applications and produce new alloys for customers' specific needs. Just as important, the increasing levels of computer controls gave Timken's steel plants the flexibility to make a wide range of alloys cost effectively. In 1989, *Computerworld* magazine ranked Timken first among industrial and automotive manufacturers and seventeenth overall in its list of the 100 companies most advanced in their application of computer technologies.[35]

Of course, Timken had a long tradition of investment in advanced manufacturing processes, sales and application engineering, new product development, and even, though it had not been called that, power density as a sales concept for

Timken bearings. Those were not new attributes, but they represented a significant renewal for a company that had lost some of its technological edge in the era of high demand. In the era of global competition they counted for a great deal. In 1988 Nihon Timken won contracts for bearings from three leading Japanese companies: Nissan Motor Company, Mazda Motor Corporation, and Mitsubishi Electric Corporation. In the United States, the company was one of the first domestic steel makers to supply Honda of America. In Europe, said Maurice Amiel, who in 1986 became head of bearing operations for Europe, Africa, and Western Asia, Timken's established reputation as "a topnotch specialist and engineering company making a precision product" was its main competitive strength.[36]

By 1988, as sales revived and Timken recorded its first significant profit in seven years, Tim Timken began to feel that a corner had been turned. The company had reestablished its decisive leadership in product quality and, with the help of its successful antidumping effort, regained much of its lost market share. *Forbes* magazine, in an admiring article of that year, said that the Timken bearing was "widely regarded as the best in the world." In contrast to many Midwestern manufacturers, including a number in Canton, whose plants were permanently closed by the late 1980s, Timken began hiring again. Then, in 1989, there was another small drop-off in sales and operating performance. The company's stock price, which had risen for the first time past 1981 levels, fell back again. That was another turning point for Tim.[37]

Tim Timken's Challenge

Two years before, in 1987, Bob Timken had retired from the board of directors after fifty years of active association with the company. On that occasion, Tim had selected a part of his father's 1972 year-end message to employees as an expression of the family's core business values. "We hope to continue to make improvements in profits and plant investments," Bob Timken had written. "Both are necessities in maintaining the success of The Timken Company. We must provide reasonable returns to our stockholders, we must ensure good wages and working conditions to our employees, and we must work toward improvement of the communities in which we live and work. The only way in which we can succeed in these three goals is by ensuring that we produce for our customers the best products we can make." Those were abiding principles, Tim asserted. But by the end of the 1980s, it appeared that Timken had fulfilled its commitment to all of the stakeholders except the owners of Timken stock. In the same era, the financial community had become focused on "shareholder value"—calculated on the basis of dividends and appreciation in stock price—as the chief measure of corporate performance. As Tim well understood, he could not truly ensure the continued independence of the company without addressing its weakness in that area.[38]

During the 1980s, Timken had made the investments it needed to regain leadership and market share in its industries. At the same time, however, the annual dividend, which had been $1.70 per share in 1981, had fallen as low as 50¢ per share in 1986 and 1987. In 1989, it still stagnated at just 92¢ per share, even though revenues were up by some 7 percent over 1981 levels. (See Table 10.1.) The company had survived. But, said Tim, "We could no longer go forward with the mentality that said things were tough out there, everybody was faring poorly, we were doing better than they were and 'Too bad, shareholders, you still have the price you had in 1981 and a lower dividend in current dollars.'"[39]

Determined to change that mentality, Tim set out to establish financial objectives for the company that would go beyond making Timken stock a good investment for the future—he wanted to make up the ground that had been lost in the 1980s. On that basis, he set ten-year objectives for growth in dividends and stock price that would—by the company's one-hundredth anniversary—provide a premium on what he judged an acceptable market return for a long-term investment in equities. If that was achieved, Tim said, "By the time 1999 came around, the shareholders who had held their stock since 1981 would feel satisfied." But meeting that goal would require significant growth in revenues and earnings. "We had to go for higher performance standards," he said. "We had to break the mentality of survival and become aggressive. That is what it was all about."[40]

Within the framework of those ten-year goals, he and Joe Toot would push through the next stage of organizational change—Tim coming at it from the shareholders' perspective, and Joe driving to achieve operational excellence. Early in 1989, the company had announced the intention to invest $1 billion in its bearing and steel businesses by 1995, a step they considered essential for maintaining Timken's leadership position in the 1990s and beyond. It would be even more essential for reaching the 1999 goals—the company would need new products, greater capacity, and more efficient manufacturing plants to increase revenues as required. As it rolled out, the investment would fund the adoption of leading-edge technologies and work practices that collectively became known in the 1990s as "lean" manufacturing, the basic principles of which (according to the authors who coined the term) were "teamwork, communication, efficient use of resources and elimination of waste, and continuous improvement."[41]

U.S. industry had begun to learn about lean manufacturing as it took a close look at Japanese companies, Toyota especially, that had assumed world leadership in their industries. In 1984, Toyota and GM had launched a joint venture—New United Motor Manufacturing, Inc. (NUMMI)—to produce a car for the U.S.

market in a domestic GM plant using Toyota production methods. Once one of the worst-performing GM plants, the Fremont, California, factory that NUMMI took over, with virtually the same shop-floor personnel as before, became the most productive in the GM system and nearly as productive as a comparable Toyota plant in Japan. It was a riveting example of what lean production methods could accomplish. The Japanese model would provide the conceptual framework for changes in Timken's manufacturing systems. Tim Timken's challenge would provide the motivating force.[42]

In the fall of 1989, the top 100 managers from Timken locations worldwide came together for the company's first "corporate forum." They heard a couple of outside speakers, experts on shareholder value and continuous improvement. But the centerpiece of the occasion was the challenge from Tim Timken to achieve his ten-year objectives. A number of significant changes would be necessary in order to meet that challenge. Managers down the line would have to become much more conscious of financial measures of performance and focus on specific targets, as opposed to the more familiar goal of simply doing better this year than last. In addition, Tim stressed that the financial goals he had set would not be achievable unless Timken could mobilize the best efforts of all its personnel. He was blunt: on a grade card for "human dignity," he gave the company no more than a D, because of the pervasiveness of "boss-subordinate" relationships that were still shaped by the command-and-control mentality and too often demeaning to the subordinate. "One thing is very clear," said Tim. "We cannot get to where we want to go without a greater amount of mutual respect for each other as people. . . . Everyone must feel a part of the effort."[43]

If Tim's role was to articulate the challenge in broad terms, it was Joe's responsibility to direct and drive the execution of the steps necessary to achieve them. The fall of 1989 was a good time to begin building mutual respect and bringing everyone in the organization on board. There were layoffs in both the bearing and the steel businesses due to lower market demand, and the strike in Canton ran for five weeks before concluding in October with a four-year contract. In late 1988, the company conducted an employee survey, the results of which had made clear the crying need for improved communications—internal publications that provided concrete information on the state of the business and a channel through which hourly employees could communicate their opinions to management. One of the results was a new internal magazine, *Exchange*—"published monthly by and for employees of The Timken Company"—launched in January 1990.[44]

But, said the first issue of *Exchange,* people also sought improved "face-to-face" communication with supervisors. "With change happening so fast in our everyday work, employees want a better understanding of the business and their place in it." That kind of change was naturally slower to develop, but another key initiative of 1989 addressed the issue. It was the Vision 2000 program, headed by Tom Strouble, developer of the UNIT-BEARING and now director of bearing manufacturing for North and South America. Numerous lean-manufacturing initiatives would be launched under the Vision 2000 banner in the 1990s—self-directed work teams, just-in-time delivery, and total quality management. But the essence was a three-step approach to engaging hourly employees in process improvement: creating awareness, providing training and development, and winning "buy-in." Linked to the $1-billion spending program, Vision 2000 would become a significant force for change within the company.[45]

The success of such programs depended on the actions and attitudes of thousands of managers and shop-floor personnel within Timken's manufacturing plants. It was driven rigorously from the top by Joe Toot, in particular through his articulation—and tireless promotion—of a corporate mission that provided the rationale for change. Timken had adopted its first formal mission statement in 1987. In 1989, it added a significant new concept (in italics): "We are an independent organization with a leadership position in high-quality anti-friction bearing and alloy steel products. To maximize shareholder value and sustain our competitive position, we will capitalize on the relationships between our businesses, emphasize the application of technology to products and processes, and combine these with unmatched customer service. *Through the strength of our people, we will strive to become the best manufacturing company in the world.*" As the organization moved through continuing changes in the 1990s, many of them exciting and many painful, it would do so under Joe's banner of becoming the best.[46]

George Foale joined British Timken as a student apprentice in the 1960s and became a plant manager at both Daventry and Duston. By 1989 he was manager of human resources, and he later recalled what it was like to be challenged by Joe Toot to become the best manufacturing company in the world. "I was sitting in the audience," said Foale. "I can remember laughing in my sleeve and thinking, 'What a stupid thing to say. We are a million miles from being the best manufacturing company. It is a hopeless dream.'" But then, he recalled, "The more you thought about it, ultimately you realized this was not a bad benchmark against which to measure yourself. Then, as you thought about new things, you asked yourself the question, 'Is this the sort of thing that the best manufacturing company in the world would do, or want to do?'"[47]

It was not an idea that would move every company, but it was a good fit with Timken's historic sense of purpose, its tradition of leadership within its narrow fields of specialization, and the culture that had grown up around them. The idea also included the critical element of benchmarking against world leaders. That was a significant break from the past and the real engine of change in the 1990s.[48]

Yet Timken would not reach the aggressive financial goals its chairman had set merely by improving its existing operations and expanding from within. Strategy also would have to shift in the 1990s toward using acquisitions and joint ventures as an avenue for growth. One minor but symbolic change helped to open the door to that shift: the 1983 acceptance by the U.S. Justice Department of the company's petition to lift the court order that had hung over its European operations for thirty-three years. Going forward, Timken, like all other U.S. corporations, would be free to organize its wholly owned subsidiaries as separate corporations if it chose to do so, making growth by acquisition more feasible. Also in the 1980s, two significant precursors to a fully developed acquisition strategy came out of the strategic management initiative launched in conjunction with the restructuring. As bearing and steel executives began to grapple with the responsibility for the long-term profitable growth of their business units, it did not take long for them to identify ways to grow at a faster rate by investment outside the company.[49]

In 1986, Timken had begun negotiations with the government of India to undertake a venture in that country. Timken's preferred practice of establishing wholly owned subsidiaries was against Indian law, so the company looked for a domestic partner. This it found in The Tata Iron and Steel Company, one of the country's leading manufacturers. Tata and Timken reached an agreement in 1986

In 1989, chairman Tim Timken and Russi Mody, chairman and managing director of Tata Iron and Steel, laid the foundation stone for the Tata Timken Limited joint venture. Tata Timken was in full operation by March 1992 and installed new processes in 1997 to increase its capacity by 50 percent.

without difficulty, but the Indian government's policy against protecting foreign trademarks stood in the way of the venture. After another year of negotiation, Timken earned a historic agreement with the Registrar of Trademarks to protect its name and thus its reputation. In 1989, the government in Delhi officially cleared the joint venture, to be known as Tata Timken Limited, with Timken a 40-percent shareholder. A Brahman priest blessed the laying of the foundation stone for a tapered roller bearing factory in Jamshedpur. The plant would become fully operational in 1992.[50]

Another initiative conceived in 1986—the acquisition of MPB Corporation—was a much more significant departure from the traditional Timken, at least symbolically. MPB was one of the leading U.S. producers of precision ball bearings for the aircraft and aerospace industries and a substantial producer of miniature bearings for precision applications. It was, in short, the very business that had been sold with Fischer Bearings Company in Great Britain roughly twenty-five years before. Timken bid on MPB when it came up for sale in 1986 but did not win. It would get another chance, and would succeed, in 1990. Though more opportunistic than part of a fully articulated acquisition strategy, the MPB purchase was a harbinger of things to come.

Acquisition of MPB

When Timken looked at MPB in 1986, Joe Toot recalled, the potential fit between the two companies was readily apparent. "MPB was a medium-sized, very successful bearing company that did not have the scale and scope to finance a research program to make it a sustainable enterprise going into the next century," said Joe. "We had a very successful research program in grinding, metallurgy, and lubrication—all those things that could make that enterprise better. Our skills were as applicable in ball bearings as they were in tapered roller bearings." MPB was also attractive for its strong presence in the aerospace market, a segment in which Timken's bearing business was attempting to expand its position. Much like Latrobe, MPB had a history of innovation and industry leadership. But it had reached the point where it was unable to sustain its independence in a consolidating industry.

MPB was the creation of a Long Island, New York, inventor, Winslow S. Pierce, Jr. In 1921, twenty-seven-year-old Pierce patented a process for fracturing bearing races without any loss of metal, so that they could be rejoined around shafts to form smooth bearing surfaces. That was the basis of his split ball bearing, patented in 1924—a significant innovation for applications in many hard-to-reach locations in industrial equipment. In 1927, Pierce purchased a controlling interest in the Niles Machine Company of Lebanon, New Hampshire, and reorganized it as the Split Ball Bearing Corporation. Niles had been producing a split ball bearing of its own design, mainly for the large regional textile industry, but it did not have a process or a product as good as Pierce's. Yet Pierce proved to be much less adept at developing a manufacturing company than at inventing new products. Split Ball Bearing would limp along unprofitably until World War II.[51]

In 1936, Pierce's inventiveness launched a second business, in miniature ball bearings. Pierce had taken a treasured silver pocket watch with a cracked jewel to a local jeweler. When he was informed that it could not be repaired, he went to the machine shop at Split Ball Bearing and made up, on a small lathe, a tiny set of bearing races, one-sixteenth inch in outer diameter. Pierce purchased balls one-sixty-fourth inch in diameter from Norma Hoffman Bearing Company in Stamford, Connecticut, and sent all the parts off to Tiffany & Company in New York to be assembled and set in his watch. He had made a miniature bearing once before, but in this case, his accomplishment achieved broader attention and became the foundation for a new line of business. The problem then was to develop production on a commercial scale. Pierce made some small-scale grinders from parts of alarm clocks. He also hired an assistant, Raymond H. Carter, a young mechanical engineering graduate from the University of New Hampshire. Those two steps, however, hardly constituted developing a manufacturing process. Between 1938 and 1939 Pierce and "Nick" Carter produced just 70 miniature bearings, which they sold for about $2.00 each, mainly to hobbyists and research engineers.[52]

One of those early customers was Carl Norden, developer of the Norden bombsight, produced by Sperry Gyroscope. In the summer of 1939, it took nine months to fill Sperry's order for 600 one-quarter-inch O.D. bearings with the crude equipment in the Split Ball Bearing machine shop. The company increased its output considerably during 1940, from 25 a week to nearly 50 a day. But as World War II progressed, the slow pace of production threatened the supply of Norden bombsights, and with it the strategy of "pinpoint bombing" with which the U.S. Army Air Force command hoped to destroy the industrial backbone of Germany and Japan. It was under those stressful conditions that Miniature Precision Bearings (MPB) was born.[53]

In January 1941, Pierce and Arthur N. Daniels, a professor of mechanical engineering at New Hampshire's Dartmouth College, established MPB as a partnership. By that time, Split Ball Bearing, under the management of Pierce's brother-in-law, T. H. Cabot, Jr., was expanding rapidly with orders for bearings for machine tools and a variety of military applications. Daniels went off to serve in the Navy, but before leaving, he hired a full-time manager, a Yale-educated engineer and attorney, Horace D. Gilbert. It was Gilbert who would provide the

Since its founding in 1941 by Winslow Pierce, Jr. (above), MPB Corporation has become a leader in super-precision bearings for the aerospace, medical, computer, and other high-technology industries. Horace Gilbert (left) was the organization-builder who oversaw its growth from 1941 to 1962. Timken acquired MPB in 1990.

managerial skills needed to put MPB on a solid footing. By July 1941, he found a separate factory space in Keene, New Hampshire, and the company moved, becoming fully independent of Split Ball Bearing. During the war, MPB was the only U.S. company to have the specialized production equipment for miniature bearings. Though it expanded dramatically, it was still not able to fill all the orders it received. British Timken, by comparison, used standard production equipment at its Fischer Bearings plant. Its output was somewhat higher (over 100,000 per year versus 90,000 for MPB). But its miniature bearings were considerably larger, with a bore of one-eighth inch and balls one-sixteenth inch in diameter—comparable to the largest of five sizes produced by MPB.[54]

After the war the partnership between Pierce and Daniels dissolved. Daniels left to form his own miniature bearings company, New Hampshire Ball Bearings, Inc., and in 1946, Pierce reorganized MPB as a corporation, with Gilbert as a minority owner and president. The applications for miniature bearings expanded steadily in the postwar era, as customers such as Bell and Howell, Eastman Kodak, General Electric, Lear, and Raytheon used MPB bearings in compasses, gauges, chronometers, and other high-precision instruments. Then, in 1948, AT&T's Bell Laboratories launched the age of miniaturization with the introduction of the transistor to replace vacuum tubes in electronic components. Winslow Pierce died in 1950, before the implications of the miniaturization revolution became clear. Yet it ensured the future rapid growth of the industry he had pioneered and the company he founded.[55]

MPB expanded dramatically in the 1950s. It served primarily military markets but also developed new nonmilitary applications—high-speed dental drills was one of the largest from the mid-1950s forward. Horace Gilbert began a modernization program to replace the equipment originally designed by Pierce—adaptations of general-purpose metalworking machinery—with new machine tools expressly designed for high-volume production of miniature bearings. The company produced more than 1 million bearings in 1955. In 1956, Gilbert moved MPB into a specially designed new factory on an eighteen-acre site in Keene that would become Precision Park. Laid out for continuous flow of material, the new plant represented a major step forward in providing a closely controlled environment, especially in the "white room," where bearings were cleaned, assembled, and packaged. MPB had recognized the need for such controls from the beginning— as Horace Gilbert noted, "a speck of dust can stop a miniature bearing the way a rock stops a wheelbarrow"—but this was the first time it had been able to enact them fully.[56]

In 1957, MPB acquired Split Ball Bearing. While that company had continued to improve its basic product, its business had remained almost wholly dependent on military customers. Thus it had expanded rapidly in wartime (World War II and the Korean War) and contracted painfully with demobilization. It was badly in need of financial resources. MPB provided them, funding a new manufacturing facility in Lebanon, New Hampshire, in 1958. By the end of the decade—with the miniature bearing industry further boosted by the revving up of the U.S. space program after the 1957 launch of Sputnik—the company expanded its new Keene plant by 50 percent and built a separate facility at Precision Park to house a centralized R&D organization. MPB had become the largest employer in Keene. It had also opened an office in Los Angeles to provide technical support and distribution to eleven western states. And Horace Gilbert was working on national publicity. In 1958, he created the MPB Miniaturization Awards, which went to Bell Laboratories for its printed circuit board in 1959. In 1961, Gilbert published *Miniaturization,* a volume of essays that he edited, with contributions from MPB employees (one was chief engineer Nick Carter) and academic experts, including the Nobel Prize-winning physicist Richard Feynman.[57]

Yet the continuing growth in demand for miniature bearings brought new competitors into the field and ushered in a period of oversupply and intense price competition in the early 1960s. Initially, the only competitors in the U.S. market were Arthur Daniels's New Hampshire Ball Bearings and Barden Corporation of Danbury, Connecticut. But by 1960 some established manufacturers of ball bearings—GM's New Departure, Federal-Mogul-Bower, Fafnir Bearing Company (which had bought Fischer Bearings from British Timken), Marlin-Rockwell (a division of TRW), and SKF Industries—had launched miniature bearings divisions to take advantage of the booming market. Then, over the next few years, Japanese producers began importing heavily into that segment of the industry. A vicious two-year price war, from 1961 to 1963, drove a number of the domestic newcomers out of the market and sent MPB into a difficult period of financial losses and retrenchment. The Split Ball Bearing division kept its parent company afloat. Its business, focused almost exclusively on bearings for sensors, engines, and gearboxes for the aerospace industry, was running at full tilt, along with the space program and the Vietnam War military buildup.[58]

In 1962, William M. Scranton succeeded Horace Gilbert as president, and Gilbert assumed the position of chairman. Under Scranton's leadership, MPB developed some improved bearings and manufacturing processes that provided a number of new business opportunities. For example, under a contract to General Dynamics, it developed a gyro-optics assembly for the guidance system of small missiles, which it began to produce in 1964. MPB also began to diversify through acquisitions. In 1961, it purchased Wafe Manufacturing Company, of Bridgeport, Connecticut, a maker of tools, dies, and miniature ball bearing races. Two other acquisitions—Joy Ball and Roller Bearing Company of Chicago (1964) and Andrews Bearings Corporation of Spartanburg, South Carolina (1967)—broadened the company's product line into ball and straight roller bearings in larger sizes as well as into lower grades of miniature ball bearings. In 1973, the acquisition of New Hampshire Industries, in Lebanon, added a line of ball bearing–equipped idler pulleys for farm and garden equipment. In 1966, MPB built new manufacturing facilities for Wafe (renamed Alinabal) and Joy Ball and Roller, expanded the Lebanon factory of Split Ball Bearing, and built a European manufacturing plant in Medemblik, Netherlands. In 1968, it opened a plant in Charlestown, New Hampshire, for expanded production of its gyro-optic products.[59]

Between 1960 and 1972 MPB's annual sales rose from $10 to $25 million, but all of its growth could not be financed internally. Though the company's stock had traded over the counter in the 1960s, it remained quite closely held. Then, in 1967, Scranton arranged a public offering of additional shares. This move increased the invested capital in the company but diluted ownership. In 1976, a group of individual investors began acquiring a significant stake in the company. Fearing a takeover by people interested in liquidating MPB rather than operating it, Scranton arranged instead for an acquisition by Wheelabrator-Frye, Inc., of Hampton, New Hampshire. Originally a company that made a metal finishing device called a wheelabrator, MPB's white knight was a highly diversified firm still growing rapidly by acquisitions in a broad range of unrelated industries. Scranton left MPB after the acquisition. But Wheelabrator provided some solid (though quite nontechnical) management from its executive ranks—Thomas Begel, from 1976 to 1981, and Steven Cerri, from 1981 to 1984—along with the financial resources required to support continued growth. It was a good period for MPB, recalled Donald Ross, the vice president in charge of Split Ball Bearing in those years. "We were beginning to take off, and they were totally supportive," said Ross. "They didn't fully understand what we were making, but could we do more of it if they gave us more capital?" Split Ball Bearing continued to enlarge its aerospace markets, and MPB successfully developed new applications and products, in particular assemblies for X-ray tubes and dental and surgical handpieces—high-value-added products in which bearings were only one part of a complete system. Total revenues hit $50 million in 1979 and doubled that by 1987.[60]

But the company's fate was now aligned with that of its corporate parent. In 1983, Wheelabrator-Frye was acquired by another diversified giant, The Signal Companies, Inc., based in La Jolla, California. Two years later, Signal merged with Allied Corporation, a large conglomerate built on the former Allied Chemical Company of Morristown, New Jersey. MPB then became part of the electronics and instrumentation sector of Allied-Signal, Inc. Donald Ross had become executive vice president of MPB in 1982 and president in 1984. Under Wheelabrator and Signal, said Ross, MPB had flourished under a regime of strong financial backing but little interference in its management. Things changed drastically under Allied-

Signal, however: "They were a $14-billion company imposing their way of doing business on tiny, little, drop-in-the-bucket MPB. We just didn't have the manpower to handle all that." And, indeed, Allied-Signal soon realized that MPB and seven other electronics and components firms it had acquired were not a good fit. It put them all up for sale in December 1986. Among the serious potential buyers of MPB were three major bearing manufacturers, Torrington, FAG, and Timken.[61]

The bidding concluded, however, with a leveraged buyout that took MPB private. It was led by Harold Geneen, who had been a pioneer in the conglomerate movement and the architect of the giant diversified firm ITT. Geneen was widely admired among U.S. corporate managers for his ability to make companies grow rapidly and profitably. At the time of the MPB acquisition, he had been retired from ITT for ten years and was nearly eighty years old. But he worked closely with Ross and his executive team to execute a plan for rapid growth of both sales and profit, which had been the basis of the buyout decision. Some $20 million of investments went into upgrading manufacturing equipment and reorganizing production to be more flexible and cost effective. In 1988, MPB opened the Precision Bearing Center to refurbish engine and gearbox bearings. It also entered an important new market with the production of computer disk-drive spindles and expanded bearing applications for commercial aircraft, both of which continued its effort to become less dependent on military customers.[62]

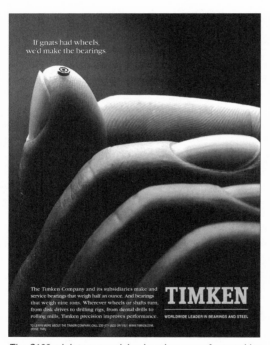

The S100 miniature precision bearing, manufactured by MPB Corporation, is found in many applications from military ordnance timing devices to equipment that bends "leads" on components for electronic circuit boards. Thirty-nine of these tiny bearings (measuring 0.100" O.D.) can fit on top of a penny.

The results were exciting. Within the first year, MPB achieved most of its three-year goals. Still, the company had to deal with the fact that it had been acquired in a classic leveraged buyout, with heavy use of high-interest junk bonds for financing—$96.5 million of discount debentures paying 14.5 percent interest. Within just two years of the deal, it became clear that, while MPB was meeting its targets for growth, it simply could not in its highly competitive markets earn the level of profits required to both service its debt and continue to invest in future growth. It was a problem common to many of the leveraged buyouts of the 1980s. Geneen and his co-investors determined to sell MPB before it began to lose its value. This time Timken came up with the winning bid, purchasing MPB for $185 million in cash, plus assumption of its debt.[63]

With its strong balance sheet and organizational resources, Timken was in a position to support MPB in continuing its push for growth. But MPB would struggle in the early 1990s, as the aerospace industry contracted sharply at the end of the Cold War. With strong direction from Canton, it responded by pursuing greater diversity in its markets, building on earlier forays into bearing service and the dental and computer industries. In 1994, Timken would open a new plant in Singapore to assemble miniature bearings in rotary actuator cartridges for computer disk drives.[64]

The acquisition of MPB was part of Timken's own drive to expand its position in countercyclical markets, in particular, aerospace. By taking the company into the manufacture of ball bearings in pursuit of that strategy, Tim and Joe moved another step beyond the narrow definition of corporate purpose that had governed from the mid-1930s into the 1980s. In their quest to improve the company's performance dramatically, they would continue on that path—reevaluating the traditional ideas and attitudes in which they had been so thoroughly schooled, and undertaking to change those that had become constraints. Timken faced its own challenges in the recession years of the early 1990s. Combined with the change effort launched with Vision 2000, the steps it took in response would be transforming.

CHAPTER ELEVEN

The New Century Approaches

*T*he pace of life—and change—at Timken picked up considerably in the 1990s, as initiatives launched in the 1980s took hold. The shift to a business unit structure and emphasis on strategic management had produced long-range plans for growth that took both Bearings and Steel into new markets. The movement of the management culture away from command-and-control progressed through the organization, spurred on by the effort to implement the principles of lean manufacturing. Triggered by recession in the early 1990s, aggressive cost-cutting programs that incorporated the lean-manufacturing philosophy of continuous improvement accelerated the pace of organizational change by emphasizing empowerment of personnel throughout the company's offices and on the shop floor. Changing—and rising—customer expectations added momentum to those initiatives. Most important, they were driven with increasing urgency from the top, as Tim Timken and Joe Toot pursued the objectives they had set—to become the best manufacturing company in the world and to produce returns for long-term shareholders that would make up for the shortfall of the 1980s.

All of this took place in the context of a remarkable period of industrial renewal within the United States generally, and in the Midwest in particular. By the mid-1990s, it was clear that intense, survival-threatening, global competition was a permanent feature of business life. But it was also clear by then that many U.S. firms had not just survived the 1980s but had grown stronger, and that they would be among the toughest competitors. Those who had proclaimed the advent of a postindustrial economy and had written off the Rust Belt as a permanently depressed region were proven wrong. Between 1987 and 1995, exports increased as a percentage of U.S. gross domestic product, from 8 to 13 percent. Exports from the Midwest grew even faster than from the nation as a whole, based largely on demand for capital goods in rapidly developing regions of the world. The steel, automotive, and automotive supply industries, which had been moving manufacturing facilities out of the Midwest for decades, began to reconcentrate in the region in the 1990s. Because of those secular trends, the recession of the 1990s did not hit the Midwest as hard as other regions. Beginning in 1991, unemployment rates there dropped below national rates. Midwest per capita income, more closely tied to manufacturing, had been below the national average since 1983 but edged above it in 1994. After more than a decade of annual net population losses, the region began to show net gains.[1]

To be sure, a complex set of economic factors influenced those changes. Yet one organizational factor was critical—the substantial increase in productivity gained through the adoption of lean-manufacturing operating principles and technologies by a significant proportion of U.S. companies. As stated in 1994 by General Electric's renowned CEO, John F. Welch, "The best companies now know, without a doubt, where productivity—real and limitless productivity—comes from. It comes from challenged, empowered, excited, rewarded teams of people." Welch continued, "The country or the company with the highest absolute productivity may be buffeted by the winds of competition or the fluctuations of currency, but in the long run it controls its own fate." That realization was the foundation of the manufacturing revival.[2]

Timken placed itself on the leading edge of that revival. Its Faircrest steel plant was a beacon in one of the worst-hit industries from the time it came on line in 1985. And, though it did not begin significant organizational change elsewhere until 1990, the company jumpstarted Vision 2000 and propelled it along at a rapid rate with its $1-billion capital spending program. By the mid-1990s, Timken would be recognized widely as a model "turnaround company." Tim Timken joined the board of the National Association of Manufacturers (NAM) in 1994 and became NAM Ohio cochairman the next year. On behalf of NAM, The Timken Company successfully petitioned Ohio governor George Voinovich to declare 1995 the Year of Manufacturing in Ohio, to be celebrated in conjunction with NAM's hundredth anniversary. Tim had a high-profile role in describing and explaining the revival of U.S. industry, particularly in the Midwest, to government and the media, and the company's Ohio plants showcased the story he was telling. In addition, by the mid-1990s, Timken would be on its way toward achieving the ambitious financial goals he had set for it.[3]

Renewal of Manufacturing

The lean-manufacturing system that Timken and other U.S. industrial companies implemented in the 1990s involved some significant new technology, in particular the application of electronic information systems and controls to a wide range of production-related tasks. One major element was computer-aided design and computer-aided manufacturing (CAD/CAM). CAD had become a familiar tool for product engineers in the 1980s. The connection to CAM not only sped the handoff to manufacturing, but also supported the all-important effort to design for manufacturability in the first place. Another critical piece was the flexible manufacturing cell, a group of production machines linked together by automated transfer equipment and electronic controls. In contrast to the highly specialized machine tools developed for high-volume production, those used for flexible manufacturing tended to be more general-purpose machines. Each cell included all the elements required to convert raw materials to finished products. Flexible manufacturing systems facilitated rapid changeover from one product to another, and they did not require long production runs to operate efficiently—in effect, they combined the advantages of batch and mass production. Other technologies included robots, both to move pieces from one step to the next and to perform machine operations, and computer control of automated materials handling systems. Networked computer systems made it possible to monitor and coordinate production throughout the entire plant.[4]

In addition to technology, there were a number of distinctive Japanese operating principles. One was "total quality," the approach to product quality that had evolved out of statistical process control. It focused on keeping processes in control, rather than inspecting for defects in final products. Generalized to the entire operation of a plant, it became total quality management. Another was the just-in-time (in Japanese, *kanban*) system for controlling the flow of materials through the production process. The object of the just-in-time system was to eliminate costly buildup of unfinished parts within the factory—for example, in buffers, as at Bucyrus. The related concept of just-in-time delivery—frequent supply of small quantities—aimed at eliminating the need for either suppliers or manufacturers to carry inventories of intermediate products, a major cost saving on both sides. Finally, lean production as practiced by Japanese companies such as Toyota included the concept of *kaizen*—continuous incremental improvement of production processes.[5]

Yet what most distinguished lean manufacturing from mainstream U.S. industrial practice was the authority and responsibility it accorded to people on the shop floor. And therein lay the real secret of its success. Paul S. Adler, a business school professor who spent two years studying the NUMMI plant in Fremont, California, noted that the dramatic turnaround there came largely through a change in the "psychology of work." In contrast to the assumption underlying command-and-control management systems—that production workers, like children, will always avoid work unless it is disguised as play—NUMMI mobilized three powerful "sources of adult motivation." Those were "the desire for excellence, a mature sense of realism [regarding the consequences of the failure to be competitive], and the positive response to respect and trust." The programmatic initiatives aimed at empowering shop-floor employees included more open communication, enhanced training, widespread adoption of a team approach to problem solving and decision making, and changes in measures of performance and rewards. But in the end, their success depended upon some significant changes in attitudes and behaviors, without which the programs came across as nothing more than "flavor of the month" management fads.[6]

As it had done at Faircrest, Timken adopted new technologies and work practices wholesale in the new bearing plants it built in the 1990s. The more challenging task, however, was to move to lean manufacturing in existing facilities. That it began to do under the banner of Vision 2000. Teams sprang up everywhere. Their work in many cases resulted in redesign of machinery and reorganization of equipment into flexible manufacturing cells. But Vision 2000 was much more about the "soft," nontechnological, aspects of organizational change. One of its most effective elements was the "centers of expertise" program, designed to speed the adoption of the many tools associated with lean manufacturing—benchmarking, team problem solving, quick changeover, and mistake proofing, to name a few—within Timken's North American plants. It assigned one or more of twenty-two such tools to each plant. Plant personnel studied the tool, learned how to use it effectively, and became the "experts," capable of training teams in other plants.[7] On the management side, Vision 2000 pushed toward more open communications and greater respect for and reliance upon plant floor personnel. In 1991, Timken took a symbolic step in that direction by generalizing the practice, adopted first at Faircrest, of calling everyone an "associate." Such changes in a tradition-bound organization were not to be enacted quickly or easily—in 1993, Tim Timken raised the company's grade on human dignity, but only to a C. Nevertheless, in a positive, reinforcing cycle of empowerment, accomplishment, and recognition, change gained momentum with the many practical successes achieved under Vision 2000 programs.

TIMKEN

The company's research and development activities are becoming increasingly global, and hundreds of customers visit the research laboratories each year. In addition to Timken Research in North Canton, Ohio, and technology centers in Latrobe, Pennsylvania, and Duston, England, Timken announced plans to open new research centers in Bangalore, India, and Yokohama, Japan, in 1999. A bearing technology center is planned at Timken Romania in 1999 as well.

A 300-square-foot commemorative wall at Timken Research recognizes every patent obtained by Timken, Latrobe, and MPB associates since Henry Timken's first tapered roller bearing patents in 1898.

Asheboro, North Carolina: Jason Brown, Wendell Murray

"There was a time in our company's history when the common belief was that a few people in management were solely responsible for making improvements. That was a static, dull time in our history when we began to lose our competitive advantage. Today we are moving forward on the power of innovation and the ideas of all our people."
—Tim Timken, addressing Timken associates in May 1998.

Colmar, France: Yves Dreyer, Christian Fardo, Gérard Bohly

*Virginia Haynes
Canton, Ohio*

*Grady Dawkins, Melissa Deal
Gaffney, South Carolina*

*Tadao Tsuneyoshi
Yokohama, Japan*

*Colleen Tomasello, Jim Maloney
Latrobe, Pennsylvania*

THE TIMKEN COMPANY

Canton, Ohio: Front row – Marilyn Welchner, Sam Williams, Michele Seymour; Back row – Rickie Mihal, Velma Riter, John Haydock

In recent years Timken associates have been outperforming such growth companies as Coca-Cola, Disney, Nucor, and Wal-Mart in ten-year compounded annual growth rate of earnings per share from 1987 to 1997.

A diverse group of 21,000 highly skilled associates make up The Timken Company. In 1998, about 30 percent of U.S. associates had twenty-five or more years of service with the company. About 60 percent of all associates worldwide were shareholders, owning 13 percent of the company's common stock.

Jamshedpur, India: Amrik Singh, Dibakar Mahto

Ron Menning
Bucyrus, Ohio

Onnette Haynes, Ricky Hall, Al Graves
Lincolton, North Carolina

Peter Cartwright
Duston, England

Timken has a long history of growth through geographic expansion and, more recently, through diversification into steel distribution and bearing service. The opening of Timken Latrobe Steel's Sandycreek Service Center in 1994 began a series of moves to strengthen the company's tool steel distribution network.

In 1995 Timken acquired Rail Bearing Service, a railroad bearing reconditioning and remanufacturing facility headquartered in Virginia. The company's railroad bearing services have grown such that, in 1998, it announced plans to build at its Timken South Africa plant a reconditioning facility to serve railroad customers in Africa, the Middle East, and West Asia. It will be the second such facility outside the United States.

Chairman, president, and CEO Tim Timken (left foreground) paused for a photo with associates during a recent visit.

Timken Latrobe Steel's Sandycreek Service Center, Pennsylvania

Timken South Africa (Proprietary) Ltd.

Yantai Timken Company Ltd., China

Timken Italia, s.r.l.

The 1990s have been a period of rapid growth for The Timken Company. In less than a decade, the company has built two new bearing plants in the United States and one in England; entered into joint ventures in India and China; announced tentative plans for its second-largest steel investment ever in a new tube mill; launched a Precision Steel Components business; announced major facility expansions in Brazil, India, Japan, Singapore, and the United States; and acquired steel distribution and bearing manufacturing facilities in the United States, the Netherlands, Poland, England, Italy, and Romania.

Left:

In 1998, Timken Company officers met with associates of newly acquired Rulmenti Grei S.A. in Romania when its official name changed to Timken Romania. Chairman, president, and CEO Tim Timken (left) and the plant's general director Constantin Trestioreanu cut the ribbon, launching the new entity.

Right:

In 1996, The Timken Company acquired FLT Prema Milmet S.A. in Sosnowiec, Poland. Renamed Timken Polska, the facility produces bearings for industries such as automotive, agricultural equipment, and industrial machinery.

Timken Romania S.A.

Timken Polska Sp.zo.o.

Below:

Since 1900, when the first Timken bearing succeeded in an automobile axle, applications for Timken bearings and steel have grown to include rolling mills and printing presses; construction and farm vehicles; energy-related equipment; computer disk drives and medical apparatus; and high-speed trains like the TGV in France, the ICE in Germany, the JR West 500 series in Japan, and Amtrak's American Flyer in the United States. From aerospace to orbiting spacecraft like the Mars Pathfinder (far right), Timken products can be found wherever wheels and shafts turn.

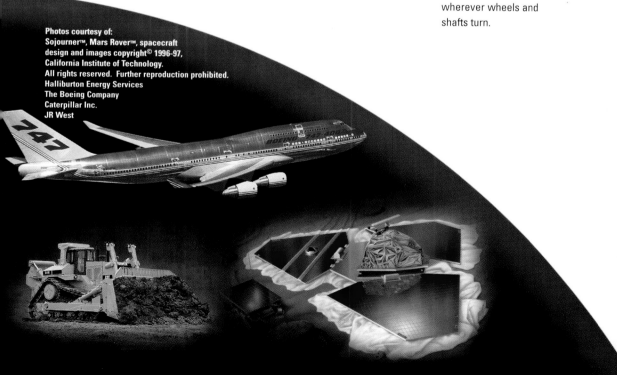

Photos courtesy of:
Sojourner™, Mars Rover™, spacecraft
design and images copyright© 1996-97,
California Institute of Technology.
All rights reserved. Further reproduction prohibited.
Halliburton Energy Services
The Boeing Company
Caterpillar Inc.
JR West

In 1998, The Timken Company had fifty-five plants and more than one hundred sales, design, and distribution centers in twenty-five countries on six continents. (See Appendix D for locations.) Timken is the world's largest manufacturer of tapered roller bearings and seamless mechanical steel tubing.

Bucyrus provided one of the first big success stories. In the mid-1980s, employees there had fully expected to see their plant permanently closed. It was a forty-year-old factory producing for the automotive industry—the most competitive segment of the bearing market. Though that had not happened, they remained fearful and demoralized. With the Vision 2000 initiative, however, Bucyrus began to undergo a conversion. As described by former general manager James Benson, it went from "a very dictatorial, very structured antichange organization to a high-involvement, high-change organization." Beginning in 1990, it moved more aggressively than any other Timken plant to implement self-directed work teams, and by 1991, it had scored numerous impressive gains in cost reduction, time to delivery, and quality, winning customer recognition awards from Nissan, Ford, GM, John Deere, Caterpillar, Borg-Warner, Chrysler, and others. One of the plant's customers said, "Trying to absorb what's happening at Bucyrus is like getting a drink of water from a fire hose. It's all happening so fast." In 1992, *Industry Week* cited Bucyrus as one of "America's Best Plants," an annual award it had devised "not only to give recognition to a selection of outstanding U.S. facilities, but also to illustrate what can be accomplished when managers and employees take up the quest for continuous improvement and world-class manufacturing."[8]

At Gaffney, plant managers committed thousands of hours to providing information on corporate objectives, training, and certification testing to men and women on the plant floor. They also created "improvement teams" to get production personnel directly involved in making changes. In the old days, said Gaffney general manager John Travers, "Supervisors would solve all of the problems if they were solvable. Now we ask for input and ideas and we realize that 90 percent of the benefits that we can achieve are achieved by our employees." By 1992, the work of the teams resulted in major improvements in flow rate through the plant and reduction of work-in-process, and a core group of production associates had begun working in self-directed teams. Designated a center of expertise for quick changeover times, Gaffney in 1990 invited Shigeo Shingo, one of the creators of the Toyota production system and president of Japan's Institute of Management Improvement, to review its set-up procedures and suggest changes. Four years later, Gaffney won the prestigious Shingo Prize for Excellence in Manufacturing, established in 1988 and awarded each year by Utah State University in recognition of "outstanding achievement in manufacturing processes, quality enhancement, productivity improvement, and customer satisfaction" among plants in Canada, Mexico, and the United States.[9]

The changes were not confined to Timken's non-union plants. For example, in 1990, $13 million of the $1-billion investment program went to modernize the Gambrinus bearing factory and consolidate production of large bearings there, transforming it into the Large Industrial Bearing Complex. That brought together green machining, heat treating, and grinding units—formerly divided between the Canton and Gambrinus plants—enabling them to work together to address issues of production schedules, delivery, and quality with improved communications and teamwork. "We now speak the same language and know how the product flows from area to area," said grinder operator Don Koffel. "If something isn't right, everyone knows to approach the team or the associate who sent them the product." In the cone assembly area for small industrial bearings, in the Canton bearing plant, a team redesigned the work and rearranged the equipment to create a manufacturing cell. The result was improved performance in meeting production requirements, fewer product defects, and "improved ergonomics" that led to less heavy lifting and less fatigue by the end of the day. Dolores Yeager, a machine operator who worked on the team, remarked, "If someone had told me five years ago that I would have been empowered to undertake such a project, I would have said 'no way.'"[10]

Timken's international plants also adopted Vision 2000 tools, or adapted them to fit their own needs and objectives. Canadian Timken became a just-in-time supplier, improving its on-time delivery rate by nearly 100 percent. A team of machine operators at Australian Timken in Ballarat achieved a 400 percent improvement in defect rate through modified tooling and process controls. At Timken France, the initiative to improve communications from management took shape under the banner *Usine Visible*—roughly translated as the transparent factory—a system by which the critical information on operation of the Colmar plant was regularly posted for all to read. After 1993, the plant reorganized its production and structured its training programs, team activities, and communications around automotive, railroad, and industrial market segments, in order to become more customer focused.[11]

British Timken, in 1992, launched Timken Tomorrow, a program that converted supervisors to team leaders and hourly employees to salaried staff in the context of Vision 2000-type efforts to raise performance. There were a number of models for such a program in Britain, notably Rover Tomorrow—at Timken's largest European customer—from which the name was borrowed. There was also a model within the company: the Timken Europa Distribution Center at Haan, Germany, had always operated with salaried staff only and a high degree of flexibility in job assignments. It was "just a common sense way of doing things," said Gerhard Reiter, general manager of the facility. But the program was a radical departure for a unionized facility like Duston, not least because it put an end to collective bargaining on wages. The union leadership at Duston supported the measure, but it did so facing the possibility of "de-recognition," which was permitted under laws passed by the Conservative Party under Margaret Thatcher. In the plant it was not an easy sell, and it required considerable adjustment—for example, to the process of individual performance reviews, an unfamiliar exercise. The overriding consideration in the end, however, was the need to remain competitive. Said Dave Martin, a twenty-two-year man in the auto shop at Duston, "When I started, Timken was the best in the world—no one could touch us. Now it's a case of fighting for market share, and if we are to get our fair percentage, there has to be change, I can see that." The shift to lean manufacturing proceeded apace in the context of Timken Tomorrow—in 1992, four teams reorganized fifty production machines into cells for gains in both productivity and quality and a projected cost saving of hundreds of thousands of dollars per year.[12]

Salaries and performance-related bonuses took hold at British Timken, but the system did not spread widely among existing company plants. By contrast, in the new bearing plants built in the 1990s—where Timken started with a clean sheet of paper in every respect—salaries for production personnel were the norm.

Twenty-First Century Plants

The facility that presented the first opportunity to adopt technology practices wholesale came on line in 1991 in Altavista, Virginia. Expectations ran high. In the words of David Hudelson, plant manager, "We believe Altavista will be the standard for the 1990s and into the twenty-first century, in the same way the 'Bucyrus Concept' revolutionized the 1950s." That was a meaningful comparison for both the similarities and the differences between the two plants.[13]

Like Bucyrus, Altavista was born in Timken's production development organization, now the advanced bearing process development group, a unit of Timken Research. Its equipment, either built or modified in-house, reflected the heavy R&D investments of the 1980s in the application of advanced computer controls and other new technologies, such as isotropic finishing. But Bucyrus had introduced straight-line automated production to bearing manufacture, while Altavista brought flexible manufacturing cells. Bucyrus had been built for high-volume output of standardized bearings, aimed at expanding Timken's market share through price reductions. The objective for Altavista was to open new market segments with high-value-added package bearings and smart bearings, produced for specific customer orders in relatively small quantities—initially just 2 million per year, versus the 30 million produced in the early years of Bucyrus (2 million was one week's output at Bucyrus in the 1990s). Its processes had to be flexible in order to operate profitably on that scale.[14]

In the automotive bearing market of the early 1980s, Timken had faced the challenge of lessening its dependence on standardized bearings, where it was suffering the most from intense competition. It also had recognized an opportunity in the trend among automakers toward de-integration—a movement to simplify and take costs out of their own operations by getting their suppliers to assume responsibility for designing and producing more complex subassemblies. In response, Timken introduced in 1982 the UNIPAC-PLUS™: a heavy-duty bearing with two cone assemblies (cone, rollers, and cage) in a single cup, prelubricated, preadjusted, and presealed, like the UNIPAC, but with the addition of a bolt-on flange. Developing the manufacturing processes for the UNIPAC-PLUS had taken Timken Research into unfamiliar territory. Altavista's production process consisted of drilling mounting holes in the forged steel flange that is part of the outer raceway of the bearing, then heat treating and grinding—including super-finishing of some surfaces—and completing the package with cone assemblies supplied by Gaffney. The time from rough forging to final product was ten minutes. On that basis, it could produce bearings to customers' exact specifications cost-effectively.[15]

In contrast to Bucyrus, however, the centerpiece of innovation was not new technology, but the reorganization of work. That was also developed at Timken Research in a pilot production program for the UNIPAC-PLUS before Altavista took over. As before, Timken Research trained a core group of production employees for the new plant, but in this case the training was aimed largely at teaching them how to function as self-directed teams. At Altavista there were no foremen or supervisors in the management structure of the plant. The computer system gave everyone access to the same information—production results, quality, machine maintenance, planning, inventory, and vacation days. Everyone was on salary. And by the mid-1990s, production teams would be conducting their own performance evaluations and participating in decisions on who would be hired or promoted.[16]

Altavista, launched with fewer than 50 people, was designed to be expanded in equal-sized increments up to five times that size as the market for its products expanded. Timken would not have to wait long—there would be expansions in 1994, 1996, and 1998. (Another is under construction, to open in 1999.) Designed specifically for independently sprung driving wheels, as in four-wheel-drive pickup trucks, the UNIPAC-PLUS became a major product for sport-utility vehicles and light trucks, two of the most popular models in the U.S. automotive market of the 1990s. SENSOR-PAC™ bearings, introduced in 1990, became increasingly important with the spread of antilock brake systems, and PINION-PAC™ opened up another niche in the market. Clearly, the trend toward de-integration in the automotive industry played to Timken's historic organizational strengths in sales and application engineering and new product development, which the move to standardization in the 1950s had made less important. Yet only by developing new capabilities in flexible manufacturing was the company able to take full advantage of that opportunity.[17]

The same kind of opportunity existed in the industrial market—if anything, to a greater degree. In 1989, Timken Research and the bearing business unit, building on their collaboration to plan Altavista, launched the "Twenty-First

The Altavista bearing plant in Virginia, opened in 1991, is highly automated to produce preset, prelubricated, and presealed (package) tapered roller bearings for light trucks and sport utility vehicles. This SENSOR-PAC™ bearing, a further enhancement to the UNIPAC bearing, incorporates an electronic sensor as part of vehicle antilock braking systems. With an active sensor that reads all speeds, this bearing allows total traction control under all conditions.

Century Business Project" to pursue that opportunity. In the 1980s, Timken's industrial customers, themselves under tremendous pressure to bring new and improved products to market, were interested primarily in reducing the eight-to-ten-month lead time required for ordering standard bearings and the year it took to develop new industrial bearings. At the same time, flexible manufacturing opened the door to significant economies in the production of specialized industrial bearings—for which lot sizes ranged from under twenty to the low thousands (as opposed to hundreds of thousands at Altavista and millions at Bucyrus). In theory, computer technology made it possible to achieve both those goals, with CAD/CAM linkages and computer control of production equipment enabling quick changeovers. Yet, as with automation technology in the late 1940s, none of that had yet been applied to a precision product such as bearings, which required heat treating and grinding as well as machining.[18]

Thus, the first phase of the twenty-first century project was necessarily a feasibility study, to evaluate both the market and the technological opportunities for success. From there a concept team developed a more concrete vision of how a new plant and a new business approach would look. Out of that came some guiding principles: to unify design and manufacturing in a single computer program; to eliminate retooling; to teach production associates new skills; and to bring them together to work in teams. In 1991, a cross-functional design team took on the task of translating the concept and principles into detailed plans, for example, equipment specifications and floor layout. The advanced bearing process development group supported that effort, first with computer simulations, and then with a cardboard 3-D model of a manufacturing cell set up at Timken Research. That enabled machine operators to have early input into the design process and resulted in a significant cost saving, through the realization that the plant would require less

Below: *The Spexx™
Performance
Bearings shown
here are new
Timken products
that typify the highly
customized bearings
produced at
Asheboro.*

*Ground was broken for the Asheboro plant in November 1991.
Chairman Tim Timken (at controls), president Joe Toot (below left),
and executive vice president Peter Ashton (right) hosted business
and education leaders, as well as government officials, including
NASCAR driver and county commissioner Richard Petty. Today, the
plant uses flexible manufacturing technology to provide speed and
flexibility in design, manufacturing, and delivery.*

floor space than had been planned. Said Harvard Business School professor David
Garvin, an expert on so-called learning organizations, it was an exemplary case of
"learning before doing."[19]

Early in 1991, Timken announced that $200 million of its $1-billion investment program would go to build two new plants on the twenty-first-century
design, one in Asheboro, North Carolina, and one in Überherrn, Germany. Both
plants were delayed by the recession of the early 1990s. Timken later abandoned
plans for Überherrn, but Asheboro came on line in September 1994.

Bucyrus had produced Green Light bearings, and Altavista had its "PAC"
series of package and smart bearings. Asheboro gave rise to Spexx™, a family of
bearings variously customized for maximum fatigue life, durability, wear resistance, advanced finishes, and other attributes required to address "problem situations" faced by Timken's industrial customers. DuraSpexx™ bearings, for
example, offered extended fatigue life for gear drives and other applications.
AquaSpexx™ bearings were engineered for high performance in equipment
exposed to high humidity or operating in wet, dirty conditions. Z-Spexx™ bearings were specialized for application in Sendzimir rolling mills. Notably, Z-Spexx

are cylindrical roller bearings. With the exception of ball bearings made briefly during World War II, they were the first non-tapered roller bearings to carry the Timken name. Certainly, developing bearings for specialized applications was not a new activity for Timken, but rapid development cycles and flexible manufacturing at Asheboro made it possible to grow that line of business substantially on a profitable basis. In 1997, Timken announced plans to expand the Asheboro plant.[20]

Asheboro and Altavista were critical elements of the company's strategy for achieving profitable growth, but not the only elements by any means. The globalization of markets for bearings and steel required advances on a broad front. In the mid-1990s, the company would launch important new initiatives in its steel business and begin to grow by acquisitions in both steel and bearings. But before that, recession forced Timken once again to grapple with the continuing need to make substantial reductions in operating costs and to improve organizational effectiveness.

Improving Performance

The worldwide recession of the early 1990s affected all of Timken's markets, beginning with a drastic drop-off in the U.S. auto industry. Steel was harder hit than bearings, but both businesses struggled with falling prices and the inefficiencies of reduced plant utilization. In 1992, the automotive industry began to revive but other key markets for bearings and steel did not. Continuing weakness in the oil industry and fierce competition from Japanese and Brazilian imports in the bar market undermined the profitability of Timken's steel sales. An antidumping protest, made jointly with Republic Engineered Steels, was unsuccessful—while the Commerce Department determined that dumping had occurred, the ITC ruled no damage had been done. MPB's business was hurt by the decline of the U.S. aerospace industry, both commercial and military. In the process of long-term restructuring as a result of the end of the Cold War, MPB saw its sales drop off sharply as the Persian Gulf War concluded. In addition, in 1992 the recession accelerated significantly in Europe and settled in for a longer stay—while Timken's U.S. and other international operations rebounded, Timken Europe had a significant operating loss in 1993.[21]

The recession brought some harsh measures reminiscent of the hard times of the 1980s, but there were significant differences between the two periods. In the fall of 1991, the company reduced the workweek for production associates worldwide, began making some layoffs, and cut salaries. Timken sustained much of its ongoing program of capital investment, but in September 1992, Joe Toot announced the delay of construction of the Asheboro and Überherrn plants. It was an appropriate time, he suggested, "to pause [and] let these events over which we have no control sort themselves out." Facing a continuing recession in Europe, Timken announced in March 1993 that it would close the Daventry plant of British Timken, consolidating 80 percent of its production and 60 percent of its personnel into the Duston plant.[22]

At the same time, however, Timken was able to mitigate the effects of recession in ways it had not done in the 1980s. In 1991, the company secured temporary price reductions from key U.S. suppliers—a move that reflected the strong relationships that had been built up over the previous decade. The following year, Timken sought and won agreement from the USW to early negotiation of a new contract. That was a move the company deemed essential to reassure customers considering long-term purchasing contracts that the disruptive strikes of the 1980s would not be repeated. In November 1992, the company and the union reached agreement on a four-year contract nearly ten months before the existing contract was to expire. In return for negotiating early and making some minor concessions to the company, the USW won cost-of-living increases to wages, greater pension and health insurance coverage, and greater job security in several areas.[23]

Another offsetting factor was the gain in productivity made as the result of the programs initiated in 1989. Timken's main response to the recession was to redouble its commitment to those changes, beginning with a major effort to reduce operating costs. That meant some reductions in personnel—restructuring charges of $27 million in 1991 and $28 million in 1993 (plus an additional write-down for losses at Tata Timken, its joint venture in India) had a great deal to do with the red ink on its bottom line in those years. (See Table 11.1.) But there were also cost reductions through changes in the way people worked, the kinds of reductions that were more important in the long run. Timken had an operating profit in 1993, and thereafter its financial performance improved steadily. Revenue growth was an indispensable part of that improvement, but it was firmly grounded in the operating efficiencies gained through the innovative programs initiated in the early 1990s.

Joe Toot in 1991 was frustrated by the slow pace of change in Timken's managerial organization and the lack of significant reductions in administrative overhead. And Timken still struggled with inefficiencies left over from the days of functional organization, in particular a bureaucratic approach to decision making that made it slow to enact new initiatives and to react to changes in the business environment. Those were "both fatal characteristics for a would-be industry leader," said Joe. In 1991, he returned to McKinsey & Company for help in developing a new approach to those problems. The result was "Breakthrough," launched in 1992.[24]

The objective of Breakthrough was to make corporate administration less costly and more efficient. Undeniably, it had a strong element of downsizing—a goal of reducing Timken's worldwide administrative staff by a little more than

TABLE 11.1

The Timken Company Comparative Financial Data, 1990–1997 (in Thousands of Dollars, except per Share Data)

	1990	1991	1992	1993	1994	1995	1996	1997
Net sales	$1,701,011	$1,647,425	$1,642,310	$1,708,761	$1,930,351	$2,230,504	$2,394,757	$2,617,562
Net income	55,242	(35,687)	4,452	(271,932)	68,464	112,350	138,937	171,419
Total assets	$1,814,909	$1,759,139	$1,738,450	$1,789,719	$1,858,734	$1,925,925	$2,071,338	$2,326,550
Total debt	266,392	273,104	320,515	276,476	279,519	211,232	302,665	359,431
Shareholders' equity	1,074,701	1,018,971	985,063	685,312	732,891	821,178	922,228	1,032,076
Return on sales	3.2%	(2.2%)	0.3%	(15.9%)	3.5%	5.0%	5.8%	6.5%
Return on assets	3.0	(2.0)	0.3	(15.2)	3.7	5.8	6.7	7.4
Return on equity	5.1	(3.5)	0.5	(39.7)	9.3	13.7	15.1	16.6
Earnings per share	$0.92	($0.60)	$0.07	($0.29)	$1.11	$1.80	$2.21	$2.73
Dividends per share	0.49	0.50	0.50	0.50	0.50	0.56	0.60	0.66
Number of employees	18,860	17,740	16,729	15,985	16,202	17,034	19,130	20,994
Number of shareholders	25,090	26,048	31,395	28,767	49,968	26,792	31,813	46,394

Source: The Timken Company Annual Reports, 1990–97.

Notes: Per share data adjusted for 2-for-1 stock split, June 1997.
Data from 1990 forward reflect acquisition of MPB Corporation.
Numbers of shareholders from 1992 forward reflect change in method of counting beginning in 1994.
Earnings per share are before cumulative effect of accounting changes.

20 percent over several years. But the process also engaged individuals through-out the organization in rethinking their work and eliminating nonessential activi-ties and redundancies of effort across the various parts of the company. After a pilot effort involving about 50 people, Breakthrough rolled out in four seven-week "waves," each wave involving a group of ten to twenty administrative units with some commonality of purpose in their operations. The waves produced thousands of cost-cutting ideas that were submitted to a steering committee of top management for a final decision.[25]

Some ideas saved as little as $2,000, such as the proposal to eliminate mail runs between Gaffney and Lincolnton. Others promised nearly a million dollars in savings, for example by moving Latrobe's data-center operations to Canton. They ranged from easily accomplished tasks, like changing computer passwords less often, to elaborate plans like computerizing engineering at MPB. The steering committee gave approval to proposals to send pay stubs to salaried associates through company mail, to use color copies instead of photographs in research reports, and to decentralize maintenance and purchasing at several plants. Altogether, Breakthrough proposals saved some $50 million by the end of 1993. But numbers did not tell the entire story, said John Schubach, vice president for strategic management and leader of the Breakthrough program, in 1994: "Beyond the financial savings, we're finding that the changes associates are making are actually improving how we run the company. We're doing many things faster than ever before and we're doing them better."[26]

From Breakthrough, Timken moved in 1994 to a comparable effort in its manufacturing plants—Accelerated Continuous Improvement (ACI). Again, the process advanced in waves, as units within each plant moved through the steps of budgeting, idea generation, idea analysis, and implementation planning. The program was even more successful than Breakthrough. By the end of 1994, with more than a third of the units still to go through the process, nearly 6,000 ideas had been approved, and the 1,500 already implemented had saved Timken $29 million. In some cases, stretch targets of 40 percent improvement in costs, quali-ty, and service had been exceeded.[27]

At least as important in the long term, ACI had moved the company further along with some of the most important changes targeted by Vision 2000—the opening of communications and building of trust between management and pro-duction personnel. Within top management, said John Schubach, ACI produced a "psychological breakthrough." In the management committee, "most of us, except for Joe, went in with the assumption that people would never give you ideas that might affect whether or not they would still have a job when they were done. That wasn't the case." In fact, he suggested, the company learned a basic truth about empowerment: "People are really dying to give you ideas. In most cases, they would say they gave us this idea 123 times in the last ten years, and now we are finally doing something about it." The shift in attitude did not go unnoticed on the shop floor, where many people began to feel that they were more than "just a clock number" to Timken management. One thirty-two-year man in the Canton bearing plant said, "The company finally realized that the people they have working for them know as much as most of the people that they have bossing them, more or less. The people on the floor make a big difference in this company, and I think there has been a vast turnaround in how well the company is doing once they realized that."[28]

The good feelings of many should not obscure the fact that there remained, inevitably, some skepticism and mistrust on both sides. As with Breakthrough, downsizing of about 20 percent of hourly personnel was a stated goal of ACI. Said John Mroczkowski, a USW leader in Canton, "They call it Accelerated Continuous Improvement, [and] it's supposed to be a way to save costs, but it seems the main thing they come up with is eliminating jobs." Union-organizing efforts at Bucyrus in 1993 and at New Philadelphia in 1995 and 1997, though unsuccessful, reminded the company of the continuing need to work on communications and address the concerns of production associates.[29]

Changing a corporate culture that had essentially remained frozen since the 1950s was an enormous undertaking and would remain a work in progress for many years to come. At the same time, however, the continuing gains from Breakthrough and ACI that helped to make Timken more competitive validated the direction of change. Timken's unionized hourly associates had made concessions in the contracts of the early 1980s that had been essential to much that the company had accomplished, particularly in its steel business. They understood as well as anyone the need to remain competitive in the 1990s, and they placed considerable weight on the fact that Timken was making the capital investments required to do so. As business picked up in 1994, Timken stopped short of the 20 percent workforce reductions planned for Breakthrough and ACI, and began to expand its employment rolls once again. Going forward, it would attempt to make continuous improvement an integral part of its day-to-day operations, a positive sign that the cultural transformation would remain on course.[30]

The steady gains in productivity that resulted from those efforts in the 1990s were a necessary element of improved performance. (See Figure 11.1.) But alone they were not sufficient to take the company where it wanted to go by the end of the decade. Profitable growth was required, and growth at a rapid pace. Tim Timken and Joe Toot set the company on a course to achieve that by recommitting to the objectives they had set four years before.

The Challenge Renewed

In 1993, coming out of the recession, it was clear that Timken had regained the position of industry leadership it had enjoyed in 1980. The investment in Faircrest had strengthened Timken steel in its traditional markets for mechanical tubing and opened up new markets in large bar products. The company had recaptured the share of the U.S. market for tapered roller bearings that it had lost to Japanese competitors and was even beginning to make headway with Japanese customers in Japan as well as in the United States. In 1992, a year of severe worldwide recession that hit both the steel and bearing industries particularly hard, Timken had earned a net profit. SKF had had a net loss that year equal to 6 percent of sales. FAG had nearly foundered under a loss equal to half its total equity. (It would survive over the next few years only by cutting 15,000 employees, 50 percent of its workforce.)[31]

Yet Timken had not progressed toward Tim's goal of providing returns to shareholders that would make up the ground they had lost in the 1980s. Indeed, its stock price had fallen from a high of $39\frac{1}{4}$ in 1989 to one of just $30\frac{1}{2}$ in 1992. Dividends had increased each year from 1989 to 1991 but had leveled off at $1.00

FIGURE 11.1

**Productivity:
Net Sales/Total Compensation, 1993–1997**

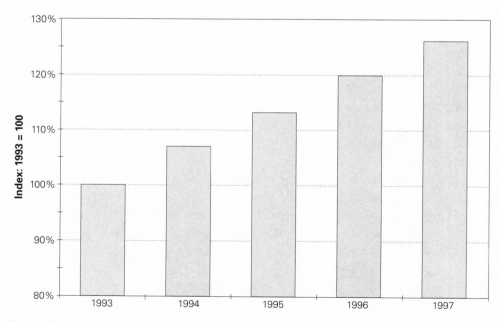

Source: The Timken Company Annual Report for 1997.

per share in 1992 with the fall in earnings per share. Those results were disappointing relative to the goals set for 1999, and they posed concerns for the company's future. One of those concerns would have been quite foreign to earlier generations of Timken executives: the performance of the company's stock affected its debt rating and consequently its cost of capital. In the 1990s Timken had become comfortable with a moderate level of debt financing as a means of sustaining its investment programs—in the early 1990s its ratio of debt to total capital averaged 22 percent, as opposed to 15 percent in the mid-1980s. A deeper concern was that indifferent financial performance posed a threat to the company's independence.[32]

Beyond that, however, Tim and Joe judged that those simply were not the kinds of results that betokened true industry leadership. "We can't just compare ourselves to our competitors. We must look at a broader constituency," said Joe. "We should focus on finding excellence and learning from it no matter where it is." The thinking of Timken's top management had evolved considerably since the late 1970s, and in the process the bar for corporate performance had been raised. Said Joe: "Some people think The Timken Company is doomed to produce mediocre or poor results because we're in the bearing and steel businesses, which have tough competitive conditions and excess capacity. That's not the case. Very good companies, even in bad industries, can and often do perform quite well."[33]

To aim the company at that higher standard, Joe unveiled a further revision of the mission statement in July 1993. Henceforth, Timken would strive to be "the best-*performing* manufacturing company in the world *in the eyes of our customers and shareholders.*" The prior version had served Timken well for three years, he said: "Our focus on being the best manufacturing company has had an impact on important measures of corporate success such as productivity, product quality and market penetration." But, going forward, the focus had to shift to other measures, in particular those, like return on capital, that were indicators of total return to shareholders. Joe added, "We would be the best-performing company in the world in the eyes of our shareholders only if their total return from owning Timken Company stock is superior to what they could earn investing in other manufacturing companies."[34]

At the same time, in the corporate forum of 1993, Tim renewed his challenge. The recession had slowed inflation, so the specific targets had changed. But the objective remained the same: to achieve a level of total return to shareholders beyond overall stock-market returns, and in that way by 1999 to make up for the poor returns of the 1980s and early 1990s. That translated into some ambitious goals—better than 50 percent growth in sales by 1999 and significant earnings improvement. As an interim target for 1996, Tim proposed $2.1 billion in revenues (an increase of 24 percent over 1992) and earnings of $3.50 per share, a level the company had not achieved since 1981.[35]

Those target numbers provided a clear point of focus for Timken's business units. As a first step toward meeting them, the business unit leaders, Charles West and Peter Ashton, undertook to restructure their organizations to share the responsibility for both growth and profits more widely. With the exception of British Timken and later Timken Europe, profit responsibility had, historically, gone no further than the president of the company. After 1986, that had broadened to include the executive vice presidents of Bearings and Steel. Now that situation changed dramatically with the creation of a second tier of business units in both Bearings and Steel, based on market segments. Within the new organizations, selling was to be clearly separated from marketing, and within marketing there was to be much greater emphasis on planning. "In the past," said Linn Osterman, marketing vice president for steel, "sales and marketing managers tended to focus mainly on sales," rather than on improving profitability. "In the new organization, if profit targets are not met for the segment . . . it is the marketing organization's responsibility to decide how to become profitable or how to sell in other market segments where the profit potential is greater."[36]

Thus, driven by a mandate from the top, Timken continued to evolve away from the centralized, top-down organization it had been and to push its engineering culture to become more business oriented. Just as significant, though, the reorganization of 1993 reinstated some parts of the old structure that had been eliminated in the earlier change. On the bearing side, market-specific divisions—automotive, industrial, and railroad—had been in place since the 1920s. Sales engineers had specialized in one field, and the chief engineers for industrial and railroad had spearheaded the push to expand applications in each area. All that had been swept away in 1986, replaced with just two large divisions, based on geography: North America, South America, and East Asia, under vice president Donald Hart; and Europe, Africa, and West Asia, led by vice president Maurice Amiel.

By 1990, however, there had been some clear signs that the change had not been all for the good. The most significant problem emerged in railroad bearings, where Timken's share of a market it had created and led for decades dropped to just 30 percent. Railroad customers had stopped specifying Timken bearings for new cars and locomotives largely because no sales engineer had paid them a call, in some cases for years. The business also had been suffering from long delivery times and a general lack of responsiveness to customer requests. "The companies were accustomed to their own sales force, not people that also visited automotive companies," said railroad marketing specialist Jacques Jones. "With restructuring in 1986, customers didn't feel they were getting the service they wanted. It looked to them as though Timken was walking away from the business."[37]

To address that problem, Ashton and Hart had developed a variation of the old formula. They created a railroad bearing business unit, pulling together marketing, sales, application engineering, and manufacturing personnel into an organization with a single market focus. The change had a dramatic impact—within a year the business unit had increased market share to 50 percent. That experience had provided some valuable learning. While such problems did not exist to the same extent in every market, it was clear from the railroad case that the changes of 1986 had undermined some of Timken's long-established competitive strengths. The immediate success of the railroad unit helped point the way to the reorganization of 1993. In Europe, Amiel carried the change even further into the plant, organizing manufacturing into teams by market segments as well.[38]

The structural changes thus reinforced the focus of the revised mission statement. Joe continued to hammer away at his message about performance—for the corporate forums of 1994 and 1995, he invited key shareholders and customers to make their case in person. The numbers Tim had proposed for 1996 provided clear-cut goals that were aggressive but achievable. All of those factors, in the context of worldwide economic recovery, contributed to success. In fact, Timken did not meet the 1996 goals—it exceeded them, with revenues of $2.4 billion and earnings per share of $4.43 (shown in Table 11.1 adjusted for a subsequent stock split). Focusing the organization ever more intensely on performance objectives drove that accomplishment. Yet it would not have been possible without some longer-term strategic initiatives in both Bearings and Steel that came to fruition in the years after 1993.

Global Growth in Bearings

As head of the bearing business unit from 1985 through 1994, Peter Ashton played an important role in transforming it from a U.S.-based multinational to a truly global operation. A British citizen, he had begun his career with British Timken in 1952 as apprentice at the Fischer Bearings Company in Wolverhampton. During the 1960s, he became manager of the Daventry plant, and in 1973, he went to Canton as assistant to James Pilz, then vice president for international. In that position, he had helped to establish Nihon Timken, and afterward he had done a tour of duty as general manager of Timken do Brasil. He was vice president for international from 1980 to 1985, when Joe and Tim chose him to be executive vice president for bearings.

Bob Leibensperger, Ashton's successor in 1995, came to the post along a very different route, through sales engineering and research. He had played a leading role in pushing for increased R&D funding in the late 1970s and had been director of Timken Research and, since 1985, vice president for technology. He was the chief architect and advocate for the concept of power density. Between them, Ashton and Leibensperger brought experience and perspective from two areas critical to long-term growth of the bearing business—the conduct of business on a worldwide scale, and the technical collaboration with customers essential to continue expanding the applications of Timken bearings.

From the early 1980s forward, the need to compete on a global basis had been a fact of life for the bearing business. On one hand, noted Tim Timken, the company's U.S. customers "could buy and were willing to buy from anywhere." On the other, those customers now had strong international competitors that in many cases had become the world market leaders. The focus on rapid growth made expansion in global markets even more important. With a better than 60 percent share of the U.S. tapered roller bearing market but less than a third of the world market—where industrial development in Latin America, Asia, and the countries emerging from communism promised a strong demand for bearings— the greatest opportunities for growth clearly lay outside the United States.[39]

Operating globally, said Ashton, meant "more than just having some plants around the world." It meant being "a company that has global systems and thinks globally." In that regard, Timken had an edge—it had some strong international institutions to build upon. One of those was its corps of sales engineers, recruited in the countries where the company did business and trained as tapered roller bearing specialists in Colmar or Canton. They gave global reach to what was historically one of Timken's greatest competitive strengths, the technical support it provided to its customers in designing their equipment to apply Timken bearings. The big advances in bearing performance made in the 1980s, plus the enhanced capabilities that came through the strengthening of Timken Research, made sales engineering all the more valuable. Said Tim Timken, "All of a sudden, bearings of smaller size can carry much greater loads, so every engineered product that our bearings go into has to be reevaluated to see how our customers can benefit from these tremendously improved product characteristics." To be sure, not every customer redesigned for power density, but among technology leaders—in Europe and Japan as well as in the United States—it was a great competitive advantage.[40]

Timken also benefited in the 1990s from having taken a rigorous approach to product uniformity. That had made the output of its plants interchangeable in the 1960s and was strengthened in the 1980s by the development of improved process controls and heightened standards for quality systems. With a network of highly automated distribution centers, built on the Bucyrus model and updated through advances in computer technology, interchangeable products made every Timken plant potentially a global supplier. Those centers included, in addition to

Bucyrus, a facility at Daventry (which remained open in the 1990s after the bearing factory closed); Timken Europa in Haan, Germany; and the newest addition, in Atlanta, Georgia, opened in 1989.[41]

For all those advantages, however, it was still a lengthy and painstaking process to gain a foothold in the market that mattered the most, at least symbolically—Japan. Peter Ashton referred to the four phases of relationship building in Japanese culture described by Patricia Gercik of the MIT Japan Program: "know me, trust me, believe me, marry me." Said Ashton, "The 'know me' stage sometimes takes a long time." An important success factor, he suggested, was the close personal attention Tim Timken paid to the issue, since many leading Japanese firms were also led by members of the founding family. By 1993, Ashton judged that Timken had reached the "trust me" stage. "They're beginning to trust us—yes, Timken does deliver on time; yes, Timken bearings don't go wrong." It was then that its business with Japan began to pick up significantly.[42]

Timken had first made inroads with Japanese manufacturers in both Japan and the United States in the 1980s. Under general manager Tadao Tsuneyoshi, Nihon Timken had begun to provide design support to Japanese industrial customers for bearing applications in construction equipment and railroad locomotives made for international markets—Hitachi locomotives built in Australia incorporated Timken bearings in 1986. In 1987, Nissan incorporated Timken bearings in some models of its cars assembled in Japan and sold both inside and outside the country. A important breakthrough in 1991 was a collaboration with Nissan on design of cars to be sold exclusively in Japan. That resulted in a front-wheel-drive application of the UNIPAC bearing on new models of some of its most popular cars in the Japanese market—the luxury cars, Cedric and Gloria. In the fall of 1991, Timken was one of twenty companies that participated in the U.S. Department of Commerce Japan Corporate Program, which brought representatives of Japan's Ministry of International Trade and Industry to Canton to visit the company. That was another important breakthrough. Timken's business in Japan increased by 50 percent in 1991. The following year the company established a design center there and doubled its engineering staff in order to provide the same kind of application engineering, and eventually physical testing, it provided to customers in the United States."[43]

Toyota first used Timken bearings in 1991 for a limited production model, the 2000GT, buying them "off-the-shelf . . . to evaluate Timken's products and services." But, said Tim Timken, "As Toyota's confidence grew, we became more involved in the design process. We started with a clean sheet of paper and worked with their engineers to provide the best bearings solution possible." Through that process, Timken bearings found applications on Toyota trucks, land cruisers, Tercels, and Corollas, plus some models made only in Japan. Toyota had a long tradition of close relationships with its suppliers, matched by Timken's well-established pattern of technical collaboration with customers. Those complementary experiences helped the relationship to blossom rapidly. In 1993, Dr. Shoichiro Toyoda, chairman of Toyota Motor Company and a member of its founding family, visited Timken in Canton to acknowledge his company's "growing reliance on Timken."[44]

In a 1994 edition of *Synergy,* a Toyota publication devoted to the topic of supplier relations, the carmaker elaborated on some of its reasons for doing business with Timken. Sales engineering was critical, in particular the staff of Japanese nationals at Nihon Timken. In addition, Timken had assigned one sales engineer to address Toyota's needs exclusively. "Working with the staff in Japan and the extensive resources in the United States, this engineer can respond more quickly to the needs of the Toyota engineering department." Another key factor was quality: "Since 1991, Timken has shipped Toyota 7.5 million pieces without a single defect—an astounding accomplishment." Toyota noted with favor the prizes Timken had won: Ford's TQE Award in 1993, given to only twenty out of 1,400 Ford suppliers in North America; the Shingo Prize won by Gaffney; and Toyota's own Superior Quality Performance Award. Finally, Toyota cited Timken for its commitment to improvement: "The company has not hesitated to embrace new concepts for manufacturing developed by Toyota. Their response times, for all their customers, have continued to improve. Timken's quality, already the best in the industry, has gotten even better. Its ability to assist clients in solving bearing and friction challenges continues to grow."[45]

Toyota's praise captured the way in which Timken's strengths—some long-established and some recently developed—combined to make it competitive in global markets. The company also made headway in the Japanese railroad industry in the 1990s. It had sold AP bearings to Japanese railroad builders since the 1970s but only for cars to be exported from Japan. In 1992, however, Nihon Timken sold AP bearings to Toshiba for railroad locomotives to be used in Japan. And in 1996, after a long courtship and technical collaboration, Timken scored another major success with the adoption of Timken bearings for the newest generation bullet train developed by Japan's second largest railroad passenger service company, Japan Railways West. It won that order with a new bearing designed specifically for the new trains to run at lower operating temperatures for a substantial savings in fuel. And, significantly, the development effort, coordinated by a railway sales engineering group based in Colmar, drew on the company's technical organizations in Japan, Ohio, and Great Britain. That kind of mobilization and coordination of resources was a central feature of Timken's increasing penetration of world markets.[46]

As part of the reorganization of 1993, the bearing business had created a new geographical organization—Asia Pacific and Latin America—as a step toward moving more aggressively into those two fast-growing regions. The new structure linked the plants in Brazil and Australia with regional marketing organizations, focusing them more on developing markets beyond their national borders. It also set Timken on a course of increasing its presence in the Pacific Rim countries, with sales organizations in South Korea, Singapore, Hong Kong, and China—in each case following the established pattern of hiring local engineers and training them in Canton. In 1994 Timken's sales office in Korea landed a major contract to supply 100 percent of the bearings used in a new passenger van produced by Ssangyong Motors. Transmissions were to be shipped from Colmar, while Australian Timken was to supply UNIPAC wheel bearings, made with its own cone assemblies and cups sent from Gaffney and Canton. Throughout the world, product uniformity and effective international linkages were important elements of Timken's market growth in the 1990s.[47]

For Latin American markets, in addition to Timken do Brasil, the company entered the 1990s with a sales unit in Florida, as well as established sales organizations in Mexico, Argentina, and Venezuela, each serving a large region encompassing neighboring countries. The automotive aftermarket was the major source of sales in those regions, and the opening of the Atlanta Export Service Center had given Timken a new edge in that segment by improving response time to the point that distributors no longer needed to maintain large inventories. The regional organizations expanded sales significantly in the 1990s and began to push into industrial and railroad applications. In Brazil, where the São Paulo plant produced bearings up to six inches in diameter, Timken was well established in diversified markets. But it was no less dependent on effective connections to U.S. facilities, from which it got all of its cages, half of its steel, and 20 percent of its rollers.[48]

Of course, success on a global scale still required growth in U.S. markets. Timken's non-U.S. sales grew by 6 percent a year in 1992–97 but remained steady at about 20 percent of total bearing sales, as expansion of business in domestic markets kept pace. There, the company advanced on many fronts. Pushing the power density concept, it developed some important new applications, for example, on truck transaxles. Timken also won back some applications that had been lost to lower-priced bearings in the 1980s—for example, the idler bearings used in engines produced by Detroit Diesel—by providing technical support in design and manufacturing. In addition to developing new product lines for Altavista and Asheboro, Timken kept older ones vital through product improvement. On a single day—September 13, 1994—the Columbus railroad bearing plant simultaneously celebrated the production of the ten-millionth AP

In 1994, veteran associate General Jefferson, Jr., was one of the speakers at the event celebrating the Columbus railroad plant's production of its ten millionth AP bearing. Akin (Chip) Muegel (background), president of the Railroad Bearing Business, also spoke to associates and visitors. General Jefferson is typical of many associates who have worked for Timken more than thirty years and also have relatives working at the company. His wife, two brothers, father, six uncles, and several cousins and their families have all worked at Timken.

bearing and the introduction of the next generation, the AP-2™ bearing, with fewer parts in a more compact design and improved seals. In addition, on the same day it announced a prototype generator bearing—an AP bearing with an electric generator built into its center, aimed at enabling the railroad industry to switch from air brakes to more effective electropneumatic brakes. Timken Research assumed a more high-profile role in selling products on the basis of such technical advances—in 1996 some 150 customers visited the facility for a close look at the support the company was able to provide.[49]

By the mid-1990s Timken was the sixth largest bearing producer worldwide, by market share, following SKF, NSK, NTN, Koyo Seiko, and FAG. Yet it held the largest share of the entire U.S. market for bearings—18 percent—followed by Torrington with 16 percent and all others below that. SKF was still the world leader, but 60 percent of its sales were in Europe. In the United States it had captured only 6 percent of the automotive market and only 12 percent overall. Naturally, the competition was not going to go away—SKF in 1996 was building a large new plant in Aiken, South Carolina, and a technical center in Michigan. Yet all the investments and changes of the 1980s and 1990s made Timken as strong a competitor as anyone. In addition, it had a unique advantage in materials. In 1986 SKF had merged its steel-making division with a Finnish company, Ovako Oy Ab, to form Ovako Steel AB, in which it retained 50 percent ownership. In 1991 it took back control of steel-making operations by re-acquiring the Swedish operations of

Ovako, but its action still left Timken as the only bearing manufacturer in the world with a sustained commitment to making its own steel. At the same time, while Steel's historic supporting role to Bearings remained critical, as a distinct business unit it was growing rapidly in some quite new directions.[50]

Timken Steel in the 1990s

In the 1980s, Timken's decision to build Faircrest aroused considerable comment, some of it skeptical. In the 1990s, both the company and Joe Toot, who had spearheaded the Faircrest project, began to gain recognition for leadership in the steel industry. The American Iron and Steel Institute (AISI), an organization representing most U.S. steel makers and the major companies in Canada and Latin America, elected Joe to a two-year term as its chairman in 1991. Though he had been a director of AISI since 1979 and a member of its executive committee since 1986, it was a departure for the chairmanship to go to someone other than an executive of one of the U.S. "Big Steel" companies. Joe's election was a sign of the extent to which smaller steel companies had become the more vital segment of the industry and to the prominent place Timken had in that segment. At the end of his term, Joe received AISI's highest honor, the Gary Memorial Medal, with the following citation: "Through his achievements both at Timken and at AISI, Joe has been a leader in modernizing and increasing the worldwide competitiveness of the North American steel industry." Also in 1993, in recognition of the company's developments in clean steel and the milestone Faircrest plant, Joe won the Medal for the Advancement of Research from the Materials Science Society of ASM International (the successor to the American Society for Metals). That was the same award William Umstattd had won in 1954, making Timken one of only seven companies in the medal's fifty-year history to win it more than once.[51]

The Faircrest plant also picked up some impressive awards. In 1994 it was one of five U.S. steel-making facilities to win the Top Operations and Plants (T.O.P.) Award from the steel industry journal *33 Metalproducing*. In the same year, *Industry Week* named it one of America's Best Plants—the first steel mill to be cited in the five years the award had been given. (Timken was one of just three companies to win twice for two separate plants, Faircrest and Bucyrus.) At the ceremony for the T.O.P. award, William Cordier, chairman and CEO of Canton Drop Forge, a Timken customer, spoke about what Faircrest had meant to the industry when it was built in the 1980s. The commitment to build a brand-new, "world-class" facility in Ohio, when it seemed that the U.S. steel industry was doomed to extinction, said Cordier, "appeared to be an unbelievable 'leap of faith'—or amazing self-confidence—or both." By completing construction of Faircrest ahead of schedule and below budget and hitting quality targets from the first day of operation, Timken had inspired other companies, like Canton Drop Forge, to set some goals beyond mere survival and to meet or exceed them. In the mid-1990s the survivors were competing successfully at home and beginning to expand abroad. "In listing the major reasons for our turnaround and that of our industry," said Cordier, "Faircrest ranks near the top."[52]

Yet Faircrest's awards were less for what it had been in the 1980s than for what it had achieved in the 1990s under the banner of continuous improvement. The plant had converted its operations entirely to self-directed teams, noted *Industry Week,* and used problem-solving teams to address specific issues. Plant manager Lee Sholley said, "If you put the best people on the job, then treat them like partners, the rest almost takes care of itself." From 1989 performance levels, it had reduced manufacturing costs by 25 percent, maintenance costs by 37 percent, electrical consumption by 18 percent, scrap and rework by 27 percent, customer rejects by 62 percent, warranty costs by 75 percent, work-in-progress inventory by 15 percent, and cycle time by 67 percent. By 1994, Faircrest's output in person hours per ton was nearly four times better than the average for U.S. and Japanese steel makers. With no major capital investment—but making the most of the extensive computerization of operations and working closely with suppliers and customers—the plant's personnel had taken a facility designed to produce 550,000 tons per year to annual production of 770,000 tons per year (a capacity increase of 38 percent), on its way toward nearly one million tons per year in 1998.[53]

Faircrest had made Timken the world leader in large alloy bars, a market it had not been in before. With Parapremium steel it also strengthened the company's leadership in mechanical tubing. Moreover, by the mid-1990s, it was the only producer of bearing grade steels, worldwide, using bottom-pour ingot casting instead of continuous casting. Timken's major U.S. competitors in mechanical tubing—CSC Industries, Inc. (formerly Copperweld) in Shelby, Ohio, and Quanex Corporation in Jackson, Michigan, and Fort Smith, Arkansas, as well as Sanyo and Sumitomo in Japan—were entirely caster based. With new casting technology they were producing bearing-grade steels of quality equal to the best that had been available in the early 1980s, but the standard had been raised. Faircrest stood alone as the top-quality steel supplier to the bearing industry. In 1993, George Matthews was part of a team that visited Sanyo in Japan, the steel maker Timken had judged the best in the world in its benchmarking exercises of 1980. "They were the high-water mark," he recalled. "Our drive was to be as good as Sanyo." But, said Matthews, when he went there, "They told me that they considered themselves the Timken of Japan. It was the highest compliment I ever received."[54]

Yet the growth of Timken's steel business did not, by any means, come from Faircrest alone. The selection of Chuck West in 1986 to be executive vice president for steel had signaled Tim and Joe's intention that the business should be taken in a new direction. West had joined Timken in 1954 with an engineering degree from Tri-State College in Indiana, and had risen through bearing research, from the physical laboratory to the lubrication laboratory in the 1960s, and to the position of chief engineer for industrial bearings in 1970. After leading the push to bring the research on the relationship between steel cleanness and bearing performance to the attention of top management, he had become director of research in 1979 and vice president for technology in 1982. Tim and Joe looked to West to strengthen the connection between Timken Research and the steel business (where there had not been much of one before) as well as the relationship between Steel and Bearings. Moreover, having committed to building a separate steel business with the investment in Faircrest, they wanted someone who could lead it down some quite untraditional avenues in search of growth.

A critical piece of the strategy was the revitalization of the Harrison Avenue steel plant. One of the fruits of collaboration between Timken Research and the steel business was the upgrading of continuous casting technology there, as part of the $1-billion capital program of the early 1990s. A new four-strand caster came on line in 1992. Built on the foundation of the old machine, it used technology from both Sumitomo and SMS Concast and produced larger blooms than the original caster (11-by-14.75 inches versus 9.5-by-12 inches). By 1994, Timken's customers had qualified the material, and virtually all of the plant's output—double what it had been in 1991—was continuously cast. Combined with an upgrade of downstream processing equipment—a small-bar rolling mill and bar-finishing operations—the caster positioned the company to expand in the medium-sized bar market. That, plus the large-bar capabilities at Faircrest, constituted a significant product-line diversification for a business that, just ten years before, had been confined almost exclusively to mechanical tubing. In 1996, Timken would push further in that direction, committing to build a new rolling mill and bar-processing facility next to the Harrison plant—in fact, on the same site where H. H. Timken had first launched steel-making operations eighty years before.[55]

Another significant new product line developed in the 1990s was precision steel components. Like package bearings, the steel components business arose from the challenges and opportunities presented by the de-integration of automotive manufacturing. Automakers wanted to reduce or eliminate the machining in their assembly operations. That trend threatened a large market for mechanical tubing, but it also opened up an avenue for higher-value-added products—either preformed shapes that still required some machining, or fully finished parts. In 1985, Timken had responded by developing three "preforms," and by 1993 it was producing more than thirty such parts. In 1993, it created Steel Parts as a discrete business, with its own general manager, marketing manager, and application engineer.

Courtesy: Mosey Manufacturing

Richard Brown, manager of the company's St. Clair plant, and George Mosey, co-owner of Mosey Manufacturing, inspect a steel component from this computer-numerically-controlled turning center. Mosey is a major supplier of machined components for the automotive and bearing industries. Timken began producing precision steel components in 1985. In 1993, the first dedicated manufacturing facility opened to meet growing customer demand. Today, four U.S. plants use technologically advanced equipment to produce precision, machined components from tubing and forgings to serve the automotive, bearing, and industrial industries worldwide.

Steel components manufacture played to Timken's strengths: it could produce parts from seamless tubing faster, more economically, and to tighter specifications than was possible with other processes; and it could draw on the company's deep technical resources for support in process and product development. Timken's bearing business knew as much about machining metal components as anyone. A new transmission developed by Ford to power its Contour, Probe, Mercury Mystique, and Mondeo models used Timken steel for fourteen of seventeen possible applications—nine of them to be sold as tubing to other Ford parts suppliers, and five as Timken steel parts. Timken's clean steel and alloy development capability were critical to that sale, as was its engineering support. Said Dan Sutter, the Detroit account manager who orchestrated it, "We capitalized on just about everything." In 1993, Steel Parts opened a manufacturing facility for finished components—St. Clair Precision Tubing Components, in Eaton, Ohio. After that the business expanded rapidly, as auto manufacturers increasingly removed machining operations from their own plants. In 1995, Timken opened the Tryon Peak plant in Columbus, North Carolina, to manufacture rings from mechanical tubing, and by the end of 1996 the business tripled in size, producing some 200 different parts. In 1997 Timken opened a second ring plant in Columbus and another facility in Winchester, Kentucky, to make forged rings from steel tubing for bearing races using a process developed at Timken Research over a period of ten years.[56] Timken renamed this business Precision Steel Components in 1998.

Timken's subsidiary, Latrobe Steel Company, also pursued some new avenues for growth in the mid-1990s. As part of the $1-billion capital spending program, Timken had invested in a new precision forging facility in 1992 that enhanced Latrobe's ability to produce bars and billets from high-strength alloy ingots for the machine-tool and aerospace markets that were its main focus. In 1994 it completed a new cold-finishing facility for round bar products for the same markets in Franklin, Pennsylvania. But in addition, Latrobe's president, former Timken chief metallurgist Phil Weigel, nurtured two small divisions—Special Products Division and Koncor Industries—that were not core businesses but were closely related and very profitable. Special Products had arisen within Latrobe in the 1960s, much like the steel components business within Timken in the 1990s, in response to its customers' need for more finished products. Koncor, located in Wauseon, Ohio, had grown out of Special Products and was both a finishing facility and a distribution center for tool steels. In 1992, when the aerospace market, Latrobe's mainstay, fell off drastically, Weigel began to develop a strategy for building upon those two divisions to make its business less cyclical in the long run.[57]

Bill Bowling followed Weigel as president of Latrobe in 1994–95 before rising to executive vice president for steel in 1996. Bowling pursued Latrobe's new strategy aggressively. In April 1996, Timken announced it would acquire Ohio Alloy Steels, in Youngstown, Ohio, a distributor of tool-steel products with a global purchasing network. Two months later, it agreed to acquire another distributor, Houghton & Richards, Inc. (H&R). H&R had a steel service center based in Marlborough, Massachusetts, and a network of distribution facilities in Massachusetts, Ohio, Illinois, Tennessee, and South Carolina. The integration of those two companies as subsidiaries of Latrobe created a distribution organization with broad geographical scope and also a good mix of products, since Ohio Alloy specialized in round products and H&R in flat sheet and plate as well as bar products.[58]

By 1996 many avenues of growth were coming together for Timken's steel business. Only one-fifth of its output now went to Timken bearing plants. In addition to its growth in bar markets, it had increased sales of mechanical tubing to the automotive industry by 100 percent over 1991. The steel components business had grown to 15 percent of total steel sales from 6 percent in 1993. Aided by the creation of a European sales office at Colmar in 1993, steel sales outside the United States had grown from just $5 million in 1990 to $30 million. Total steel revenues approached $1 billion. (See Figure 11.2.) The acquisitions in steel distribution merely increased the pace of growth and change. In fact, both Bearings and Steel were in a striking new pattern of growth by acquisition, hot in pursuit of their objectives for 1999.[59]

Accelerating Growth through Acquisitions

Between December 1995 and the end of 1997, Timken completed nine acquisitions and one joint venture. That was an extraordinary concentration of activity, though much of it was the result of plans in the works for several years. It reflected two main strategic thrusts: to grow rapidly and to mitigate the cyclical nature of Timken's core businesses. A strategy of aggressive growth by acquisition was a significant departure, to be sure. Yet it was clearly an extension of the broader phenomenon of opening up to outside influences and new ideas.

Part of that phenomenon with a special relevance to strategy was the shifting makeup of Timken's board of directors. By 1996, a majority of board members were outsiders. But there was already a critical mass by 1992, including the

FIGURE 11.2

**Timken Bearing and Steel Sales
1988–1997**

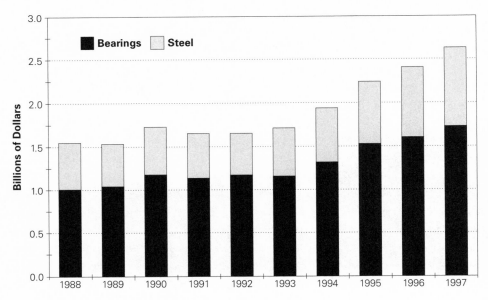

Source: The Timken Company Annual Report, 1997.

chairmen and former chairmen of some leading corporations with global reach—Robert Anderson of Rockwell International, Stanley C. Gault of Goodyear (and formerly of Rubbermaid), Robert W. Mahoney of Diebold, and Alton W. Whitehouse of Standard Oil. (See Appendix A.)

The urgency behind the strategies came from the aggressive goals for financial performance that had been set for the 1990s. Joe Toot explained, "We came to realize that we could not fulfill our financial expectations if we stuck to our traditional businesses alone. We began to move, therefore, from a strict, traditional product orientation toward the application of certain skills which we believed we possessed in an exceptional way—for example, in clean steels, rolling motion, surface finishes." The direction Timken moved with those skills was into the service sector of its core businesses.[60]

Latrobe's expansion in steel distribution was one move in that direction. Within months of completing its initial acquisitions, Latrobe pushed its new distribution business into international markets, with the acquisition of Sanderson Kayser, Ltd., in December 1996. Based in Sheffield, England, the heart of Britain's steel industry, Sanderson had deep roots in steel making and had been in the distribution business since 1957. It shipped to some 2,000 customers around the world from facilities in Sheffield, three other British cities—Birmingham, London, and Wigan—and Glasgow, Scotland. In mid-1997, Latrobe merged its two distribution subsidiaries, Ohio Alloy and H&R, into a single unit, OH&R Special Steels Company. In November, it announced that OH&R would build a new distribution facility in Greer, South Carolina, to serve growing markets in the U.S. Southwest.[61]

Timken also made acquisitions in the service sector of the bearing industry. In December 1995 it purchased Rail Bearing Service, Inc. (RBS), a Virginia-based company with seven facilities around the country for servicing and reconditioning railway bearings. For a time in the 1970s, Timken had itself been in the business of reconditioning its railroad bearings. But it had not been successful, and in 1977 had authorized RBS to do the work. Part of the intent at the time of the acquisition was to expand RBS outside the United States as a unit for both sales and service of Timken bearings. In August 1996, Timken established an RBS operation near British Timken in Northampton, England, to serve the newly privatized British rail system and to provide a base for expanding sales and service into Europe. Yet another move into the service sector came in May 1997, when MPB acquired Handpiece Headquarters, a repairer and rebuilder of dental handpieces, located in Orange, California. Dental handpieces had long been an important nonmilitary application of miniature bearings. The acquisition allowed MPB not only to apply its bearing knowledge to grow the distribution business but also to learn about and expand its bearing sales into that market, which Handpiece Headquarters served on an international scale.[62]

Rapid growth in non-U.S. markets was a second major theme of the acquisition program. Besides being countercyclical, it was an essential step for a company seeking worldwide leadership, especially after the end of the Cold War dramatically opened up the opportunities for expansion. In planning its move into the economies emerging from communism, Timken had the benefit of counsel from a distinguished group of international advisors. That was an institution that had grown out of a long-standing relationship between British Timken and the former son-in-law of John Pascoe, Lord John Eden. Elected a member of the British Parliament in 1958, Eden had served Pascoe as an advisor in the post of non-executive director—a position that many British corporate executives used to get advice from outsiders. He had continued the relationship with Umstattd, Bob and Henry Timken, and their successors, not as a director, but in an advisory role based on the same idea. As Eden said, there was "value in being able to talk freely to people who had no personal interest to promote or defend." In the 1980s he worked with Joe, Tim, and Maurice Amiel to develop strategy for the business in Europe. In the 1990s, the international advisory group included Madame Marie-France Garaud, president of the Institut Geopolitique and former counselor to French president Georges Pompidou, and Sigismund von Braun, former ambassador to France from the Federal Republic of Germany. In 1996, when von Braun retired, Carl H. Hahn joined the group. Hahn was former chairman of the board of management of two leading German companies, Volkswagen AG and Continental Tire. The group's role became especially important as Timken devised its strategy for entering the markets of Eastern Europe and China.[63]

As it had done in India, the company went into China in a joint venture. But in this case, its partner was a bearing company—Shandong Yantai Bearing Factory, located in Yantai, a city of 600,000 on the eastern coast of China, north of Shanghai. Timken took a 60 percent stake in the new venture, Yantai Timken Company Limited, created in March 1996. Timken was only one of many international companies rushing to gain a foothold in the huge Chinese market—SKF, for example, was another. Yet it had taken more than two years to choose its partner. Among the sixty manufacturers of tapered roller bearings in China, Shandong Yantai was, like Timken, a specialist in tapered roller bearings. A forty-year-old company, it was a leader in the field, with an established customer base in automotive, truck, and agricultural equipment markets. Those were the kinds of characteristics Timken looked for in all of its acquisitions, to provide a solid foundation on which it could expand through application of its financial resources as well as its technological and organizational capabilities.[64]

The company moved into Eastern Europe in March 1996 with the acquisition of the tapered roller bearing business of FLT Prema Milmet S.A., in Sosnowiec, Poland. This business was wholly owned by Timken and renamed Timken Polska

Sp.z.o.o. Maurice Amiel negotiated that deal, the first in which Poland agreed to privatize a state-owned manufacturer with 100 percent foreign ownership. The establishment of Timken Polska was an important first step into the bearing markets of Central Europe and beyond that, potentially, into Russia. At the end of 1997, Timken continued its push in that direction by acquiring a 70 percent stake in Rulmenti Grei S.A., a Romanian manufacturer of a full line of anti-friction bearings, with a plant near Bucharest, in Ploiesti.[65]

Of course, as in China, Timken's competitors were on the move as well. SKF became a major partner in a Polish company in 1995 and had expanded its presence in Asia by building factories in Thailand, Malaysia, Indonesia, and South Korea. NSK acquired Britain's largest bearing manufacturer, RHP, to become the second largest company in the industry after SKF. In short, consolidation was continuing at a rapid pace. In the 1960s, Timken had stood on the sidelines as SKF grew by acquisition to be the largest company in the worldwide industry. In the 1990s, it pursued growth as aggressively as anyone.[66]

In February 1997, Timken acquired the bearing assets of Gnutti Carlo S.p.A., in Cogozzo, Italy. A medium-sized producer of tapered roller bearings, competing successfully in the European truck, railroad, and industrial markets, Gnutti simply lacked the scale and resources to thrive on its own, long-term, in a consolidating industry. Yet it was a good strategic fit with Timken, selling to many of the same customers but producing a wider range of ISO (metric) bearings. There was a certain irony in the purchase—Gnutti was one of a number of Italian companies that had gone into the business of making inch-sized tapered roller bearings in the 1960s, capitalizing on the success of Timken's Green Light series. Another purchase with historic as well as strategic significance was a Torrington factory in Wolverhampton, England, which became MPB UK Ltd. in July 1997. That facility, producing super-precision ball and roller bearings for the aerospace market, was the same Fischer Bearings Company plant that had been owned and operated by British Timken and sold in 1959 in a swift exit from the ball bearing industry. It was a neat bit of symbolism for the shift in strategic thinking that had occurred in the company since then.[67]

Joe Toot, who had shared in the development and led the execution of the strategy of the 1990s, retired as president and CEO at age sixty-two at the end of 1997. (In support of the policy of promotion from within, Tim and Joe had established incentives to advance the normal retirement age for executives.) Like Umstattd and Markley, Joe would stay involved on the board of directors as chairman of the executive committee. He would also continue to help Timken nurture the important relationships he had forged in China, Poland, and elsewhere in the 1990s. Under his presidency, since 1979, Timken's revenues had more than doubled, most of that growth coming in the last ten years. Indeed, Timken's ten-year rate of growth in earnings per share exceeded that of some of the best-known U.S. growth companies, such as Coca-Cola, WalMart, Walt Disney, and Nucor. Also during the 1990s, its return on capital doubled, its market value nearly tripled, and its dividends increased by more than 40 percent. In the five years from 1992 through 1997, the company outperformed its bearing and steel competitors and the S&P 500 in total returns. (See Figure 11.3.)[68]

Those were only the most easily measured achievements Joe's leadership had helped to produce. In the Faircrest project, he had established an approach to stimulating higher performance that involved, in his own words, "setting high standards and expectations; convincing people they could meet or exceed them; rallying a large constituency around a common cause; then reporting, recognizing, and celebrating results." Carried forward into Breakthrough, ACI, and the mission to be the world's best-performing manufacturing company, his approach became a formula not only for improving performance but also for driving the organizational change on which improved performance depended. To skeptics who questioned the company's seriousness in pursuing its mission of being the best, Joe liked to say, "Somebody is going to be first; why not us?" That spirit was a big part of what made Timken, after nearly one hundred years, as dynamic as it had ever been.[69]

FIGURE 11.3

**Shareholder Returns
1992–1997**

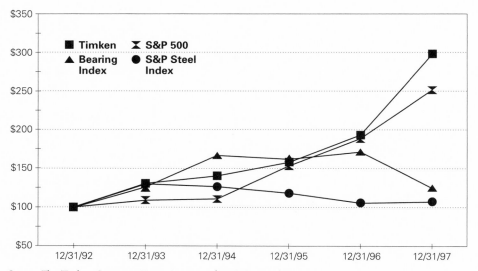

Source: The Timken Company, Proxy Statement for 1998 Annual Meeting.

It is the genius of the Timken family, and of the modified form of managerial enterprise they developed, to maintain an active role and still create an environment in which such talented professional managers could flourish. The continuity of leadership has been extraordinary: from H. H. to Tim, just four individuals have led the firm for one hundred years. They have guided the company's strategy, and, more important, they have infused it with the meaning of fundamental corporate purpose and values. The family's role has been in one sense conservative—it has preserved the traditions that have provided strength over the years. Yet many of the most significant initiatives and changes have originated in the chairman's office. Now Tim, having presided over the most sweeping changes of all, will—with a new management team—take Timken into its second century.

Timken at Ninety-Nine: Continuity and Change

*I*n the spring of 1982, as it became clear that the company was in a down year, *Business Week* printed an article titled "Why Timken's 'Stability' Will Save its Bottom Line." Timken executives had not agreed to be interviewed for the piece, but customers, competitors, and industry analysts had assured the magazine that Timken would "weather the storm." Their reasons touched upon a number of historic strengths. One was its steadfast commitment to its core businesses. "Timken refuses to accept the idea of 'maturity' in its sector," said *Business Week*, "choosing instead to invest steadily in research and new facilities." As a specialist in tapered roller bearings, it had remained "in the forefront of that technology." That, plus the extraordinary technical support provided to customers through its sales and service engineers, had earned it "a unique spot in the industry." Another strength was its cadre of managers, who made lifetime careers with the company and, *Business Week* said, "proudly identify with Timken's premier status, both in [Canton] and in its industry." Faircrest at that time was still a "costly and risky" investment amid a declining market and heightened competition. Yet there was a general expectation that the new steel mill would "go a long way" toward enabling Timken to emerge from the slump with its market leadership intact. Among "envious" competitors there was consensus that the company's ability to take such a long-term view was largely a factor of the sustaining role of the Timken family as owner-managers.[1]

At the same time, this portrait of Timken captured some of the historic idiosyncrasies of an industry leader still riding the wave of the era of high demand. Its technically advanced products and technical support had enabled it to "lock in many of its customers." But, noted *Business Week,* "Timken expects much from its customers, too." One of them cited an instance in which the company had rejected a large order because the buyer had not specified part numbers in the proper sequence. *Business Week* said, "It refuses to deviate even slightly from standard procedures . . . [and it] has consistently raised prices and stuck with them, no matter what." The magazine also drew a contrast between Timken's "ultramodern" products and "management practices" that seemed "antiquated"—epitomized by its hardball approach to dealings with its unionized workforce and its executives punching in and out every day on time clocks. Finally, *Business Week* noted the company's apparent imperviousness to the opinions of the financial community.[2]

After fifteen years of crisis and renewal, it is instructive to look back on that snapshot from the other side. On one level, the notion that the company could "weather the storm" by maintaining "stability" seems as outdated as a time clock— eliminated for Timken executives in 1986 and replaced with computerized record keeping for hourly associates in 1994.[3] Those aspects of the 1982 culture that simply had to change are clearly recognizable in the *Business Week* portrait. And, indeed, change has been the dominant theme in the company's experience since then. In the midst of it all, however, the persistence and importance of historic strengths should not be underestimated. Both continuity and change are central features of the success story of recent years, and maintaining an effective balance between them remains a challenge for the future.

One thing is certain—changes will continue, because the forces driving them are unabated. The conditions that allowed Timken to resist change for so long are gone forever. The all-important development of customer focus, for example, is necessary to survival but does not guarantee it. One triumph of the 1990s was to win back a large part of lost business with Caterpillar, one of Timken's long-time best customers for both bearings and steel. In the old days, recalled Jack Porter, Caterpillar's director of centralized purchasing, Timken had been "the only game in town in terms of tapered roller bearings." Its pricing had been changeable and invariably too high, and it had been intractable on issues important to Caterpillar, such as branding. Caterpillar was accustomed to putting its own name on parts, and to taking the replacement business that resulted. That was not acceptable to Timken. Their relationship was adversarial, and when, in the mid-1980s, Japanese bearing makers began to offer tapered roller bearings in the larger sizes that Caterpillar used, at lower prices, it switched a good portion of its business.[4]

Yet that was not what either company wanted, and they had begun to turn it around in 1990. After a series of "candid" talks, Caterpillar signed a multiyear agreement to buy 100 percent of certain bearing sizes from Timken. In 1991 it also signed its first-ever multiyear steel contract with Timken. Those agreements concluded, the two companies began a technical collaboration—for example, exchanging expertise on heat treating and grinding—while the commercial staffs continued to work on pricing and other tough issues. At the end of 1995, they resolved the branding dispute, with Timken consenting to produce bearings for Caterpillar carrying both trademarks and a Caterpillar part number—a significant departure in practice for both companies. Remarked Porter about Timken, "They have become—in my opinion, anyway—very, very, very customer focused." By the late 1990s, between bearings and steel, Timken would be Caterpillar's largest supplier.[5]

Bearing shipments to Caterpillar increased by 180 percent between 1991 and 1995. But even so, reported Gene Martin, district manager for bearing sales in Peoria, Timken has lost business on applications—for which it had provided considerable technical support—to competitors offering the bearings at a lower price. The company has given up some other bearing sales because it could not keep up production in pace with Caterpillar's increasing demand. In the new industrial landscape, Timken must, in Martin's words, "run just as hard as everyone else to deliver on time at competitive prices"—even while chasing demand.[6]

In every respect, the company has become more driven—a change kept in motion by its opening up to the outside. One area in which that is noticeable is in relations with the investment community. Now, as in mainstream corporate America, the job descriptions of Timken's chairman and its CEO include getting the company's message out to Wall Street. In no way has Tim Timken had to break the family mold more decisively than in his effort in the 1990s to fill that role of communicator. As late as December 1996, the *New York Times* reported continuing complaints from analysts that the company did not give them "the red carpet treatment" when in Canton. Yet both Tim and Joe by then had taken to giving interviews and addressing analysts' gatherings in London, Zürich, and Singapore as well as in New York. And, in June 1997, they hosted a large gathering at the New York Stock Exchange to celebrate Timken's seventy-fifth year on the exchange and three-hundredth consecutive dividend paid.[7]

In other ways as well, Timken's top managers have begun to project an image more in line with that of other large public corporations. In 1991, they moved into new corporate offices *across* Dueber Avenue from the bearing plant.

The spaces on "the third floor" are modest by contemporary standards. There are no corner offices and little privacy—each office has windows in all four walls, echoing the original design of H. H. Timken. Yet they are a far cry from the austere surroundings of Mahogany Row. Another notable change: after so many years of publishing the minimum amount of financial information required, Timken in November 1996 earned recognition from large institutional investors for its reporting on revenues and profits by business and geographical segments. Philosophical changes are in evidence as well, for example, in a 1997 piece written by Tim Timken for the company newspaper, *Timken World*. "Critics decry Wall Street's emphasis on quarterly results," Tim wrote. "Yet in our economic system, the ability to attract investors over the long haul is the yardstick measuring our future." In fact, said Tim, "Wall Street puts more pressure on all of us, and that's good. It helps keep companies competitive."[8]

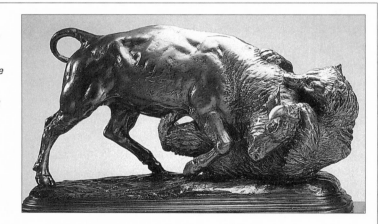

The bull defeating the bear is a symbol of the New York Stock Exchange. The sculpture was presented to Timken in June 1997 at a ceremony in New York to commemorate The Timken Company's seventy-fifth year as a member of the Exchange and to celebrate the company's three-hundredth consecutive dividend paid to shareholders. In the same month, Timken common stock split, two-for-one, for the fifth time in its history.

The leadership of Tim and Joe Toot, particularly in the 1990s, has been largely about putting that kind of pressure on the organization, focusing it more on financial goals. That has meant a continuing transformation of the management culture. As in most large U.S. corporations, Timken's managerial hierarchy is smaller in size and flatter than it was a decade ago. The workload is greater, scrutiny of performance is more intense, raises are no longer automatic, and job security is less certain. That was one of the major outcomes of the 1980s crisis, Tim explained: "Associates had to take more responsibility to fight for their jobs. If they wanted to be paid more, they had to be more productive than people in Japan and

Germany." Accordingly, the compensation system has moved away from the idea of pay as reward "for a job well done," and the expectation of regular increases. Now a significant portion of all salaries is tied to specific goals for financial performance—the type of compensation system, according to Joe Toot, "prevalent in the outstanding firms, no matter what industry they are in." Such changes have extended the drive, begun with the reorganization of 1986, to make the engineering culture more businesslike.[9]

The company's embrace of lean manufacturing has also been a force for cultural change. Associate empowerment and team problem-solving inevitably have undermined the acceptance of authoritarianism and territorialism that allowed the "bulls of the woods" to flourish. Tim and Joe are both too intense and hands-on to have abandoned top-down management entirely. Yet from the top they have driven initiatives that will continue to move the organization away from command-and-control in the years to come. Chief among those is the commitment to the discipline of continuous improvement, a fundamental precept of which is to enlist and honor the contributions of all personnel.[10]

To be sure, Timken management remains predominantly an organization of engineers, with its strong apprenticeship and training programs intact. The policy of promotion from within also is still in force. "Ultimately," said Joe Toot, "we believe we will get better performance that way." Yet, in a departure from the rigid adherence of the past, he and Tim have bent that rule in a growing number of cases to recruit people in areas such as communications and marketing, where they perceived the need to go outside for expertise and experience the company lacked. They also hired a corporate director of finance, Sallie Ballantine, from outside as part of a broader effort to push along the advancement of women into leadership positions. That has been a difficult change to enact, said Joe, simply because "the institution was so male oriented." Nevertheless, there has been progress throughout the company. Bucyrus, New Philadelphia, and the Canton bearing plant all have had women managers in recent years, and on the steel side Deborah Anderson became plant manager at Faircrest in mid-1998. The highest-ranking woman in a line position, Donna Demerling, became president of MPB in 1997.[11]

In that area, and in general, maintaining the policy of promotion from within has undoubtedly slowed the pace of change. Yet historically the policy played a central role in creating and sustaining shared values and sense of mission, and that remains an essential function today. Career paths for rising executives now include not only international postings but in many cases also assignments that cross the line between Bearings and Steel. That change, plus geographical expansion and the elaboration of the business unit structure, has created many more opportunities for managers to hold positions of real authority. With the greater uncertainty of financial rewards, ensuring that kind of opportunity for advancement seems more important than ever. In an age when the career advice in most professional fields is to anticipate multiple job changes in a lifetime, Timken remains a company in which careers of twenty-five years or more are common. That fact speaks volumes about the importance Tim and Joe have placed upon maintaining a cohesive management culture.

At the same time, however, they have pushed to extend the shared values and mission onto the shop floor. Said one long-time associate in the Canton bearing plant, "There is a lot more pride now in working for Timken than there was twenty years ago. [Then] you had a job, you made big money, but you didn't talk about your job once you left. I think it has evolved to the point now where The Timken Company makes money because *everybody* at The Timken Company is good at what they do." As a result, he said, the feeling now is, "'We are members of The Timken Company.' Before it was just, 'I work for The Timken Company.'" The fundamental shift in attitude reflected in those remarks is surely the most dramatic aspect of the cultural changes in progress.[12]

Timken management in Canton remains resolutely anti-union, and where unions exist, union sentiment remains strong. But both sides have begun to show greater acceptance: the company of the fact that the union is not going to go away, and the union of the fact that Timken is not going to be like other companies. "We work more closely with the union than twenty years ago," said Tim Timken. There is no chance in the foreseeable future, however, that the company will attempt to work in partnership with the USW, as some in the steel and auto industries have done with their unions. The political divisions between corporate management and the unionized workforce in Ohio are still clear-cut. *New York Times* reporter Michael Winerip lived in Canton and covered politics and society in Stark County in the presidential election year of 1996. He found that there, as elsewhere, support for the Democratic party is no longer as solid among union members as it once was. But in the company, Winerip reported, "there is an expectation that top corporate managers will take an active interest in the Republican party." Tim and other members of his family are Republican stalwarts. Timken's stand on dumping of imports has aligned it with organized labor on that issue. But, said one union member at Faircrest, on most issues of concern to labor, such as workers' compensation, "the union is on one side and they are on the other. Maybe it isn't talked about as much, but it will always be there."[13]

Nevertheless, there is simply not the kind of adversarial relationship that characterized earlier periods. "There is not the union bashing or the company bashing that you used to see years ago," said one Canton union member. The crisis of the 1980s and the revival of the 1990s have undoubtedly played the major role in that change. The concessions the union made to enable the Faircrest plant to be built were pivotal. Since then, while Timken has continued to build new plants in non-union environments in the U.S. South, it has also invested in Canton—between

1990 and 1996, nearly $50,000 for each of the 6,500 associates working in the area. Those investments, together with the cultural change associated with the move to lean manufacturing, have formed the practical basis for greater alignment around corporate objectives that has reduced the passion in ideological differences.[14]

As in every other area, there is an interesting mix of the old and the new in the programs that aim to build alignment on that broader front. In 1995, Timken introduced the Dedication to Excellence Award—"the highest corporate distinction an associate can attain." It is conferred twice yearly on teams that achieve outstanding performance in continuous improvement. Yet it coexists with the long-established program of awards "for years of loyal service"—the company's attempt in 1993 to cut back on service awards having met with a strong outcry of protest at all levels. Company publications—*Exchange* for U.S. personnel, *Contact* for European personnel, and *Timken World* for both U.S. and international associates—are a humanizing and unifying element in an organization no longer just hierarchical, but geographically dispersed as well. They still provide a vehicle for management's message, but they also now offer a level of concrete information on corporate strategy, competition, and results that would have been unthinkable just a decade ago.[15]

No integrating force in the company is more traditional than the role of the Timken family. Yet in that, too, there are elements of change as well as continuity. In the 1990s, Tim has acted as much like an activist shareholder as a fourth-generation owner-manager. In the longer term, he has presided over, in his own words, the "building [of] a modern, stand-alone, public corporation." Between personal holdings and those of the Timken Foundation, the family controls 19 percent of Timken stock. But, in addition, 60 percent of all Timken personnel are now shareholders. As of early 1998, they collectively owned 13 percent of the company, a figure likely to increase, since Timken has cleared the way for stock-holding by non-U.S. associates in some countries. The family block is thus no longer the only bulwark protecting the company's independence. Three Timkens are currently board members—Tim, his younger brother Jack Timken, and their cousin, John M. Timken, Jr. However, in contrast to 1975, when Tim became chairman of an all-insider board, outside directors are now in the majority. "The dominance of the Timken family perspective has diminished," said Tim, "during this long transition from a family company."[16]

The outside directors will have an important role to play as the transition continues. Tim will be sixty years old when the company reaches its one-hundredth anniversary—he expects to retire at sixty-five. It is as yet unclear who will succeed him as chairman. Like other families still active as owner-managers in public companies, the Timkens require family members to have skills and training comparable to non-family executives. But they must also be willing to take on a heavy burden of leadership. One of Tim's sons, Henry H. (Kurt) Timken II, worked for five years in the company, then completed an MBA degree and went to work for Rockwell International, "to see how other companies did things." Ultimately, however, he decided on a non-business career. Jack's thirty-year-old son, Ward J. (Tim) Timken, Jr., is now the only member of the next generation active in the company. He recently advanced to the position of vice president for the bearing business in Latin America but has yet to take a seat on the board. At the same time, Joe Toot has retired without a successor—Tim has taken on the titles of president and CEO and created an office of the chairman with Bill Bowling and Bob Leibensperger serving as co-chief operating officers in addition to their duties as business unit presidents. Helping the company work out a solid, long-term succession plan will be an important task for the board in the next five years.[17]

Whatever the exact course the changing of the guard may take, family members remain convinced that the best outcome would be to retain the formula of a Timken as chairman with a non-family president. That formula, said Tim, "offers the opportunity for people who have become professional managers to rise to the very top, get the rewards, and exercise the power that goes with it." At the same time, he noted, "We believe that the continuity of family involvement by people who are committed to working in the company has been an important asset."[18] Looking back over recent history, it would be hard to argue against that assertion. Family shareholders provided the patient capital that permitted Timken to make the investments needed to reassert industry leadership and lay the foundation for renewal of profitable growth. Just as important, within the corporate culture, sustained family engagement ensured a stable center around which essential change could take place.

Tim's highly visible role as chairman has, of course, been critical. Jack Timken's role has been less visible but also essential. In addition to being a corporate vice president, he is president of The Timken Company Charitable Trust and of The Timken Company Educational Fund, which provides college scholarships to the children of associates. Yet one of his most important corporate roles is the most informal one. By getting out and meeting people in Timken offices and plants, Jack has provided the kind of down-to-earth personal connection to the family that was one of his uncle Henry Timken's greatest contributions. Said Joe Toot, "He has come to know nearly every associate in this company." As necessary as it has been to make Timken more like other large public corporations in governance and outward image, the inner life of the organization has surely benefited from the persistence of that touch of the traditional family firm.[19]

The Timken family's commitment to community also has persisted as a defining aspect of its role in the company. While the fortunes of many of America's industrial elite have gone into charitable foundations supporting a wide range of social and cultural causes, the heirs of H. H. Timken have continued to honor his wish that the major portion of the family's philanthropy should be focused on the communities in which the company operates. In Bob Timken's generation, it was he among the three Timken brothers who assumed the most direct responsibility for the work of the family foundations. In the next, it has been Jack, who divides his time between the company and his duties as president of the Timken Foundation. A local journalist commented in 1987 on the contrasting roles of the Timken brothers in the Canton community: "Tim is the one who makes the announcement when the company lays off 100 workers, but Jack gets to tell people they're going to get $1 million for their charity."[20] Those are two sides of the coin of duty that Bob inherited from his father and passed along to his sons. They also reflect a third generation of Timken brothers working out complementary ways to contribute to the family enterprise.

In the annals of U.S. business, the achievement of such continuity is rare. In only a very few long-lived U.S. industrial firms are the fortunes and careers of the founding family still tied up in the company. As the *New York Times*'s Winerip noted, that family character and the conservative business principles it has fostered—the financial conservatism, the investments for the long term, the focus on maintaining technological leadership in chosen industries, and the commitment to community—seem "out of step" to many observers of the U.S. business scene. "The rap on The Timken Company from Wall Street analysts," he wrote, "is that it could be even more profitable if it would only be more aggressive about downsizing its work force . . . if it were not so preoccupied with striving to produce the top quality bearing and steel products in the world and if it was less worried about its responsibility to the people of Canton."[21]

But those characteristics are more common and more highly regarded in other parts of the world. As Maurice Amiel has noted, they made the company "not entirely American," an advantage in Europe. In 1991, the government of François Mitterrand gave Tim Timken France's highest recognition for service, appointment to membership in the French Legion of Honor. William Umstattd had received that award in 1961; Amiel received it in 1993; and Joe Toot, in 1998. Those repeated distinctions over so many years speak well for the traditions on which The Timken Company has been built. To be sure, public honors do not guarantee competitive success. Yet the respect the company has earned abroad for being both an industry leader and a good corporate citizen is an advantage in an era when growth worldwide will depend to a great degree on succeeding with joint ventures and acquisitions.[22]

There is also, however, a certain irony in juxtaposing those awards, since the trick for Tim and Joe has been to maintain continuity with the best of the Umstattd era while shaking off the rigidities it created. As times change, successful organizations with strong traditions must sift through them to determine which are the

In the 1990s, dramatic change has renewed The Timken Company's historic sense of purpose and identity, a central element of which has been commitment to plant communities. Seen here are its corporate headquarters, based in Canton, Ohio, since 1901.

core strengths and which are simply old. Timken has been deeply engaged in that task in the 1980s and 1990s. The effort has brought renewal through cultural change. It has also prompted a rethinking of strategy and ultimately a cautious but significant adjustment of corporate identity and mission. One result: Steel has become a full partner with Bearings. That has opened up for the first time the opportunity to capture the full value of the synergies that have resulted from the company's unique marriage of steel making and precision manufacturing and its long-term quest for competitive advantage through material quality. The power density concept—which applies to both steel and bearing products—and the rise of Precision Steel Components provide examples of those synergies at work. At the same time, the company has opened up to looking at opportunities for growth in terms of organizational capabilities, not just products, a change that has taken it into bearing service and steel distribution. Thus far, those have been invigorating changes. Their full significance will become clear as Timken moves into its second century.

Naturally, some in the company worry that its venture into some market and geographical niches for ball bearings (through the acquisitions of MPB and Rulmenti Grei) and the development of a cylindrical roller bearing (Z-Spexx) to be sold under the Timken name are steps onto a slippery slope leading away from technological leadership in tapered roller bearings. That is a legitimate concern for those responsible for balancing continuity and change in the future. Timken's history forcefully demonstrates the ways in which focus can help a company avoid falling into the trap of making product maturity a self-fulfilling prophecy. Yet there is little in that history to suggest that Timken will cede leadership in tapered roller bearings anytime soon. The concept of value in the reduction of friction remains as valid and powerful today as ever. The dramatic improvement in bearing performance and advances in manufacturing technology have given new life to the drive to expand applications and to the technical collaboration with customers that has played such a large role in product innovation over the years.

The story of the recent past is not one of abandoning the historic sense of purpose but of refreshing it and building upon it. In the long run, of course, the capacity for such renewal through change is as necessary to survival as is the steady adherence to guiding principles. It is through both that the Timken name has taken on a life of its own, not just as a trademark, but as a focus of pride in product for the company's associates around the world.

Appendix A

The Timken Company Officers and Directors, 1899–1998

Name	Office	Dates of Tenure
Henry Timken	President	1899–1909
	Director	1899–1909
Henry H. Timken	Director	1899–1940
	Vice President	1906–09
	President	1909–29
	Chairman	1929–40
William R. Timken	Director	1899–1938
	Secretary/Treasurer	1906–14
	Treasurer	1914–17
	Vice President/Treasurer	1917–20
	Vice President	1920–38
G. C. Kimbark	Director	1904–6
	Secretary/Treasurer	1905
Georgia Timken Fry	Director	1904–6
	Director	1914–21
A. R. Demory	General Superintendent	1906–9
	Director	1906–10
C. W. Lewis	Assistant Secretary and Manager—Sales	1906–9
	Director	1906–10
*Austin Lynch	Director	1909
Heman Ely	Secretary	1914–20
	Director	1914–25
	Vice President & Treasurer	1920–25
J. George Obermier	Director	1914–35
	Vice President	1920–35

Notes:
*Denotes outside director.

Official listings of officers before 1905 and directors before 1904 not found; official listings of officers and directors for 1910–13 and 1915–16 not found.

Name	Office	Dates of Tenure
J. Fred Strough	Secretary	1920–25
	Director	1922–30
	Secretary/Treasurer	1925–30
Marcus T. Lothrop	Vice President	1925–29
	Director	1925–32
	President	1929–32
Harry J. Porter	Vice President	1925–38
Tracy V. Buckwalter	Vice President	1925–45
W. A. Brooks	Assistant Secretary/Treasurer	1927–29
Freeman F. Tudor	Assistant Secretary	1929
Louis M. Klinedinst	Vice President	1930–48
	Director	1934–51
R. Charles Brower	Assistant Secretary/Treasurer	1929
	Secretary/Treasurer	1930–52
	Director	1935–52
Judd W. Spray	Vice President	1928–34
	Director	1929–34
Henry H. Timken, Jr.	Director	1930–68
	Vice President	1934–40
	Chairman & Vice President	1940–43
	Chairman & Executive Vice President	1943–59
	Chairman	1959–68
William E. Umstattd	Executive Vice President	1931–34
	Director	1933–73
	President	1934–59
	Chairman, Executive Committee	1959–73
John A. Riley	Assistant Secretary/Treasurer	1933–52
	Secretary/Treasurer	1952
*Alwin C. Ernst	Director	1929–33
	Ernst & Ernst (Cleveland, Ohio)	
Frederick J. Griffiths	Director	1932–36
	(President—Timken Steel & Tube Company)	

Name	Office	Dates of Tenure
William R. Timken	Director	1936–87
	Vice President	1941–59
	President & Chairman—Finance Committee	1959–64
	President	1964–68
	Chairman	1968–75
	Vice Chairman & Chairman Executive Committee	1975–78
	Chairman of the Board Emeritus	1987–90
John E. Fick	Director	1940–66
	Vice President	1943–61
	Vice President—Steel & Tube Operations	1961
Albert M. Donze	Director	1940–59
	Vice President	1943–58
Albert L. Bergstrom	Vice President	1945–61
	Director	1952–65
	Vice President—Engineering	1961
Whitley B. Moore	Vice President	1948–58
	Director	1952–59
Dwight A. Bessmer	Vice President	1952–57
	Director	1952–60
	Executive Vice President	1957–59
	President	1959
Herbert E. Markley	Secretary	1953–55
	Assistant to the President	1955–58
	Vice President	1958
	Executive Vice President	1959–68
	Director	1959–83
	President	1968–79
George L. Deal	Treasurer	1953–55
	Secretary/Treasurer	1955–64
	Director	1960–76
	Vice President—Finance	1964–73
John M. Timken	Director	1956–71
Paul J. Reeves	Vice President	1958–61
	Director	1960–72
	Vice President—Sales	1961–70

Name	Office	Dates of Tenure
Herchel M. Richey	Vice President	1958
Henry A. Tobey	Vice President	1959–61
	Director	1960–66
	Vice President—Bearing & Rock Bit Operations	1961–63
	Vice President—Bearing Operations	1963–66
Sir John Pascoe	Director (Chairman—British Timken)	1959–62
Richard L. Frederick	Vice President	1960
	Vice President—International Division	1961–67
	Vice President—Industrial Relations & Services	1967–75
Richard A. Gulling	Controller & Assistant Treasurer	1960–64
	Treasurer	1964–74
	Vice President—Finance & Treasurer	1974–85
	Director	1976–93
	Vice President—Finance	1985
Brooks R. Powell	Assistant Secretary	1960–64
	Secretary	1964–79
Edwin S. Hoopes, Jr.	Vice President—Steel & Tube Operations	1962–71
	Director	1966–72
Stephen F. Bennett	Director (Managing Director—British Timken)	1962–76
Harley J. Urbach	Vice President—Engineering	1962–64
	Vice President—Engineering & Research	1964–72
	Director	1966–74
David N. Borden	Assistant Secretary	1964–67
Clyde L. Van Horn	Assistant Treasurer	1964–73
William R. Timken, Jr.	Director	1965–Present
	Corporate Vice President	1968–73
	Vice Chairman	1973–75
	Chairman	1975–98
	Chairman, President, & CEO	1998–Present
James E. O'Connor	Vice President—Bearing Operations	1966–83
	Director	1972–84

Name	Office	Dates of Tenure
Norman H. Peterson	Vice President—Corporate Services	1965–78
	Vice President—Corporate Relations	1978–83
Joseph F. Toot, Jr.	Vice President—International Division	1967
	Corporate Vice President	1968–73
	Director	1968–Present
	Executive Vice President	1973–79
	President	1979–92
	President & CEO	1992–98
	Chairman, Executive Committee	1998–Present
Dewitt C. Cox	Assistant Secretary	1967–73
James W. Pilz	Vice President—Marketing	1970–73
	Director	1972–96
	Vice President—International Operations	1973–77
	Senior Vice President	1977–79
	Executive Vice President	1979–86
Ward J. Timken	Director	1971–Present
	Vice President	1992–Present
Ralph T. Shipley	Vice President—Steel Operations	1971–80
	Director	1973–81
Ralph E. McKelvey	Vice President—Engineering & Research	1972–80
	Director	1974–80
Wyn E. McCoy	Vice President—Marketing	1973–77
	Director	1976–83
	Vice President—International Operations	1977–80
	Vice President—Engineering & Research	1980–82
Robert W. Lang	Vice President—Industrial Relations	1975–78
	Vice President—Personnel Administration	1978–85
	Vice President—Personnel Administration & Logistics	1985–89
E. Ronald Knapp	Director (Managing Director—Timken Europe)	1976–85
John H. Fellows	Vice President—Marketing	1977–85
	Director	1980–88
	Vice President—Marketing—Steel	1985–87
Donald L. Hart	Vice President—Communications & Logistics	1978–85
	Vice President—Bearings— North/South America	1985–95

Name	Office	Dates of Tenure
*Robert G. Wingerter	Director Retired Chairman of the Board Libby–Owens–Ford Company (Toledo, Ohio)	1978–89
*Joseph S. Hoover	Director Retired Vice Chairman & Secretary The Hoover Company (North Canton, Ohio)	1978–89
J. Kevin Ramsey	Secretary Secretary/Treasurer Vice President—Finance & Law, Secretary/Treasurer Vice President—Finance	1979–85 1985–86 1986–90 1990–92
Peter J. Ashton	Vice President—International Operations Vice President—Bearing Operations Director Executive Vice President—Bearings Executive Vice President & President—Bearings	1980–83 1983–85 1983–95 1985–92 1992–95
Leo A. Fiedorek	Vice President—Steel Operations	1980–82
Alfred B. Glossbrenner	Vice President—Steel Operations Vice President—Steel	1982–85 1985–87
Charles H. West	Vice President—Engineering & Research Director Vice President—Technology Executive Vice President—Steel Executive Vice President & President—Steel	1982–85 1984–Present 1985–86 1986–92 1992–96
Charles E. Craig	Vice President—International Operations Executive Vice President—Steel Director	1983–85 1985–86 1985–86
John J. Schubach	Vice President—Strategic Management Vice President—Strategic Management & Continuous Improvement Senior Vice President—Strategic Management & Continuous Improvement	1984–96 1996–98 1998–Present
John M. Timken, Jr.	Director	1986–Present
*Alton M. Whitehouse	Director Retired Chairman & CEO The Standard Oil Company (Cleveland, Ohio)	1986–Present

Name	Office	Dates of Tenure
Robert L. Leibensperger	Vice President—Technology	1986–95
	Executive Vice President & President— Bearings	1995–98
	Executive Vice President, Chief Operating Officer, & President—Bearings	1998–Present
*Stanley C. Gault	Director Retired Chairman & CEO, The Goodyear Tire & Rubber Company (Akron, Ohio) and Rubbermaid Inc. (Wooster, Ohio)	1988–Present
*Robert Anderson	Director Chairman Emeritus, Rockwell International Corporation (Costa Mesa, California)	1988–98
Maurice Amiel	Vice President—Bearings—Europe, Africa, & West Asia	1988–94
	Vice President and Chairman—Bearings— Europe, Africa, & West Asia	1994–96
Bill J. Bowling	Vice President—Human Resources & Logistics	1990–93
	Executive Vice President & President—Steel	1996–98
	Executive Vice President, Chief Operating Officer, & President—Steel	1998–Present
Larry R. Brown	Vice President & General Counsel	1990–98
	Senior Vice President & General Counsel	1998–Present
Gene E. Little	Treasurer	1990–92
	Vice President—Finance	1992–98
	Senior Vice President—Finance	1998–Present
*Robert W. Mahoney	Director Chairman & CEO, Diebold, Incorporated (Canton, Ohio)	1992–Present
*J. Clayburn La Force, Jr.	Director Emeritus Dean & Professor, Anderson Graduate School of Management, University of California, Los Angeles	1994–Present
Stephen A. Perry	Vice President—Human Resources & Logistics	1993–98
	Senior Vice President—Human Resources, Purchasing, & Communications	1998–Present

Name	Office	Dates of Tenure
*Martin D. Walker	Director Principal, MORWAL Investments (Westlake, Ohio) & Retired Chairman & CEO, M. A. Hanna Company (Cleveland, Ohio)	1995–Present
Jon T. Elsasser	Vice President—Bearings—Europe, Africa, & West Asia Group Vice President—Bearings—Rail, Europe, Africa, & West Asia	1996–98 1998–Present
James W. Griffith	Vice President—Bearings—North American Automotive, Rail, Asia Pacific, & Latin America Group Vice President—Bearings— North American Automotive, Asia Pacific, & Latin America	1996–98 1998–Present
Salvatore J. Miraglia	Vice President—Bearings—North American Industrial & Super Precision Group Vice President—Bearings—North American Industrial & Super Precision	1996–98 1998–Present
Thomas W. Strouble	Vice President—Technology Senior Vice President—Technology	1995–98 1998–Present
*Jay A. Precourt	Director Vice Chairman & CEO, Tejas Gas, LLC (Houston, Texas)	1996–Present
Karl P. Kimmerling	Group Vice President—Alloy Steel	1998–Present
Hans J. Sack	Group Vice President—Specialty Steel & President—Latrobe Steel Company	1998–Present

Appendix B

History of Sales, Income, and Stock Prices for The Timken Company

Year	Net Sales (millions of dollars)	Net Income (Loss) (millions of dollars)	Stock Price Range [a] High	Stock Price Range [a] Low
1922	$19.7	$7.7	$1.094	$0.852
1923	25.5	8.1	1.406	1.031
1924	22.2	5.8	1.281	0.984
1925	26.4	8.1	1.860	1.180
1926	26.4	8.5	2.670	1.400
1927	27.7	9.6	4.453	2.438
1928	38.2	13.7	4.840	3.543
1929	42.7	14.2	8.711	3.656
1930	27.4	7.5	5.578	2.508
1931	16.6	2.6	3.688	1.031
1932	9.2	0.5	1.438	0.480
1933	15.8	2.2	2.219	0.860
1934	22.2	3.5	2.563	1½
1935	31.3	7.5	4.531	1.770
1936	39.6	9.3	4.656	3½
1937	46.7	10.8	4.938	2¼
1938	24.5	1.4	3.469	1.953
1939	40.1	7.3	3.391	2.141
1940	59.1	9.0	3.281	2.196
1941	90.0	9.5	3.203	2.396
1942	101.2	6.5	2.703	1.969
1943	108.7	6.4	3⅛	2.539
1944	112.7	6.3	3.281	2.719
1945	89.3	5.4	4⅛	3⅛
1946	80.5	5.5	4.142	2.391
1947	107.8	11.1	3.359	2.532
1948	120.5	13.2	3.438	2½
1949	99.4	3.5	2.703	2½
1950	144.1	15.4	2.797	2.071
1951	188.7	14.1	3.234	2.688
1952	169.6	10.6	3³⁄₁₆	2.469
1953	178.2	10.9	2.922	2.188
1954	135.6	10.7	3.274	2.258
1955	196.1	22.1	4.719	3.000
1956	214.5	21.8	6.422	3.891
1957	205.2	20.7	6.719	3¾
1958	155.2	11.2	5.781	3.875
1959	262.1	29.9	8.719	5.641
1960	244.8	19.2	8.594	5.532

Note: This table covers the years The Timken Company has been publicly traded on the New York Stock Exchange.
Source: The Timken Company corporate records; *New York Times* (January 1, 1926; January 1, 1927).

Year	Net Sales (millions of dollars)	Net Income (Loss) (millions of dollars)	Stock Price Range [a] High	Stock Price Range [a] Low
1961	$240.0	$16.0	$7.407	$6 1/16
1962	277.2	25.1	7.156	5.625
1963	292.5	31.0	9.235	6.703
1964	334.4	39.8	11.407	8.938
1965	375.7	48.8	12.719	10.000
1966	392.9	48.5	12.469	8 1/4
1967	355.1	35.5	11.844	8.407
1968	351.4	34.1	10.907	8.813
1969	399.4	34.7	10.156	6.782
1970	389.2	28.6	8.281	6.283
1971	410.6	38.1	11.094	8.344
1972	470.8	42.3	11.188	9 3/8
1973	567.5	53.0	10.688	7.283
1974	738.9 [b]	56.0 [c]	8.875	6 1/32
1975	804.5	61.3	10.656	6 5/16
1976	884.4	60.9	14.844	9 5/16
1977	974.4	74.4	13.875	10.688
1978	1105.8	88.6	13.469	10 1/4
1979	1282.1	102.1	15.875	12 1/16
1980	1338.5	92.6	17 1/8	11 1/4
1981	1427.2	101.1	19 1/2	14.283
1982	1014.4	(3.0)	16 1/4	10.094
1983	937.3	0.5	17 1/16	12 1/16
1984	1149.9	46.1	16.813	12 5/16
1985	1090.7	(3.9)	13 1/4	10.344
1986	1058.1	2.7 [d]	13.344	9.875
1987	1230.3	10.3	20 1/16	10.657
1988	1554.1	65.9	20.656	13 1/8
1989	1533.0	55.3	19.625	12 3/4
1990	1701.0 [e]	55.2	18 1/8	10.000
1991	1647.4	(35.7) [f]	15.000	10 5/16
1992	1642.3	4.5	15 1/4	11.563
1993	1708.8	(271.9) [g]	17 7/16	13 1/4
1994	1930.4	68.5	19.625	15.625
1995	2230.5	112.4	24.000	16 1/4
1996	2394.8	138.9	23.813	18 1/4
1997	2617.6	171.4	41 1/2	22 5/8

[a] Years 1922–28 adjusted for 2-for-1 stock split of January 1929; 1922–56 adjusted for 2-for-1 stock split of June 1957; 1922–64 adjusted for 2-for-1 stock split of April 1965; 1922–87 adjusted for 2-for-1 stock split of August 1988; and 1922–96 adjusted for 2-for-1 stock split of June 1997.

[b] On April 25, 1975, Latrobe Steel Company was acquired. Financial data for 1974 forward includes Latrobe Steel Company.

[c] Effective with 1974, LIFO method of valuing inventory was adopted with effect of reducing net income by $5.6M.

[d] Includes effect of changing to Straight Line depreciation method of $71.2M, which includes cumulative effect on prior years of $59.5M and $11.7M for 1986 operations. Adoption of FASB No. 87 increased income $5.8M and FASB No. 88 increased income $26.0M. These gains were offset by a $43.2M charge for restructuring of operations.

[e] On May 25, 1990, MPB Corporation was acquired. Financial data include MPB Corporation figures.

[f] The 1991 loss includes a provision for restructuring of $41.0M; $26.6M net of tax.

[g] The 1993 loss includes a provision for restructuring of $48.0M for operating income ($33.1M net of tax) and the cumulative effect of accounting changes of $254.2M, net of income tax, for net income.

Appendix C

The Timken Company—Timeline of Key Events

Date	Corporate Milestones	Product/Process Milestones	Plants and Facilities
1898	First patents issued for Timken tapered roller bearing		
1899	The Timken Roller Bearing Axle Company incorporates		
1901	The company moves to Canton, Ohio		The Canton plant opens to produce bearings and bearing-equipped axles
1907		Timken patents and begins using a one-piece cage, an improvement in bearing design and the economics of production	
1908		Timken introduces Short Series bearings, which are more compact, suitable for application in automotive transmissions	
1909	• The corporate name is changed to The Timken Roller Bearing Company • The axle business is separated as Timken-Detroit Axle Company • Timken enters overseas markets through a licensing agreement with Vickers subsidiary, Electric & Ordnance Accessories, Ltd., in England		Electric & Ordnance Accessories launches bearing production in Birmingham, England

Date	Corporate Milestones	Product/Process Milestones	Plants and Facilities
1913		Timken establishes a metallurgical and chemical laboratory for materials evaluation and control	
1915			Steel tube piercing mill begins operation
1916	Timken forms Bearing Service Company jointly with Hyatt Roller Bearing Company and New-Departure Bearing Company		Timken commits to steel making with installation of four 5-ton electric furnaces
1917	Electric & Ordnance Accessories transfers Timken license to another Vickers subsidiary, Wolseley Motors		Harrison steel plant in Canton pours its first heat of steel
1918	• Wolseley Motors licenses La Société de Mécanique de Gennevilliers to assemble Timken bearings in Paris, France (original license granted during World War I) • Wolseley sublicensee Max Prausnitzer incorporates Deutsche Timken GmbH in Berlin, Germany		
1919		Timken organizes the Industrial Division to push expansion of bearing applications in nonautomotive fields	
1920	Wolseley Motors incorporates British Timken, Ltd., and transfers Timken license to the new entity		• Columbus, Ohio, bearing plant opens • Treatment plant for waste acid opens in Canton

Date	Corporate Milestones	Product/Process Milestones	Plants and Facilities
1922	• Public offering of Timken stock, which begins trading on the New York Stock Exchange • Timken acquires 100 percent of Bearing Service Company; forms The Timken Roller Bearing Service and Sales Company		Bearing assembly plant opens in Walkerville, Ontario, Canada
1923		First application of Timken bearings to railroad cars on the Cleveland-Canton interurban streetcar	
1924		• Following acquisition of the Neal patent, Timken establishes the modern design of the Timken bearing • Nickel-molybdenum steel replaces chrome-nickel steel as the basic Timken bearing material	
1925	Timken acquires The Gilliam Manufacturing Company in Canton, Ohio		
1926	Timken acquires The Bock Bearing Company in Toledo, Ohio	Timken offers three new types of bearings to expand applications: large bearings for steel and other mills; all-thrust bearings for industrial equipment such as valves and pivots; and double-row bearings for motors, turbines, pumps. This is the beginning of a long stream of bearings designed for specific industrial applications.	
1927	The Timken Company and Michael Dewar jointly purchase British Timken, Ltd., from Wolseley Motors. Timken is the majority shareholder.		Timken enlarges the Harrison steel plant, replacing the original furnaces with three larger electric furnaces and one 100-ton open-hearth furnace

Date	Corporate Milestones	Product/Process Milestones	Plants and Facilities
1928	• British Timken creates La Société Anonyme Française Timken, a new manufacturing and sales subsidiary in France • Timken forms a sales subsidiary in Canada, Timken Roller Bearing Company, Ltd. • Timken acquires Weldless Tube Company in Wooster, Ohio, which becomes the Wooster steel plant		• La Société Anonyme Française Timken begins operation in Asnières • Deutsche Timken begins bearing production in Berlin • Expansion of the Harrison steel plant continues with the addition of three open-hearth furnaces and a 100-ton electric furnace, the largest in the world
1929		Timken establishes a metallurgical laboratory and alloy development program under Martin Fleischmann	Gambrinus bearing and steel plants open
1930		The Four Aces locomotive goes into service to demonstrate railroad bearing and steel applications	
1931		Timken introduces its first graphitic tool steels and high-strength, high-temperature alloys	
1932	British Timken forms a South African sales subsidiary, British Timken S.A. Proprietary, Ltd., in Johannesburg	• Timken develops a removable steel bit for drilling equipment—the Timken Rock Bit • Walter Assel develops an experimental process for elongation rolling of seamless tubes	
1935			The Mount Vernon, Ohio, rock bit plant opens

Date	Corporate Milestones	Product/Process Milestones	Plants and Facilities
1936			Deutsche Timken closes its Berlin plant
1937	Deutsche Timken ceases all operations	Timken's product testing and bearing-life testing programs move into a new laboratory with new, large-scale testing equipment	Timken starts up its first Assel mill for production of seamless tubing in converted Wooster steel plant
1940		• Timken introduces Alloy 16-25-6 (Super Steel) for high-temperature aircraft engine applications • Timken develops a process for making large gun barrels from seamless tubing	
1941			The Timken Ordnance Company begins production of gun barrels for World War II, in Canton
1942			British Timken opens the Duston bearing plant
1943		Timken establishes the Division of Development and Research for bearing process development at its Savannah Avenue plant (formerly the Gilliam Manufacturing Company plant)	Zanesville, Ohio, bearing plant begins operation
1944	Timken organizes a sales subsidiary in São Paulo, Brazil—The Timken Roller Bearing Company of South America		
1946			New bearing plant opens in St. Thomas, Ontario, Canada

Date	Corporate Milestones	Product/Process Milestones	Plants and Facilities
1947		Timken begins development of an automated, high-volume-production bearing factory, to be located in Bucyrus, Ohio	
1948			Timken rock bit plant opens in Colorado Springs, Colorado
1951	• Timken attains ownership of 100 percent of La Société Anonyme Française Timken and 53 percent of British Timken by acquiring shares owned by Michael Dewar following his death (December 1950) • The U.S. Supreme Court resolves an antitrust suit brought against Timken in 1947 with an order requiring the company to compete with its British and French associate companies		• Bucyrus, Ohio, bearing plant comes on line • British Timken S.A. opens a bearing plant in Benoni, South Africa
1952		Timken removes the last of its open-hearth furnaces and produces electric-furnace steel only	
1953	Timken forms a sales subsidiary in Mexico, Timken de Mexico		New Philadelphia, Ohio, plant opens for production of precision bearings
1954		• Timken introduces the AP™ bearing, designed for railroad freight cars • Timken introduces a new line of standardized automotive bearings, produced at Bucyrus and marketed to automotive and industrial customers as Green Light bearings	Daventry plant of British Timken begins operations

Date	Corporate Milestones	Product/Process Milestones	Plants and Facilities
1956	Timken forms a sales subsidiary, Timken Rollenlager GmbH, in Cologne, Germany (moved to Düsseldorf the same year)		Bucyrus Distribution Center begins operation with newly developed automated handling and packing technology
1957	Timken establishes a new manufacturing and sales subsidiary, Australian Timken Proprietary, Limited		
1958	Timken reorganizes La Société Anonyme Française Timken as Timken France, a division of the U.S. company		• Australian Timken begins bearing production in Ballarat • Columbus, Ohio, railroad bearing plant begins automated, high-volume production of AP railroad bearings
1959	• Timken acquires the publicly held shares of British Timken and consolidates it as a division of the U.S. company • Timken establishes a sales subsidiary in Buenos Aires, Timken Argentina S.r.l.	Timken product development, metallurgical research, and product testing groups move into expanded facilities in three new laboratories in Canton	• Zanesville bearing plant closes
1960	Timken forms a manufacturing and sales subsidiary, Timken do Brasil, in São Paulo		São Paulo, Brazil, bearing plant comes on line
1961			Timken France plant in Colmar, France, begins operation
1962			Timken opens its fourth Assel tube mill in Canton
1963			Asnières plant of Timken France closes
1964		First vacuum degasser starts up at Harrison steel plant	

Date	Corporate Milestones	Product/Process Milestones	Plants and Facilities
1965		Addition of a second vacuum degasser: all steel produced in Harrison steel plant is now degassed	
1966		Timken Research, a new centralized R&D organization, moves into new laboratory facilities in North Canton, Ohio	Gambrinus roller plant begins operations
1967		• Timken introduces the UNIT-BEARING™ for automotive and industrial applications • Timken introduces the SP™ bearing for railroad applications, with improved seal and shorter cup	Daventry Distribution Center of British Timken opens
1968		• Timken brings on line a continuous caster in its Canton steel plant • British Timken introduces a metric SP™ bearing	
1969			Timken opens a plant in Ashland, Ohio, to produce specialty tooling for its bearing and steel plants
1970	The corporation changes its name to The Timken Company	Timken introduces Set-Right™ assemblies for automotive bearings	
1971		• Timken introduces the XP™ railroad bearing, developed to be maintenance-free for ten years • Timken expands its line of through-hardened bearing steel with TBS-9™, a lower-cost alternative to the standard material for ball bearings	Gaffney, South Carolina, automated mass-production bearing plant comes on line

Date	Corporate Milestones	Product/Process Milestones	Plants and Facilities
1972		• Introduction of the Hydra-Rib™ bearing for machine tools • Development of polyethylene reactor tubing, a new steel product	
1974	Timken establishes a sales subsidiary in Japan: Nihon Timken K.K.	Development of thrust bearings with pin-type cages	
1975	Timken acquires Latrobe Steel Company in Latrobe, Pennsylvania		
1978		• Introduction of super precision "000" class bearings • Timken Steel initiates a clean steel program based on research findings correlating clean steel with bearing performance	Canton water purification plant opens
1979		Introduction of the UNIPAC™ bearing for automotive wheel applications	• Lincolnton, North Carolina, bearing plant opens for medium-volume production of industrial bearings • Timken opens distribution center in Haan, Germany • Tube Mill No. 5 begins operation in Canton
1980		Harrison steel plant begins making BSP (Bearing Steel Practice) steel using precipitation deoxidation	
1982		• Introduction of UNIPAC-PLUS™ and Wheel-Pac™ bearings • Harrison steel plant commissions the continuous thermal treatment facility	

Date	Corporate Milestones	Product/Process Milestones	Plants and Facilities
1983		Timken Research doubles in size	
1984		Ladle refiner comes on line in Harrison steel plant, the next step in the clean steel program	
1985		• Timken Research develops computer optimization of bearing contours for specific load cycles, the Select-A-Nalysis℠/Bearing System Analysis program, and a prototype manufacturing system • Introduction of the Hydrodynamic Labyrinth (HDL™) seal for UNIPAC-PLUS bearings • Timken introduces TMS 80™ non-heat-treatable microalloy steel	Faircrest steel plant comes on line in Canton with technologies for a major step forward in the clean steel program
1986	• Timken sells the Rock Bit Division • A corporate reorganization creates two business units, Steel and Bearings, to be supported by five corporate centers	• Timken Research begins finite element modeling in bearing design • Timken introduces Parapremium™ steel, a family of MPP (maximum performance practice) steels, the culmination of the clean steel program	
1987		• Introduction of eccentric bearings for high-speed printing presses • Introduction of trailer wheel bearing kits • Development of a two-element seal for UNIPAC and UNIPAC-PLUS bearings	

Date	Corporate Milestones	Product/Process Milestones	Plants and Facilities
1988	Timken opens sales offices in Italy, Korea, Singapore, and Venezuela	• Introduction of P900™ bearings • Development of helicopter blade root bearing	
1989	Timken enters a joint venture for bearing production in India with Tata Iron and Steel Company, creating Tata Timken Ltd.	• Introduction of the first of several high-toughness steel alloys for perforating gun tubing • Introduction of Precision Plus™ bearings • Introduction of low-energy AP bearing	• Atlanta Export Service Center opens in Georgia • Columbus, Ohio, bearing plant closes; Columbus railroad bearing plant remains open
1990	• Timken acquires MPB Corporation in New Hampshire • Timken opens a sales office in Hungary	Introduction of SENSOR-PAC™ bearings	
1991	Timken forms a sales subsidiary in Spain, Timken España S.A.		• Altavista, Virginia, bearing plant comes on line, a flexible manufacturing facility for package bearings • New corporate office building opens in Canton
1992		• New continuous caster comes on line in Harrison steel plant • Introduction of rivet pin cage bearings for helicopters	• Tata Timken plant in Jamshedpur, India, reaches full production status • Latrobe precision forging facility starts up
1993	• Timken opens a sales office in Hong Kong • Timken opens Shanghai representative office in China	• Launch of the Steel Parts Business (renamed Precision Steel Components in 1998) • Development of cold ring rolling for precision auto parts • Development of heavy truck SENSOR-PAC™ bearing	• St. Clair Precision Tubing Components opens in Eaton, Ohio • Daventry bearing plant closes; Daventry Distribution Center remains open

Date	Corporate Milestones	Product/Process Milestones	Plants and Facilities
1994	Timken opens MPB Singapore Pte. Ltd., for production of rotary actuator cartridges for computer disk drives	• Introduction of AP-2™ bearing for improved service life with fewer parts in a more compact design • Development of Dynametal™ good-machining, lead-free steel	• Asheboro, North Carolina, plant opens for flexible production of industrial bearings • Latrobe opens the Sandycreek Service Center in Pennsylvania, expanding its facilities for distribution of tool and die steels
1995	Timken acquires Rail Bearing Service, Inc., in Richmond, Virginia	• Development of AP generator bearing • Development of Spexx™ family of application-specific industrial bearings • Introduction of encapsulated bearings for airplane wheels • Development of AdvanTec™, patented heat-treatment process for making steels tougher	Tryon Peak plant begins ring operations in Columbus, North Carolina
1996	• Timken completes four acquisitions: - Ohio Alloy Steels in Youngstown, Ohio - Houghton & Richards, Inc., of Marlborough, Massachusetts - Sanderson Kayser Ltd. in Great Britain - FLT Prema Milmet S.A. in Poland • Timken forms joint venture for bearing production in China: Yantai Timken Company Ltd. • Timken opens office in Beijing, China • Timken opens Moscow office		Timken de Mexico begins distribution of Timken steel

Date	Corporate Milestones	Product/Process Milestones	Plants and Facilities
1997	• Timken completes four acquisitions: - Bearing assets of Gnutti Carlo S.p.A., Italy - Aerospace bearing operations of The Torrington Company Ltd. in Wolverhampton, England - Handpiece Headquarters, Inc. in Orange, California - Rulmenti Grei S.A. in Romania • Ohio Alloy Steels and Houghton & Richards merge to form OH&R Special Steels Company • Timken opens office in Istanbul, Turkey	• Radiation-type wall thickness gauge goes into service in Gambrinus steel plant for in-process control of tube production • Introduction of new line of automotive service parts	• Timken opens a railroad bearing repair facility in Duston, England • Winchester, Kentucky, steel parts plant opens • Singapore Logistics Center opens • Profile ring mill starts up at Tryon Peak plant in North Carolina
1998	Timken acquires an industrial bearing repair business, Bearing Repair Specialists, in South Bend, Indiana	Launch of Timken IsoClass™ line of metric tapered roller bearings	• Greer, South Carolina, Tool and Alloy Steel distribution center opens • Advanced Package Bearings plant opens in Duston, England • Construction of rolling mill completed at Harrison steel plant • Timken announces tentative plans to build a new steel tube mill—site undetermined

Appendix D

Offices and Plants of The Timken Company
As of June 1998

CORPORATE HEADQUARTERS
1835 Dueber Avenue, S.W.
Canton, Ohio 44706–2798
P.O. Box 6932
Canton, Ohio 44706–0932
U.S.A.

www.timken.com

OFFICES

Argentina
Buenos Aires

Australia
Ballarat
Brisbane
Melbourne
Perth
Sydney

Brazil
São Paulo

Canada
Edmonton
St. Thomas
Toronto

China
Beijing
Shanghai

England
Duston
Pontefract
Sheffield
Wolverhampton

France
Bourron Marlotte
Colmar
Paris

Germany
Gemuenden
Haan
Hannover
Stuttgart

Hong Kong
Hong Kong

Hungary
Budapest

Italy
Cogozzo
Milan

Japan
Yokohama

Korea
Seoul

Mexico
Mexico City

Netherlands
Medemblik

Poland
Sosnowiec

Romania
Ploiesti

Russia
Moscow

Singapore
Singapore

South Africa
Benoni

Spain
Madrid

Turkey
Istanbul

United States
Atlanta, Ga.
Boca Raton, Fla.
Charlotte, N.C.
Chicago, Ill.
Cincinnati, Ohio
Cleveland, Ohio
Columbus, Ohio
Dallas, Tex.
Detroit, Mich.
Hartford, Conn.
Houston, Tex.
Kansas City, Kans.
Keene, N.H.
Knoxville, Tenn.
Latrobe, Pa.
Lebanon, N.H.
Los Angeles, Calif.
Marlborough, Mass.
Milwaukee, Wis.
Moline, Ill.
Peoria, Ill.

Philadelphia, Pa.
Pittsburgh, Pa.
Richmond, Va.
Seattle, Wash.
Wauseon, Ohio
Youngstown, Ohio

Venezuela
Caracas

PLANTS

Australia
Ballarat

Brazil
São Paulo

Canada
St. Thomas

England
Duston (2)
Northampton
Sheffield
Wolverhampton

France
Colmar

Italy
Cogozzo

Netherlands
Medemblik

Poland
Sosnowiec

Romania
Ploiesti

Singapore
Singapore

South Africa
Benoni

United States
Altavista, Va.
Asheboro, N.C.
Ashland, Ohio
Bucyrus, Ohio
Canton, Ohio (6)

Carlyle, Ill.
Columbus, N.C.
Columbus, Ohio
Eaton, Ohio
Franklin, Pa.
Gaffney, S.C.
Greer, S.C.
Keene, N.H. (3)
Knoxville, Tenn. (4)
Latrobe, Pa.
Lebanon, N.H. (2)
Lenexa, Kans.
Lincolnton, N.C.
New Philadelphia, Ohio
North Little Rock, Ark. (2)
Ogden, Utah (2)
Orange, Calif.
Richmond, Va.
South Bend, Ind.
Wauseon, Ohio
Winchester, Ky.
Wooster, Ohio

Tata Timken Limited

India

Offices
Bangalore
Bombay
Calcutta
Jamshedpur
New Delhi

Plant
Jamshedpur

Yantai Timken
Company Limited

China

Office
Yantai

Plant
Yantai

A Note on Sources
and List of Interviewees

Most of the internal company sources that are the foundation for this history are stored in The Timken Company Archives in Canton, Ohio. That collection includes a rich body of correspondence from a number of key corporate executives, concentrated in the years from 1909 to about 1936. Another particularly valuable source in the archives is the successive company magazines published between four and twelve times a year from 1912 to 1920 and from 1942 to the present. In addition, the archives includes significant collections of Timken advertisements, catalogs, engineering journals, press releases, informational pamphlets on the company and its products, and related newspaper clippings. There are also invaluable materials from prior history projects, including transcripts and notes of interviews conducted in the early 1970s, departmental histories compiled at that time, and a privately printed commissioned history of the company's activities during World War II—Edward Hungerford, *Timken at War* (1945). Finally, the archives houses an extensive photographic collection, including photos donated by many Timken associates through the years.

A second important source of internal documents was a file cabinet of papers belonging to H. H. Timken, which the family opened to the author. That included some helpful correspondence on his philanthropy and noncompany investments. The family also provided copies of correspondence from Edmund Heinzelman that were essential in reconstructing the story of the development of the Timken bearing by Henry Timken and Reginald Heinzelman.

Timken corporate documents that have not been collected in the archives but are held by individuals or departments within the company are identified in the notes as Timken Company corporate records. Where those are found in the offices of British Timken or Timken France, they have been identified as records of those divisions. The materials on patents are maintained as a discrete collection at Timken Research. One serious gap in the records should be noted. In 1975, the company inadvertently destroyed its historical collection of Treasurer's Reports, the principal internal compilation of financial data. Since it closely controlled the circulation of those reports and collected and destroyed all but one central copy, the loss of information was considerable. Early in the history project, W. R. (Bob) Timken gave the author a copy of the 1936 year-end Treasurer's Report, which he had happened to save in his personal files. That report, plus a limited amount of financial reporting in the correspondence between the company treasurers and H. H. and W. R. Timken in the 1920s and early 1930s, made it possible to discuss topics such as bearing sales by market segment and levels of employment in different departments, which unfortunately could not be addressed for other eras of the company's early history. In addition, the company maintained summary tables of selected financial data, including some items such as operating income that it did not include in annual reports prior to 1988. Those provided the information on revenues and net income for 1919–21 in Table 3.1 and formed the basis for the graph on operating margins in Chapter 10.

In addition to internal sources, this history draws on collections of materials in the Stark County Historical Society in Canton, and in the Canton Public Library. Of particular significance were the library's microfilm files of the daily newspaper, the *Canton Repository*, and notes of interviews conducted by Edward Thornton Heald for his series of historical essays, *The Stark County Story as Told in Radio Broadcasts*, published by the historical society in the 1950s. Other public sources for the history include material published in industry and business journals and the technical publications of Timken personnel, as cited in the footnotes. Historical studies of the automotive industry and the more limited literature on the U.S. automotive supply industry provided the essential context for the company's evolution in the early decades of the twentieth century. There is also one published, though rare, history of anti-friction bearings that was invaluable: Hudson T. Morton, *Anti-Friction Bearings* (Ann Arbor: Hudson T. Morton, 1965).

A final major source of information: the oral history interviews conducted between 1993 and 1998 with current and retired Timken personnel, and with some of the company's customers, distributors, and suppliers. In addition to the author, three members of The Winthrop Group, Inc., conducted interviews in 1993–96: Barbara Griffith, Davis Dyer, and Virginia Dawson. Interview citations in the notes provide exact date of interview and indicate the interviewer, if other than the author. The list of interviewees includes names and titles only. All titles refer to positions within The Timken Company except where otherwise noted.

1993

Peter J. Ashton	Executive Vice President and President—Bearings
Frederick C. Crawford	Retired Chairman of TRW
George L. Deal	Retired Vice President—Finance
Robert L. Leibensperger	Vice President—Technology
Norman H. Peterson	Retired Vice President—Corporate Relations
Ward J. Timken	Vice President
William R. Timken, Jr.	Chairman—Board of Directors
Joseph F. Toot, Jr.	President and Chief Executive Officer
Charles H. West	Executive Vice President and President—Steel

1994

Raymond J. Addicott	Retired Senior Scientist
Maurice Amiel	Vice President and Chairman—Bearings—Europe, Africa, and West Asia
James Bennett	Managing Director, McKinsey & Company, Inc., Cleveland, Ohio
Kendall Brooke	Retired Managing Director—Timken South Africa
George L. Deal	Retired Vice President—Finance
Harold E. Forrest	Retired Office Manager—The Timken Family Office and Secretary/Treasurer of the Timken Foundation of Canton
Richard L. Frederick	Retired Vice President—Industrial Relations and Services
Richard A. Gulling	Retired Vice President—Finance
Thomas W. Hannon	Chief Executive Officer of Hannon Electric Company
Wyn E. McCoy	Retired Vice President—Engineering and Research
Ralph E. McKelvey	Retired Vice President—Engineering and Research
Sheila M. Markley	Partner—Day, Ketterer, Raley, Wright & Rybolt Law Firm
William H. Murphy, Jr.	Principal Standards and Patents Engineer
James L. Nickas	Retired Supervisor—Technical Administration
William J. C. North	Retired Managing Director—Australian Timken
Charles Nouhaud	Retired Chief Engineer—Timken France
James E. O'Connor	Retired Vice President—Bearing Operations
James W. Pilz	Retired Executive Vice President
Brooks R. Powell	Retired Secretary
John C. Richey	Retired Product Engineer
Robert M. Rybolt	Retired Partner—Day, Ketterer, Raley, Wright & Rybolt Law Firm

Marshall Schober	Retired President of Latrobe Steel Company
Ralph T. Shipley	Retired Vice President—Steel Operations
Robert L. Sisson	Retired Assistant General Manager—Bearing Operations
Franklin Slayman	Retired Development Engineer
Mrs. H. H. Timken, Jr.	Wife of the late H. H. Timken, Jr.
William R. Timken	Retired Chairman—Board of Directors and Chairman Emeritus
Harley J. Urbach	Retired Vice President—Engineering and Research
C. Philip Weigel	Retired President of Latrobe Steel Company
Robert G. Wingerter	Former Member—The Timken Company Board of Directors

1995

Stanley Aitken	Retired Director—Human Resources—British Timken
Dennis Ashton	Retired Managing Director—British Timken
Mrs. Stephen Bennett	Wife of the late Stephen Bennett, Retired Managing Director—British Timken
George Bentley	Retired Chief Engineer—British Timken
Bruce Campbell	General Manager—Manufacturing—British Timken
Raymond H. Carter	Retired Chief Engineer—MPB Corporation
Yves Chapotot	Retired General Foreman—Timken France
Michael Clements	Regional Sales Manager—UK and Scandinavia
Lucien Dambrin	Director—Human Resources and Logistics— Europe, Africa, and West Asia
Roberto Dotti	Sales Manager—Timken Italia
John H. Fellows	Retired Vice President—Marketing—Steel
George Foale	Manager—Human Resources—British Timken
Edmond Gerrer	Mayor of Colmar, France
Bela Gold	Fletcher Jones Professor of Technology and Management, The Claremont Graduate School
Hubert Adrien Hamilton	Retired General Manager—Société Anonyme Française Timken
Raymond J. Howes	Manager—Distribution and Logistics Project
E. Ronald Knapp	Retired Managing Director—Timken Europe
Richard Kopp	Project Leader—Total Quality Advancement—Timken France
Robert W. Lang	Retired Vice President—Personnel Administration and Logistics
Jacques Lesage	Retired Manufacturing Director—Timken France

Sheila M. Markley	Partner—Day, Ketterer, Raley, Wright & Rybolt Law Firm
Louis Matler	Headmaster, Colmar Technical High School, France
Harry Mayfield	Retired Timken Associate and District Director for the United Steelworkers of America
Claude Perret	Retired Director, Marketing and Sales—Europe, Africa, and West Asia
James F. Ragazino	Retired Motor Inspector
J. Kevin Ramsey	Retired Vice President—Finance
Gerhard Reiter	General Manager—Aftermarket and Distribution—Europe
Robert M. Rybolt	Retired Partner—Day, Ketterer, Raley, Wright & Rybolt Law Firm
Klaus Schulze	Director—Marketing and Sales—Europe, Africa, and West Asia
Donald W. Simonson	Director—Industrial Relations
John Thorpe	Director of the Nene Foundation, England
Joseph F. Toot, Jr.	President and Chief Executive Officer
Henri Trepier	Retired Director—Customer Services—Continental Europe
Ian Tucker	General Manager—Materials Management and Customer Service
Raymond Tuckey	Retired Director of Sales—British Timken
James Umstattd	Son of William E. Umstattd, Retired President
Roger Violy	Director—Manufacturing—Timken France
Isabelle Yau	Technician—Human Resources—Timken France
Jack Zutavern	Retired Scheduler—Machine Shop

1996

John Askew	Sales Administration Manager—Desford Tubes, England
Alberto Bianchi	President—Bianchi Cuscinetti S.p.A., Italy
Jack Bond	Retired Manager—Central Purchasing, Caterpillar Inc.
John Bostock	Retired Production Services Director—Desford Tubes, England
Jean Bouley	Former Secretary General of the International Union of Railways (UIC) and Former Motive Power and Rolling Stock Director, French National Railways (SNCF)
Bill J. Bowling	Executive Vice President and President—Steel
Frank A. Cope	Manufacturing & Personnel Director—Desford Tubes, England
John Davenport	Technical Director—Desford Tubes, England

George L. Deal	Retired Vice President—Finance
The Rt. Hon. Lord Eden of Winton	International Advisor to The Timken Company
David Eley	Retired Chief Engineer for Transmission Design—Land Rover, England
Alberto Fauda	Director—Marketing, Bianchi Cuscinetti S.p.A., Italy
Albrecht Fischer	Retired Head of Chassis Engineering/Passenger Cars—Volkswagen A.G., Germany
Erich Fischer	Former Consultant to The Timken Company
Maria Luisa Garavaglia Fuchs	Capo Area Regional Manager—Bianchi Cuscinetti S.p.A., Italy
James A. D. Geier	Retired Chairman—Cincinnati Milacron
George Jones	Retired Chief Engineer—Transmission Design—Austin Rover, England
William E. Judy	Retired Director of Sales—Timken Europe
George LaMore	Retired Chair and Chief Executive Officer of Bearings, Inc.
William J. Lhota	Executive Vice President—American Electric Power
Michael J. Mahoney	Director—Corporate Communications, American Electric Power
Scott Mathot	President—MPB Corporation
Alan Padgett	Logistics Director—Desford Tubes, England
Jack Porter	Manager—Central Purchasing, Caterpillar Inc.
Donald Ross	Retired President—MPB Corporation
John J. Schubach	Vice President—Strategic Management and Continuous Improvement
Samuel R. Williams	Chief Engineer—Railroad Bearing Business

GROUP INTERVIEWS

Bucyrus Bearing Plant

Group 1	Group 2	Group 3
Edgar R. Bealer	Carl F. Leonberger	Steven D. Barnes
Robert L. Gulling	Donald R. Leonberger	Jack L. Cress
Leonard E. Kocher, Jr.	Lee A. Orewiler	Paul J. Ebbeskotte
Richard D. Makeever	Leland M. Orewiler	Tom Emerson
Robert L. Makeever	Dale E. Smith	Phil Harris
	Jack L. Stockmaster	Nancy B. Herschler
		Marilyn J. Holdcraft
		Mark A. McMichael

Columbus Railroad Bearing Plant

William A. Hughes

General Jefferson, Jr.

Linda L. Markham

Douglas Poe

Samuel R. Williams

Columbus Railroad Bearing Plant Retirees

John F. Byrom

Thomas C. Keller

James E. McCort

Rodney E. Martinsen

James E. Wise

1997

Bill J. Bowling	Executive Vice President and President—Steel
Arthur L. Christenson	Retired Director—Research
Russell P. Fowler	Retired Plant Manager—Bucyrus Bearing Plant
Robert L. Leibensperger	Executive Vice President and President—Bearings
Gene E. Little	Vice President—Finance
George T. Matthews	General Manager—Quality Assurance—Steel
James K. Preston	Retired Plant Manager—Faircrest Steel Plant
Robert M. Rybolt	Retired Partner—Day, Ketterer, Raley, Wright & Rybolt Law Firm
John J. Schubach	Vice President—Strategic Management and Continuous Improvement
Donald W. Simonson	Director—Industrial Relations
Eugene L. Stewart	Senior Partner Emeritus, Stewart and Stewart Law Firm
Jack D. Stover	Retired Senior Research Specialist
William R. Timken, Jr.	Chairman—Board of Directors
Joseph F. Toot, Jr.	President and Chief Executive Officer

GROUP INTERVIEWS

Faircrest Steel Plant

Lynn Campbell

Don Childress

Mary L. Eibel

John W. Fick

Jim Marvin

Richard S. Miller

Timothy S. Morris

Connie E. Thomas

Howard D. Walters

Ronald Michael Wilson

Bill Withers

Canton Bearing Plant

Linda Adorisio

Enzo Bagnoli

Richard S. Kaufman

Helen D. Koah

Gus Reale

Michael W. Roberts

James A. Sims

Naomi M. Vance

Charles R. Walters

1998

Russell P. Fowler	Retired Plant Manager—Bucyrus Bearing Plant
James D. Holderbaum	Vice President—Business Advancement and Controller—Steel
Robert L. Leibensperger	Executive Vice President, Chief Operating Officer, and President—Bearings
Kai Licht	Retired Manager—Product Acceptance—Bearings
Gene E. Little	Senior Vice President—Finance
James E. Oberlander	Retired Plant Superintendent—Bucyrus Bearing Plant
Donald W. Simonson	Director—Industrial Relations
Jack D. Stover	Retired Senior Research Specialist
Thomas W. Strouble	Senior Vice President—Technology
Connie E. Thomas	Senior Human Resources Analyst—Faircrest Steel Plant
William R. Timken, Jr.	Chairman, President, and Chief Executive Officer
Joseph F. Toot, Jr.	Chairman—Executive Committee, Board of Directors
Ronald L. Widner	Director—Steel Development

Notes

Notes to Introduction

1. See Alfred D. Chandler, Jr., *Scale and Scope: The Dynamics of Industrial Capitalism* (Cambridge, Mass.: Harvard University Press, 1990), Appendix A.2, 649, for Timken's position in 1929. On the *Fortune* 500 list of U.S. industrial companies for 1993, the last year before *Fortune* combined the lists for industrial and service firms, Timken ranked 226 in assets and 249 in sales (*Fortune* [April 18, 1994]: 228). On the combined list for 1997, Timken ranked 509. [(See *Fortune* [April 27, 1998]: F54.)] On life expectancy of firms, see Arie de Geus, *The Living Company: Habits for Survival in a Turbulent Business Environment* (Boston: Harvard Business School Press, 1997), 1–2; and "How to Live Long and Prosper," *Economist* (May 10, 1997): 59.

2. There are meaningful parallels between this part of Timken's history and development of aluminum and its applications by another venerable U.S. corporation, Aluminum Company of America (Alcoa). On sales engineering linked to research, see Bettye H. Pruitt and George David Smith, "The Corporate Management of Innovation: Alcoa Research, Aircraft Alloys, and the Problem of Stress-corrosion Cracking," in Richard S. Rosenbloom, ed., *Research on Technological Innovation, Management and Policy* (Greenwich, Conn.: JAI Press, 1986): 33–81; and on the broader technical history of Alcoa, Margaret B. W. Graham and Bettye H. Pruitt, *R&D for Industry: A Century of Technical Innovation at Alcoa* (New York: Cambridge University Press, 1990).

3. Studies of that subject in other companies include, in addition to Graham and Pruitt, *R&D for Industry*, Leonard S. Reich, *The Making of American Industrial Research: Science and Business at GE and Bell, 1876–1926* (New York: Cambridge University Press, 1985); David A. Hounshell and John Kenly Smith, Jr., *Science and Corporate Strategy: Du Pont R&D, 1902–1980* (New York: Cambridge University Press, 1988).

4. On the severity of competitive pressures in Timken's industry segments, see Alfred D. Chandler, Jr., "The Competitive Performance of U.S. Industrial Enterprises since the Second World War," *Business History Review* (Spring 1994): 25, 43–57.

5. This abbreviated overview follows that provided by Chandler, in "Competitive Performance," but that, in turn, rests on *Scale and Scope* as well as Chandler's earlier study of managerial capitalism: *The Visible Hand: The Managerial Revolution in American Business* (Cambridge, Mass.: Harvard University Press, 1977).

6. James C. Collins and Jerry I. Porras, *Built to Last: Successful Habits of Visionary Companies* (New York: HarperCollins, 1994); and de Geus, *The Living Company*. A number of historians in the field of business history have expressed the need to give greater consideration to cultural issues, and some have begun the work of reconsidering Chandler's theses in that light. See, for example, two articles in *Business and Economic History* (Winter 1995): Kenneth Lipartito, "Culture and the Practice of Business History," 1–42; and Naomi R. Lamoreaux, "Constructing Firms: Partnerships and Alternative Contractual Arrangements in Early Nineteenth-Century American Business," 43–73. See also Charles Dellheim, "The Creation of a Company Culture: Cadburys, 1861–1931," *American Historical Review* (Februrary 1987): 13–44; and Jonathan Rees, "Cultural Influences on Labor Policy: American Steel Manufacturers in the Nonunion Era," *Essays in Economic and Business History* (1998): 197–214. This broadening of focus took place earlier in the management field, which was strongly influenced by Chandler, *Strategy and Structure: Chapters in the History of the American Industrial Enterprise* (Cambridge, Mass.: The M.I.T. Press, 1962). Thomas J. Peters and Robert H. Waterman, Jr. (*In Search of Excellence: Lessons from America's Best-Run Companies* [New York: Harper & Row, 1982], 4–11) describe the intellectual process by which management consultants at McKinsey & Company began to consider cultural issues as a necessary addition to Chandler's strategy-structure model in the analysis of what makes companies successful.

7. Collins and Porras, 48; and on financial performance, 5–7, 54–72; and de Geus, *The Living Company*, 11, 177.

8. De Geus, *The Living Company*, 103; and Collins and Porras, *Built to Last*, 122–6, and Chapter 8.

9. De Geus, *The Living Company*, 9; and Collins and Porras, *Built to Last*, 82, 137–9, and Chapter 7.

10. On the hierarchical nature of managerial capitalism and some of its advantages, see Herman Daems, "The Rise of the Modern Industrial Enterprise: A New Perspective," in Alfred D. Chandler, Jr., and Herman Daems, eds., *Managerial Hierarchies: Comparative Perspectives on the Rise of the Modern Industrial Enterprise* (Cambridge, Mass.: Harvard University Press, 1980), 203–23. On the historical origins and implications of the rigidities in managerial hierarchies, see William Lazonick, *Competitive Advantage on the Shop Floor* (Cambridge, Mass.: Harvard University Press, 1990), chapters 7–9, and "Organizational Capabilities in American Industry: The Rise and Decline of Managerial Capitalism," background paper for the Business History Conference (March 23, 1990); and Michael H. Best, *The New Competition: Institutions of Industrial Restructuring* (Cambridge, Mass.: Harvard University Press, 1990).

11. Of the 508 U.S. corporations equal in size to or larger than Timken on the *Fortune* 1,000 list for 1997, only 18 had a higher annual rate of growth in earnings per share, 1987 to 1997. More than half of those were in the financial services or computer industries. See *Fortune* (April 27, 1998): F44–66.

Chapter 1: Henry Timken

1. Henry Timken's words as paraphrased by his son, Henry H. Timken, quoted in O. D. Foster, "This Business Grew Nearly 200-Fold in 20 Years," *Forbes* (November 15, 1924): 229–31, 236.

2. Ibid.

3. Ibid. On the central role of improved mechanical efficiency in the transformation of industry, see Chandler, *The Visible Hand*, 241–4. In particular, improved bearings contributed to increases in throughput, that is, to the all-important economies of speed. According to Chandler (p. 244), "It was not the size of a manufacturing establishment in terms of number of workers

and the amount and value of productive equipment but the velocity of throughput and the resulting increase in volume that permitted economies that lowered costs and increased output per worker and per machine."

4. Hudson T. Morton, *Anti-Friction Bearings*, 2d ed. (Ann Arbor: Hudson T. Morton, 1965), 1–6. On the spread of ball bearings through their introduction on bicycles, see David A. Hounshell, *From the American System to Mass Production, 1800–1932* (Baltimore: Johns Hopkins University Press, 1984), 190–2, 194–6. On production of ball-bearing-equipped axles in 1895, see "A Man of Ideas: The Story of Henry Timken, Carriage Builder and Founder of a World-Wide Enterprise," *The Carriage Journal* 17:4 (Spring 1980): 187. It mentions the Meeker Ball Bearing Axle and the Crawford Axle as "two of several similar types" available at that time.

5. On the family's work on bearing development: Edmund Gooding Heinzelman, "The Story of the Creation of the Timken Roller Bearing Company," (1947?), MS in Timken Family Papers; and the account by H. H. Timken in Foster, "This Business Grew Nearly 200-Fold," 230–1.

6. Foster, "This Business Grew Nearly 200-Fold," 230.

7. Chandler, *The Visible Hand*, 356. On the importance of materials and materials understanding, see Cyril Stanley Smith, "Materials and the Development of Civilization and Science," *Science* (May 1965): 901–20; and "The Interaction of Science and Practice in the History of Metallurgy," *Technology and Culture* 2:4 (1961): 357–67; and Pruitt and Smith, "Corporate Management of Innovation," 39, 50–4, and Table 1, 56–8.

8. The Timken Company Annual Report for 1997; and on market share, Gene E. Little, speech at New York Stock Exchange (June 1997).

9. On the implications of the Mars mission for the future of space exploration, see Timothy Ferris, "Some Like it Hot," *The New York Review of Books* (September 25, 1997): 16–20. And on current bearing applications, The Timken Company Annual Reports for 1996 and 1997.

10. Quotations from Richard O'Connor, *The German-Americans: An Informal History* (Boston: Little, Brown and Company, 1968), 68–70. See also Theodore Huebner, *The Germans in America* (Philadelphia: Chilton Company, 1962).

11. Patricia Timken Blodgett, "The Timken Family in Germany," typescript in Timken Family Papers (1993) provides the facts underlying this paragraph.

12. Quotation and description of the journey from Walter O. Forster, *Zion on the Mississippi: The Settlement of the Saxon Lutherans in Missouri, 1839–1941,* (St. Louis: Concordia Publishing House, 1953), 206–10.

13. Forster, *Zion on the Mississippi*, 377–84, 433–40; Ed Heinzelman to Louis Klinedinst (July 22, 1949), in Timken Company Archives. The application of Timken and four other families from Hanover who joined the Stephanites in St. Louis is reproduced and discussed in Forster, *Zion on the Mississippi*, 361, 555.

14. Blodgett, "The Timken Family in Germany," 4–5 provides the details on the Timkens' land purchases.

15. Blodgett, "The Timken Family in Germany," 5.

16. This description of St. Louis draws primarily on Forster, *Zion on the Mississippi*, 229–33, 250–3.

17. Quotation from "Henry Timken," *The Hub* (November 1895): 1; on the state of the industry and the skills of a carriage maker, see Joanne Abel Goldman, "From Carriage Shop to Carriage Factory: The Effect of Industrialization on the Process of Manufacturing Carriages," *19th Century American Carriages: Their Manufacture, Decoration and Use* (Stony Brook, N.Y.: The Museums of Stony Brook, 1987), 9–10. According to Henry's great-nephew he was a wheel-

wright "by trade" (Heinzelman to Klinedinst, July 22, 1949); I have added metalworking because it was a central element of all of his patented inventions.

18. Missouri, Vol. 37, 479, 484, R. G. Dunn & Co. Collection, Baker Library, Harvard University Graduate School of Business Administration; and "A Man of Ideas," 185. On Belleville, see O'Connor, *The German-Americans*, 79–80; and John A. Hawgood, *The Tragedy of German-America: The Germans in the United States of America during the Nineteenth Century—and After* (New York: G. P. Putnam's Sons, 1940), 125–8.

19. "Biography of Henry Timken," typescript (November 12, 1897); and M. R. Drummond to C. F. Farnham (September 1, 1945), in Timken Company Archives; Heinzelman to Klinedinst (July 22, 1949).

20. O'Connor, *The German-Americans*, 136–42; "Biography of Henry Timken;" Drummond to Farnham (September 1, 1945).

21. Quotation from Goldman, "From Carriage Shop to Carriage Factory," 15–17. According to Goldman, the industry grew with its market, from roughly 6,000 producers and a total value of $18 million in 1850 to 15,500 producers and $102 million in 1890. At the same time its center of gravity shifted from the East Coast, which accounted for nearly 90 percent of the horse-drawn vehicles produced in 1850, to the Midwest, where some 60 percent of vehicle production was located by 1880. However, she cautions that those statistics, drawn from federal census data, are useful mainly for indicating trends. See also the discussion of the carriage industry and the preeminent manufacturer, Studebaker Brothers Manufacturing Company, in Hounshell, *From the American System to Mass Production*, 148–51. I am grateful to Thomas A. Kinney, Case Western Reserve University, for sharing with me his work in progress on the carriage industry, now completed as "From Shop to Factory in the Industrial Heartland: The Industrialization of Horse-drawn Vehicle Manufacture in the City of Cleveland" (Ph.D. dissertation, Case Western Reserve University, 1997).

22. *The Hub* 19:4 (July 1877): 169; and "Does Machinery Pay?" *The Hub* 17:1 (April 1875): 5–6. On the fire in 1864, see "Biography of Henry Timken." Some other sources date it as 1874, but none provide evidence to contradict his memory of events (see "Henry Timken," *The Hub* 37:8 [November 1895]:1).

23. Quotations from H. H. Timken obituary, *Canton Repository* (October 14, 1940); and "Representative Carriage Factories," *The Hub* 26:6 (September 1884): n.p. On Studebaker's factory in the late 1870s, see Hounshell, *From the American System to Mass Production*, 147.

24. This paragraph is based on Naomi Lamoreaux and Kenneth Sokoloff, "Inventors, Firms, and the Market for Technology in the Late Nineteenth and Early Twentieth Centuries," NBER Historical Working Paper No. 098 (1997).

25. Tom Ryder, "Steel Carriage Springs, Part IV—American Designs," *The Carriage Journal* 16:3 (Winter 1978): 141–4.

26. *The Hub* (November 1881): 418, and (December 1881): 482; Edward Thornton Heald, *The Stark County Story as Told in Radio Broadcasts*, Vol. III (Canton, Ohio: The Stark County Historical Society, 1952), 10; and "A Man of Ideas," 186.

27. I am indebted to Thomas P. Hannon of the Hannon Electric Company, Canton, Ohio, for sharing with me his knowledge of carriage history and for helping with the research on this critical phase of Henry Timken's career. Charles E. Tuttle, "Columbus Buggy Company—Part I," *The Carriage Journal* 15:4 (Spring 1978): 386–91; and "Columbus Buggy Company—Part II," *The Carriage Journal* 16:1 (Summer 1978): 7–14. See also "A Man of Ideas," 186; and for an example of Timken's victory announcement, see *The Hub* (January 1885): 715.

28. *Supreme Court of the United States, Olin et al.* v. *Timken*, November 19, 1894, in *Decisions of the Commissioner of Patents and of United States Courts in Patent Cases, 1894* (Washington: Government Printing Office, 1895), 645–56; and U.S. Circuit Court—Southern District of Ohio, Western Division, *Timken* v. *Olin et al.*, January 15, 1890, in *Decisions of the Commissioner of Patents and of United States Courts in Patent Cases, 1890* (Washington: Government Printing Office, 1891), 393–5.

29. *The Hub* is quoted in "A Man of Ideas," 186–7. The art collection of William R. Timken and Lillian Guyer Timken was divided between the National Gallery of Art and the Metropolitan Museum of Art, as described in obituaries at the time of her death (see, for example, the *Cleveland Plain Dealer*, November 11, 1959).

30. "Biography of Henry Timken," 2. It was likely on his travels in this period that Timken acquired land in Rush County, Kansas, which he sold to the Railroad Town Site Company with the understanding that the new town, along the route of the Acheson Topeka and Santa Fe Railroad, would be named Timken, Kansas ("Timken Named for Roller Bearing Family," n.p., n.d., in Timken Company Archives). The Timkens' fondness for European travel comes through in a note, written late in life, by Fredericka to her son Will: "I wish I could go with you when you go to Germany. I can beat Pa altogether in that language, even if I do say it. He does not use good grammar." Fredericka Timken to William R. Timken (August 26, 1908), in Timken Company Archives.

31. *The Hub* (November 30, 1893): 306.

32. Information on W. R. Timken's involvement in Mutual Wheel Company and St. Louis Carriage Manufacturing Company from the corporate minute books of the St. Louis Carriage Manufacturing Company, Timken Corporate Archives.

33. H. H. Timken is quoted in Foster, "This Business Grew Nearly 200-Fold." The information on the pattern of deafness in the family is from W. R. Timken, Jr., written comments.

34. Timken Carriage Company and St. Louis Carriage Manufacturing Company minute books, in Timken Company Archives; and "A Man of Ideas," 167.

35. Jean-Pierre Bardou, Jean-Jacques Chanaron, Patrick Fridenson, and James M. Laux, *The Automobile Revolution: The Impact of an Industry*, James M. Laux, trans. (Chapel Hill: University of North Carolina Press, 1982), 12, 14–20. See also Robert Paul Thomas, "An Analysis of the Pattern of Growth of the Automobile Industry, 1895–1929," unpublished Ph.D. dissertation, Northwestern University, 1965, 9–13.

36. H. H. Kohlsaat, "America's First Horseless Carriage Race, 1895," *Saturday Evening Post* (January 5, 1924): 21. Kohlsaat was the editor of the *Times Herald* and chief organizer of the race. Two accounts of the race that differ somewhat in details are provided by Thomas, "Analysis," 21–3; and Allan Nevins, *Ford: The Times, The Man, the Company* (New York: Charles Scribner's Sons, 1954), 139–41.

37. Kohlsaat, "Horseless Carriage Race," 89; and Nevins, *Ford*, 133, 141, 146. A well-known first-hand comment on the emergent American technical community in the early 1890s is by Hiram Percy Maxim (quoted in Nevins, *Ford,* 133) : "As I look back I am amazed that so many of us began work so nearly at the same time, and without the slightest notion that others were working on the same problem. In 1892, when I began my work on a mechanical road vehicle, I suppose there were fifty persons in the United States working on the same idea. Why did so many different and widely separated persons have the same thought at the same time?" Even that retrospective comment shows the lack of awareness of developments in Europe, where Daimler and Benz had both patented motorized vehicles by 1886.

38. Foster, "This Business Grew Nearly 200-Fold." On the bicycle sulky and its impact: "A Man of Ideas," 187–8; and "The Sulky," *The Hub* (October 1892): 242–3.

39. This paragraph relies on Morton, *Anti-Friction Bearings*, 1–7; 443–5; 467; and E. Sachs, "Ball Bearings: Origin, Manufacture, Design, and Application," *The Automobile* 20 (May 13, 1909): 787–9. The equipment sold by the Cleveland Screw Machine Company was developed under patents it had acquired from a Massachusetts firm, the Waltham Emery Wheel Company, and from John J. Grant.

40. Morton, *Anti-Friction Bearings*, 9; and Heinzelman, "The Story of the Creation of the Timken Roller Bearing Company."

41. Heinzelman, "The Story of the Creation of the Timken Roller Bearing Company." Heinzelman, understandably, expressed regret that they chose not to pursue the original design for an annular ball bearing.

42. Morton, *Anti-Friction Bearings*, 10–12, 16–21, 456.

43. Morton, *Anti-Friction Bearings*, 456–7. On the development of grinding machines and their importance for bearing production, see Nathan Rosenberg, "Technological Change in the Machine Tool Industry, 1840–1910," *Journal of Economic History* 23 (1963): 434–5, including the following excerpt from Robert S. Woodbury, *History of the Grinding Machine* (Cambridge, Mass.: MIT Press, 1959), which refers to ball bearings but was equally true for roller bearings: "The successful ball bearing depends upon having the balls themselves perfectly spherical and all of identical diameter. The ball must run in races perfectly circular, perfectly concentric, and of exact dimensions. Not only must the balls and their races be machined to a fine surface finish, but all these dimensions must be held to close tolerances, and all these parts must be hardened. Only grinding could deal with this problem."

44. Company tradition places this event in 1895, but logically it could just as well have occurred at a later time, when the development of a distinctive design was further along. A review of St. Louis papers from 1895 through 1899 turned up no mention of the incident to date it and prove conclusively that it took place.

45. Morton, *Anti-Friction Bearings*, 16–22 provides a review, with drawings, of numerous early roller bearing patents. On tapered roller bearing patents preceding those of Henry Timken, see also correspondence between The Timken Company and its patent attorneys Carr & Carr & Gravely, of St. Louis; see J. J. Gravely to G. H. Turner (June 28, 1938), in Timken Company Archives.

46. The distinction between the Timken-Heinzelman design and others is clarified in Herbert W. Alden, "Self-Aligning Taper Roller Bearings," *The Automobile* (February 27, 1908): 281–2.

47. Alden, "Self-Aligning Taper Roller Bearings," 281. The ten-month process of rejection, amendment, and final granting of the bearing patents is detailed in correspondence between the commissioner of patents and Carr & Carr (predecessor to Carr & Carr & Gravely). The relationship of the designs embodied in the Timken-Heinzelman patents to subsequent evolution of the Timken bearing is covered in "History," unpublished MS (August 1, 1974), a document prepared by Timken Company engineers as part of a corporate initiative to compile a history of the company. According to Edmund Heinzelman ("History of the Creation of the Timken Roller Bearing Company"), the addition of the intermediate rollers was the contribution of Henry Timken, while the basic design was conceived by Reginald Heinzelman; but none of the contemporaneous documents give any indication of authorship of specific ideas.

48. State of Missouri, Certificate of Incorporation No. 11262 (December 15, 1899).

49. Foster, "This Business Grew Nearly 200-Fold," 230.

50. Ibid.

51. H. H. Timken to Cora Burnett (October 21, 1935), in Timken Family Papers; Henry Timken obituary, *San Diego Union* (March 18, 1909), 3; and Earl Goris, *With Dignity and Respect and Reverence for Age: The Eighty-five Year History of a Precedent-setting Retirement Community, Fredericka Manor* (San Diego: Pacific Homes/ Fredericka Manor, 1996). One of the family's most significant contributions was its sale to the city of a large tract of land on San Diego Bay, at less than its book value, which the city set aside for the location of a United States naval base. In addition, H. H. Timken personally gave $5,000 to help the city purchase the land from the family's investment company. (H. H. Timken to Senator Warren G. Harding [December 30, 1916] and reply [January 1, 1917]; and Timken to Colonel Edward G. Fletcher [September 9, 1919] in Timken Family Papers.)

52. H. H. Timken to A. C. Ernst (January 2, 1936), in Timken Family Papers.

Chapter 2: "Famous Automotive Brothers"

1. R. L. Cusick, "Famous Automotive Brothers, Part II," *Automotive Industries* (December 31, 1927): 970–2; 981.

2. H. H. Timken to W. R. Timken (May 9, 1917), in Timken Company Archives.

3. In 1920, each of the Timken brothers and Hugh Chalmers had pledged equal shares in a $1 million underwriting syndicate for Maxwell-Chalmers. The Chase National Bank joined this syndicate in 1921, taking over 60 percent of the total subscription (Agreement between H. H. Timken, W. R. Timken and Hugh Chalmers and The Chase National Bank of the City of New York [June 23, 1921], in Timken Company Archives). On the role of the Chase syndicate in the reorganization of Maxwell-Chalmers and the emergence of Chrysler, see John B. Rae, *American Automobile Manufacturers: The First Forty Years* (Philadelphia: Chilton Company, 1959), 143–5. A frequent co-investor with H. H. was Edward A. Langenbach, who played a central role in making Canton a center of alloy steel production as an organizer and manager of several of the companies that later became Republic Steel. He was general manager of United Steel Company when it developed production of vanadium steel for Henry Ford in 1906. That alloy, with a higher ratio of strength to weight than other steels commercially available at the time, gave Ford the material he sought to develop the Model T. See Heald, "Edward A. Langenbach—Steel Industrialist, 1886," in *The Stark County Story*, Vol. II, 187–99; and "The Henry Ford Steel Tests at Canton, 1906–1907," *The Stark County Story*, Vol. III, 33–9.

4. Information on ownership is from The Timken Roller Bearing Axle Company stock book, in Timken Family Papers. Of the original 1,000 shares of stock, 150 shares were divided among Henry Timken's three daughters and the remainder equally among Heinzelman, Henry Timken, H. H., and W. R. Subsequently the shares acquired from Heinzelman were distributed among the three remaining cofounders, the Timken sisters, and other family members, including Fredericka, Mabel Bridges (daughter of Amelia), Valerie Timken (daughter of W. R.), and three of Henry Timken's nephews who were then employed in the company: John Ringen, Cord Ringen, and O. Heinzelman. Reginald Heinzelman's third roller bearing patent is No. 698,944, issued April 29, 1902; he died of tuberculosis in 1921.

5. Hosfeld is quoted in the *Timken Triangle* 3 (July 1920): 2. H. H. Timken's reputation for physical aggressiveness is also noted in Leland G. Stanford, "San Diego Lawyers You Should Have Known," from a San Diego paper, n.d., a clipping in Timken Family Papers; and in his obituary, *Canton Repository* (October 14, 1940). In 1947 Reginald's brother, Edmund Heinzelman, wrote to Mrs. H. H. Timken, asking what "mistake" his brother had made that had "caused him

the loss of his one-quarter interest in the Timken Company." His "Story of the Creation of the Timken Roller Bearing Company," which chronicles the important role that Reginald played in the development of the Timken bearing, was likely written at about the same time.

6. Timken Roller Bearing Company Catalogue No. 4 (1901), in Timken Company Archives.

7. Timken Roller Bearing Axle Company Catalogue (1901), in Timken Company Archives. Testimonial letters formed a large part of all the early catalogs.

8. Timken Roller Bearing Axle Company ledger for 1899–1901, and contract with Wolf & Colthar (March 12, 1901), in Timken Company Archives. This one ledger book is, unfortunately, the only surviving financial record from the company's early years.

9. Timken Roller Bearing Axle Company sales catalogs and ledgers 1900–1901, in Timken Company Archives.

10. Correspondence discussing a possible venture in automaking was provided by George P. Dorris, III, president, Dorris Company, Inc.: W. R. Timken to G. P. Dorris (June 20, 1903) and reply (June 28, 1903). The timing of these early automotive purchases is documented in Timken Roller Bearing Axle Company ledger for 1899–1901 and sales catalog for 1901. Essential information on Dorris and the early automotive industry in St. Louis was provided by Charles L. Rhoads, automotive historian, in correspondence with The Timken Company, 1995–96, including "St. Louis, Missouri, Early Automotive History," unpublished MS (1996). Mr. Rhoads also supplied copies of pages from the 1903 St. Louis Motor Carriage Company catalog, which advertises the use of Timken roller bearing axles and includes the testimonial from Henry Timken. See also *George Dorris and the St. Louis Auto Industry*, pamphlet (St. Louis: The National Park Service, 1988).

11. Foster, "This Business Grew Nearly 200-Fold," 236.

12. Heald, *The Stark County Story*, Vol. III, 70; *Canton Repository* (February 16, 1904): 4.

13. For a colorful description of McKinley's 1896 Front Porch Campaign and the "replay" in 1900, see H. W. Brands, *The Reckless Decade: America in the 1890s* (New York: St. Martin's Press, 1995), 271–6, 340.

14. The *Canton Repository* (July 29, 1901) quoted Dougherty as saying that they had turned down offers from Middletown, Connecticut, of a building site plus $10,000 bonus and from Beaver Falls, Pennsylvania, of a factory building ready for occupancy. During this period of rapid growth, the city produced a number of pamphlets detailing its advantages for industry, including: *The Industrial Advantages of Canton, Ohio, and Environs, Alliance, Ohio, and Massillon, Ohio, And A Series of Comprehensive Sketches of their Representative Manufacturing and Mercantile Enterprises* (Rochester: James P. McKinney, 1894); and *Canton, City of Diversified Industries* (Canton: The Caxton Press, ca. 1922).

15. On the rise of the machine-tool industry in Ohio and its significance for further industrial development and the region, see Rosenberg, "Change in the Machine Tool Industry," 420–6; and Jon Glasgow, "The Westward Expansion of the Manufacturing Belt: The Ohio Machine Tool Industry in the Late Nineteenth Century," *Ohio History* 10 (Winter/Spring 1991): 20–3. On the automotive industry, see Thomas, "Analysis," 56, 321; and Nevins, *Ford*, 189, 192–209.

16. Monnot is quoted in the *Canton Repository* (June 29, 1902): 10.

17. The *Canton Repository* (July 29, 1901): 1, and (December 1, 1901): n.p.; Map of Dueber Avenue lots, Contract between Canton Board of Trade and Timken Roller Bearing Axle Company, and C. A. Dougherty to Timken Roller Bearing Axle Company (August 30, 1901), in Timken Company Archives; *Timken* 19:4 (1978): 12.

18. On the state of the auto industry in these years, see Thomas, "Analysis," 42–3, 47–50; figures

on annual production of horse-drawn vehicles from U.S. Bureau of the Census, *Historical Statistics of the United States, Colonial Times to 1970*, Bicentennial Edition, Part 2 (Washington, D.C., 1975), 696.

19. H. H. Timken to Henry Timken (December 3, 1902), in Timken Company Archives.

20. Quoted in Eugene W. Lewis, *Motor Memories: A Saga of Whirling Gears* (Detroit: Alved Publishers, 1947), 167–8.

21. Ibid., 24, 39–42.

22. Ibid., 24–5, 195–203; and David Hochfelder and Susan Helper, "Suppliers and Product Development in the Early American Automobile Industry," *Business and Economic History* 25:2 (Winter 1996): 39–51. See also Hiroyuki Itami, *Mobilizing Invisible Assets* (Cambridge, Mass.: Harvard University Press, 1987) 25–6. This important work on the subject of what are commonly called core competencies uses Timken's sales engineering function as an example of a differentiating capability.

23. Lewis, *Motor Memories*, 41.

24. Quotation from Foster, "This Business Grew Nearly 200-Fold," 230. The earliest extant company catalog mentioning case-hardened steel is from 1901, in Timken Company Archives. Timken's manufacturing processes are described, with special emphasis on the adoption of nickel steel, in a special Industrial Edition of the *Canton Repository* (September 5, 1909). This paragraph also draws on "The Metallurgy of the Timken Bearing," unpublished paper (July 24, 1924), in Timken Company Archives.

25. Quoted in the *Canton Evening Repository* (November 13, 1903): 13; on the 1903 project to develop a new axle design, H. H. Timken obituary, the *Canton Repository* (October 14, 1940); on the World's Fair exhibition, *Canton Repository* (March 6, 1904): 3.

26. On Alden's quite notable career both before and after joining Timken, see *Timken Detroit Axle News* 18:3 (1950): 2. This source says that Alden started at Timken in 1907, but Timken letterhead, dated 10-31-06, shows Alden as Mechanical Engineer. Alden held U.S. Patent No. 921,656 on the one-piece cage, applied for April 15, 1907. He also undoubtedly contributed in the area of axle design and was perhaps also responsible for the fact that the company was selling steering knuckles and brakes after 1906 (see Timken ads in *Cycle and Automobile Trade Journal*, 1906–7).

27. Quotations from H. H. Timken to The Adams Company (December 15, 1909), in Timken Company Archives. Information on early bearing applications is from *Timken Tapered Roller Bearings: Bearing Applications in Passenger Cars, Trucks, Buses, Tractors, Farm Implements* (Canton: The Timken Roller Bearing Service & Sales Company, 1930). According to that source, the first automaker to use Timken bearings for differential and steering mechanisms (worm shafts or bevel pinions) was Columbia, of Hartford, Connecticut. Other early users included Dorris, Olds, and Winton. Chalmers and Autocar were among the first to adopt them for transmissions.

28. Alfred P. Sloan, Jr., *Adventures of a White Collar Man* (New York, 1934), 38–9. This paragraph draws largely on Hounshell, *From the American System to Mass Production*, 6, 80–2, 221, 372, n.45.

29. H. H. Timken obituary, *Canton Repository* (October 14, 1940); and Hugh Dolnar, "The Timken Roller Bearing and the Timken Factory," *Cycle and Automobile Trade Journal* 11:11 (1907): 112–26.

30. The sale to Cadillac is noted in H. H. Timken to W. R. Timken (July 16, 1907), in Timken Company Archives. Leland's standards are noted in Sloan, *Adventures of a White Collar Man*, 38. On machine tools available in 1908, see Woodbury, *History of the Grinding Machine*, 136–9.

31. Thomas, "Analysis," 131–41; Nevins, *Ford*, 447–511; and Hounshell, *From the American System to Mass Production*, 10–11, 223–4.

32. Jeffrey R. Yost ("Components of the Past, Assemblages of the Future: The United States Automobile Supply Industry, 1895–1930 [Ph.D. dissertation, Case Western Reserve University, 1998]), discusses Timken's broad customer base and its significance; *Bearing Applications in Passenger Cars, Trucks, Buses, Tractors, Farm Implements*, lists car and truck manufacturers using Timken bearings, 1904–1930; *Canton Repository,* Industrial Edition (September 5, 1909).

33. W. R. Timken to Electric & Ordnance Accessories, Ltd. (December 28, 1909), in Timken Company Archives; Yost dissertation.

34. W. R. Timken to Electric & Ordnance Accessories Co. (February 8, 1910), in Timken Company Archives. Lawrence H. Seltzer, *A Financial History of the American Automobile Industry* (Boston: Houghton Mifflin, 1928), 21, indicates that this form of financing for automakers remained viable until 1909. For a more extensive discussion of credit policy, see Yost dissertation.

35. H. H. Timken to Electric & Ordnance Accessories Co. (January 12, 1910) and W. R. Timken to same (December 28, 1909), in Timken Company Archives. On American Ball Bearing, see Yost dissertation; on the patents covering annular bearings, see Morton, *Anti-Friction Bearings*, 9–10.

36. The best source on Hyatt in this era is Sloan, *Adventures of a White Collar Man*. On New Departure, see Morton, *Anti-Friction Bearings*, 458–9. Charles E. Duryea, "The Battle of the Bearings is Still in Progress," *The Automobile* (December 31, 1908): 965, describes the competition between ball and roller bearings in this era.

37. Quotations from the *Canton Repository* (January 13, 1909): 1; and from the *Detroit Journal*, reprinted in *Canton Repository* Industrial Edition (September 5, 1909).

38. Agreement Relating to Foreign Patents, The Timken Roller Bearing Company and The Electric & Ordnance Accessories Company, Ltd. (July 16, 1909), in Timken Company Archives.

39. On the circumstances of Timken's death, see his obituary, *San Diego Union* (March 18, 1909): 3.

40. H. H. Timken to Electric & Ordnance Accessories Co. (January 12, 1910), in Timken Company Archives.

41. H. H. Timken obituary, *Canton Repository* (October 14, 1940).

42. Chandler, *The Visible Hand*, 412–3, 415. Timken's pattern of adoption of advanced management practices combined with sustained family involvement places it with DuPont on the spectrum of leading industrial firms described by Chandler (*The Visible Hand*, 451–2).

43. See JoAnne Yates, *Control through Communication: The Rise of System in American Management* (Baltimore: Johns Hopkins University Press, 1989), chapters 1 and 2.

44. H. H. Timken to A. R. Demory (September 4, 1915), in Timken Company Archives. In other correspondence Timken described his system for keeping track of work in the metallurgical department and his plans to implement "a more scientific method of handling our shop supplies, that is, keeping a record of the supplies used in each department . . . and thus have year by year the comparative figures so that we can watch each department and see if its use of supplies is going up or down" (H. H. Timken to W. R. Timken [November 11, 1914], in Timken Company Archives). Yates emphasizes the critical role of leadership such as H. H. provided in implementing these systems. It was necessary to have a powerful champion, she suggests, because the costs were significant and resistance from middle managers, who stood to lose a fair degree of autonomy, was inevitable. She also points out that companies frequently started internal magazines, along with other policies aimed at counteracting the

depersonalizing effects of systematic management. Just such a magazine, the *Timken Triangle,* was launched in Canton in 1919. (Yates, *Control through Communication,* 16, 273–4.)

45. *Timken Magazine*: "Automatic Roller Making," (May 1913): 200; and "Closing in the Cages of Timken Roller Bearings," (October 1913): 280. On the development of machine tools for bearing and auto manufacturing in this era, see Woodbury, *History of the Grinding Machine* 114–40. On precision manufacturing at Timken-Detroit, "Foundations of Timken-Detroit Accuracy," *Timken Magazine* (December 1912): 102–3.

46. This paragraph draws on a series of articles on manufacturing processes in *Timken Magazine*: "Automatic Roller Making" (May 1913): 200–1; "Cage Making in Canton" (December 1914): 137–9; "Timken Grinding A Fine Art" (July 1914): 49–52. Much of Timken's process improvement in this era was achieved by developing specialized jigs, fixtures, and gauges for its machine tools. On the fundamental role of such devices in precision manufacturing, see Hounshell, *From the American System to Mass Production,* 6.

47. "Some of the Why and the How of the Timken Magazine," *Timken Magazine* (October 1914): 10–11; A. R. Demory to W. R. Timken (April 21, 1914); W. R. Timken to Heman Ely (September 28, 1916); and Ely to W. R. Timken (November 16, 1916), in Timken Company Archives.

48. Chandler, *The Visible Hand,* 356–7, emphasizes that only a few leading metal fabricators developed in-house sales capabilities by 1917.

49. H. Vanderbeek, "Report on Visit to the Packard Motor Company" (June 6, 1911) and Herbert W. Alden to Heman Ely (June 24, 1911), in Timken Company Archives, describe the conditions under which Timken decided to develop a special bearing for a proposed Packard 5-ton truck. On the 1915 application of Timken bearings to the pinion shaft: "How Many Car Builders Use Timken Bearings—Where Do They Use Them and Why?" *Timken Magazine* (March 1916): 428. On the intent to pursue industrial applications: Jack F. Flaherty to H. H. Timken (March 13, 1915); and Heman Ely to W. R. Timken (September 23, 1915), in Timken Company Archives. Hochfelder and Helper, "Suppliers and Product Development," indicate that the decline of the supplier's role in design began in the decade 1910–19 and became complete in the next decade.

50. H. H. made his position on wage systems clear in a letter to A. R. Demory (September 3, 1915) in which he stated, "For a number of years I have been trying to get you to install a premium system in one or more of your departments to show you how much superior it is to a piecework system." On labor conflict in Canton in 1914–16, see numerous articles in the *Canton Repository,* including the following: "Stark Phone Girls Go Out" (February 14, 1914); "Dozen Union Labor Organizers Coming Here in a Few Days" (March 11, 1914); "I.W.W. Chiefs Coming, A.F.L. Leader Hears" (March 17, 1914); and others in the *Canton Daily News*: "Canton Steel Workers Refuse Offer" (February 20, 1915); "Local Strikers Attend Meeting in Massillon" (February 23, 1915); and "May Import Men to End Strike in Massillon Mill" (February 25, 1915). H. H. Timken noted in May 1916 a recent across-the-board pay increase of 10 percent, which, he believed, had helped the company avoid trouble as strikes continued in the area (H. H. Timken to A. R. Demory [May 5, 1916]), in Timken Company Archives.

51. H. E. Ely to H. H. Timken (March 21, 1917); H. H. Timken to S. S. Marquis (April 27, 1917); F. T. Mackay to H. H. Timken (December 6, 1917), in Timken Company Archives.

52. Mackay to Timken (December 6, 1917). Apparently, Mackay was the head of the Advisory Department. His overview of the operation of the program in 1917 provides some insight into its perceived shortcomings. One of the major causes of complaint among employees subject to

the plan, he indicated, was the company's reassessment of skill levels at the plan's inaugura-
tion. Many saw their previous level reduced, so that their wages did not advance as expected
under the new plan. Others were unhappy when the company set different levels for individuals doing the same job, based on productivity. These complaints suggest why it made sense
to return to the old system, with an hourly rate plus premiums based on piecework calculations, simply raising the hourly rate and paying overtime rates for shifts that exceeded eight
hours. On the hourly rate for the screw-machine department in 1920, J. G. Obermier to H. H.
Timken (March 19, 1920), in Timken Company Archives.

53. Sloan, *Adventures of a White Collar Man*, 77; and H. H. Timken to Heman Ely (March 27,
1917), in Timken Company Archives. The historian Daniel Raff has drawn the connection between investment in manufacturing processes—both machinery and management systems—
profitable growth, and high wages, for example at Ford. See Daniel M. G. Raff, "Making Cars
and Making Money in the Interwar Automobile Industry: Economies of Scale and Scope and
the Manufacturing behind the Marketing," *Business History Review* 65 (Winter 1991): 726–7,
729–31.

54. W. R. Timken to H. H. Timken (March 2, 1912), in Timken Company Archives.

55. Quotation from W. R. Timken to E. B. Lausier (July 12, 1915), in Timken Company Archives;
William R. Timken interview (May 3–4, 1994).

56. Sloan, *Adventures of a White Collar Man*, 93; W. R. Timken to H. H. Timken (February 9 and
March 3, 1915), in Timken Company Archives.

57. H. H. Timken to W. R. Timken (January 20, 1915), in Timken Company Archives. In March
1915, W. R. reported that Timken had won a contract for 1916 for the front axle bearings of
Willys-Overland's most popular car, Model 83, but had cut its price by 27 percent to do so.
Hyatt, he noted, had already closed a contract for the rear axle, "so you see we could not get
all their business" (W. R. Timken to H. H. Timken [March 3, 1915]). For the Bock bearing, see
U.S. Patent 1,144,751, granted June 29, 1915, to Henry L. Bock, of Toledo, Ohio.

58. H. H. Timken to W. R. Timken (February 7 and 12, 1912; and February 24, 1915) and to John
N. Willys (February 25, 1915), in Timken Company Archives.

59. H. H. Timken to W. R. Timken (January 20, 1915).

60. W. R. Timken to H. H. Timken (March 16 and April 15, 1915) and H. H. Timken to W. R.
Timken (March 25, 1915), in Timken Company Archives.

61. W. R. Timken to H. H. Timken (April 15 and November 26, 1915), in Timken Company
Archives; Thomas, "Analysis," 321.

62. Heman Ely to W. R. Timken (January 13, 1916), in Timken Company Archives. H. H.'s view of
Sloan's diversion from the bearing business was remembered by his son (William R. Timken
interview).

63. Sloan, *Adventures of a White Collar Man*, 23.

Chapter 3: H. H. Timken, Organization Builder

1. H. H. Timken to F. J. Fisher (September 10, 1926), in Timken Company Archives.

2. The figures on industry growth and consolidation are from Thomas, "Analysis," and Yost dissertation. The latter provides a thorough discussion of its impact on Timken's pricing policies in this era.

3. H. H. Timken to A. R. Demory, Eugene W. Lewis, Herbert W. Alden (January 20, 1915), in
Timken Company Archives.

4. "Timken Steels Take the Third Degree," *Timken Magazine* (February 1913): 146–7; Marcus
Thompson Lothrop, biographical file in Timken Company Archives.

5. For this paragraph and the next: "Timken Steels Take the Third Degree;" "Weirick—Lightning

Laboratorian," *Timken Magazine* (July 1914): 66–7; "The Most Complete Bearing Plant in the World," *Timken Magazine* (April 1917): 660; "The Timken Steel and Tube Division," *News from Timken* (June 19, 1949), and "The Story of Timken Steel," *Timken Magazine* (November 1916): 562.

6. McCool would go on to a Timken career of more than thirty years. H. H. Timken to W. R. Timken (December 3, 1915); Heman Ely to W. R. Timken (December 11, 1915); and H. Y. Mc-Cool to J. E. Fick (January 20, 1947), in Timken Company Archives; Heald, *The Stark County Story*, Vol. III, 23–4.

7. See *The McGraw Hill Encyclopedia of Science and Technology*, 8th ed. (New York: McGraw Hill, 1997), Vol. 6, 17–18; and Vol. 17, 385–90.

8. M. T. Lothrop to H. H. Timken (March 27, 1914), in Timken Company Archives.

9. H. H. Timken to W. R. Timken (January 4, 1916), in Timken Company Archives. Central Steel was in this period a competitor to Canton's United Steel, the more so because it lured away one of United's top managers, Fred J. Griffiths. In 1926, however, the two companies merged to form Central Alloy Steel Company. During the 1920s, Central Alloy placed increasing emphasis on electric-furnace steel and pioneered the production of stainless steel in the United States. In 1930, when it was taken over by Republic Steel Corporation, Central Alloy was hailed by Republic's chairman as having "the largest capacity in America for making electric furnace steel." Thomas M. Girdler, from his autobiography, *Bootstraps*, quoted in Edward Thornton Heald, *The Stark County Story*, Vol. IV, 64.

10. W. R. Timken to H. H. Timken (December 29, 1915), in Timken Company Archives.

11. H. H. Timken to W. R. Timken (December 20, 1915), in Timken Company Archives.

12. H. H. Timken to W. R. Timken (December 29, 1915, and January 4, 1916), in Timken Company Archives. *Timken Magazine* put the scrap rate at 80 percent in 1916–17: "The Story of Timken Steel," *Timken Magazine* (November 1916): 561–4; and "Steel that Never Leaves the Plant," *Timken Magazine* (April 1917): 661.

13. H. H. Timken to W. R. Timken (April 17, 1918), to M. T. Lothrop (February 5, 1916), and to A. R. Demory (May 5, 1916), in Timken Company Archives.

14. H. H. Timken to W. R. Timken (April 17, 1918).

15. Chandler, *Scale and Scope*, 231, 317, 492, 559–60; and Maurice Lévy-Leboyer, "The Large Corporation in Modern France," in Chandler and Daems, eds., *Managerial Hierarchies*, 119. Chandler (p. 560) notes that Ford "and possibly one or two others" were the exceptions in the United States.

16. J. G. Obermier to H. H. Timken (February 17, 1916), in Timken Company Archives. Chandler, *Scale and Scope*, 38, 494–5, says that manufacturers generally preferred to buy raw materials where they were available at reasonable prices. Naomi R. Lamoreaux, *The Great Merger Movement in American Business, 1895–1904* (New York: Cambridge University Press, 1985), 145, notes the absence of production economies and discusses other motivations for vertical integration.

17. *The Story of SKF* (Göteborg: SKF, 1982), 6. "Much of [SKF's] success was, and still is, due to strict quality control at every stage of manufacture. . . . But while it is relatively simple to maintain high standards in the laboratory and on the shop floor, it is not so easy to apply them to bought-in materials such as steel. It was this thinking that prompted SKF to buy its own steel works."

18. W. R. Timken to C. H. Wills (December 7, 1917), in Timken Company Archives.

19. Allan Nevins and Frank Ernest Hill, *Ford: Expansion and Challenge, 1915–1933* (New York: Charles Scribner's Sons, 1957), 9; Thomas, "Analysis," 178–9.

20. C. H. Wills to H. H. Timken (February 22, 1917), and Heman Ely to H. H. Timken (March 23

and 28, 1917), in Timken Company Archives. Ford's opposition to the adjustable feature of Timken bearings is reported in Charles Balough to H. H. Timken (February 26, 1918), in Timken Family Papers.

21. H. H. Timken to H. C. Wills (May 20, 1919 and July 25, 1917), in Timken Company Archives.

22. H. H. Timken to Joseph Galamb (December 27, 1917), in Timken Company Archives. Another investor in Hercules who played an active role in running it was Edward A. Langenbach (see Chapter 2, note 3).

23. Charles Balough to H. H. Timken (February 26, 1918).

24. H. H. Timken to Heman Ely (February 4, 1918), in Timken Company Archives.

25. Heman Ely to H. H. Timken (March 1, 1918); H. H. Timken to W. R. Timken (January 16 and May 19, 1919) in Timken Company Archives.

26. The correspondence indicating that Timken had extensive contracts includes W. R. Timken to H. H. Timken (September 10, 1917); H. H. Timken to W. R. Timken (November 11, 1917); and H. H. Timken to Stockholders of the Company (December 16, 1918), in Timken Company Archives.

27. H. H. Timken to H. W. Alden (October 19, 1918), in Timken Company Archives. On the distinctions among batch, bulk, and mass production, see Philip Scranton, "Diversity in Diversity: Flexible Production and American Industrialization, 1880–1930," *Business History Review* (Spring 1991): 27–33. Although Timken made very large batches, it produced to order, not for inventory as in bulk production. It presents an excellent example of the "batch specialists" producing for the auto industry that Scranton notes (57, n. 63) but does not discuss.

28. H. H. Timken to W. R. Timken (May 15, 19, 26, and June 2, 1919), in Timken Company Archives. According to this correspondence, Timken-Detroit Axle was the first Detroit company to have a strike in this period, precipitated by the attempt of management there to create and work with an internal, elected employee committee along the lines of a plan developed by Bethlehem Steel.

29. H. H. Timken to W. R. Timken (August 19 and 26, 1919), in Timken Company Archives.

30. H. H. Timken to J. G. Obermier (January 29, 1920); on labor issues at the steel plant, H. H. Timken to W. R. Timken (October 3, 1919) and H. H. Timken to M. T. Lothrop (February 9, 1920); M. T. Lothrop to H. H. Timken (February 26, 1920), in Timken Company Archives.

31. Despite Ely's wishes, Timken would borrow again a few years later to finance the purchase of the Gilliam Company. H. H. Timken to W. R. Timken (January 29 and May 20, 1920); and Heman Ely to W. R. Timken (September 20, 1921), in Timken Company Archives. By H. H.'s calculation the Columbus plant cost $1.5 million and the Maryland Road development an equal amount.

32. These events are detailed in regular correspondence between W. R. and Heman Ely during this period, in Timken Company Archives. On the impact of the recession on other companies, see Chandler, *The Visible Hand*, 456–60; and John B. Rae, *The American Automobile Industry* (Boston: G. K. Hall & Company, 1984), 50–7.

33. H. H. Timken letters to Watt L. Moreland (December 5, 1921) and W. C. Chrysler (May 2, 1921) indicate the amount of research that had been done and describe the processes in detail. Cups and cones were burnished in the green "by means of a fixture having rolls, with the right angle and taper." To prevent warpage in hardening, "we force by pressure a tapered plug in this already expanded hot cup [just out of the hardening furnace], and expand it further from twenty to forty thousandths, and instantly quench. The result is a perfectly true cup with really a smoother surface than the ordinary ground surface."

34. W. R. Timken to H. H. Timken (May 20, 1919), in Timken Company Archives.

35. H. H. Timken stated the level of family investment in "Reasons Why My Salary Was Increased" (January 31, 1922), part of the documentation provided in connection with the sale of shares to the public, in Timken Family Papers.

36. W. R. Timken to H. H. Timken (March 24, 1920); H. H. Timken to W. R. Timken (July 13, 1922); and Agreement between Hornblower & Weeks and Timken Roller Bearing Company (July 20, 1922), in Timken Company Archives.

37. H. H. Timken to F. J. Fisher (September 10, 1926). For Timken's ranking, see Chandler, *Scale and Scope*, Appendix A.2, 645.

38. H. H. Timken to R. E. MacKenzie (October 12, 1920), in Timken Company Archives.

39. On getting the negative report from Reo, Heman Ely reported that Lothrop and chief engineer Tracy Buckwalter were going to visit the customer: "I am sure the session will do us both good." Ely to H. H. Timken (March 23, 1921); and on Gilliam, H. H. Timken to W. R. Timken (August 26, 1919), in Timken Company Archives.

40. On the extent of the reduction in friction, The Timken Roller Bearing Company Annual Report for 1924, 1. George Lee Miller's story as recounted here was told by Miller to George Deal, a personal friend and executor of his estate. In later years Miller was reconciled with the company, became a stockholder, and regularly attended annual meetings. (George L. Deal interview, October 16, 1996.)

41. On the development of Marlin-Rockwell at this time, see Morton, *Anti-Friction Bearings*, 447–50. The significance of the changes encompassed by the Neal and Miller patents is discussed in "History" (unpublished MS, August 1, 1974), an overview of Timken bearing evolution prepared by Timken Company engineers for a history of the company; also "The Metallurgy of the Timken Bearing" (July 24, 1924), in Timken Company Archives.

42. H. H. Timken to W. R. Timken (May 14, 1925); and on the Bock acquisition, J. F. Strough to W. R. Timken (August 10 and August 21, 1926), in Timken Company Archives. Correspondence of 1921 provides detail on the suit against Gilliam.

43. H. H. Timken to W. R. Timken (July 14, 1926), in Timken Company Archives.

44. H. H. Timken to F. J. Fisher (September 10, 1926).

45. The changes instituted in the 1920s by Louis Klinedinst are described in "Contribution of the Timken Roller Bearing Company to Industry during the 1920s," unpublished MS (n.d.), in Timken Company Archives.

46. The Timken Roller Bearing Company Annual Report for 1925, 2.

47. Examples of other companies that hired engineers for sales in the 1920s are Alcoa, for aircraft applications of aluminum alloys, and Bailey Boiler Meter: Pruitt and Smith, "Corporate Management of Innovation," 46–47; and Virginia P. Dawson, "Knowledge is Power: E. G. Bailey and the Invention and Marketing of the Bailey Boiler Meter," *Technology and Culture* (July 1996): 522–24. On the larger pattern of engineers entering corporations at this time, see David F. Noble, *America by Design: Science, Technology, and the Rise of Corporate Capitalism* (New York: Oxford University Press, 1977), 39–49.

48. The Timken Roller Bearing Company Annual Reports for 1926 and 1928; and L. M. Klinedinst to Arthur Kessel (March 8, 1945), in Timken Company Archives. With the exception of data on the 1930s, presented in Chapter 4, there is no extant information on the breakdown of bearing sales until the 1970s, so it is impossible to know in what year automotive bearings sales first fell below 50 percent of the total. In 1976, however, they accounted for just under 30 percent of U.S. bearing revenues ("Analysis of Operating Income—Bearings, U.S. Division," in Timken corporate records).

49. *Timken Trading Post*, 50th Anniversary Issue (June 1949): 18, 27–9; and "Timken Steel and Tube Company," *Blast Furnace and Steel* (October 1928): 1329–30.

50. M. T. Lothrop, "An Extensively Electrified Steel Plant," *Electrical World* (July 30, 1927): 207; and "Timken Forms Steel Subsidiary," *Iron and Trade Review* (September 20, 1928): 737.

51. *Timken Trading Post* (June 1949): 29; Interview with H. C. McCollum, The Timken Company, by Anthony Florence (July 11, 1968), in Timken Company Archives.

52. H. H. Timken to W. R. Timken (June 1, 1925), in Timken Company Archives.

53. Fred Glover to W. R. Timken (May 29, 1925); and H. H. Timken to Fred Glover (December 1, 1927), in Timken Company Archives; Timken-Detroit Axle Company Annual Report for 1929, in Timken Company Archives; *The New York Times* (May 25, 1953): 33–6; and *Dictionary of American Biography*, Supplement 10 (New York: Charles Scribner's Sons, 1995), 691–2.

54. For the industry ranking, see Chandler, *Scale and Scope*, Appendix A.4, 662. According to Morton, *Anti-Friction Bearings*, 468, the Hoover Steel Ball Company, which had been supplying Ford 150,000 bearings per month, manufactured under the Bock patent, simply opted out of the tapered roller bearing line when Ford adopted Timken bearings for the Model A in 1928. Morton was a metallurgist with Hoover at that time.

55. Albro Martin, *Railroads Triumphant: The Growth, Rejection, and Rebirth of a Vital American Force* (New York: Oxford University Press, 1992), 80–9.

56. "T. V. Buckwalter: Chief Engineer, Timken Roller Bearing Company," *Timken Magazine* (April 1917): 680–1; and "Company Consultant Honored," *Timken Trading Post* (February 1946): 5.

57. "Roller Bearings on Freight Cars," *Railway Age* (June 18, 1932): 1032–3.

58. H. H. Timken to W. R. Timken (July 14, 1926), in Timken Company Archives. The plan was to cover the inboard truck with patents and gain an advantage through control of that key improvement. H. H. wrote, "We feel that this inboard truck may be the real reason why the anti-friction bearings will be adopted to a considerable extent."

59. Samuel R. Williams, interview with Barbara Griffith, April 16, 1996.

60. H. H. Timken to W. R. Timken (July 14 and October 9, 1926); and Russell J. Carnes, "Early History of the Railway Division" (n.d. but likely 1937–40); and unidentified newspaper clippings from May 1927, in Timken Company Archives.

61. Robert L. Leibensperger, written comments, provided essential information on Buckwalter's central role and the farsightedness of his thinking about the Four Aces.

62. "A Hundred Thousand Miles for the Timken Locomotive," *Railway Mechanical Engineer* (March 1932): 94; "Roller Bearings Performance on Locomotives," *Railway Age* (August 20, 1932): 255–6; and "'Four Aces' Set Records as It Rolled," *Timken Trading Post* (May/June 1958): 12.

63. "A Hundred Thousand Miles for the Timken Locomotive," 92; "'Four Aces' Set Records as It Rolled," 13; and photo with caption showing the three Chicago women pulling the engine in the Pennsylvania Railroad demonstration, in Timken Company Archives.

64. "A Hundred Thousand Miles for the Timken Locomotive," 92–3; and "Roller Bearings Performance on Locomotives," 256, 258.

65. "Results with Roller-Bearing Equipped Locomotive," *Machinery* (April 1932): 611; Buckwalter's award came in April 1946, just one year after his retirement, as reported in *Timken Trading Post* (February 1946): 5.

Chapter 4: Crisis and Transition

1. H. H. Timken to Mrs. Don R. Mellett (May 23, 1927), in Timken Company Archives.

2. "Cousin Recalls Timken's Tries for 'Instant Cures,'" unidentified news clipping [1980s], in

Timken Company Archives. Cunningham's extravagant claims for hyperbaric medicine were discredited in the late 1930s, but the concept survived and later expanded greatly as a field of treatment for wounds, burns, and related problems (Michael S. Smookler and Paul Cianci, "New Horizons in Hyperbaric Medicine," *Sea Technology* (January 1986): 61–2. Cunningham's tank in Cleveland was torn down and used for scrap metal during World War II.

3. "Bearing Man," *Time* (August 19, 1935): 48.

4. H. H. Timken to H. Vanderbeek (November 24, 1922); and Cora Burnett to H. H. Timken (October 28, 1935), in Timken Family Papers. Said Cora, "It left a queer picture in one's mind of you pacing around on velvet carpets, throwing lighted cigarettes all over like a crazy man."

5. J. F. Strough to H. H. Timken (April 16, 1929), in Timken Company Archives.

6. R. C. Brower to W. R. Timken (June 29, 1932); H. H. Timken to John W. Prentiss (April 21, 1932); William E. Umstattd, interview with Anthony Florence, ca. 1970; Martin Fleischmann, former director, Metallurgical Department, The Timken Company, interview with Anthony Florence, ca. 1970, in Timken Company Archives; Heald, "The Griffiths Brothers–Alloy Steel Pioneers," *The Stark County Story*, Vol. IV, 97–105.

7. "W. E. Umstattd Celebrates 50th Anniversary with the Company," *Timken* 10:7 (1969): 5; "W. E. Umstattd Dies at the Age of 79," *Timken* 14:6 (1974): 4; Citation from The Presentation of the Chevalier of the French Legion of Honor to W. E. Umstattd (January 31, 1962), in Timken Company Archives; Joseph F. Toot, Jr., interview with Davis Dyer and Bettye Pruitt, September 22, 1993; James Umstattd, interview with Barbara Griffith, June 14, 1995; William R. Timken, interview.

8. J. F. Strough to W. R. Timken (April 12, 1928); and F. J. Fisher to H. H. Timken (September 22, 1926), in Timken Company Archives.

9. Morton, *Anti-Friction Bearings*, 465, 467–8 [Morton was a metallurgist with Hoover in 1927]; J. F. Strough to W. R. Timken (April 12, 1928); Bower Roller Bearing Company Annual Report for the Year Ending December 31, 1931.

10. M. T. Lothrop to H. H. Timken (December 24, 1930; January 22 and February 6, 1931); H. H. Timken to M. T. Lothrop (January 5, 1931); W. R. Timken to H. H. Timken (September 15, 1932); The Timken Roller Bearing Company Board of Directors meeting minutes (August 6, 1935), in Timken Company Archives. The board minutes noted, "Chrysler has been very insistent that they be protected by a second source of supply and that this new program would work out to the best interests of Chrysler." It was further noted that Timken was to retain Chrysler's business for the Plymouth, De Soto, and Chrysler cars and for Dodge trucks, hence "the financial effect of this switch will depend entirely upon the popularity of the various models."

11. According to testimony by Louis Klinedinst in the Smith-Leterstone trial, the companies making tapered roller bearings in 1936 (with date of start-up in parentheses) were the following: Bantam (1921); Orange Bearing Company (1922); Hoover (1924); Tyson (1927); Pratt; Bower; and Tapered Roller Bearing Company of America. From 1939 through World War II, Timken's revenue from bearings was four times greater than Bower's, according to data summarized in H. A. Norden to R. C. Brower, "Comparison Sales, Profits, Etc., Timken with Bower" (November 19, 1946), in Timken Company Archives.

12. United States District Court for the Northern District of Illinois, Eastern Division, No. 14348, *The Timken Roller Bearing Company* vs. *Leterstone Sales Co.*, transcript, in Timken Company Archives.

13. According to testimony in the Smith-Leterstone case, replacement bearings constituted roughly

5 percent of bearings sold; but so-called service sales constituted 10 to 15 percent of bearing revenues through the 1930s. The court document indicates that Leterstone Sales had lost a previous case to Timken and in 1926 had been enjoined from the same activities complained of in the 1936 case.

14. Morton, *Anti-Friction Bearings*, 22, 485; and *Story of SKF*, 2–10. According to Morton (485), SKF was the first bearing company "to undertake systematic theoretical and experimental research in ball and roller bearing engineering" and was responsible for establishing the critical relationship between bearing life and load-carrying capacity that provided the foundation for calculating and interpreting bearing performance ratings. SKF Industries launched manufacturing operations by building a plant in Hartford, Connecticut, and by purchasing the Hess-Bright Manufacturing Company (Morton, *Anti-Friction Bearings*, 9–10).

15. *Story of SKF*, 3–4, 9–11.

16. Patent drawings in Morton, *Anti-Friction Bearings*, 22, permit comparison between Palmgren's design (DRP patent 331,651 held by SKF) and the Timken bearing based on the Neal patent. Its distinguishing feature appears to be the inner surface of the cup, which was slightly convex and did not contact the roller along its full length. Unfortunately, the Timken correspondence sheds no light on the rationale for making acquisition of this patent part of the negotiations.

17. J. F. Strough to W. R. Timken (May 6, 1929); Marcus Lothrop to All the Boys (August 22, 1930); summary of internal correspondence on discussion with SKF (December 8, 1930–April 27, 1931), in Timken Company Archives; and *Story of SKF*, 10.

18. H. H. Timken to Mark Lothrop (January 5, 1931), in Timken Company Archives.

19. "Agreement between Timken Roller Bearing Company and Wolseley Motors Limited" (April 6, 1920); and "History of British Timken," *Timken Times* (December 1959), in British Timken Archives; "International Timken," *Timken Magazine* (July–August 1920): 417–18, in Timken Company Archives; and Bardou, et al., *The Automobile Revolution*, 71. Chandler, *Scale and Scope*, 201, states that Timken built its first manufacturing plants abroad after World War I, either not knowing of the activities of E&OA before and during the war or discounting them, perhaps because E&OA was operating as a licensee with no direct investment from U.S. Timken. Be that as it may, the manufacturing activities of E&OA were certainly significant in expanding the market for the Timken bearing.

20. H. H. Timken to W. R. Timken (December 3, 1919), in Timken Company Archives; interview with Charles Nouhaud, former Chief Engineer, Timken France, by Gérard Palenstijn (February 19, 1995). I am grateful to Timken associates Klaus Schulze and Hans J. Lehmann for the research that established the facts of Deutsche Timken's original incorporation in 1918, as well as for additional documentation on this early Timken presence in Germany. The incorporation records list Max Prausnitzer as the general manager (Geschäftsführer) of Deutsche Timken in 1918; in addition, Prausnitzer was a party with Dewar and Timken to a 1928 agreement to reorganize the German company. On the European recognition of Timken bearings and H. H. Timken's reaction to it, see "Proper Bearings for Automotive Vehicles, by Government Architect Dierfeld," *Timken Magazine* (March 1920); and H. H. Timken to Rollin H. White (August 11, 1920), in Timken Company Archives. An important element of the successful rearrangement of Timken's licensing agreements in 1920 was Wolseley's willingness to accept a new provision allowing U.S. car manufacturers to import Timken bearings into its territory. The original agreement had precluded importation of any Timken bearings except in complete vehicles. This had loomed as an onerous constraint in the years following World War I,

as the major U.S. car makers made plans to set up new plants in Europe. In order to use Timken bearings they would have been forced to buy from British Timken, which had considerably higher production costs and therefore higher prices. Such a development, Timken feared, might provoke them to switch all their contracts to other tapered roller bearing suppliers not hampered in the same way. H. H. Timken to W. R. Timken (December 3, 1919), in Timken Company Archives; and "Agreement between Timken Roller Bearing Company and Wolseley Motors Limited" (April 6, 1920), in British Timken Archives.

21. British Timken raised its capitalization, from £50,000 to £100,000 in 1926; British Timken corporate records. Wolseley was bought by William Morris, Viscount Nuffield, a key figure in the early British auto industry. (See R. J. Overy, *William Morris, Viscount Nuffield* [London: Europa Publications Limited, 1976], 28.) A version of the story told at British Timken is that Morris believed he was purchasing British Timken along with Wolseley Motors and that, furious to find out that was not the case, he vowed never to use Timken bearings on any of his cars. Unfortunately, Overy's detailed study of Morris and his business does not consider bearings.

22. Some company sources say that Dewar was vice chairman of Wolseley Motors prior to buying British Timken, but the official biographies note only that Dewar was managing director of Leeds Forge, Ltd., from 1919 to 1922 and of the Metropolitan Carriage Wagon and Finance Company, Ltd., from 1922 to 1927. "Dewar, Michael Bruce Urquhart," *Who Was Who*, 1941–1950, Vol. IV (London: Adam & Charles Black, 1951); obituary of Michael Dewar, *Timken Times* (January 1951), in British Timken Archives; B. R. Powell to C. P. Kindelberger (November 3, 1972), in Timken Company Archives.

23. J. F. Strough to H. H. Timken (March 27, 1929); B. R. Powell to C. P. Kindelberger (November 3, 1972); Nouhaud interview; "History of British Timken"; The Timken Roller Bearing Company Annual Report for 1928. Prausnitzer's continuing role is inferred from the fact that the official record of Deutsche Timken in Berlin lists only two general managers (Prausnitzer and Dr. Ing. Max Wrba) and from his being a party to an agreement with U.S. Timken, British Timken, and Dewar "to take necessary procedure for reconstitution of German Company and to secure completion of agreement between Mr. Prausnitzer and the German Company," in British Timken Archives. The general manager recruited from Société de Mécanique de Gennevilliers was a Monsieur de Beauvivier. He held that position until 1937 and was succeeded by Hubert Adrien Hamilton, who had served as French Timken's chief accountant since 1933. Hubert Adrien Hamilton interview with Maurice Amiel, July 28, 1995.

24. For tax purposes, in 1929 Timken organized a separate corporation, Industrial and Commercial Investments, Inc. (ICI), to hold the shares of French Timken and Deutsche Timken. Timken made the loans to the European subsidiaries through ICI, receiving preferred stock in return for this investment. J. F. Strough to H. H. Timken (March 15, 1929); Strough to W. R. Timken (April 26 and August 13, 1929), in Timken Company Archives.

25. Curriculum vitae of Dr. Ing. Max Wrba, in files of Timken Europa; J. F. Strough to H. H. Timken (March 15, 1929) and to W. R. Timken (April 26 and August 13, 1929); D. P. Hess to M. L. Lothrop (February 11, 1931); R. C. Brower to H. H. Timken (September 8, 1932 and April 30, 1934), in Timken Company Archives. See Timken Roller Bearing Company Board of Directors meeting minutes for December 3, 1929 and March 4, 1930, in Timken Company Archives.

26. "History of British Timken"; J. F. Strough to H. H. Timken (April 8, 1929); J. F. Strough to W. R. Timken (January 29, 1930), in Timken Company Archives.

27. The calculation of the value of the public sale is based on the sale of 125,000 shares at an issue price of 35 shillings per share and an exchange rate of $5.86 per £1 sterling, figures provided

in the following correspondence: R. C. Brower, "Memorandum: British Timken Refinancing" (January 24, 1935); D. P. Hess, "Memorandum Re: New British Timken Deal" (February 12, 1935); and D. P. Hess to W. R. Timken (August 14, 1935), in Timken Company Archives. By 1935, Timken had organized three separate holding companies for its investments in Britain and Europe: Industrial and Commercial Investments, Inc.; Foreign Patents and Investments, Inc.; and International Bearings Investments, Inc. These were merged into a single entity, Continental Bearings, Inc. (CBI), at the time of the public offering of British Timken stock. CBI then became the holding company for Timken's and Dewar's shares in British Timken and its European subsidiaries. See "Agreement of Merger" (April 24, 1935); and Brower, "Memorandum: British Timken Refinancing," in Timken Company Archives.

28. J. C. Sanders, "Introductory Comments on Reports in Two Sections: The Timken Roller Bearing Company" (October 26, 1931); R. C. Brower to W. R. Timken (May 14, 1936), in Timken Company Archives; Bardou, et al., *The Automobile Revolution*, 144–5; Morton, *Anti-Friction Bearings*, 483.

29. R. C. Brower to W. R. Timken (August 7, 1930), in Timken Company Archives; Timken Company Annual Reports; and Standard Corporation Records, Vol. 11, No. 2054 (Hudson, New York: Standard Statistics Co., 1933).

30. The Timken Roller Bearing Company Treasurer's Report (December 1936); R. C. Brower to H. H. Timken (February 22, 1939 and March 1, 1940); and "Comparison of Gross Bearing Sales by Classification" (May 1935[?]), in the files of R. C. Brower, in Timken Company Archives. One measure of relative impact of the Depression is that personal income in the United States declined 42 percent between 1929 and 1932, while auto sales declined 75 percent in the same period. See Nevins and Hill, *Ford: Expansion and Challenge*, 574n. For GM's performance in the Depression, see Table 4.2. Nevins and Hill, 596, reported that Ford lost a total of $125 million over the three years 1930–32.

31. The Timken Roller Bearing Company Treasurer's Report (December 1936); and R. C. Brower to H. H. Timken (February 22, 1939 and March 1, 1940). By 1939 total company sales revived to 94 percent of the 1929 high, while bearing sales remained at just 67 percent of the 1929 level.

32. Quotations from articles published in the *Magazine of Wall Street*: Ferdinand Otter, "In a Class by Itself" (February 6, 1932): 481; William Wren Hay, "Attractive as a Long-Term Holding" (June 24, 1933): 230; and "Timken Roller Bearing Co." (January 7, 1933): 339.

33. R. C. Brower to Marcus Lothrop (June 20, 1930); R. C. Brower to W. R. Timken (June 26 and July 3, 1930).

34. R. C. Brower to W. R. Timken (September 19 and October 4, 1930); M. L. Lothrop to W. R. Timken (November 6, 1930); and M. L. Lothrop to H. H. Timken (December 24, 1930), in Timken Company Archives.

35. H. H. Timken to Marcus Lothrop (December 8, 1930); Lothrop to Timken (December 30, 1930, and February 3, 1931), in Timken Company Archives.

36. R. C. Brower to W. R. Timken (October 24, 1931); and H. H. Timken to Alois Hauser (February 11, 1932), in Timken Company Archives.

37. The Timken Roller Bearing Company Board of Directors, meeting minutes (February 2, 1932); H. H. Timken to Mrs. J. C. Burnett (May 14 and May 20, 1932), in Timken Company Archives.

38. H. H. Timken to Mrs. J. C. Burnett (May 20, 1932), in Timken Family Papers.

39. H. H. Timken to John W. Prentiss (March 21 and June 13, 1932), in Timken Company Archives;

H. H. Timken to A. C. Ernst (January 2, 1936); and H. H. Timken to W. R. Timken (September 21, 1939), in Timken Family Papers; Harold E. Forrest interview with Barbara Griffith, September 26, 1994.

40. R. C. Brower to H. H. Timken (July 1 and August 16, 1933); and Timken Roller Bearing Company, Treasurer's Report (December 1936), in Timken Company Archives.

41. This brief overview follows Louis Galambos and Joseph Pratt, *The Rise of the Corporate Commonwealth: United States Business and Public Policy in the 20th Century* (New York: Basic Books, Inc., 1988), 98–9; and George David Smith and Davis Dyer, "The Rise and Transformation of the American Corporation," in Carl Kaysen, *The American Corporation Today* (New York: Oxford University Press, 1996), 48–9.

42. Prior to 1949, Timken reported operating profit only. R. C. Brower to H. H. Timken (December 7, 1935), in Timken Company Archives; Smith and Dyer, "Rise and Transformation of the American Corporation," 48; Galambos and Pratt, *Rise of the Corporate Commonwealth*, 103–4.

43. This paragraph and the following based on Sanford M. Jacoby, *Employing Bureaucracy: Managers, Unions, and the Transformation of Work in American Industry, 1900–1945* (New York: Columbia University Press, 1985), 223–42; and Galambos and Pratt, *Rise of the Corporate Commonwealth*, 114–6.

44. R. C. Brower to W. R. Timken (October 26, 1933), in Timken Company Archives.

45. Donald W. Simonson interview, December 16, 1997; Brower to H. H. Timken (March 21, 1934 and March 29, 1935), in Timken Company Archives.

46. W. E. Umstattd to Senator Donashey (April 19, 1935), in Timken Company Archives; Harry Mayfield, interview with Barbara Griffith, October 21, 1995; Roosevelt quoted in William E. Leuchtenburg, *Franklin D. Roosevelt and the New Deal, 1932–1940* (New York: Harper Torchbook, 1963), 183–4.

47. H. H. Timken is quoted in William R. Timken interview.

48. Quotation from "Steelworkers' Hard-nosed Boss," *Life* (June 25, 1965): 45–7; and I. W. Abel biography in *Current Biography Yearbook 1965* (New York: H. W. Wilson Company, 1965), 3–5. On management attitudes toward labor unions similar to those at Timken, see Howell John Harris, *The Right to Manage: Industrial Relations Policies of American Business in the 1940s* (Madison: University of Wisconsin Press, 1982), 23–32.

49. Mayfield interview; Jacoby, *Employing Bureaucracy*, 2–6. On the issue of the foreman's power in two cases of unionization efforts with different outcomes, see also Nevins and Hill, *Ford: Expansion and Challenge*, 589–91; and Davis Dyer, *TRW: Pioneering Technology and Innovation since 1900* (Boston: Harvard Business School Press, 1998), Chapter 4.

50. Mayfield interview.

51. William R. Timken interview.

52. William R. Timken interview; biographies of H. H. Timken, Jr., and John M. Timken, in Timken Company Archives.

53. W. R. Timken to J. F. Strough (May 2, 1929), in Timken Company Archives.

54. H. H. Timken to Gordon M. Mather (January 27, 1931), in Timken Company Archives. On the purchase of the plant, R. C. Brower wrote to W. R. Timken (January 24, 1930): "Young Henry, I believe, wanted a sportier model but H. H. decided on the safer type of machine. A year ago H. H. declared up and down he would not buy the boy an airplane but I offered to bet him a good hat that he would eventually be talked into it."

55. Quotation from H. H. Timken to C. F. Kettering (October 11, 1920), in Timken Family Papers.

On Canton Vocational High, H. H. Timken obituary, *Canton Repository* (October 14, 1940): 1; Heald, *The Stark County Story,* Vol. IV, 50; and "New Timken Vocational School Has Print Shop," *The Inland Printer* (December 1939): 104.

56. In writing to W. R. to persuade him to try his new listening device, H. H. said, "You can't tell me you have no mental inquisitiveness to listen to some of these senators, foreign statesmen, etc., who are now talking over the radio every day." H. H. Timken to W. R. Timken (October 10, 1939), in Timken Company Archives. On the September 1939, meeting convened by H. H.: Edward Hungerford, *Timken at War* (Canton: The Timken Roller Bearing Company, 1945), 9.

Chapter 5: Timken at War

1. Hungerford, *Timken at War*, 27.

2. Testimony to the fact that many manufacturing companies sustained developmental work in the crisis is the following note from The Timken Roller Bearing Company Annual Report for 1932: "general engineering work in industry has continued during this period, with the result that a vast number of new developments and new machines have been designed, tested and made ready to be marketed."

3. William Umstattd interview; John C. Richey interview with Bettye Pruitt and Barbara Griffith, November 30, 1994.

4. Woodbury, *History of the Grinding Machine,* 151–4; *Cincinnati Milacron, 1884–1984: Finding Better Ways* (Cincinnati: Cincinnati Milacron, Inc., 1984), 53–5; and James A. D. Geier interview, November 20, 1996. Thanks also to James E. Schwartz of the Midwest History Workshop and Paul Gruber of Cincinnati Milacron for participating in the discussion of centerless grinding.

5. Geier interview.

6. "Assel Elongator Installed at Canton," *Timken Trading Post* (May 1953): 14–15.

7. "Assel Elongator Installed at Canton;" and William Umstattd interview.

8. Information on alloy development in this paragraph and the next is drawn from Ralph L. Wilson to E. E. Thun (December 19, 1947); and "Developments and Contributions to Steel Knowledge," *Timken Trading Post* (June 1949), in Timken Company Archives.

9. For a parallel in the Depression-era technical program of Alcoa Research Laboratories, see Graham and Pruitt, *R&D for Industry,* 205–17.

10. Hungerford, *Timken at War,* 40–8; Fleischmann interview; and "Ex-German Flier Invents Special Steel to Aid Fight Against Axis," unidentified news clipping in Timken Company Archives. Fleischmann worked with Allis-Chalmers on the development of a turbojet engine in the 1940s. On the role of Allis-Chalmers, see Edward W. Constant II, *The Origins of the Turbojet Revolution* (Baltimore: Johns Hopkins University Press, 1980), 222–23, 225. Constant unfortunately does not give much attention to the role of improved materials in that innovation.

11. *Timken Roller Bearing Company vs. Leterstone Sales Co.*, transcript, 137–40; and Timken Roller Bearing Company, Treasurer's Report (December 1936). The seven engineering departments were Railroad Development, Bearing Design & General Engineering, Diesel Pump Engineering, Bearing Factory Engineering, Diesel Plant Engineering, Steel Mill Engineering, Tool Design. On the widespread closing of R&D laboratories, see Margaret B. W. Graham, "Industrial Research in the Age of Big Science," Richard S. Rosenbloom, ed., *Research on Technological Innovation, Management and Policy* 2 (Greenwich, Conn.: JAI Press, 1985), 51.

12. Fleischmann interview; *A Trip through the Timken Plants: Camera Studies of the Manufacture of Timken Steel, Timken Carbon and Alloy Seamless Steel Tubing, Timken Bearings, Timken Rock Bits, and Timken Fuel Injection Equipment* (Canton: The Timken Roller Bearing Company, 1939), 76–80.

13. "Bearing Manufacturer Expands Research and Testing Facilities," *Steel* (April 12, 1937): 50–4; and similar articles in *Railway Age* (April 24, 1937), *Automotive Industries* (March 27, 1937), and *Iron Age* (July 8, 1937). On the life-testing program and its significance, J. D. Stover, "History of Timken Rating Formula, Bearing Fatigue Life Testing, Modes of Fatigue and Their Causes," presentation to The Timken Company International Chief Engineers (November 11, 1971), in Timken Company corporate records; and Jack D. Stover interview, December 6, 1997.

14. "Bearing Manufacturer Expands Research and Testing Facilities," 52–53; and Robert L. Leibensperger interview, January 16, 1998.

15. On the national experience, see Graham, "Industrial Research in the Age of Big Science." A company with a similar experience in the 1930s and World War II, though a dramatically different postwar experience, was Aluminum Company of America (Alcoa): see Graham and Pruitt, *R&D for Industry*, 183–271.

16. Richard Overy, *Why the Allies Won* (New York: W. W. Norton, 1995), 192.

17. Overy, *Why the Allies Won*, 192–3; 200–1. Overy notes that more than four-fifths of all war contracts went to the largest one hundred industrial companies.

18. Hungerford, *Timken at War*, 11.

19. Hungerford, *Timken at War*, 17–21; and D. C. Ladd, typescript statement on the history of Timken Ordnance Company (July 17, 1968), in Timken Company Archives.

20. Hungerford, *Timken at War*, 17–21; Ladd typescript; Deal interview, 1996.

21. Andrea Gabor, *The Man Who Discovered Quality* (New York: Times Books, 1990), 15, 40–56, 73.

22. Overy, *Why the Allies Won*, 198.

23. Hungerford, *Timken at War*, 75–7; "Timken Steel and Tube Division Contributions to the War Effort" (March 8, 1943); and "Timken Steel and Tube Division" (June 19, 1949), in Timken Company Archives.

24. "Some Outstanding Developments for War Emergency" (March 8, 1943); J. F. Leahy to H. M. Richey, "Contributions to War Effort" (May 24, 1944); and S. C. Partridge to W. B. Moore, "Some Outstanding Jobs for the War Effort" (April 24, 1945), in Timken Company Archives.

25. W. Robert Timken to Donald S. Carmichael (May 4, 1945), in Timken Company Archives. Figures on wartime production of trucks and jeeps from Rae, *American Automobile Industry*, 91.

26. "Some Outstanding Developments for War Emergency"; and W. Robert Timken to Donald S. Carmichael (May 4, 1945). According to the official history of the U.S. Air Force in World War II, Schweinfurt was singled out because the concentration of bearing plants was so heavy and because "their destruction would have immediate and critical effects that would pervade the enemy's entire industrial system." USAF Historical Division, *The Army Air Forces in World War II*, Vol. III (Chicago: University of Chicago Press, 1951), 800.

27. Hungerford, *Timken at War*, 14–15, 23–4.

28. Hungerford, *Timken at War*, 10–13; Ladd typescript; Robert Sisson interview with Bettye Pruitt and Barbara Griffith, June 16 and August 8, 1994.

29. On the CIO vote, see the *Canton Repository* (July 15, 1942): 1.

30. *Canton Repository*, page 1 articles on March 15, March 18, and April 3, 1943; Mayfield interview; Sisson interview.

31. *Canton Repository*, page 1 articles on June 8, June 9, July 1, and July 3, 1944.

32. On British productivity compared to German, see Overy, *Why the Allies Won*, 198.

33. "History of British Timken," *Timken Times* (December 1959): 2–3.

34. Obituary of Michael Dewar, *Times* (London) (December 29, 1951); *Who Was Who*, Vol. VI, 1961–70 (London: Adam & Charles Black, 1971), 873.

35. Peter Hennessy, *Never Again: Britain 1945–1951* (New York: Pantheon, 1993), 46–7; E. Ronald Knapp interview with Bettye Pruitt and Barbara Griffith, October 26, 1995.

36. *Timken Times and "FBC" Bulletin* (September 1946): 2–5; Knapp interview; Stanley Aitken interview with Bettye Pruitt and Barbara Griffith, October 26, 1995; Mrs. Stephen Bennett interview with Bettye Pruitt and Barbara Griffith, October 27, 1995; The Rt. Hon. Lord Eden of Winton interview, July 17, 1996.

37. Nouhaud interview.

38. Nouhaud interview; Hamilton interview; and Yves Chapotot, Henri Trepier, and Jacques Lesage interview with Bettye Pruitt and Barbara Griffith, October 25, 1995.

39. Nouhaud interview.

40. Ibid.

41. Ibid.

42. Ibid.

43. Don Cook, *Charles De Gaulle: A Biography* (New York: G. P. Putnam's Sons, 1983), 253; Nouhaud interview; W. E. Umstattd interview.

44. Cook, *Charles De Gaulle*, 288–95.

45. W. E. Umstattd interview.

46. Nouhaud interview.

47. *Timken Trading Post* (November 1949); 8.

48. Melvyn Dubovsky, *The State and Labor in Modern America* (Chapel Hill: University of North Carolina Press, 1994), 193–202; and Harris, *The Right to Manage*, 105–29. The *Canton Repository* covered these Timken strikes in detail in numerous articles, 1945–46; see also Neil W. Chamberlain, *The Union Challenge to Management Control* (New York: Harper & Brothers, 1948), 131, 294, which describes Timken's position in a case heard by the National Labor Relations Board in August 1946.

49. The report of Timken's arbitrator, Herman A. Grey, is quoted in the *Canton Repository* (January 12, 1945), 12.

50. John G. Ketterer, "Staff Meeting Notes," May 15, 1973, in Day, Ketterer, Raley, Wright & Rybolt archives; and U.S. Cartel Suit Charges Timken," *Canton Repository* (July 31, 1946). Thanks to Robert Rybolt and Sheila Markley for sharing some of the law firm's documentation on the antitrust suit.

51. Ketterer, "Staff Meeting Notes."

52. W. R. Timken, Jr., "Take-over Bids in England," unpublished paper (1962) in Timken Family Papers; *Timken Roller Bearing Co.* v. *United States*, opinions of the Supreme Court, 341 U. S. 593 (1951); W. E. Umstattd to F. J. Pascoe (April 9, 1950), in Timken Company Archives; Ketterer, "Staff Meeting Notes;" Robert M. Rybolt and Sheila M. Markley interview with Barbara Griffith (February 2, 1995).

Chapter 6: Timken at Midcentury

1. Galambos and Pratt, *Rise of the Corporate Commonwealth*, 158–66. According to Galambos and Pratt (161), "By the end of the 1950s, this phase of the managerial revolution had reached deeply into the business system."

2. Alfred D. Chandler, *Scale and Scope*, 41–5, describes how the potential for economies of scope residing in the organizational capabilities built up in functionally organized firms drove strategies of diversification. For comparisons to Timken, see recent histories of TRW, which diversified and reorganized in the postwar years, and Cummins Engine, which did not: Dyer, *TRW*; and Jeffrey L. Cruikshank and David B. Sicilia, *The Engine That Could: Seventy-Five Years of Values-Driven Change at Cummins Engine Company* (Boston: Harvard Business School Press, 1997).

3. The quotation is from *Timken Trading Post* (June 1949): 5, the anniversary volume; the July edition describes the open house, in Timken Company Archives.

4. *Timken Trading Post* (July 1949).

5. *Canton Repository* (June 17, 1949).

6. *Timken Trading Post* (July 1949): 7; *The State of the Company* (Canton: The Timken Roller Bearing Company, 1947); and "Roller Bearing Manufacturer Marks Fiftieth Anniversary," *Rock Products* (August 1949): 157.

7. *State of the Company*, 3; and, for a broad discussion of the role of in-house magazines, Yates, *Control through Communication*, 74–7, 192–9.

8. *Timken Trading Post* published seventy-five articles between January 1947 and May 1953 describing the many departments in the company. On Departments 60 and 61 at Gambrinus and the main grinding room in the Canton bearing plant, see the *Timken Trading Post* (October 1949): 13–24 and (January 1951): 20–7.

9. The story of William Powell, who built a public golf course so that he and other African-Americans in the area would have a place to play, is featured in Michael Winerip, "His Most Powerful Drive Was to Play, with Pride," *New York Times* (June 28, 1996): 14. Photos in *Timken Trading Post* and from plant files at Columbus verify the predominance of African-Americans in the sanitation department and the existence of the black Timken softball team.

10. Ralph T. Shipley interview with Barbara Griffith, September 27, 1994; *Timken Trading Post* (July 1946; September 1948; March 1952), in Timken Company Archives.

11. Mrs. H. R. Grable, "Counseling Women at Timken," *The State of the Company*, 145–6.

12. On the Timken Charitable Trust, see *Timken Trading Post* (January 1956): 8; and on Helen Keller's visit, *Canton Repository* (July 22, 1945): 1. In the 1950s, the company received at least two national citations for its employment of the handicapped: the Blinded Veterans Association Employer of the Year Award in 1952 and a Commendation from the President's Committee on Employment of the Physically Handicapped in 1956 (*Timken Trading Post* [September 1952]: 6; and [March 1956]: 15.)

13. "One of the Problems American Manufacturers Have Solved," *Timken Magazine* (November 1918): 129; and "Training at The Timken Company," *Timken Trading Post* (August 1959): 13. On the origin of the suggestion system, see *Exchange* (March 1990): 5; and on the awards given in a typical year in the Umstattd era, *Timken Trading Post* (March 1949): 5–6.

14. *Timken Trading Post* (July 1952).

15. Sisson interview. Timken's incentive system is described in "Grinding: Incentives Up Accuracy," [unidentified magazine clipping in Timken Company Archives] (September 23, 1954): 71.

16. W. E. Umstattd interview.

17. W. E. Umstattd interview. On the fundamental nature of the battle between skilled machine operators and management, see David F. Noble, *Forces of Production: A Social History of Industrial Automation* (New York: Alfred A. Knopf, 1984), 33–4.

18. *Timken Trading Post* (February 1956): 15; and (March 1951): 24.

19. *Timken Trading Post* (September 1959): 18-20; and *Timken* (November 1961): 14–16; and James L. Nickas interview, June 8–9, 1994.

20. *Timken Trading Post* (February 1956): 13–15.

21. Ibid. and *Timken Magazine* (November 1960): 14.

22. *Timken Trading Post* (November 1955): 20–4; and (December 1955): 20–3.

23. *Timken Trading Post* (December 1955): 20–3; and (June 1956): 6–7.

24. *Timken Trading Post* (January 1956): 9–11.

25. *Timken Trading Post* (November 1959): 20–22.

26. Michael Useem, "Corporate Education and Training," in Kaysen, ed., *The American Corporation Today*, 295.

27. Nickas interview; Richey interview; Shipley interview.

28. Richey interview; Sisson interview. On the importance of relationships between R&D and operating divisions, see Graham and Pruitt, *R&D for Industry*, 154–5, 208–11, 214–16. On the contributions of the sales engineering function as described in this paragraph, see Itami, *Invisible Assets*, 26. The sales engineer's close involvement with customers, says Itami, "creates the opportunity to learn about customers' operations and their needs, present and possibly future, and to gather valuable information on the performance of Timken's products in customer applications." In addition, it sets up a flow of information from Timken to the customer through which additional sales can be made; and through regular contact, it "helps maintain a customer-oriented culture at Timken."

29. George L. Deal interview with Davis Dyer and Bettye Pruitt, May 2, 1994; *Timken Trading Post* (January 1947): 24.

30. Deal interview, 1994; Shipley interview; and interview with James D. Holderbaum, May 29, 1998.

31. On Timken's relative size in the steel industry, see *Canton Repository* (March 12, 1951): 1; *Story of SKF*, 13; interview with George T. Matthews, general manager—quality assurance—steel, October 16, 1997.

32. *Timken Trading Post* (February 1956): 13–15.

33. James W. Pilz interview, May 24, 1994; Matthews interview.

34. On the ASM award to Umstattd, see *Canton Repository* (October 13, 1954): 1. Steel Mill innovations are described in the following issues of *Timken Trading Post*: (January 1953): 4–5; (March 1953): 4–5; and (February 1954): 4–5.

35. Division of Development and Research, meeting minutes (October 20, 1943), in Timken Company Archives.

36. "Increase Capacities for Timken Bearings," *Blast Furnace and Steel Plant* (August 1957): 904; Jack D. Stover, "History of Timken Rating Formula, Bearing Fatigue Life Testing, and Modes of Fatigue and Their Causes," paper to The Timken Company's International Chief Engineers (November 11, 1971); Nickas interview.

37. "Company Announces $3 Million Expansion," *Timken Trading Post* (May 1957): 4–5; Deal interview, 1994; Shipley interview; Pilz interview.

38. Pilz interview; Nickas interview.

39. Sisson interview.

40. Mrs. H. H. Timken, Jr., interview, August 11, 1994; Deal interview, 1994; Sisson interview.

41. R. C. Brower to H. H. Timken (March 1, 1937), in Timken Company Archives; Pilz interview, Deal interview, 1994.

42. Deal interview, 1994.

43. Mrs. H. H. Timken, Jr., interview.

44. George Dippel, "A History of The Timken Company Corporate Aviation Department" (January 30, 1995), in Timken Company Archives; William R. Timken, Mrs. H. H. Timken, Jr., interviews.

45. H. H. Timken to E. G. Heinzelmann (December 5, 1923), in Timken Family Papers. Sisson interview; Ward J. Timken interview with Davis Dyer and Bettye Pruitt, October 14, 1993; Richard L. Frederick interview, July 1, 1994.

46. William R. Timken interview; Erich A. Fischer interview, June 20, 1996.

47. *Canton Repository* (March 17, 1946): 10 noted, "The two brothers figured prominently in last fall's five-week Timken Strike . . . when they publicly defended the strike position of Mr. Umstattd." In 1957, accepting an award for the Timken Foundation, Bob Timken took pains to note that Umstattd was his and his brother's "most trusted adviser": *Canton Repository* (October 10, 1957): 10.

48. Deal interview, 1993; Sisson, Shipley, Nickas interviews; James E. O'Connor interview with Barbara Griffith, September 26, 1994.

49. W. R. Timken, James Umstattd, O'Connor, Sisson interviews; Deal interview, 1993; Norman H. Peterson interview with Davis Dyer, Bettye Pruitt, and Virginia Dawson, September 22, 1993.

50. Various company publications give the story of the early misquote, for example, *History of The Timken Company* (Canton: The Timken Company, 1991), 9. W. E. Umstattd interview; Mayfield interview; George LaMore interview, November 14, 1996; Umstattd obituary, *Canton Repository* (December 3, 1973): 6.

51. "Countertrend," *Forbes* (July 1, 1958): 17–8; Timken Company Annual Report for 1957.

52. H. H. Timken to Mrs. J. C. Burnett (January 6, 1932), in Timken Family Papers.

53. Frederick C. Crawford interview with Davis Dyer and Bettye Pruitt, November 3, 1993.

54. Nickas interview.

55. Deal interview, 1993; Nickas interview.

56. *Timken Trading Post* (February 1949): 5; and Deal interview, 1994.

57. John Dos Passos, "Where Do We Go From Here?" *Life* (January 27, 1947): 96.

58. File of advertisements, in Timken Company Archives; and "Memo from the President," *Timken Trading Post* (April 1958): 3, and (June 1958): 3.

59. William E. Umstattd to C. M. Goethe (April 14, 1952); and file of advertisements in Timken Company Archives.

60. On the broad phenomenon, described as "a conservative counter-offensive . . . waged by business," see David Vogel, "Why Businessmen Distrust Their State: The Political Consciousness of American Corporate Executives," *British Journal of Political Science* (January 1978): 63–5. "Radio Script" (July 9, 1950), in Timken Company Archives; and various issues of *Timken Trading Post*, 1947–59.

61. Harris, *The Right to Manage*, 28–9, 132–3, 157–8; and Frederick interview.

62. W. R. Timken, Jr., written comments; and *Canton Repository* (October 1 and December 13, 1949).

63. Donald W. Simonson interview with Barbara Griffith, April 11, 1995; and Robert W. Lang interview with Barbara Griffith, June 2, 1995.

64. *Canton Repository* (July 2, July 7, and August 21, 1952) and (August 26, 1956); Simonson interview, 1995.

Focus Chapter: Bucyrus

1. Carroll W. Pursell, Jr., *The Machine in America: A Social History of Technology* (Baltimore: The Johns Hopkins University Press, 1995), 287–8; Noble, *Forces of Production*, 60–1, 66–7.

Noble's book touches on the excitement over computerized controls and on automation using traditional mechanical devices, as at Timken, but focuses mostly on something in between: the development of numerical controls for machine tools in the 1960s. On the central role of the moving assembly line in creating mass production, see Hounshell, *From the American System to Mass Production*, 10–13, 237. See also James R. Bright, "The Development of Automation," in Melvin Kranzberg and Carroll W. Pursell, Jr., eds., *Technology in Western Civilization*, Vol. 2 (New York: Oxford University Press, 1967), 635–51; and John Diebold, *Automation: The Advent of the Automated Factory* (New York: D. Van Nostrand Company, Inc., 1952), 54–89.

2. Pursell, *The Machine in America*, 282–7; Noble, *Forces of Production*, 57–67.

3. Ladd typescript. James Bright ("The Development of Automation," 651) describes a similar early use of automated handling in a 155-mm shell plant put into operation by the U.S. Army just at the end of World War II. There were many similarities between that and the Timken gun barrel plant: the pieces handled were large; mechanical handling made it possible for women to run the plant; the process steps included heat treatment and grinding. However, the army plant had some features—for example, automatic gauging and inspection and "trouble-indicator" lights—designed to make the plant operable by unskilled workers.

4. "Division of Development & Research, First Meeting" (October 2, 1943), in Timken Company Archives.

5. W. E. Umstattd interview. On Taylor and Scientific Management, see Robert H. Guest, "The Rationalization of Management," in Kranzberg and Pursell, eds., *Technology in Western Civilization*, 52–64; and Pursell, *The Machine in America*, 210–13. I am grateful to Carroll Pursell for pointing out the connections to Taylorism in much of Timken's thinking about production during this era.

6. H. H. Timken to W. R. Timken (December 20, 1915), in Timken Company Archives; and Richey and Nickas interviews on the development of cost-estimating methods and the calculation of hourly machine-operating costs during and just after World War II. H. Thomas Johnson and Robert S. Kaplan, *Relevance Lost: The Rise and Fall of Management Accounting* (Boston: Harvard Business School Press, 1987), especially Chapter 6, discusses the general trend away from detailed cost accounting after 1920.

7. W. E. Umstattd interview; and "BU-CY-RUS," text of slide presentation, n.d., in Timken Company Archives.

8. On the introduction of tungsten-carbide tooling to the automotive industry, see William J. Abernathy, *The Productivity Dilemma: Roadblock to Innovation in the Automobile Industry* (Baltimore: The Johns Hopkins University Press, 1978), 189–90. W. E. Umstattd interview; E. S. Newman, "Mechanized Roller Bearing Plant," *Mechanical Engineering* 79 (October 1957): n.p.; H. J. Urbach [executive engineer, The Timken Roller Bearing Company], "Why and How the Timken Company Built an Automatic Bearing Plant," paper presented to the Society of Automotive Engineers National Production Meeting, March 19, 1959, 5.

9. W. E. Umstattd interview. On the negative implications of Taylorism for skilled machine operators, see Guest, "The Rationalization of Management," 55–61.

10. W. E. Umstattd interview; Russell P. Fowler interview, February 6, 1998; K. W. Sullivan, "Introduction/Welcome to Bucyrus Operations" (November 2, 1993), in Timken Company Archives.

11. "The Supplier's Role in Standardization," *Purchasing* (April 28, 1958): 77–8; Richey interview; Pilz interview; Timken advertising materials (1948); and "The Bucyrus Concept," press release (1957), in Timken Company Archives.

12. "The Bucyrus Concept"; and Urbach, "Why and How," 2–3, 5–6.

13. "The Bucyrus Concept"; Newman, "Mechanized Roller Bearing Plant"; and Anderson Ashburn,

"America's Automatic Factory," *American Machinist* 101 (September 23, 1957): 156.

14. James E. Oberlander, one of the Smith Tool and Engineering Company employees hired in 1948, who went on to become Bucyrus plant superintendent (1963–76), helped with this section in both written comments and a phone interview, February 6, 1998. See also "The Bucyrus Concept"; and Charles A. Weinert, "Secrecy Wraps Taken Off Automatic Plant," *Automotive Industries* 117 (October 1957): 985.

15. Oberlander comments; Weinert, "Secrecy Wraps Taken Off," 985.

16. Leo H. Everitt and O. E. Cullen, "Heat Treating of Roller Bearings Is Geared to Automatic Production," reprint from *Metal Progress* (n.d.), in Timken Company Archives.

17. Everitt and Cullen, "Heat Treating of Roller Bearings"; and "The Bucyrus Concept."

18. *Bucyrus Telegraph Forum* (May 19, 1950) and (June 21, 1971), clippings, in Timken Company Archives.

19. "The Computer and The Shipping Center," Timken press release (September 1957), in Timken Company Archives; and Bucyrus group interviews with Barbara Griffith, April 16–17, 1996.

20. Written comments from Glen Wilson, Retired Machine Repair Supervisor—Bucyrus Bearing Plant (1997); "America's Automatic Factory"; "The Bucyrus Concept"; and Bucyrus group interviews.

21. "America's Automatic Factory"; "The Bucyrus Concept"; Bucyrus group interviews.

22. Bucyrus group interviews. This discussion of improved working conditions follows Abernathy's analysis of Ford's automated engine plant, in *Productivity Dilemma*, 88, 105–7; but contrasts with David Noble's view, which emphasizes the deskilling effects of automation (*Forces of Production*, 335–9).

23. Form letter of invitation to journalists (n.d.), in Timken Company Archives; Fowler phone interview.

24. Peter Trippe, "Russia's 'Automatic Factory,'" *American Machinist* (January 14, 1957), reprint in Timken Company Archives.

25. "Timken Officials Will Fly to Moscow," *Canton Repository* (June 16, 1945): 3.

26. "America's Automated Factory," 155–6.

27. Joseph Geschelin, "Million and a Half Automotive Bearings A Month," *Automotive Industries* (August 1, 1948): 26–30; John Squire, "Automated Lines for Heat Treating Bearings," *Automotive Industries* (December 15, 1957): 48–52; "The Supplier's Role in Standardization," *Purchasing* (April 28, 1958): 77–8; "America's Automated Factory," 153; "Bucyrus Press Conference," *Timken Trading Post* (October 1957): 4–5; and "BU-CY-RUS." When Fafnir Bearing Company built a new plant in Newington, Connecticut, that did *not* incorporate significant automation, it was described as purposely bucking the prevailing industry trend: "New Plant By-Passes Full Automation," *Steel* (March 11, 1957): 196–7.

28. Everitt and Cullen, "Heat Treating of Roller Bearings"; Pursell, *The Machine in America*, 287–9; Noble, *Forces of Production*, 63–6; 69–70.

29. "The Bucyrus Concept."

Chapter 7: Timken Bearings on a Roll

1. "Memo from the President," *Timken Trading Post* (April 1951): 3; *Canton Repository* (March 12, 1951; August 20, 1953; and October 3, 1955).

2. *Timken Trading Post* (September 1953): 26–7; Robert L. Leibensperger interview, February 13, 1998.

3. "Company Marks Fifth Anniversary of First AP Bearing Put into Service," *Timken Trading Post*

(August 1959): 7; "What is an AP Bearing?" *Timken* (September 1963): 11; Nickas interview.

4. *Canton Repository* (November 22, 1955): 1; "Columbus Discovers Bucyrus," *Timken* (November 1962): 31–4; Nickas interview.

5. "Columbus Discovers Bucyrus," 32; "Roller Bearings Take Hold," *Modern Railroads* (September 1959): n.p.; "One Millionth 'AP' Bearing Made at Columbus," *Timken* (September 1963): 8–11; "Two Millionth 'All Purpose' Railroad Bearing Produced at Columbus," *Timken* (June 1966): n.p.

6. "Company Marks Fifth Anniversary," 8; "25 Years Ago, The Timken 'AP' Bearing Revolutionized Rail Freight," *Timken* (June 1979): 6; and "The Elmer A. Sperry Award," *Timken* (January 1978): 4–5. On Timken's share of the rail freight market in the early 1960s, and its size, see "One Egg, Many Baskets," *Forbes* (May 1, 1963): 21. On Brenco's position in the market: J. W. Pilz, "Marketing Objectives," *Passport to Progress: Timken 1967 International Sales Conference*, in Timken Company Archives.

7. "One Egg, Many Baskets."

8. "Timken to Spend $51 Million," *Canton Repository* (June 6, 1958): 1; and "Countertrend."

9. "One Egg, Many Baskets"; "Bearing Makers Face Earnings Improvement," *Financial World* (March 25, 1959): 11, 31; and "Bearing Sales Roll Toward New Record," *Steel* (August 8, 1960): 121–2. My thanks to Jack Stover for tracking down this information on Tyson: Heald, *The Stark County Story*, Vol. IV, 63–71.

10. *Timken Trading Post* (December 1946): 5–6.

11. This paragraph draws largely on articles in *Timken Trading Post*, as follows: (December 1946): 5–6; (January 1947): 14–5; "Memo from the President," (February 1948): 3, and (June 1948): 3. Other sources are H. C. Sauer, "The Foreign Division," *The State of the Company*, 138–40; Deal interview, 1994; Joseph F. Toot, Jr., interview with Barbara Griffith, July 18, 1995.

12. E. Fischer interview.

13. "International Sales Conference," unpublished document (October 23–28, 1955), in Timken Company Archives; *Timken Trading Post* (November 1955): 28–9 and (December 1957): 5–6; Henry F. Altorfer, "History of Timken Germany," typescript (September 19, 1995), in Timken Company Archives; E. Fischer interview.

14. Mira Wilkins, *The Maturing of Multinational Enterprise: American Business Abroad, 1914–1970* (Cambridge, Mass.: Harvard University Press, 1974), 331–4, 375–9; and Mira Wilkins, "America and the World Economy," in Robert H. Bremner, Gary W. Reichard, and Richard J. Hopkins, eds., *American Choices: Social Dilemmas and Public Policy since 1960* (Columbus: Ohio State University Press, 1986), 219–46; Toot interview, 1995.

15. *New York Times* (May 25, 1953): 33–6; biography of Willard F. Rockwell in *Dictionary of American Biography*, Supplement 10 (New York: Charles Scribner's Sons, 1995), 691–2; and Pilz interview.

16. William R. Timken interview; Altorfer, "History of Timken Germany"; E. Fischer interview; *Timken Trading Post* (March 1956): 11; *Timken* (April 1965): 6; and William E. Judy interview, July 9, 1996.

17. Altorfer, "History of Timken Germany"; Judy interview; E. Fischer interview.

18. William J.C. North, interview with Bettye Pruitt and Barbara Griffith, November 29, 1994; and the following issues of *Timken Trading Post* (August 1957): 6–7, 14; (May/June 1958): 8–9; and (September/October 1958): 8–9.

19. North interview.

20. *Timken Trading Post* (December 1959); *Story of SKF*, 14; Sisson interview.

21. "Timken's Progress," typescript (1959), in British Timken Archives.

22. *Timken: British Timken*, company publication ca. 1960, in British Timken Archives.

23. *Timken: British Timken*.

24. Aitken, Knapp, Frederick interviews.

25. Aitken, Knapp, Frederick, Eden interviews.

26. Knapp interview.

27. "History of British Timken"; Knapp interview; George Bentley interview with Bettye Pruitt and Barbara Griffith, October 26, 1995; and Joseph F. Toot, Jr., written comments.

28. *Timken Times and "FBC" Bulletin* (September 1946): 2–5; Knapp, Aitken, Bennett, Eden interviews.

29. Knapp and Frederick interviews; Raymond Addicott interview, June 9, 1994; and Raymond Tuckey interview with Bettye Pruitt and Barbara Griffith, October 27, 1995. Dick Frederick, director of labor relations for U.S. Timken in the 1950s, confirmed that the spirit of labor relations was one of the major differences between the two Timken companies at that time.

30. Hennessy, *Never Again*, 46–7, 51, 276, 309; Paul Addison, *Churchill on the Home Front, 1900–1955* (London: Pimlico, 1963), 99–100; Bentley interview; and Dennis Ashton interview with Bettye Pruitt and Barbara Griffith, October 26, 1995.

31. "History of British Timken"; From *Timken Times and FBC Bulletin*: "Bearing Design at Aston" (April 1954): 28–31; and "Presenting Timken to Timken and the Rest of the World" (January 1950). Aitken, Bentley, D. Ashton interviews.

32. Roland Treen, "Impressions in America," *Timken Times and FBC Bulletin* (March 1954): 32–3; D. Ashton, Tuckey, Aitken interviews.

33. "History of British Timken"; Addicott interview.

34. For the general view of U.S. companies in Britain, see John H. Dunning, *American Investment in British Manufacturing Industry* (London: George Allen & Unwin, Ltd., 1958), 164–74, 310.

35. Tuckey interview.

36. "History of British Timken"; Aitken, Bentley, D. Ashton interviews.

37. D. Ashton interview. For a contemporary British view of the effects of U.S. antitrust law, see Dunning, *American Investment in British Manufacturing Industry*, 316–21.

38. "Control Inspection and Quality Control Engineering," *Timken Trading Post* (July 1951): 18, 23; and interview with Kai Licht, February 11, 1998.

39. Gabor, *The Man Who Discovered Quality*, 57–8; Licht interview. See also the discussion in Lazonick, *Competitive Advantage on the Shop Floor*, 286–8.

40. From the *Timken Times and FBC Bulletin*: "Statistical Quality Control: Timken-Fischer Course at Leicester" (September–October 1952): 22; and "Statistical Training at Duston" (November 1954): 4; Knapp and Addicott interviews.

41. Knapp interview.

42. "History of British Timken"; articles from the *Timken Times and FBC Bulletin*: "Birth of a Baby" (June 1953):12–3; C. R. Dunn, "A Survey of the Miniature Bearing Market"; and G. Marchant, "FBC Set out to Make Miniatures" (May 1954): 30–5.

43. Kendall Brooke, interview with Barbara Griffith, September 1994; Aitken, Bentley interviews; "History of British Timken"; and three articles in the *Timken Times and FBC Bulletin*: Santosh Bagchi, "Centenary of the Indian Railways" (September/October 1953): 6–7; "Overseas: Satisfactory Increase in Exports during 1954" (February 1955); and Richard Howard, "Railways and Timken Applications" (February 1954): 28–31.

44. Knapp, Bentley interviews.

45. W. R. Timken, Jr., "Take-over Bids in England," unpublished paper (1962), in Timken Family Papers.

46. *Timken* (January 1960): 1; Timken, "Take-over Bids in England."

47. Nouhaud interview; Toot written comments.

48. Nouhaud interview; W. R. Timken, Jr., written comments.

49. Nouhaud interview. Said one historian, "After 1949 West German politics were, frankly, unexciting—which was perhaps a sign of their efficacy" (Norman Davies, *Europe: A History* [New York: Oxford University Press, 1996], 1074).

50. Cook, *De Gaulle: A Biography*, 321–7.

51. Nouhaud interview; Maurice Amiel interview, May 3, 1994; Edmond Gerrer and Louis Matler interview with Bettye Pruitt and Barbara Griffith, October 24, 1995.

52. Gerrer-Matler interview; and text of speech by Gerrer at Timken plant opening in Colmar, June 1961, in Timken Europe corporate records.

53. Gerrer-Matler interview; "Zone industrielle, Transaction Immobilière Timken," report of Mayor Rey to Colmar Municipal Council (November 3, 1958); Toot written comments.

54. Gerrer-Matler interview.

55. Gerrer-Matler interview; *Timken* (March 1969), 9–11.

56. Timken, "Take-over Bids in England."

57. Ibid.

58. *Timken Trading Post* (February 1953): 6; William R. Timken interview; Deal interview, 1994.

59. Toot interview, 1995.

Chapter 8: Competition on an International Scale

1. "Move from Strength," *Forbes* (December 1, 1964): 44; and T. M. Rohan, "Bearing Makers Roll to Big Year," *Iron Age* (December 31, 1964): 27.

2. "Move from Strength"; Rohan, "Bearing Makers Roll to Big Year"; and comparative rates of growth presented by W. R. Timken, Jr., in *Passport to Progress*.

3. Lawrence G. Franko, "Multinationals: The End of U.S. Dominance," *Harvard Business Review* (November–December 1978): 96. See also Wilkins, *Maturing of Multinational Enterprise*, 375–9.

4. Deal interview, 1993.

5. Deal interview, 1993; Toot interview, 1993.

6. Career biography of Markley in *Timken* (May 1979): 6; Amiel interview.

7. Sisson interview.

8. Sisson interview; Joseph F. Toot, Jr., interview, September 23–24, 1997.

9. William R. Timken interview; Toot interview, 1993.

10. Timken quotation from Michael Winerip, "Canton's Biggest Employer is Out of Step, and That's Fine with Him," *New York Times* (December 2, 1996): B8; Sisson interview.

11. William R. Timken interview.

12. Toot interview, 1995.

13. Ibid.

14. W. E. Umstattd, "Summary and Concluding Remarks," *First International Conference for General Managers* (April 19–22, 1960), 147, in Timken Company Archives.

15. Amiel interview.

16. Wilkins, *Maturing of Multinational Enterprise*, 416ff.

17. Umstattd, "Summary and Concluding Remarks," 146.

18. Joseph Selby, "The Problems of Quality in International Operations," *First International Conference for General Managers*, 134–6.

19. Ibid.

20. Ibid; and Robert L. Leibensperger and Thomas W. Strouble written comments.

21. Selby, "The Problems of Quality in International Operations"; and Joseph Selby, "Interchangeability," in *International Scope of the Timken Roller Bearing Company, Bearing Divisions* (Canton: The Timken Roller Bearing Company, 1966), 3.

22. *First International Conference for General Managers*, 113–4, 121; Knapp interview.

23. Knapp interview; John Bostock interview, July 18, 1996.

24. C. H. McCollam, "Report of Meeting with VAL-TI [*sic*]" (August 4, 1966); and Lord Plowden to H. H. Timken, Jr. (July 11, 1967), in Timken Company Archives; Bostock interview.

25. E. H. Hughes, "Supply and Demand," *Passport to Progress*; W. R. Timken, Jr., written comments.

26. Claude Perret interview with Bettye Pruitt and Barbara Griffith, October 23, 1995.

27. Perret interview; Michael Clements interview with Bettye Pruitt and Barbara Griffith, October 26, 1995.

28. North interview; and W. H. Shealor, "International Sales," *Passport to Progress*; and "Profile of our Competitors," presentation to Timken International Sales Conference, June 1972, in Timken Company Archives.

29. Shealor, "International Sales"; and Brooke interview.

30. Brooke interview.

31. Judy interview; Gerhard Reiter interview with Bettye Pruitt and Barbara Griffith, October 23, 1995.

32. Judy, Reiter interviews.

33. *Story of SKF*, 13–16. Said William Umstattd of SKF's growth strategy, so different from Timken's, "The S.K.F. company claims to be the biggest manufacturer of anti-friction bearings in the world; and this claim may be true, as they make almost every type of anti-friction bearing conceivable" ("Worldwide Bearing Competition," *Passport to Progress*).

34. Shealor, "International Sales."

35. Toot interview, 1995; Perret interview; A. J. Grainger, "European Sales Situation" (October 20, 1966), in Timken Europe corporate records.

36. Toot interview, 1997; Chapotot-Trepier-Lesage interview.

37. Ibid.

38. R. A. Gulling to A. J. Grainger (October 13, 1966) and reply (October 31, 1966), in Timken Europe corporate records.

39. Ibid.; Maria Luisa Garavaglia Fuchs and Alberto Fauda interview, July 15, 1996; Roberto Dotti interview with Bettye Pruitt and Barbara Griffith, October 23, 1995.

40. D. L. Hart, "Timken Europe" (May 8, 1970), in Timken Europe corporate records.

41. E. Wooler, "Tapered Roller Bearing Standardization" (January 6, 1932), in Timken Company Archives.

42. Wooler, "Tapered Roller Bearing Standardization"; and C. R. D. Tuckey, "The Metric System," *Passport to Progress*; Fayette Leister and R. M. Riblet, "American and Foreign Standards for Ball and Roller Bearings," *Magazine of Standards* 20 (November 1949): 292–3, 307.

43. Tuckey, "The Metric System"; and Leibensperger written comments.

44. Tuckey, "The Metric System."

45. Grainger, "European Sales Situation"; and "Timken Europe's Annual Report for 1966," n.d., in Timken Europe corporate records; and *Passport to Progress*.

46. *Passport to Progress*.

47. J. Seiwerts, "The ISO Bearing Market," *Papers Presented at the International Distributor Conference* (November 1978), in Timken Company Archives.

48. *Passport to Progress.*

49. Seiwerts, "The ISO Bearing Market"; Perret interview.

50. Albrecht Fischer interview, July 21, 1996.

51. A. Fischer interview.

52. *Story of SKF*, 9; Strouble interview (February 10, 1998); *Passport to Progress.*

53. Grainger, "European Sales Situation;" Jean Bouley interview, July 16, 1996; *Tomorrow's Railway*, SNCF publication (ca. 1975), 2–3.

54. Bouley interview.

55. On development of the European network of high-speed trains, "The High Speed Trains," a publication of GEC Alsthom Transport (1994). A history of the development of the TGV is available in French: Jean-François Picard et Alain Beltran, "D'ou viens-tu TGV?" *La Revue Générale des Chemins de Fer* (Août-Septembre 1994), a publication of Association pour l'histoire des chemins de fer en France. My thanks to Yves Peyronnaud, Timken director of sales for France and Benelux, and to Jean Bouley for assistance in obtaining those publications.

56. David Eley interview, July 19, 1996; George Jones interview, July 19, 1996; and "Leyland Cars 77 mm Gearbox Details," MS supplied by David Eley.

57. Citation from The Presentation of the Chevalier of the French Legion of Honor; and "W. R. Timken, Jr., Receives France's Legion of Honor Distinction," Timken news release (August 26, 1991).

58. *Colmar* (Colmar: S.A.E.P. Ingersheim, 1989).

59. Gerrer, Amiel interviews; Alberto Bianchi interview, July 15, 1996. On the Nene Foundation: John Thorpe interview with Bettye Pruitt and Barbara Griffith, October 26, 1995; and *The Nene Foundation, 1965–1977*, pamphlet (n.d.) in British Timken corporate records.

60. Amiel interview.

61. Amiel interview; Gerrer interview.

62. Brooke interview.

63. Wilkins, "America and the World Economy," 224; and William J. Lederer and Eugene Burdick, *The Ugly American* (New York: W. W. Norton & Company, 1958).

Chapter 9: Chasing Demand

1. Henry Timken was responsible for the location, which is next to the Akron-Canton airport. He had led the movement to establish a municipal airport immediately after World War II. He wished to ensure its future by encouraging industrial rather than residential development of the surrounding area, to minimize complaints about airport noise. (W. R. Timken, Jr., written comments; Mrs. H. H. Timken, Jr., interview.)

2. R. E. McKelvey, W. F. Green, R. L. Wilson, H. R. Neifert, E. S. Rowland, "A Study of Research and Development: Appraisal of the Present Program; Proposals for the Future" (March 30, 1964), in Timken Company Archives; Toot written comments.

3. Galambos and Pratt, *Rise of the Corporate Commonwealth*, 140–1, 172–4; Graham, "Industrial Research in the Age of Big Science," 47–79, especially Table 1.

4. McKelvey, et al., "A Study of Research and Development"; Leibensperger interview; *Story of SKF*, 13; on tribology, *Timken* (June 1972): 12; and, on the work of SKF and the general indifference to tribology in U.S. industry, Raymond J. Larsen, "Tribology: The Little Known Science of Friction and Wear," *Iron Age* (November 6, 1978): 51–4.

5. McKelvey, et al., "A Study of Research and Development"; Leibensperger interview, 1998; Ralph E. McKelvey interview with Virginia Dawson, June 10, 1994; phone interview with Tom Strouble and Ron Widner (February 17, 1998).

6. McKelvey, et al., "A Study of Research and Development."

7. Ibid.; and W. R. Timken, Jr., written comments.

8. McKelvey, et al., "A Study of Research and Development."

9. Ibid.; Leibensperger interview.

10. McKelvey, et al., "A Study of Research and Development"; Leibensperger interview, 1998; McKelvey interview; Strouble and Widner interview.

11. McKelvey interview; Robert L. Leibensperger interview, October 15–16, 1997; Arthur L. Christenson interview, October 9, 1997.

12. *Canton Repository* (March 16, 1968); *Timken* (April 1968): 4–5; W. R. Timken, Jr., interview, October 16, 1995.

13. W. R. Timken, Jr., interview, September 23, 1997. Pilz's comments and information on the beginning of information systems development from *Passport to Progress*; text of speech by William R. Timken (January 3, 1967), in Timken Company Archives.

14. Nickas interviews; Richard A. Gulling interview, June 16, 1994; and J. Kevin Ramsey interview with Bettye Pruitt and Barbara Griffith, May 4, 1995.

15. Ramsey, Sisson, Christenson interviews; W. R. Timken, Jr., interview, February 19, 1998.

16. Quotation from W. R. Timken, Jr., in *Passport to Progress*; Ramsey interview.

17. Pilz interview.

18. Toot interview, 1997.

19. W. R. Timken, Jr., written comments.

20. Herbert E. Markley, "From the President," *Timken* (May 1979): 3–4; and "The Development of Management Philosophy and Policy," six-volume video set, in Timken Company Archives.

21. Foster, "This Business Grew Nearly 200-Fold," 230. One manuscript history ("The Timken Company" [1972,] in Timken Company Archives) states at the end, in reference to the independence quote, "That is The Timken Company Tradition. That is the keystone to Timken Company management. That, in effect, is the principle [*sic*] element in The Timken Company history." The interviews that Anthony Florence conducted with Umstattd and others were done at this time; see also "History for W. E. Umstattd, 1969," and N. H. Peterson, "Company History Project Review" (September 11, 1974), in Timken Company Archives.

22. Toot written comments; "The Cost of Being Involved," *Timken* (June 1972): 24–5; "Company to Spend $14 Million in Canton for Clean Air," *Timken* (March 1973): 12; "Canton Water Purification Plant Dedicated," *Timken* (April 1978): 24–5.

23. Robert G. Wingerter interview with Barbara Griffith, December 19, 1994.

24. Interview with Robert M. Rybolt, November 25, 1997; W. R. Timken, Jr., written comments.

25. D. O. Scheetz, "Japan—Our Newest Competitor," *International Operations and General Managers Conference*, 1968, n.p., in Timken Company Archives.

26. W. R. Timken, Jr., written comments; and Eugene L. Stewart interview, October 6, 1997.

27. J. F. Toot, Jr., "From the President," *Timken* 11:7 (1970): 3; and *Timken* 15:5 (1974); Stewart interview; Toot written comments.

28. Deal interview, 1994; and Markley quotation from "Timken Steers its Own Course—Successfully," *Iron Age* (May 10, 1978): 33–6. The Timken Company Annual Report for 1975 (p. 3) takes care to note that the bonds the company was issuing did "not constitute any change in

our basic philosophy and attitude toward the use of debt or borrowings."

29. "The Development of Management Philosophy and Policy"; "Timken Steers its Own Course—Successfully."

30. "Timken Steers its Own Course—Successfully"; Richey interview; Marshall Schober interview with Bettye Pruitt and Barbara Griffith, November 15, 1994; group interview, Canton Bearing Plant, October 16, 1997.

31. W. R. Timken, Jr., interview, 1997.

32. Ibid.; and "Gaffney: A New Bearing Plant for The Timken Company," *Timken* (January 1970): 4–5.

33. M. N. Laronge, "Life and Death Race," *Iron Age* (February 27, 1969): 48–9; James M. Beattie, "Bearings Industry Won't Cry Wolf—Yet," *Iron Age* (April 29, 1974): 32–3; "Higher Tariffs Fail to Cheer U.S. Bearings Manufacturers," *Industry Week* (April 15, 1974): 17, 19, 22.

34. Beattie, "Bearings Industry Won't Cry Wolf—Yet;" "A Low-profit Boom for Makers of Bearings," *Business Week* (October 15, 1979): 160, 165–6; and Robert E. Harvey, "Bearing Firms Not Slowed by Friction Here, Abroad," *Iron Age* (August 13, 1979): 43.

35. "Why Timken's 'Stability' Will Save its Bottom Line," *Business Week* (May 17, 1982): 107–8; and "A Low-profit Boom for Makers of Bearings." Other sources for this paragraph: "Timken Rolling at a Fast Clip," *Financial World* (February 14, 1973): 20; and Wyn E. McCoy, "New Company in Japan" (July 17, 1974), in Timken Company Archives.

36. W. R. Timken, Jr., written comments; and "Competitive Race Proves too Much for Federal's Bearings," *Iron Age* (November 4, 1971): 53.

37. *Timken* (May 1967): n.p.; (April 1979): 4–5; and (June 1972): 11–12; "Timken's New Ratings and Bearings," *Automotive Industries* (January 1, 1968): 129, 156; and "Computer Rolls into Bearing Selection," *Iron Age* (January 25, 1973): 51–2.

38. Bruening quote from Harvey, "Bearing Firms Not Slowed by Friction Here, Abroad," 45; W. R. Timken, Jr., interview, 1997; Timken Company Annual Reports.

39. W. R. Timken. Jr., interview, 1997.

40. Timken Company Annual Reports. The company began reporting financial results by line of business in 1977.

41. Timken Europe Annual Reports, 1971–79, in Timken Europe corporate records. On investments by SKF and FAG in the 1970s, see *Story of SKF*, 17–18; "Still on Top," *Forbes* (August 1, 1971): 18–19; and the following in the *Economist*: "Rolling SKF into a New Shape" (April 11, 1970): 60–1; "Bearings: Seizing Up" (October 2, 1971): 83; "Sunrise in Düsseldorf" (October 21, 1972): 89; and "SKF's Smooth Move" (October 26, 1974): 96.

42. Timken Europe Annual Reports for 1976–79, in Timken Europe corporate records.

43. Timken Europe Annual Reports; *Timken Bearing News*, International Edition (February 1979), n.p.; and H. J. Lehmann, "Haan—What It Means to You," papers presented at the International Distributor Conference, 1979, in Timken Company Archives.

44. James K. Preston interview, September 22, 1997.

45. Preston interview.

46. J. T. Cook, L. D. Peterson, E. S. Hoopes, "Report on Trip to Western Europe and England to Investigate Continuous Casting of Steel" (May 10–24, 1964), in Timken Company Archives; *Timken* (September 1965): 8–9; Knapp interview. For information on the minimill and the adoption of continuous casting by Nucor Corporation, see Richard Preston, *American Steel: Hot Metal Men and the Resurrection of the Rust Belt* (New York: Prentice Hall, 1991).

47. Matthews interview; Preston interview.

48. Preston interview; Matthews interview.

49. Matthews interview.

50. Preston interview; Matthews interview; Timken Company Annual Report for 1980, with a special segment on the steel business.

51. Matthews interview.

52. William R. Timken interview; Schober interview; Toot written comments.

53. *50-Year Journey: The Story of Latrobe Steel Company on Its 50th Anniversary* (Latrobe: Latrobe Steel Company, 1963), 3.

54. Ibid., 6.

55. Ibid., 7–8; Schober interview.

56. *50-Year Journey*, 11–15.

57. Ibid., 17–18.

58. Schober interview; *50-Year Journey*, 21; Latrobe Steel Company Annual Reports for 1962 (p. 8), 1964, and 1967; and John Davenport, "The Special Case of Specialty Steels," *Fortune* (November 1968): 129–30.

59. Latrobe Steel Company Annual Reports for 1966 and 1968; Schober interview.

60. Latrobe Steel Company Annual Reports for 1970–74; Schober interview.

61. Schober interview.

62. Ibid.; and Toot written comments.

63. Latrobe Steel Company Annual Report for 1968; Schober interview.

64. Schober interview; Toot written comments.

65. Schober interview; *50-Year Journey*, 18.

66. Schober interview; Coyne is quoted in "How Changes in Work Rules Sparked a Walkout," *U.S. News & World Report* (April 17, 1978): 84.

67. "How Changes in Work Rules Sparked a Walkout"; *Business Week* (February 27, 1978): 43.

68. Schober interview; *Wall Street Journal* (May 2, 1978): 14.

69. Matthews interview. On the prospects for the 1980s, see Timken Company Annual Report for 1979, 2–3.

70. John Schubach interview, December 16, 1997; Gene E. Little interview, February 4, 1998; The Timken Company and SKF Annual Reports, 1968–80.

71. Leibensperger interview, 1997; phone interview with Jack D. Stover, January 8, 1998; phone interview with Ronald Widner, February 12, 1998.

72. Leibensperger (1997), Stover, Widner interviews; and Jack D. Stover and Robert V. Kolarik II, "The Evaluation of Improvements in Bearing Steel Quality Using an Ultrasonic Macro-Inclusion Detection Method," Timken Company Technical Note (January 1987).

73. Leibensperger (1997), Stover interviews.

74. T. W. Strouble, R. J. Addicott, C. A. Moyer, W. J. Timken, C. P. Weigel, C. H. West, "A Study of Research, Development and Technical Departments" (October 26, 1978) in Timken corporate records.

75. Strouble, et al., "A Study of Research, Development and Technical Departments;" W. R. Timken, Jr., interview, 1997.

76. Several works by Margaret B. W. Graham chart these changes in the national climate for R&D: "Industrial Research in the Age of Big Science," 47–79; "Corporate Research and Development: the Latest Transformation," *Technology in Society* 7 (1985): 183–4; and on the disenchantment

of the 1960s, *RCA and the Videodisc: the Business of Research* (New York: Cambridge University Press, 1986), 104–9. On a technology company that diversified into nontechnological fields, see Dyer, *TRW*.

77. H. H. Timken to W. R. Timken (May 14, 1925), in Timken Company Archives.

78. "Joseph F. Toot, Jr., Elected President to Succeed Herbert E. Markley," *Timken* 20:5 (1979): 6–7.

Focus Chapter: Faircrest

1. J. F. Toot, Jr., various discussions and written comments; W. R. Timken, Jr., interview, 1997.

2. Schubach interview.

3. Toot written comments.

4. Toot interview, 1997; Preston interview; Shipley interview; Bill J. Bowling interview, December 5, 1996. Although imports of specialty steel increased dramatically in the 1960s and 1970s, this competition was less pronounced and detrimental to the domestic industry than that suffered by U.S. basic carbon-steel producers. With the exception of two years (1971 and 1975), imports of specialty steel to the United States during these two decades were less than 15 percent of the domestic market. *United States Senate, Hearing Before the Committee on Banking, Housing, and Urban Affairs, Economic Conditions in Specialty Steel Industry* (Washington, D.C.: U.S. Government Printing Office, January 5, 1982); Paul A. Tiffany, *The Decline of American Steel: How Management, Labor, and Government Went Wrong* (New York: Oxford University Press, 1988), 167–184; Robert W. Crandall, *The U.S. Steel Industry in Recurrent Crisis: Policy Options in a Competitive World* (Washington, D.C.: The Brookings Institution, 1981).

5. Schubach interview, 1996; Bowling interview, 1996.

6. Bowling interview, 1996; Preston interview.

7. Bowling interview, 1996; Schubach interview, 1996.

8. Matthews, Schubach interviews.

9. Bowling interview, 1996; Matthews interview and written comments.

10. Bill J. Bowling interview, October 15, 1997.

11. Schubach interview, 1996; and Dravo Engineers and Constructors, *The Timken Company, Canton, Ohio, Feasibility Study for a Steelmaking Facility, Final Report, Volume 1, Gambrinus Farm Site* (January 30, 1981).

12. On the comparative rates of adoption of continuous casting technology and discussion of its significance, see Michael L. Dertouzos, Richard K. Lester, and Robert M. Solow, *Made in America: Regaining the Productive Edge* (Cambridge, Mass.: The MIT Press, 1989), 279–82.

13. Ibid.; Matthews interview.

14. Dravo, *Feasibility Study for a Steelmaking Facility*; Toot written comments.

15. Schubach interview, 1996.

16. Dravo, *Feasibility Study for a Steelmaking Facility*.

17. Bowling interview, 1996; Schubach interview, 1996.

18. "OK Indicated on Timken Package," *Canton Repository* (November 1, 1981): 1, 8.

19. "OK Indicated on Timken Package"; and "Timken Talks Tough to Win Concessions," *Business Week* (November 9, 1981): 43.

20. Schubach interview, 1996; Toot written comments.

21. Schubach interview, 1996; and a case study on the Faircrest project in Robert T. Lund, Albert B. Bishop, Anne E. Newman, and Harold Salzman, *Designed to Work: Production Systems and People* (Englewood Cliffs, N.J.: PTR Prentice Hall, 1993), 123.

22. Tim Timken quotations from Michael Winerip, "Canton's Biggest Employer is Out of Step, and That's Fine with Him."

23. Timken's ratio of debt to total capital (equity plus debt) in 1983 was 13.3 percent. Comparisons at that time were made on debt-to-equity: Timken's debt-to-equity ratio was 15 percent, compared with the average for U.S. industrial firms of 100 percent ($1 of debt for every $1 of equity). Said an industry analyst of Timken: "Strategically and financially they're in better shape than anybody else in the steel industry. Nobody else has any money in that industry." Timken presents a strong case for the conservative financial policy advocated by Arie de Geus (*The Living Company*, 171–86). See Mark Potts, "Timken Jolts Steel Industry by Building Ohio Plant," a *Washington Post* wire service dispatch printed in the *Columbus Dispatch* (July 5, 1984), n.p.; "A Perilous Swing to Short-term Debt," *Business Week* (July 9, 1984), n.p.; Kathy Rebello, "Steel Firm's New Mill Bucks Trend," *USA Today* (May 23, 1984); and "Reagan: Tax Plans Sparked New Plant," *Canton Repository* (September 26, 1984).

24. "Recession Buying Bee Speeds Timken's Automatic Look," *Business Week* (September 20, 1958): 160–2.

25. Bowling interview, 1996.

26. Toot and Leibensperger written comments.

27. Lund, et al., *Designed to Work*, 118–9; Mark Breibart, "Fit to be Tied," *Computerworld* (April 3, 1989): 63–4.

28. Richard Creal, "Quality, Efficiency Highlight Timken's New Canton 'CTTF,'" unidentified clipping in Timken Company Archives.

29. Preston interview; Lund, et al., *Designed to Work*, 122, 124–6.

30. Faircrest group interviews (October 19, 1997).

31. Bowling interview, 1996.

32. Faircrest group interviews; Toot written comments; Connie E. Thomas interview, June 5, 1998.

33. Preston interview.

34. Toot written comments; Toot interview, 1997.

35. Lund, et al., *Designed to Work*, 127; Matthews interview.

36. Charles H. West interview with Davis Dyer and Bettye Pruitt, October 14, 1993; Timken Company Annual Report for 1986.

Chapter 10: Crisis and Transition

1. On comparative levels of capital spending as a percentage of sales, Timken Company Annual Report for 1982, 6.

2. W. R. Timken, Jr., interview, 1997.

3. Ibid., and Ward J. Timken biography (February 5, 1996) from The Timken Company.

4. Ibid., and Toot interview, 1997.

5. On productivity and competitiveness, Steven S. Cohen and John Zysman, *Manufacturing Matters* (New York: Basic Books, 1987), 61–6; and Dertouzos, et al., *Made in America*, 29–31. On the currency issue, see Jack L. Hervey and William L. Strauss, "A Regional Export-Weighted Dollar: A Different Way of Looking at Exchange Rates," *Assessing the Midwest Economy*, Working Paper Series, no. GL-2 (Federal Reserve Bank of Chicago, 1996), 10–12.

6. Diane C. Swonk, "The Great Lakes Economy Revisited," *Assessing the Midwest Economy*, Working Paper Series, no. SP-2 (Federal Reserve Bank of Chicago, 1996), 2–4, 8; and *Assessing the Midwest Economy: Looking Back for the Future* (Federal Reserve Bank of Chicago, 1997), 5–7.

7. Pilz interview; and on the same pattern in other industries, Dertouzos, et al., *Made in America*, 56.

8. Jerry Flint, "Paint the Devil," *Forbes* (May 11, 1981): 187–8; and Mark Webster, "Bearing Up under the Japanese," *Financial Times* (May 14, 1982), 32.

9. Licht interview; "The Word is Quality," *Timken* (April 1982): 6–8; and "SPC," *Timken* (June 1983): 14–7; and "Quality: It's the Name of the Game," *Timken* (May 1986): 9.

10. Licht interview.

11. "Quality: It's the Name of the Game," 9–12; William H. Miller, "Timken Jumps into Tomorrow," *Industry Week* (September 2, 1991): 73; and Timken Company Annual Reports for 1990–97.

12. For the Dana official quote, Thomas M. Rohan, "Imports Sting U.S. Bearings," *Industry Week* (March 31, 1986): 68. On market share of imports in 1986, "Marketplace: Roller Bearings," *Purchasing* (September 11, 1986 and July 16, 1987); and *Encyclopedia of American Industries* (1994), 958. Published sources on Timken's share of the U.S. tapered roller bearing market in the 1980s include "Why Timken's 'Stability' Will Save Its Bottom Line," 107; Ralph King, Jr., "You Do the Job or You're Dead," *Forbes* (October 3, 1988): 56; and "Marketplace: Roller Bearings" (September 11, 1986).

13. Rohan, "Imports Sting U.S. Bearings," 66–8; and Joseph F. Toot, Jr., letters to employees (August 5 and December 26, 1985; January 9, 1986), in Timken Company Archives.

14. R&D spending figures from Timken Company Annual Reports; comparison to technology leaders from King, "You Do the Job or You're Dead," 56; and to the steel industry from Robert L. Leibensperger, "Power Density: Product Design for the 21st Century," *International Journal of Technology Management, Special Publication on the Role of Technology in Corporate Policy* (1991): 221. On investments in computerization, see "Timken Expands, Seeks to Attack Specialty Steel Biz," *Business Marketing* (May 1985): 114; and articles in *Timken*: "OPAC" (July 1982): 4, 12–13; "Company Operations Just Seconds Apart" (June 1985): 14–16; and "Making Real Changes" (June 1987): 16–19.

15. W. R. Timken, Jr., interview, 1997; and on the antitakeover measure, David Hagelin, "Timken Takes Action Intended to Protect Self Against Takeover," *Canton Repository* (December 20, 1986): 5.

16. Michael Hattersley, "The Timken Company," Harvard Business School Case No. 9-387-035 (Boston: Harvard Business School, 1986), 5.

17. W. R. Timken Jr., interview, 1997; Toot interview, 1997; and Toot written comments.

18. James Bennett interview with Barbara Griffith, December 16, 1994; Leibensperger and Toot written comments.

19. Peter Ashton interview; and Peters and Waterman, *In Search of Excellence*, 8–12.

20. Schubach interview, 1997; P. Ashton, J. Bennett interviews.

21. J. Bennett, West interviews.

22. "'Best Ever' Pact Hailed by Unionists," *Canton Repository* (October 12, 1968): 1, 8; "Timken Doing What Has to be Done," *Canton Repository* (August 25, 1985): 33; Hattersley, "The Timken Company," 3; Simonson interview, 1997.

23. Robert W. Lang interview with Barbara Griffith, June 2, 1995; Simonson interview, 1995.

24. Hattersley, "The Timken Company," 4; Mayfield interview; "Work Continues at Timken for Less Pay," *Canton Repository* (August 29, 1983): 1.

25. Hattersley, "The Timken Company," 6; "5,800 Off Jobs After Timken Vote," *Akron Beacon Journal* (September 15, 1986): A1; and Jim Quinn, "The Timkens: Canton's First Family," *Akron Beacon Journal* (March 15, 1987): 14.

26. "Timken Strikers Criticize Offer," *Canton Repository* (October 21, 1989): 1; Lang interview; Bowling interview, 1996; Schubach interview, 1996; Faircrest group interview.

27. Toot written comments; Stewart interview.

28. Toot interview, 1995; "W. R. Timken, Jr. Is a 'Missionary' on Capitol Hill," *Canton Repository* (March 8, 1986): 2; and W. R. Timken, Jr., written comments.

29. "Toot: Japan Undercuts Timken," *Canton Repository* (October 4, 1985): 1; Joseph F. Toot, Jr., "Executive Exchange," *Industry Week* (January 26, 1987): 14; and "Sales, Profit Margins, Jobs Increasing after Anti-dumping Wins," *Timken* (December 1987): 10–11.

30. "Timken Wins Bearing-dumping Claim," *Canton Repository* (September 16, 1987): 1; Stewart interview.

31. Toot interview, 1995.

32. Matthews interview; Timken Company Annual Report for 1986, 10.

33. Timken Company Annual Reports for 1986 and 1989; Leibensperger, "Power Density"; and Leibensperger written comments. The close relationship between Chrysler and Timken is described in various sources: Robert A. Lutz, "Interfacing at the Interface," *UMTRI Research Review* (September–December 1991): 7; "Thomas T. Stallkamp, 1996 Executive of the Year," *Automotive Industries* (February 1996): 80; "Timken Bridges Tiers With SCORE To Save $2.6 Million Annually," *Chrysler Corporation Supplier* (July/August 1997); and Robert L. Leibensperger, "A Supplier's View of The Extended Enterprise," speech to the International Congress on Target Costing, The University of Akron (October 27, 1997).

34. "Timken: Bearings Straight," *Purchasing* (June 13, 1985); "Timken: New Bearing Gets the Job Done for Less Money," *Purchasing* (April 28, 1988); and "P900—a Powerful Weapon," in *Timken: Winning the Transaxle Wars*, Timken pamphlet (1996).

35. Michael L. Sullivan-Trainor, "A Gamble and a Long-term View Pay Off," *Computerworld Premier 100* (September 11, 1989): 66–7.

36. Sullivan-Trainor, "Gamble," 66; "Three U.S. Companies to Supply Steel Bar Products to Honda of America for Engine Drivetrain Production," *PR Newswire* (March 6, 1989); and Amiel interview.

37. King, "You Do the Job or You're Dead," 56.

38. "W. R. Timken To Leave The Timken Company Board," news release (April 21, 1987), in Timken Company Archives; and W. R. Timken, Jr., interview, 1997. The seminal work on shareholder value is Alfred Rappaport, *Creating Shareholder Value: The New Standard for Business Performance* (New York: The Free Press, 1986); but see also "Shareholder Value: The Alchemy of the 80s," a special edition of *Planning Review* 16 (January–February 1988).

39. W. R. Timken, Jr., interview, 1997.

40. Ibid., and Gene E. Little, "Outline of Thoughts Regarding Long-term Financial Objective" (April 18, 1993), in Timken Company corporate records.

41. The term as it was first used was "lean production." See James P. Womack, Daniel T. Jones, and Daniel Roos, *The Machine That Changed the World* (New York: Rawson Associates, 1990). See also "Billion Dollar Capital Investment Program Envisioned," Timken news release (March 6, 1989), in Timken Company Archives.

42. On NUMMI, see Paul S. Adler, "Time-and-Motion Regained," *Harvard Business Review* (January–February 1993): 97–108. Japanese manufacturing practices had begun receiving attention well before the publication of that article, for example in Michael Cusumano, *The Japanese Automobile Industry* (Cambridge, Mass.; Harvard University Press, 1985) and after 1986 in accounts about NUMMI's achievements. The comparative study conducted by MIT on the Japanese automotive industries on which Womack, et al., *The Machine That Changed the World*

reported, was launched in 1985. On diffusion of the ideas, see Lazonick, *Competitive Advantage on the Shop Floor*, 286, 402, note 56.

43. W. R. Timken, Jr., interview, 1997; interview with Gene E. Little, September 24, 1997; *Exchange*, Timken employee magazine (January 1990): 1; and "Tim Timken on Human Dignity," *Forum Forward*, Timken newsletter (August 1993).

44. *Exchange* (January 1990): 1; and on the 1989 strike and layoffs in Canton steel plants, *Akron Beacon Journal* (November 1, 1989): 1, 14; on layoffs at Gaffney and Lincolnton, *The Greenville News* (October 26, 1989): D8.

45. *Exchange* (January 1990): 2; and on Vision 2000, Gary S. Vasilash, "Timken: Targeted on the 21st Century," *Production* (June 1992): 44; and John H. Sheridan, "America's Best Plants: Timken," *Industry Week* (October 19, 1992): 53–4.

46. For comparison, see versions of the mission statement in "Joseph Toot Talks Mission," *Timken* (June 1987): 8; and "Not Flying by the Seat of Our Pants," *Exchange* (January 1990): 1, 3.

47. George Foale interview with Bettye Pruitt and Barbara Griffith, October 25, 1995.

48. This mission is a good example of a BHAG (Big Hairy Audacious Goal), as described by Collins and Porras, *Built to Last*, 91–114.

49. On the end of the court order, "Timken Freed from Restrictions," *Canton Repository* (May 21, 1983): 2; and Ramsey interview.

50. "The Timken Company and the Tata Iron and Steel Company to Establish a Joint Venture in India," Timken Company Update, November 10, 1986; "Tata Timken Limited Joint Venture for Manufacture of Tapered Roller Bearings in India Cleared by Delhi Government," Timken news release (January 31, 1990); and P. Ashton interview.

51. Evan Hill, *Beanstalk: The History of Miniature Precision Bearings, Inc., 1941–1966* (Keene: Miniature Precision Bearings, Inc., 1966), 15–18; and "Split Ball Bearings," *Steel* 118 (April 11, 1946): 137.

52. "Smallest Bearing in the World!" *Machinery* (January 1937), n.p., quoted in Hill, *Beanstalk*, 22–3; and Hill, *Beanstalk*, 29–30.

53. Ibid., 33–9; interview with Raymond H. Carter, May 25, 1995; and "Success of AAF in Bombing Enemies Once Threatened by Small Bearings Shortage," *Steel* 116 (February 5, 1945): 108.

54. Hill, *Beanstalk*, 47–64; and "Maker of Tiny Bearings is Only Company Affected by WPB Order Which It Helped to Draft," *Business Week* (June 17, 1944): 41–2; Marchant, "FBC Set Out to Make Miniatures," 30.

55. Hill, *Beanstalk*, 85; and Horace D. Gilbert, ed., *Miniaturization* (New York: Reinhold Publishing Corporation, 1961), 2–12; Carter interview.

56. Quotation from "Very Tiny," *The New Yorker* (August 9, 1958): 18. Also, Hill, *Beanstalk*, 100–6; *MPB Corporation 50th Anniversary, 1941–1991*, pamphlet (Keene: MPB Corporation, 1991).

57. Hill, *Beanstalk*, 107–23; *MPB Corporation 50th Anniversary*; Gilbert, *Miniaturization*.

58. Hill, *Beanstalk*, 144–5; Donald Ross interview with Bettye Pruitt and Jeffrey P. Moran, February 6, 1997; and "Miniature Precision Bearings Enjoys Snappy Comeback in Sales, Earnings," *Barron's* (November 21, 1966): 24.

59. Hill, *Beanstalk*, 149; *MPB Corporation 50th Anniversary*; Ross interview.

60. *MPB Corporation 50th Anniversary*; and Ross interview.

61. Ross interview; Toot written comments; and John H. Stevens, "MPB 'Excited' by Geneen Acquisition," *New Hampshire Business Review* (June 5, 1987): 19.

62. Ross interview; and "Timken Purchases MPB," *Metalworking News* (April 30, 1990), n.p.

63. Ross interview; "MPB Completes Placement of $96,500,000 of Debentures," *PR Newswire* (November 20, 1987); and "Timken Purchases MPB."

64. Timken news release (May 29, 1990); "Company to Buy Bearing Maker," *Exchange* (May 1990): 1; interview with Joseph F. Toot, Jr., the *Wall Street Transcript* (May 27, 1996): 122; and Toot written comments.

Chapter 11: The New Century Approaches

1. *Assessing the Midwest Economy: Looking Back for the Future*, 4–6, 14–15, 18–20. See also, as a sampling of writings on the revival of U.S. industry, the following articles from the *Wall Street Journal*: Robert L. Rose, "Once the 'Rust Belt,' Midwest Now Boasts Revitalized Factories" (January 3, 1994): 1; Daniel Strickberger, "The Other American Dream Team" (February 15, 1995): 18; and John F. Welch, "A Matter of Exchange Rates" (June 21, 1994): 16.

2. Welch, "A Matter of Exchange Rates." See also John H. Sheridan, "Lessons From the Best," *Industry Week* (February 15, 1993): 54–5, which describes the characteristics of the finalists for the magazine awards to America's Best Plants, a program it launched as an effort "to encourage competitive renewal of U.S. industry."

3. See *Exchange* articles: "Tim Timken Joins NAM Board" (April 1995): 1; and "U.S. Manufacturers Climb Back on Top" (June 1995): 1, 6.

4. Thomas A. Klier, "Structural Change and Technology in the Manufacturing Sector," *Assessing the Midwest Economy*, Working Paper Series, no. SP-6 (Federal Reserve Bank of Chicago, 1986), provides an overview of technologies and charts the rate of their adoption in various industries, grouped by SIC codes. Because of the nature of flexible manufacturing, the machine tools in Timken's flexible manufacturing plants, especially for green machining, tended to be more off-the-shelf (less "Timkenized") than usual—a real departure from the company's historic pattern. (Thanks to Carroll Pursell for raising this question and to Bob Leibensperger for answering it.)

5. Womack, et al., *The Machine That Changed the World*, describes these operating principles and their origins at Toyota. See also Cusumano, *The Japanese Automobile Industry*, for lean-production practices at both Toyota and Nissan.

6. Quotation from Paul S. Adler, "Time-and-Motion Regained," 105. Klier, "Structural Change and Technology," 11–12, discusses the importance of nontechnological factors in lean manufacturing and makes the point about the cumulative nature of the change: "restructuring with the goal of implementing best practices requires an ongoing process rather than a one-time adjustment."

7. On centers of expertise, "Bearing Plants Focus on Experience," *Exchange* (November 1993): 1, 4.

8. John H. Sheridan, "America's Best Plants: Timken," *Industry Week*, (October 19, 1992): 54; and "Bucyrus Bearing Plant Named One of Nation's Best," *Exchange* (October 1992): 1, 4.

9. Vasilash, "Timken: Targeted on the 21st Century," 43; "Gaffney Plant Honored for Excellence," *Exchange* (May 1994): 1.

10. Stories and quotations from *Exchange* articles: "Large Bearing Production to be Consolidated at Gambrinus Plant" (September 1990): 1, 6; "At LIB Complex, Silence Isn't Golden Anymore" (November 1995): 4l; and "Teams: Key to the Company's Future" (October 1993): 2.

11. Timken Company Annual Report for 1992; Richard Kopp and Isabelle Yau interview, and Roger Violy interview with Bettye Pruitt and Barbara Griffith, October 23, 1995.

12. Foale interview; *Timken Tomorrow: Associates Handbook* (1992); and two special editions of British Timken employee magazine, *Contact* (April and May 1992); Timken Company Annual Report for 1992.

13. "Company Dedicates Flagship Plant," *Exchange* (October 1991): 1; and "Manufacturing for the 21st Century," *Exchange* (June 1992): 4–5. See also William H. Miller, "Timken Jumps into Tomorrow," *Industry Week* (September 2, 1991): 72–80.

14. "Manufacturing for the 21st Century," 5; Miller, "Timken Jumps into Tomorrow," 74; Leibensperger interview, 1998.

15. "Manufacturing for the 21st Century"; and Miller, "Timken Jumps into Tomorrow," 74. On changes in the auto supply industry underlying the growth in importance of package bearings, see Tim Keenan, "Supplier Sequel?" *Ward's Auto World* (May 1996): 79–81.

16. "Manufacturing for the 21st Century"; and "Teamwork Spreads at Altavista," *Exchange* (December 1994): 1, 3.

17. "Manufacturing for the 21st Century"; and "New 'Smart' Bearings Introduced," *Exchange* (March 1990): 1.

18. "New Bearing Plants Planned for North Carolina and Europe," and "Global Leadership in Next Century," *Exchange* (February 1991): 1, 2; *Learning before Doing*, Harvard Business School Video (1995); Leibensperger interview, 1998.

19. *Learning before Doing*.

20. "New Spexx Bearings Seen as Giant Leap Forward in Productivity," *Timken World* (December 1995): 5; "The Timken Company Launches Spexx Family of Performance Bearings," Timken news release (October 16, 1995); and Timken Company Annual Report for 1995, 3.

21. Timken Company Annual Reports for 1991–93; "ITC Finds No Injury to U.S. Steelmakers from Brazilian Dumping," joint news release from Republic Engineered Steels and The Timken Company (July 2, 1993); and "Steelmakers Appeal ITC Ruling on Brazilian Dumping," joint news release from Republic Engineered Steels and The Timken Company (September 13, 1993).

22. Quotation from "The Timken Company Delays Project Due to Uncertain Economy," Timken news release (September 23, 1992); and "British Timken Plants Consolidate at Duston," *Exchange* (April 1993): 5. On salary reductions, "The Timken Company Announces Temporary Reduction in Pay for Salaried Employees, Lessened Use of Contingent Work Force," Timken news release, (August 9, 1991).

23. "Company Seeks Price Reductions from Suppliers to Match Salary Cuts," *Exchange* (September 1991): 1; and "Early Settlement Reached at Timken," *Monthly Labor Review* 116 (February 1993): 63.

24. Joseph F. Toot, Jr., written communication (February 6, 1998); Schubach interview, 1996.

25. "Breakthrough Bulletin" (July 15, 1992) and (May 13, 1994), in Timken corporate records.

26. "Breakthrough Bulletin" (January 14, 1994), in Timken corporate records.

27. "ACI Leadership Meeting" (December 14, 1994), in Timken corporate records.

28. Schubach interview, 1997; Canton Bearing Plant group interview.

29. Quotation from Michael Winerip, "Early, in a Bellwether City, Democrats Have an Edge," *New York Times* (February 12, 1996): A1; "Timken Company Associates Reject Union Representation for Bucyrus Operations," Timken news release (March 12, 1993).

30. On associates' opinions, Canton Bearing Plant and Faircrest Steel Plant group interviews and results of an "Associate Alignment Survey" conducted in 1997, which indicated that more than 90 percent of Timken associates worldwide "understand why continuous improvement is

important to the company's success," reported in *Timken World* (March 1998): 1.

31. "Company Fares Well Against Competition," *Exchange* (May 1993): 1, 7; "Joe Toot Describes Company Vision as Best-performing Manufacturer," *Exchange* (July 1993): 7; SKF Annual Report for 1992. On FAG, "Kugelfischer Comes Back from the Brink," *Financial Times* (May 2, 1997): 29.

32. Timken Company Annual Reports for 1984, 1990–91, and 1996; and Gene E. Little interview, September 24, 1997.

33. Quotation from "Joe Toot Describes Company Vision as Best-performing Manufacturer."

34. "Joe Toot Describes Company Vision as Best-performing Manufacturer."

35. W. R. Timken, Jr., interview, 1997; Little interview.

36. "Marketing Reorganizations Give Clearer Picture of Customer," *Timken World* (December 1993): 6; and Little interview.

37. "Railroad Unit on Track Toward First Place," *Exchange* (January 1991): 4–5; and "A Look Back at a Year of Progress," *Exchange* (February 1992): 2.

38. "Railroad Unit on Track Toward First Place"; "Bearing Business Strengthens Focus on Customers," *Exchange* (October 1993): 3; and "Marketing Reorganizations Give Clearer Picture of Customer," 1, 6.

39. Quotation from W. R. Timken, Jr., interview, 1993. Also Timken interview, *Wall Street Transcript*, 2; and Peter Ashton interview.

40. Timken interview, *Wall Street Transcript*, 6; P. Ashton interview.

41. On interchangeable product and distribution centers, see "Turning the Wheels of the World," *Exchange* (September 1994): 4–5; and "Why it Pays to Span the Globe," *Timken World* (June 1996): 3.

42. P. Ashton interview; and Patricia Gercik, *On Track with the Japanese: A Case-by-Case Approach to Building Successful Relationships* (New York: Kodansha International, 1992), vii–viii. The Timken Company was a member of the MIT Japan program.

43. This paragraph draws on the following *Exchange* articles: "Design Efforts Mark First with Nissan" (August 1991): 1, 4; "Top MITI Official Makes Visit" (October 1991): 1; and "Tech Center Planned for Nihon Timken" (June 1992): 1, 3.

44. "This Relationship Has a Strong Bearing on Quality," *Synergy* (Toyota Motor Sales, U.S.A., Inc., Summer 1994), 14–18; "Toyota Visit Strengthens Relationship," *Exchange* (August 1993): 1. On Toyota's tradition of supplier relationships, see Womack, et al., *The Machine That Changed the World*, 60–62. I am grateful to Carroll Pursell for pointing out the significance of this similarity of company experiences.

45. "This Relationship Has a Strong Bearing on Quality."

46. "Toshiba to Use AP Bearings," *Exchange* (May 1992): 1; "Japanese 'Bullets' Will Glide on Timken Bearings," *Timken World* (March 1997): 2.

47. "Turning the Wheels of the World," *Exchange* (September 1994): 4–5; "Making a Commitment to Customers and Associates," *Timken World* (June 1997): 5; and "Why it Pays to Span the Globe," *Timken World* (June 1996): 3.

48. "Turning the Wheels of the World."

49. "Competitor Out, Timken Company In," *Exchange* (October 1994): 6; "10 Millionth Timken AP Railroad Bearing Comes Off Line," and "Timken Company Prototype Bearing Points to Improved Railroad Performance," Timken Company news releases (September 13, 1994); and "Timken Research Helps Keep Company Out Front," *Exchange* (September 1997): 1.

50. "Good Bearings," *Forbes* (September 23, 1996): 52; and on market shares, "U.S. Ball and Roller

Bearings, Market Shares," Snapshots International, Ltd. (June 1997); and "World Bearings to 2001," The Freedonia Group, Inc. (August 1997). On SKF and Ovako, see "History" at the Internet address *www.SKF.com*; and "Ovako Steel to Build New Tube-Rolling Plant in Hofors for SEK 0.5 Billion," SKF press release (May 10, 1996).

51. "Joe Toot Elected AISI Chairman," *Exchange* (June 1991): 1; "Toot Receives AISI Highest Honor," Timken Company news release (May 20, 1993); and "Award Honors Company Commitment to Research," *Timken World* (December 1993): 3.

52. "CEO Applauds Company's Faircrest Initiative," *Exchange* (August 1994): 3; "Industry Week's 5th Annual Salute," *Industry Week* (October 17, 1994): 31–2; and "The Timken Company's Faircrest Steel Plant Wins 33 *Metalproducing*'s T.O.P. Award," Timken Company news release (May 23, 1994).

53. "Industry Week's 5th Annual Salute."

54. Ibid.; Matthews interview; "Bar Mills: Moving Up the Value-added Ladder," *Iron Age* (February 1989): 20–4, 29; and George W. Hess, "Specialty Producers Are Fit to Spend," *Iron Age* (September 1992): 32–5.

55. Matthews interview; Norman L. Samways, "Timken Increases Continuous Casting Capacity by 100%," *Iron and Steel Engineer* (September 1992): 37; John Schriefer, "Continuous Bloom Casting in Ohio," *New Steel* (April 1996): 38–40; "The Timken Company Continues Transformation of its Steel Business," Timken Company press release (September 9, 1996); and *Exchange* articles: "$170 Million Goes to Steel Projects" (October 1990): 1, 3; and "Steel Business Strives for Competitive Edge" (July 1992): 2.

56. "St. Clair Precision Tubing Components Celebrates 'Year 1 of Success,'" Timken Company news release (June 15, 1994); Matthews interview; *Exchange* articles: "Steel Business Moves into New Markets" (February 1993): 3, 7; "Steel Business Drives in New Directions—Faster" (February 1997): 1, 3.

57. "Latrobe Steel Announces New Finishing Facility," Latrobe Steel Company news release (July 6, 1993); "Steel Firm to Build in Sandycreek," *Franklin News-Herald* (July 7, 1993): 1; Latrobe Steel Company Annual Report for 1967.

58. Thomas W. Gerdel, "Timken to Buy Steel Distributor," *Cleveland Plain Dealer* (April 4, 1996): C1; and "Timken Company Acquisition to Expand Tool Steel Customer Services," Timken Company news release (June 27, 1996).

59. "The Timken Company's Steel Business Establishes European Sales Unit," Timken Company news release (April 19, 1993); and "Steel Business Drives in New Directions—Faster."

60. Joseph F. Toot, Jr., to author (February 6, 1998).

61. "Welcome to the Newest Members of the Timken Team," *Timken World* (June 1997): 3; "Company Mobilizes to Improve Customer Service," *Timken World* (September 1997): 2; and "The Timken Company Announces Tool Steel Distribution Facility in Greer, S.C.," Timken Company news release (November 17, 1997).

62. "Timken Company Railroad Bearing Business Finalizes Purchase of Remanufacturing Services," Timken Company news release (January 11, 1995); and "Welcome to the Newest Members of the Timken Team."

63. Eden interview; and "International Advisors Bring Wisdom, Add Value," *Timken World* (June 1996): 2.

64. Thomas W. Gerdel, "China's New 'Gold Rush,'" *Cleveland Plain Dealer* (May 21, 1996): C1; on SKF in China, "Good Bearings," 53; and *Exchange* articles: "From Ohio to China: Company Growth Crosses Continents" (June 1996): 5; and "Yantai Timken Venture Gives Important Foothold" (August 1996): 3.

65. Timken Company news releases: "The Timken Company Announces Acquisition in Poland" (January 12, 1996); and "The Timken Company Acquires Romanian Bearing Maker" (December 17, 1997). Also, "1996—A Year of Robust Growth for The Timken Company," *Timken World* (March 1997): 5; and Toot written comments.

66. "Good Bearings"; and "NSK: A Growing Presence in Europe through NSK-RHP," *Automotive Components Analysis*, newsletter (May 1, 1997): 8–9.

67. "World List of Anti-Friction Bearing Manufacturers and Steel Ball Manufacturers," Anti-Friction Bearing Manufacturers Association, Inc. (October 1964), in Timken Company Archives; "Welcome to Newest Members of the Timken Team"; "Company Mobilizes to Improve Customer Service," *Timken World* (September 1997): 2; and "The Timken Company Acquires Bearing Business in Italy," Timken Company news release (February 21, 1997).

68. *Fortune* (April 27, 1997): F45, 50, 53, 54, 57.

69. Interview with Joseph F. Toot, Jr., *Wall Street Transcript* (May 27, 1996), reprint, 6; and Toot written comments.

Conclusion: Timken at Ninety-Nine

1. "Why Timken's 'Stability' Will Save its Bottom Line," 107–8.

2. Ibid.

3. Eliminating time clocks was a cost-saving measure initiated under Breakthrough: "Time and Attendance System Debuts at Plants," *Exchange* (April 1994): 1, 4.

4. Interview with Jack Porter and Jack Bond, October 22, 1996.

5. Ibid.

6. Gene Martin, "Happy Customers Make for a Happy Company," *Exchange* (June 1996): 2.

7. Winerip, "Canton's Biggest Employer Is Out of Step," B8; and Michael R. Sesit, "Disclosure Fails to Satisfy Big Investors," *Wall Street Journal* (November 4, 1996): B10B.

8. Tim Timken, "The Wall Street Factor," *Timken World* (September 1997): 3.

9. Timken is quoted in "U.S. Manufacturers Climb Back to the Top," *Exchange* (June 1995): 1; Toot is quoted in "New Performance-based Pay Plan," *Timken World* (December 1995): 3, 5.

10. "Special Continuous Improvement Bulletin," *Timken World* (March 1998), including "Tim Timken Issues C.I. Challenge," 4; and Schubach interview, 1997. "The Timken Company Launches Worldwide Associate Recognition Award," Timken Company news release (May 1, 1995).

11. Toot interview, 1997.

12. Canton Bearing Plant group interview.

13. W. R. Timken, Jr., written comments; Donald W. Simonson interview, June 1, 1998; Canton Bearing Plant group interview; Faircrest Steel Plant group interview; and Michael Winerip, "An American Place," *New York Times* (September 30, 1996): B6. On labor-management partnerships in the steel industry, including some problems, see Brian Berry, "George Becker: Compassion vs. the God of the Bottom Line," *New Steel* (May 1996): 30; and Nancy Pieters, "From Partnerships to Confrontation," *New Steel* (June 1996): 80.

14. Canton Bearing Plant group interview. On investments in Canton, "Company Leads the Pack in Worldwide Race," *Exchange* (June 1996): 3.

15. Alex Markels and Joann S. Lublin, "Longevity-Reward Programs Get Short Shrift," *Wall Street Journal* (April 27, 1995): B1; "Service Recognition Program Reinstated," *Exchange* (February 1994): 5.

16. W. R. Timken, Jr., interview, 1997.

17. Ibid.

18. Ibid.

19. Ward J. Timken, biography; and Toot written comments.

20. Quinn, "The Timkens: Canton's First Family,": 8.

21. Winerip, "Canton's Biggest Employer Is Out of Step."

22. Amiel interview; "W. R. Timken, Jr., Receives France's Legion of Honor Distinction," Timken Company news release (August 26, 1991); and "Amiel Receives French Honor," *Timken World* (December 1993): 2, 6.

Index

A. O. Smith Company, 198
Abel, I. W., 127, 191, 344
Adler, Paul S., 366
aerospace industry, as market for
  Latrobe steel, 391
  MPB bearings, 354, 358, 360, 373, 395
  See also bearings, Timken (tapered roller) applications and markets
African-Americans, 150–151, 170–172
aircraft industry, British, 230
aircraft industry, U.S., 10, 140, 148, 204
  jet engines, 10, 140, 181, 234
Alden, Herbert W., 27, 46, 52, 54, 57, 62, 90, 142
Alexander Proudfoot engineering firm, 341–342
Allied Chemical Company, 359
Allied Corporation, 359
Allied-Signal, Inc., 359–360
Allis Chalmers, 265
Altorfer, Henry, 223
American Ball Bearing Company, 51
American Car and Foundry Company, 97
American Federation of Labor (AFL), 125
American Iron and Steel Institute (AISI), 387
American Locomotive Company, 99
American Machinist, 197, 208
American Society for Metals, Medal for the Advancement of Research awarded to Timken, 183, 387

American Society of Mechanical Engineers, 216
Amiel, Maurice, 252, 274, 349, 380, 381, 407, 417
  business strategy, 394, 395
  receives French Legion of Honor award, 407
Anderson, Deborah, 403
Anderson, Robert, 393, 417
Andrews Bearing Corporation, 358
anti-friction bearings.
  See bearing design and types; bearings (general discussion); bearings, Timken
antitrust actions against Timken, 134, 157, 159–160, 185, 192, 212, 220, 231, 232, 236, 248, 263, 426
Antitrust Division, Department of Justice, 128
antitrust laws, 111, 117, 123, 296, 337
Antonopoulos Brothers, 221
Apperson brothers, 33
Arnold, Thurman, 128
Arthur, Joseph, 177
Ashton, Dennis, 232
Ashton, Peter J., 227, 232, 342, 372, 380–383, 416
Assel, Walter, 138, 139, 181, 424
Assel tube mill (Assel Elongator)
  in Britain, 256–257
  in Canton, Ohio, 139, 300, 424, 425, 427
  development of, 138
  the dominant technology, 181

Atlantic Coast Line Railroad, 213
Atlas Steels, Ltd. of Canada, 298
Atomic Energy Commission, 278
AT&T, 145, 233, 278
  Bell Laboratories, 357, 358
Austin, Edgerly, 223
Austin, Herbert, 52
automated production technologies, 197–199, 208, 209–210, 233
automobile industry, European, 22, 23, 49, 52, 112, 115, 116–117, 252
automobile industry, German, 223, 260
automobile industry, Japanese, 350–351, 365, 383–384
automobile industry, U.S., 35–36, 38, 41, 42, 87, 260, 336, 364
  automated production technologies, 198
  business environment and change, 311
  competition and markets, 50, 94, 313, 369
  consolidation of, 66, 69, 95
  de-integration of, 369, 370, 389
  economies of scale, 75–76
  emergence of, 22–23
  growth, 6, 44, 49–50, 52, 53, 77, 212
  precision manufacturing, 48–49
  unionization, 125, 404
  (*See also* United Auto Workers)

automobile industry, U.S.,
  (continued)
  vertical integration, 61, 64,
    66, 69, 73
Automotive Industries, 33
automotive supply industry,
  364, 433
axles, 6, 18, 23, 46
  bearings for, 25, 189, 267,
    269
  for railroad cars, 97, 98, 99,
    101, 112
  for trucks, 78, 79
axles, Timken, 27, 35, 36, 37,
  38, 45, 95
  applications to automobile
    and truck industry, 37,
    39, 40, 46

Bailey, F. O., 36–38
Ballantine, Sallie, 403
Balough, Charles, 79
Barden Corporation, 358
Bartholdi, Auguste, 272, 273
Barwick, Edward, 206
batch production, 80–82, 198,
  458n27
bearing design and types, 7,
  63, 66, 76, 78, 88, 90–92
  annular ball, 24, 51, 58, 77,
    112, 148
  ball, 5–6, 7, 23–24, 52, 65,
    68, 78, 89, 108, 110, 147,
    190, 191
  bicycle-type ball, 51
  cageless tapered roller, 217
  cartridge, 270, 271
  double-row, self-aligning
    ball, 110
  double-row ball, 51–52
  flexible (wound) roller, 25,
    66, 97, 108, 112
  miniature, 246, 292,
    354–361, 393
  miniature (FJP1), 234–235
  needle, 7, 191, 309
  plain (friction), 5, 52, 93, 97
  precision of, 47–49
  roller alignment, 26–27, 87,
    89
  spherical roller, 7, 110, 112

split ball, 354
straight (cylindrical) roller,
  6, 7, 9, 25, 64, 68, 97
tapered roller, 6, 7, 25–26,
  36, 63, 64, 89, 96, 104,
  107, 108, 110, 147, 148,
  190, 219, 264, 289, 309
See also bearings, Timken
  (tapered roller)
bearing industry, European,
  23, 112–117, 147, 148,
  241, 263
bearing industry, international, 9, 111
  consolidation of, 395
  shortages, 293–295
bearing industry, Japanese,
  292–293, 336–337, 378,
  401
  miniature bearing
    production, 358
  price competition and
    markets, 292–293,
    338–340, 358
  statistical process control
    (SPC) and quality,
    337–338
bearing industry, Russian, 147
bearing industry, U.S., 378
  antitrust litigation, 159
  competition and markets, 9,
    51, 104, 109, 292–293,
    337–340
  dumping of imports in,
    288–289, 292, 345–346
  effect of Japanese competi-
    tion on, 289, 292–293,
    358
  government regulation of,
    292, 345
  oversupply, 358
bearings (general discussion),
  6, 24–26, 36, 97, 139
  friction-reducing function,
    4–6, 7, 9, 23, 38, 51, 89,
    97, 98, 101, 113, 279
  hot box problem, 97, 98,
    101, 215, 259
  military use of, 148, 355,
    357–358, 360
  performance, related to

material quality, 8, 45
  (*See also* bearings,
  Timken (tapered roller):
  performance, related to
  material quality)
  tribology (friction, wear,
    lubrication technology),
    279, 293
Bearings, Inc., 293
bearings, Timken (ball), 148,
  372–373
bearings, Timken (cylindrical
  roller)
  Z-Spexx, 372, 409
bearings, Timken (tapered
  roller), 8, 35, 46, 66,
  163–165, 190, 259
  adjustable, 26, 57, 77,
    268–269, 293
  capacity ratings, 183, 245
  crowned rollers in, 183,
    255
  design, 2, 46–49, 50, 57, 59,
    87–89, 90–92, 93, 183,
    232, 421, 423
  development of, 23–28
  friction-reducing function,
    1, 4, 5, 28, 93, 103, 183,
    198, 235, 252, 265, 409
  life, 245, 271, 293, 309–310,
    312, 315, 425
  load-bearing capacity, 7,
    89, 92, 93, 97, 255, 267,
    269, 329
  metric standard and, 252,
    260, 263–267
  nickel-molybdenum alloy
    steel, 76, 88, 89, 235,
    241, 256, 257, 423
  patents, 1, 2, 19
  performance, 88–89, 112,
    141, 348
  performance, related to
    material quality, 68,
    69–77, 302, 309–312, 317,
    328–329, 388–389, 409
  performance testing, 70, 72,
    76, 92, 134, 141, 233,
    281, 309–310, 312, 425
  precision manufacturing of,
    48–49, 56, 92

price of, 36, 38, 85, 89, 94, 97, 101, 189, 200, 209, 213, 216, 217, 219, 245, 260, 261, 296–297

production costs, 337

production output, 337

quality/quality control, 216, 219, 318, 331, 337

ratings/performance, 347

replacement, 65, 77, 79, 110, 113, 116, 119, 147, 400

standardization of, 165, 200, 202–203, 210, 213, 232, 245, 252, 263–267, 314, 337, 369

ultrasonic inspection of, 310, 317

See also Timken Bearing Business unit

bearings, Timken (tapered roller) applications and markets, 5, 6, 10, 52, 53, 68, 119, 183, 382

aerospace/aircraft industry, 10, 147, 230, 354, 432

automobile industry, 5, 38, 44–45, 47, 49, 50, 51, 53, 58–59, 89, 117, 141, 142, 165, 200–203, 209, 261, 281, 293, 336, 348, 369–370, 380, 383–384

carriage industry, 36–38

competition and, 2, 216–219, 310, 378

industrial, 59, 92–94, 95, 116, 117–119, 142, 165, 252, 265, 266, 281, 293–295, 310, 368, 370–371, 380, 423, 432

machine tools, 49, 147, 157, 212

military, 80, 112, 147, 148

non-automotive, 5, 86, 89, 101, 117, 141, 203, 266

price competition, 252, 292, 295–296, 338–340

railroad industry, 94, 96–101, 116, 119, 134, 157, 165, 182, 230, 232, 235, 259, 270, 281, 293, 380–381, 386, 393, 423, 428

railroad industry (AP bearings), 212, 213–216, 427

railroad industry, Japanese, 383, 384

steel industry, 94, 97, 157, 182

tractors and agricultural machinery, 59, 80, 81–82, 92, 93

transaxles, 347, 385

transmissions, 5, 39, 46, 47, 182, 183, 269, 271, 390

truck industry, 46, 77, 80, 81–82, 107, 113, 143, 148, 211, 385

wheel(s), 5, 15, 189, 203, 260, 261, 268, 269, 271, 370

bearings, Timken (tapered roller) types and trademarks

all-thrust, 94, 423

AP (All-Purpose), 212–216, 259, 270, 340, 384–386, 426, 431, 432

AP-2, 386, 432

double row, 94, 423

generator, 386

Green Light (continuously operating), 205, 209, 259–261, 265, 266, 271, 290, 372, 395, 426

Hydra-Rib, 293, 294, 348, 429

IsoClass, 433

J-line, 265–266

Performance-900 (P900) series, 347, 348

PINION-PAC, 294, 370, 372

precision, 212, 348

roll-neck, 94, 97

SENSOR-PAC, 294, 370, 371, 372, 431

SET-RIGHT mountings for, 268, 293, 428

Short Series, 47, 50, 421

smart bearings, 348, 369, 372

Spexx family of industrial bearings, 372, 432

tapered-cup axle bearing, 72, 78, 81

trademark/branding dispute with Caterpillar, 400–401

ultra-high-speed, 281

UNIPAC, 39, 293, 294, 370, 371, 372, 383, 385, 430

UNIPAC-PLUS, 370, 372, 429, 430

UNIT BEARING, 269, 293, 428

value-added package, 369, 372, 389, 433

Wheel-Pac, 429

XP (Xtended Performance), 293, 428

Bearing Service Company, 65–66, 423

Begel, Thomas, 359

Bell, Davitt, 304

Bell and Howell, 357

Bell Laboratories, 145

Bennett, James, 343

Bennett, Stephen F., 228, 229, 233, 241, 248, 414

Benson, James, 367

Bentley, George, 235–236

Benz, Karl, 22, 23

Bergstrom, Albert L., 197, 199, 201, 202, 207, 213, 238, 413

Berliet truck manufacturer, 157

Bessemer process, 5, 72

Bessmer, Dwight A., 242–243, 248, 413

Bethlehem Steel, 75, 193–194

Betts, George, 56

Bhatia, Ravi, 347

Bianchi, Luigi, 263

Bianchi Cuscinetti S.p.A., 262–263

bicycles, 22–23, 23, 25

Big Steel. *See* steel industry, U.S.; *specific corporations*

Blackburn, Larry, 327

Bloom, Ray, 316

BMW, 260

Bock Bearing Company, The, 63, 64, 80, 88, 108, 423

Borden, David N., 414

Borgward automobiles, 260

Borg-Warner, 367

Boston & Maine Railroad, 100

Bouley, Jean, 270

Bower Roller Bearing Company, 64, 108, 109, 111, 112, 125, 209, 293

Bowling, Bill J., 316, 319–320, 322, 324, 327, 339, 391, 406, 417

Brenco bearing manufacturer, 216

Brewster, James B., 18, 20

Bridges, Amelia (née Timken), 122

Bridges, Appleton S., 20

British Aerospace, 230

British Leyland, 271

British Rail Company, 232

British Timken Limited, 113–117, 128, 130, 155, 157, 159, 160, 165, 210, 220, 222, 223, 235, 252, 298, 352, 358, 383, 384, 395, 422, 423, 424, 425, 428

  apprenticeship programs, 226–227

  Aston (Birmingham) plant, 112, 114, 116, 152, 228, 230

  Bucyrus concept at, 231

  competition and markets, 235, 246

  competition with U.S. Timken, 220, 221, 232, 235, 260, 426

  consolidation with U.S. Timken, 212, 219, 225, 236–241, 259

  Daventry Distribution Center, 383, 428

  Daventry plant, 226, 228, 232, 273, 426

  Daventry plant closure, 374, 431

  during World War II, 133, 151–153

  Duston plant, 152, 228, 231, 273, 425, 433

  integration with Timken Europe, 296

  manufacture of UNIT-BEARING, 269

  metric standard and, 264, 265

  in the 1950s, 225–230

  precision ball bearings, 232, 235

  products/production output, 230–232, 357

  profitability and revenues, 380

  quality/quality control, 256, 257, 310

  statistical process control at, 232–233, 338

  steel supply to, 256–257

  stock, 116, 240, 241

  subsidiary, British Timken S.A. Proprietary, Ltd. (South Africa), 116, 235, 259, 424, 426

  subsidiary, Fischer Bearings Company, 152, 234, 357, 358, 381

  Timken Tomorrow program, 368, 369

British Timken Show, 153, 229

Brock, R. E., 71

Brooke, Kendall, 259, 274–275, 275

Brooks, W. A., 412

Brower, R. Charles, 106, 122, 130, 132, 185, 187, 412

Brown, Larry R., 417

Brown, Richard, 390

Brown & Sharpe, 41, 48

Bruening, Joseph M., 293

Buckeye Buggy Company, 38

Buckeye Manufacturing Company, 39

Buckwalter, Tracy V., 96–97, 98–99, 101, 412

Bucyrus, Ohio, automated high-volume bearing plant, xvi, 161, 165, 176, 280, 290, 292, 338, 365, 403, 426

  compared to Altavista, 370–372

  development of technology for, 203–205

  Distribution Center, 205, 255, 283, 382–383, 427

  spread of Bucyrus technology, 219, 231

  standardization of production, 197–203, 210, 243, 369

  teamwork policies, 366–367

  training, working conditions, 202, 206, 209–210

  unions and labor relations, 288, 343, 377

Bucyrus concept (standardization and high-volume production), 210, 369

  as corporate strategy, 216–219, 243, 252, 314

  international applications, 258–262

Buick, 49, 50, 73

Burness, Jack, 256

Burnett, Cora (née Timken), 106, 121, 122

business environment and change, 104

  anti-big business, 123

  diversification strategies and, 311

  during the Depression, 161

  following the Depression, 123–128

  oversupply, 336, 341

  post-World War II, 157–161

  unionization and, 128

business units. *See* Timken Bearing Business unit; Timken Steel Business unit

Business Week, 399, 400

Cabot, T. H., Jr., 355

Cadillac Automobile Company, 47, 49, 72, 108

Canton, Ohio, 30, 34, 35, 40–42, 61, 105, 107, 168, 287, 407

  during the Depression, 121–122

  population, 170

race relations, 171
unionization activities, 127, 128
Canton, Ohio, locations of The Timken Company, 2, 112, 113, 116, 120, 121, 167–170, 336
Canton bearing plant (*See* Timken Company, The, U.S. locations and plants)
corporate headquarters, 190, 274, 278, 279, 408, 431, 435, 437
Engineering Laboratory, 279, 280, 282, 427
Harrison Avenue steel plant, 71, 279, 307, 322, 329, 389, 422, 433
Maryland Road housing development, 82, 83
Metallurgical Laboratory, 70, 85, 94, 139–141, 147, 178, 181, 184, 279–281, 298–299, 325, 422, 424, 427
Physical Laboratory, 279, 280, 281, 427
recreation and sports facilities, 171, 172, 207
recycling, waste treatment operations, 287, 422, 429
"Savannah Avenue," 150, 183, 199, 200–204, 206, 212, 231, 279, 280, 425
tube mills, 71–72, 82, 85, 94, 422, 425, 429
unions, labor relations, and strikes, 125, 126, 127, 128, 151, 191–192, 320, 343, 344, 351, 404
See also Faircrest steel plant; Timken Research, Canton, Ohio
Canton Drop Forge, 148, 387, 388
Canton Steel Company, 41
Card, D. T., 13
Carnahan Tin Plate and Steel, 41
Carnegie Institute of Technology, 145

Carriage Builders National Association, 18, 20, 22
carriage industry, 10, 14–15, 17–18, 20–21, 23, 25, 35, 49
Carriage Monthly, The, 18
Carter, Raymond H. (Nick), 355, 358
Caterpillar, Inc. construction equipment, 212, 221, 246, 265, 279, 328, 367
as customer of Timken, 294, 400–401
Central Steel Company, 73
Cerri, Steven, 359
Chalmers Motor Company, 34
Chandler, Alfred, xiii, 8, 54, 74–75
Chapotot, Yves, 154, 155
chemical industry, 300, 313
Chesapeake & Ohio Railroad, 100
Chevrolet, 108
Christenson, Arthur L., 282
Chrysler, Walter, 35
Chrysler Corporation, 35, 108, 109, 120, 182, 190, 261, 367
as customer of Timken, 184, 347, 348
Platinum Pentastar award given to Timken, 339
Cincinnati Milling Machine Company, 135, 265
Citroën automobiles, 114, 115, 155
Civil War, 14, 15
Clark, Claude L., 181–182
Clayton Act, 111
Cleveland Axle Company, 38, 40, 54
Cleveland Machine Screw Company, 24
Cold War, 221, 278, 361, 373, 394
Colmar, Alsace. *See* Timken France, Colmar plant
Columbus Buggy Company, 18–19
Common Market, 238, 270, 296

communism, 158, 236, 237, 382, 394
competition and markets (general discussion)
domestic, 313, 336
global, 311, 322, 336, 349, 363–364
international, 336
post–World War II, 199
price, 160
world, 313
See also specific companies
computer-aided design (CAD), 365, 371
computer-aided manufacturing (CAM), 365, 371
computer industry, 198, 206
See also Timken Company, The: computer and electronic systems
Congress of Industrial Organizations (CIO), 125, 126, 127, 128, 150, 151, 193
Conrad, Robert, 51
Contact, Timken publication, 58, 405
Continental Tire, 394
Coolidge, Calvin, 123
Corbett, George, 174
Cordier, William, 387, 388
Coty, René, 237
Cox, Dewitt C., 415
Coyne, James N., 305
Craig, Charles E., 416
Crawford, Frederick C., 190
Crosby Company, 38
CSC Industries, Inc. (formerly Copperweld), 388
Cullen, O. E., 205
Cummins engines, 328
Cunningham, Orval H., 105
Curtis, Mike, 256

Daimler, 22, 23
Dallow, William, 115
Dana Corporation, 212, 221
Daniels, Arthur N., 355, 357, 358
David Brown & Sons, 62
Davidson brothers, 33

Deal, George L., viii, 180–181, 185, 188, 189, 191, 248, 283, 289, 413
de Beauvivier, Maurice, 154
de Beauvivier, Robert, 157
Dedication to Excellence Award (awarded by Timken), 405
Defense Plant Corporation, 149–151, 161
de Gaulle, Charles, 156–157, 237–238, 239
Demerling, Donna, 403
Demetrakis, Stavros (Steve), 170
Deming, W. Edwards, 145, 338
Democratic party, 404
Demory, A. R., 52, 54, 57, 62, 95, 411
Detroit Diesel, 385
Deutsche Timken GmbH, 113–117, 264, 422, 424, 425
Dewar, Michael Bruce Urquhart, 113–117, 130, 152, 160, 225, 241, 423, 426
Diebold Company, 148, 393
Digest of Steels for High-Temperature Applications, 182
diversification strategies, 163, 165, 311
Djupedal, Lars, 316
Doebereiner, James, 338
Dodge, 85, 109, 120
Donze, Albert M., 199, 413
Dorris, George P., 38–39
Dos Passos, John, 192
Dotti, Roberto, 263
Dougherty, Charles A., 40, 41, 238
Dravo Engineers and Constructors, 317, 319, 320, 322, 328
Drummond, Ring, 186–187
Duden, Gottfried, 11
Duggan, Gregory W., viii
DuPont, 86, 278
Durant, William, 49, 65, 85
Duryea, Charles, 23, 33

Duryea, J. Frank, 22, 23, 33
Duryea Motor Wagon Company, 22
Dziggle, Karl, 260

Eastburg, Clifford, 213, 215, 216
Eastman Kodak, 357
Eastmet Corporation, 304
Eaton Corporation automotive parts, 212, 338
economy, European, 221
economy, U.S., 68
  direct overseas investment, 221
  government role in, 123–124
  Great Depression, 101, 104, 107, 115–123, 133, 134, 139, 141, 161, 189
  post–Vietnam War recession, 303
  post–World War II, 195, 198, 210, 211, 246
  recession (1920s), 82, 85, 86, 87
  recession (1938), 119, 123
  recession (1958), 195
  recession (1979), 331
  recession (1980s), 311, 313, 322–323, 324, 326, 331, 336
  recession (1990s), 361, 363, 364, 372, 373–374, 378
  recovery (mid-1990s), 364
  recovery after Great Depression, 122–123
  stagflation (1970s), 295
Eden, Lord John, 228, 394
Edgewater Steel, 304
Edison, Thomas, 44, 45
Edwards, Herbert C., 183
Edwards, Paul, 150
Ehlers, Norm, 339
Electric & Ordnance Accessories Company, Ltd. (E&OA), 52–53, 56, 112, 114, 159, 421
Electric Vehicle Company, 46
electronics industry, 357, 359–360, 365

Eley, David, 271
Elmer A. Sperry Award, 215, 216
Elsasser, Jon T., 418
Ely, Heman, 54, 57, 60, 65, 71, 77, 79, 83, 87, 93, 106, 130, 411
engines, 39
  diesel, 215
  gasoline, 46
  jet, 10, 140, 181, 234
  turbocharged, 140
environmental concerns, 286–287
Erie Railroad, 100
Ernst, Alwin C., 106, 109, 122, 187, 248, 412
European Economic Community, 236, 240
Everitt, Leo, 205
Exchange, Timken publication, 58, 351, 405
export/import balance, 336
exports, 116, 216, 364

Fafnir Bearing Company, 358
FAG bearing manufacturer, Germany, 116–117, 152, 222, 261, 296, 307, 360, 378, 386
  metric standard and, 265, 267
Faircrest steel plant, xvi, 8, 44, 181, 297, 312, 313–329, 331, 334, 337, 341–343, 378, 387, 399, 430
  capital spending program, 364
  computerized efficiency programs, 324–325, 327
  continuous improvement strategy, 329
  large alloy bar production, 328, 388, 389
  Parapremium steel production, 346–347, 388, 430
  production output, 388
  teamwork strategy, 326, 327, 345
  unions and labor relations, 404

Federal-Mogul-Bower, 217, 245, 246, 259, 293, 307, 358

Federal-Mogul Corporation, 209

Federal Reserve Board, 123

Federal Trade Commission, 123

Fellows, John H., 415

Feynman, Richard, 358

Fiat, 260

Fick, John E., 178, 413

Fiedorek, Leo A., 416

financial services industry, 311, 313

Finch, Mary, 153

Firestone, C. D., 18, 19, 33

Firestone, Harvey, 18, 19, 33

Firestone Rubber Company, 125

Fischer, Albrecht, 267–268

Fischer, Erich, 220, 223

Fischer, Friedrich, 23, 24, 33

Fischer, Phillipp, 23, 33

Fischer Bearings Company, 152, 233, 234, 354, 357, 358, 381

Fisher, Frederick J., 67, 68, 86, 108

Fisher, Ronald A., 145

Fisher Body Company, 67

Flaherty, Jack, 56

Fleischmann, Martin, 139, 140, 181, 424

flexible manufacturing, 9, 284, 297–300, 348, 365, 366, 368–371, 373

FLT Prema Milmet S.A., Poland, 394–395

Foale, George, 352

Forbes magazine, 3, 46, 217, 286, 349

Ford, Henry, 6, 22, 41, 60, 75–77, 96, 108, 109

Ford Motor Company, 51, 61, 65, 75, 76, 85, 117, 190, 367

assembly line mass production, 50, 80, 108, 198

automated production technologies, 197

as customer of Timken, 58, 66, 76–82, 108, 109, 116, 117, 135, 181, 184, 216, 221, 223, 311, 390

design engineering, 63

European manufacturing, 222

Model A, 108

Model T, 49, 50, 58, 77, 78, 79, 108

profitability and revenues, 246

statistical process control (SPC), 338

Total Quality Excellence (TQE) Award given to Timken, 339, 384

unionization, 126

vertical integration, 69

Ford Motor Company, Britain, 116

Forrest, H. Edward, 122

Foster, O. D., 3, 5, 6

Four Aces demonstration locomotive (TRBX1111), 96, 99–101, 424

Fowler, Russell P., 206

Franklin Institute, 101

Fredell, Steve, 295

Frederick, Richard L., 414

Fredericka Home for Aged Women, 30

free trade policies, 288

French National Railways (SNCF), 270–271

friction-reducing devices. *See* bearing design and types; bearings (general discussion); bearings, Timken (tapered roller)

Fry, Georgia (née Timken), 86, 411

Fuchs, Maria Luisa Garavaglia, 262–263

fuel-injection equipment, 119, 134

Fujikoshi (Nachi), 292, 337

Galamb, Joseph, 78

Gamet, Monsieur, 154–155, 237

Garaud, Madame Marie-France, 394

Garcia, Frank, 324

Garvin, David, 372

Gary Memorial Medal, 387

Gault, Stanley C., 393, 417

gears, 18, 39, 88, 182, 183, 299

Geier, Frederick A., 135

Geier, James A. D., 138

Geneen, Harold, 360, 361

General Agreements on Tariffs and Trade, 221

General Dynamics, 340, 358

General Electric, 340, 357, 364

General Electric and Aluminum Company of America, 159

General Motors (GM), 47, 49–50, 61, 63–66, 67, 68, 85, 117, 143, 367

automated production process, 208

ball bearing manufacture, 97, 108

as customer of Timken, 64, 65, 108, 221, 223, 245

Detroit Diesel Allison division, 338

joint venture with Toyota, 350–351

New Departure division, 358

New Departure-Hyatt division, 103, 108, 168, 180, 208, 217, 245, 292, 307–309

organizational structure, 86

profitability and revenues, 246

quality/quality control, 338

unions, labor relations, and strikes, 126, 158

vertical integration, 69

Gercik, Patricia, 383

Gerrer, Edmond, 239

Gilbert, Horace D., 355–357, 358

Giles, David J., 302

Gilliam Manufacturing Company, 87–89, 117, 150, 423

Gilliam Manufacturing
Company *(continued)*
See also Canton, Ohio,
locations of The Timken
Company: "Savannah
Avenue"
Girardi, Daniel J., 281, 282
Glossbrenner, Alfred B., 416
Glova, Greg, 306
Glover, Frederick, 95
Gnutti Carlo S.p.A., Italy, 395,
433
Gonzales, Diego, 170
Goodrich, 125
Goodyear Tire & Rubber
Company, 107, 125, 393
Grainger, Tony, 262, 265
Grant, Arthur W., 25
Grant Axle and Wheel
Company, 25, 64
Great Depression.
See economy, U.S.: Great
Depression
Green, Walter F., 180, 183, 281
Gregg, Joseph R., 304
Griffith, James W., 418
Griffiths, Frederick J., 107,
181, 412
Griswold, Dean, 288
Gulling, Richard A., 283, 284,
414
Gurney bearings, 77, 79
Guttzeit, Charles W., 301–302
gyro-optics technology, 358,
359

Hahn, Carl H., 394
Halcomb Steel Company, 54
Hamilton, Hubert Adrien, 154
Handpiece Headquarters, 393,
433
Harding, Warren G., 123
Harley Davidson, 33
Harrisberger, Elnora, 143
Hart, Donald L., 380, 381, 415
Harvard Business School, 129,
179, 220, 248, 249, 250,
274, 314, 372
Harvard University, 129, 178
heat treatment technology,
204–205, 207

Heinzelman, Edmund, 24, 186
Heinzelman, John, 13, 24
Heinzelman, Louisa, 14
Heinzelman, Reginald, 6, 24,
25, 26, 36, 69, 437
Helflinger, Charles, 21
Henderson Medal, 101
Hercules Motor Company, 79,
148
Heroult, Paul L. T./Heroult
furnace, 72, 94
Hess-Bright Manufacturing
Company, 51
H.F. Borbein & Company, 39
Hitachi, 383
Honda of America, 349
Hoopes, Edwin S. (Sarge), Jr.,
178, 299, 414
Hoover, Herbert, 123
Hoover, Joseph S., 286, 416
Hoover Company, The, 286
Hoover Steel Ball Company,
108
Horger, Oscar, 141, 182, 207,
216
Hosfeld, William, 36
Houghton & Richards, Inc.
(H&R), 391, 393
Houpt-Rockwell automobile,
52
Howland, James, 70
Hub, The, 15–16, 18, 19, 20, 21
Hudelson, David, 369
Hudson, William, 316
Hudson automobiles, 109
Hughes, J. H., 25
Hunt, John, 271
Hyatt, John Wesley, 25
Hyatt Roller Bearing
Company, xiv, 47, 51, 52,
57, 62–63, 64–65, 65–66,
68, 69, 112, 119
bearings for railroad
industry, 97, 98
See also General Motors
(GM): New Departure-
Hyatt division

IBM, 246
Imperial Bearing Company,
108

Industry Week, America's Best
Plants citation, 209, 387,
388
Ingersoll-Rand, 309
In Search of Excellence (Peters
and Waterman), 342
Institute of Management
Improvement (Japan),
367
Institut Geopolitique, 394
interchangeable products.
See standardization of
products and production;
Timken Company, The:
interchangeable prod-
ucts; Timken Roller Bear-
ing Company, The: inter-
changeable products
International Harvester, 223,
265
International Monetary Fund,
221
International Nickel
Company, 279
International Standards Asso-
ciation (ISA), 263–264
International Standards
Organization (ISO), 263,
264–265, 266–267
International Trade
Commission (ITC), 289,
345, 346, 373
Interstate Commerce
Commission, 123
ITT, 360

Japan Railways West, 384
Jefferson, General, Jr., 386
Jefferies, Ressie, 295
Jehu, Walter, 224
jet engines. *See* aircraft
industry
John Deere agricultural
machinery, 212, 221, 223,
367
Johns, John S., 191, 343
Jones, Jacques, 380
Jouve, Monsieur, 154, 155,
156
Joy Ball and Roller Bearing
Company, 358, 359

Judy, William E., 222, 260, 262
just-in-time manufacturing and
    delivery systems, 205,
    284, 352, 365

kaizen continuous improve-
    ment strategy, 365
kanban concept. *See* just-in-
    time manufacturing and
    delivery systems
Keim, Edward, 258
Keller, Helen, 173, 174
Kimbark, G. C., 411
Kimmerling, Karl P., 418
Kirby, Bob, 291
Klinedinst, Louis M., 92–93,
    94, 132, 182, 187, 412
Knapp, E. Ronald, 153, 227,
    228, 234, 235, 415
Knauer, Jürgen, 223
Knoell, Rudi, 223
Knudsen, William S., 143
Koffel, Don, 368
Korean War, 182, 195, 210,
    358
Koyo Seiko, 292, 293, 337, 386
Krupp Stahltechnik GmbH,
    324
Krupp steel producer, 200
Kugelfischer Georg Schaefer
    AG (FAG). *See* FAG bear-
    ing manufacturer,
    Germany

labor market, postwar, 157
labor unions and strikes, 60,
    80, 81, 82, 104, 123–127,
    150, 151, 191–195, 198,
    305–306, 320, 343–345,
    351, 404
  business environment and
    change, 128
  France, 274
  postwar, 159
  See also Canton, Ohio, loca-
    tions of The Timken
    Company: unions, labor
    relations, and strikes;
    Timken Company, The:
    unions, labor relations,
    and strikes; Timken

Company, The, U.S.
    locations and plants:
    unions, labor relations,
    and strikes; Timken
    Roller Bearing Company,
    The: unions, labor rela-
    tions, and strikes
La Force, J. Clayburn, Jr., 417
Landon, Alf, 126
Lang, Robert W., 415
Latrobe, Pennsylvania, 305
Latrobe Steel Company (later
    Timken Company sub-
    sidiary), 9, 300–307, 348,
    354, 391, 393
  Cast Masters, Koncor Indus-
    tries, and Special Prod-
    ucts divisions, 303,
    391–392
  precision forging facility,
    391, 431
Lausier, E. B., 57
L.C. Smith Bearings and Parts
    Company, 109
lean manufacturing concept,
    350–352, 363–366, 369,
    403, 405
Lear, 357
Leibensperger, Robert L., 310,
    339, 347, 348, 381–382,
    406, 417
Leland, Henry M., 47, 49
Leterstone Sales Company, 109
Levassor, Emile, 22
leveraged buyouts, 360–361
Lewis, C. W., 411
Lewis, Eugene W., 44–45, 52,
    54, 57, 62, 95
Libbey-Owens-Ford, 286, 289
Life magazine, 192
Little, Gene E., 417
Litton Industries, 246
Lorist, Rudi, 270
Lothrop, Marcus T., 54, 55,
    72–74, 76, 78, 79, 82,
    94–96, 106–107, 109, 111,
    120, 121, 181, 412
  as president of The Timken
    Roller Bearing Company,
    96
Lynch, Austin, 411

machine-tool industry, 234,
    336, 391
  technology, 25, 30, 49, 50,
    280, 293, 365
  See also Cincinnati Milling
    Machine Company;
    Timken Roller Bearing
    Company, The:
    centerless grinding
    technology
Mack Truck Company, 33, 95,
    328
Mahoney, Robert W., 393, 417
Malcolm Baldrige National
    Quality Award, 338
Markley, Herbert E., 248–249,
    282, 304, 413
  antidumping petition and,
    288–289, 345
  industrial engineering
    strategy, 341–342
  management philosophy
    and style, 285, 289–290
  research and development
    programs, 310
  retirement, 312, 334, 395
  role in international
    operations, 223–224, 238
Marlin-Rockwell Corporation,
    87, 88
Marshall Plan, 157, 223
Mars Pathfinder, 10
Martin, Dave, 369
Martin, Gene, 401
Massey Ferguson, 223
Mather, Gordon, 40, 79, 131
Matler, Louis, 239
Matthews, George T.,
    298–299, 307, 316–317,
    346, 388
Maxim, Hiram Percy, 22
Maxwell automobiles, 50
Maxwell-Chalmers, 35
Mayfield, Harry, 127, 128, 191,
    343–344
Mazda Motor Company, 349
Mazeraud, Pierre, 270
McCool, Harry Y., 71
McCoy, Wyn E., 415
McKelvey, Ralph E., 269, 282
McKinley, William, 40

McKinsey & Company, 342–343, 374
McNicoll, David, 228, 230
Mercedes Benz, 261
Mercy Hospital (formerly the Timken mansion), Canton, Ohio, 186
Miami Cycle & Manufacturing Company, 38, 41
Middletown Cycle Company, 38, 41
Miller, George Lee/Miller bearing, 87, 88, 96, 108
Milwaukee & St. Paul Railroad, 98
Miraglia, Salvatore J., 418
missile industry. *See* aerospace industry; National Aeronautics and Space Administration
MIT Japan Program, 383
Mitsubishi Electric Corporation, 349
Mitterrand, François, 407
Monnot, John E., 41
Monz, Karl, 260
Moore, Whitley B., 413
Moreland, Jules A., 219–220, 261, 263
Moriarty, John Paul, 174
Morris Maxi, 271
Mosey, George, 390
Mosey Manufacturing, 390
Mott, Charles, 68
MPB Corporation (Miniature Precision Bearings) (later Timken Company subsidiary), 9, 10, 354–361, 373, 393, 408, 431
MPB Singapore Pte., Ltd., 361, 432
MPB UK Ltd., Britain, 395
Mroczkowski, John, 377
Muegel, Akin (Chip), 386
Mueller, H., 22
Mulroney, M. J., 233
multinational corporations, 221, 236, 247, 265, 288, 381
Murphy, Josephine, 167
Mutual Wheel Company, The, 21

Nash Motors, 95
Nashua Corporation, 338
National Aeronautics and Space Administration (NASA), 278, 279, 281
National Association of Manufacturers (NAM), 126, 312, 364
National Industrial Recovery Act, 124
National Labor Relations Act (Wagner Act), 124–125, 126, 158
National Labor Relations Board, 125
National Machinery Company, 185
National War Labor Board, 123
Neal, Elmer/Neal bearing patent, 87, 88, 89, 96, 108, 109, 423
Nene Foundation, 273
Nevins, Allan, 77
New Deal programs, 104, 123–128, 143, 159, 193
New Departure Company, xiv, 51–52, 57, 63–65, 119
New Departure-Hyatt, 245. *See also* General Motors (GM): New Departure-Hyatt division
New Hampshire Ball Bearings, Inc., 357, 358
New Hampshire Industries, 359
New Haven Railroad, 100
New United Motor Manufacturing, Inc. (NUMMI), 350–351, 366
New York Central Railroad, 100
New York Times, 401, 404, 407
Nickas, James L., 179, 184, 190, 214
Niles Machine Company, 355
Nissan Motor Company, 349, 367, 383
Norden, Carl, 355
Norma Hoffman Bearing Company, 355
North, William J. C., 224

North American Rockwell, 286
Northern Pacific Railroad, 99, 101, 215
Nouhaud, Charles, 115, 154–156, 233, 237, 238
NSK company, Japan, 337, 386, 395
NTN bearing company, Japan, 261, 337, 386

Obermier, J. George, 54–55, 74, 76, 79, 81, 89, 93, 106, 107, 131, 188, 411
O'Connor, James E., 414
offshore manufacturing, 288, 331
Ohio Alloy Steels, 391, 393, 433
OH&R Special Steels Company, Greer, South Carolina, 393, 433
oil industry, 295, 300, 307, 313, 373
Olds, Ransom, 41
Oldsmobile, 41, 49
Olin, Edwin D., 19
Olin, Thomas D., 19
Ordnance Department, U.S., 144
Osterman, Linn, 380
Otto Konigslow, 38, 41
Ovako Steel AB, 386–387

Palmgren, Arvid, 110
Pascoe, Frederick John (Sir John), 115, 152, 153, 222
  director of British Timken Limited, 225, 227–229, 233, 237, 241, 248, 259, 394, 414
  miniature bearing design (FJP1), 234–235
Pasquale, Armando, 263
patent law, 16–17
patents
  bearing, 51, 87–88, 96, 97, 108–112, 217, 354, 421
  grinding, 135
  litigation, 64, 109, 110
  process technology, 68, 199

See also Timken, Henry:
carriage patents
Pennsylvania Railroad, 97, 100
Perret, Claude, 223, 258
Perry, Stephen A., 417
Persian Gulf War, 373
Peters, George M., 18
Peters, Oscar G., 18
Peters, Thomas J., 342
Peterson, Donald, 175
Peterson, Frank, 175
Peterson, Harold, 175
Peterson, Norman H., 415
Petty, Richard, 372
Phillips, S. E., 38
Piatt, Mark, 328
Pierce, Winslow S., Jr.,
354–355, 356, 357
Pilz, James W., 182, 184, 283,
284, 316, 337, 381, 415
Pinay, Antoine, 237, 238
Pioneer Limited train, 98
polyethylene, 300, 429
Pompidou, Georges, 394
Pope Manufacturing
Company, 22, 46
Porter, Harry J., 106, 412
Porter, Jack, 400, 401
Powell, Brooks R., 414
Powell, William/Powell
family, 170, 171
power density. *See* Timken
Company, The: power
density concept
Prausnitzer, Max, 113, 115,
422
Précision Industrielle, La,
236–237
precision manufacturing
bearings, 357, 371
grinding, 135
machine tools, 147, 157,
203–204
technology, 47, 49, 56, 68,
80–82, 94, 180, 232, 268
See also bearing design and
types: miniature
Precision Steel Components
business. *See* Timken
Steel Business unit: com-
ponents (parts) business

Precourt, Jay A., 418
Preston, James K., 297, 315,
316, 325, 327
Prytz, Björn G., 111
Pullman railroad cars, 96, 98
Pursell, Carroll W., Jr., 198

quality revolution, 338
Quanex Corporation, 388

Rail Bearing Service, Inc.
(RBS), 393, 432
railroad industry, British, 393
railroad industry, French
high-speed *Train à Grande
Vitesse* (TGV), 270–271
railroad industry, U.S., 94,
96–101
hot box problem (*See* bearings (general discussion):
hot box problem)
See also bearings, Timken
(tapered roller) applica-
tions and markets; bear-
ings, Timken (tapered
roller) applications and
markets: railroad industry
Ramsey, J. Kevin, 284, 416
Raytheon, 357
RCA, 278
Reagan, Ronald, 323, 326,
337, 345
Reeves, Paul J., 266, 413
Reiser, Fred, Jr., 222
Reiter, Gerhard, 260, 368
Renault automobiles, 75, 157
SNR bearing subsidiary,
252, 260, 261
Republican party, 404
Republic Engineered Steels,
373
Republic Steel, 126, 148, 250,
279, 300, 303
research and development,
311, 336
government funding, 278,
281
See also Timken Research,
Canton, Ohio
Rey, Joseph, 238–239, 272
RHP bearing company, 395

Richey, Herchel M., 175, 176,
177, 202, 206, 414
Richey, John C. (Jack), 180,
203
Riley, Bernard, 156, 157, 237
Riley, John A., 412
Ringen, Adelheid (née
Timken), 11, 12, 13
Ringen, Cord, 21
Ringen, Gerhard, 13, 14
Ringen, John, 14
RIV bearing company, Italy,
260–261
robotics, 365
Rockwell, Albert F., 51–52
Rockwell, Edward D., 51–52
Rockwell, Walter F., 95, 221
Rockwell, Willard F., 95,
221–222
Rockwell Cab, 52
Rockwell International, 222,
286, 393, 406
Rockwell Spring and Axle
(renamed Rockwell
Standard), 221, 222
Rockwell Standard Company,
286
Rolls Royce, 230, 234
Roosevelt, Franklin D., 104,
123, 126, 142
Roosevelt, Theodore, 46
Ross, Donald, 359–360
Rotol Company, 230, 235
Rover automobiles/Rover
Group (British Leyland),
271, 368
Rowland, Elbert S., 182, 281,
282
Rulmenti Grei S.A., 9, 395,
409, 433
Russia, 147, 160. *See also*
Soviet Union
Rybolt, Robert M., 288

Sack, Hans J., 418
Samuel Fox & Company, Ltd.,
257
Sanderson Kayser, Ltd., 393
Santa Fe Railroad, 215
Sanyo, 388
Sauer, Howard C., 220

Saxman, Marcus W., 301, 302

Saxman, Marcus W. III/ Saxman family, 303, 304, 305

Schaefer, Georg, 24

Schober, Marshall, 301, 304–306

Schubach, John J., 314–317, 319, 322, 329, 342, 346, 376–377, 416

scientific management concept, 199, 202

Scranton, William M., 358, 359

seamless tubing steel production, 66, 67, 70–71, 78, 119, 138, 144–145, 181–182, 299–300, 307, 328, 390

Securities and Exchange Commission (SEC), 124, 248

securities industry, 124

Selby, Joseph, 255, 256

Shandong Yantai Bearing Factory, 394

Shelby Steel Company, 71

Sheldon Axle Company, 38

Sherman Act, 111

Shewhart, Walter, 145

Shingo, Shigeo/Shingo Prize for Excellence in Manufacturing, 291, 367, 384

Shipley, Ralph T., 181, 188, 415

Sholley, Lee, 388

Signal Companies, Inc., 359

Simca automobiles, 261

Sisson, Robert L., 150, 175, 180, 185, 188, 249, 262

SKF (Svenska Kullagerfabriken), Sweden, 110–112, 156, 222

 as competitor, 98, 104, 116, 224, 231, 259, 260–261, 270, 307, 332

 international markets and expansion, 394, 395

 metric standard and, 263–265, 267

 parent company of Volvo, 269

 production output, 337

profitability, 307, 309, 332, 334, 378

steel production, 76, 181, 386–387

SKF Industries, Inc. (U.S. subsidiary), 97, 110, 112, 125, 217, 292, 337, 358, 386

Sloan, Alfred, 47, 61, 62, 65–66, 68, 126

Smith, Henry K., 88

SMS Concast, 389

SNR. *See* Société Nouvelle de Roulements (SNR)

Société Anonyme Française Timken, La, 115, 236, 424, 426, 427. *See also* Timken France

Société de Mécanique de Gennevilliers, La, 113, 422

Société Nouvelle de Roulements (SNR), 237, 252, 260, 261, 265, 270

Society of Automotive Engineers, 46

South African Railways, 235, 259

Soviet Union, 116, 192, 193

 bearing industry, 208

 space program, 278, 358

space program

 Soviet, 278, 358

 U.S., 10, 358

Sperry Gyroscope, 355

Split Ball Bearing Corporation, 355, 357–358, 359

Spray, Judd W., 412

springs, carriage, 17–18, 19

springs, Timken, 44

Sputnik, 358

Ssangyong Motors, Korea, 385

St. Louis automobile, 39

St. Louis Carriage Manufacturing Company, 21

St. Louis Motor Carriage Company, 38, 39

Standard Bearing Company, 87

standardization of products and production, 50

See also bearings, Timken (tapered roller): standardization of; Bucyrus, Ohio, automated high-volume bearing plant; Bucyrus concept; Timken Company, The: interchangeable products; Timken Roller Bearing Company, The: interchangeable products

Standard Oil, 393

Standard Roller Bearing Company, The, 64–65, 72

Standard Steel Spring Company, 222

Stark Rolling Mill, 41

statistical process control (SPC). *See* Timken Company, The: statistical process control; Timken Roller Bearing Company, The: statistical process control

steel industry, Japanese, 316–317, 319, 388

steel industry, U.S., 300, 303, 323, 328–329, 336, 364, 378, 387

 effect of Japanese competition on, 313, 315

 global competition and markets, 303, 317

 mini-mills, 298, 318

 research and development expenditures, 340

 unions, labor relations, and strikes, 82, 193–194, 305–306, 404

 vertical integration, 74–76

 See also United Steelworkers (USW)

steel types

 alloy, 107, 119, 138, 181, 298

 alloy 16-25-6 (Super Steel), 140, 147, 181

 carbon-vanadium, 99

 case-hardened, 45–46, 53, 88, 235, 255, 256

 chrome, 235, 241, 256, 257

chromium-molybdenum alloy, 139
corrosion-resistant, 281
Desegatized, 302
free-machining, 302
graphitic, 140
high-strength, 232, 281, 298, 424, 431, 432
high-temperature, 140, 147, 181, 281, 424
low-tungsten alloy, 302
molybdenum steel alloy, 76
nickel-alloy, 99
nickel-chromium-molybdenum alloy, 140
nickel-molybdenum, 235, 241, 256, 257, 423
through-hardened, 235, 255, 428
tool, 302–303
Steinmetz, Charles, 44
Stephan, Martin, 12
Stewart, Eugene L., 288–289, 346
stock market crash, 104, 115, 117, 122, 123. *See also* economy, U.S.
Stover, Jack D., 309, 310
Strickland, Silas A., 108
Strouble, Thomas W., 269, 310, 352, 418
Strough, J. Fred, 106, 108, 111, 115, 130, 412
Studebaker automobiles, 16
Studebaker brothers, 33
Sullivan Principles, 275, 286
Sumitomo Metal Industries, 317, 318, 388, 389
Surface Combustion Corporation, 204–205
Svenska Kullagerfabriken. *See* SKF
Sweitzer, Elmer, 223, 224

Taft-Hartley Act, 158
taper-measuring devices, 255–256
Tata Iron and Steel Company, 353
Tata Timken Limited joint venture, 353–354

taxation, 82, 85, 126, 167, 169, 192, 289
Taylor, Frederick W., 199, 202
Thatcher, Margaret, 368
Thompson Products, Inc., 190
Timken, Amelia, 16, 20
Timken, Cora, 16, 20, 106
Timken, Edith M., 250, 344
Timken, Edith (née Kitzmiller), 40, 105
Timken, Fredericka (née Heinzelman), 13, 16, 17, 30
Timken, Georgia, 16, 20
Timken, Gerhard, 12
Timken, Henry, 2, 17, 39, 286, 411
  advertising and promotion strategies, 18, 44, 57
  automobile industry and, 5, 22–23
  carriage business, 2, 5, 6, 10, 13–16, 17–18, 20–21, 38, 43, 49, 53
  carriage patents, 16–20, 20–21
  death, 53
  induction into National Inventors Hall of Fame, 8
  invention and patenting of the Timken bearing, 5–6, 23–27, 36
  investment strategy, 28, 30, 43–44
  personal life and career in carriage industry, 10–16, 20, 21, 22, 28
  vision and legacy, 1–10, 28–31, 53
Timken, Henry H. (Kurt) II, 405–406
Timken, Henry Heinzelman (H. H.), 2, 16, 23, 28, 75, 185, 186, 190, 192, 312, 389, 397, 402, 411
  character of the organization and, 3–4, 29, 104, 132, 161, 189
  competitive strategy, 51, 62–64, 65–66, 69, 87, 108–109, 111–112, 217

corporate purpose/identity, 3–6, 8, 29, 30, 31, 286
cost-reducing policies, 120, 121
development of manufacturing processes, 38, 45–46, 54–56, 78
economy of production strategy, 199–200, 421
efficiency strategy, 5, 47, 49, 112
employee relations, 174
Ford Motor Company and, 78–80
growth strategy, 5, 62, 64–65, 66, 67–68, 69, 71, 82
induction into Automotive Hall of Fame, 8
investment strategy, 35, 43–44, 68, 73, 78–79, 85–86, 311
patents, 36, 85, 88, 109
personality and private life, 21, 34, 104–106, 129, 130–132, 188, 191
philanthropy, 30, 121–122, 131–132, 272, 406–407
quality control and, 47, 64, 69, 89
salary, 120
teamwork and collaboration with brother, 33, 34–35, 36
Timken-Detroit Axle Company and, 52, 62, 95
unions and labor relations, 126, 187
vertical integration into steel strategy, 66, 68, 69–77, 297
wage policy, 60–61, 82
work ethic, 29
Timken, Henry Heinzelman, Jr., 2, 3, 129, 130, 165, 187, 242, 251, 394, 412
  Bucyrus and, 197, 199, 205
  competition and markets strategy, 217, 240
  continuous casting and, 298–299

Timken, Henry Heinzelman, Jr., *(continued)*
death of, 282, 299
personal and management style, 184–185, 186, 190–191, 248, 406
philanthropy, 272
research and development programs, 280
Timken Ordnance Company and, 144–145
Timken, Jacob, 11, 12, 13
Timken, Johann, 11, 12
Timken, John M., 248, 272, 413
Timken, John M., Jr., 405, 416
Timken, John Marter, 129
Timken, Louise (née Blyth), 186
Timken, Mary (née Jackson), 186
Timken, Trine Mahnken, 11
Timken, Ward J. (Jack), 8, 39, 334, 405–407, 415
Timken, Ward J. (Tim), Jr., 2, 406
Timken, William Robert (W. R.), 2, 4, 8, 17, 21, 25, 28, 43, 44, 46, 142, 217, 272, 411
financial management and function, 50–51, 65, 73, 74, 85, 86, 109, 122, 130
leadership position, 106, 130
patents and, 36, 109
personality and private life, 20, 34, 61–62, 66, 68, 130
sales, administration, and finance function, 35, 52, 54, 57, 61
on steel production, 73–74
teamwork and collaboration with brother, 33, 34–35, 36
Timken-Detroit Axle Company and, 52
Timken, William Robert (Bob), 2, 129, 132, 165, 187, 222, 240, 242, 254, 272, 273, 291, 333, 394, 413

acquisition of Latrobe Steel Company, 300–307
corporate mission/purpose, 184
creation of Timken Research, 277–282
financial management, 129, 130, 185
mandating change, 282–283, 314
personal and management style, 185–186, 190–191, 242–243, 349
philanthropy, 272, 273, 407
Timken France and, 237
training programs, 249–251
Timken, William R., Jr. (Tim), 2, 39, 243, 253, 275, 291, 339, 353, 364, 372, 397, 405, 407, 414
antidumping petition and, 288
business strategy, 316, 394
communications policy, 401
continuous improvement strategy, 325
corporate mission/purpose, 361
cost-reducing policies, 340
excellence strategy, 379
Faircrest steel plant and, 319–322
financial growth strategy, 290–292, 293–295, 349–354, 363, 378, 381, 388–389, 402
on global strategy, 382, 383
investment strategy, 323
Japanese automobile market and, 383–384
leadership roles, 282, 285, 406
management strategy, 345, 403
management team with Toot, 312, 334–335
market research programs, 314–315, 316, 317
personnel policies, 397
research and development programs, 310, 311

restructuring and, 341–342
teamwork strategy, 341
training and early assignments, 249–251, 285
work ethic, 251
Timken Automatic stove, 95
Timken Bearing Business unit, 329, 342, 363, 370–371, 380, 381, 387, 430
acquisitions and mergers, 373, 392
Timken Bearing Business unit, divisions
Asia Pacific and Latin America, 385, 431
Europe, Africa, West Asia, 380, 431, 433
North America, South America, and East Asia, 380
relationship with Timken Steel Business unit, 389, 409
See also bearings, Timken (tapered roller)
Timken-Brewster Combination Spring, 20
Timken Carriage Company, The, 21
Timken Company, The, 1
acquisition of Latrobe Steel Company, 300–307
acquisitions and mergers, 9, 300–307, 353–354, 392–397, 407, 433
antidumping campaigns, 288–289, 293, 345, 349, 373, 404
awards and presentations, 209, 215, 268, 272–273, 287, 324, 339, 384, 387–388, 402, 405, 407
business environment and change, 3, 8, 290, 307, 313–314, 341, 374, 400, 401, 405, 407–408
business strategy, 6, 8, 314, 329, 392–393, 399
business unit structure, 363, 380, 403 (*See also* Timken Bearing Business

unit; Timken Steel Business unit)

communication systems and policies, 351–352, 366, 376–377, 405, 406

computer and electronic systems, 254, 293, 297, 324–325, 338, 340, 348, 365, 371, 382, 388, 400

continuous improvement strategy, 325, 327, 363, 365, 367, 377, 384, 388, 403, 405

continuous improvement strategy/Breakthrough/ Accelerated Continuous Improvement (ACI), 374–376, 377, 396

corporate mission/purpose, 3, 6, 8, 10, 285–286, 314, 325–326, 329, 335, 343, 352, 377, 379, 397, 404, 406–409

customer base, 336, 378

customer relations, 294–295, 363, 374, 400–401

discrimination suit against, 288

distribution centers, 382–383 (*See also* Bucyrus, Ohio, automated high-volume bearing plant: Distribution Center)

environmental programs, 286, 289, 429

flexible manufacturing, 297–300, 348, 365, 366, 369–371, 373

government regulations and, 286, 288–289

growth strategy, 6, 9, 290, 297, 343–344, 353, 373, 380, 406 (*See also* Bucyrus concept: as corporate strategy)

growth through acquisitions strategy, 392–397

information systems, 325, 340, 365, 370

interchangeable products, 382, 385

just-in-time manufacturing and delivery, 352, 365

leadership succession, 406

lean manufacturing initiatives, 350–351, 352, 363, 365, 366, 403

marketing research and programs, 317, 346–347, 380, 385

as model turnaround company, 364

as multinational corporation, 381

new product lines, 311, 385, 389

1999 Centennial, 405, 409

organizational structure, 314, 348, 363, 366, 374, 380, 381, 385, 391, 409

outside influences, consultants, and board members, 38, 286, 338, 341–342, 392–393, 405

planning function/strategy, 315, 317, 341, 380

power density concept, 347–349, 382, 385, 409

process control and innovation, 314, 338, 382, 390, 433

product innovation and development, 385, 390, 409

production output, 9, 290, 292–300, 314, 318, 365, 369, 371

quality/quality control, 8, 36, 56, 315, 327, 329, 338, 349, 352, 365, 368, 382, 384

research and development, 310–311, 348, 354 (*See also* Timken Research, Canton, Ohio)

restructuring, 353, 373, 374, 380, 381, 385

restructuring into business units, 341–345 (*See also* Timken Bearing Business

unit; Timken Steel Business unit)

sales and sales engineering, 300, 348, 380, 382, 384–385, 399, 419–420

service engineering, 399, 403, 408

statistical process control (SPC), 337–338, 365

steel-making capability, 6–9, 54, 300, 312, 314, 315, 317, 318, 350, 388

stock, 68, 304, 332, 340, 346, 349–350, 378–379, 396, 401–402, 405, 419–420, 423

technical collaboration with customers, 382, 384, 386, 389, 399, 401, 409

trademark, 109, 110, 354, 401, 409

training programs, 285, 293, 326–327, 366, 370, 382, 385, 403

unions, labor relations, and strikes, 325–327, 343–345, 351, 374, 377, 378, 400, 404–405

value concept and strategy, 4, 5, 30–31, 33, 289–290, 348, 349, 352, 402–403, 404, 407, 408

Vision 2000 reorganization and modernization program, 352, 361, 364, 366–367, 368, 376

wages and benefits, 60, 320, 327, 340, 341, 343, 344, 369, 373, 374, 402–403

women employees, 403

Timken Company, The, competition and markets, 6, 8, 9, 312, 317, 347–349, 378, 385

aerospace industry, 391

automotive industry, 369, 373

Chinese, 394, 395

domestic, 307–309, 316, 385, 386, 388

Timken Company, The, competition and markets, *(continued)*
Eastern European, 394–395, 431
European, 315, 316
German, 402–403
global, 331–332, 373, 381–387
international, 394
Japanese, 246, 288–289, 292–293, 307, 315, 316–317, 331, 337–338, 345, 346, 383, 388, 400, 402
Russian, 395
See also bearings, Timken (tapered roller) applications and markets; Timken Roller Bearing Company, The, competition and markets; Timken steel products and markets
Timken Company, The, finances
asset turnover (sales/assets ratio), 294
cost-reducing policies, 309, 311, 315, 331, 338, 340, 341, 363, 388
cost-reducing policies/Breakthrough/ACI, 374–376, 377, 396
debt rating/cost of capital, 379
growth strategy, 289, 322–323, 349–354, 364, 393
pricing policies, 337, 346, 400, 401 (*See also* bearings, Timken (tapered roller): price of; Timken Roller Bearing Company, The: pricing policies)
production costs, 331
profitability and revenues, 8–9, 289, 296, 307, 322, 331–332, 340, 349, 378–381, 391–392, 395–396, 419–420

profitability and revenues, annual reports, 308, 309, 334, 375, 378, 392, 396, 402, 438
research and development expenditures, 310–311, 340
Timken Company, The, investments
capital expenditure, 323, 350, 364, 373, 378, 379, 406
equipment, 297, 298, 366
facilities, 312, 313, 315, 322–323, 350, 372, 378, 389, 399
long-term, 407
manufacturing, 341
outside the company, 353
research and development, 341, 369, 399
strategy, 30, 34–35, 35, 53, 60, 290, 311, 327, 332, 350, 386
technology and modernization, 314, 328–329, 350, 365–369
Timken Company, The, joint ventures, 353, 392, 407
Tata Timken Limited, India, 353–354, 374, 431
Yantai Timken Company Limited, China, 394, 432
Timken Company, The, management, 399
culture, 189–191, 289–290, 342, 343, 363, 402, 404, 406
decision making, 314, 315–316, 329, 335, 341, 374
downsizing, 374–376, 377
hierarchy, 289–290, 314, 326, 402
independence, philosophy of, 286–290, 350, 379, 405
information systems, 285
personnel policies, 288, 326–327, 344, 366–367, 370, 396, 402–404

strategic, 329, 341, 353, 363, 376, 397
teamwork strategy, 352, 366–367, 369, 371, 388, 403
See also Timken Roller Bearing Company, The, management
Timken Company, The, subsidiaries and wholly owned companies
Australian Timken Proprietary Limited (Ballarat plant), 165, 219, 223–224, 231, 248, 252, 256–259, 368, 385, 427
Canadian Timken Limited, 165, 166, 219–220, 252, 256, 257–258, 368, 424, 425
competition among, 296–297, 426
Nihon Timken K.K., Japan, 293, 349, 381, 383, 384, 429
Timken Argentina S.r.l., 427
Timken de Mexico, 426, 432
Timken do Brasil, 165, 224, 225, 248, 252, 256, 259, 381, 385, 427
Timken Italia, 395, 433
Timken Polska Sp.z.o.o, 394–395, 395
Timken Roller Bearing Company of South America, The, Brazil, 219, 221, 425
Timken Romania, 395, 433
Timken South Africa, 252, 259, 274–275, 426
See also British Timken Limited; Handpiece Headquarters; Latrobe Steel Company; MPB Corporation; OH&R Special Steels Company; Rulmenti Grei S.A.; Timken France; Timken Rollenlager GmbH
Timken Company, The, U.S. locations and plants, 82, 166

Altavista, Virginia, bearing
plant, 369–373, 385, 431
Asheboro, North Carolina,
bearing plant, 9, 372,
373, 385
Atlanta Export Service
Center, 382–383, 385,
431
Canton bearing plant,
41–42, 52, 53, 54–56,
80–82, 123, 169–171, 175,
212, 217, 290, 368, 403,
421
centers of expertise
program, 366, 367
closures, layoffs, and
downsizing, 85, 120–123,
125, 340, 343–344, 351,
373, 374, 407
Colorado Springs,
Colorado, 166, 426
Columbus, Ohio, bearing
plant, 81, 82, 85,
120–121, 122–123, 125,
127, 149, 151, 161, 171,
213–215, 232, 280, 338,
340, 343, 385–386, 422
culture and organization,
169–176
Detroit, Michigan, sales
department, 82
Franklin, Pennsylvania,
cold-finishing plant, 391
Gaffney, South Carolina,
bearing plant, 290–292,
293, 338, 367, 370, 384,
428
Gambrinus, Ohio, bearing
and steel plants, 94, 150,
168, 169–172, 175, 211,
217, 297, 367, 424, 428,
433
Gambrinus, Ohio, Large
Industrial Bearing
Complex, 367–368
Lincolnton, North Carolina,
bearing plant, 295, 297,
314, 429
New Philadelphia, Ohio,
bearing plant, 212, 348,
377, 403, 426

non-union, 210, 343, 344,
367
sales divisions, 110, 119
St. Clair Precision Tubing
Components, Eaton,
Ohio, 390, 431
St. Louis, Missouri, 15, 16,
18
Tryon Peak ring plant,
Columbus, North
Carolina, 390–391, 432,
433
tube mills, 138–139, 144,
145, 319, 422
unions, labor relations, and
strikes, 124–128, 151,
305–307, 320, 343–344,
344, 351
Wooster, Ohio, tube mill,
120, 128, 138, 140, 171,
424, 425
working conditions, 193
Zanesville, Ohio, finishing
plant, 149, 161, 223, 425,
427
See also Bucyrus, Ohio,
automated high-volume
bearing plant; Canton,
Ohio, locations of The
Timken Company; Fair-
crest steel plant
Timken Company Charitable
Trust, The, 406
Timken Company Educational
Fund, The, 406
Timken Cross Spring, 17–21
Timken-David Brown worm
gears, 77
Timken-Detroit Axle
Company, The, 34, 35,
53, 54, 61–62, 65, 66, 85,
421
advertising and promotion
strategies, 57–58
during World War I, 74
expansion to 1915, 62
labor strike at, 81
merged with Rockwell
Spring and Axle Com-
pany, 221–222
in the 1920s, 95

pricing strategy, 69
sales, 57
stock, public sale, 86
Timken Engineering Journal,
93
Timken Europa Distribution
Center (Haan, Germany),
297, 368, 383, 429
Timken Europe, 251
creation, 262–263
lean manufacturing
principles, 368–369
management and organiza-
tional structure, 296–297,
316, 380
metric standard and,
263–267
profitability and revenues,
373, 380
Timken Foundation, 30, 122,
129, 131, 173, 186,
272–273, 305, 332, 405,
407
Timken France, 114–116, 128,
151, 159, 160, 165, 220,
233, 235, 248, 251, 252,
268, 272
Asnières bearing plant, 115,
154–157, 236–237, 251,
424, 427
competition and markets,
220, 221, 296, 426
consolidation with U.S.
Timken, 212, 219, 225,
236–241, 274
customers, 258, 261,
262–263
as division of The Timken
Roller Bearing Company,
212, 219
during World War II, 133,
153–157
unions, labor relations, and
strikes, 237
Timken France, Colmar plant,
338, 427
location decision, 238–240
production and pricing
issues, 261–262, 296
sales and application engineering at, 258

Timken France, Colmar plant, *(continued)*
  steel supply, 255, 257, 310
  unions, labor relations, and strikes, 274
Timken & Heinzelman, 14
Timken-Heinzelman bearing patents and design, 26, 27–28
Timken International Fund, 272–273
Timken Investment Company, 28
Timken Magazine, 57, 58, 70
Timken Management Institute, 285
Timken Ordnance Company, 145, 150, 199, 232, 425
Timken, publication, 58
Timken railroad bearing business unit, 381
Timken Research, Canton, Ohio, 278–282, 311, 316, 332, 428, 430
  advanced bearing process development group, 369, 371
  alloy development, 300
  bearing-life studies, 309–310
  clean steel technology, 310, 429, 430
  collaboration with Timken Steel Business unit, 389
  continuous casting technology, 389
  creation of, 277–282
  new product development, 370–371
  production process technology, 391
  technology-based sales strategy, 386
  ultrasonic inspection of bearings, 310, 317
  work reorganization program, 369
Timken Rock Bit, 119, 134, 166, 424, 430

Timken Rollenlager GmbH, Germany, 222, 251, 260, 262, 316, 427
  integration with Timken France and British Timken Limited, 296
Timken Roller Bearing Axle Company, The, 28, 36, 41, 43, 50–51, 421
  competition and markets, 42–44, 52
  creation and early development, 1–3, 5–6, 28, 35–40
  customer base, 50, 52
  demand for products, 46
  growth strategy, 50, 51, 52
  in-house production, 42, 45–46, 49
  investments, 41–42, 44–49, 51
  product design, 46, 50, 51
  profitability and revenues, 42–43
  quality/quality control, 45
  sales engineering, 44–45, 50
  separation of axle and bearing businesses, 52
Timken Roller Bearing Charitable Trust, The, 173
Timken Roller Bearing Company, The, 34, 35, 52, 61, 237, 421, 423
  acquisitions, sales, and mergers, 62–66, 67, 69, 88, 94, 107, 108–109, 111, 217, 252
  advertising and promotion strategies, 35, 57–58, 59, 63, 109, 119, 134, 140, 207–208
  agents and distributors, 219, 220–221
  antitrust proceedings against, 134
  awards to, 173
  business environment and change, 104, 108–112, 157–161, 165, 210, 277–279
  business strategy, 189–190,

216–219, 246, 251, 252, 258, 270
  centerless grinding technology, 135, 140
  communication systems, 55–56
  computerization, 283–284
  continuous process production, 198, 200–202, 203–204, 206
  corporate mission/purpose, 103, 141–142, 165, 184, 217–219, 254, 281
  cost-reducing policies, 138, 199–200
  customer base/customer relations, 63, 69, 85, 93, 165, 180, 221, 258–259, 261, 265, 280
  Department 36 technology, 259, 261
  divisional jealousies (steel versus bearings), 180–181, 184
  during the Depression, 104, 117–123, 133, 134, 139, 141, 189
  during World War I, 80, 112–113
  during World War II, 132, 133, 142–157, 232
  employee relations, 60–61, 149–151, 169–176, 180
  engineering organization, 119, 178, 184
  European operations (*See* British Timken Limited; Timken Europe; Timken France)
  fiftieth anniversary, 166–169
  foreign division, 220
  foreign licensing agreements, 52–53, 56, 111, 112, 128, 160, 421
  General Motors and, 67, 108
  growth strategy, 34, 42, 60, 76, 80–82, 94, 112–113, 141, 163–166, 195, 210, 252, 277 (*See also*

Bucyrus concept: as corporate strategy)
handicapped employees, 173, 174
Industrial Division, 92, 93, 94, 422
integration strategy, 252–258, 275–276
interchangeable products, 255, 257–258, 266
international sales conferences, 221
joint ventures, 65–66
leadership transition, 104–107, 128–132
manufacturing processes, 40, 54, 56, 74, 78, 80, 85, 87, 89, 132, 165, 169
as multinational corporation, 246, 258, 275–276
name changed to The Timken Company (1970), 285, 428
organizational structure, 46, 53–61, 86, 103, 107, 132, 133, 144, 163, 169, 179, 180, 254, 258, 267, 277–278
patent litigation, 109–110
political advertising, 192–193, 208
precision manufacturing, 94, 180, 255, 268
pricing policies, 184, 189, 245
process engineering, 199–202
product engineering and focus, 86, 93–94, 96, 110, 119, 132, 143–144, 147, 163–165, 217–219
production output, 53, 55–56, 63, 80, 81, 94, 95, 108, 110–111, 121, 135, 143, 148, 161, 166, 175, 176, 198, 199, 202, 208, 214, 233, 267, 283, 311
product testing, 183, 184, 270
profitability and revenues, 38, 53, 60–61, 93, 94, 96,

105, 117, 189–190, 245–247, 254, 419–420
profitability and revenues, annual reports, 84, 116, 118, 120, 124, 130, 164, 218, 246, 247, 308, 333, 375
quality/quality control, 69–70, 109, 141, 183, 184, 233, 255–256, 277
recycling system, 204
research and development, 70, 72, 76, 134, 139, 180, 181, 183, 184, 199, 277 (*See also* Timken Research, Canton, Ohio)
Sales and Service Division, 66
sales/sales engineering, 57, 59, 68, 82, 85, 92, 93–94, 103, 141, 147, 178, 180, 182, 209, 223, 232, 252, 254, 267, 269–270, 271
seamless tubing production, 71, 165, 422
service engineering, 254, 270
statistical process control (SPC), 145, 147, 232–234
steel-making capability, 103, 119, 144, 147, 168, 181, 182, 210, 297–298
steel production and sales, 53, 67, 69–74, 76, 77, 87, 89, 92–96, 121, 134, 138–139, 143–144, 147, 180–182, 184
steel purchases, 70–71, 72–73, 76, 256
stock, 85–86, 105, 106, 117, 119, 122, 124, 129, 160, 186, 190, 217, 222
technical innovation and strengths, 134–142, 145–148, 180, 197–210, 219, 252, 258, 267–271
technical support policies, 269, 270
trademark, 159, 192, 235, 240
training programs, 93,

173–180, 188, 202, 206, 212, 249, 274, 285
unions, labor relations, and strikes, 124–126, 150–151, 158, 159, 168–169, 173, 187, 191–195, 202
vertical integration, 67–68, 74–76
wages and benefits, 82–83, 120, 121, 122, 127, 158, 173–176, 178, 179, 193–194, 206–207
women employees, 143, 149–150, 172–173, 178, 179, 206, 227, 262–263
working conditions, 207, 210
Timken Roller Bearing Company, The, competition and markets, 96, 104, 107–112, 210, 245
automotive, 34–35, 82–85, 86–89, 117 (*See also* Ford Motor Company: as customer of Timken)
competition with Timken France and British Timken Limited, 117, 134, 153, 220, 221, 232
global, 176, 195, 241, 290
international, 104, 111, 112–113, 160, 165
railroad (the Four Aces demonstration locomotive), 96–101
See also bearings, Timken (tapered roller) applications and markets; Timken Company, The, competition and markets; Timken steel products and markets
Timken Roller Bearing Company, The, investments
capital expenditures, 183, 189
equipment, 80–82, 89, 143–144, 183, 185, 189, 190, 216, 241
facility expansion, 141

Timken Roller Bearing
Company, The,
investments *(continued)*
strategy, 53, 80, 82–85,
115–116, 134
technology, 163, 165,
182–183, 210, 278
Timken Roller Bearing
Company, The, manage-
ment, 86, 104, 106, 107,
126–128, 132, 159, 164,
169, 175–176, 187,
246–252
conference of international
management (1960),
252–254
culture, xv–xvi, 142, 165,
179–184
hierarchy, 176–179, 194
independence, philosophy
of, 28–29
information systems,
283–284
personnel policies, 158,
176–180, 188, 199, 243,
250–251, 274–275, 285
right-to-manage issues, 194,
274
strategy, 202, 248–249, 277,
282 (*See also* Bucyrus
concept: as corporate
strategy)
Timken Roller Bearing
Service and Sales
Company, 110
Timken Steel and Tube
Company, 95, 107, 119,
129, 256
Timken Steel Business unit,
329, 342, 380, 381, 387,
430
acquisitions and mergers,
373, 392
clean steel production, 387,
389, 390
clean steel program,
310–311
components (parts)
business, 9, 389–391,
409, 431, 433
contributions to steel

technology, 138–141,
181–183
distribution business, 9,
391, 393, 409
personnel policies, 403
profitability and revenues,
373
relationship to bearing
division, 180–181, 182
relationship with Timken
Bearing Business unit,
389, 409
Timken steel production and
processes
Bearing Steel Practice
(BSP), 429
bottom-pouring ingot
casting, 317–318, 322,
388
clean steel technology, 310,
317 (*See also* Timken
Company, The: power
density concept; Faircrest
steel plant: Parapremium
steel production; Timken
Steel Business unit: clean
steel program)
continuous casting technology, 298–299, 315, 318,
388, 389, 431
electric-furnace, 72–73, 74,
75, 94, 181, 182–183,
298, 300, 301, 302, 317,
324, 426
ingot, 298, 317, 318
open-hearth, 72, 73, 94,
182, 424, 426
process-control capabilities,
324, 326
slow-cool furnace, 183, 257
synergies with bearing production, 68, 297–298, 409
vacuum-arc/electric-arc
remelting, 298, 301–303,
307, 315
See also Timken company,
The: steel-making capa-
bility; Timken Roller
Bearing Company, The:
steel-making capability;
Timken Roller Bearing

Company, The: steel pro-
duction and sales; Timken
Roller Bearing Company,
The: vertical integration
Timken steel products and
markets, 297–298
bar, 299, 328, 378, 391
bearing industry, 95, 147,
184, 388
large bars, 328, 347 (*See also*
Faircrest steel plant: large
alloy bar production)
mechanical tubing, 182, 347,
388, 389, 392
product mix, 391
See also steel types
Timken Trading Post, 58, 168,
169, 171, 172, 175, 176,
177, 178, 179, 180, 193,
233
Timken Triangle, 58, 83
Timken World, 58, 402, 405
Timoshenko, Stephen, 141
Tobey, Henry A., 414
Toot, Joseph F., Jr., 243, 251,
253, 286, 310, 314, 324,
372, 401, 406, 415
acquisitions and mergers,
305, 354
antidumping petition and,
289, 345–346
business strategy, 315–316,
322, 393, 394
communications policy, 401
continuous improvement
and efficiency strategies,
324–325, 328
corporate mission/purpose,
352, 361
cost-reducing policies, 340
director of European operations, 251, 262
excellence strategy, 350,
363, 379, 381, 396
Faircrest steel plant and,
319, 320–322, 324–325,
328, 387, 396
financial function, 374,
402–403
growth strategy, 293–294,
379, 388–389

Latrobe Steel Company
and, 305, 306
leadership positions, 282,
285, 312
management policies, 345,
403
management team with
Tim Timken, 312,
334–335
market research programs,
315–316
receives French Legion of
Honor award, 407
restructuring and, 341–342
retirement as president and
CEO, 396, 406
teamwork strategy,
325–326, 341
at Timken Europe (Colmar,
Alsace), 261–262
training and early assignments, 249–252, 285
Top Operations and Plants
(T.O.P.) Award (given by
33 Metalproducing
journal), 387
Torrington bearing company,
309, 360, 386, 433
Toshiba, 384
Toyo Bearing Manufacturing
Company, 292, 293
Toyoda, Shoichiro, 384
Toyota Motor Company, 365,
383–384
joint venture with General
Motors (GM), 350–351
Superior Quality Perfor-
mance Award, 384
Travers, John, 367
Trotman, Alex, 339
TRW, 190, 340
Marlin-Rockwell division,
358
Tsuneyoshi, Tadao, 383
Tube Investments, 256–257
Tubes, Ltd., 257
Tuckey, Raymond, 152, 229,
232, 265
Tudor, Freeman F., 412
Twenty-First Century Business
Project, 370–372

Tyson, Frank, 217
Tyson Bearing Company, 217

Überherrn, Germany (pro-
posed Timken bearing
plant), 372, 373
Ugine steel company, 257
Umstattd, William, Jr., 192
Umstattd, William Earle, 107,
138, 144, 174, 177, 183,
250, 253, 272, 286, 319,
344, 387, 394, 412
business strategy, international, 217, 219, 220, 222,
237, 239, 240–241
character of the organization, 184, 189, 254
Cold War production, 207
at European Timken plants
after World War II,
152–153, 157
growth strategy, 165, 222
influence and achieve-
ments, 242, 243, 312
inspiration and vision, 252,
289
investment strategy, 237,
239, 323
leadership collaboration
with Henry and Bob
Timken, 187, 190–191,
242–243, 246–248, 251
leadership transition and,
128, 129, 132
organizational structure
and, 181, 202
personal and management
style, 187–191, 222,
246–248, 396
production output and, 209
receives French Legion of
Honor award, 272, 407
retirement as president, 242
training programs, 175–176,
206, 251
unions and labor relations,
126, 191–195
United Auto Workers (UAW),
125, 126
United Mine Workers, 125
United Motors Company, 65

United States Steel
Corporation, 83
United Steel Companies, Ltd.,
298
United Steel Company, 72
United Steelworkers (USW),
104, 126, 127, 151, 158,
191–192, 193, 194, 305,
319, 320, 343–344, 374,
377, 404
University of Michigan, 139,
182
Urbach, Harley J., 213, 215,
216, 238, 281, 414
U.S. Steel, 126
Useem, Michael, 179

Vallourec steel company, 257
VALTI steel company, 257
Vanderbeek, Herbert, 57, 74,
91, 97
Van Horn, Clyde L., 414
Vickers, Ltd., 52, 53, 112, 113,
230, 421
Vietnam War, 274, 298, 300,
358
Voest company, Austria, 236
Voinovich, George, 364
Volkswagen, 260, 261, 394
as customer of Timken,
267–269, 271, 293
Volvo, 269
von Braun, Sigismund, 394

Wafe Manufacturing Company
(later Alinabal), 358, 359
Wagenalls, Robert, 232
Wagner Act, 124–125, 126,
158
Walker, Martin D., 418
Waltham Watch Company, 198
Walton, Edwin, 57
War Labor Board, 151
War Labor Relations Board,
158
War Manpower Commission,
151
Waterman, Robert H., Jr., 342
Weckstein, Samuel M., 182,
236
Weigel, C. Philip, 282, 391

Welch, John F., 364
Wellington, Duke of, 229
West, Charles H., 310, 328,
    329, 380, 388–389, 416
West, John, 291
Western Automatic Machine
    Screw Company, 38, 41
Western Electric, 145
Westinghouse, 148
Weston-Mott Axle Company,
    51, 62, 68
Wheelabrator-Frye, Inc., 359
Whitehouse, Alton W., 393,
    416
Whitney, Valerie Timken, 130
Widner, Ronald L., 309–310,
    347
Wilkins, Mira, 275–276
Wills, C. Harold, 76, 77, 78
Willys, John, 64
Willys-Overland automobiles,
    50, 64, 65, 120
    manufacture of bearings, 73
Wilson, Glenn, 206

Winerip, Michael, 404, 407
Wingerter, Robert G., 286,
    289, 416
Wingquist, Sven, 110, 269
Winton, Alexander, 41, 44
Wiseman, Paul C., 262
Wolf & Colthar, 38
Wolseley Motors, 52, 112, 113,
    422, 423
Wooler, Ernest, 264
World Bank, 221
World War I, 34, 59, 65, 68,
    75, 112, 123, 302
    effect on U.S. industry,
    70–72, 74, 80
World War II, 117, 128, 132,
    142, 148, 152, 278
    airplane industry, 140, 147,
    148
    bearing demand, 355–357,
    373
    British Timken Limited,
    133, 151–153
    production output, 142–143

steel production, 155–156,
    302
Timken France, 133,
    153–157
    See also Timken Roller
    Bearing Company, The:
    during World War II
Wrba, Max, 115, 222
Wright, Wilbur, 34
Wuletich, Peter, 170

Xerox, 246

Yantai Timken Company
    Limited, 394
Yeager, Dolores, 368
Yellow Taxicab Company, 52
Yom Kippur War, 300
Young, Arthur, 126

Zahnradfabrik
    Friedrichshafen, 223
Zampetos, Theodore, 170